Gift: Lord Howe of Aberavon

Tolley's Tax Guide 2010–11

Tolley's
Tax Guide
2010–11

by
Arnold Homer

Rita Burrows

Claire Hayes

Ruth Newman

Consultant Editor:

Francesca Lagerberg

Members of the LexisNexis Group worldwide

United Kingdom	LexisNexis, a Division of Reed Elsevier (UK) Ltd, Halsbury House, 35 Chancery Lane, London, WC2A 1EL, and London House, 20–22 East London Street, Edinburgh EH7 4BQ
Argentina	LexisNexis Argentina, Buenos Aires
Australia	LexisNexis Butterworths, Chatswood, New South Wales
Austria	LexisNexis Verlag ARD Orac GmbH & Co KG, Vienna
Benelux	LexisNexis Benelux, Amsterdam
Canada	LexisNexis Canada, Markham, Ontario
China	LexisNexis China, Beijing and Shanghai
France	LexisNexis SA, Paris
Germany	LexisNexis Deutschland GmbH, Munster
Hong Kong	LexisNexis Hong Kong, Hong Kong
India	LexisNexis India, New Delhi
Italy	Giuffrè Editore, Milan
Japan	LexisNexis Japan, Tokyo
Malaysia	Malayan Law Journal Sdn Bhd, Kuala Lumpur
New Zealand	LexisNexis NZ Ltd, Wellington
Poland	Wydawnictwo Prawnicze LexisNexis Sp, Warsaw
Singapore	LexisNexis Singapore, Singapore
South Africa	LexisNexis Butterworths, Durban
USA	LexisNexis, Dayton, Ohio

© Reed Elsevier (UK) Ltd 2010

Published by LexisNexis
This is a Tolley title

[Twenty-ninth edition]   ISBN 978 0 7545 3908 7

Printed in the UK by CPI William Clowes Beccles NR34 7TL

Visit LexisNexis at www.lexisnexis.co.uk

About this book

This is the twenty-ninth edition of Tolley's Tax Guide, which is one of the range of Tolley annuals on all aspects of taxation.

The Guide is updated annually to incorporate the changes in law and practice that occur each year, and is published this year soon after the passing of Finance Act No.2.

The aim of the book is to provide clear and concise guidance on all aspects of taxation that are likely to be encountered day-to-day by tax advisers and personal and business taxpayers. It deals with income tax and capital gains tax (including self-assessment), corporation tax, inheritance tax, value added tax and stamp taxes. There are also chapters on council tax and business rates, national insurance contributions and statutory sick pay, statutory maternity pay, adoption and paternity pay. There are numerous examples to demonstrate how the provisions work in practice.

Tax planning opportunities in the various areas are highlighted as 'tax points' at the end of most chapters.

This edition gives the position for the tax year 2010/11 and covers all legislation, HMRC's published guidance and other relevant sources of information including the provisions of Finance Act 2010 and Finance (No.2) Act 2010. In addition, we have included relevant commentary on the third Finance Bill of 2010 which is scheduled to be published and receive Royal Assent towards the latter part of 2010. Where appropriate the position for earlier years is also explained.

All chapters have been revised to incorporate the many changes that have taken place since the previous edition, and there is a useful summary of the main changes.

The general law, as opposed to tax law, is not always the same in Scotland and in Northern Ireland as in England and Wales. Except where otherwise stated, this book is concerned with the law in England and Wales. Readers in Scotland and Northern Ireland should take advice if in any doubt.

Any comments on this publication will, as always, be welcomed by the publishers.

LexisNexis

Contents

Contents

Abbreviations

CAA 2001	Capital Allowances Act 2001
CFC	Controlled foreign company
CGT	Capital gains tax
CPA 2004	Civil Partnership Act 2004
CRCA 2005	Commissioners for Revenue and Customs Act 2005
CTA 2009	Corporation Tax Act 2009
CTA 2010	Corporation Tax Act 2010
CTFA 2004	Child Trust Funds Act 2004
EEA	European Economic Area
EIS	Enterprise Investment Scheme
ESC	Extra-statutory concession
FA	Finance Act
FYA	First-year allowance
F(No.2)A	Finance (No.2) Act
HMRC	Her Majesty's Revenue and Customs
IHT	Inheritance tax
IHTA 1984	Inheritance Tax Act 1984
ISA	Individual Savings Account
ITA 2007	Income Tax Act 2007
ITEPA	Income Tax (Earnings and Pensions) Act 2003
ITTOIA 2005	Income Tax (Trading and Other Income) Act 2005
LLPA 2000	Limited Liability Partnerships Act 2000
MIRAS	Mortgage interest relief at source
NIC	National insurance contributions
NICA 2008	National Insurance Contributions Act 2008
PAYE	Pay As You Earn
reg	Regulation
s	Section

SA 1891	Stamp Act 1891
SAYE	Save As You Earn
Sch	Schedule
SI	Statutory instrument
SP	HMRC Statement of Practice
SSCBA 1992	Social Security Contributions and Benefits Act 1992
TA 1988	Income and Corporation Taxes Act 1988
TCA 2002	Tax Credits Act 2002
TCEA 2007	Tribunals, Courts and Enforcement Act 2007
TCGA 1992	Taxation of Chargeable Gains Act 1992
TIOPA 2010	Taxation (International and Other Provisions) Act 2010
TMA 1970	Taxes Management Act 1970
VAT	Value added tax
VATA 1994	Value Added Tax Act 1994
VCT	Venture Capital Trust

Table of rates and allowances

(Correct to 27 July 2010)

Income and corporation tax

Personal reliefs (see chapter 2)

	2008/09 £	2009/10 £	2010/11 £
Personal allowance			
general	6,035	6,475	6,475
aged 65–74	9,030	9,490	9,490
aged 75 and over	9,180	9,640	9,640
personal allowance income limit	n/a	n/a	100,000
age allowance income limit	21,800	22,900	22,900
minimum where income exceeds age allowance limit (but not personal allowance limit where applicable)	6,035	6,475	6,475
Married couple's allowance			
either partner born before 6 April 1935 but aged less than 75	6,535*	n/a	n/a
either partner aged 75 or over	6,625*	6,965*	6,965*
age allowance income limit	21,800	22,900	22,900
minimum where income exceeds limit	2,540*	2,670*	2,670*
Blind person's allowance	1,800	1,890	1,890

*These allowances attract tax relief at only 10%.

Income tax rates on taxable income (see chapter 2)

Rate	2008/09		2009/10		2010/11	
	Band £	Tax £	Band £	Tax £	Band £	Tax £
Starting for savings income (10%)	0–2,320		0–2,440		0–2,440	
Basic (20%)	0–34,800	6,960.00	0–37,400	7,480.00	0–37,400	7,480.00

| Higher (40%) | Over 34,800 | Over 37,400 | 37,401–150,000 |
| Additional (50%) | | | Over 150,000 |

A general 10% starting rate was abolished for 2008/09 onwards but was replaced by a new 10% starting rate for savings income, which applies only if non-savings income is within certain limits. See **2.24** and **2.25** for full details of the rates of tax on savings and dividend income.

Company cars – private use benefit (see chapter 10)

The taxable benefit is the appropriate percentage of the lower of (a) the list price of the car plus certain accessories or (b) £80,000. The percentage for cars registered after 31 December 1997 which have an approved carbon dioxide emissions figure can be found using the table below.

2008/09 to 2009/10 g/km	% of price taxable	2010/11 g/km	% of price taxable
		0	0
		75	5 *
120	10 *	120	10 *
135	15 *	130	15 *
140	16 *	135	16 *
145	17 *	140	17 *
150	18 *	145	18 *
155	19 *	150	19 *
160	20 *	155	20 *
165	21 *	160	21 *
170	22 *	165	22 *
175	23 *	170	23 *
180	24 *	175	24 *
185	25 *	180	25 *
190	26 *	185	26 *
195	27 *	190	27 *
200	28 *	195	28 *
205	29 *	200	29 *
210	30 *	205	30 *
215	31 *	210	31 *
220	32 *	215	32 *
225	33 **	220	33 **

2008/09 to 2009/10 g/km	% of price taxable	2010/11 g/km	% of price taxable
230	34 ***	225	34 ***
235	35 ****	230	35 ****

*Add 3% if car runs solely on diesel.

**Add 2% if car runs solely on diesel.

***Add 1% if car runs solely on diesel.

****No diesel supplement.

For 2010/11 there are discounts for certain alternative fuel cars. See **10.29** regarding these and other rates and discounts, and changes to company car tax from 6 April 2010 onwards.

Cars first registered before 1 January 1998, and cars which have no approved carbon dioxide emissions figure, are taxed as follows.

Engine size	% of price taxable	
	Pre-1.1.98 cars	Post-31.12.97 cars with no emissions figure
0–1,400 cc	15	15*
1,401–2,000 cc	22	25*
2,001 cc and over	32	35

*Plus 3% supplement for diesel cars.

Company cars – car fuel benefit (see chapter 10)

The fuel benefit is calculated by reference to CO_2 emissions, where the car was new on or after 1 January 1998 and has an approved CO_2 emissions figure. The same percentage as for car benefit (ranging from 0% to 35% depending on CO_2 emissions) is applied to the fixed sum of £18,000 (£16,900 for 2009/10).

Where the car has no approved CO_2 emissions figure, the same percentage figure used to calculate company car benefit is used.

Company cars – advisory fuel rates from 1 June 2010 (see chapter 10)

	Petrol	Diesel	LPG
1400cc or less	12p	11p	8p
1401cc to 2000cc	15p	11p	10p
Over 2000cc	21p	16p	14p

Use of own transport – authorised mileage rates (see chapter 10)

Cars

	First 10,000 business miles	Additional business miles
All cars	40p	25p
Each passenger making same business trip	5p	5p

Cycles

The authorised mileage rate for cycles is 20p per mile for all business miles.

Motorcycles

The authorised mileage rate for motor cycles is 24p per mile for all business miles.

Official rate of interest: cheap loans (see chapter 10)

From 6 April 2010	4% p.a.
From 1 March 2009	4.75% p.a.
From 6 April 2007	6.25% p.a.

Interest on unpaid tax (income tax and capital gains tax) (see chapter 2)

From 29 September 2009	3% p.a.
From 24 March 2009	2.5% p.a.
From 27 January 2009	3.5% p.a.
From 6 January 2009	4.5% p.a.
From 6 December 2008	5.5% p.a.
From 6 November 2008	6.5% p.a.
From 6 January 2008	7.5% p.a.

Interest on overpaid tax (income tax and capital gains tax) (see chapter 2)

From 29 September 2009	0.5% p.a.
From 24 March 2009	0% p.a.
From 27 January 2009	0% p.a.

From 6 January 2009	0.75% p.a.
From 6 December 2008	1.5% p.a.
From 6 November 2008	2.25% p.a.
From 6 January 2008	3% p.a.

Note

The rates of interest on unpaid and overpaid income tax and capital gains tax also apply, where appropriate, to national insurance contributions (see CHAPTERS **13** and **24**), stamp duty and stamp duty reserve tax (see CHAPTER **6**).

Interest on unpaid corporation tax (see chapter 3)

From 29 September 2009	3% p.a.
From 24 March 2009	2.5% p.a
From 27 January 2009	3.5% p.a
From 6 January 2009	4.5% p.a
From 6 December 2008	5.5% p.a
From 6 November 2008	6.5% p.a
From 6 January 2008	7.5% p.a.

Interest on overpaid corporation tax (see chapter 3)

From 29 September 2009	0.5% p.a.
From 24 March 2009	0% p.a
From 27 January 2009	0% p.a
From 6 January 2009	1% p.a
From 6 December 2008	2% p.a
From 6 November 2008	3% p.a
From 6 January 2008	4% p.a.

Interest on unpaid instalment payments for 'large companies' (see chapter 3)

From 16 March 2009	1.5% p.a.
From 16 February 2009	2% p.a.
From 19 January 2009	2.5% p.a.
From 15 December 2008	3% p.a.
From 17 November 2008	4% p.a.
From 20 October 2008	5.5% p.a.
From 21 April 2008	6% p.a.

From 18 February 2008   6.25% p.a.

Interest on overpaid instalment payments for 'large companies' and on early payments by other companies (see chapter 3)

From 21 September 2009	0.5% p.a.
From 16 March 2009	0.25% p.a.
From 16 February 2009	0.75% p.a.
From 19 January 2009	1.25% p.a.
From 15 December 2008	1.75% p.a.
From 17 November 2008	2.75% p.a.
From 20 October 2008	4.25% p.a.
From 21 April 2008	4.75% p.a.
From 18 February 2008	5% p.a.

Corporation tax rates (see chapter 3)

Year beginning	1 April 2008	1 April 2009	1 April 2010
Full rate	28%	28%	28%
Small profits rate	21%	21%	21%
—upper profit limit	£300,000	£300,000	£300,000
—marginal relief upper profit limit	£1,500,000	£1,500,000	£1,500,000
—marginal relief fraction	7/400	7/400	7/400
—effective marginal rate	29.75%	29.75%	29.75%

The full rate will be reduced to 27% from 1 April 2011, when it is also proposed to reduce the small profits rate to 20%.

Capital gains are included in profits and therefore chargeable at the applicable corporation tax rate.

Capital gains tax (see chapter 4)

For 2010/11 for individuals, capital gains remaining after deduction of the annual exemption will be taxed at a flat rate of either 18% or 28% depending on their personal tax position (see **4.2**). For 2008/09 and 2009/10, capital gains remaining after deduction of the annual exemption were chargeable at a flat rate of 18%. For 2010/11 for personal representatives and trustees, gains arising on or after 23 June 2010 are taxed at 28%; gains arising before 23 June 2010 are taxed at 18%. The annual exemption for individuals, personal representatives and trustees for disabled people is:

2010/11	£10,100
2009/10	£10,100
2008/09	£9,600

See **4.34** and **4.35** regarding personal representatives and trustees.

Retail prices index (for indexation allowance)

	1982	1983	1984	1985	1986	1987	1988	1989	1990
January		82.61	86.84	91.20	96.25	100.0	103.3	111.0	119.5
February		82.97	87.20	91.94	96.60	100.4	103.7	111.8	120.2
March	79.44	83.12	87.48	92.80	96.73	100.6	104.1	112.3	121.4
April	81.04	84.28	88.64	94.78	97.67	101.8	105.8	114.3	125.1
May	81.62	84.64	88.97	95.21	97.85	101.9	106.2	115.0	126.2
June	81.85	84.84	89.20	95.41	97.79	101.9	106.6	115.4	126.7
July	81.88	85.30	89.10	95.23	97.52	101.8	106.7	115.5	126.8
August	81.90	85.68	89.94	95.49	97.82	102.1	107.9	115.8	128.1
September	81.85	86.06	90.11	95.44	98.30	102.4	108.4	116.6	129.3
October	82.26	86.36	90.67	95.59	98.45	102.9	109.5	117.5	130.3
November	82.66	86.67	90.95	95.92	99.29	103.4	110.0	118.5	130.0
December	82.51	86.89	90.87	96.05	99.62	103.3	110.3	118.8	129.9

	1991	1992	1993	1994	1995	1996	1997	1998	1999
January	130.2	135.6	137.9	141.3	146.0	150.2	154.4	159.5	163.4
February	130.9	136.3	138.8	142.1	146.9	150.9	155.0	160.3	163.7
March	131.4	136.7	139.3	142.5	147.5	151.5	155.4	160.8	164.1
April	133.1	138.8	140.6	144.2	149.0	152.6	156.3	162.6	165.2
May	133.5	139.3	141.1	144.7	149.6	152.9	156.9	163.5	165.6
June	134.1	139.3	141.0	144.7	149.8	153.0	157.5	163.4	165.6
July	133.8	138.8	140.7	144.0	149.1	152.4	157.5	163.0	165.1
August	134.1	138.9	141.3	144.7	149.9	153.1	158.5	163.7	165.5
September	134.6	139.4	141.9	145.0	150.6	153.8	159.3	164.4	166.2
October	135.1	139.9	141.8	145.2	149.8	153.8	159.5	164.5	166.5
November	135.6	139.7	141.6	145.3	149.8	153.9	159.6	164.4	166.7
December	135.7	139.2	141.9	146.0	150.7	154.4	160.0	164.4	167.3

	2000	2001	2002	2003	2004	2005	2006	2007	2008
January	166.6	171.1	173.3	178.4	183.1	188.9	193.4	201.6	209.8
February	167.5	172.0	173.8	179.3	183.8	189.6	194.2	203.1	211.4

March	168.4	172.2	174.5	179.9	184.6	190.5	195.0	204.4	212.1
April	170.1	173.1	175.7	181.2	185.7	191.6	196.5	205.4	214.0
May	170.7	174.2	176.2	181.5	186.5	192.0	197.7	206.2	215.1
June	171.1	174.4	176.2	181.3	186.8	192.2	198.5	207.3	216.8
July	170.5	173.3	175.9	181.3	186.8	192.2	198.5	206.1	216.5
August	170.5	174.0	176.4	181.6	187.4	192.6	199.2	207.3	217.2
September	171.7	174.6	177.6	182.5	188.1	193.1	200.1	208.0	218.4
October	171.6	174.3	177.9	182.6	188.6	193.3	200.4	208.9	217.7
November	172.1	173.6	178.2	182.7	189.0	193.6	201.1	209.7	216.0
December	172.2	173.4	178.5	183.5	189.9	194.1	202.7	210.9	212.9

	2009	2010
January	210.1	217.9
February	211.4	219.2
March	211.3	220.7
April	211.5	222.8
May	212.8	223.6
June	213.4	224.1
July	213.4	
August	214.4	
September	215.3	
October	216.0	
November	216.6	
December	218.0	

The post-April 1998 figures are relevant only for calculating capital gains of companies. The index was re-referenced in January 1987 from 394.5 to 100.

National insurance contributions

Employers and employees: class 1 NICs (see chapter 13)

	2009/10	2010/11
Lower earnings limit per week (LEL)	£95	£97
Upper earnings limit per week (UEL)	£844	£844
Primary threshold	£110	£110
Secondary threshold	£110	£110

Rates: 2009/10 and 2010/11

Not contracted out

Band of weekly earnings	Employee	Employer
£0 to £110	—	—
£110.01 to UEL	11%	12.8%
Over UEL	1%	12.8%

Contracted out

The 'not contracted out' rate of contribution for employees is reduced for earnings between £110 per week and the UEL by 1.6% to 9.4%. In addition, employees receive a rebate of 1.6% on earnings from the LEL up to £110 per week. Where the rebate exceeds the employee's liability, the excess goes to the employer. For employers, the 'not contracted out' rate is reduced on the band of earnings from £110 per week to the UEL by 3.7% (to 9.1%) for employees in salary-related schemes and by 1.4% (to 11.4%) for employees in money purchase schemes. In addition, employers receive a rebate of 3.7% or 1.4%, as appropriate, on earnings from the LEL up to £110 per week.

Reduced rate for certain married women and widows

Payable on earnings in the band £110.01 to UEL	4.85%
Over UEL	1%

Employers: class 1A NICs on benefits in kind (see chapter 13)

12.8% of the taxable benefit

Self-employed: class 2 and class 4 NICs (see chapter 24)

	2009/10	2010/11
Class 2 contributions per week	£2.40	£2.40
small earnings exception	£5,075	£5,075
Class 4 contributions rate	8%	8%
on profits between	£5,715 and £43,875	£5,715 and £43,875
Class 4 contributions rate	1%	1%
on profits over	£43,875	£43,875

Voluntary: class 3 NICs (see chapters 13 and 24)

	2009/10	2010/11
Class 3 contributions per week	£12.05	£12.05

Statutory sick pay from 6 April 2010 (see chapter 14)

Average weekly earnings	£97 and over
SSP flat weekly rate	£79.15

Statutory maternity pay, statutory paternity pay and statutory adoption pay from 4 April 2010 (see chapter 14)

The lower of £124.88 and 90% of average weekly earnings.

Main state benefits (see chapter 10)

	2009/10 £	2010/11 £
Taxable (weekly rates)		
Retirement pension*		
—single	95.25	97.65
—based on husband's contributions	57.05	58.50
Old person's pension*		
—higher rate	57.05	58.50
Bereavement (widow's) benefits		
—widowed parent's (mother's) allowance	95.25	97.65
—bereavement allowance / widow's pension standard rate	95.25	97.65
Employment and support allowance (contribution-based)**		
—main phase rate (work-related)	up to 89.80	up to 91.40
—main phase rate (support group)	up to 95.15	up to 96.85
Carer's allowance		
—single	53.10	53.90
Jobseekers allowance (taxable maximum)		
Single		
—under 25	50.95	51.85
—25 or over	64.30	65.45

Non-taxable (weekly rates)
(excluding income-related benefits)

Child benefit		
—eldest child	20.00	20.30
—other children	13.20	13.40
Maternity allowance		
—standard rate	123.06	124.88
Employment and support allowance (contribution-based)**		
—assessment phase rate (under 25)	50.95	51.85
—assessment phase rate (25 and over)	64.30	65.45
Disability living allowance		
care component		
—higher rate	70.35	71.40
—middle rate	47.10	47.80
—lower rate	18.65	18.95
mobility component		
—higher rate	49.10	49.85
—lower rate	18.65	18.95
Severe disablement allowance		
—single (standard rate)	57.45	59.45

* A taxable age addition of 25p per week is payable to persons aged 80 or over with any one of these benefits.

** Employment and support allowance replaced incapacity benefit and income support, paid because of illness or disability, for new claims from 27 October 2008. See www.jobcentreplus.gov.uk. Claimants entitled to the income-related allowance may receive more than the contribution-based amounts and the rates vary.

Tax Credits (see chapter 2)

	2009/10 £ p.a.	2010/11 £ p.a.
Working tax credit		
— basic	1,890	1,920
— additional couple's and lone parent element	1,860	1,890
— 30 hour	775	790
— disabled worker	2,530	2,570
— addition for severe disablement	1,075	1,095

— 50 plus return to work 16 to 29 hours	1,300	1,320
— 50 plus return to work 30+ hours	1,935	1,965
— childcare: maximum eligible cost	300pw	300pw
— childcare: maximum eligible cost (one child)	175pw	175pw
— percent of eligible costs recovered	80%	80%
Child tax credit		
— family (only one family element per family)	545	545
— baby addition	545	545
— child	2,235	2,300
— disabled child addition	2,670	2,715
— severely disabled child addition	1,075	1,095
For both working credit and child credit		
— first income threshold	6,420	6,420
— first withdrawal rate	39%	39%
— second income threshold	50,000	50,000
— second income withdrawal rate	6.67%	6.67%
— first threshold (those entitled to child credit only)	16,040	16,190
— income disregard	25,000	25,000

Value added tax (see chapter 7)

	From 1 Jan 2010	From 4 Jan 2011
Standard rate	17.5%	20%

	From 1 May 2009	From 1 April 2010
Registration threshold		
taxable supplies		
—in last 12 months	More than £68,000	More than £70,000
—in next 30 days	More than £68,000	More than £70,000
unless taxable supplies in next year not expected to exceed	£66,000	£68,000
Deregistration		
taxable supplies in next year	£66,000 or less	£68,000 or less

VAT—private motoring—car fuel scale rates from 1 May 2010

CO_2 emissions, g/km	Annual returns £	Quarterly returns £	Monthly returns £
120 or less	570	141	47
125	850	212	70
130	850	212	70
135	910	227	75
140	965	241	80
145	1,020	255	85
150	1,080	269	89
155	1,135	283	94
160	1,190	297	99
165	1,250	312	104
170	1,305	326	108
175	1,360	340	113
180	1,420	354	118
185	1,475	368	122
190	1,530	383	127
195	1,590	397	132
200	1,645	411	137
205	1,705	425	141
210	1,760	439	146
215	1,815	454	151
220	1,875	468	156
225	1,930	482	160
230 or more	1,985	496	165

Interest payable on VAT (default interest)

From 29 September 2009	3% p.a.
From 24 March 2009	2.5% p.a.
From 27 January 2009	3.5% p.a.
From 6 January 2009	4.5% p.a.
From 6 December 2008	5.5% p.a.
From 6 November 2008	6.5% p.a.
From 6 January 2008	7.5% p.a.

Repayment supplement

Repayment supplement of 5% of the tax due (or £50 if greater) is paid on overpaid VAT if the return was made by the due date, the return did not overstate the amount repayable by more than the greater of £250 and 5% of the amount due, and directions for repayment are not issued by HMRC within 30 days from the day following the return due date, or the date the return was received if *later*.

Statutory interest payable by HMRC on overpaid VAT in cases of official error

From 29 September 2009	0.5% p.a.
From 27 January 2009	0% p.a.
From 6 January 2009	1% p.a.
From 6 December 2008	2% p.a.
From 6 November 2008	3% p.a.
From 6 January 2008	4% p.a.

Inheritance tax (see chapter 5)

Rate of tax

A single rate of inheritance tax of 40% (20% for lifetime transfers), applies to the excess of gross cumulative chargeable transfers over the 'nil rate' threshold shown below:

Transfers between 6 April 2009 and 5 April 2015	£325,000
Transfers between 6 April 2008 and 5 April 2009	£312,000
Transfers between 6 April 2007 and 5 April 2008	£300,000

Interest on unpaid inheritance tax

From 29 September 2009	3% p.a.
From 24 March 2009	0% p.a.
From 27 January 2009	1% p.a.
From 6 January 2009	2% p.a.
From 6 November 2008	3% p.a.
From 6 January 2008	4% p.a.

Interest on overpaid inheritance tax

From 29 September 2009	0.5% p.a.

From 24 March 2009	0% p.a.
From 27 January 2009	1% p.a.
From 6 January 2009	2% p.a.
From 6 November 2008	3% p.a.
From 6 January 2008	4% p.a.

Stamp duty (see chapter 6)

Interest on unpaid stamp duty, stamp duty land tax and stamp duty reserve tax

From 29 September 2009	3% p.a.
From 24 March 2009	2.5% p.a.
From 27 January 2009	3.5% p.a.
From 6 January 2009	4.5% p.a.
From 6 December 2008	5.5% p.a.
From 6 November 2008	6.5% p.a.
From 6 January 2008	7.5% p.a.

Interest on overpaid stamp duty, stamp duty land tax and stamp duty reserve tax

From 29 September 2009	0.5% p.a.
From 24 March 2009	0% p.a.
From 27 January 2009	0% p.a.
From 6 January 2009	0.75% p.a.
From 6 December 2008	1.5% p.a.
From 6 November 2008	2.25% p.a.
From 6 January 2008	3% p.a.

Main Tax Changes

There will be three Finance Acts in 2010 once the third Finance Bill of the year receives Royal Assent in the Autumn. The main changes that have either been enacted by the first two Acts or will be enacted in the third Finance Bill (as announced in the June 2010 Emergency Budget) and thought likely to be of relevance to most readers, are outlined below.

Income tax and tax credits (chapter 2)

The basic rate of income tax remains at 20%, and dividends within the basic rate band remain chargeable at 10%. The rates for income above the basic rate limit and up to the higher rate limit remain unchanged at 40% for non-dividend income and 32.5% for dividend income. The rates above the higher rate limit are 50% for non-dividend income and 42.5% for dividend income. The basic rate limit remains at £37,400 and the higher rate limit is £150,000.

The basic personal allowance remains unchanged at £6,475. Personal allowances for those over 65 remain at £9,490 for those aged up to 74 and £9,640 for those aged 75 and over. The personal allowance for those over 65 is restricted to the extent that income exceeds £22,900, but will not fall below £6,475, unless the individual's income exceeds £100,000, in which case the personal allowance is restricted for all individuals regardless of age and can be reduced to zero. It is proposed to increase the personal allowance to £7,475 from 6 April 2011, but higher rate taxpayers will be prevented from benefiting from the increase by a reduction in the basic rate limit. There are changes to some elements of child tax credit and working tax credit.

Corporation tax (chapter 3)

The small profits rate of corporation tax remains at 21%, but will be reduced to 20% from 1 April 2011. The main rate remains at 28%, but will be reduced to 27% from 1 April 2011. It was also announced at the June 2010 Emergency Budget that there will be progressive further reductions in the main rate to 24% by April 2014.

The Corporation Tax Act 2010 and the Taxation (International and Other Provisions) Act 2010 completed the rewrite of corporation tax law.

Capital gains tax (chapter 4)

The annual exemption for individuals and personal representatives remains at £10,100, with corresponding exemptions for trustees remaining unchanged. The entrepreneurs' relief limit was increased to £2m from 6 April 2010 and again to £5m from 23 June 2010. The capital gains tax rate applying to gains above the basic rate limit for individuals, and all gains arising to trustees and personal representatives, increased to 28% from 23 June 2010.

Inheritance tax (chapters 5 and 42)

The inheritance tax nil threshold remains at £325,000 for 2010/11, the planned increase to £350,000 having been reversed. New rules were introduced in connection with the tax treatment of certain interest in possession trusts.

Value added tax (chapter 7)

The VAT registration limit was increased to £70,000 and the deregistration limit to £68,000, with effect from 1 April 2010. The standard rate of 15% applied for the period 1 December 2008 to 31 December 2009 before reverting to 17.5% on 1 January 2010. F(No.2)A 2010 included detailed anti-forestalling rules for supplies 'spanning' 4 January 2011 when the rate will increase to 20%. Changes to the place of supply rules were introduced from 1 January 2010, with further changes to be introduced in 2011 and 2013 with the ongoing aim of applying VAT in the place of consumption.

Dealing with HMRC (chapter 9)

The unified regime of penalties for late filing of returns and late payment of tax, was partially introduced from 1 April 2010 for a number of specified taxes. The regime will be extended to other taxes (including various indirect taxes) from a date yet to be announced.

FA 2009 introduced a provision enabling HMRC to enter into voluntary 'managed payment plans' with taxpayers which were due to apply from April 2011. It was, however, announced at the June 2010 Emergency Budget that this scheme will be deferred for the time being.

From 1 April 2010 the time limit in which many claims etc can be made has been reduced to four years from the end of the tax year or relevant accounting period (previously six years).

HMRC have published a charter setting out the standards of behaviour and values to which they aspire when dealing with people in the exercise of their functions.

Employments (chapters 10 and 13)

FA 2010 introduced changes to the car benefit calculations, introducing lower percentages for zero and low emission cars. There are proposed changes in national insurance rates and thresholds from 6 April 2011.

Pension provision (chapter 16)

Tax relief on pension contributions made by persons with gross income of £150,000 or more will be restricted to the basic rate of tax from 6 April 2011 with anti-forestalling measures applying from 22 April 2009. FA 2010 modified the FA 2009 provisions. The requirement to buy an annuity is deferred until age 77.

Capital allowances (chapter 22)

The Annual Investment Allowance was increased from April 2010 to £100,000 but it is proposed to be reduced to £25,000 from 2012. A 100% first year allowance is to be introduced from 1 April 2010 for new zero-emission goods vehicles. The main rate of writing down allowances is to be reduced to 18% and the special rate reduced to 8% for chargeable periods ending on or after April 2012.

Main anti-avoidance provisions (various)

FA 2010 included rules to counter avoidance involving capital allowances buying by companies, and property loss relief and sideways loss relief for individuals.

Introduction

introduction

1

Introduction

[1.1] Tolley's Tax Guide first appeared 28 years ago — this is in fact the 29th edition because two books were published when there was a change of government in 1997. The tax world has changed out of all recognition over the last quarter of a century and the book has expanded from its original 333 pages to more than 800 pages.

The volume of legislation has been considerably increased over recent years because of the recent project to rewrite tax law in simpler language. Making it simpler unfortunately resulted in using a lot more words. The Income Tax Act 2007 completed the work on the income tax legislation. The corporation tax legislation was rewritten to the Corporation Tax Act 2009, Corporation Tax Act 2010 and the Taxation (International and Other Provisions) Act 2010. Her Majesty's Revenue and Customs (HMRC) announced in July 2009 that the rewrite project would end in 2010.

[1.2] UK tax law applies throughout the United Kingdom, but there are sometimes specific provisions that recognise the different legal systems in Scotland and, to a lesser extent, in Northern Ireland. These differences are not dealt with in this book.

UK tax law must comply with the regulations and directives of the European Commission. EU member states must allow members of other EU states freedom of establishment and not tax them at higher rates than their own nationals. One EU state may require another state to take proceedings to recover both direct and indirect taxes owed in the first state, and an EU state may ask the UK tax authorities to deliver documents to a UK taxpayer on their behalf in relation to a tax liability in that EU state. UK tax law must also be compatible with the European Convention on Human Rights and the Human Rights Act 1998.

The Scottish Parliament has the power to increase or decrease the basic rate of income tax by up to 3%. This power has been available since 2000 but has not yet been exercised.

[1.3] The work of HMRC was done by the Inland Revenue and HM Customs and Excise until those departments merged in 2005.

The merger was followed by the establishment of an independent authority, the Revenue and Customs Prosecutions Office, to deal with prosecution work. In January 2010 the RCPO merged with the Crown Prosecution Service to become a specialist Revenue and Customs Division within the CPS. The RCD works with HMRC investigators in the same way that the CPS operates with the police.

HMRC are allowed to disclose information to the police in the UK and abroad in connection with criminal investigations and also to the intelligence services. Information is also available to government departments as a result of the money laundering regulations — see **CHAPTER 9**.

[1.4] Knowing how the UK system works, what taxes can be charged and what deductions and allowances are available, as well as the tax effect of alternative courses of action, will help a taxpayer cope with his responsibilities and make sure that all relevant tax reliefs and allowances are obtained.

The first part of this book contains a brief outline of all the various taxes covered, including council tax. The following sections go on to deal with specific subject areas such as employment, pensions, trades, land, tax and the family, and choosing investments. Tax saving opportunities and possible problems are highlighted in the form of 'tax points' at the end of each chapter.

Statutory references will help to track down the relevant legislation if a topic needs to be researched in more depth. The main Acts dealing with taxation are the Inheritance Tax Act 1984, the Income and Corporation Taxes Act 1988, the Taxation of Chargeable Gains Act 1992, the Value Added Tax Act 1994, the Capital Allowances Act 2001, the Income Tax (Earnings and Pensions) Act 2003, the Income Tax (Trading and Other Income) Act 2005, the Income Tax Act 2007, the Corporation Tax Act 2009, the Corporation Tax 2010 and the Taxation (International and Other Provisions) Act 2010. In addition there are annual Finance Acts which alter some of the existing provisions and bring in new ones.

Statutory instruments are increasingly being used to provide detailed regulations on various aspects of the main Acts but also to make changes to the provisions of the Acts, partly because legislation is often introduced in haste and without the benefit of detailed consultation and/or parliamentary scrutiny. In the June 2010 Budget, the Government announced that it intends to impose 'sunset clauses' on regulations, under which they will cease to be law after seven years unless Parliament has confirmed that they are still necessary and proportionate, or they were explicitly set to have a longer timeframe.

Published statements of practice and extra-statutory concessions set out HMRC's views on particular aspects and sometimes allow matters to be treated more sympathetically than the strict letter of the law allows. Some concessions are now being written into legislation, while others are being withdrawn.

Much of the published material is posted on the HMRC website well in advance of the paper versions. Indeed some publications, including the self-assessment Help Sheets and Revenue and Customs Briefs, are only available online. It is the Government's declared aim to increase the use of electronic communication with taxpayers.

A number of consultations were announced in the June 2010 Budget. Of particular interest is the discussion document entitled 'Tax Policy Making: A New Approach'. This is intended 'to improve the way tax policy is made', and to support the objectives of predictability, stability and simplicity. Comments are invited by 22 September 2010. The Government has also confirmed its intention to create an independent Office of Tax Simplification, and will announce further details shortly.

[1.5] Despite the vast array of tax statutes and supplementary material, it is not always clear what the law means. Alternatively, the meaning of the law may not be in doubt, but the facts of the case may be unclear. It is therefore possible to take a different view from the tax authorities either on the interpretation of the law, or on the facts, or a mixture of the two.

As far as income tax, capital gains tax and corporation tax are concerned, since they are self-assessed it is up to the taxpayer to calculate how much tax is owed based on their view of the law. If there are areas of doubt, these should be drawn to the attention of HMRC. If a self-assessment tax return is completed, HMRC will initially deal with points of difference by raising an enquiry into the return, at the end of which they have the right to make amendments if they disagree with the taxpayer's figures. They also have the right to issue assessments themselves in cases of careless or deliberate actions of the taxpayer or if inadequate information is provided.

Appeals may be made to an independent appeals tribunal in cases of disagreement with an HMRC assessment etc. The distinction between questions of law and fact is important, because what an appeal tribunal decides on questions of fact is generally binding on both the taxpayer and HMRC. A tribunal's decision on points of law, however, can be referred by the losing party to the courts. It is important, however, to think very carefully before taking an appeal on a question of law to the appeal tribunal, because it may take a very long time before it is settled, it will cost a lot of time and money, and at the end of the day the case may still be lost.

In addition, a taxpayer's victory may be short-lived if the Government decide to change the law to reverse the effect of the court's decision. For example, in December 2004 the Government took the unprecedented step of announcing that future legislation to counter arrangements aimed at frustrating the Government's intention 'that employers and employees should pay the proper amount of tax and NICs on the rewards of employment' would take retrospective effect from that date. The Government announced their intention to change the 'settlement' rules, following the taxpayer's victory in the *Arctic Systems* case (see **12.10**), to counter so-called 'income shifting', but it announced later that proposed reforms would be delayed to allow for further consultation.

[1.6] The Tribunals, Courts and Enforcement Act 2007 provided for the functions of the general and special commissioners, and those of the VAT tribunals, to be transferred to a new tribunals service administered by the Ministry of Justice. The new system comprises a First Tier Tribunal and an Upper Tribunal. In the event of an appeal from the Upper Tribunal, the appeal will go to the Court of Appeal rather than the High Court. Where leave is granted, further appeal may be made to the Supreme Court. There is the further possibility of going to the European Court on the grounds that UK law is not in accordance with European Union rules. Most referrals to the European Court relate to VAT, but some relate to direct taxes. There is also the possibility of appealing to the European Court of Human Rights if it is felt that rights under the European Human Rights Convention have been breached.

Taxpayers and their advisers wishing to undertake tax planning need to bear in mind that HMRC have a good deal of 'anti-avoidance' legislation at their disposal. They may also be able to challenge a series of transactions with a tax avoidance motive so that only the end result of the series is taken into account. Broadly speaking, advance planning by way of a series of transactions is still possible providing the transactions are not so pre-ordained and interlinked that they can only really be regarded as a single transaction.

Such advance planning is, however, affected by further significant measures to counter tax avoidance, introduced in 2004, which require promoters of tax avoidance schemes, and in some cases the taxpayers using such schemes, to provide details to HMRC.

[1.7] Most people do not want to be involved in disputes with the tax authorities, and merely wish to make sure that they comply with their obligations without paying more than is legally due. It is necessary, however, to understand the difference between tax avoidance and tax evasion. Tax avoidance means using the tax rules to best advantage, whereas tax evasion means illegally reducing tax bills, for example by understating income, over claiming expenses or deliberately disguising the true nature of transactions. It seems reasonable to distinguish tax avoidance from more straightforward tax planning or mitigation, with some avoidance being regarded as unacceptable by HMRC — some 'structured avoidance' schemes might be regarded, for example, as setting out to defeat the purpose of the legislation — and planning or mitigation being regarded as acceptable. However, there are no firm definitions in this area.

Some ministers and HMRC officials have been accused of blurring the distinction between evasion and avoidance in an effort to highlight what they have regarded as unethical practice on the part of some taxpayers and professional advisers engaged in 'aggressive' or 'artificial' avoidance schemes.

There is an increased public awareness of the issue of tax avoidance following a series of reports investigating the 'tax gap', published by *The Guardian* in February 2009, and the widespread publicity given to the practice of some MPs, already under media scrutiny over their parliamentary expenses claims, who 'flipped' the designation of their main homes to save capital gains tax (see **30.3**).

Although the MPs made and then varied their main residence elections as permitted under a longstanding tax relief for private residences, apparently in accordance with HMRC guidance, their actions were widely criticised. During the Finance Bill 2009 debates a minister indicated that the Government regards 'flipping' to obtain the benefit of the CGT relief as an abuse of the relief.

A further indication of the Government's determination to tackle tax avoidance came with the publication of a code of practice on tax for the UK's banks. The voluntary code, which was finalised in late 2009, requires a bank to undertake not to promote arrangements that 'will give a result contrary to the intentions of parliament'.

Where tax has been illegally evaded, it can result in criminal prosecution as well as payment of the relevant tax plus interest and penalties. The tax authorities collect billions of pounds from their investigation, audit and review work, and undertake a number of major criminal prosecutions.

The UK also has wide-ranging international arrangements to help combat tax evasion, and information is exchanged with countries with whom the UK has double taxation agreements or tax information exchange agreements. A country with which the UK has a double taxation or tax information exchange agreement may also ask HMRC to require a UK taxpayer to provide information relating to tax liabilities with the overseas country.

The sensible course for taxpayers to follow is to try to understand what their liabilities are and to seek professional advice on non-straightforward matters. It is important to consider all the risks including any chance of retrospective legislation. This book aims to explain the basic rules on how tax liabilities are calculated and how they can be managed without falling foul of the law.

Outline of UK tax system

2

Income tax and tax credits: general principles

Basis of income tax charge (ITA 2007, Pts 1 and 2)

[2.1] In order to establish an individual's income tax position it is necessary to understand what 'income' is. Tax law classifies amounts received under various headings, and an item must come within one of these headings to be charged as income. The main income headings are set out in **2.7**.

Capital receipts are dealt with under the capital gains tax rules (see **CHAPTER 4**). Sometimes tax law requires capital items to be treated as income. For example, when a landlord charges a tenant a premium in return for the grant of a short-term lease, part of the lump sum is taxed as income (see **32.18**). Generally, however, an amount cannot be charged to income tax unless it has the quality of income. Usually commissions, cashbacks and discounts received by ordinary retail customers are not taxable, but such amounts may be taxable when received by employees or traders. See **7.2** for the VAT position and **37.5** for the tax treatment of cash received on building society mergers, takeovers etc.

Tax credits are welfare benefits and do not enter into the calculation of taxable income, but they are dealt with by HMRC and are means-tested by reference to a claimant's annual income — see **2.33** to **2.40**.

Exempt income

[2.2] Certain types of income are specifically exempt from tax, notably the following, most of which are dealt with in other chapters as indicated:

11

	Chapter
Income within individual savings accounts (ISAs)	**36, 38**
Income within personal equity plans (PEPs)	**38**
Income and gains of a child trust fund	**33**
Increase in value of national savings certificates	**36**
Premium bond prizes	**36**
Other prizes and betting winnings	**4**
Bonuses and profits on life assurance policies (subject to detailed anti-avoidance rules)	**40**
The capital element in amounts received from a purchased life annuity	**34**
Financial support received by adopters and foster carers from local authorities and adoption agencies	**20**
Local authority home improvement grants	
Income (and gains) arising in specified circumstances to householders who have installed microgeneration systems in their homes	
Some social security benefits (but others are taxable)	**10**
Benefits payable under sickness and unemployment insurance policies	**10**
Damages and compensation for personal injury (whether received as a lump sum or by periodic payments), including payments from the Thalidomide Children's Trust	
Save As You Earn account bonuses	**11**
Shares and share options allocated by an employer under HMRC-approved schemes	**11**
Educational grants and scholarships	
Statutory redundancy pay and certain amounts received from an employer on termination of employment	**15**
Maintenance payments following divorce or separation	**33**
Certain payments to members of the Armed Forces	
Compensation paid by UK or foreign banks and building societies on frozen accounts of Holocaust victims	
Compensation for mis-sold pensions products	**17**
Profits from commercial occupation of woodland	**31**

FA 2009 introduced a new income tax exemption for low-income employees meeting certain conditions, for example migrant workers who are employed in seasonal work in the agricultural or service sectors in both the UK and in other countries in the same tax year, whose overseas income is taxed where it is earned. The change removes the requirement to file a self assessment return in most cases where there would be little or no UK tax liability.

It is proposed that trustees of certain trusts specifically set up before 24 March 2010 as part of an arrangement made by a company with its creditors to pay compensation to asbestos victims will be exempt from tax.

Persons chargeable

[2.3] Each individual, whether man, woman or child, is chargeable to tax on his/her own income. The income of a child under 18 may be treated as the parent's income if it, or the capital which produces it, comes from the parent (see 33.10). Personal representatives and trustees pay income tax on estate and trust income (see CHAPTER 42). Companies generally pay corporation tax instead of income tax (see CHAPTER 3).

Income tax is charged broadly on the income of UK residents, whether it arises in the UK or abroad, subject to special rules for individuals who are not ordinarily resident or not domiciled in the UK. Non-residents are liable to income tax only on income that arises in the UK. Double tax relief is available where income is taxed both in the UK and abroad. Overseas aspects are discussed in CHAPTER 41.

Rates of tax payable by individuals (ITA 2007, ss 6–21)

[2.4] The rates of tax payable depend on the type of income, which for this purpose is divided into three classes, namely dividends, other savings income and non-savings income.

Tax rates — 2010/11

[2.5] For 2010/11 the rates of income tax on non-savings income are:

* the basic rate of 20% on the first £37,400;
* the higher rate of 40% on income above the 'basic rate limit' of £37,400 and up to the 'higher rate limit' of £150,000;
* the additional rate of 50% on income above the 'higher rate limit' of £150,000.

It is proposed that the basic rate limit will be reduced from 6 April 2011 to prevent higher rate taxpayers benefiting from the proposed increase in the personal allowance (see 2.16). The amount of the reduction will be confirmed after the September 2010 retail prices index figure is known.

There is a 10% 'starting rate for savings', which applies to savings income other than dividends. This is not the same as the general starting rate that applied for 2007/08. HMRC guidance on the operation of this 10% starting rate for savings, as it applied for 2008/09, was published at www.hmrc.gov.uk/tdsi/ten-per-cent-guidance.htm.

The starting rate for savings applies to so much of income, up to a 'starting rate limit' of £2,440, as is savings income. However, for this purpose savings income is treated as the highest part of total income (except where an individual has dividend income, in which case the dividend income is treated as the highest part. There are also exceptions in relation to tax payable on certain lump sum termination payments and benefits (see 15.6) and on a chargeable event gain on a life policy (see 40.9)).

This means that this 10% rate will apply only if the £2,440 band is not already used against non-savings income such as earnings and pensions — see Examples 1 and 2.

Example 1

In 2010/11 tax will be charged at the rates shown below where the taxable income is £2,940 (the non-savings income having been reduced by the personal allowance) and it includes savings income of (a) £500, (b) £1,500 and (c) £2,000.

	(a) £		(b) £		(c) £	
Non-savings income	2,440	@ 20%	1,440	@ 20%	940	@ 20%
Savings income	500	@ 20%	1,000	@ 10%	1,500	@ 10%
			500	@ 20%	500	@ 20%
Taxable income	2,940		2,940		2,940	

In short, the 10% starting rate for savings is not available where non-savings income exceeds the amount of the personal allowances plus £2,440.

Savings income within the basic rate band is taxed at 20%, as illustrated in Example 1. On dividend income, the rates are 10% (called the dividend ordinary rate) on income up to the basic rate limit, 32.5% (the dividend upper rate) on income above the basic rate limit up to the higher rate limit, and 42.5% (the dividend additional rate) on income above the higher rate limit— see **2.21** to **2.25**.

Tax rates — earlier years

[2.6] For 2009/10 the rates of income tax on non-savings income were:

• the basic rate of 20% on the first £37,400 (the basic rate band), and
• the higher rate of 40% on income above the 'basic rate limit' of £37,400.

The starting rate limit in relation to the 10% starting rate for savings (see **2.5**) was £2,440.

The tax rates and income bands for 2008/09 are shown in the Table of Rates and Allowances under 'Income tax rates on taxable income'.

Calculating taxable income

[2.7] The tax year runs from 6 April in one year to 5 April in the next, the current year from 6 April 2010 to 5 April 2011 being known as 2010/11.

Taxable income is broadly worked out by adding together the amounts under the headings listed below to arrive at 'total income', then deducting certain reliefs (for example for trade losses or interest payments) to arrive at 'net income', then deducting the personal allowance (and blind person's allowance if relevant) to arrive at the income on which tax is calculated at the rates indicated in **2.5**.

There is then an entitlement to deduct from the calculated amount certain 'tax reductions' which save a specified amount of tax. Tax reductions include age allowances for married couples or civil partners (see **2.18**), and double tax relief (see **41.26**), which is deducted after all other tax reductions. The resulting amount is the income tax liability for the year, unless there is a liability to pay additional tax under a specific provision (such as where the amount of tax treated as deducted from gift aid donations made exceeds the tax liability for the year — see **43.23**). In that event the appropriate amount is added to arrive at the final income tax liability.

Unless there is a specific provision to the contrary, reliefs, allowances and tax reductions are deducted in the way which results in the lowest tax bill, as illustrated later in this chapter.

The main headings under which income is charged are as follows:

* Employment income, pensions and some social security benefits (see **CHAPTERS 10** to **16**).
* Trading income, including profits from trades, professions or vocations (see **CHAPTERS 18** to **29**).
* Property income (see **CHAPTERS 30** to **32**).
* Savings and investment income (see **CHAPTERS 36** to **40**).
* Miscellaneous income (see **19.1**).

The amount chargeable is sometimes affected by the taxpayer's residence, ordinary residence and domicile. The meaning of these terms and their effect on UK tax liability is dealt with in **CHAPTER 41**.

How is tax collected?

[2.8] Tax is collected from most individuals without the need for any direct contact with HMRC. The most common sources of income are earnings from employment, savings interest and dividends on shares. Tax on earnings, and on occupational and personal pensions, is collected through the Pay As You Earn (PAYE) system (see **CHAPTER 10**). Tax on some small items of other income received in full (such as interest from National Savings Income Bonds) may be collected through an adjustment in the PAYE code.

Deduction of tax from savings income and dividend tax credits

[2.9] Tax on bank and building society interest (except some interest paid by National Savings & Investments) is deducted by the payer at the savings rate of 20%, and there is nothing more to pay unless the individual is liable to tax at higher rates. Tax is not deducted if the individual has certified that he is entitled to receive the interest in full because he is not liable to pay *any* tax on income — see **37.4**. Tax is not deducted from interest on any security issued by a company that is listed on a stock exchange (including building society permanent interest-bearing shares), nor from most interest on Government stocks — see **37.6** and **38.4**.

[2.10] There are various finance arrangements, in particular those designed to meet the requirements of Islamic law, that do not involve paying or receiving interest but have a similar effect. Special rules equate the tax treatment of such payments and receipts with the treatment of interest.

[2.11] Dividends from UK companies carry a tax credit equal to 1/9th of the dividend (representing 10% of the tax credit inclusive dividend). Thus a dividend of £90 carries a tax credit of £10, giving income of £100. The tax credit of £10 covers the dividend ordinary rate tax of 10%, but a further 22.5%, amounting to £22.50, is payable by a higher rate taxpayer liable at the dividend upper rate of 32.5% (see **2.5**). A further 32.5%, amounting to £32.50 is payable by an additional rate taxpayer liable at the dividend additional rate of 42.5%. Dividend tax credits are not repayable to non-taxpayers.

Dividends from non-resident companies did not carry a tax credit prior to 2008/09. A tax credit of 1/9th of the dividend is now available, subject to certain conditions (see **41.13**).

Companies sometimes give shareholders the opportunity of taking shares instead of dividends (i.e. scrip dividends). The shareholders are treated as receiving dividends with a notional tax credit (see **38.3**).

Paying tax directly to HMRC

[2.12] A minority of employees and pensioners, and all self-employed people, are required to fill in tax returns and pay some or all of their income tax directly to HMRC. Those with capital gains above the annual exempt limit are also required to fill in tax returns and pay the tax directly. Tax that is due to be paid direct to HMRC is normally collected by means of two half-yearly payments on account, payable on 31 January in the tax year and the next 31 July, based on the total income tax payable directly for the previous tax year. A balancing payment, plus the first payment on account for the following tax year, is payable on the next 31 January. Any capital gains tax due is included in the balancing payment. This is dealt with in more detail at **9.7** to **9.10**. See also **2.29**.

Deductions (ITA 2007, Pt 8; FA 2004, ss 188–195A)

[2.13] Certain payments made are allowable as 'reliefs' in arriving at net income (see **2.7**), saving tax at the top rate.

The allowable interest payments dealt with in **2.14** (other than home income plan interest, see below) are made in full (i.e. without deduction of tax), and relief is given at the top tax rate by having the tax code adjusted or in working out the self-assessment.

An individual is entitled to tax relief on pension contributions paid under an occupational or personal pension scheme, subject to a contributions limit of the higher of 100% of 'relevant earnings' and £3,600 gross, overriding annual and lifetime allowances and a 'special annual allowance charge'. The special annual allowance charge will limit tax relief from 6 April 2011 broadly to the basic rate of tax on pension contributions made by individuals with gross income of £150,000 or more and relevant income of not less than £130,000. For further details see CHAPTERS **16** and **17**.

Pension contributions are not usually deducted as 'reliefs' in calculating net income. If an employee is in an occupational pension scheme, his contributions will reduce his taxable pay (but not his pay for national insurance contributions).

As far as personal pension scheme contributions are concerned, employees pay the contributions net of basic rate tax, and any higher rate relief to which they are entitled is given by means of a PAYE coding adjustment. Self-employed people and those without earned income also obtain basic rate relief by deducting it from their contributions, and higher rate relief where relevant is given in their self-assessment.

Premiums on pre-1 July 1988 pension contracts (retirement annuity policies) may still be paid gross, in which case they reduce the taxpayer's taxable earnings, relief being given in the self-assessment or by coding adjustment. For further discussion of pension provision see CHAPTERS **16** and **17**.

An individual can also save tax at the top tax rate if he gives quoted shares or securities, land and buildings, or certain other investments to charity. The amount of the net benefit to the charity, which is normally the market value of the investment, is deducted in arriving at net income.

Relief is also available at the top tax rate on all 'gift aid' cash donations to charities and registered community amateur sports clubs. The cash amount donated is treated as being paid net of basic rate tax and the individual normally retains the tax deducted as the tax relief. If he is taxable at higher rates (either on income or on capital gains), he will get the extra relief to which he is entitled by an adjustment in his coding or self-assessment. If the individual does not pay enough tax to allow him to retain all the tax relief on his charitable payments, he may have to account to HMRC for the shortfall — see **43.23**.

An individual is entitled to tax relief at a specified rate (a 'tax reduction' — see **2.7**) on certain other payments, as follows:

Interest on the first £30,000 of a pre-9 March 1999 loan to a borrower aged 65 or over to buy a life annuity, the loan being secured on the borrower's home (home income plans — see **34.12**)	23%

Up to £2,670 of qualifying maintenance payments to former or   10%
separated spouse where either spouse was born before 6 April
1935 (see **34.6**)

Venture Capital Trust (VCT) subscriptions up to £200,000 (see   30%
29.26)

Enterprise Investment Scheme (EIS) subscriptions up to £500,000   20%
(see **29.17**)

Amounts invested in Community Development Finance Institu-   5%
tions (CDFIs — see **29.31**), relief being 25% of the investment
spread over five years, giving an annual relief of

The limited tax relief for the over 65s on interest paid on pre-March 1999
home income plans is usually given by deduction of tax before the payment is
made. Maintenance payments, VCT and EIS subscriptions and CDFI investments are paid in full and the tax saving is given by an adjustment in the coding
or self-assessment. The tax saved on such payments cannot exceed the tax
payable on income.

Allowable interest (ITA 2007, ss 383–412)

[2.14] Interest relating to let property is usually deductible from rental
income, saving tax at the top tax rate (see **30.20** and **32.5**). Relief at the top tax
rate is also allowed, the payments being deducted in arriving at the taxable
income, for interest paid on a loan to:

(a)   buy a partnership share, to introduce capital to a partnership or to lend
money to it, providing that the individual is not a limited partner or a
partner in an 'investment' limited liability partnership (i.e. one whose
business consists wholly or mainly of making investments) and providing he is still a partner when the interest is paid (see **20.16** and **23.12**).

(b)   buy shares in or lend money to a trading company controlled either by
its directors or by five or fewer people (known as a close company), so
long as, at the time the interest is paid, either the individual owns more
than 5% of the issued ordinary share capital or he owns any part of the
ordinary share capital, however small, and work for the greater part of
his time in the management or conduct of the company or an associated
company. If he or his spouse has claimed income tax relief or capital
gains deferral relief in respect of shares acquired under the Enterprise
Investment Scheme, he cannot also claim interest relief on a loan to buy
the shares.

(c)   buy plant or machinery, other than cars, vans, motor cycles or bicycles,
for use in the individual's partnership or employment (see **10.15**).

(d)   personal representatives of a deceased person to pay inheritance tax (see
42.4).

(e)   acquire shares in an employee-controlled trading company.

(f)   acquire one or more shares in, or to lend money to, a co-operative.

Relief under (a), (b), (e) and (f) is restricted if the shares are sold or the partnership, close company or co-operative repays all or part of the loan, without the borrowing being reduced by an equivalent amount. Interest is allowable on loans which replace existing qualifying loans. Relief is only available as the interest is paid. It is not spread over the period of accrual and will not be allowed if it is never paid.

Bank overdraft interest is never allowed as a deduction from *total* income. Relief is only available where the overdraft is part of the funding of a trade or property letting and therefore allowable as an expense in arriving at trading or rental profits.

As indicated in **2.13**, relief is available for pre-9 March 1999 home income plan loans to the over 65s, interest on the first £30,000 of such loans qualifying for tax relief at 23% (not the basic rate of 20%). Relief for such interest continues if the individual moves home, or remortgages, or goes into a nursing home (see **34.12**).

There are provisions to block the artificial creation of allowable interest and to prevent tax relief being obtained on interest that would not otherwise qualify for tax relief by means of various devices such as converting the interest into an annuity.

See **2.10** for the treatment of special finance arrangements such as those designed to meet the requirements of Islamic law.

Personal reliefs (ITA 2007, Pt 3)

[2.15] In addition to claiming a deduction for particular payments etc. as indicated above, an individual may reduce his taxable income, or the amount of tax payable as the case may be, by certain personal reliefs, as detailed below. The amounts stated relate to the tax year 2010/11. For the rates of allowance for earlier years, see the Table of Rates and Allowances under 'Personal Reliefs'. Personal reliefs are available only to UK residents and, for years prior to 2010/11, specified categories of non-resident (see **41.27**).

The personal allowance and blind person's allowance are deducted from net income and save tax at the highest tax rate. This is subject to the restriction in the value of the personal allowance for individuals with income over £100,000 (see **2.16**). The married couple's allowance (which applies both to married couples and civil partners where certain conditions are satisfied) saves tax at only 10% and is given by reducing the amount of tax payable (but it cannot create a repayment). For the way in which relief is given under PAYE, see **10.47**.

An individual is not entitled to personal reliefs for any tax year for which he claims the remittance basis (see **41.14**).

Personal allowance (ITA 2007, ss 35–37)

[2.16] The personal allowance depends on age, and is increased if an individual is aged 65 or over at any time in the tax year (subject to an income limit, see **2.19**), the amounts for 2010/11 being as follows:

Under 65	Age 65 to 74	Age 75 and over
£6,475	£9,490	£9,640

However, the amount of the personal allowance otherwise available is reduced where 'adjusted net income' (calculated as in **2.19** for age-related allowances) exceeds £100,000. The reduction will be one half of the excess until the allowance is reduced to nil. See www.hmrc.gov.uk/budget2009/additional-rate-examples.pdf for HMRC examples of the calculations.

The personal allowance for those under 65 is proposed to be increased from 6 April 2011 to £7,475. However, the basic rate limit is also proposed to be reduced so that higher rate taxpayers cannot benefit from the increase (see **2.5**).

Blind person's allowance (ITA 2007, ss 38–40)

[2.17] An allowance of £1,890 for 2010/11 is available to a person who is registered blind (in England and Wales) or is ordinarily resident in Scotland or Northern Ireland and unable because of blindness to do any work for which eyesight is essential. The allowance saves tax at the individual's highest tax rate. A married couple or registered civil partners who are both blind may each claim the allowance. A married blind person or blind civil partner may transfer unused blind person's allowance to the spouse/partner (whether or not the spouse/partner is blind).

Married couple's allowance (ITA 2007, ss 42–55)

[2.18] Married couple's allowance is available to married couples and to civil partners, providing at least one spouse or partner was born before 6 April 1935 (i.e. was 65 before the start of tax year 2000/01). A spouse or partner who was born before 6 April 1935 will be 75 or over by the end of 2009/10, so the allowance will be the amount for those 75 or over, i.e. £6,965. The allowance saves tax at 10%, not at the individual's top rate of tax.

Where a married couple has been entitled to the allowance since before 5 December 2005, the allowance is given to the husband (subject to any claim by his wife — see below). For marriages or civil partnership registrations taking place on or after that date, the allowance is based on the income of, and given to, the spouse or partner with the higher income (subject to a claim by the other spouse or partner).

A couple who were married before 5 December 2005 may elect for the new rules to apply to them instead of the old rules. However, where a wife has the higher income, the effect of the election may be a reduction in the tax saved.

As with the personal allowance, the allowance is restricted if income exceeds a certain limit (see **2.19**).

The married couple's allowance is given in full in the year of divorce, or dissolution of civil partnership, and in the year of separation or death of either spouse/partner. When a spouse/partner dies, the surviving spouse/partner will get the benefit of any part of the allowance that has not been used by the deceased spouse/partner.

A married woman (for pre-5 December 2005 marriages) or lower income spouse/partner (for marriages or civil partnership registrations on or after 5 December 2005) is entitled as of right to claim one half of a specified amount of the married couple's allowance (half of £2,670, i.e. £1,335 for 2010/11). Alternatively the couple may jointly claim for an allowance equal to the whole of the specified amount, i.e. £2,670, to be given to the wife or lower income spouse/partner as the case may be. In either case the allowance available to the other spouse/civil partner is reduced accordingly.

If either spouse or civil partner pays insufficient tax to use the married couple's allowance, he/she may notify HMRC (not later than four years after the end of the relevant tax year) that the unused amount is to be transferred to the other spouse/partner. The unused amount is *not* transferred automatically. Provision for transferring surplus allowances is made in tax returns.

The allowance starts in the year of marriage or registration as civil partners, but in that year the available allowance (after taking into account the income restriction where appropriate) is reduced by one-twelfth for each complete tax month (ending on the 5th) before the date of marriage/registration.

Income limit

[2.19] Both the personal allowance and the age-related personal allowance are reduced by £1 for every £2 by which 'adjusted net income' (i.e. taking account of any allowable reliefs and the gross amount of charitable donations and pension contributions, but before deducting personal and blind person's allowances) exceeds the relevant limit. For the personal allowance the limit is £100,000. For the age-related personal allowance the limit is £22,900. However, the age-related personal allowance cannot fall below the amount the individual would be entitled to if he were aged under 65. This means that for an individual with income of £100,000 or less it cannot fall below £6,475 which is the basic personal allowance for 2010/11. Where the individual's income exceeds £100,000 there is the possibility that the allowance could be reduced to nil as for individuals aged under 65.

For couples married before 5 December 2005, the married couple's allowance is similarly reduced by half of the excess of the husband's total income over £22,900 which has not already been taken into account to reduce his personal allowance, but it cannot fall below a specified minimum amount, which is £2,670 for 2010/11. The wife's income is not taken into account, even if the allowance is given because of her age rather than the husband's, or if the tax saving is transferred to the wife because the husband's income is too low to use it. This treatment does not apply to those marrying or registering as civil partners on or after 5 December 2005. The main person claiming the allowance will be the partner with the higher income, and it will be that person's income that will be taken into account to calculate any reduction in the married couple's allowance.

For examples and detailed information on the tax treatment of people over 65, see CHAPTER 34.

Life assurance relief

[2.20] Life assurance relief is no longer available for contracts made after 13 March 1984 but it continues for policies made on or before that date. The relief is 12½% of qualifying premiums, subject to a limit on allowable premiums of either one-sixth of total income or £1,500, whichever is greater. The relief is deducted when the premium is paid, and may be retained whether you are a taxpayer or not.

There were many restrictions on which policies qualified for relief, and there are anti-avoidance rules under which HMRC recover excess relief. The provisions are dealt with in detail in CHAPTER 40.

Tax relief for life cover for a limited period (term assurance) was available for contributions within a personal pension plan, including those under the new pension scheme provisions introduced from 6 April 2006. This relief was withdrawn following FA 2007, subject to certain transitional provisions (see 40.2).

Calculating tax on taxable income (ITA 2007, Pt 2; IT-TOIA 2005, s 397)

[2.21] As indicated in 2.4, there are different rates of tax payable depending on whether the income is dividend income, other savings income or non-savings income. The main types of income within each of these three categories are as follows.

Non-savings income (possible rates for 2010/11: basic rate 20%, higher rate 40% and additional rate 50%)

[2.22] Income from employment and self-employment

Pensions from the state and from occupational and personal pension schemes

Taxable social security benefits (see 10.5)

Property income

[2.23] The income chargeable at the 'non-savings income' rates includes both interest and dividends from abroad taxable on the 'remittance basis' (applicable to someone who is resident but not ordinarily resident and/or not domiciled in the UK. Such individuals are not taxed on such foreign income unless it is brought into the UK (see 41.14).)

Savings income other than dividends (possible rates: 'starting rate for savings' 10%, basic rate 20%, higher rate 40%, additional rate 50%)

[2.24] Interest arising on bank and building society accounts, government stocks, private loans etc., both in the UK and abroad (other than that charged on the remittance basis as indicated above)

The income element of a purchased life annuity (see **34.9**)

Accrued income charges on the sale/purchase of interest-bearing securities (see **36.19**)

Dividend income (possible rates: dividend ordinary rate 10%, dividend upper rate 32.5% and dividend additional rate 42.5%)

[2.25] UK and foreign dividends (other than that charged on the remittance basis as indicated above).

Taxable income, deductions and allowances

[2.26] The legislation treats savings income as the top slice of the taxable income apart from dividend income (subject to the exceptions mentioned below). An illustration of how this works is in Example 2.

Example 2

In 2010/11 tax will be charged at the rates shown below where a taxpayer's taxable income is as indicated. Dividends are shown inclusive of tax credits, the non-savings income has been reduced by the personal allowance and the additional rate does not apply as the income does not exceed £150,000.

	(a) £		(b) £		(c) £	
Non-savings income	1,000	@ 20%	17,000	@ 20%	23,000	@ 20%
Non-dividend	1,440*	@ 10%	5,000	@ 20%	8,000	@ 20%
savings income	13,560	@ 20%				
	16,000		22,000		31,000	
Dividends	3,000	@ 10%	3,500	@ 10%	6,400 **	@ 10%
					37,400	
Dividends (balance)					600	@ 32½%
Taxable income	19,000		25,500		38,000	

* In (a) the non-dividend savings income is £15,000 and there is £1,440 of the 10% 'starting rate for savings' band of £2,440 (see **2.5**) available to be allocated against that income, giving rise to a tax refund claim if 20% tax has been deducted at source and tax has already been accounted for on the non-savings income.

** Total tax-credit inclusive dividends in (c) are £7,000, of which only £6,400 is within the basic rate band. The balance of £600 is taxable at the dividend upper rate of 32.5% against which there is a 10% tax credit.

There are two instances where savings income is not treated as the top slice of income, namely the receipt of a lump sum taxed under the 'golden handshake' rules (see **15.6**) and a chargeable event gain on a life policy (see **40.5**).

Before applying the different tax rates to income in the order shown in Example 2, however, it is necessary to decide which sources of income have been reduced by deductions and allowances and to what extent. Deductions and allowances can be set against income in the order that saves most tax, which normally means setting them against non-savings income first, then savings income other than dividends, then dividends. If the taxable income remaining after deductions and allowances is less than the tax-credit inclusive dividend income, the dividend tax credit that can be set against tax payable is restricted to 10% of taxable income because the tax credit is not repayable.

Effect of rate charging structure on marginal tax rates

[2.27] The complex rate charging structure means that although the higher rate of tax is 40%, the marginal rate of tax payable if taxable income increases may be higher than that, as illustrated in Example 3.

Example 3

An individual has taxable income in 2010/11 of £37,400 (i.e. equal to the basic rate limit) as follows:

	£
Salary	41,875
Dividends (1,800 + tax credits 200)	2,000
	43,875
Personal allowance	6,475
Taxable income	37,400

Tax payable:				
	Salary	35,400	@ 20%	7,080
	Divi-dends	2,000	@ 10%	200
		37,400		7,280

If his dividends increase by £90, giving a tax credit inclusive amount of £100, an extra £32.50 tax will be payable (of which £10 is covered by the dividend tax credit). If, however, the *salary* increases by £100, the extra salary will be taxed at 20% but £100 of dividends will be taxed at 32.5% instead of 10%, so that the total tax on the extra £100 will be £42.50, giving a marginal tax rate of 42.5%.

If the taxable salary had already been above the basic rate limit, extra salary would cost extra tax of 40% and extra dividends would cost extra tax of 32.5% (of which 10% would be covered by the tax credit).

Looked at from the opposite point of view, the marginal rates of tax illustrated in Example 3 will be *saved* by making a payment qualifying for tax relief (such as a personal pension contribution or a gift aid donation to charity) so that taxable income moves from a point above the basic rate limit to a point below it. Where the taxpayer is entitled to tax credits (see **2.33** onwards) the payment would also reduce income for tax credits purposes, possibly saving a further 39% (see Example 7 in **2.40**).

Losses from miscellaneous transactions (ITA 2007, ss 152–155, 1016; FA 2009, s 69)

[2.28] An individual, or a partnership of which he is a member, may make a claim for loss relief if a loss is sustained in a miscellaneous transaction (i.e. one which falls within ITA 2007, s 1016). The relief may only be given against the amount of any miscellaneous income arising from any other miscellaneous transactions in respect of which he is assessable for the same tax year. Any unrelieved loss is carried forward against miscellaneous income in future years.

Relief must be claimed within four years of the end of the tax year of loss, but a separate claim may be made within the time limit in relation to the question of whether, and if so how much, loss relief should be given. FA 2009 confirmed that the relief does not arise from offshore life insurance policies.

Payment of tax, interest on tax paid late and interest on tax overpaid (TMA 1970, Pts VA and IX, and Sch 3ZA; TA 1988, s 824)

[2.29] As indicated in **2.8**, much of the tax due on income is deducted before the income is received, under the PAYE system for employees and those receiving occupational and personal pensions, and by deduction at source from savings interest. Dividends received are accompanied by a dividend tax credit.

Tax that is not deducted or credited at source in this way is payable to HMRC under the self-assessment system. Interest is charged on tax paid late, and HMRC pays interest on tax overpaid. The rates are adjusted frequently in line with commercial interest rates — for details of recent rates see the TABLE OF RATES AND ALLOWANCES. Interest on unpaid tax is not deductible in calculating the tax liability, and tax is not due on any interest received on overpaid tax.

A claim that results in tax relief being given in relation to an earlier tax year (e.g. because of a claim to carry back a trading loss in a new business — see **25.8**) takes effect by means of an adjustment to the tax liability for the year of claim, so that interest is payable only by reference to the balancing payment date (see **2.12**) for the claim year. For example, where a claim is made in 2010/11 affecting the tax liability of 2007/08, the repayment would be calculated according to the 2007/08 tax position, but interest would be payable only from 31 January 2012. Carry-back claims also have an anomalous effect in relation to payments on account (see **9.6**).

[2.30] If an individual is required to fill in a self-assessment tax return he is also required to work out his tax liability. However, HMRC will do the calculation if a paper return is filed by 31 October after the end of the tax year. If the return is filed online, the calculation is done automatically.

HMRC are able to 'determine' the tax owed if a return is not submitted, but their tax figure will be replaced by the self-assessment when it is received. If HMRC enquire into a return, the taxpayer has the right to appeal against any amendments they make to the figures, and also to apply to postpone payment of any disputed amount until the appeal is settled.

In some circumstances claims are made separately from returns and there is a right to appeal against HMRC amendments to such claims, although not to postpone payment of the tax. There are some limited circumstances where HMRC still issue assessments outside the self-assessment system and tax on such assessments is payable 30 days after the issue of the assessment. Interest on such assessments, however, runs from 31 January following the tax year to which the assessment relates, regardless of when the assessment was issued. Apart from such exceptions, HMRC will not make assessments themselves unless they discover that tax has been underpaid through a taxpayer's omission brought about carelessly or deliberately, or because of inadequate disclosure of information (see **9.35**). See **CHAPTER 9** for detailed information on appeal and postponement procedures, claims made outside returns and HMRC enquiries.

[2.31] Payments on account are payable for the current tax year on 31 January in the tax year and 31 July following the tax year, each payment equal to half the total net income tax and self-employed class 4 national insurance contributions (see **24.6**) payable for the previous tax year *unless* the amount due is less than the limits stated below. The balance of tax due, including capital gains tax if any, should then be paid on the following 31 January, or a refund claimed if tax has been overpaid. At any time before that 31 January date a claim may be made to reduce the payments on account (or get a refund) if the taxpayer thinks the current year's tax will be lower (subject to penalties if the claim has a careless or deliberate inaccuracy). Interest is charged on underpaid payments on account and balancing payments from the due dates, and HMRC pay interest on tax overpaid from the date of the overpayment to the date of repayment.

If a claim is made to reduce payments on account, interest will be charged from the due dates on any shortfall compared with the *lower* of half of the previous year's tax and half the current year's tax (excluding capital gains tax in each case). If the final income tax bill is less than the payments on account (net of any repayments already claimed), HMRC will pay interest on half of the difference from the date each payment on account was made. See Example 4.

Example 4

Assume payments on account are made on the due dates. Total income tax payable directly to HMRC for 2008/09 is £15,000, so that the payments on

---

account for 2009/10 should be £7,500 on each of 31 January 2010 and 31 July 2010. The due date for the final payment/repayment is 31 January 2011. If no claim is made to adjust payments on account, no interest will be charged on them if final tax exceeds £15,000; if final tax is less than £15,000, interest will be allowed on half of the difference from each of the 31 January 2010 and 31 July 2010 payment dates.

Let us suppose that the taxpayer, having made the first 2009/10 payment on account of £7,500 on 31 January 2010, applies to reduce the payments to £6,000 each because he thinks the 2009/10 tax liability will be around £12,000. The overpayment of £1,500 on the first instalment will be refunded with interest from the payment date to the date of repayment. If the final 2009/10 tax liability (excluding any capital gains tax) turns out to be:

(a) £16,000

A balancing payment of £4,000 will be due on 31 January 2011 and interest will be charged from that date if it is paid late.

Interest will in any event be charged on the difference between the payments on account that should (with hindsight) have been paid, i.e. £7,500 each, and the £6,000 actually paid. The interest will therefore be:

On £1,500 re 1st payment on account from 31 January 2010 to 31 January 2011.

On £1,500 re 2nd payment on account from 31 July 2010 to 31 January 2011.

(b) £14,000

The balancing payment due on 31 January 2011 will be £2,000, and the interest charges re each payment on account will be based on £1,000 (since the payments should only have been reduced to £7,000 each instead of the £6,000 which has been paid).

(c) £10,000

The taxpayer would be entitled to a refund of £2,000, with interest on £1,000 from 31 January 2010 and £1,000 from 31 July 2010 to the date of repayment.

A taxpayer does not have to make payments on account if the previous year's income tax bill (excluding tax deducted at source) was below £1,500, or if more than 80% of the tax due was collected at source.

A surcharge is payable if the balancing payment for the year is more than a month late (see **9.11**). Where there is a repayment of tax deducted at source (including over-deductions under PAYE), interest is payable from 31 January following the relevant tax year.

Repayment claims

[2.32] People often overpay tax because, for example, tax has been deducted at source from much of their income and they have not received the full benefit of their personal allowances and/or lower rates of tax, or because they have incurred losses in a business that can be set against income on which tax has been paid. They are entitled to claim repayment of the overpaid amount, although many of those entitled do not put in claims. Repayment claims cannot be made in respect of tax credits on dividends.

Example 5

Income of taxpayer aged 67 in 2009/10 comprises pensions of £8,500 and net bank interest of £1,200. Tax can be reclaimed as follows:

			Tax paid
		£	£
Pensions		8,500	—
Bank interest (net)	1,200		
Tax deducted	300	1,500	300
		10,000	300
Age allowance		9,490	
Taxable income		510	
Tax thereon @ 10% (starting rate for savings, see 2.5)			51
Repayment due			£249

Notes

(i) The taxpayer was not entitled to apply to receive his bank interest in full, because this is only possible for someone who expects to pay no tax at all. Had he received the interest in full he would have owed tax of £51.

(ii) No repayment could have been claimed if the savings income was dividend income.

(iii) If the repayment is made after 31 January 2011, HMRC would pay interest from that date.

If a taxpayer does not receive a tax return, he may use form R40, available at www.hmrc.gov.uk/forms/r40.pdf, to claim repayment. The general time limit for making a repayment claim (i.e. where no specific time limit applies) is four years from the end of the tax year.

Vouchers or certificates of tax deducted do not need to be sent with a claim.

Tax credits (TCA 2002)

[2.33] The main legislation relating to child tax credits and working tax credit is contained in the Tax Credits Act 2002, but most of the detail is contained in statutory instruments. Although tax credits are welfare benefits, they are administered by HMRC and a good deal of guidance is available at www.hmrc.gov.uk/taxcredits. For a summary of the proposed changes for 2011/12 see www.hm-treasury.gov.uk/d/junebudget_press_notice2.pdf. It is estimated that nine out of ten families with children qualify for tax credits.

To qualify, the individual must be aged 16 or over and must normally live in the UK (although some non-residents qualify). For married couples, civil partners, couples living together as husband and wife and co-habiting same-sex couples, a joint claim must be made.

Tax credits are means-tested, so they are progressively withdrawn from claimants with incomes above a stipulated income threshold. The rate of withdrawal where income exceeds the threshold is 39%. It is proposed that this will be increased to 41% from 6 April 2011.

Payments of tax credit are not backdated for more than three months, so claims for 2010/11 should have been made by 5 July 2010.

Credits are normally awarded for a tax year, i.e. the year ending on 5 April. The maximum tax credit entitlement is worked out on a daily basis according to the claimant's circumstances during the year (see **2.36**), and the amount payable is then restricted where appropriate to take account of income.

The amount of the tax credit for a tax year is initially based on the previous year's income. After the end of the tax year, the claim is finalised on the basis of either the previous year's income or the current year's income (i.e. the income for the year of the claim). The previous year's income is used where income has increased by no more than £25,000 (proposed to be reduced to £10,000 from 6 April 2011). The current year's income less £25,000 is used where the current year's income exceeds the previous year's income by more than £25,000, and the current year's income is used if it is less than the previous year's income.

After the end of the tax year HMRC send claimants a renewal notice. For claimants entitled to only the family element of child tax credit (see **2.39**), the award will be automatically renewed and they only have to respond to the renewal notice if their income and/or personal circumstances have changed. Other claimants must confirm or amend the information in the notice by 31 July following the tax year, or the payment of tax credits may stop. As far as income is concerned, where final figures are not available at that date, an estimate must be given, with the final figures being notified by the following 31 January at the latest (i.e. by 31 January 2011 for 2009/10). A penalty may be charged if the declaration is not submitted (see **2.37**). HMRC have published guidance which explains how the tax credit annual review process works and advises the action which should be taken at various times, see www.hmrc.gov.uk/leaflets/tax-credit-renew.pdf.

Definition of income

[2.34] Income for tax credit purposes is defined in the Tax Credits (Definition and Calculation of Income) Regulations 2002 (SI 2002/2006) as amended by later statutory instruments. Where there are joint claimants, the joint income is taken into account. The definition of income equates fairly closely with taxable income, but there are many differences both in the income and the deductions that may be made, and the detailed provisions need to be studied carefully.

Income is reduced by the gross amount of all pension contributions and gift aid donations to charity in the tax year (but there is no provision for carrying contributions and donations back to an earlier year). The first £300 of the total income (or the joint total income for joint claimants) that falls within one or more of five categories is ignored. Those categories are pension income, investment income (which includes chargeable event gains on life policies), property income, foreign income and notional income.

Notional income covers amounts that are specifically included in taxable income, such as premiums on let property and scrip dividends, and also income someone has deliberately deprived himself or herself of, or failed to apply for, or could have received for services he or she provided (other than for voluntary or charitable bodies) cheaply or without charge.

If a trading loss is incurred in the year, it is deducted from the total income of the claimant (or the combined total income where there are joint claimants) for that year. Any balance of loss not relieved against the total income of the current year is carried forward to set against the *trading* income in future years. (Note that losses may be treated differently for income tax, and different rules apply for Class 4 national insurance contributions (see CHAPTER 25)).

Notification of changes in income

[2.35] A claimant is not *required* to notify changes in income levels during the tax year. He is, however, required to notify certain other changes in circumstances (see **2.37**). If he does not notify changes in income, then when he sends in his renewal notice showing the actual amount (see **2.33**) his entitlement for the year will be revised using actual income if it is lower than the previous year's income. Any underpaid tax credits will then be paid to him.

If actual income exceeds the previous year's income by more than £25,000 (proposed to be reduced to £10,000 from 6 April 2011), an overpayment of tax credits may arise. An overpayment is normally recovered from future tax credits or, if that is not possible, by direct payment to HMRC (see HMRC's Code of Practice booklet COP 26).

One point that needs care, however, is that when the renewal notice is submitted showing the income increase, this will usually be several months into the *next following* tax year (see **2.33**). By that time credit will have been overpaid for that *later* year, because until the revised information is received the credit will have been based initially on the income for the last but one year. See Example 6.

Example 6

Income for 2009/10 is £20,000 more than 2008/09 income. The renewal notice is submitted in July 2010 showing this increase. There is no revision of the tax credit award for 2009/10 because of the £25,000 'disregard'. But the 2010/11 award will be revised at this stage — it will be reviewed after 5 April 2011 — to reflect the 2009/10 income. Tax credits will have been overpaid from April to July 2010, because the award will have been based initially on the 2008/09 income.

For self-employed people, the current income (based normally on the profits of the accounting year ended in the tax year — see **21.2**) will not be known early enough to decide whether credits will be available, and as indicated in **2.33**, awards are not backdated for more than three months. The self-employed should therefore make claims at the appropriate time, even though their previous year's income would not give them any entitlement. HMRC will then issue a nil award, which will then be adjusted after the end of the tax year in the light of actual income and any other change in circumstances. HMRC are obliged to permit such 'protective claims'.

Calculation of entitlement

[2.36] The calculation of the amount of tax credit available is relatively straightforward where the claimant's maximum entitlement remains unchanged throughout the tax year. HMRC provide an online calculator to calculate roughly how much tax credit an individual might be entitled to, see www.hmrc.gov.uk/taxcredits/payment-entitlement/entitlement/question-how-much.htm. Where entitlement starts part way through the year, or ends part way through the year, or circumstances change during the year, the year will be split into 'relevant periods', with the maximum available credits for each period being calculated according to the daily amounts for the credits available in the period multiplied by the number of days in each period.

Income, on the other hand, is not looked at according to the amounts arising in the relevant periods. It is calculated over the whole year and then apportioned on a time basis to each of the relevant periods. The relevant income thresholds for withdrawing credits are similarly reduced according to the days in each relevant period. The credits due for each period are then added together to give the total credit award for the year. For simplicity, annual figures are used in the rest of this section.

Changes in circumstances, interest and penalties

[2.37] Certain changes in circumstances may be notified in advance, such as for working tax credit (see **2.38**) where someone expects to start work within seven days, or for child tax credit where a child nearing age 16 is going to continue in non-advanced full-time education (see **2.39**).

The following changes in circumstances *must* be notified within one month after the date of the change, or within one month after becoming aware of the change (except for changes under (f), where this later date does not apply):

(a)   A claimant no longer counts as a single claimant, or is no longer part of a claimant couple.

(b)   One member of a claimant couple goes abroad either permanently or for longer than a specified period.

(c)   Approved childcare costs either cease or decrease by £10 or more a week for more than four consecutive weeks, or there are certain changes involving the childcare provider in particular with regard to their registration or approval.

(d)   A claimant's working hours fall to less than 16 or 30 hours a week as the case may be (see **2.38**).

(e)   A claimant ceases to be responsible for one or more children.

(f)   A child ceases to be a qualifying child (other than by reaching age 20).

(g)   A child dies. Child tax credit continues for eight weeks following the child's death, or until the date the child would have reached age 20 if earlier.

Registration of a same-sex couple as a civil partnership, or entering into an unregistered same-sex partnership, comes within heading (a).

A penalty of up to £300 may be imposed for failure to notify within the time limit.

Other changes in circumstances need not be notified immediately, but if they increase the tax credits payable the increase will not be backdated for more than three months and if they decrease the credits they take effect from the date of the change.

In some circumstances (e.g. following a separation) a claimant may be liable to repay an overpaid amount plus a penalty, while at the same time being entitled to a new claim which cannot strictly be backdated more than three months. HMRC may be prepared to work out the amount the claimant is required to pay using a fully backdated figure for the new claim.

A penalty of up to £300 may also be imposed for failing to provide information or evidence relating to a claim, including failing to send in the year-end renewal notice. If the failure continues, a further penalty of up to £60 a day may be charged.

A penalty of up to £3,000 may be charged for fraudulent or negligent claims.

Interest is chargeable on any unpaid penalties and also on any tax credit overpaid through the claimant's careless or deliberate actions.

Working tax credit

[2.38] Working tax credit (WTC) is available to employees and the self-employed who usually do 16 hours or more paid work a week (the work being expected to last for at least four weeks), and who are aged 16 or over and are either responsible for one or more children or are disabled, or are aged 25 or over and usually work at least 30 hours a week, or are aged 50 or over and have recently been receiving a specified benefit. If both members of a couple satisfy the conditions, there is only one credit and they may decide which of them will receive it. From 6 April 2011 individuals aged 60 or over will qualify for WTC if they work at least 16 hours per week, regardless of whether they have dependent children.

WTC is calculated by adding together the following amounts (from 6 April 2010):

	Maximum annual amount £
Basic element	1,920
Addition for couple or single parent §	1,890
Additional element for those working 30 or more hours a week	790
Additional element for disability*	2,570
Additional element for severe disability*	1,095
Additional element (payable for 12 months only) for those aged 50 or over who have recently received a specified benefit* —	
working 16–29 hours a week	1,320
working 30 or more hours a week	1,965

* Two elements are payable if both claimant and partner satisfy conditions.

§ Not available in addition to 50 plus element unless claimant or partner is *either* working 30 hours or more a week *or* responsible for a child *or* entitled to disability element.

The WTC may be increased by a childcare element for working claimants who pay for childcare, subject to detailed conditions. The claimant must work at least 16 hours a week (or for joint claimants each must work 16 hours a week unless one is incapacitated). The childcare element amounts to 80% of eligible costs up to £175 per week for one child (giving a maximum £140 per week), or up to £300 per week for two or more children (maximum £240 per week). The childcare element is not available after 1 September following the child's 15th birthday (or 16th birthday if the child is blind or disabled). See **10.26** for the interaction of the childcare element of WTC with childcare vouchers provided by the employer.

The WTC is reduced by 39p (proposed to be 41p from 6 April 2011) for every £ of income above an annual income threshold of £6,420 (for both single and joint claims). The non-childcare element of WTC is withdrawn before the childcare element. For those entitled to both WTC and child tax credit (see **2.39**), the same income threshold of £6,420 applies to the child element of child tax credit and the WTC is withdrawn first.

WTC for both employees and the self-employed is paid directly by HMRC (into a bank, building society, NS&I or post office card account), except for the childcare element, which is paid direct to the main carer along with CTC.

Child tax credit

[2.39] Child tax credit (CTC) replaces all the previous child elements within social security payments, except child benefit, which continues to be paid to anyone with eligible children regardless of income. An individual qualifies for CTC if they are responsible for at least one child under 16 or under 20 if still in full-time non-advanced education (or undergoing unpaid work based training). For children not in full-time non-advanced education or unpaid training CTC ends on 1 September after the 16th birthday unless they have ceased full-time education and registered for work or training with the Careers Service, in which case CTC will continue for up to 20 weeks. (Those with children in this position may notify HMRC in advance to ensure there is no interruption in receiving CTC — see **2.37**.)

CTC comprises a family element and a child element. The family element is paid to any family responsible for one or more children, and it is paid at a higher rate (the baby element) if there is a child under the age of one (although it is proposed that this element will be removed from 6 April 2011). The child element is payable for each qualifying child, higher rates applying for children with a disability (the disabled child element). If a child dies, the entitlement for that child ends eight weeks after death, or the date when the child would have reached age 20 if earlier. CTC is payable direct to the main carer — usually the mother.

The maximum amounts of CTC from 6 April 2010 are as follows:

		Maximum annual amount £
Family element (one only):		
Either	Standard amount	545
Or	Baby element for those with child under 1	1,090
Child element (per child):		
Either	Standard amount	2,300
Or	Amount for disabled child	5,015
Or	Amount for severely disabled child	6,110

CTC is withdrawn progressively from claimants on higher incomes. As indicated in **2.38**, for those entitled to both WTC and CTC, the annual income threshold for both WTC and the child element of CTC is £6,420, and WTC is withdrawn first. For those entitled to CTC only, the income threshold for

2010/11 is £16,190. The child element of CTC is withdrawn at the rate of 39p (proposed to be 41p from 6 April 2011) for each £1 of excess income over the threshold.

Once the child element of CTC has been fully withdrawn, there is no further withdrawal of CTC unless annual income exceeds a second income threshold of £50,000 (proposed to be reduced to £40,000 from 6 April 2011). The rate of withdrawal on income in excess of that amount is £1 for each £15 of excess income, i.e. 6.67% (proposed to be increased to 41% from 6 April 2011). But if CTC and/or WTC amounts to £26 or less no award is made. If the amount due exceeds £26 but is less than £2 a week it is paid in a lump sum.

The June 2010 Emergency Budget proposed various changes to CTC and WTC, most of which have been outlined above. In addition it is proposed to increase CTC by £150 above the consumer price index from 6 April 2011.

Conclusion

[2.40] The above summary only scratches the surface of the tax credits provisions, which represent a minefield for everyone involved — taxpayers, non-taxpayers, tax advisers and welfare rights advisers. Example 7 below gives a very basic illustration of some of the principles. Example 8 illustrates the possible combined tax/tax credit effect of making payments, such as pension contributions or gift aid payments, that reduce taxable income.

Example 7

Married couple are both full-time employees and have two children aged 2 and 4. They make childcare payments of £340 a week. Their final entitlement to tax credits for 2010/11 will be as follows, given joint income for 2010/11 (after excluding £300 of their investment income) at the following levels:

(a) £36,000   (b) £56,000

Tax credits maximum amount (worked on annual basis for simplicity):

	£
WTC:	
Basic	1,920
Couple addition	1,890
30 hour element	790
	4,600
Childcare element (max. 80% × £300 × 52)	12,480
	17,080
CTC:	
Child element (2 × 2,300)	4,600
Family element	545

Maximum amount		22,225

	(a)	(b)
	£	£
Maximum credits excluding CTC family element	21,680	21,680
Restrict according to income:		
(36,000 – 6,420 =) 29,580 × 39%	(11,536)	
(56,000 – 6,420 =) 49,580 × 39%		(19,336)
	10,144	2,344
CTC family element	545	545
Tax credits payable to main carer	10,689	2,889

Notes

(i) Credits would initially have been based on 2009/10 income, and adjusted to actual income after the year-end if necessary.

(ii) If circumstances had changed in year, say because one partner became unemployed, the year would be split into separate 'relevant periods' and credits calculated separately according to the days in each period, with income for the year being split pro-rata between the separate periods.

(iii) The income threshold for the CTC family element in this example is £62,010, i.e. the lowest amount of income that would result in the tax credits other than the CTC family element being reduced to nil.

Example 8

The couple in part (b) of Example 7, who had income of £56,000 in 2010/11, lost £19,336 of the maximum tax credits available, i.e. 39% of £49,580. If say the husband had paid a personal pension contribution in the year of £2,000 gross, the tax credit entitlement would have increased by 39% of £2,000, i.e. £780. The payment would also reduce his tax bill by 40% if he were a higher rate taxpayer (or possibly more depending on the mix of his income — see Example 3), so that the 'net of tax' cost of the pension contribution would be around £420.

3

Corporation tax: general principles

Basis of charge (CTA 2009, ss 2–8, 931A–931W)

[3.1] Corporation tax is charged on the profits of companies and of unincorporated bodies that are not partnerships, for example members' clubs (see **3.32**). The term profits includes all sources of income and capital gains. From 1 July 2009 this also includes dividends (UK and overseas), although most will not be taxable (see **3.18**). Before 1 July 2009 profits did not include dividends from UK companies. However, dividends from foreign companies were taxable, subject to relief for foreign tax paid.

Corporation tax is charged on the worldwide profits of UK-resident companies. Non-resident companies carrying on a trade in the UK through a 'permanent establishment' are charged on the income arising from the permanent establishment and on capital gains on the disposal of assets in the UK used for the purposes of the trade or otherwise for the permanent establishment. Double taxation relief is available where profits are taxed twice. Some changes to the basis of taxation of the foreign profits of UK companies and groups came into effect on 1 July 2009. Overseas aspects are dealt with in CHAPTER 41.

Notification of liability (FA 2004, s 55)

[3.2] A company must give written notice to HMRC when it first comes within the charge to corporation tax. The notice must be given not later than three months after the beginning of the accounting period. Similar notice must be given of the beginning of any accounting period that does not immediately follow the end of a previous accounting period. A penalty may be imposed if the notice is not given as required, unless the company had a reasonable excuse for not doing so and complied without reasonable delay after the excuse ceased. The penalties regime is discussed in CHAPTER 9.

Self-assessment (TMA 1970, ss 59D, 59E; FA 1998, s 117 and Sch 18)

[3.3] The corporation tax provisions are broadly the same as those that apply for income tax self-assessment, subject to the following exceptions. Companies are required to self-assess their corporation tax (they do not have the option of asking HMRC to work out the tax (see **9.17**)) and they must pay the amount due within nine months and one day after the end of the accounting period, except for certain large companies which are required to pay their tax by instalments (see **3.22**). They must file a statutory return (CT 600) with supporting accounts and computations within 12 months after the end of the accounting period. Automatic penalties apply for late returns. From 1 April 2011, for any accounting period ending after 31 March 2010, company tax returns must be filed online. As well as this, companies must file accounts and computations in a set format — Inline eXtensible Business Reporting Language (iXBRL).

The detailed provisions on returns, assessments and penalties are in CHAPTER 9. The payment provisions are dealt with at **3.22** and interest on underpaid or overpaid tax is discussed at **3.24**.

Calculation of profits (CTA 2009, Pts 2–10; TCGA 1992, ss 8, 16A)

[3.4] Business profits are calculated in accordance with generally accepted accounting practice (see CHAPTER 20). A company's taxable income is computed using the rules applying to each source of income. The sources are as follows:

(a)   Trading income (see **20.2**)
(b)   Property income (see CHAPTER 32)
(c)   Non-trading profits from loan relationships, and relationships treated as loan relationships (see **3.5**)
(d)   Profits from derivative contracts (see **3.7**)
(e)   Non-trading gains on intangible fixed assets (see **20.31**)
(f)   Intellectual property: Disposals of know-how and sales of patent rights

(g)   Miscellaneous income including estate income of corporate beneficiaries; income from holding an office, distributions from unauthorised unit trusts, sale of foreign dividend coupons, and annual payments and other income not otherwise charged to tax.

Different rules from those for income tax apply to interest paid and received by companies. Interest on underpaid corporation tax is allowable as a deduction from profits and interest on overpaid corporation tax is taxable, and is taken into account under the 'loan relationships' rules (see **3.5**).

Dividends paid by a UK resident company do not reduce the company's taxable profits, because they represent a distribution of profit. Most dividends *received* by a company from both UK resident and non-UK resident companies are in practice exempt from corporation tax (see **3.1**) (unless they are trade receipts of a company other than a general insurance company). The tax treatment of dividends paid and received is dealt with at **3.17**. Special rules apply to certain dividends from authorised investment funds (see **38.26**).

In computing the company's trading profits, capital allowances are deducted as trading expenses, and balancing charges treated as trading income (see **CHAPTER 22**). Expenditure of a revenue nature (see **20.10**) incurred not more than seven years before the trade started is treated as incurred on the first day of trading (see **21.8**).

A company's chargeable gains are broadly computed using capital gains tax principles, but the gains are charged to corporation tax and there is no annual exemption (see **CHAPTER 4**). Furthermore, profits and losses on a company's capital transactions relating to loans, certain derivative contracts and foreign exchange are brought into account in calculating income rather than chargeable gains (see **3.5** and **3.7**). Profits and losses on intangible assets created or acquired on or after 1 April 2002, such as goodwill and intellectual property, are also brought into account in calculating income (see **20.30** to **20.36**). A special 'substantial shareholdings exemption' applies where trading companies dispose of holdings of 10% or more in other trading companies (see **3.31**). In arriving at chargeable gains, allowable capital losses of the current period and unrelieved losses from earlier periods are deducted.

There are a number of anti-avoidance provisions relating to company losses, particularly for companies that are members of a group (see **3.29**, **26.19**, **45.9** and **45.10**). Since 5 December 2005 companies have been specifically denied relief for a loss that arises as a result of arrangements made to secure a tax advantage. This provision was extended from 6 December 2006 to apply to individuals, trustees and personal representatives as well as to companies.

None of the significant changes made to capital gains tax in 1998 and 2008 in relation to taper relief, indexation allowance and share pooling apply to companies.

Treatment of interest paid and received and profits and losses on loans (CTA 2009, Pts 5 and 6; ITA 2007, Pt 15)

[3.5] Special rules apply to a company's 'loan relationships', which covers all loans made both by and to the company, excluding trading transactions for goods and services. Loans to the company include bank overdrafts and loans by the company include holdings of gilt-edged securities and corporate bonds. Gains and losses on building society permanent interest-bearing shares (PIBS, dealt with in **37.6**) are included within the loan relationships rules. Subject to special provisions concerning particular types of security, all UK and foreign interest paid and received by companies is brought into account in calculating profits, normally on an accruals basis (i.e. taking into account amounts in arrear and advance). The accrued income scheme (see **36.19**) does not apply to companies. Interest on underpaid and overpaid corporation tax is taken into account in calculating profits, and it is treated as non-trading interest.

Profits or losses made on loans (whether as borrower or lender) are treated as income or expenses. The amounts are arrived at using 'generally accepted accounting practice' (see **20.2**). Special rules apply where a connected creditor company is resident in, or managed in, a 'non-qualifying' territory. Foreign exchange differences on loan relationships and other monetary debts are dealt with under the loan relationships rules. For brief notes on foreign exchange aspects see **41.63**.

Amounts that relate to the trade are taken into account in arriving at the trading profit or loss. (Interest receivable and profits/losses on loans will not normally relate to the trade, except for financial businesses). As far as non-trading profits, losses, interest paid and interest received are concerned, they are all aggregated and merged with any financial instruments, non-trading debits and credits (see **3.7**). An overall profit is chargeable to corporation tax. If there is an overall loss (a 'non-trading deficit'), relief is available similar to that available for trading losses. For the treatment of company losses in relation to money borrowed or lent, see CHAPTER 26.

Income tax is not deducted from most interest paid and received by companies. Where tax is deducted, it is at the basic rate of 20% (see **3.21**).

There are numerous provisions designed to counter complex avoidance transactions in relation to the loan relationship rules. These provisions are complex, the detail of which is outside the scope of this book.

Alternative finance arrangements (CTA 2009, ss 501–521)

[3.6] There are various finance arrangements, in particular those designed to meet the requirements of Islamic law, that do not involve paying or receiving interest but have a similar effect. Provisions were introduced with effect from 6 April 2005 to equate the tax treatment of such payments and receipts with the treatment of interest, so that they are brought into account for companies under the loan relationships rules. The range of alternative finance arrangements covered by the legislation has been extended by later Finance Acts and further amendments may be made by Treasury Order.

Derivative contracts (CTA 2009, Pt 7)

[3.7] There are separate provisions to deal with profits and losses on 'derivative contracts' (i.e. options and futures). This area is extremely complex and highly technical. It covers a wide range of instruments used by companies for managing interest rate and currency risk. The rules are closely aligned with the loan relationships rules dealt with in **3.5**. Foreign exchange gains and losses on currency contracts are included within the provisions. Profits are charged (and losses allowed) in calculating income, being brought into account either as trading debits and credits or non-trading debits and credits as the case may be. Non-trading debits and credits are brought into account as if they related to loan relationships of the company (see **3.5**). They are accordingly treated as part of an overall non-trading deficit on loan relationships where appropriate (see **26.5**).

Again, as for loan relationships there are detailed anti-avoidance provisions which are outside the scope of this book.

Qualifying charitable donations (ITA 2007, Pt 15; CTA 2010, Pt 6)

[3.8] Having arrived at the company's total profits (both income and capital), qualifying charitable donations (referred to as charges on income prior to the rewrite to CTA 2010) are deducted to arrive at the profits chargeable to corporation tax. For details of what constitutes a qualifying charitable donation see **CHAPTER 43**. The amount deducted from profits is the amount of the qualifying charitable donations paid in the accounting period.

If the qualifying charitable donations exceed profits, no relief is available unless the company is one of a group of companies, in which case group relief may be available (see **26.16**).

Periods of account and chargeable accounting periods (CTA 2009, ss 9–12, 52)

[3.9] A company's taxable profits are computed for a chargeable accounting period, which normally means the period for which the company's accounts are made up, no matter how short it is. If, however, a company makes up an account for a period greater than 12 months, it is split into one or more chargeable accounting periods of 12 months plus a chargeable accounting period covering the remainder of the period of account.

In arriving at the split of profits for an account exceeding 12 months, the trading profit is usually split on a time basis. Capital allowances (see **CHAPTER 22**) are calculated for each chargeable accounting period, so that if for example an account was made up for the fifteen months from 1 July 2009 to 30 September 2010 and plant was bought in August 2010, the first allowance for the new plant would be given against the profit of the three months to 30 September 2010.

Interest received or paid that relates to the trade is taken into account in arriving at the trading profit of the period of account, and is normally time apportioned in the same way as the trading profit. Non-trading interest is also time apportioned. Rental income is calculated in the same way as trading profits, so that it is split on a time basis (see **CHAPTER 32** and also **CHAPTER 41** for overseas aspects of rental income). If there are any other sources of income they are allocated to the chargeable accounting period in which they arise.

Chargeable gains are similarly allocated to the chargeable accounting period in which the disposal occurs, and qualifying charitable donations (see **3.8**) to the chargeable accounting period in which they are paid.

If a company ceases to trade, the date of cessation marks the end of a chargeable accounting period even if the period of account continues to the normal accounting date. The commencement of winding-up also marks the end of a chargeable accounting period, accounting periods then running for successive periods of 12 months until the winding-up is completed. These rules are varied in some circumstances for companies in administration. If a company enters administration, an accounting period will end immediately before that date. An accounting period will also end when the period of administration ends. If immediately before a company enters administration it is in the course of being wound up, the normal rule about accounting periods running for successive 12-month periods during the winding up will not apply. See **3.25**.

Losses (CTA 2010 ss 37–47; CTA 2009, ss 456–463; FA 2009, s 23 and Sch 6)

[3.10] When a company incurs a trading loss, it may set the loss against any other profits of the same accounting period, both income and capital, and then, if it wishes, carry any balance back against the total profits of the previous 12 months so long as the trade was carried on in that year. However, the carry back period is extended to the previous three years in respect of a limited amount of loss incurred in accounting periods ending after 23 November 2008 and before 24 November 2010. A three year carry back is also available if the loss occurs in the last 12 months of trading.

The loss set-off is proportionately restricted to exclude profits of an accounting period falling partly outside the one year or three year carry-back period. For a continuing trade, any balance of loss remaining (or the whole loss if the company does not wish to claim the current set-off and carry-back) is carried forward to set against later profits of that trade. These loss reliefs are not available for trades carried on *wholly* abroad.

Where a non-trading deficit arises under the loan relationships rules (see **3.5**), the relief available is similar to that for trading losses.

Capital losses are set against capital gains of the same chargeable accounting period (or in certain circumstances relieved intra-group, see **4.33**), any excess being carried forward to set against future gains. Capital losses cannot be carried back.

For detailed notes on trading losses and non-trading deficits, including transferring loss reliefs within groups, see **CHAPTER 26**. The treatment of losses on UK rented property is dealt with in **CHAPTER 32**. For foreign property letting businesses and losses on trades carried on wholly abroad see **CHAPTER 41**. Capital losses are dealt with in **CHAPTER 4** and in context in other chapters.

Rates of tax (CTA 2009, ss 7, 8)

[3.11] Corporation tax rates are fixed for financial years ending 31 March. Financial years are identified by the calendar year in which they commence, so the financial year 2010 is the year to 31 March 2011. Where the tax rate changes during a company's chargeable accounting period, the total profits are apportioned on a time basis (in days) and charged at the respective rates in calculating the corporation tax payable for the period. For details of the corporation tax rates in recent years, see the TABLE OF RATES AND ALLOWANCES.

Main rate (FA 2008, s 6; FA 2009, s 7; FA 2010 s 2; F(No.2)A 2010, s 1)

[3.12] The main rate of corporation tax is currently 28% (except for 'ring fence' profits from oil activities which is 30%). Each Finance Act fixes the main rate for the next following financial year because certain large companies have to pay corporation tax by instalments in advance (see **3.22**). The main rate for financial year 2011 has been set at 27% and it was announced in the June 2010 Emergency Budget that there will be further reductions to 24% by 1 April 2014. The main rate for 'ring fence' profits from oil activities is to remain at 30%.

Small profits rate (CTA 2010, Pt 3; FA 2008, s 7; FA 2009, s 8 and Sch 14; FA 2010 s 3)

[3.13] A lower, small profits rate of corporation tax (referred to as the small companies' rate prior to the rewrite to CTA 2010) is payable where a company's profits are below £300,000. (Note the small profits rate does not apply to close investment-holding companies, whose profits are always charged at the full rate (see **3.26**)).

The small profits rate is, for financial year 2010, 21% (19% on 'ring fence' profits from oil activities), having been at this level since 1 April 2008. It was announced at the June 2010 Emergency Budget that this will be reduced to 20% from 1 April 2011, although the rate for 'ring fence' profits from oil activities is to remain at 19%.

There is a special definition of profits for the small profits rate. It includes not only the profits chargeable to corporation tax but also dividends received from other UK resident and non-UK resident companies plus their related tax credits (the dividends plus the credits being called 'franked investment income'). The tax credit is at the rate of 1/9th of the cash dividend, so that a cash dividend of £900 carries a tax credit of £100 and thus represents franked investment income of £1,000. The inclusion of franked investment income in the calculations means that it is not possible for a company with a large amount of income in that form to obtain the benefit of the small profits rate on only a small amount of profits chargeable to corporation tax.

[3.14] Where a company's profits fall between £300,000 and £1,500,000, marginal relief ensures that the corporation tax rate on the profits is gradually increased to the full 28% level.

The marginal relief is given by calculating tax on the profits chargeable to corporation tax at the full corporation tax rate and reducing it by an amount arrived at by the following formula:

$$F \times (U-A) \times \frac{N}{A}$$

where F = The standard fraction (i.e. the marginal relief fraction set by Parliament)

U = Upper limit

A = Profits as defined for small profits rate purposes, i.e. income and gains chargeable to corporation tax plus franked investment income

N = taxable total profits, i.e. income and gains chargeable to corporation tax

The current upper limit is £1,500,000 and the marginal relief fraction is $^7/_{400}$. For historical details see 'Corporation tax rates' in the TABLE OF RATES AND ALLOWANCES.

The marginal relief ensures that the corporation tax rate on the profits is gradually increased to the full 28% level, but the effect is that profits lying between the lower and upper limits suffer a tax rate in excess of the full rate (currently this is 29.75%). This is the marginal rate where there is no franked investment income — where there is such income the marginal rate works out to a lower percentage.

Example 1

A company with no franked investment income has profits chargeable to corporation tax in financial year 2010 (the year to 31 March 2011) of either (i) £300,000, or (ii) £310,000.

The tax position is as follows:

		£
(i) £300,000 @ 21%		63,000
(ii) £310,000 @ 28%	86,800	
Marginal relief		
$(\frac{7}{400} \times (1,500,000 - 310,000) \times \frac{310,000}{310,000}$	20,825	65,975
Additional corporation tax on extra £10,000 profits (29.75%)		2,975

To the extent that a company is able to reduce its profits within the marginal rate band, it can thus save tax at the higher marginal rate.

The £300,000 and £1,500,000 limits are annual limits and they are scaled down proportionately if an accounting period is less than 12 months. They are also scaled down where for any part of a chargeable accounting period a company has associated companies. Associated companies include both companies that are associated through being members of the same group and companies controlled by the same persons. If, for example, there are five associated companies, the present limits for each company are £60,000 and £300,000. If four companies have profits of £70,000 and one £20,000 the small profits rate will only apply to the last one, and the others will have profits subject to the marginal relief. On the other hand if, say, there were two companies associated with each other and one's profits were £1,800,000 and the other's £150,000, the company with £150,000 profits would qualify for the small profits rate even though the combined profits greatly exceeded the upper maximum.

If a company's accounting period does not end on 31 March and there is a change either in the marginal relief fraction or in the marginal relief limits or both (as there was from 1 April 2008), the profit figures have to be apportioned to apply the respective figures for the different financial years.

Example 2

Say a company with no franked investment income had profits chargeable to corporation tax in the year to 31 December 2008 of either (i) £300,000, or (ii) £310,000. The tax position is as follows:

(i) *3 months to 31 March 2008*   £

$$300,000 \times \frac{3}{12} =$$ 75,000 @ 20%   15,000

9 months to 31 December 2008

$$300,000 \times \frac{9}{12} =$$ 225,000 @ 21%   47,250

                                                                                                        ──────
                                                                                                        62,250

(ii) 3 months to 31 March 2008

$$310,000 \times \frac{3}{12} =$$ 77,500 @ 30%   23,250

Marginal relief:

$$\frac{1}{40} \times (1,500,000 - 310,000) \times \frac{310,000}{310,000} \times \frac{3}{12}$$ 7,438   15,812

---

9 months to 31 December
2008

$$310,000 \times \frac{9}{12} = \qquad 232,500 \ @ \ 28\% \qquad 65,100$$

Marginal relief:

$$\frac{7}{400} \times (1,500,000 - 310,000) \times \frac{310,000}{310,000} \times \frac{9}{12} \qquad 15,619 \quad 49,481$$

65,293

Additional corporation tax on extra £10,000 (65,293 – 62,250)   £3,043

For accounting periods ending on or after 1 April 2010 (for corporation tax purposes) and for tax years 2010–11 onwards (for income tax purposes) there is no need to make a formal claim for the small profits rate or marginal relief. For earlier periods both had to be specifically claimed in the self–assessment return.

Bank payroll tax (FA 2010, s 22 and Sch 1)

[3.15] Bank payroll tax (BPT) was introduced by FA 2010 and charges tax at 50% on all bonuses in excess of £25,000 paid by UK resident banks or building societies to employees during the chargeable period beginning at 12.30 pm on 9 December 2009 and ending on 5 April 2010. The tax does not apply to regular salary, wages or benefits or any shares awarded/granted under an approved SIP or SAYE scheme.

The companies to which the tax applies are detailed in the legislation, but essentially it will apply to UK resident banks and building societies; foreign banks and building societies trading in the UK through a permanent establishment; and companies that are members of banking groups where they are either UK resident investment companies, UK resident financial trading companies or relevant foreign financial trading companies.

It must be stressed that BPT has no effect on the employee receiving the bonus, who is taxed in the normal way on the income he/she receives. However as BPT is not deductible against corporation tax, the real cost is the 50% BPT, plus 28% corporation tax on the amount of the tax — at least where the institution is profitable. For details as to when BPT must be paid see **3.23**.

Bank levy

[3.16] It was announced in the June 2010 Emergency Budget that a levy based on banks' balance sheets will be introduced from 1 January 2011. This is intended 'to encourage banks to move to less risky funding profiles'. The final details of the levy will be published later this year, following consultation. It is proposed that it will be set at a rate of 0.07%, with a lower initial rate of 0.04% in 2011.

Dividends and other distributions (FA 1998, ss 31, 32)

[3.17] From 1973 to 5 April 1999, companies had to pay some of their corporation tax in advance when they paid dividends. Advance corporation tax (ACT) was abolished with effect from 6 April 1999, but companies with profits above the upper limit for the small profits rate are now required to pay their corporation tax by quarterly instalments (see **3.22**).

Many companies were not able to offset all the ACT they had paid against their tax bills, giving rise to surplus (unrelieved) ACT at 5 April 1999. They still have the right to offset any remaining surplus ACT even though ACT has been abolished, but only under the provisions of a shadow ACT system, which will still leave many companies with large unrecovered amounts. The detailed provisions of the shadow ACT system are dealt with in earlier editions of this book.

Corporate recipients (CTA 2010, ss 931A–931W, 1109)

[3.18] Distributions paid by a UK or overseas company are chargeable to corporation tax on the recipient unless the distribution is exempt. Although the detail of the provisions are complex, in practice most distributions will fall to be exempt. Where an exempt qualifying (**3.20**) distribution is paid to a UK resident company the recipient is entitled to a tax credit equal to 1/9th of the dividend (representing 10% of the tax credit inclusive dividend) which is not repayable to *any* taxpayer. The distribution, together with the tax credit, is franked investment income in the hands of the UK-resident recipient company and will be taken into account when calculating the corporation tax liability of the company (**3.14**).

Non-corporate recipients (ITTOIA 2005, ss 383–385, 397–397C; ITA 2007, s 8)

[3.19] As for corporate recipients, distributions to non-corporate recipients also carry a tax credit equal to 1/9th of the dividend (representing 10% of the tax credit inclusive dividend) which is not repayable to *any* taxpayer. The shareholder is liable, where appropriate, to the excess of the dividend additional rate (42.5%) or upper rate (32.5%) over the dividend ordinary rate of 10%. The dividend additional rate applies to distributions otherwise taxable at the 50% additional rate of tax. The dividend upper rate applies to distributions otherwise taxable at the 40% higher rate of tax. See **2.5**.

Qualifying and non-qualifying distributions (CTA 2010, ss 1101, 1136; ITTOIA 2005, ss 399–401)

[3.20] The legislation distinguishes between 'qualifying distributions' and 'non-qualifying distributions'. Non-qualifying distributions are broadly those that confer a future rather than a current claim on the company's assets, such as a bonus issue of redeemable shares (with qualifying distributions being chargeable distributions that are not non-qualifying distributions).

When the non-qualifying distribution shares are redeemed, the redemption is a qualifying distribution, but any tax paid by the shareholder on the non-qualifying distribution may be set against any tax due from him on the later qualifying distribution.

The company is required to notify HMRC within fourteen days after the end of the quarter in which the non-qualifying distribution is made.

Where a company supplies goods or services to a shareholder for more than cost but at a price concession, this is not treated as a distribution because there is no cost to the company, as distinct from a reduction in profit margins, so that no part of the company profits has been distributed.

Deduction of income tax from patent royalties, interest, etc (ITA 2007, Pt 15)

[3.21] Companies do not have to deduct tax from interest or patent royalties (or from annuities or other annual payments, although such payments are rare) if they reasonably believe that the recipient is a company liable to corporation tax on the amount received, a local authority, or a body exempt from tax (such as a charity, pension fund or an ISA fund manager). These provisions enabling payments to be made gross also apply (subject to various conditions) to payments of interest, patent royalties etc to companies of another EU state, or a permanent establishment in an EU state of such a company.

If it turns out that tax should have been deducted, the payer is liable to pay the tax plus interest, but no penalty will be charged unless it should have been clear to the payer that it should have deducted tax. Tax must still be deducted from payments of interest, patent royalties etc by companies and local authorities that do not come within the above provisions, unless covered by a specific exception.

As far as payments to individuals are concerned, tax is not deducted from interest on 'quoted Eurobonds', which are interest-bearing securities issued by a company (or unincorporated association such as a building society) and listed on a recognised stock exchange. Nor is tax deducted from bank and building society interest paid to those who have certified that they are non-taxpayers (see **37.4**). Tax at 20% (i.e. at the basic rate) is deducted from other interest paid to individuals, and tax at the basic rate is deducted from patent royalty payments to individuals. Similarly, where a company *receives* patent royalties from an individual, they will be received net of 20% tax. Interest received from individuals will usually be received gross.

Where companies are required to deduct income tax from payments made, they have to account to HMRC for the tax deducted. Any income tax deducted from a company's income may be offset against the tax deducted on the company's payments if any. Where income tax suffered on a company's income is not recovered in this way, it will be set against the company's corporation tax liability, or if that is insufficient it will be repaid.

Tax payable is accounted for at the appropriate rate on form CT 61. Returns are made to 31 March, 30 June, 30 September and 31 December, the tax being due within 14 days after the quarter ends. Where a company's accounting year does not end on one of the four calendar quarter days the company has five return periods, the first running from the first day of the account to the next calendar quarter day and the last ending at the end of the accounting period.

Date of payment of corporation tax (TMA 1970, ss 59D, 59DA and 59E, 98; SI 1998/3175 as amended)

[3.22] Companies are required to self-assess their corporation tax, as indicated in **3.3**. Companies with profits at or above the upper limit for small profits relief, i.e. £1.5 million (reduced pro rata where there are associated companies and for accounting periods of less than 12 months — see **3.14**), are required to pay their corporation tax by equal quarterly instalments (see below). Companies not required to pay by instalments are due to pay their corporation tax nine months and one day after the end of the accounting period. They must, however, account on a quarterly basis for any income tax they have deducted from interest payments etc as indicated in **3.21**.

Example 3

A company pays interest to and receives interest from other companies and pays patent royalties to an individual. The company's results for the year to 31 March 2011 are:

		£
Trading profits, net of allowable expenses other than interest and patent royalties (see below)		311,000
Rental income, net of allowable expenses		14,000
Interest received:	June 2010	15,000
	December 2010	15,000
Chargeable gains		104,000
Patent royalties paid (gross amount):	May 2010	20,000
	November 2010	28,000
Loan interest relating to the trade, paid February 2011		10,000

Interest received and interest receivable are the same amounts. The interest payable for the year exceeds the interest paid during the year by £3,000. Patent royalties paid in the year exceed patent royalties payable by £2,000.

The company paid a dividend of £100,000 in December 2010.

There were no amounts brought forward from earlier years.

Corporation tax computation for year to 31 March 2011	£
Trading profits, net of £13,000 interest and £46,000 patent royalties payable	252,000
Interest received	30,000
Rental income	14,000
Chargeable gains	104,000
Profits chargeable to corporation tax	400,000
Corporation tax on £400,000 @ 28%	112,000
Less marginal relief for small profits rate $(1,500,000 - 400,000) \times {}^7/_{400}$	19,250
	92,750
Corporation tax payable	92,750

Income tax is accounted for as follows:

CT 61 return for quarter to 30 June 2010	
Income tax deducted from patent royalties paid May 2010: 20,000 @ 20%	4,000
Income tax payable by 14 July 2010	4,000
CT 61 return for quarter to 31 December 2010	
Income tax deducted from patent royalties paid November 2010: 28,000 @ 20%	5,600
Payable by 14 January 2011	5,600
Corporation tax payment	
Corporation tax as shown above payable 1 January 2012	92,750

No tax was deducted from the interest paid to and received from other companies. There were no taxed payments or taxed income in the quarters to 30 September 2010 and 31 March 2011, so CT 61 returns were not required for those quarters. The payment of the dividend does not affect the computation.

At any time before the corporation tax liability is finally determined, companies may claim repayments if they consider they have overpaid tax, but interest will be charged from the normal due date on any tax finally found to be due (or allowed on overpayments) — see **3.24**.

The instalment paying provisions for companies with profits above the small profits rate upper limit affect only around 20,000 out of some 700,000 corporation tax-paying companies. The detailed provisions are in regulations, and companies are liable to penalties if they fail to provide, or provide incorrect, information, records, etc.

The first instalment is due 14 days after the end of the sixth month of the accounting period and the remaining three instalments at quarterly intervals thereafter. The instalments are based on the company's estimated corporation tax liability for the accounting period (including, where appropriate, amounts payable under the provisions relating to loans to directors (see **12.13** to **12.15**) and under the controlled foreign companies rules (see **45.15**)). Companies can recover quarterly payments if they decide they should not have been paid.

If a company's profits are below the small profits rate upper limit in one year, they will not have to make quarterly payments in the following year if their profits in that year do not exceed £10 million (reduced pro rata where there are associated companies). A company with profits chargeable to corporation tax of less than £10,000 is not required to make quarterly payments, even though its profits exceed the marginal relief limits because of the number of its associated companies or because of its dividend income.

Groups of companies may pay their corporation tax on a group-wide basis, without needing to allocate instalments paid to particular companies until the respective liabilities are formalised.

Bank Payroll Tax (FA 2010, s 22 and Sch 1)

[3.23] Companies that are liable to bank payroll tax (BPT) (see **3.15**) must pay it on or before 31 August 2010. A bank payroll return (whether or not BPT applies) must be delivered to HMRC on or before 31 August 2010 self-assessing any BPT due. If a return is filed without a self-assessment, HMRC may make the assessment on the company's behalf, based on the information in the return. If no return is filed, HMRC may determine to the best of their knowledge and belief the amount of BPT due. Penalties apply to late filed returns (see **9.49**) or incorrect returns (see **9.44**). Interest (see **9.42A**) and penalties (see **9.50**) apply to late paid BPT .

Interest on overdue and overpaid tax (TMA 1970, ss 87A, 90; TA 1988, ss 826, 826A; FA 1989, s 178)

[3.24] Interest is charged on overdue corporation tax and allowed on overpaid corporation tax. The latest rates of interest are shown in the TABLE OF RATES AND ALLOWANCES. The interest is brought into account as non-trading interest under the 'loan relationships' provisions (see **3.5**) in computing profits chargeable to corporation tax, subject to what is said at **3.25** concerning companies in liquidation or administration.

The fact that interest is taken into account in calculating profits is reflected in the formula for determining interest rates. For companies required to make quarterly payments, however, a different formula is used in order to reduce the differential between the two rates during the period from the first instalment date (14 days after the end of the sixth month of the accounting period) to the date nine months and one day after the end of the accounting period, after which the normal rates apply. This is intended to avoid penalising companies who make mistakes in their estimates. For companies not required to pay tax by instalments, interest on overdue tax runs from the normal due date of nine months and one day after the end of the accounting period, and interest on overpaid tax runs from the payment date. If, however, tax is paid early, repayment interest is not payable from any earlier date than the first instalment date for instalment paying companies, the interest rate from that date to the normal nine months due date being the same as for instalment paying companies.

If a company makes quarterly payments in the mistaken belief that its profits will exceed the upper small profits rate limit, it will be entitled to interest on the overpayment from the payment date. Where a company is entitled to a refund of income tax suffered on its taxed income (see **3.21**), interest will be paid on the refund from the day after the end of the accounting period.

A company that pays its instalments late may be liable to a penalty not exceeding twice the amount of interest payable, but this penalty is unlikely to be imposed other than in exceptional circumstances.

If a company is late paying the income tax due under the CT 61 quarterly accounting procedure (see **3.21**), interest is charged from the due date for the quarterly return until the payment date. If any of the tax becomes repayable in a subsequent return period, some of the interest already charged is repaid, but only from the date the later return is due or, if earlier, from the date the later return is actually filed.

Liquidation and administration (CTA 2010, ss 626–633; CTA 2009, ss 9–12)

[3.25] A company liquidation is usually preceded by a cessation of trade. The cessation of trade triggers the end of a chargeable accounting period, and a chargeable accounting period also ends at the commencement of winding-up (and at 12-monthly intervals until the winding-up is completed, subject to what is said below about companies in administration). Self-assessment returns must be completed accordingly. To help liquidators who want to finalise matters before formal completion of the winding-up, HMRC will accept an informal return, such as a letter, and will also, where appropriate, provide a clearance that they will not open an enquiry into the return. See also tax point at **28.13** re HMRC concession C16 on the use of the 'defunct company' procedure as an alternative to a formal liquidation.

The above rules are varied if a company goes into administration. An accounting period will end immediately before the commencement of the administration and also at the date the company comes out of administration. Unlike the rule for companies in liquidation (see above), there is no requirement for accounting periods to run for 12 months during the administration period and the normal accounting date may be retained. Under the insolvency procedures, certain creditors or the liquidator of a company that is in the process of winding-up may apply to the court for an administration order instead. If the order is granted the winding-up order will be discharged and the rule that accounting periods must end at 12-monthly intervals until the winding-up is completed will cease to apply.

Under self-assessment, interest on underpaid and overpaid tax is taken into account in calculating taxable profits (see **3.24**). If interest on overpaid tax is received or receivable by a company in liquidation in its final accounting period, however, the interest will not be included in taxable profits if it does not exceed £2,000. The same provisions apply in respect of the final accounting period where a company is in administration if the company moves from administration to dissolution.

Problems can arise when a company that has been making trading losses realises chargeable gains on the sale of its assets, because if the gains are realised after the trade ceases there will be no current trading losses to offset them, but it is not possible to part with the assets until the trade has ceased. This problem can be avoided if an unconditional contract for sale of the assets takes place before ceasing to trade, with completion taking place subsequently. The contract date is the relevant disposal date for capital gains purposes, and any trading losses occurring in the accounting period in which the trade ceases will then be available to reduce the gains. The gains cannot, however, be reduced by trading losses brought forward (see CHAPTER 26 for the detailed provisions on company losses).

Close companies (CTA 2010 ss 34, 438–465)

[3.26] A close company is a company under the control of five or fewer participators (which broadly means shareholders, although it is defined more widely), or under the control of its directors. In considering what rights an individual has in a company, the rights of his 'associates' are included, which covers close family, spouses, civil partners, business partners and the trustees of any family settlements.

As well as being subject to the normal corporation tax rules, close companies are subject to additional requirements.

Benefits in kind to participators are treated as distributions (except where already treated as earnings under the benefits rules, see CHAPTER 10) and loans to participators attract a tax liability. These provisions are dealt with in CHAPTER 12.

If the company is a 'close investment-holding company', tax is charged at the full rate of corporation tax (currently 28%) rather than at the lower small profits rate, whatever the level of the company's profits. A company is not a close investment-holding company if it is a trading company (including companies that deal in land, shares or securities) or a member of a trading group, or if it carries on the business of property investment on a commercial basis.

Close company liquidations

[3.27] Where a close trading company ceases to trade and goes into liquidation, it will not be treated as a close investment-holding company for the accounting period beginning at the commencement of winding-up, providing it was within the definition of a close trading company for the previous accounting period. This provision will strictly only be of use when there is no gap between ceasing to trade and commencing winding-up, thus preventing that gap being treated as a separate accounting period (see **3.25**). HMRC may, however, ignore the strict rule if a company could not avoid a short gap and would suffer significantly if the rule were applied (see HMRC's Company Taxation Manual CTM 60780). Otherwise the full corporation tax rate will apply to the period in which the winding-up commences as well as to later chargeable accounting periods during the winding-up process.

Groups of companies (CTA 2010, ss 97–188, 973–980; TCGA 1992, ss 170–175, 179–181, 190 and Schs 7A, 7AA, 7AB; FA 1998, Sch 18 paras 66–77A; CTA 2009, s 457; TIOPA 2010, ss 260–353)

[3.28] The Taxes Acts do not treat a group of companies as one taxable entity. The corporation tax position of each company in the group is computed independently (small profits rate and various other limits being scaled down according to the number of associated companies). There are, however, various provisions as indicated below that recognise the group structure and give special treatment in the appropriate circumstances. It is also provided under the self-assessment regime that if group companies are required to pay their tax in instalments, the tax may be paid on a group-wide basis (see **3.22**). See **6.25** for stamp duty provisions relating to groups.

The group provisions are not restricted to UK resident companies. Groups and consortia may be established through non-resident companies, enabling the benefit of the provisions to be claimed providing the companies concerned are within the charge to UK corporation tax. As a corollary, tax payable by a non-resident company may be recovered from another group company. See **41.58** for special provisions applicable when companies operating in different European Union member states merge to form 'European Companies' (SEs) or 'European Cooperative Societies' (SCEs).

Parent company and its 75% subsidiaries

[3.29] The following issues are important when considering the tax treatment of a company and its 75% subsidiaries:

(a)   Trading losses (and UK property business losses and qualifying charitable donations in excess of other profits) can be surrendered to other group members for use against total profits (including capital gains) of the corresponding accounting period. The same applies to an excess of non-trading losses/payments on loans over non-trading income on loans. (Trading interest paid and losses on trade loans are treated as trading expenses and thus form part of a trading loss). These 'group relief' provisions are dealt with in CHAPTER 26.

(b)   For capital gains purposes, assets transferred from one group company to another are treated as transferred on a no gain/no loss basis.

Where a chargeable gain or allowable loss accrues to one group company it can elect to transfer part or all of that gain or loss to another group member. This election (which must be made by both companies concerned) can only be made at a time when both companies are members of the same group, and a disposal of the asset between them would otherwise be on a no gain/no loss basis. Special rules apply where the transferee company is an insurance company.

(c)   A chargeable gain made by one group company on a business asset qualifying for rollover relief may be rolled over or held over against an acquisition by another group company. Rollover relief is dealt with in CHAPTER 4.

(d)   For accounting periods beginning on or after 1 January 2010, the tax deduction for finance expenses, (such as payments of interest), of groups of companies with either a UK or foreign parent may be restricted. The restriction applies to UK companies of 'large worldwide groups' where certain conditions are met. Where the restriction applies the aggregate UK tax deduction for the UK members of a group of companies that have net finance expenses will be limited to the consolidated gross finance expense of that group.

The group provisions have frequently been manipulated in order to make tax savings over and above that intended by the legislation, and there are numerous anti-avoidance provisions. These include provisions denying group relief for losses where there are 'arrangements' under which some or all of a company's shares could be disposed of to another party (see **26.19**), provisions preventing groups reducing their capital gains liability by acquiring companies with capital losses or by bringing companies with capital gains into a group that has unrelieved capital losses (see **45.10**). There are also anti-avoidance provisions deeming a gain to arise where a company leaves a group within six years after acquiring an asset intra-group on a no gain/no loss basis (known as the degrouping charge). All or part of the gain (or loss, if the event triggers a loss) may, however, be reallocated to one or more companies in the same group. A company that is chargeable in respect of a degrouping gain may defer the charge by claiming capital gains rollover relief (see **29.11**) if the asset on which the charge arises is within the allowable rollover relief categories and replacement assets have been acquired within the appropriate period. Degrouping charges also apply under the intangible fixed assets provisions (see **20.35**) and the same provisions apply to enable the charge to be rolled over or reallocated within the group.

Transfer pricing (TIOPA 2010, ss 146–230)

[3.30] To prevent groups reducing their taxable profits by having a high level of debt to equity, the transfer pricing provisions require non-arm's length interest payments between connected companies to be treated as distributions and therefore not deductible in arriving at profits. Similarly, the transfer pricing rules require prices between non-arm's length companies to be adjusted to an arm's length price. The rules apply not only to transactions between UK and overseas companies but also between UK companies. There are exemptions for most small and medium-sized companies. The provisions are covered briefly in **45.19**.

Disposals of substantial shareholdings (TCGA 1992, s 192A and Sch 7AC)

[3.31] Where a trading company (operating independently or as part of a trading group) disposes of all or part of a substantial shareholding in another trading company (or holding company of a trading group), any gain on the disposal is exempt from tax (and any loss is not an allowable loss). The exemption applies to qualifying holdings in overseas companies as well as UK companies. 'Substantial' means the company disposing of the shares must have owned 10% or more of the ordinary shares in the other company (and be entitled to 10% or more of the company's profits available for distribution and of its assets on a winding-up) throughout a period of at least 12 months in the two years before the sale. There are provisions to aggregate the shares held by companies and their 51% subsidiaries. HMRC gave detailed comments on their understanding of the meaning of 'trading company' and 'trading group' in their December 2002 Tax Bulletin. The exemption is subject to anti-avoidance provisions, and HMRC issued Statement of Practice 5/02 in this connection. Detailed guidance is provided in HMRC's Capital Gains Manual at CG 53100.

Members' clubs

[3.32] As stated at **3.1**, the profits of members' clubs are chargeable to corporation tax. This does not apply to clubs that are registered as community amateur sports clubs, which are treated in a similar way to charities. For further details see **43.33**.

The corporation tax charge on clubs applies only to profits from transactions other than between the club members themselves, so it covers such items as interest received on deposits of the club's funds, and any trading profits on transactions with non-members, no matter how small such income may be.

The fact that clubs are within the definition of companies for corporation tax means that banks and building societies are able to pay interest to them without deducting tax, so the clubs are due to account for tax on the full amount of the interest at the appropriate rate of corporation tax under the self-assessment system. By concession, HMRC will normally treat a club as dormant if its annual corporation tax liability is not expected to exceed £100, and the club is run exclusively for the benefit of its members. This is subject to various conditions, which are set out at www.hmrc.gov.uk/ctsa/small-tax-liabilities.htm. Where dormant status has been granted, clubs will not normally need to complete corporation tax returns, although HMRC will review the situation at least every five years. If a club is not already treated as dormant but considers it meets the conditions, it should contact its tax office. Clubs must notify HMRC within 12 months after the end of the relevant accounting period if their circumstances change.

HMRC operate a special simplified scheme for investment clubs (i.e. people who join together to invest on the Stock Exchange), allowing them to submit less detailed calculations of members' gains and income than are strictly required by law if the club satisfies certain criteria.

Encouraging business investment, enterprise and efficiency

[3.33] Various measures are available to enable companies to operate in a tax-efficient manner and to stimulate investment in new and expanding ventures, including:

- Capital gains tax entrepreneurs' relief
- Rollover relief on replacement of business assets
- Corporate venturing
- Venture capital trusts
- Demergers

These are dealt with separately in **CHAPTER 29**.

4

Capital gains tax: general principles

Introduction

[4.1] Capital gains tax (CGT) is a tax on the chargeable gains of individuals, personal representatives and trustees. Most of the basic CGT rules apply to companies as well, but there are some important differences, and a company's gains are charged to corporation tax and not CGT (see **4.7**). The law was consolidated in the Taxation of Chargeable Gains Act 1992 (TCGA 1992) but has been substantially amended since then.

Finance Act 2008 enacted a major reform of CGT. There is now a flat 18% tax rate (rising to 28% in some circumstances, see **4.2**), but in computing gains realised by individuals there is no longer any entitlement to the pre-April 1998 'frozen' indexation allowance or taper relief. To compensate the business community for the loss of these reliefs, entrepreneurs' relief was introduced which allows up to £5m of gains on qualifying business disposals to be taxed at an effective rate of 10% (see **29.3**). Furthermore, a number of measures were enacted in FA 2008 to simplify CGT, for example in relation to assets held at 31 March 1982.

Basis of charge for individuals, personal representatives and trustees (TCGA 1992, Pts 1 and 2; FA 1995, s 113; FA 1998, s 122; FA 2008, s 8 and Sch 2; F(No.2)A 2010, s 2 and Sch 1)

Rate of tax

[4.2] CGT applies to a disposal of chargeable assets. The first £10,100 of an individual's net chargeable gains in 2010/11 are exempt. For gains realised on or after 23 June 2010, the balance is taxed at 18% for gains that fall within the individual's otherwise unused basic rate income tax band (currently £37,400) and 28% thereafter. Gains realised prior to 23 June 2010 were taxed at a flat rate of 18% irrespective of the level of the individual's other income. For 2010/11 onwards, the annual exemption and losses can be applied in a way that produces the lowest possible tax charge. Therefore where, for example, a 40% taxpayer has gains both before and after 23 June 2010, the exemption and any losses should be applied to the gains arising on or after 23 June 2010 in priority. This is subject to any existing legislation that limits the way in which certain losses may be set off.

Example 1

In 2010/11 X's taxable income, after all allowable deductions and the personal allowance, is £27,400. The upper limit of the income tax basic rate band is £37,400. X sells an asset in May 2010 and realises a chargeable gain of £17,000. In November 2010 X sells another asset, realising a chargeable gain of £25,100. X has no allowable losses to set against these gains, and the annual exemption for 2010/11 is £10,100. Neither of the gains qualifies for entrepreneurs' relief.

X's taxable income is £10,000 less than the upper limit of the basic rate band (£37,400 – £27,400). X sets the annual exemption against the later gain (because part of that gain is liable to tax at the higher CGT rate), leaving £15,000 taxable (£25,100 – £10,100). The first £10,000 of the £15,000 is taxed at 18% and the remaining £5,000 is taxed at 28%. The £17,000 chargeable gain that X realised in May 2010 before the change of rates on 23 June 2010 is taxable at the old 18% rate.

The tax position of personal representatives and trustees is dealt with at **4.34** and **4.35**.

Chargeable gain

[4.3] Gains and losses are calculated separately for each asset. In general, the cost of an asset acquired before 31 March 1982 is taken to be its value on that date. For disposals prior to 6 April 2008 there were provisions to use original cost instead of the March 1982 value in some circumstances. If allowable losses exceed chargeable gains, the excess is carried forward to be used against later gains. Losses are not allowable losses if they arise through arrangements to secure a tax advantage.

The gains and losses arising on all disposals of chargeable assets during a tax year are aggregated to give the net chargeable gains or allowable losses for the year. Broadly, if losses exceed gains, the losses are carried forward without time limit, to set against later gains to the extent that those gains are not covered by the annual exemption (see **4.21**).

Relief for losses is usually claimed in tax returns, with an overall time limit to make the claim of 5 years 10 months from the end of the tax year in which the loss occurred (but this has no effect on the time for which losses may be carried forward). Where brought-forward losses are used to reduce gains, losses in years from 1996/97 onwards are regarded as set off before pre-1996/97 losses. This could delay, or at worst prevent, a pre-1996/97 loss on a transaction with a connected person being set off against later gains on transactions with that person (see **4.8**), since any post-1996/97 losses would have to be set off first.

Trading losses

[4.4] Sole traders and partners may set off unrelieved trading losses against their capital gains in certain circumstances (see **25.7**).

Residence, ordinary residence and domicile (TCGA 1992, ss 2, 9–12)

[4.5] Individuals who are either resident or ordinarily resident in the UK (see **41.5**) are liable to CGT on all gains wherever they arise if they are also UK domiciled (see **41.8**). Non-domiciled individuals or 'non-domiciles', i.e. those who do not have a UK domicile, are liable on gains arising in the UK, but their liability on foreign gains is limited to gains brought into the UK if the remittance basis applies (see **41.14**).

Non-resident individuals carrying on a trade in the UK are liable on gains arising on the disposal of business assets in the UK.

Individuals who become non-resident and not ordinarily resident may escape CGT unless they return to the UK and their period of non-residence is less than five complete tax years. In that event they will be liable to tax on gains arising during their absence.

The overseas aspects are dealt with in CHAPTER 41. For the treatment of non-resident companies with interests in the UK see **41.49**.

Spouses and civil partners (TCGA 1992, ss 2, 58)

[4.6] The gains of spouses or civil partners living together are calculated and charged separately, each being entitled to the annual exemption (£10,100 for 2010/11). Losses of one may not be set against the other's gains. Disposals between husband and wife or civil partners in a tax year when they are living together are, however, treated as made on a no gain/no loss basis (see **4.33**), and it should be possible through advance planning and transfers of assets between spouses/partners to ensure that one is not left with unrelieved losses while the other has gains in excess of the annual exemption.

The above treatment of assets acquired from the other spouse or civil partner has no relevance to assets acquired on a spouse's or civil partner's death. Any such assets are treated for CGT as acquired at market value at the date of death. See **33.13** for the CGT treatment on breakdown of the marriage or civil partnership.

Basis of charge for companies (TCGA 1992, ss 8, 16A, 184G-184I; CTA 2009, s 4)

[4.7] The capital gains of companies are broadly computed on CGT principles but are charged to corporation tax and not CGT. The gains for an accounting period are reduced by current and brought forward allowable capital losses. Companies are not entitled to an annual exemption. The abolition of indexation does not apply to companies, which remain entitled to indexation allowance. Companies are also treated differently in relation to gains on stocks and shares (see **CHAPTER 38**).

Capital losses on disposals made on or after 5 December 2005 are not allowable if they arise through arrangements to secure a tax advantage. Specific anti-avoidance provisions counter arrangements to secure a tax advantage by converting an income receipt into a capital receipt in order to secure a deduction for capital losses (provided HMRC have given the company notice in relation to the arrangements). Similarly arrangements aimed at using capital losses to reduce a chargeable gain, can be countered where the transaction that produced the gain resulted in expenditure that reduced income profits (again provided HMRC have given the company notice in relation to the arrangements).

A 'substantial shareholdings exemption' applies to trading companies disposing of holdings of 10% or more in other trading companies — see **3.31** for brief details. There are also separate 'intangible fixed assets' rules for companies under which gains and losses on such assets (notably goodwill) are dealt with in computing income profits and losses rather than capital gains and losses — see **20.30** to **20.36**. Other differences in the capital gains provisions for companies are mentioned in context as they occur. See **3.29** in relation to the capital gains of groups of companies.

Transactions with connected persons (TCGA 1992, ss 18–20, 286)

[4.8] All transactions made between connected persons, or made not at arm's length, are regarded as made for a consideration equal to open market value (subject again to the special treatment for transfers between spouses or civil partners living together). Broadly, a person is connected with his spouse or civil partner; his or his spouse's or civil partner's close relatives (see below) and their spouses or civil partners; with business partners and their spouses or civil partners and relatives (except in relation to normal commercial transactions). The relatives that are taken into account are brothers and sisters, ancestors (i.e. parents, grandparents, etc.), and lineal descendants (i.e. children, grandchildren, etc.). Companies under the same control are connected with each other and with the persons controlling them. The trustee of a settlement is connected with the settlor (if an individual) and with any person connected with the settlor.

Where an asset is disposed of to a connected person (other than the individual's spouse or civil partner) and a loss arises, the loss may not be set against general gains but only against a later gain on a transaction with the same connected person. See **4.2** for the possible adverse effect of the set-off order for brought forward losses. Where someone disposes of assets (for example, unquoted shares) on different occasions within a period of six years to one or more persons connected with him, and their value taken together is higher than their separate values, then the disposal value for each of the transactions is a proportionate part of the aggregate value, and all necessary adjustments will be made to earlier tax charges.

Chargeable assets and exempt assets (TCGA 1992, ss 21–27, 251–253)

[4.9] All forms of property are chargeable unless specifically exempt. A disposal of a chargeable asset may give rise to a chargeable gain or allowable loss. A chargeable gain or allowable loss may also arise when a capital sum is realised without any disposal taking place (for example if compensation is received for damage to an asset, although if the compensation is used to restore the asset no gain arises).

Where an asset is exempt, no chargeable gain or allowable loss can normally arise, although there are some special rules about losses on chattels (see the table below). As indicated in **4.7**, there is a special exemption for the disposal by trading companies of substantial shareholdings in other companies.

Exempt assets		
	TCGA 1992 reference	*See chapter*
An individual's only or main residence — all or part of the gain may be exempt.	ss 222, 223	30
Chattels which are wasting assets, unless used in a business and capital allowances have been, or could have been, claimed	s 45	39

Non-wasting and business chattels where disposal proceeds do not exceed £6,000	s 262	39
Government securities and qualifying company loan stock	s 115	38
SAYE contracts, savings certificates and premium bonds	s 121	11, 36
Prizes and betting winnings (see below)	s 51	
Private motor cars, including veteran and vintage cars	s 263	39
Sterling currency, and foreign currency for an individual's own spending and maintenance of assets abroad	ss 21, 252, 269	39
Foreign currency bank accounts (see below)	ss 251, 252, 252A, Sch 8A	
Decorations for valour if disposed of by the original holder or legatees but not by a purchaser	s 268	
Compensation or damages for personal or professional wrong or injury (and by HMRC concession D50, certain compensation from the UK or a foreign government for property lost or confiscated)	s 51	
Rights to receive compensation from UK or foreign banks and building societies on frozen accounts of Holocaust victims	s 268A	
Life assurance policies but only in the hands of the original owner or beneficiaries	s 210	40
Gifts of assets that are considered by the Treasury to be of pre-eminent national, historic or scientific interest, but breach of any conditions imposed will nullify the CGT exemption	s 258	
Gifts to charities and certain amateur sports clubs	s 257	43

Prizes and betting winnings

If a lottery prize is won, it is exempt from CGT, as indicated in the table. If playing as a member of a group, the group should draw up an agreement setting out how the group will operate, who will buy tickets and claim prizes, and how any prize money is to be shared, otherwise a group claimant passing on shares of prize money to other group members could be regarded as making gifts for inheritance tax (see **CHAPTER 5**) purposes. The same would apply to similar group arrangements, such as for football pools. There would not, however, be any inheritance tax to pay unless the person who passed on the shares of prize money died within seven years, and even then there may be exemptions available to cover the gifts.

Foreign currency bank accounts

Where a foreign currency bank account includes amounts for personal expenditure outside the UK (of the account holder, his family or dependants) any deposits or withdrawals are exempt and do **not** give rise to chargeable gains or allowable losses. As in the case of foreign currency itself, personal expenditure includes the costs of providing or maintaining a residence outside the UK. However where a foreign currency bank account includes amounts that are not for personal expenditure outside the UK, those amounts are treated as debts which are chargeable assets. Deposits and withdrawals are separate acquisitions and disposals respectively and should be converted into sterling in each case at the currency exchange rates prevailing at the date of the particular deposit or withdrawal. Where a person has multiple accounts (situated outside the UK) denominated in the same foreign currency they can be treated as one. This means that direct transfers between such accounts can be ignored for CGT purposes.

For 2008/09 onwards, where the amount of net gains from transfers from overseas non-sterling bank accounts which an individual remits (**41.14**) to the UK is less than £500 in any tax year in which they are taxed on the remittance basis, they will not be required to report such gains on their tax returns.

For remittances of income on or after 16 December 2009, anti-avoidance provisions prevent the interaction of the capital gains tax rules and the rules for the remittance basis of taxation from resulting in allowable losses for CGT purposes that do not reflect economic losses. HMRC have issued a technical note providing examples of how this restriction will operate, available at http://www.hmrc.gov.uk/cnr/fcba-technical-note.pdf.

Treatment of loans

[**4.10**] For companies, capital transactions relating to loans are brought into account for income purposes (see **3.4**). For individuals, trustees and personal representatives, a debt is not within the capital gains provisions unless it is a 'debt on a security' (which broadly means marketable loan stock). Even then, most loan stock is within the definition of a 'qualifying corporate bond' (see **38.6**), and is exempt from CGT. The effect is that if capital gains or losses arise on simple debts, or on qualifying corporate bonds, no relief is available for the losses (subject to some special rules for loans to UK traders — see **4.28** and **38.36**), and gains are exempt. For the treatment of loan stock that is outside the definition of qualifying corporate bonds see **38.6**. Where a simple debt has been assigned other than to someone with whom the creditor is 'connected' (see **4.8**), the debt is a chargeable asset for the assignee, thus giving rise to a chargeable gain or allowable loss on a disposal by the assignee.

Computation of gains and losses (TCGA 1992, ss 2, 2A, 15–17, 35–57 and Schs A1, 2–4)

[**4.11**] Gains and losses on individual assets are worked out by deducting from the sale proceeds or, in some instances, from the market value at the time of disposal (see **4.8** and **4.23**) the following amounts:

(a)   Original cost and incidental costs of acquisition

(b)   Expenditure that has increased the value of the asset

(c)   Incidental costs of disposal

For companies, an indexation allowance (see **4.13**) may then be given to reduce or eliminate a gain, but the allowance cannot create or increase a loss. For individuals, personal representatives and trustees, capital gains are taxed at a flat rate (no indexation allowance is available) and entrepreneurs' relief may be available (see **4.22**). Taper relief applied for disposals made prior to 6 April 2008 (and after 5 April 1998). For details of the taper relief regime see earlier editions of this book.

Effect of capital allowances (TCGA 1992, s 41)

[4.12] A taxpayer's business or rental income may be reduced by capital allowances (see **CHAPTER 22**). Capital gains on some assets that qualify for capital allowances are exempt from CGT, such as gains on items of movable plant and machinery sold for less than £6,000 (see **39.4**). Where an asset is not exempt, capital allowances are not deducted from the cost in computing a capital gain (though they will be recovered by way of a balancing charge in the capital allowances pool (**22.17**)). This means that there will be a gain only if the asset is sold for more than its original cost. Capital allowances are, however, taken into account in computing a capital loss. Capital allowances (that have not been recovered by way of a balancing charge) are deducted from the original acquisition cost. This means in practice that capital losses on such disposals do not normally arise since the capital allowance system has usually covered any drop in value. This will change for industrial and agricultural buildings as a result of the planned withdrawal of industrial and agricultural buildings allowances in the period up to 1 April 2011 (see **CHAPTER 22** for details). For an example, see **22.41**.

Indexation allowance (TCGA 1992, ss 53, 54; FA 1998, s 122)

Individuals, trustees and personal representatives

[4.13] The indexation allowance (see **4.11**) was abolished for individuals, trustees and personal representatives with effect for disposals after 5 April 2008. From this date, capital gains are taxed at a flat rate.

Companies

[4.14] Indexation remains available to companies. The allowance is calculated by applying to each item of expenditure the increase in the retail prices index between the month when the expenditure was incurred, or March 1982 if later, and the month of disposal of the asset. That increase is expressed as a decimal and rounded (up or down) to three decimal places. The movement in the index is published monthly and the figure for each month since March 1982 is in the **TABLE OF RATES AND ALLOWANCES** under 'Retail prices index'. The formula for working out the increase is:

$$\frac{RD - RI}{RI} \text{ or put more simply } \frac{RD}{RI} - 1$$

RD is the index for the month of disposal and RI the index for the month in which the expenditure was incurred. For example, using the figures in the 'Retail prices index' table in the Table of Rates and Allowances, the increase from November 1982 to April 1998 is

$$\frac{162.6}{82.66} - 1 = .967 \text{ (or as a percentage, 96.7\%)}$$

The indexation allowance can only reduce or eliminate a gain and cannot create or increase a loss.

Where the expenditure was incurred before 31 March 1982, the indexation calculation is made by reference to the value of the asset at 31 March 1982 if the taxpayer has elected to be treated as if he had acquired all the assets he owned on 31 March 1982 at their market value on that day (see **4.15**). If the election has not been made, the 31 March 1982 value is still used to calculate the indexation allowance unless using original cost would give a higher figure, in which case that higher figure is taken.

Assets held on 31 March 1982 (TCGA 1992, ss 35, 36 and Schs 3, 4; FA 2008, s 8 and Sch 2)

[4.15] Originally, CGT applied to gains or losses made on or after 6 April 1965, and there were special rules relating to assets already owned on that date to ensure that pre-6 April 1965 gains and losses on such assets were excluded. Since 6 April 1988 broadly speaking only gains or losses arising since 31 March 1982 have been taken into account.

Individuals, trustees and personal representatives

[4.16] For individuals, trustees and personal representatives (for disposals after 5 April 2008) there is an automatic 'rebasing' of allowable expenditure to 31 March 1982. This means that all assets owned on 31 March 1982 are automatically treated as having been acquired at their market value on 31 March 1982.

Companies

[4.17] Companies, however, have the option to make an irrevocable 'rebasing' election for all assets owned on 31 March 1982 (except plant and machinery on which capital allowances have been, or could have been, claimed) to be treated as having been acquired at their market value on that day.

The time limit for making the rebasing election dates from the *first disposal after 5 April 1988*, and must be made no later than two years after the end of the accounting period of disposal. Most disposals that normally result in no chargeable gain or allowable loss are not, however, treated as triggering the time limit (see HMRC Statement of Practice SP 4/92).

If the rebasing election is not made, the 31 March 1982 value is still used to calculate gains and losses, unless using original cost would show a lower gain or lower loss, in which case the lower figure is taken. If one method shows a gain and the other a loss the result is neither a gain nor a loss. In making these calculations indexation allowance is always based on the higher of cost and 31 March 1982 value (see **4.14**).

For many assets it may be costly to find out their value at 31 March 1982, but this has to be done whether the election to use 31 March 1982 value is made or not.

Example 2

A chargeable asset was bought for £20,000 in 1980 and was worth £24,000 on 31 March 1982. It was sold in February 2010. The company had made no other disposals since 5 April 1988, so it can make a rebasing election, which will then apply to all subsequent disposals of chargeable assets owned on 31 March 1982.

The retail prices index for February 2010 is 219.2. This gives an index increase from March 1982 of:

$$\frac{219.2}{79.44} - 1 = 1.759, \text{i.e. } 175.9\%$$

Indexation allowance (based on 31 March 1982 value, since higher than cost) is therefore £42,216.

The position is as follows.

	(a) £	(b) £	(c) £
Sale proceeds, say	80,000	19,000	22,000
31.3.82 value (giving lower gain)	(24,000)		
Cost (giving lower loss)	—	(20,000)	
Unindexed gain (loss)	56,000	(1,000)	
Indexation allowance	(42,216)	—	No gain,
Chargeable gain (allowable loss)	13,784	(1,000)	no loss

If rebasing election is made

	(a) £	(b) £	(c) £
Sale proceeds as above	80,000	19,000	22,000

31.3.82 value	(24,000)	(24,000)	(24,000)
Unindexed gain (loss)	56,000	(5,000)	(2,000)
Indexation allowance	(42,216)	—	—
Chargeable gain (allowable loss)	13,784	(5,000)	(2,000)

Rebasing election is either neutral or favourable in relation to this asset, depending on sale proceeds.

Example 3

Using the same figures as in Example 2, but assuming that cost price was £24,000 and 31.3.82 value was £20,000, i.e. figures are reversed, the position is as follows.

If general rebasing election is not made

The outcome will be the same as in Example 2, since the lower gain or loss is always taken, and there is no gain or loss where one computation shows a gain and the other a loss.

If general rebasing election is made

Cost of £24,000 becomes irrelevant. Indexation allowance on 31.3.82 value of £20,000 is £35,180.

	(a)	(b)	(c)
	£	£	£
Sale proceeds as above	80,000	19,000	22,000
31.3.82 value	(20,000)	(20,000)	(20,000)
Unindexed gain (loss)	60,000	(1,000)	2,000
Indexation allowance	(35,180)	—	(2,000)
Chargeable gain (allowable loss)	24,820	(1,000)	—

Rebasing election is unfavourable or neutral in relation to this asset, depending on sale proceeds.

Where the right to make a rebasing election is still available, it is not possible to be selective. If it is made at all, it applies to all chargeable assets owned on 31 March 1982 (except plant and machinery) and it cannot be revoked. The election does simplify the calculations and it makes it unnecessary to maintain pre-31 March 1982 records.

Various reliefs allow gains to be deferred to a later time, either by treating the gains as reducing other expenditure, or by treating them as arising at a later time. Where gains were deferred before 31 March 1982, the effect of using

31 March 1982 value to calculate later gains is that these deferred gains will escape tax altogether, since the cost from which the deferred gain was deducted is no longer used.

Where an asset acquired after 31 March 1982 but before 6 April 1988 has been disposed of after 5 April 1988, and the gain related wholly or partly, directly or indirectly, to an asset acquired before 31 March 1982 (in other words, where a claim for deferral was made between 31 March 1982 and 5 April 1988 that related to an asset acquired before 31 March 1982), the taxpayer is able to make a claim for one-half of the gain to be exempt from tax. The purpose of this 'halving relief' is to compensate the taxpayer for the fact that part of the gain charged on his disposal related to gains accruing in the period up to 31 March 1982.

Assets held on 6 April 1965 (TCGA 1992, s 35 and Sch 2)

[4.18] Assets already owned on 6 April 1965, the original start date for CGT, are treated as acquired at market value on 31 March 1982 if either the rebasing election is made or automatic rebasing applies on a post-5 April 2008 disposal by an individual, trustee or personal representative (see 4.16).

Where rebasing does not apply the position is more complicated. The old rules for calculating the position on assets owned on 6 April 1965 contained separate provisions for land with development value, for quoted securities and for all other assets.

The gain or loss on land with development value was calculated by comparing the proceeds either with the original cost or with the value at 6 April 1965, whichever showed the lower gain or loss. If one method showed a gain and the other a loss, there was neither gain nor loss. The same rules applied to quoted securities, except that it was possible to elect for quoted securities to be treated as having been acquired on 6 April 1965 at their value on that date and pooled with later acquisitions of shares of the same class in the same company. The detailed provisions for shares are in CHAPTER 38.

Where an asset other than quoted securities or land with development value was acquired before 6 April 1965, only the time proportion of the gain falling after 6 April 1965 was chargeable, although the earliest date that could be used in a time apportionment calculation was 6 April 1945. It was possible to elect to work out the gain by using the 6 April 1965 value as the cost instead of using time apportionment, but once made this election was irrevocable, even if it resulted in more tax being payable.

Following the 1988 changes (see 4.15), in the absence of a rebasing election (where available) the above rules are modified to bring the 31 March 1982 value into the calculation. The calculation is first made using the old rules for assets owned on 6 April 1965 but with indexation allowance based on 31 March 1982 value if higher. When making the time apportionment calculation for assets other than quoted securities and land with development value, indexation allowance is deducted before the gain is time apportioned. The resulting gain or loss is compared with the result using 31 March 1982 value. The lower gain or loss is then taken and if one calculation shows a gain and the other a loss, the result is neither gain nor loss. If, however, the old 6 April 1965 rules have already resulted in a no gain/no loss result, that position is not disturbed.

Example 4

A company has owned a chargeable asset since 6 April 1964, which it sells in 2010. The gain will be calculated as follows:

Cost of antique 6.4.64	£4,250
Value at 6.4.65	£4,500
Value at 31.3.82	£10,000
Sale proceeds 6.4.10	£44,705

If no election is made to use 31.3.82 value for all assets

Calculation using 6 April 1965 rules:

	£	£
Sale proceeds	44,705	44,705
Cost	(4,250)	
6.4.65 value		(4,500)
Indexation allowance on 31.3.82 value of £10,000 (say)	(15,705)	(15,705)
Overall gain	£24,750	

Time proportion since 6.4.65

$$\frac{45}{46} \times 24,750 = \qquad 24,212$$

	Gain	£24,212	or	£24,500

Therefore no election would be made to use 6.4.65 value and gain under 6 April 1965 rules is £24,212.

Calculation using March 1982 rules	£
Sale proceeds	44,705
31.3.82 value	(10,000)
Indexation allowance (say)	(15,705)
Gain under March 1982 rules	£19,000

Chargeable gain is the lower of £24,212 and £19,000, i.e. £19,000.

If election made to use 31.3.82 value for all assets

> Chargeable gain is not affected, since the 31 March 1982 value is used in any event.

Part disposals (TCGA 1992, ss 42, 242)

[4.19] Where part only of an asset is disposed of, the cost of the part disposed of is worked out by taking the proportion of the overall cost that the sale proceeds bear to the sum of the sale proceeds plus the market value of what remains unsold. Any indexation allowance is calculated on the apportioned part of the cost and not on the total.

Where part of a holding of land is sold for £20,000 or less, and the proceeds represent not more than 20% of the value of the whole holding, the taxpayer may claim not to be treated as having made a disposal, but the amount received reduces the allowable cost of the remaining land for a future disposal. Any available indexation allowance on a subsequent disposal is calculated on the full cost in the usual way, but is then reduced to take account of the previous part disposal. This claim may not be made if other disposals of land are made in the same year, and the total proceeds for all disposals of land exceed £20,000.

Leases (TCGA 1992, s 240 and Sch 8)

[4.20] The grant of a lease at a premium gives rise to a CGT liability, and if the term is 50 years or less there is also an income tax liability. The calculation of the income and capital elements is shown in CHAPTER 32. Where a tenant assigns a lease at a premium to another tenant, the premium is charged to CGT in the normal way if the lease has more than 50 years to run at the time of the assignment. If, however, it has 50 years or less to run, it is a wasting asset and the cost has to be depreciated over those 50 years according to a table in Sch 8 which ensures that the cost is depreciated more slowly during the early part of the 50-year period than during the later years.

Annual exemption (TCGA 1992, s 3 and Sch 1)

[4.21] The annual CGT exemption is £10,100 for 2010/11 (it was the same amount for 2009/10), available to each individual, whether single, married or a civil partner. If an individual's gains for a tax year are below this amount, no capital gains tax is payable. Any unused exemption cannot be carried forward and set against future gains.

Provision is made for the exempt amount to be increased each year in line with increases in the retail prices index unless Parliament decides otherwise. The annual exemption is not available to companies.

For the annual exemption available to personal representatives and trustees, see **4.34** and **4.35**.

Reliefs

[4.22] Specific reliefs, which either reduce the CGT liability or defer it, are available. The following reliefs relating to businesses are examined in CHAPTER 29:

(a) entrepreneurs' relief for qualifying business disposals after 5 April 2008;
(b) rollover relief on the replacement of business assets; and
(c) reliefs under the enterprise investment scheme, the venture capital trusts scheme and the corporate venturing scheme.

Incorporation relief on the transfer of a business to a company is examined in CHAPTER 27. Chattel relief and private residence relief are discussed in CHAPTER 30 and CHAPTER 39 respectively. The remainder of this chapter includes a brief description of:

(i)   holdover relief for gifts of certain assets (**4.24**);
(ii)   relief for assets of negligible value (**4.27**);
(iii) relief for losses on certain loans (**4.28**).

In addition anti-avoidance provisions apply to prevent taxpayers escaping tax by abusing a concession which permits a deferral of CGT (**4.29**).

Gifts (TCGA 1992, ss 17, 67, 165–169G, 258–261, 281 and Sch 7)

[4.23] For CGT purposes a gift of a chargeable asset is regarded as a disposal at open market value (except for transfers between spouses or civil partners living together, see **4.6**), and the chargeable gain or allowable loss is computed in the usual way, unless gift relief (see below) is avaliable.

Gift relief (TCGA 1992, ss 165–169G, 260, 281 and Sch 7)

[4.24] Where a gain arises on the gift of an asset by an individual or trustees, a claim may be made to defer the gain if the asset qualifies for gift relief (subject to various anti-avoidance provisions mentioned below). Gift relief is also available where assets are not given outright but are disposed of for less than their value. If, however, the amount received exceeds the original cost a chargeable gain will arise.

Gift relief used to be available on virtually any asset, but the gifts that now qualify for relief are as shown below (although note that relief for gifts of shares or securities under (a)(iii) and (iv) is not available if the gift is to a company):

(a) Gifts of business assets, which comprise:
    (i) assets used in the donor's business or in his personal 'trading company' (i.e. one in which he owns at least 5% of the voting rights), or used by a company in a 'trading group' of which the 'holding company' is the donor's personal trading company;

(ii)   farm land and buildings that would qualify for inheritance tax agricultural property relief (see **5.43**); note that this enables relief to be claimed on agricultural land held as an investment, providing the appropriate conditions are satisfied;

(iii)   unquoted shares or securities in trading companies;

(iv)   shares or securities in the donor's personal trading company or personal holding company of a trading group (relief being restricted proportionately if not all the company's assets are business assets).

(b)   Gifts that:

(i)   are *immediately* chargeable to inheritance tax (or would be immediately chargeable if they were not covered by the inheritance tax annual exemption); or

(ii)   fall within certain specified inheritance tax exemptions (i.e. gifts of heritage property (works of art, historic buildings, etc.), gifts to funds for the maintenance of heritage property or gifts to political parties).

A 'trading company' is a company carrying on trading activities whose activities do not include 'to a substantial extent' activities other than trading activities. A 'holding company' is a company with one or more 51% subsidiaries. A group of companies (i.e. a company and its '51% subsidiaries') is a 'trading group' if one or more of its members carries on trading activities and the activities of all members taken together do not include to a substantial extent activities other than trading activities.

The relief under heading (a)(i) also applies where the business is carried on by trustees or by a beneficiary with a life interest in the trust. For the detailed provisions, see **CHAPTER 42**.

[4.25] Where gift relief is claimed, the donor is not charged to tax on the gain and the value at which the donee is treated as having acquired the asset is reduced by the gain, so that the donee will make a correspondingly larger gain (or smaller loss) when he disposes of the asset. HMRC have stated that in most circumstances it will not be necessary to agree market values at the time of the gift relief claim. Establishing the market value at the date of the gift can normally be deferred until the donee disposes of the asset (HMRC Statement of Practice SP 8/92).

There are provisions to ensure that gift relief is not used to avoid tax altogether, for example where the donee is not resident in the UK. If the donee is an individual resident in the UK at the time of the gift, but becomes non-resident before disposing of the asset and within six years after the end of the tax year in which the gift was made, the gain is then charged to tax. This charge will not apply if the asset has previously been disposed of, the donee is leaving the UK to take up an overseas employment or the donee resumes UK residence within three years of the initial change of residence. (Note, this provision does not apply to trustees, because separate rules impose a tax charge on all trust assets when a trust becomes non-resident — see **41.65**.) Gift relief is not available on disposals to trusts in which the settlor has an interest (see **42.14**). There are also provisions to prevent the exploitation of the interaction between gift relief and the private residence exemption dealt with in **CHAPTER 30** (see **30.9**).

[4.26] Claims for gift relief to apply must be made by the donor and donee jointly except where the donees are trustees, in which case only the donor need make the claim. Under self-assessment, claims will usually be sent in with tax returns. There is a form for making the claim in HMRC help sheet HS295. The overall time limit for claims is (from 1 April 2010) four years from the relevant year of assessment. Prior to 1 April 2010, the time limit was five years from the 31 January following the tax year to which the claim relates.

Where a gift on which the gift holdover relief is claimed attracts inheritance tax, either immediately or as a result of the donor's death within seven years, the donee's base cost for CGT is increased by the inheritance tax (but not so as to create a loss on future disposal). If, however, a lifetime gift does not qualify for holdover relief and CGT is paid, there is no direct inheritance tax relief for the CGT paid if the gift becomes chargeable for inheritance tax because of the donor's death within seven years (although the CGT paid has reduced the wealth of the donor and therefore the amount liable to inheritance tax on his death).

Where tax remains payable after gift relief, it may be paid by ten annual instalments if the gift was one of land, a controlling shareholding in a company, or minority holding of unquoted shares or securities in a company. Interest is, however, charged on the full amount outstanding and not just on any instalment which is paid late.

Assets of negligible value (TCGA 1992, s 24)

[4.27] If an asset is lost, destroyed or extinguished, it is treated as disposed of at that time, even if no compensation is received. This means, for example, that shareholders of a company that goes into liquidation, will be regarded as disposing of the shares when the liquidation is completed, and relief may be claimed for the loss.

It is, however, possible to get relief before an asset is lost or destroyed if its value has sunk to a negligible level. (HMRC maintain a list of quoted shares which are accepted as being of negligible value. A claim is automatically accepted for any shares on this list). A claim can be made for the asset to be treated as sold and reacquired at that negligible value, establishing an allowable loss accordingly. The disposal will be deemed to take place either on the date of the claim or on an earlier date indicated in the claim. The earlier date must fall within the two years before the tax year or accounting period in which the claim is made, and the asset must have been of negligible value on that earlier date (whether or not it was of negligible value before then). There is no requirement to make a negligible value claim so that, for example, a claim should not be made if it would mean wasting the annual exemption.

Relief for losses on loans (TCGA 1992, ss 251–253)

[4.28] Relief is available to the lender or guarantor for losses on loans or guarantees if the borrower is UK resident and uses the money lent wholly for the purposes of a trade carried on by him. Upon an appropriate claim by the lender or guarantor, an irrecoverable loan or payment under guarantee gives rise to an allowable loss for CGT, provided that the debt or the rights acquired by the guarantor following the guarantee payment are not assigned. If any amount is subsequently recovered (whether from the borrower or from any co-guarantor) it will be treated as a capital gain. The loss under these provisions is treated as a loss at the date of the claim, unless the claim stipulates an earlier time falling not more than two years before the beginning of the tax year of the claim, and providing the amount was irrecoverable at the earlier date.

This relief is not available if the loss arises because of something the lender, or guarantor, has done or failed to do, or where the amount has become irrecoverable in consequence of the terms of the loan, nor is it available where the claimant and borrower are husband and wife or civil partners.

For the treatment of loans generally see **4.10**.

Abuse of concessions (TCGA 1992, s 284A)

[4.29] Where someone defers a gain under the capital gains provisions under a concession first published before 9 March 1999, or a later replacement concession with substantially the same effect, then if the deferred gain becomes chargeable (e.g. on the disposal of the asset) and the person on whom the gain arises seeks to avoid bringing it into charge, he is treated as having made a chargeable gain equal to the deferred gain in the tax year or company accounting period in which the deferred gain should have been brought back into charge. The person on whom the charge arises could be the same taxpayer or another taxpayer to whom the asset had been transferred with the benefit of capital gains deferral.

An example of the sort of abuse these measures counter is where a trader makes a gain on the sale of a business asset and incurs enhancement expenditure on an existing asset rather than buying another asset. Rollover relief to defer the gain (see **29.11** onwards) is not strictly available in these circumstances, but concession D22 enables the enhancement expenditure to be treated as the acquisition of a qualifying asset. Since the gain is deferred only by concession, the trader could not, without this provision, be compelled to bring it into account on the disposal of the asset on which the enhancement expenditure was incurred.

Returns, due date of payment, interest on overdue tax and repayment supplement (TCGA 1992, ss 3A, 283; TMA 1970, ss 59B, 86)

[4.30] Under the self-assessment system, the annual tax return contains details of capital gains, although in some instances the capital gains pages of the return do not have to be completed. The same payment date and interest rules apply for both income tax and CGT (see **2.29**), except that CGT is not included in payments on account and is payable in full on 31 January following the end of the tax year. Interest on underpaid tax is charged from the due date and repayment supplement is paid on overpaid tax from the date of overpayment to the date the repayment is made. For the latest interest rates see the TABLE OF RATES AND ALLOWANCES.

For companies, any capital gains are charged to corporation tax. For details see CHAPTER 3.

Payment by instalments (TCGA 1992, s 280)

[4.31] CGT may, at the taxpayer's option, be paid by instalments where the proceeds are being received by instalments over 18 months or more. The instalments run over eight years, or until the last instalment of the price is received if sooner, with relief for bad debts being available if part of the amount due proves irrecoverable. Interest is charged on any instalments paid late (but only on the instalment and not on the full amount outstanding).

CGT is also payable by instalments on certain gifts, but interest is then payable on the full amount outstanding, not just on overdue instalments.

Quoted and unquoted shares and securities

[4.32] Special rules apply to the CGT treatment of both quoted and unquoted shares and securities. The freezing of indexation allowance for individuals, personal representatives and trustees, and the introduction of taper relief, with the existing provisions being retained for companies, made these rules particularly complex. The abolition of indexation and taper relief for disposals after 5 April 2008 by taxpayers other than companies was accompanied by measures to simplify the CGT treatment in relation to such assets — see CHAPTER 38.

No gain/no loss disposals

[4.33] Special provisions apply to certain disposals, the main ones being:

(a)   Transfers on company reconstructions (TCGA 1992, s 139).

(b)   Transfers within a 75% group of companies (TCGA 1992, s 171). Companies in a 75% group may make a joint election under TCGA 1992, s 171A to set one group company's loss against another group company's gain without actually transferring assets intra-group under TCGA 1992, s 171 (see 3.29).

(c)   Transfers between spouses and civil partners living together (TCGA 1992, s 58).

The disposal is effectively treated as giving rise to neither gain nor loss, and the transferee's acquisition cost is the original cost plus any available indexation allowance. (Any indexation allowance added to cost cannot, however, create or increase a loss on ultimate disposal but this rule does not apply to indexation allowance that had been added to cost up to the time of the last no gain/no loss transfer made before 30 November 1993).

A wide-ranging anti-avoidance provision was introduced from 6 December 2006 (5 December 2005 for companies) to deny relief for losses arising from arrangements made to secure a tax advantage. The Government has stated that taking advantage of a statutory relief, such as that in (c) above for spouses and civil partners, does not come within this anti-avoidance provision.

Death (TCGA 1992, ss 3(7), 4, 62; F(No.2)A 2010, s 2 and Sch 1)

[4.34] No CGT charge arises on increases in value of assets up to the point of death. If losses arise in the year of death these may be carried back and set against gains chargeable to tax in the three previous tax years, latest first (with the set-off being made only against any gains not covered by the annual exemption in those years). Tax will be refunded accordingly, with repayment supplement where appropriate running from the payment date for the tax year of death (see **9.42**).

The personal representatives or legatees are treated as acquiring the assets at the market value at the date of death. When personal representatives dispose of assets at values in excess of the values at death, gains arising will be charged to tax (and exemptions the deceased could have claimed may not be available, for example on a private residence) but they may claim the annual exemption, currently £10,100, in respect of disposals by them in the tax year of death and in each of the following two tax years. For 2010/11, any remaining gains realised on or after 23 June 2010 are taxed at 28% (gains realised prior to 23 June 2010 were taxed at 18%).

Where within two years after a death the persons entitled to the estate vary the way in which it is distributed, they may specify in the variation that it is to apply for CGT. The variation is then not regarded as a disposal by those originally entitled but as having been made by the deceased at the date of death so that no CGT charge arises on any increase in value since death — see **35.14** to **35.16**.

Trusts (TCGA 1992, ss 3, 4, 68–98 and Schs 1, 5; F(No.2)A 2010, s 2 and Sch 1)

[4.35] Trustees are chargeable persons for CGT. Trustees are entitled to an annual exemption of £5,050 for 2010/11 unless the trust is for the disabled, in which case the exempt amount is £10,100. The exemption is divided where there are several trusts created by the same settlor, but with each trust getting a minimum exemption of £1,010. The exemption is usually increased each year in line with the retail prices index. For 2010/11, any remaining gains realised on or after 23 June 2010 are taxed at 28% (gains realised prior to 23 June 2010 were taxed at 18%).

The detailed CGT provisions for trusts are dealt with in CHAPTER 42, with the overseas element being dealt with in CHAPTER 41.

Options (TCGA 1992, ss 114, 143–148)

[4.36] The grant of an option is treated as a disposal of an asset (i.e. the option). It is not a part disposal of the underlying asset. Therefore the full amount of the consideration for the grant of the option is chargeable as a gain (less any costs associated with the grant).

Options with a life of 50 years or less are treated as wasting assets, so that their cost wastes away over their life, restricting loss relief accordingly if they lapse or become valueless. If such options are abandoned, no allowable loss can arise. The forfeiture of a deposit is treated as the abandonment of an option.

The following options however are not treated as wasting assets:

(a)   quoted options to subscribe for new shares (usually called share warrants);

(b)   traded options to buy or sell shares or other financial instruments quoted on a recognised stock exchange or futures exchange and 'over the counter' financial options; and

(c)   options to acquire assets for use by the option holder in his business.

This means that when they are disposed of or abandoned, an allowable loss or chargeable gain may arise.

On the exercise of the option the price paid for the option is incorporated with that of the asset to form a single transaction both as regards the seller and the buyer. In the case of a put option, the cost of the option is netted off against both the grantor's cost of acquiring the asset and the grantee's disposal proceeds. Where a call option is exercised and settled in cash, rather than by delivery of the asset, the grantor of the option is treated as having disposal proceeds equal to the price paid by the grantee for the option, less the cash payment made by the grantor, and the grantee is treated as having disposal proceeds equal to the cash received less the cost of the option. An exercise of an option to acquire an asset on non-arm's length terms is treated as if it were a sale of the underlying asset at market value. The exercise price and any consideration given for the option will be ignored.

For individuals, the disposal of an option to buy or sell gilt-edged securities or qualifying corporate bonds is exempt. For companies, such options are taken into account in calculating profits under the 'loan relationships' rules (as to which see **3.5**).

There are special rules concerning options connected with employment (see **CHAPTER 11**). For companies, options in connection with financial instruments, such as currency options and interest rate options, are taken into account in calculating income (see **3.7**) and are not subject to the CGT provisions outlined above. Anti-avoidance provisions impose an income tax charge rather than a CGT charge where transactions in futures and options produce a guaranteed return.

Deferred consideration

[4.37] Transactions are sometimes structured along lines where only part of the consideration is received at the time of the sale, with further amounts depending upon later events, for example profit performance in the case of the sale of a family company. This aspect is dealt with briefly in CHAPTER 28.

5

Inheritance tax: general principles

Introduction

[5.1] Inheritance tax is charged on transfers of capital by individuals. It may be payable on certain lifetime gifts, on wealth at death, on certain transfers into and out of trusts and on certain transfers made by close companies. The law is contained in the Inheritance Tax Act 1984 (abbreviated in this book to IHTA 1984). The tax was introduced in 1975 to replace estate duty, and was called capital transfer tax until 1986.

Persons liable (IHTA 1984, ss 1–6, 267)

[5.2] UK domiciled individuals are chargeable to inheritance tax in respect of property anywhere in the world, and non-UK domiciled individuals are chargeable in respect of property in the UK. Spouses and civil partners are chargeable separately, so that any available exemptions apply to each of them and each can make transfers free of tax up to the nil rate threshold (see **5.21**).

Where a surviving spouse or civil partner dies after 8 October 2007 a claim may be made for any part of the nil rate band unused on the death of the first spouse or civil partner to die to be added to the survivor's own nil rate band on his or her death (see **35.3**).

Domicile is a legal term that is not easy to define but essentially it means the country an individual regards as 'home'. The term has an extended meaning for inheritance tax, so that broadly speaking, even if an individual does not have a UK domicile under general law, he will be treated as UK domiciled if:

(a)   he was UK domiciled within the three years immediately preceding the transfer; or

(b)   he was resident (as determined for income tax) in the UK in at least 17 of the 20 tax years ending with the year of transfer.

Double taxation relief is given where the transfer of assets attracts foreign tax as well as UK tax.

Exempt transfers etc

[5.3] Certain transfers are not taken into account for inheritance tax. These include the following:

Transfers 'not intended to confer gratuitous benefit' (IHTA 1984, s 10)

[5.4] Such a transfer is not taken into account providing it was either an arm's length transaction between unconnected persons or it was on terms similar to those that would be expected in an arm's length transaction.

Capital transfers for family maintenance (IHTA 1984, s 11)

[5.5] It may sometimes be necessary to make transfers of capital in order to provide for family, for example, following divorce or dissolution of a civil partnership, when the usual exemption for transfers between spouses or civil partners (see **5.11**) no longer applies, or to make reasonable provision for a dependent relative. Such transfers do not attract inheritance tax. 'Dependent relative' is defined as a relative of either spouse or civil partner who is incapacitated by old age or infirmity, or the parents of either spouse or civil partner.

Waivers of remuneration and dividends (IHTA 1984, ss 14, 15)

[5.6] A waiver or repayment of remuneration that would have been employ-ment income for income tax does not attract inheritance tax. Nor does a waiver of dividends made within 12 months before any right to the dividend arises.

Small gifts to same person (IHTA 1984, s 20)

[5.7] Any outright lifetime gifts to any one person in any one tax year are exempt if the total gifts to that person do not exceed £250 in that year.

Gifts in consideration of marriage or civil partnership (IHTA 1984, s 22)

[5.8] Gifts of up to £5,000 by a parent, £2,500 by a grandparent, £2,500 by one party to the marriage or civil partnership to the other, or £1,000 by anyone else are exempt.

Normal expenditure out of income (IHTA 1984, s 21)

[5.9] To obtain this exemption the gift must be part of the donor's normal expenditure. It must, taking one year with another, be made out of the donor's income and must not reduce his available net income (after all other transfers) below that required to maintain his usual standard of living. The exemption will often apply to life insurance policy premiums paid for the benefit of someone else. HMRC require details of income and expenditure for the seven years before death in support of a claim to this exemption (see **9.22**).

Where a loan is made free of interest, there is no transfer of capital and it is usually possible to regard the interest forgone as being normal expenditure out of income and thus exempt. If, however, a loan is made for a fixed period, or is not repayable on demand, it may be treated as a transfer of value equal to the difference between the amount lent and the present value of the future right to repayment.

Annual transfers not exceeding £3,000 (IHTA 1984, s 19)

[5.10] The first £3,000 of lifetime transfers in any tax year are exempt. Any unused portion of the exemption may be carried forward for one year only for use in the following tax year after the exemption for that following tax year has been used.

Transfers between spouses or civil partners (IHTA 1984, s 18)

[5.11] Such transfers are exempt. Where a spouse or civil partner domiciled in the UK makes a transfer to a foreign domiciled spouse or civil partner the exemption is limited to £55,000 less the amount of any previous transfers covered by the same exemption.

Gifts to charities etc (IHTA 1984, s 23)

[5.12] Gifts to charities, either outright or to be held on trust for charitable purposes, and gifts to registered community amateur sports clubs, are exempt.

Gifts to political parties (IHTA 1984, s 24)

[5.13] Gifts to political parties that qualify by having either at least two MPs in the House of Commons, or one MP and at least 150,000 votes in their candidates' favour at the last general election, are exempt.

Gifts of land to registered housing associations (IHTA 1984, s 24A)

[5.14] Gifts of land in the UK to registered social landlords or registered housing associations are exempt.

Gifts for national purposes (IHTA 1984, s 25 and Sch 3)

[5.15] Gifts to any of the bodies listed in IHTA 1984, Sch 3 (for example, the National Gallery, the National Trust and any UK university) are exempt.

Conditional exemption for heritage property (IHTA 1984, ss 30–35A, 78–79A)

[5.16] Providing various undertakings are given, for example in relation to public access, a conditional exemption applies to the transfer of property which is designated by the Treasury as of pre-eminent national, scientific, historic, artistic, architectural or scenic interest (e.g. works of art and historic buildings). A claim for such designation must be made not later than two years after the date of the transfer, or where a potentially exempt transfer (see **5.23**) becomes chargeable, the date of the donor's death or in either case within such longer period as HMRC may allow. If there is any breach of an undertaking, inheritance tax becomes payable by the donee.

Maintenance funds for heritage property (IHTA 1984, s 27)

[5.17] A transfer into a settlement established for the maintenance, repair or preservation of heritage property is exempt providing a Treasury direction is in effect, or is given after the time of the transfer. A claim for a direction must be made not later than two years (or such longer period as HMRC may allow) after the date of the transfer.

Late compensation for World War II claims

[5.18] By HMRC concession F20, payments under various schemes established to provide compensation for wrongs suffered during the World War II era, made either to the victim or the surviving spouse, are excluded from inheritance tax.

Mutual transfers (FA 1986, s 104)

[5.19] Where a potentially exempt transfer (see **5.23**) or a chargeable transfer is made and the donee then makes a gift back to the donor, there are provisions to avoid a double charge to tax if the donor dies within seven years.

Excluded property (IHTA 1984, ss 3, 5, 6, 48)

[5.20] Inheritance tax is not chargeable on lifetime transfers of excluded property, nor is such property taken into account in valuing an estate at death. Excluded property includes:

(i)   property situated overseas where the person beneficially entitled to it is not domiciled in the UK;

(ii)   a reversionary interest in trust funds (i.e. the right to the capital when the rights to the income come to an end);

(iii)   certain government securities;

(iv)   savings owned by persons domiciled in the Isle of Man or the Channel Islands;

(v)   decorations awarded for valour or gallant conduct providing they have never been sold. If they have been sold at any time, the exclusion does not apply.

In limited circumstances, excluded property may need to be taken into account in valuing lifetime transfers of other property, but in general excluded property is treated in the same way as property that is exempt.

Basis of charge (IHTA 1984, ss 1–8 and Sch 1; FA 2006, s 155; FA 2010, s 8)

[5.21] A running total is kept of chargeable lifetime transfers and no tax is payable either on the lifetime gifts or on wealth at death until a threshold is reached. The thresholds from 6 April 2007 have been fixed as follows:

	Threshold
6 April 2007 to 5 April 2008	£300,000
6 April 2008 to 5 April 2009	£312,000
6 April 2009 to 5 April 2015	£325,000

The threshold is able to be increased annually and at least in line with increases in the retail prices index unless Parliament decides otherwise (as it has done for the years shown above). Any annual increases do not enable tax paid on earlier transfers to be recovered.

The full rate of tax on transfers above the threshold is 40%. Chargeable lifetime transfers above the nil rate threshold are charged at only 20% (but see **5.26**). The rates and thresholds for earlier years are shown in the Table of Rates and Allowances under 'Inheritance tax'. Transfers are excluded from the running total seven years after they are made.

Lifetime transfers

[5.22] Most of the transfers a person is likely to make in a lifetime will be wholly exempt from tax (see **5.3** to **5.19**). Transfers that do not fall within those categories will either be potentially exempt (**5.23**) or a chargeable lifetime transfer (**5.24**).

Potentially exempt transfers (IHTA 1984, s 3A)

[5.23] Potentially exempt transfers are only chargeable to tax if the donor dies within seven years of making them (subject to what is said at **5.36** about retaining a benefit). Even then, there will be no tax to pay on a potentially exempt transfer unless, when added to reckonable chargeable transfers in the seven years before it (see **5.24**), it exceeds the nil rate threshold at death. Potentially exempt transfers that become chargeable will, however, be taken into account to establish how much, if any, of the nil rate band is available to set against the value of an estate at death. Clearly, a very wealthy individual who had made no chargeable transfers could make a series of annual gifts, each of which (after exemptions) equalled the threshold at that time. If he survived the last of the series by seven years, a substantial amount would have been given away with no inheritance tax consequences. If, however, he died, say, within eight years after the first gift, an extremely large inheritance tax bill would arise in respect of the lifetime gifts before considering the estate at death (although tapering relief would apply on gifts made more than three years before death (see **5.27**)).

Example 1

The only lifetime transfer made by a widower is a gift of £100,000 on 10 June 2008 to his daughter towards the cost of buying a house. He dies in May 2010, leaving an estate at death of £300,000.

After deducting two years' annual exemptions totalling £6,000 (see 5.10), there is a potentially exempt transfer of £94,000 on 10 June 2008, which becomes chargeable because of the widower's death within seven years. No tax is payable on that transfer because it falls within the £325,000 nil rate threshold applying at the date of death. There is then, however, only £231,000 of the nil rate threshold remaining, so that £69,000 of the death estate of £300,000 is chargeable to tax at 40%.

If the widower had survived until 10 June 2015 the lifetime gift would have been completely exempt, and tax would only have been payable if the estate at death had exceeded the nil rate threshold at that time.

A potentially exempt transfer which becomes chargeable on death within seven years of the original transfer is brought into account at the value of the gift when it was originally made. Tax is calculated taking into account any chargeable transfers (including potentially exempt transfers that have become chargeable) within the seven years before that transfer. The nil rate threshold and rate of tax used are, however, those in force at the date of death.

It is therefore possible to fix the value of the transfer by giving in lifetime and this may be particularly useful where there are appreciating assets, since any later growth in value is in the hands of the donee. The capital gains tax effect must also be considered, however, because a lifetime gift of a chargeable asset will be liable to capital gains tax unless the gain can be deferred (see **CHAPTER 4**), whereas if the asset is held until death the increase in value up to that time escapes capital gains tax. Any capital gains tax paid on a gift that is a potentially exempt transfer cannot be offset in calculating any inheritance tax that becomes payable, but the wealth of the donor will have been depleted by the capital gains tax paid, thus reducing the inheritance tax liability.

If capital gains tax gift relief *is* available, and the potentially exempt transfer becomes liable to inheritance tax, that tax will be payable by the donee and will be deducted in computing the donee's capital gain (but cannot create a loss) when he eventually disposes of the asset.

See **5.26** for the treatment of a gift that has fallen in value by the time of the donor's death. See CHAPTER 42 for specific transfers into interest in possession trusts that are treated as potentially exempt.

Chargeable lifetime transfers (IHTA 1984, ss 2, 3, 5)

[5.24] The value of a chargeable lifetime transfer is the difference between the value of the donor's estate before and after the transfer, reduced by any available exemptions (see **5.3** to **5.19**) and ignoring disposals of excluded property (see **5.20**). This is referred to as the 'loss to the donor' principle. In many cases the value of the transfer will be the same as the market value of the asset transferred, but this is not always the case, particularly when unquoted shares are disposed of. In some instances other 'related property' also has to be taken into account (see **5.31**).

From 22 March 2006 the main category of transfers which are immediately chargeable in lifetime are those to all lifetime trusts except disabled trusts (see CHAPTER 42 for details). (Prior to 22 March 2006, the main category were transfers to discretionary trusts (i.e. trusts in which no-one has a right to the income, and it is up to the trustees how much of the income is distributed).

The annual exemption and the nil rate threshold of £325,000 are available providing they have not already been used against earlier chargeable transfers. As with potentially exempt transfers, chargeable lifetime transfers are taken into account in the running total at death if the donor dies within seven years after making them. Tax is recalculated on them at the full rate, taking into account any chargeable transfers (including potentially exempt transfers that have become chargeable) within the seven years before the transfer.

If the gifted asset was a chargeable asset for capital gains tax, and the gain had been deferred under the capital gains gift relief provisions (see **4.24** to **4.26**), any inheritance tax paid immediately or on the donor's death within seven years is deducted in computing the donee's capital gain when he eventually disposes of the asset.

The inheritance tax on a chargeable lifetime gift is usually paid by the recipient, but it may be paid by the donor. In that event, the amount chargeable to tax is found by grossing up the amount of the gift to allow for the tax which the donor has to pay.

Example 2

Donor makes a chargeable lifetime transfer of £8,000 when the nil rate threshold had already been used, so that the rate of tax is 20%. He pays the tax.

The value for inheritance tax is £8,000 × 100/80 = £10,000.

Being:	The chargeable transfer	10,000
	Tax payable @ 20%	2,000
	Leaving for the donee	£8,000

If the donor fails to pay the capital gains tax on a gift, it may be collected from the recipient, and in that event it is deducted from the value of the gift in calculating the value for inheritance tax.

Transfers on death (IHTA 1984, s 4)

[5.25] On death, the individual is treated as making a final transfer of the whole of his estate. The tax charged depends on the value of the estate plus the total of chargeable lifetime transfers and potentially exempt transfers within the previous seven years. No account is taken of 'excluded property' (see **5.20**).

In arriving at the value of an estate, any liabilities at the date of death are deducted (unless they are excluded under the anti-avoidance provisions), and also reasonable funeral expenses, mourning expenses and the cost of a headstone.

The estate is the total of all the property to which the individual was beneficially entitled (with the exclusion of any powers over trust property (see **42.8**)). The estate also includes:

(a)   any interests held as a joint tenant. Such an interest is automatically transferred to the other joint tenant(s) on death, but it still forms part of the estate for tax purposes (this differs from a share as a tenant in common, where each person has a separate share which he may dispose of as he wishes, and which therefore counts as his own property for all purposes); and

(b)   the capital value of a trust fund where the individual was entitled to the trust income (called an interest in possession or a life interest) if the interest in the trust arose before 22 March 2006, or arose on or after that date and comes within certain limited categories.

The inclusion of the capital value in a trust fund in an estate ((*b*) above) means that on death, the beneficiary is treated as making a chargeable transfer of the capital in the fund, although the tax on that amount is paid by the trustees.

On the other hand, if, because of the beneficiary's entitlement to the income, the capital is treated for inheritance tax purposes as part of his estate already, there is no charge to tax if in his lifetime he was allocated part of the capital which supports his life interest.

Where assets in the estate at death are left to a spouse or civil partner, no tax is payable (unless the spouse or civil partner is not domiciled in the UK, in which case the exempt amount is limited to £55,000). The other exempt transfers listed at **5.3** to **5.19** are also left out of account. For more detailed points relating to the death estate, see **CHAPTER 35**.

Transfers made within the seven years before death (IHTA 1984, s 7)

[5.26] Where a chargeable lifetime transfer has been made, all or part of which has been charged at the 20% rate, and the donor dies within seven years of making it, additional tax may be payable. This is because the tax is recomputed at the full scale rate applicable at the date of death, taking into account other chargeable transfers (including potentially exempt transfers that have become chargeable) within the seven years before the transfer and using the nil rate threshold applicable at the date of death. The donee has to pay the amount by which the tax at the appropriate percentage of the full-scale rate exceeds any tax paid on the gift in lifetime. If, however, the lifetime tax exceeds the death tax, no repayment is available.

If any potentially exempt transfers have been made in the seven years before death, they become chargeable and are taken into account in the running total, along with any chargeable lifetime transfers, according to the date each transfer was made. The re-allocation of the nil rate threshold may mean that some or all of it is no longer available against a chargeable lifetime transfer, causing tax, or more tax, to be payable.

Example 3

Donor who died on 25 May 2010 made the following gifts in lifetime (after taking annual and other exemptions into account):

9 April 2003	To brother	£40,000
26 July 2003	To son	£70,000
15 September 2004	To daughter	£75,000
10 April 2008	To discretionary trust (tax paid by trustees)	£322,000
30 June 2009	To sister	£20,000

The only chargeable lifetime gift was the gift to the discretionary trust on 10 April 2008, on which, using the nil rate band at that date, the tax was:

(£322,000 − £312,000 nil rate band) = £10,000 @ 20%	£2,000

On death on 25 May 2010:

The gift on 9 April 2003 to brother is not taken into account, since it was more than seven years before donor's death. Gifts to son, daughter and sister become chargeable, but no tax is payable on gifts to son and daughter, since those two gifts together are below the nil rate threshold. The threshold remaining is, however, (£325,000 − £145,000) = £180,000.

Tax on gift to trust	
(£322,000 − £180,000) = £142,000 @ 40%	56,800
Less paid in lifetime	2,000

Tax payable by trustees		£54,800
Tax payable by sister on gift to her	£20,000 @ 40%	£8,000

Tax @ 40% will also be paid on the estate at death.

Had the gift on 9 April 2003 been to a discretionary trust, it would have been a chargeable transfer at that time, although no tax would have been payable since it would have been below the nil rate threshold. It would have been taken into account in calculating whether tax was payable on the other lifetime transfers, since it was made within the seven years before each of them. It would, however, have been excluded from the running total seven years after it was made, i.e. at 9 April 2010, and would not, therefore, have been taken into account in calculating tax on the death estate.

If the value of a gifted asset that is not a 'wasting asset' has fallen between the time of the gift and death, the lower value may be used to calculate the tax. If the donee had sold the asset before the donor's death in an arm's length, freely negotiated sale, to an unconnected person, the sale proceeds may be used instead if they are lower than the value when the gift was made.

Tapering relief

[5.27] When working out the tax, or additional tax, payable on gifts within the seven years before death, the tax is reduced if the donor survives the gift by more than three years. The percentage of the full scale rate payable following the reduction is as follows:

Time between chargeable gift and death	% payable
Up to 3 years	100
More than 3 but not more than 4 years	80
More than 4 but not more than 5 years	60
More than 5 but not more than 6 years	40
More than 6 but not more than 7 years	20

Example 4

The only chargeable transfer made by a taxpayer in lifetime is a transfer to a discretionary trust of £375,000 (after exemptions) on 30 September 2010. The tax payable by the trustees is (£375,000 – £325,000 nil rate band = £50,000 @ 20%), i.e. £10,000.

Assuming that the tax rate and threshold remained unchanged, so that £20,000 was in fact the amount of tax at the full rate of 40%, the effect of the tapering relief would be as follows:

If taxpayer died in	Time between gift and death	% of £20,000 payable	Amounting to
			£
October 2011	Less than 3 yrs	100	20,000
December 2013	3 to 4 yrs	80	16,000
January 2016	5 to 6 yrs	40	8,000

Therefore:

Extra tax payable if death had occurred in October 2011 would be £10,000.

Extra tax payable if death had occurred in December 2013 would be £6,000.

No extra tax would be due if death occurred in January 2016 because the reduced tax of £8,000 would be less than the tax already paid of £10,000. No tax would, however, be repayable.

If the lifetime gift had been to an individual it would have been potentially exempt, and no tax would have been paid on it in lifetime, but the calculation of the tax at death would be as shown above.

Valuation of property (IHTA 1984, ss 160–198)

[5.28] The value of property for inheritance tax is the amount it might reasonably be expected to fetch if sold in the open market. The price is not, however, to be reduced on the grounds that the whole property is placed on the market at one time.

If the asset to be transferred will give rise to a capital gains tax liability, and the donee agrees to pay that tax, then the value transferred is reduced by the capital gains tax paid. However, capital gains tax may sometimes not arise on gifts because of the availability of gift holdover relief. See 4.24 to 4.26.

Valuation on death

[5.29] The way in which the death estate is valued, and the reliefs which are available, are dealt with below. The various exemptions that may be available are dealt with at 5.3 onwards.

Transfers of 'excluded property' are ignored in valuing the death estate (see 5.20).

Apart from life insurance policies (see 5.32), the value of property to be included in the estate at death is that immediately before death. Changes in the value of the estate as a result of the death are taken into account, for example the increased value of life insurance policies and the reduction in the value of goodwill which depends upon the personal qualities of the deceased. Allowance is made for reasonable funeral expenses, mourning expenses and the cost of a headstone. In the case of overseas property, allowance is also made for additional expenses incurred because of its situation, subject to a limit of 5% of the value of the property.

Quoted securities and land transferred on death

[5.30] Where an estate on death includes quoted securities, and they are sold by the personal representatives within 12 months after death for less than their value at death, then the total sales proceeds before expenses may be substituted for the death value. A revised value may also be included for quoted securities that are cancelled, or in which dealings are suspended, within the 12 months after death. In claiming this relief, *all* sales in the 12 month period, including those at a profit, must be taken into account in the total proceeds figure. The relief is restricted if any purchase of quoted securities takes place in the period from the date of death to the end of two months after the last sale within the 12 months after death.

HMRC have announced (at http://www.hmrc.gov.uk/inheritancetax/solicitors-advisers/bb-shares.htm) that for deaths on or after 5 July 2010, the right to receive compensation in respect of Bradford and Bingley shares may be included at a nil value. For deaths occurring before 5 July 2010, where the holding is of 1,000 shares or less, the right to receive compensation may be included at a nil value; if the holding is 1,000 or more taxpayers are advised to contact the Shares and Assets Valuation Helpline.

If the estate includes land which is sold by the personal representatives within four years after death, a claim may be made, subject to certain restrictions, to substitute the total sale proceeds before expenses for the value at death.

Related property

[5.31] If an individual owns part of an asset, (and part is owned by a spouse or civil partner), or an individual has made an exempt transfer of part of an asset to a charity, political party or national heritage body and it is still owned by that body or has been so owned at any time within the previous five years, the related property provisions apply. These provisions are mainly relevant to valuing transfers of unquoted shares and where freehold or leasehold property is owned jointly.

The value of a part of related property is taken as an appropriate portion of the total value of all the property if it produces a higher value than its unrelated value.

Example 5

The shareholders of Related Ltd, an unquoted company, are Mr R 40%, Mrs R 25%, others 35%. Shareholdings are valued as follows:

65% holding   £117,000

40% holding	£48,000
25% holding	£30,000
Inheritance tax values are:	
Mr R 40/65 × £117,000	£72,000 (being greater than £48,000)
Mrs R 25/65 × £117,000	£45,000 (being greater than £30,000)

Business property relief may be available (see **5.40**).

If related property is sold within three years after death to an unconnected person, a claim may be made for the tax at death to be recomputed using its unrelated value (not its sale value).

Life insurance policies

[5.32] The valuation of life insurance policies depends on whether the transfer is during the lifetime or on the death of the donor. Policies transferred in lifetime are valued at the greater of the surrender value and the premiums paid. Sometimes it is the policy premiums, rather than the policy itself, which are transfers of value (e.g. where a policy is written in trust for another person and the premiums are paid by the person whose life is assured). In such cases, depending on the policy arrangements and conditions, each premium payment may be a potentially exempt transfer unless it is already exempt as a gift out of income or as a small gift or because of the annual exemption.

On death the maturity value of a policy taken out by a person on his own life will be included in his estate unless it has been assigned to someone else in lifetime (when it will be reckoned as a lifetime transfer), or it has been written in trust for the benefit of someone else.

Survivorship clauses (IHTA 1984, s 92)

[5.33] Although the tax on successive transfers may be reduced by quick succession relief (**5.45**) where death occurs within five years after the first transfer, this is not so beneficial as the value not being included at all. It is possible to include a survivorship clause in a will stipulating that assets do not pass to the intended beneficiary unless he/she survives the deceased by a prescribed period, limited to a maximum of six months (see **35.13**). This avoids the double charge to tax.

Varying the distribution of the estate (IHTA 1984, ss 17, 142, 218A)

[5.34] The way in which the estate liable to inheritance tax at death is distributed may be varied by those entitled to it, and legacies may be disclaimed wholly or in part. Where this happens within two years after the death, the variation or disclaimer takes effect for inheritance tax purposes as if it had applied at the date of death. The variation or disclaimer must not be for consideration. For variations (but not disclaimers) this is subject to the proviso that those making it (and the personal representatives if additional inheritance tax is payable) state in the variation that they intend it to have this effect. Where additional tax is payable, then within six months after the date of the variation the personal representatives must notify HMRC of the amount of extra tax and send a copy of the variation. Following the variation/disclaimer inheritance tax will be payable as if the revised distribution had operated at death. Similar provisions apply for capital gains tax (see **4.34**). For further details, see CHAPTER 35.

The effect of the transitional rules following the amendment in Finance Act 2006 of the taxation treatment of trusts is dealt with in CHAPTER 42.

Anti-avoidance provisions

[5.35] Anti-avoidance provisions have been introduced to prevent exploitation of potentially exempt transfers, in particular where taxpayers give property away in a series of connected operations (known as associated operations), or where property is gifted but the donor retains a benefit. The main anti-avoidance provisions are discussed below.

Gifts with reservation of benefit (FA 1986, ss 102–102C and Sch 20; FA 2004, s 84 and Sch 15)

[5.36] Property that is given away is treated as still belonging to the donor if he continues to enjoy any benefit from it (or the donee does not assume possession and enjoyment of it). This rule does not apply if the gift qualifies for one of the exemptions listed at **5.3** onwards (with the exclusion of the normal expenditure out of income exemption, the £3,000 annual exemption, the conditional exemption for heritage property and the World War II compensation exemption).

Where the property given is an interest in land, the donor will be regarded as having retained a benefit if there is some interest, right or arrangement which enables or entitles him to occupy the land to a material degree without paying full consideration, and the gift is made within seven years after the interest, right or arrangement is created or entered into. If the donor still retains a benefit at the time of his death, the property is treated as remaining in his estate and is taxed accordingly.

Example 6

A donor gives away his house but continues to live in it rent free. His continued occupation is a reservation of benefit. He will be treated as making a second gift at the time when he ceases to occupy the house or starts to pay a proper rent for his occupation, so that inheritance tax may be payable if he does not then survive for a further seven years.

The donor will not be treated as retaining an interest if an unconditional gift of a *share* in the home is made and both donor and donee continue to live there and each pays a *full* share of the outgoings.

The gifts with reservation rules were extended to apply to certain life interests in trusts that come to an end on or after 22 March 2006, where the former holder of the interest continues to enjoy a benefit from the trust assets.

The rules about retaining a benefit can result in a double inheritance tax charge and there are special rules to eliminate any double charges that occur.

This is a complex aspect of inheritance tax. Detailed guidance is available in HMRC's Inheritance Tax Manual at IHTM14301.

Various schemes have been devised to circumvent the gifts with reservation rules. An *income tax* 'pre-owned assets' charge is made where someone has disposed of assets since *18 March 1986* but retains a benefit. The charge is based on the annual value of the use of the assets. If the total annual value amounts to £5,000 or less, however, no income tax charge will arise (see **5.37**).

Pre-owned assets (FA 2004, s 84 and Sch 15; SI 2005/724; SI 2005/3441; SI 2007/684)

[5.37] Provisions were introduced with effect from 2005/06 to impose an income tax charge where a taxpayer has the benefit of free or low-cost use of an asset that he has previously owned. The intention of the provisions is to counter schemes which avoid the inheritance tax (IHT) charge on gifts with reservation, but it is widely considered that the measures are ill-considered and in many instances unfair, particularly as they relate to transactions that may have been undertaken as long ago as 1986.

The provisions apply to land, chattels and gifts into trusts of intangible assets (which include cash). The charge for land is based on the rental value and the charge for other assets is calculated by applying the official rate of interest to the value of the asset, reduced in the case of chattels by any payments made for use of the asset and reduced in the case of intangible assets by any income tax or CGT payable in respect of the assets. Land and chattels are valued at 6 April 2005 (or when the asset first becomes chargeable) for the purpose of arriving at the first and subsequent annual charges and revaluations will be made at 6 April every five years. There is no charge if the value of the benefit is £5,000 per annum or less.

The provisions do not apply to property:

(a)   that ceased to be owned before 18 March 1986;
(b)   sold for an arm's length price;
(c)   given outright to the former owner's spouse or civil partner (or former spouse or civil partner);
(d)   that was a cash gift towards the purchase of land or chattels, made at least seven years before the individual occupied the land or had use of the chattels (excluding outright cash gifts made before 6 April 1998);
(e)   where the transfer is within the IHT annual or small gifts exemptions (see **5.10**) or the 'gifts for family maintenance' exemption (see **5.5**);

(f)   that is still included in the estate of the taxpayer or his/her spouse or civil partner for IHT, for example because the property has been transferred to a trust in which the transferor has an interest in possession which is reckoned for IHT at his death, or because of the gifts with reservation rules (as to which see **5.36**); this exemption does not apply where a taxpayer has disposed of an asset and continues to benefit from it through an interest in possession which escapes IHT on his death because the asset then reverts to the settlor;

(g)   previously owned only by virtue of a will or intestacy which has subsequently been varied by agreement between the beneficiaries.

The provisions do not affect bona fide equity release schemes made at arm's length, or in some instances otherwise than at arm's length (see **34.11** onwards). Life policies put into trust before 22 March 2006 (see **40.14**) are not within the provisions, nor are nil rate band trusts created by will (see **35.4**).

The provisions do not apply to those who are not resident in the UK, nor to overseas property in relation to someone who is UK resident but domiciled abroad.

There are basically three ways of dealing with the pre-owned assets provisions:

(a)   Leave the provisions in place and pay the annual income tax charge (or a market rent). This means that the asset will not form part of the estate for IHT (providing the taxpayer survives the gift by seven years).

(b)   Leave the provisions in place but notify HMRC on or before the filing date for the self-assessment return that the gift is to be treated as within the gifts with reservation rules (see **5.36**). From 21 March 2007 HMRC may accept elections made after the filing date, even if the filing date was before 21 March 2007. The notification is made on form IHT 500. This avoids the income tax charge but for IHT the asset is then still treated as part of the estate at death. Furthermore, for CGT the donee will have acquired the asset at the market value at the date of the gift, so may face a large CGT bill when it is sold.

(c)   Unravel the scheme. This may be quite complicated, and the costs involved may be significant. There is relief for double charges where the value is included for IHT under more than one provision.

Associated operations (IHTA 1984, s 268)

[5.38] There are rules to enable HMRC to treat a series of connected operations as a single transfer of assets made at the time of the last of them.

Reliefs

[5.39] There are a number of reliefs available either to reduce the amount chargeable to IHT or to reduce the amount of tax due. The main reliefs are discussed below.

Business property relief (IHTA 1984, ss 103–114)

[5.40] Business property relief is available on the value of transfers of business property (in the UK or elsewhere), providing certain conditions as to the length of ownership and type of business are satisfied. The relief is given at the following rates:

A business or interest in a business (including a partnership share)	100%
Transfers out of a holding of unquoted shares	100%
Transfers out of a holding of unquoted *securities* in a company which, together with any unquoted *shares* in the company (including in both cases 'related property' holdings), gave the holder control of the company	100%
Transfers out of a controlling shareholding in a quoted company (including control through 'related property' holdings)	50%
Land or buildings, machinery or plant used for a business carried on by a company of which the donor had control; or a partnership in which he or she was a partner; or the donor, where the property was settled property in which he or she had an interest in possession	50%

Shares on the Alternative Investment Market (AIM) are treated as unquoted shares.

The property transferred must normally have been owned by the donor throughout the previous two years. Business property relief is not available where the business consists of dealing in stocks and shares (except market makers on the Stock Exchange and discount houses), dealing in land and buildings or holding investments (including land which is let).

The relief is applied automatically without a claim and is given after agricultural property relief (see below) but before available exemptions.

Binding contract for sale (IHTA 1984, ss 113, 124)

[5.41] Property does not qualify for business or agricultural relief (**5.43**) if it is subject to a binding contract for sale (except a contract relating to the conversion of an unincorporated business to a company, or a company reconstruction). A 'buy and sell' agreement made by partners or company directors to take effect on their death is considered by HMRC to constitute such a contract, but not a double option agreement whereby the deceased's personal representatives have an *option* to sell and the surviving partners or directors an *option* to buy.

Calculation of tax on lifetime transfers following death within seven years (IHTA 1984, ss 113A, 113B, 124A, 124B)

[5.42] In computing the tax payable as a result of death, business and agricultural property relief is applicable so long as:

(a)   the original property (or qualifying property which has replaced it) was owned by the donee throughout the period beginning with the date of the transfer and ending with the death of the donor; this condition will be regarded as satisfied if there is a period of up to three years between the sale of one qualifying property and the acquisition of another; and

(b)   immediately before the death of the donor, the property (or any replacement property) is qualifying business or agricultural property (this may not apply because, for example, there might have been a change of use, or at the time of death there might be a binding contract for sale). In order for unquoted shares to be qualifying business property they must still be unquoted when the donor dies.

If the donee died before the donor, the periods at (a) and (b) are from the date of the gift to the date of death of the donee.

Proportionate relief is available where only part of the property continues to qualify, for example, where part of the property has been sold.

Since any increase in the value of assets up to the date of death is also exempt from capital gains tax (see **4.34**), the availability of the 100% business or agricultural property relief is an important influence in estate planning, because where it applies there will be no tax benefit from making potentially exempt transfers in lifetime. On the other hand, it cannot be certain that the tax regime will remain as favourable as it is now.

Agricultural property relief (IHTA 1984, ss 115–124C)

[5.43] Agricultural property relief is available on the transfer of agricultural property situated in the UK, Channel Islands, Isle of Man or (from 22 April 2009) in any country that is a member of the European Economic Area, so long as various conditions are met. The extension to EEA countries also applies to any earlier chargeable occasion where inheritance tax in respect of that occasion was due or paid on or after 23 April 2003.

Agricultural property is agricultural land or pasture (including short rotation coppice land and farmland dedicated to wildlife habitats under Government Habitat Schemes), woodland and buildings used for rearing livestock or fish where the occupation of the woodland and buildings is ancillary to that of the agricultural land, and cottages, farm buildings and farmhouses occupied with the agricultural land. The relief only applies to the agricultural value of the property, and in arriving at that value any loan secured on the agricultural property must be deducted.

The agricultural property must at the time of the transfer have been either occupied by the donor for agriculture throughout the two years ending with the date of transfer or owned by the donor throughout the previous seven years and occupied for agriculture by him or someone else throughout that period. This enables relief to be given on agricultural investment property. In certain circumstances these rules are modified if the property transferred was acquired as a replacement for other agricultural property.

Relief is available both on the transfer of agricultural property itself, and on the transfer of shares out of a controlling holding in a farming company to the extent of the underlying agricultural value.

The rates of relief are:

(c)   100% where the donor had the right to vacant possession immediately before the transfer, or the right to obtain vacant possession within the next 12 months. By HMRC concession F17, the 100% rate is given on tenanted agricultural property where vacant possession is obtainable within 24 months, or where the property is valued broadly at vacant possession value despite the tenancy.

(d)   100% for other tenanted agricultural property where the letting commenced on or after 1 September 1995 (including successions to tenancies following the death of the previous tenant on or after that date).

(e)   50% for transfers of property let before 1 September 1995.

(f)   100% on tenanted agricultural property where the donor had been beneficially entitled to his interest in the property since before 10 March 1981 and would have been entitled to the higher rate of relief (then 50%) under the provisions for agricultural relief which operated before that date.

Where agricultural property satisfies the conditions for business property relief, agricultural property relief is given first and business property relief is given on the non-agricultural value. As with business property relief, agricultural property relief is given without the need for a claim.

The provisions discussed at **5.41** and **5.42** apply equally to agricultural property relief.

Growing timber (IHTA 1984, ss 125–130)

[5.44] Where an estate on death includes growing timber, an election may be made to leave the timber (but not the land on which it stands) out of account in valuing the estate at death. The relief is dealt with in **31.30**.

Quick succession relief (IHTA 1984, s 141)

[5.45] Where a donee dies after receiving a chargeable transfer, the transfer will have increased his estate at death and therefore attracts tax in his estate as well as tax possibly having arisen on the earlier transfer. Relief is given where the death occurs within five years after the earlier transfer. There is no requirement to retain the actual asset obtained by that transfer.

The total tax on the chargeable estate is calculated in the normal way and reduced by the quick succession relief. The relief is arrived at by first making the following calculation:

$$\frac{\text{Previous transfer net of tax}}{\text{Previous gross transfer}} \times \text{Tax paid on previous transfer}$$

The relief is the following percentage of the calculated amount:

Years between transfer and death	Percentage relief
Up to 1 year	100%
More than 1 but not more than 2	80%
More than 2 but not more than 3	60%
More than 3 but not more than 4	40%
More than 4 but not more than 5	20%

Example 7

Thomas, who died on 28 June 2010 leaving an estate of £400,000, had received a gift of £50,000 from his father on 30 October 2007, on which he had paid tax of £20,000 following his father's death on 26 May 2009.

Tax on Thomas's estate will be reduced by quick succession relief as follows (Thomas having died more than two years but not more than three years after gift):

$$\frac{\text{Net transfer } 30,000}{\text{Gross transfer } 50,000} \times \text{Tax } £20,000 \times 60\% = £7,200$$

Quick succession relief is also available where there are successive charges within five years on trust property which has been reckoned for inheritance tax by reference to the death of the person entitled to the income. The rates of relief are the same as those quoted above, with the percentage relief depending on the period between the successive charges.

It may be that at the time the donee dies, the transfer to him is still classed as a potentially exempt transfer because the donor is still alive, but the donor may then die, after the donee but within the seven-year period, so that the potentially exempt transfer becomes chargeable by reference to the donor's estate, with the personal representatives of the donee being liable to pay any tax. Quick succession relief will then be available in the donee's estate by reference to that tax.

Administration

[5.46] IHT is administered by the Inheritance Tax Offices. Unlike other taxes, IHT is not based on an annual process. Instead the tax will only arise when a transfer of value is made either during the lifetime of an individual or on his death. The main payment provisions are discussed below.

Date of payment; interest on overdue or overpaid inheritance tax; penalties (ss 226–236)

[5.47] The normal due dates of payment are as follows.

Chargeable lifetime transfers between 6 April and 30 September	Chargeable lifetime transfers between 1 October and 5 April	Death — including additional tax on chargeable lifetime transfers and tax on potentially exempt transfers which become chargeable
30 April in following year	6 months after end of month in which transfer was made	6 months after end of month in which death occurs

The personal representatives of a deceased's estate must, however, pay any tax for which they are liable, and which may not be paid by instalments, at the time they apply for probate, even if this is before the due date as shown above. If the personal representatives take out a loan to pay the inheritance tax, relief for the interest paid on the loan is given in calculating the tax payable on the income of the estate (see **42.4**).

If there are funds on bank or building society accounts belonging to the deceased, the personal representatives may arrange for a direct transfer to HMRC before probate is granted rather than taking out a loan to pay the inheritance tax (see **42.2**).

Interest is payable on overdue tax (or repayable on overpaid tax). For recent rates see the Table of Rates and Allowances under 'Interest on overdue/overpaid inheritance tax'. Interest on overdue tax is not deductible in arriving at income tax payable by the personal representatives and interest on overpaid tax is tax-free. Overpayments carry interest from the date of payment.

Where tax has not been paid because a transfer was conditionally exempt, the due date is six months after the end of the month in which the event by reason of which it is chargeable occurs (e.g. breach of an undertaking in respect of heritage property).

Payment by instalments

[5.48] Inheritance tax may be paid by equal yearly instalments over ten years on qualifying assets. This applies where the assets are transferred on death, and also to chargeable lifetime transfers if the *donee* pays the tax. The option to pay by instalments also applies to a potentially exempt transfer of qualifying property which becomes a chargeable transfer on the death of the donor within seven years after the gift, so long as the donee still owns the gifted property (or, for transfers of property qualifying for business or agricultural relief, replacement property) at the time of the donor's death. The first instalment is due on chargeable lifetime transfers on the normal due date and in the case of tax payable in consequence of death, six months after the end of the month in which the death occurred.

The instalment option applies to land wherever situated, to a business or interest in a business, to timber when it becomes chargeable after being left out of account on a previous death, to controlling shareholdings, and to unquoted shares if certain conditions are met. For unquoted shares, the instalment option is not available for tax payable as a result of the donor's death, unless the shares are still unquoted when the donor dies (or, if earlier, when the donee dies).

Interest normally runs only from the date the instalment falls due and not on the full amount of the deferred tax. This does not apply in the case of land, other than land included in a business or partnership interest and agricultural land, nor in the case of shares in an investment company. Interest in those two cases is charged on the total amount remaining unpaid after the normal due date, the interest being added to each instalment as it falls due.

If the asset is sold, the outstanding tax becomes payable immediately.

Penalties

[5.49] In addition to interest on overdue tax, various penalties may be charged. For details see **9.51**.

Liability for tax (IHTA 1984, ss 199–214, 237)

[5.50] On lifetime transfers of property which are immediately chargeable, other than transfers of property in a trust fund, primary liability for payment rests with the donor. The donor and donee may, however, agree between them who is to pay, the transfer having to be grossed up if the donor pays (see Example 2 at **5.24**).

In the case of lifetime chargeable transfers of property which is within a trust, the primary liability is that of the trustees.

On death, the personal representatives are liable to pay the tax on the assets coming into their hands, while the liability for tax on trust property which becomes chargeable at death rests with the trustees. See the example at **42.23**.

Where, as a result of the death of the donor within seven years, additional tax becomes payable on a lifetime transfer, or a potentially exempt transfer becomes liable to tax, the primary responsibility for paying the tax is that of the donee. The personal representatives are only liable if the tax remains unpaid 12 months after the end of the month in which the donor died, or to the extent that the tax payable exceeds the value of the gifted property held by the donee.

In addition to the persons mentioned, certain other people may be liable to pay inheritance tax, but usually only where tax remains unpaid after the due date. Where tax is unpaid HMRC are usually able to take a legal charge on the property concerned.

The person who is liable to pay inheritance tax is not necessarily the person who ultimately bears the tax. The trustees of a settlement are liable to pay any tax arising on trust funds, but those next enjoying the income or receiving the capital bear the tax because the trust funds are correspondingly lower. Personal representatives are liable to pay the tax on the assets of the deceased at death, but the residuary legatees (those who receive the balance of the estate after all other legacies) will suffer the tax by a reduction in the amount available for them, the other legatees receiving their legacies in full unless the will specifies that any particular legacy should bear its own tax.

Personal representatives, trustees and others liable to pay inheritance tax have to deliver an account to HMRC Inheritance Tax. For details see **9.21**.

Use of insurance

[5.51] There are many instances in the inheritance tax provisions where the potential liability to tax is not known at the time of the transfer, notably when potentially exempt transfers are made, but also when chargeable transfers are made, because if the donor dies within seven years additional tax may be payable. Temporary insurance cover may be taken out by the donee on the life of the donor to provide for the possible tax liability, with the policies being tailored to take account of the reduction in potential liability once the donor has survived the gift by three years. See also CHAPTER 40.

6

Stamp taxes

Background

[**6.1**] Stamp taxes have been charged since the seventeenth century. Stamp duty is a fixed or ad valorem charge on documents and duty is not payable if there is no document. A separate charge — stamp duty reserve tax — was introduced in 1986 to cover share transactions that escaped stamp duty (see **6.6**). The Electronic Communications Act 2000 made it possible to remove the legal requirement for transactions to be evidenced by paper documents, and the electronic transfer of land and buildings was facilitated by the introduction of a separate tax — stamp duty land tax — which replaced stamp duty on land and buildings from December 2003. Following the introduction of stamp duty land tax, stamp duty applies only to stock and marketable securities and certain transfers of interests in partnerships (see **6.23**).

Stamp duties and taxes are administered by HMRC Stamp Taxes. Stamp duty is dealt with in **6.2** to **6.5**, stamp duty reserve tax in **6.6** and **6.7**, and stamp duty land tax in **6.8** to **6.21**. Paragraphs **6.22** to **6.26** deal with topics affected by both stamp duty and stamp duty land tax.

Stamp duty

Instruments chargeable and rates (FA 1999, ss 112, 113 and Schs 13–16)

[**6.2**] Stamp duty applies in the following situations:

(a)   to transfers of stock and marketable securities (executed in the UK or relating to UK property, wherever executed) and to certain transfers of interests in partnerships (**6.23**). The rate of stamp duty is ½%;

(b)   to bearer instruments issued in the UK or by a UK company. The rate of stamp duty is 1¹/₂%;

(c)   to deposit certificates in non-UK companies or bearer instruments issued by non-UK companies. The rate of stamp duty is 0.2%;

(d)   to the issue of depository receipts or shares put into a duty free clearance system (other than between corporate nominees or between a depositary receipt system and a clearance service (or vice versa)). The rate of stamp duty is 1¹/₂%.

For instruments executed on or after 12 March 2008, stamp duty is not chargeable where the amount or value of the consideration is less than £1,000. No duty arises on transactions carried out orally. No duty is payable in connection with British Government stock, including gilt warrants, nor on a conveyance, transfer or lease to the Crown. There are special exemptions from duty for financial intermediaries trading in UK securities and in connection with stock borrowing and sale and repurchase arrangements. Furthermore FA 2009 provided relief from stamp duty (and SDRT) where, under a stock lending or sale and repurchase arrangement, securities are not returned to the originator because of the insolvency of one of the parties. Where the lender or seller buys securities to replace those lost the purchase is relieved from stamp duty and SDRT. HMRC subsequently confirmed that any person who has paid stamp duty in such circumstances (and where the relevant insolvency occurred on after 1 September 2008), is entitled to a repayment.

Generally, documents should be stamped before they take effect, although in practice stamping is permitted within 30 days without any penalty being charged.

Duty is either fixed or based on value depending on the heading under which the transaction falls. Ad valorem duties are rounded up to the nearest multiple of £5.

Adjudication and valuation (SA 1891, ss 12–13B)

[6.3] Adjudication is the assessment by a Stamp Office of how much duty, if any, is payable on a document and also the amount of any penalty payable for late stamping (as to which see **6.4**). Additionally, if after adjudication an unstamped or insufficiently stamped document is not duly stamped within 30 days, a penalty of up to £300 may be charged. Adjudication may be voluntary or compulsory. Anyone may ask a Stamp Office to state whether a document is chargeable, and if so, how much duty is payable. Sometimes, adjudication is compulsory, for example where exemption from duty is claimed on a company reconstruction without change in ownership.

Having considered the document the Stamp Office will either stamp it 'adjudged not chargeable with any stamp duty' or they will assess the duty and when it is paid, they will stamp the document 'adjudged duly stamped'. An adjudication stamp is normally conclusive evidence of due stamping.

An appeal may be made against an adjudication. Such an appeal must be made within 30 days and the duty plus any interest or penalty must be paid first. Appeals relating to late stamping penalties go first to the first tier tribunal and other appeals to the High Court.

Interest and penalties (SA 1891, ss 15–15B; FA 1989, s 178; FA 1999, ss 110, 114 and Sch 17)

[6.4] Where documents are submitted late for stamping, interest and penalties may be charged, as follows.

Interest is chargeable on all documents liable to ad valorem duty that are not stamped within 30 days of execution, but rounded down to a multiple of £5 and not charging amounts of £25 or less. Interest is also chargeable on stamp duty penalties (other than late stamping penalties).

Interest will be paid on repayments of overpaid duty from 30 days after execution or from the date of payment if later (except for repayments of less than £25).

The rates of interest are the same as for income tax.

If documents are submitted for stamping more than 30 days after execution a (mitigable) penalty may be charged.

The maximum penalty is £300 or the amount of the duty if less for documents submitted up to one year late. For documents submitted later than that, the maximum is £300 or the amount of the duty if more. There is a penalty of up to £300, or up to £3,000 in cases of fraud, for various administrative offences.

The above provisions are modified slightly in relation to bearer instruments, depository receipts and clearance systems.

Anti-avoidance provisions (FA 2000, ss 117–122 and Sch 33)

[6.5] The sharply increasing rates of stamp duty over recent years have led to an increase in devices to avoid stamp duty. FA 2000 introduced a general provision that regulations may be issued to block such devices as they arise, where they relate to any extent to land, stock or marketable securities. Such regulations will cease to be valid after 18 months unless they have been included in a Finance Act. These anti-avoidance provisions are relevant only to stock and marketable securities and certain partnership transactions from 1 December 2003 following the introduction of stamp duty land tax.

Various specific anti-avoidance provisions were also introduced by FA 2000. Duty is charged at the shares rate where marketable securities are transferred in exchange for property that is exempt from stamp duty reserve tax. Stamp duty is also chargeable at the shares rate where the consideration for a sale is the right to a future issue of securities.

Stamp duty reserve tax (FA 1986, ss 86–99; FA 1990, ss 110, 111; FA 1997, ss 100, 101; FA 1999, s 122 and Sch 19; FA 2001, s 94; FA 2010, s 54; SIs 1986/1711; 1997/1156; 1999/3262; 2001/964)

[6.6] Stamp duty reserve tax is dealt with mainly by Stock Exchange brokers and financial intermediaries. The following is a brief outline of the tax.

Stamp duty reserve tax (SDRT) at the rate of $\frac{1}{2}$% applies to:

(a) share transactions which escape stamp duty, for example, sales of renounceable letters of allotment and transactions within the same Stock Exchange account. Following the introduction of the CREST system of paperless share dealing on the Stock Exchange, CREST transactions that would have attracted stamp duty now attract SDRT instead;

(b) transfers of units in unit trust schemes or shares in Open Ended Investment Companies (OEICs). Transfers of units in unit trusts and surrenders of shares in open ended investment companies are exempt where they are held within individual pension accounts (see **17.1**);

(c) transfers of foreign currency bearer shares and of sterling or foreign currency bearer loan stock that is convertible or equity related. This charge does not apply if the securities are listed on a recognised stock exchange and the transfer is not made as part of a takeover.

SDRT also applies to shares converted into depositary receipts or put into a duty free clearing system. The rate of tax on these transactions is $1\frac{1}{2}$%. This higher rate acts as a 'season ticket' with subsequent transfers within the $1\frac{1}{2}$% system being exempt from the ordinary $\frac{1}{2}$% charges. Where securities that have been subject to a $1\frac{1}{2}$% entry charge are subsequently transferred to another $1\frac{1}{2}$% regime, relief is available to ensure that there is no double charge. On 1 October 2009, the European Court of Justice (ECJ) held that this higher rate charge on issues of chargeable securities to clearance services in the EU is incompatible with EU law. As a result, it became possible, from that date, for shares intended for non-EU markets to be issued initially to an EU clearance service or depositary receipt issuer, and then transferred to a non-EU clearance service or depositary receipt issuer, under cover of the existing exemptions for transfers between such systems, thereby avoiding all SDRT charges. Legislation was therefore introduced to ensure that where securities enter a clearance service or depositary receipts scheme without Stamp Duty or SDRT being due in accordance with the ECJ decision, a subsequent transfer of those securities into a clearance service or depositary receipts scheme no longer benefits from the exemptions designed to prevent a double charge.

There are several exceptions to this charge (e.g. it does not apply to transfers between certain corporate nominees, it does not apply on the issue or transfer of UK bearer instruments (unless they are renounceable letters of allotment and the rights are renounceable within six months of issue or they are foreign currency instruments which do not raise new consideration) etc.).

Clearing systems are able to elect to pay stamp duty or SDRT in the normal way on their transactions, and in that event, the $1\frac{1}{2}$% charge does not apply when chargeable securities are put into the system.

SDRT does not apply to gilt-edged stocks, traded options and futures, non-convertible loan stocks, foreign securities not on a UK register, depositary interests in foreign securities, transfers of units in foreign unit trusts, the issue of new securities and purchases by a charity. There are also special exemptions for financial intermediaries. Furthermore FA 2009 provided relief from SDRT (and stamp duty) where, under a stock lending or sale and repurchase arrangement, securities are not returned to the originator because of the insolvency of one of the parties. Where the lender or seller buys securities to replace those lost the purchase is relieved from stamp duty and SDRT. HMRC subsequently confirmed that any person who has paid stamp duty in such circumstances (and where the relevant insolvency occurred on or after 1 September 2008), is entitled to a repayment.

Liability to SDRT arises at the date of the agreement (or if the agreement is conditional, at the date the condition is satisfied). For transactions via an exchange (in particular CREST transactions), the tax is payable on a date agreed with HMRC (or if there is no agreed date, the fourteenth day after the transaction). For other transactions the due date is the seventh day of the month following the month in which the transaction occurred and the person liable to pay the tax (i.e. the broker, dealer or purchaser) must give notice of the charge to HMRC on or before that date.

SDRT is only payable to the extent that it exceeds any ad valorem stamp duty on the transaction, and where the ad valorem duty exceeds the amount of SDRT, no SDRT is payable. If duty is paid after SDRT has been paid, the SDRT is refunded (plus income tax free interest on refunds over £25).

HMRC guidance on SDRT is available at www.hmrc.gov.uk/so/sdrt.

Interest and penalties (SI 1986/1711 reg 20 and Sch)

[6.7] Interest is charged on overdue SDRT (or paid on SDRT repayments) from 14 days after the transaction date for exchange transactions and otherwise from seven days after the end of the month of the transaction, and there are various penalties for defaults, including a mitigable penalty of £100, plus £60 a day following a declaration by HMRC, where the appropriate notice of liability has not been given and the tax has not been paid.

The rates of interest are the same as for income tax.

Stamp duty land tax (FA 2003, ss 42–124 and Schs 3–19; FA 2010 s 6)

[6.8] Stamp duty land tax (SDLT) was introduced from 1 December 2003 to charge tax on transactions relating to UK land whether or not any party to the transaction is present or resident in the UK and whether or not a document is used. If a document is used, SDLT is charged whether or not it is executed in the UK. If a contract for a land transaction is 'substantially performed' (broadly when most of the consideration is paid or possession is taken of the property) before being formally completed, SDLT arises at that time. Otherwise it arises at the time of completion.

The consideration for an SDLT transaction is the amount payable in money or moneys' worth. Where consideration is contingent, tax is payable on the assumption that the consideration will be payable. Where consideration is uncertain, a reasonable estimate must be made. Where all or part of contingent or uncertain consideration is payable more than 18 months after the effective date of the transaction, an application may be made to defer the appropriate amount of tax. Provision is made for the tax to be adjusted upwards or downwards when the contingency occurs (or it is clear it will not occur), or when uncertain consideration is ascertained. Where a company purchases land from a connected person, the purchase price is deemed to be not less than the market value.

Certain transactions are exempt from SDLT, as indicated in **6.17** to **6.19** and **6.24**. HMRC guidance on SDLT is available at www.hmrc.gov.uk/sdlt.

Rates of tax etc

[6.9] The rates of SDLT are set out below:

Non-residential or mixed property:	Up to £150,000	Nil
	£150,001 to £250,000	1%
	£250,001 to £500,000	3%
	Over £500,000	4%
Residential property:	Up to £125,000	Nil
	£125,001 to £250,000: first time buyer*	Nil
	£125,001 to £250,000: non-first time buyer	1%
	£250,001 to £500,000	3%
	Over £500,000	4%
	Over £1,000,000**	5%

* *Where the effective date of the transaction is on or after 25 March 2010 and before 25 March 2012.*

** *Where the effective date of the transaction is on or after 6 April 2011.*

Special rules apply to equate the SDLT payable in relation to Sharia-compliant mortgages with the tax payable in relation to conventional mortgages.

Leases of land and buildings (FA 2003, ss 55, 56, 77, 120 and Schs 5, 17A)

[6.10] SDLT applies both to lease premiums and to the rental element of a lease. Lease premiums are charged at the same rates as for freehold transfers (see **6.9**). The SDLT payable on the rental element of leases is 1% of the excess of the net present value (NPV) of the rental payments over the thresholds of £125,000 for residential property or £150,000 for non-residential property.

All variations of a lease in the first five years that increase the rent (other than to reflect changes in the retail prices index) are treated as the grant of a new lease. SDLT applies to a capital payment by a landlord where the term of a lease is reduced, and to a capital payment by a tenant to commute all or part of the rent.

[6.11] After the first five years of a lease, then unless an increase is regarded as 'abnormal', any rent increases are ignored in calculating NPV and the rent value used for later periods is the highest rent in any 12 months in the first five years. Where rent is uncertain (e.g. related to turnover), the NPV is originally based on a reasonable estimate. If the rent is still uncertain after five years, a single additional land transaction return is required in which the NPV will be based on the actual rent in the first five years and the highest rent in any 12 months during those years, as above, for the remaining years of the lease. If the rent becomes certain within the five years the single additional return will be required at that time.

[6.12] Where a lease is surrendered, SDLT is payable on any consideration paid by the landlord as for a sale. If a reverse premium is paid by the tenant, SDLT is not chargeable. Where a lease is surrendered in return for a new lease, the grant of the new lease does not count as chargeable consideration for the surrender, and the surrender does not count as chargeable consideration for the new lease. Furthermore, credit is given in computing the SDLT on the new lease for the amount of rent due for the surrendered years.

[6.13] The grant of a lease for less than seven years or the assignment of such a lease only has to be notified to the Stamp Office if there is tax to pay or a relief to be claimed. Other grants/assignments of leases up to seven years may be self-certified.

Value added tax

[6.14] The value on which SDLT is charged on sales and leases of land and buildings includes any value added tax on the transaction. Where, however, a landlord has the option to charge VAT, but has not chosen to do so by the date of the transaction, VAT will be excluded from the chargeable consideration for the lease. For further details on the VAT position on property, see **CHAPTER 32**.

Part exchanges, sale and leaseback and other reliefs (FA 2003, ss 57A, 58A and Sch 6A)

[6.15] Relief is available, subject to various conditions, where a builder takes a home in part exchange, or where someone buying a new home from a builder sells their old home to a property trader, or where a property trader buys a home from someone whose sale of the property has fallen through to enable that person to proceed with the purchase of another property. Where the conditions are satisfied, the acquisition by the builder or property trader is exempt from SDLT.

Relief for sale and leaseback transactions is available for both commercial property and residential property. The effect of the relief is that the 'leaseback' element of the transaction is exempt from SDLT.

Rents to mortgages scheme (FA 2003, Sch 9.6)

[6.16] Where council house tenants buy their homes under a 'rents to mortgages scheme', SDLT is charged at the time they enter the scheme, on the then market value of the property, less any discount under the 'right to buy' provisions. If that amount is less than £125,000 no SDLT is payable. 'Rents to mortgages' schemes enable tenants to buy their homes for an initial payment, which may be financed by a mortgage and repaid in place of rent, plus a balance provided by way of interest-free loan. The amount payable when the purchaser is ready to repay the loan depends on the market value of the property at that time.

Transfers and leases of land and buildings by and to Registered Social Landlords (FA 2003, ss 49, 71 and Sch 3)

[6.17] Land transactions under which property is acquired by Registered Social Landlords (RSLs) or registered providers of social housing (e.g. Housing Associations) are, in specified circumstances, exempt from SDLT.

Leases by RSLs or registered providers of social housing are also exempt from SDLT if the lease is for or an indefinite term or terminable by notice of a month or less and it is provided under contracts with local authorities to house the homeless (the RSL itself having obtained the property on a lease of five years or less).

Transfers and leases of property in disadvantaged areas (FA 2003, s 57 and Sch 6; SI 2003/1056)

[6.18] Sales and leases of residential property in designated disadvantaged areas (referred to as Enterprise Areas) are exempt from SDLT if the consideration, or the relevant rental value for leased property, does not exceed £150,000. This exemption does not apply in the case of leased property where a premium is payable and the annual rent exceeds £600. In that event there is still no charge on the rental value but SDLT is chargeable on the premium. The part of the premium that would otherwise have fallen within the zero rate band is chargeable at the 1% rate. Provision is made for apportionment where only part of the property is within a disadvantaged area, or where property is only partly residential.

Relief for new zero-carbon homes (FA 2003, ss 58B, 58C)

[6.19] Specific provisions reduce or eliminate the SDLT charge on a new dwelling which is a 'zero-carbon home'. The relief is available from 1 October 2007 to 30 September 2012, and there is no SDLT charge for a qualifying new house/flat bought for up to £500,000. Where the price exceeds £500,000, the SDLT liability is reduced by £15,000.

Returns etc (FA 2003, ss 76–78, 81, 82A, Schs 10, 11A)

[6.20] Purchasers (or agents on their behalf) must send the Stamp Office a return notifying a land transaction within 30 days after the effective date of the transaction. With limited exceptions this applies even if no tax is payable.

A return is not, however, required in certain circumstances (for example there is a notification threshold of £40,000 for most freehold and leasehold transactions). In such cases a self-certificate must be submitted stating that no land transaction return is required. Where tax is payable, the land transaction return must include a self-assessment and payment must be made on or before the filing date for the return (i.e. 30 days after the effective date of the transaction).

A further return will be required within 30 days after any event causing SDLT relief to be withdrawn under, for example, the groups or charities provisions, accompanied by the tax due.

It is now possible in most circumstances to complete SDLT returns online via www.hmrc.gov.uk/so/online/menu.htm and in that event the tax will normally be automatically calculated. If the online service is used, the return *must* be filed online, and a paper printout should not be submitted. A unique transaction reference number (UTRN) will be provided when the return is filed. HMRC strongly recommend electronic payment for returns filed online, but other payment methods are acceptable.

There are provisions similar to the income tax self-assessment rules providing for separate claims to be made where they cannot be made in an SDLT return or amended return, requiring records to be kept and providing for HMRC enquiries into returns, HMRC determinations and assessments, and appeals against HMRC decisions. (HMRC have produced a booklet SD8 explaining how settlements are negotiated at the end of an enquiry under SDLT). There are also similar penalties for failing to deliver a return, failing to preserve records etc. Penalties may also be imposed under the penalty regime originally introduced by FA 2007 (**9.43**) in relation to carelessly or deliberately delivering an incorrect return or under the information and inspection powers, originally introduced by FA 2008 (**9.29**) for failing to comply with notices to provide documents or information, assisting in incorrect returns etc. Criminal proceedings may be taken for fraudulent evasion of SDLT. Interest is payable on overdue SDLT and on overdue penalties, and interest is payable to taxpayers on overpaid tax. The rates of interest are the same as for income tax.

When registering land transactions with the Chief Land Registrar, purchasers must produce either an HMRC certificate that a land transaction return has been delivered or a self-certificate that no land transaction return is required. There are provisions requiring records to be kept and there are related penalty provisions.

Anti-avoidance provisions

[6.21] Various SDLT anti-avoidance provisions were introduced from 17 March 2005, including measures affecting groups, partnerships and leases — see **45.25**. In addition, disclosure requirements were introduced from 1 August 2005 relating to certain SDLT schemes and arrangements — see **45.2**.

Transfers of interests in partnerships (FA 2003, Sch 15, Pt 3)

[6.22] SDLT applies to partnership transactions in the following circumstances:

(a)   where there are land transfers to or from an unconnected third party by the partnership; SDLT applies in the usual way, including any applicable reliefs;

(b)   where land is transferred to a partnership by a partner (or a person who becomes a partner in return for the land or the land is transferred by a person connected with either person); the amount chargeable is the proportion of the market value of the land that has been transferred;

(c)   where there is a transfer of a partnership interest in a property investment partnership, but not in any other form of partnership, when the partnership property includes land (whether any consideration is given). The chargeable consideration is based on the market value of the relevant partnership property, although the precise calculation differs depending upon whether there is consideration or not for the transfer. A property investment partnership is a partnership whose sole or main activity is investing in or dealing in land whether that involves carrying out construction operations on land or not.

[6.23] Stamp duty continues to apply to instruments effecting transfers of partnership interests, but only on the amount of consideration equal to the value of any stock or marketable securities included in the transfer.

Distribution of a deceased's estate; transfers of property on break-up of marriage or civil partnership (FA 1985, ss 83, 84; FA 2003, ss 49, 58A and Schs 3, 6A)

[6.24] All qualifying variations of the distribution of a deceased's estate (see CHAPTER 35) and deeds conveying property under an order on divorce or dissolution of a civil partnership, or on separation, are exempt from stamp duty and SDLT where the property concerned is an interest in land and buildings.

No charge to SDLT arises when property passes to a beneficiary under a will or intestacy, nor when personal representatives dispose of a deceased's home to a property trader.

Intra-group transfers and company reconstructions etc. (FA 1930, s 42; FA 1967, s 27; FA 1986, ss 75–77; FA 2002, ss 111, 113 and Schs 34, 35; FA 2003, s 62 and Sch 7; FA 2007, s 73)

[6.25] Stamp duty is not chargeable on transfers of property between companies within a 75% group, nor on company reconstructions without a change of ownership. These provisions are subject to stringent anti-avoidance provisions. For transfers of shares and securities not within these provisions (takeovers etc.), stamp duty is charged at 1/2%.

Similar reliefs and restrictions apply in respect of stamp duty land tax. There are also specific anti-avoidance provisions to prevent transactions avoiding the clawback of group relief.

Foreign exchange currency rules (SA 1891, s 6; FA 2003, Sch 4 para 9)

[6.26] All foreign currency amounts on which duty is payable are converted to sterling at the rate applying on the date of the document. For stamp duty land tax, foreign currency amounts are converted to sterling at the London closing exchange rate on the effective date of the transaction, unless the parties have used a different rate.

7

Value added tax: general principles

Basis of charge (VATA 1994, ss 1, 2, 4; F(No.2)A 2010, s 3)

[7.1] Value added tax (VAT) is charged on the supply of goods and services in the UK and on the import of goods into the UK from outside the European Union. It is charged either at the standard rate of 17.5% (rising to 20% from 4 January 2011), reduced rate of 5% or the zero-rate (see **7.14**). In addition certain supplies are specifically exempt from VAT (see **7.18**).

VAT applies to taxable supplies made in the course of a business by a taxable person, i.e. an individual, firm or company registered, or liable to be registered, for VAT (see **7.6**). Special rules apply to transactions within the European Union (see **7.29**). See **32.37** for VAT on transactions relating to land and buildings.

The principal legislation is contained in Value Added Tax Act 1994 (VATA 1994), but many of the detailed rules are in regulations. European Union law on VAT, including Directive 2006/112/EC, takes precedence over UK law in the event of any inconsistency.

How the VAT system works (VATA 1994, Pt 1, s 51B, Schs 6 and 10A)

[7.2] VAT is an indirect tax on the supply of goods and services. Each person in the chain between the first supplier and the final consumer is charged VAT (input tax) on taxable supplies to him and charges VAT (output tax) on taxable supplies made by him. The excess of output tax over input tax is paid over to HMRC. If input tax exceeds output tax, a refund is made by HMRC. The broad effect of the scheme is that businesses are not affected by VAT except in so far as they are required to administer it, and the burden of the tax falls on the consumer.

However, VAT does represent a cost to any business that cannot set off or recover all of its input tax. Non-VAT registered businesses cannot recover any VAT at all, partially exempt businesses (i.e. those making taxable and exempt supplies, see **7.19**) cannot recover all their VAT, and VAT on certain items cannot be recovered at all (see **7.4**).

For income tax and corporation tax purposes, input tax that cannot be recovered forms part of the related expenditure, which may be allowed as a deduction in calculating profits or may qualify for capital allowances.

VAT repayments are likely to arise where most supplies are zero-rated, since input tax is likely to exceed output tax.

Output tax

[7.3] Output tax must be charged on all taxable supplies, including, for example, sales of fixed assets like plant and machinery. In most situations, this is a fairly straightforward calculation, however some transactions are less clear cut, as detailed below.

If a discount is offered for prompt payment, VAT is charged only on the discounted amount whether or not the discount is taken. This is subject to exceptions in relation to payment by instalments and contingent discounts.

The treatment of face value vouchers (such as gift vouchers and 'phone' cards) is broadly as follows, but those issuing vouchers need to study the detailed rules carefully. Retailers issuing vouchers which they will exchange for goods or services do not have to account for VAT until the vouchers are redeemed. Intermediate suppliers who sell vouchers are, however, liable to account for VAT when the vouchers are sold, subject to the normal rules concerning recovery of input tax. Sales of postage stamps at or below face value are disregarded for VAT purposes.

Where a manufacturer gives 'cashbacks' to his customers, he is entitled to reduce his output tax providing he charged VAT on the original supply. The cashback reduces the taxable value of the supply to the customer, who must reduce his input tax accordingly.

Where business cars on which no input tax was recovered are sold, VAT is not normally chargeable. Where business cars on which any input tax was recovered are sold, VAT is payable on the full selling price.

There is a supply of services where business goods are used privately. The value of the supply for VAT purposes, where there is no actual consideration, is normally the cost of the goods to the business.

A gift of business assets is a supply of goods unless the total value of gifts given to the same person in the same year does not exceed £50 or one of a number of other exemptions applies. There is not usually a VAT liability on a gift of services. HMRC guidance on business gifts and samples is available in VAT Notice 700/35.

Particular care is needed with licensing and franchise arrangements, and even if someone is regarded as self-employed, they may be treated as the agent of the licensor/franchisor, so that the VAT liability depends on the licensor's/franchisor's VAT status. VAT tribunals have often come to conflicting decisions about people doing similar work, particularly in cases relating to driving instructors and hairdressers, some of whom have been held to be self-employed principals and some to be acting as agents. Even if regarded as a principal, a hairdresser will usually be treated as paying for composite supplies chargeable at the standard rate of VAT rather than merely renting space.

Input tax

[7.4] Subject to the restrictions for partially exempt businesses, input tax can be recovered on goods purchased for resale and on business expenses and capital expenditure. Where there is mixed business and non-business use, an adjustment needs to be made (see **20.22** onwards).

Even when VAT incurred is attributable to a fully taxable supply, it is not possible to recover input tax in respect of business entertaining (see **20.14**), most cars and related supplies (see **20.23**). Special rules apply in relation to input tax recovery for business vehicle fuel bills (see **7.5**). Companies cannot recover input tax on repairs, refurbishments and other expenses relating to domestic accommodation provided for directors or their families.

Business vehicle fuel bills

[7.5] A business may recover all of the input tax incurred on the purchase of fuel if all of the fuel is used for a business purpose, or the business accounts for output tax in respect of private motoring in accordance with the fuel scale rates (based on the car's CO_2 emissions) set out in the TABLE OF RATES AND ALLOWANCES.

Alternatively, input tax may be recovered on the basis of detailed mileage records which separate business and private motoring costs. HMRC provide detailed guidance in VAT Notice 700/64.

Where employees buy fuel for their employers and are reimbursed, either on an actual cost or mileage allowance basis, the employers can recover the VAT on the fuel so long as the employee has provided them with a VAT invoice and the fuel is used in making taxable supplies. Other acceptable ways for employees to purchase fuel for the employer are by use of an employer's credit or debit card, or by charging the fuel to an employer's account at the garage.

If the business vehicle fuel bills include fuel for private use, an adjustment must be made in respect of the non-business proportion unless, in the case of employees, they have paid for it in full, including VAT, in which case the business must account for the output tax. For commercial vehicles, the adjustment is made by disallowing the private proportion of the input tax. For cars, a private use fuel scale charge applies.

Although employees earning less than £8,500 per annum are not charged to income tax on the benefit of private use of a car, employers have to pay the VAT fuel scale charge for *all* employees. Furthermore, it applies whether the car is provided by the employer or owned by the employee. The VAT charged on car fuel bills is fully recoverable, but a tax-inclusive supply equal to the car fuel scale charge is regarded as made in each return period for the appropriate number of cars. By concession, the scale charges do not apply if HMRC are notified that an input tax deduction is not going to be claimed for *any* fuel (including fuel used in commercial vehicles). The scale charges also do not apply if the input tax claimed relates only to business mileage (this being supported by detailed records).

Input tax on repair and maintenance costs paid by the business is fully recoverable, and no private use adjustment is required, except that input tax cannot be reclaimed if a proprietor uses a vehicle solely for private purposes.

Registration (VATA 1994, Schs 1–3A)

Compulsory registration

[7.6] From 1 April 2010 'persons' who are in business and make or intend to make taxable supplies are liable to be registered for VAT at the end of *any month* if the taxable supplies of all business activities in the year ended on the last day of that month exceeded £70,000 (previously £68,000), unless they can satisfy HMRC that the taxable supplies in the next 12 months will not exceed £68,000 (previously £66,000). HMRC must be notified within 30 days of the end of the month in which the yearly limit was exceeded, and registration is compulsory from the beginning of the next month or such earlier date as is agreed with HMRC.

Liability to register also arises at any time if taxable supplies in the next 30 days are expected to exceed £70,000. HMRC must be notified within the 30 day period and registration is compulsory from the beginning of the 30 days.

Example 1

Turnover for the 12 months ended 31 October 2010 is £71,000, having been below the yearly limit at the end of previous months. HMRC must be notified by 30 November 2010 and registration must be from 1 December 2010 (or from an earlier date agreed with HMRC) unless it can be shown that turnover in the year to 31 October 2011 will not exceed £68,000.

Example 2

On 16 December 2010 trading commences and it is expected that the first month's turnover will be £71,000. Liability to register must be notified by 14 January 2011 and the business will be registered from 16 December 2010.

Registration may also be required in relation to acquisitions from other countries in the European Union (see **7.29**). Farmers are able to avoid VAT registration if they opt to become 'flat rate farmers' (see **31.17**). Small businesses may join an optional flat-rate scheme, but they will still be required to be registered for VAT (see **7.23**). See also **7.7** and **7.41** below as regards voluntary registration and selling a business as a going concern.

An application for registration is made on form VAT 1 and HMRC will issue a certificate of registration VAT 4 showing the VAT registration number. Application for registration may be made online via www.hmrc.gov.uk/vat. Groups of companies may register as a single taxable person (see **7.40**).

HMRC have discretion to exempt a business from registration if they are satisfied that only zero-rated supplies (see **7.16**) are made. In such cases HMRC must be notified within 30 days of a material change in the nature of supplies made, or within 30 days after the end of the quarter in which the change occurred if the day of the change is not identifiable.

There are provisions to prevent the splitting of businesses in order to stay below the VAT registration threshold. HMRC have the power to direct that where two or more persons are carrying on separate business activities which are effectively parts of the same business, they are to be treated for VAT purposes as the same business, e.g. where one spouse is a publican and the other runs the catering within the public house. Such a direction only affects future supplies and is not retrospective.

There are anti-avoidance provisions requiring non-UK registered overseas businesses to register in the UK if they sell goods in the UK on which they have claimed a refund of UK VAT under the EU or export/import provisions.

Voluntary registration

[7.7] HMRC will allow a person to register voluntarily if the business makes taxable supplies even though its turnover is below the statutory limits. Once a business is registered, it will then charge VAT on its supplies and recover input tax suffered. This may be beneficial if its customers are mainly taxable persons, but not where they are the general public. Registration will bring an administrative burden so it may not be considered worthwhile in some cases, even though a price advantage may arise.

Example 3

A person is in business as a handyman and incurs input tax of £1,000 on business expenses in the quarter to 30 September 2010. Turnover is £30,000, of which £1,000 covers the input tax that cannot be recovered because he is not registered for VAT.

If he registers voluntarily for VAT, he need only charge £29,000 for the same supplies and turnover will then be:

£29,000 + VAT at 17.5% (£5,075) = £34,075.

HMRC will be paid £5,075 less £1,000 = £4,075, leaving the business with £30,000 (including £1,000 to cover the VAT suffered) as before. If the customers are the general public, prices to them will be higher, but if they are VAT registered persons they will recover the VAT. The services provided by the handyman will thus be more expensive to the general public but less expensive to the business community.

* Note that the standard rate of VAT increases to 20% from 4 January 2011.

Intending trader registration

[7.8] If a business is not currently making taxable supplies, but intends to do so in the future, it may apply for registration and HMRC are required to register it. This enables such businesses to recover any input tax suffered even though no taxable supplies are being made. Evidence of the intention to trade may be required.

Variation or cancellation of registration (SI 1995/2518 Part II)

[7.9] If there is a change in the name, constitution or ownership of a business or any other change in circumstances that may require registration to be varied or cancelled, HMRC must be notified within 30 days of the change.

A registration will require cancellation when business ceases, a partner is taken in (or a partnership reverts to a sole proprietor), the business is incorporated/disincorporated or the business ceases to make taxable supplies. In some circumstances it is possible to transfer the registration number to the new business.

Many changes require amendment to a registration, such as changes in the composition of a partnership, change of business name, changes in a group of companies, change of address and so on.

De-registration

[7.10] From 1 April 2010, a business is no longer liable to be registered if taxable supplies in the next 12 months will be £68,000 or less (previously £66,000), unless the reason for taxable supplies not exceeding that amount is that the business will cease making taxable supplies in that year, or will suspend making them for 30 days or more. It is, however, possible to remain voluntarily registered (see **7.7**) so long as the trade continues.

Within 30 days of ceasing to make taxable supplies HMRC must be notified and the registration will be cancelled from the date of notification or a later date agreed with HMRC. VAT will be payable on a deemed supply of goods (with certain exceptions) forming part of the business assets, at their value at the time of deregistration. This charge does not apply if the business is transferred as a going concern (see **7.41**) or the VAT would not exceed £1,000. Goods on which no input tax was recovered (see **7.4**) are excluded if they were not acquired on the transfer of a going concern.

Time of supply (tax point) (VATA 1994, s 6)

[7.11] The basic tax point is normally when goods are made available or services are performed, unless they are invoiced and/or paid for earlier, in which case the earlier date is the tax point. Where goods or services are invoiced within 14 days after supply, the later date is the tax point and if a business invoices monthly it can adopt a monthly tax point. In any case the tax point will still be the date payment is received if earlier. Where payment is made online by credit or debit card when the goods are ordered, the tax point is the payment date, even though the customer has the right under the distance selling regulations to cancel the contract. For certain continuous supplies (including electricity, gas and water, management services) the tax point is normally the date of invoice or the payment date if earlier. To combat exploitation of these rules by connected businesses, some of which cannot recover all their input tax, annual tax points apply in certain circumstances for connected persons and groups of companies to ensure that VAT payments are not indefinitely or excessively delayed.

Place of supply (VATA 1994, ss 5, 7–9A and Sch 4A)

[7.12] VAT applies to supplies 'made in the UK'. From 1 January 2010 business-to-business supplies of services are taxed at the place where the customer is established. There are exceptions in relation to certain supplies, such as passenger transport, cultural, educational and entertainment services, restaurant and catering services, short-term hire of means of transport and the provision of telecommunication and broadcasting services. The place of supply for business-to-consumer supplies of services is the place where the supplier is established. (Prior to 1 January 2010, services were normally supplied where the supplier's business was established, although this general rule was subject to a large number of exceptions listed in Sch 5, where the service was treated as supplied in the country in which it was received). The main outcome of these place of supply changes is that many more services to EU customers will be dealt with under the 'reverse charge' system (see **7.28**).

Goods are normally supplied where they are physically located when they are allocated to a customer's order.

Further changes are to be introduced in 2011 and 2013 with the aim of continuing the policy of applying tax in the place of consumption. HMRC provides initial guidance and updates at www.hmrc.gov.uk/vat/cross-border-changes-2010.htm. Further guidance is provided in VAT Notice 741A.

Taxable supplies (VATA 1994, Sch 4)

[7.13] All supplies in the UK of goods and services to UK or overseas customers (including goods taken for own use) are taxable supplies, apart from items which are specifically exempt (see **7.18**). Special 'place of supply' rules to determine whether a supply is made 'in the UK' (see **7.12**).

Rates of VAT (VATA 1994, s 2; F(No.2)A, s 3 and Sch 2)

[7.14] There are three rates of VAT:

(a)   a standard rate of 17.5% (rising to 20% from 4 January 2011);
(b)   a reduced rate of 5% (see **7.15**); and
(c)   the zero rate (see **7.16**).

The distinction between exempt supplies (**7.18**) and zero-rated supplies is important. Those who make exempt supplies do not charge VAT, and can only recover any VAT suffered on expenses and purchases (input tax, see **7.2**) by adjusting their selling prices. Those making zero-rated supplies are charging VAT, albeit at a nil rate, and can recover the related input tax.

The VAT fraction used in calculating the VAT element in tax-inclusive supplies at the 17.5% rate is 7/47. The fraction at the 20% rate is 1/6 and at the 5% reduced rate it is 1/21.

F(No.2)A 2010 includes provisions to counter schemes that purport to apply the 17.5% rate of VAT to goods or services delivered or performed on or after 4 January 2011, the date on which the standard rate increases to 20%. The legislation, which has effect for transactions on or after 22 June 2010, provides that, in certain circumstances, a supplementary VAT charge of 2.5% is due on supplies of goods or services on which VAT has been declared at 17.5%. This charge will apply where the customer cannot recover all the VAT on the supply and one of the following conditions is met:

(a)   the supplier and customer are connected parties;
(b)   the supplier, or someone connected with him, funds a prepayment;
(c)   an advance VAT invoice is issued where payment is not due in full within six months (except for hire purchase invoices issued in accordance with normal commercial practice);
(d)   the value of the supply (and any related supplies) exceeds £100,000 (this does not apply if a prepayment, or the issue of an advance VAT invoice, is normal commercial practice).

The supplementary charge does not apply to prepaid or invoiced rentals of land, buildings or other assets if the period concerned does not exceed one year and the payment or invoicing method is normal commercial practice. The supplementary charge also applies to rights and options.

HMRC guidance on the change of rate to 20% can be found at http://www.hmrc.gov.uk/vat/forms-rates/rates/rate-rise-guidance.pdf.

Reduced rate (VATA 1994, s 29A and Sch 7A)

[7.15] The items charged at the reduced rate of 5% are:

(a)   Supplies of domestic fuel or power
(b)   Installation of energy-saving materials
(c)   Heating equipment or security goods or connection of gas supply (grant-funded installation)
(d)   Women's sanitary products
(e)   Children's car seats
(f)   Residential conversions, renovations and alterations (see 32.38)
(g)   Contraceptive products
(h)   Welfare advice or information
(i)   Installation of mobility aids for the elderly
(j)   Smoking cessation products

Zero rate (VATA 1994, s 30 and Sch 8)

[7.16] There are 16 groups of zero-rated items, as follows (see also CHAPTER 43 re charities):

(a)   Food
(b)   Sewerage services and water
(c)   Books etc
(d)   Talking books for the blind and handicapped and wireless sets for the blind
(e)   Construction of buildings etc
(f)   Protected buildings
(g)   International services
(h)   Transport
(i)   Caravans and houseboats
(j)   Gold
(k)   Bank notes
(l)   Drugs, medicines, aids for the handicapped etc
(m)   Imports, exports etc (but see 7.29 re the European Union)
(n)   Charities etc
(o)   Clothing and footwear
(p)   Emissions allowances (but see 7.42 re anti-avoidance to counter missing trader intra-community fraud)

These are only broad categories. There are very detailed rules setting out which heading an item falls under. Many disputes between HMRC and the taxpayer have been settled by VAT tribunals or the courts.

Mixed and composite supplies

[7.17] Supplies may sometimes be a mixture of various elements. There is a distinction between supplies treated as mixed or multiple supplies, i.e. a combination of two separate supplies each taxable at its own rate, and composite supplies, which are held to be a single supply, with any ancillary elements being taxed at the same rate as the main supply. Disputes as to the appropriate treatment have led to a large number of court cases, and the European Court has laid down various tests that need to be considered.

Exempt supplies (VATA 1994, s 31 and Sch 9)

[7.18] Supplies under the following headings (i.e. groups 1–15 in Sch 9) are exempt, detailed rules applying as to what comes under each heading:

(a) Land
(b) Insurance
(c) Postal services — although it has been announced that from 31 January 2011 this exemption will be restricted only to supplies of public postal services by Royal Mail. Other services (such as those made by Parcelforce) will become standard rated from that date. See also HMRC Brief 64/09
(d) Betting, gaming and lotteries
(e) Finance
(f) Education
(g) Health and welfare
(h) Burial and cremation
(i) Subscriptions to trade unions, professional and other public interest bodies
(j) Sport, sports competitions and physical education
(k) Works of art etc
(l) Fund-raising events by charities and other qualifying bodies
(m) Cultural services etc
(n) Supplies of goods where input tax cannot be recovered
(o) Investment gold

Partial exemption (SI 1995/2518 Pt XIV; SI 2009/820)

[7.19] If only exempt supplies are made VAT is not charged. This means however that input tax cannot be recovered, so any prices on onward supplies must include an element to recover the VAT suffered. Some businesses make both taxable and exempt supplies and are thus partially exempt.

If a business is partially exempt it can still recover all input tax suffered despite the exempt supplies if the de minimus threshold is not exceeded. For VAT periods starting on or after 1 April 2010, the de minimus threshold will not be exceeded if:

(a) main test: the input tax on exempt supplies does not exceed £625 a month on average and does not exceed 50% of total input tax; or
(b) simplified tests: (test 1) its total input tax is no more than £625 per month on average and the value of exempt supplies is no more than 50% of the value of all supplies, or (test 2) its total input tax less input

tax directly attributable to taxable supplies is no more than £625 per month on average and the value of exempt supplies is no more than 50% of the value of all supplies.

For VAT periods starting before 1 April 2010 only (a) above was used to calculate the threshold. The stated purpose of introducing the additional test is to simplify matters by saving some businesses the need to carry out a full partial exemption calculation to confirm their de minimis status.

If the de minimis limits are exceeded, there are rules to determine how much input tax can be recovered. Only the input tax directly attributable to taxable supplies plus a proportion the input tax that relates to overheads can be recovered.

Under the standard method this proportion is calculated on the amount that taxable supplies bear to total supplies. It is expressed as a percentage, rounded up to the nearest whole number, or to two decimal places if the relevant input tax exceeds £400,000 per month on average. The standard method covers input tax on all supplies except for input tax incurred in relation to investment gold. Input tax which relates to supplies of certain financial instruments or supplies which are made from overseas establishments are included in the standard method, but instead of using the values-based calculation, input tax incurred on these supplies must be attributed using a method based on use.

The proportion of input tax a business may claim for each VAT period is an estimated figure. At the end of the VAT year the position must be recalculated for the whole of that VAT year and an annual adjustment made.

Businesses using the standard method must adjust their deductible input tax if the method produces an amount which does not properly reflect the extent to which the goods and services are used to make taxable supplies, and the difference is 'substantial', defined as (i) more than £50,000 or (ii) more than 50% of the residual input tax and not less than £25,000. This does not apply where the *total* residual input tax does not exceed £50,000 (£25,000 for a company that is part of a group that is not a VAT group — see **7.40**).

For VAT returns for periods commencing on or after 1 April 2009:

(a)   a business may use the previous year's recovery percentage to fix a provisional recovery rate for each VAT return, and make an annual adjustment;

(b)   a business may bring forward its annual adjustment calculation to the last VAT return of its tax year;

(c)   a new partly exempt business may recover input tax on the basis of the use or intended use of 'input tax bearing costs' in making taxable supplies.

Detailed guidance is provided in HMRC's VAT Information Sheet 4/09.

Alternatively, a 'special method' can be agreed in writing with HMRC. Certain exempt supplies can be ignored in these calculations, for example where they are supplies of capital goods used for the business or are 'incidental' to the business activities. There is a right of appeal against the decision of HMRC on the proportion of input tax which is recoverable. A business wishing to use a special method must submit a declaration that its proposed special method is fair and reasonable before gaining approval from HMRC. Businesses that make overseas supplies will be able to apply for a 'combined method' enabling them to recover the input tax on those supplies.

Where businesses use a special method, and the method does not fairly and reasonably reflect the proportion of VAT relevant to taxable supplies, an override notice may be served either by HMRC or by the business to correct the results of the special method until a replacement method is implemented. This will apply only where it is considered that a new method would not be agreed quickly and either HMRC or the business would lose out.

Capital goods scheme (SI 1995/2518 Pt XV)

[7.20] Input tax recovery on certain capital items does not depend just on the initial use of the asset but must be adjusted over a longer period where use changes between exempt and taxable supplies.

The assets concerned are computer hardware with a tax-exclusive value of £50,000 or more per item, and land and buildings (including refurbishment costs to existing buildings), or civil engineering works, with a tax-exclusive value of £250,000 or more. The adjustment period is ten years except for computers and leases for less than ten years, where the adjustment period is five years. The adjustments are reflected in the business capital allowances computations for the calculation of tax on profits (see **22.19**).

Lost goods (VATA 1994, s 73) and bad debts (VATA 1994, ss 26A, 36)

[7.21] If goods are lost or destroyed before being sold, output tax is not chargeable. But once a supply has been made, VAT is generally chargeable.

If a customer fails to pay, VAT may be reclaimed on any debt which is more than six months old and has been written off in the accounts. VAT must be accounted for on any part of the debt that is later recovered. If the debt has been assigned to someone else, payments received by the assignee are not taken into account unless the assignor and assignee are connected. If the debtor is declared insolvent, the claim in the insolvency will be the VAT-inclusive amount, because VAT will have to be accounted for on any debt recoveries.

Debtors must repay to HMRC input tax they have reclaimed on supplies if they fail to pay the supplier within six months after the date of invoice (or after the date on which payment was due, if later), regardless of whether the supplier claims bad debt relief.

Where the goods were supplied on credit, the credit element is exempt from VAT, so that appropriate adjustments need to be made on the basis of the commercial method used by the supplier to allocate payments between the goods and the credit element. Guidance on bad debt relief is provided in HMRC's VAT Notice 700/18.

Alternative accounting methods/schemes

Second-hand goods (VATA 1994, s 50A)

[7.22] Many second-hand goods sold in the course of business have been obtained from the general public rather than from VAT registered traders, and if there were no special rules, the dealer buying the second-hand goods would have to charge VAT on the selling price without having any input tax to recover. EU countries operate a margin scheme which may be used for the sale of all second-hand goods, works of art, antiques and collectors' items except precious metals, investment gold and gemstones, unless VAT was charged on the invoice under which the goods were acquired. Where goods are sold under the margin scheme, VAT is charged on each item only on the excess of the selling price over cost (i.e. the dealer's margin). VAT must not be shown separately on the invoice, and no input tax is recoverable by the purchaser. Where individual items cost £500 or less and are purchased in bulk, businesses may also adopt 'global accounting', under which they work out the margin on the difference between total purchases and sales rather than item by item. Global accounting cannot be used for aircraft, boats and outboard motors, caravans, horses and ponies and motor vehicles, including motor cycles. The margin scheme does not have to be used for all second-hand sales, so that VAT may be charged in full under a normal VAT invoice on sales to VAT-registered businesses.

Anti-avoidance provisions prevent the scheme being abused where goods that would not otherwise have been eligible are transferred under the provisions for transfers of going concerns (see **7.41**) and where goods have been acquired through the assignment of rights under hire purchase or conditional sale agreements. Goods acquired under such transfers are not eligible unless they would have been eligible in the hands of the transferor.

EU margin scheme sales are charged to VAT in the country of origin rather than the country of destination. This means that UK margin scheme sales to someone from a country within the EU are taxed only in the UK (exports outside the EU are zero-rated). Acquisitions from countries in the EU are dealt with in the same way as purchases in the UK. VAT is not charged on acquisitions from private EU individuals, and the margin scheme may be used when the goods are sold in the UK. Acquisitions from EU VAT registered businesses may either be made through the scheme (so that the scheme may be used on resale), or outside the scheme, in which case VAT will be recoverable but the scheme cannot be used for the resale.

Imports of second-hand goods from outside the EU are subject to import VAT in the normal way (see **7.27**), except that imports of certain works of art, antiques and collectors' items are charged at an effective import VAT rate of 5%.

Optional flat-rate scheme (VATA 1994, s 26B; SI 1995/2518 Pt VIIA; SI 2009/586)

[7.23] Under the flat-rate scheme the business continues to charge VAT on its taxable supplies but, instead of paying over to HMRC the output tax (less recoverable input tax) in the normal way, the business pays an amount equal to the appropriate flat-rate percentage of turnover (as listed in VAT Notice 733).

A business may apply to use the scheme if there are reasonable grounds for believing that taxable supplies (excluding VAT) in the next year will not exceed £150,000. Those using the scheme cannot also use the cash accounting scheme (**7.25**), margin scheme (**7.22**) or retail scheme (**7.24**). They can, however use the annual accounting scheme (**7.26**) at the same time.

A business may opt to leave the flat-rate scheme at any time. It is required leave the scheme if, on the anniversary of joining the scheme, total income (including VAT) in the previous year exceeded £225,000 (£230,000 with effect from 4 January 2011) or there are reasonable grounds to believe that income for the next 30 days (excluding sales of capital assets) will exceed that amount. The business may be allowed to continue in the scheme, however, if HMRC are satisfied that income in the next year will not exceed £187,500 (£191,500 with effect from 4 January 2011).

Where a business includes two or more trade sectors (e.g. a pub that also supplies food), the percentage for the trade sector with the higher turnover is taken. Businesses who register for VAT and join the flat-rate scheme will pay 1% less than the flat-rate percentage for their trade sector for the first year from the date of their VAT registration. HMRC provide an online ready reckoner to help businesses and their advisers decide whether the flat-rate scheme will be beneficial.

When invoicing supplies to their customers, flat-rate scheme traders add VAT in the normal way showing the normal VAT rate. The trader retains any VAT charged to his VAT registered customers but does not normally make a separate claim for input tax which is covered by the flat-rate percentage. If, however, the trader has acquired capital goods in the period with a tax-inclusive value of more than £2,000, he may recover the input tax on them. If such goods are subsequently sold, VAT must be accounted for at the full rate rather than the flat-rate.

See **20.25** for the way flat-rate scheme traders deal with VAT in their business accounts.

Special schemes for retailers

[7.24] The normal VAT procedure requires records to be kept of every separate transaction. Some retailers would find it virtually impossible to keep such detailed records, so there are special schemes which enable retailers to calculate output tax in a way that suits their particular circumstances. Such schemes are restricted to businesses that cannot be expected to account for VAT in the normal way. There are three types of published retail schemes, namely point of sale, apportionment and direct calculation (see VAT Notice 727). Any retailer with annual turnover in excess of £130 million is, however, required to arrange a bespoke scheme with HMRC (see VAT Notice 727/2). Businesses using one of the retail schemes can use the annual accounting scheme (**7.26**) at the same time.

Cash accounting (VATA 1994, s 25; SI 1995/2518 Pt VIII)

[**7.25**] Businesses with a tax-exclusive turnover of not more than £1.35 million may use the cash accounting system providing they are up-to-date with their VAT returns and have either paid over all VAT due or have arranged to pay any overdue amount by instalments. HMRC guidance is contained in VAT Notice 731. Businesses using cash accounting can use the annual accounting scheme (**7.26**) at the same time.

Tax invoices still have to be issued but output tax does not have to be accounted for until the cash is received. On the other hand, input tax is not recoverable until suppliers are paid. Businesses that have many bad debts may find the scheme particularly useful. Certain transactions are excluded from the scheme, including hire purchase and similar transactions, supplies of goods and services invoiced in advance, and supplies for which payment is not due in full within six months after the invoice date. HMRC can refuse entry to the scheme, or withdraw the scheme, if they think it necessary to protect tax revenue.

A business can leave the scheme voluntarily at the end of any tax period. A business is required to stop using the scheme in specified circumstances, including where taxable supplies have exceeded £1.6 million in a period of one year. HMRC may be prepared to allow the business to remain in the scheme in the event of a large 'one-off' increase in sales arising from genuine commercial activity.

A business that leaves the cash accounting scheme in a VAT period may either account for all outstanding VAT due in the return for that period or opt to account for it over a period of six months.

Annual accounting (SI 1995/2518 Pt VII)

[**7.26**] Businesses with an annual tax-exclusive turnover of not more than £1.35 million may apply (on form VAT 600) to join the annual accounting scheme under which they are required to make payments on account of their VAT liability during the year. New businesses may join the scheme as soon as they are registered. The annual return and balancing payment have to be made within two months after the end of the year. Once in the scheme, a business may remain in it unless annual turnover reaches £1.6 million. HMRC guidance is provided in VAT Notice 732.

Transactions outside the EU (VATA 1994, ss 30, 37)

Goods

[7.27] When goods are imported from outside the European Union (see 7.29 for special rules relating to the EU), the importer normally has to pay VAT on the goods at that time. VAT is charged at the rate that would apply had the goods been supplied in the UK (subject to the various reliefs that are available). Subject to any restriction for partial exemption etc., the importer gets a credit for the input tax on his next return, thus cancelling or reducing the VAT cost to him. If the goods are for resale, output tax will be accounted for in the normal way when they are sold. There is a deferment scheme enabling importers to pay both Customs duty and VAT monthly on paying an amount as security. No VAT is payable on goods temporarily imported for repair, processing or modification, then re-exported. Goods which have been temporarily exported and are re-imported by the same person after repair, process, or modification bear VAT only on the value of the repair, etc. plus freight and insurance.

Exports outside the EU are generally zero-rated provided the exporter complies with several conditions (in relation to, for example, record keeping requirements, use of goods prior to export etc.).

Services

[7.28] The liability of overseas services depends upon the place of supply rules (see 7.12). If the place of supply is outside the UK the services are outside the scope of UK VAT. If the place of supply is in the UK, the services are subject to the normal UK provisions.

For services from abroad that are treated as supplied in the UK and liable to VAT a 'reverse charge' procedure applies. The reverse charge procedure requires a UK business to account for VAT on the supplies, with a corresponding deduction for input tax on the same return. Similarly if supplies are treated as supplied in the EU, the EU customer will account for VAT using a reverse charge procedure.

Transactions within the EU (VATA 1994, Sch 2)

Goods

[7.29] Supplies of goods between EU countries are not referred to as imports and exports, but as 'acquisitions' and 'supplies'.

Acquisitions

[7.30] If a non-VAT registered person in the UK makes acquisitions of goods from an EU supplier, the supplier will be liable to register in the UK if his supplies (known as 'distance sales') to such non-registered persons exceed

£70,000 in a calendar year. The supplier must register in the UK within 30 days of exceeding the limit, registration taking effect from the date the limit is exceeded. His supplies will then be subject to UK VAT. The supplier may opt to register in the UK even if he does not exceed the £70,000 limit. If, however, he is neither required to register in the UK nor wishes to register in the UK, he must charge VAT at the rate applicable in the country where he is registered.

If the non-registered person's acquisitions exceed the registration thresholds (see **7.6**) he will become liable to register in his own right. The cumulative turnover limit for such acquisitions relates to the calendar year, i.e. to acquisitions from 1 January to the end of the relevant month. Goods subject to excise duty and new means of transport are not taken into account because they are subject to separate rules.

When a UK VAT registered person makes acquisitions from a supplier who is registered for VAT in another EU country, the supplier will zero-rate his supply. Output tax must be accounted for on the UK registered person's next VAT return, but with an equivalent amount being deducted as input tax in the same return (subject to any partial exemption or other restriction).

Supplies

[7.31] Supplies of goods by a VAT registered UK business to VAT registered EU customers are zero-rated, but VAT is accounted for on the acquisition of those goods by the customer at his country's VAT rate, i.e. the country of destination. Special rules apply to new motor vehicles, motor cycles, boats and aircraft, under which VAT is charged at the rate applicable in the purchaser's country. Supplies to non-VAT registered EU customers are at the rate applicable in the UK, although if sales to an EU country exceed that country's stipulated limit the distance selling rules apply and the seller must register for VAT in that country or he may appoint a tax representative to act for him; that country will then become the place of supply. Again, the seller may opt to register in the country of the customer if the limit is not exceeded.

There are special rules where there is an intermediate supplier between the original supplier and the customer.

For supplies to VAT registered EU customers, a UK seller must state both his own and the customer's VAT number on VAT invoices. In addition to making his normal VAT returns, he also has to submit a return of all supplies to VAT registered customers in the EU for each calendar quarter (known as EU sales statements).

Larger businesses (acquisitions above £600,000 or supplies above £250,000) are required to complete supplementary declarations under the Intrastat system. See **7.22** for the EU treatment of second-hand goods and **7.36** for EU provisions relating to invoicing. HMRC guidance on the single market and Instrastat is provided in VAT Notices 725 and 60.

Services

[7.32] The provisions at **7.28** apply equally to intra-EU supplies of services. From 1 January 2010 business-to-business supplies of services are generally taxed at the place where the customer is established (see **7.12**). Consequently, from this date, the EU sales statements regime also applies to intra-EU supplies of services subject to a reverse charge in the customer's member state.

Administration

Tax periods, VAT account and tax returns, default surcharge, re-payment supplement (VATA 1994, ss 59, 79; SI 1995/2518 Pt V; FA 2008, ss 121, 135)

[7.33] A tax period is normally three months, but if VAT repayments are regularly claimed (for example because mainly zero-rated supplies are made) it is possible to have a one-month period. The advantage of earlier repayments in those circumstances must be weighed against the disadvantage of having to complete 12 returns annually.

Quarterly return dates are staggered over the year depending on the business classification. The dates can be changed to coincide with the businesses accounting period.

The transactions for each tax period must be summarised in a VAT account. Returns are made to HMRC on form VAT 100 for each tax period, showing the VAT payable or repayable and certain statistical information (including specific entries for European Union sales and purchases). For businesses with turnover in excess of £100,000, returns must be filed online and VAT paid electronically for accounting periods that start on or after 1 April 2010. For businesses registering for VAT on or after 1 April 2010, returns must be filed online and VAT paid electronically irrespective of turnover levels.

The submission and payment deadline for paper returns is one month after the end of the tax period (the payment deadline is extended by seven days if payment is made electronically). For online filing the submission and payment deadline is one month and seven days after the end of the tax period. These rules do not apply for businesses in the annual accounting and payments on account schemes (see **7.26**, **7.34**).

A late claim to recover input tax can only be made within four years after the due date for the return in which the claim should have been made. This time limit was disapplied in relation to input tax deductible before 1 May 1997 following a House of Lords decision, and HMRC invited claims to repayment of (a) output tax overpaid in accounting periods ending before 4 December 1996 as well as (b) input tax for accounting periods ending before 1 May 1997 (see Revenue & Customs Brief 07/08). Finance Act 2008 allowed a transitional period up to 31 March 2009 for businesses to make such claims for those periods.

A 'default surcharge' is payable if two or more returns within a year are not made on time. When a return is late, a 'surcharge liability notice' is issued. The notice remains in force for a period of one year, unless a further return is made late, in which case the surcharge liability period is extended for a year from the last day of the period covered by that return and so on. The surcharge is 2% of the tax due for the first late return in the surcharge liability period, then 5%, 10% and a maximum 15% for subsequent late returns. The 2% and 5% surcharges will not be collected if they are less than £400. The minimum surcharge at 10% or 15% is £30. If no VAT is due, or the VAT is paid on time even though the return is late, then although the late return affects the surcharge liability period, the surcharge does not apply and the rate for subsequent late returns is not increased. If HMRC accept that a business has a reasonable excuse for late payment no default will be recorded.

Where there is an unreasonable delay on the part of HMRC in making a VAT repayment, a repayment supplement amounting to an extra 5% (or £50 if more) will be added to the repayment, providing the return claiming the repayment was made on time (see **7.38**).

These provisions are, from a date to be announced, to be replaced by a unified penalty regime for late filing of returns and late payment of taxes (see **9.49** and **9.50**). The provisions for imposing penalties for errors in relation to VAT legislation are detailed at **9.44** onwards.

Monthly payments on account for large VAT payers (VATA 1994, s 28; SI 1993/2001; SI 1995/2518 Pt VI)

[7.34] Traders who make quarterly VAT returns and pay VAT of more than £2 million a year have to make payments on account at the end of the second and third months of each VAT quarter. A balancing payment is made with the quarterly VAT return.

HMRC calculate the payments on account. Each payment is fixed by dividing by 24 the annual VAT liability in the 12-month period in which the business exceeded the threshold. Future payments on account are determined by reference to an annual cycle and a reference year.

Payments on account must be made by electronic transfer and there is no seven-day period of grace. Traders may elect to make monthly VAT returns, or to make monthly payments of VAT based on the actual liability for the preceding month without making a monthly VAT return. One of these options may be preferable where there are seasonal variations in turnover. HMRC guidance is provided in VAT Notice 700/60.

Records and returns (VATA 1994, Sch 11)

[7.35] VAT registered businesses must supply tax invoices in respect of taxable supplies, keep a VAT account showing the calculations of the VAT liability for each tax period, keep all invoices received and copies of all VAT invoices issued, retain all business and accounting records, and make returns to HMRC showing the VAT payable or repayable (see **7.33**).

VAT invoices (SI 1995/2518 Pt III)

[7.36] Where a taxable supply is made to another taxable person a VAT invoice must be provided showing the following details:

(a)   A sequential number that uniquely identifies the document
(b)   Time of supply, or tax point (see **7.11**)
(c)   Date of issue of the invoice
(d)   Trader's name, address and VAT registration number
(e)   Customer's name and address
(f)   Description of goods or services supplied, and for each description the quantity or extent, the rate of VAT and the VAT-exclusive amount payable
(g)   Total amount payable excluding VAT and, for countable goods or services, the unit price (for example, in the case of services, the hourly rate)
(h)   Rate of any cash discount offered
(i)   A reference or indication, where appropriate, that a margin scheme (see **7.22**) has been applied
(j)   A reference or indication, where appropriate, that the invoice relates to a supply where the person supplied is liable to pay the tax
(k)   Total VAT chargeable

There are special rules for supplies to persons in other EU member states. Retailers may provide a less detailed invoice omitting the customer's name and address and the amount (but not the rate) of VAT, if the VAT-inclusive price is £250 or less. Copies of these less detailed invoices need not be kept.

Provision is made for customers to self-bill their suppliers, subject to specified conditions. Provision is also made for electronic invoicing (see HMRC guidance in VAT Notice 700/63).

Assessments (VATA 1994, ss 73, 76, 77; FA 2008, Sch 39 para 34)

[7.37] If a taxpayer fails to make returns, or HMRC consider returns are incomplete or incorrect, they may issue assessments of the amount of VAT due. Assessments cannot be made later than four years after the end of the return period, except in cases involving loss of VAT brought about deliberately or resulting from failure to comply with certain obligations, when the period is increased to 20 years. Where the taxpayer has died, no assessment can be made later than four years after the death.

Repayments, repayment supplement and statutory interest (VATA 1994, ss 78–81; FA 1996, s 197; CTA 2009, s 1286; ITTOIA 2005, ss 54, 869)

Repayment supplement

[7.38] A repayment supplement of 5% of the tax due (or £50 if greater) is paid on overpaid VAT if the return was made by the due date, the return did not overstate the amount repayable by more than the greater of £250 and 5% of the amount due, and repayment has been unnecessarily delayed by HMRC. Unnecessary delay is defined as more than 30 days from the day following the end of return period, or the date the return was received if later. This supplement is not chargeable to income tax or corporation tax.

Statutory interest

[7.39] Where overpaid VAT has not been recovered through the normal accounting procedures, a claim may be made for a refund, which is increased by statutory interest where the overpayment is a result of error by HMRC. Unlike the repayment supplement, statutory interest is chargeable to direct tax, i.e. income tax or corporation tax. A claim to interest under this heading must be made within four years after the end of the 'applicable period'. (See also Revenue & Customs Brief 14/09).

For the latest rates of interest see 'Statutory interest payable by HMRC in cases of official error' in the TABLE OF RATES AND ALLOWANCES.

Groups of companies (VATA 1994, ss 43, 43A–43D, 44 and Sch 9A; SI 2004/1931)

[7.40] Two or more companies that are established or have a fixed establishment in the UK may apply to be treated as a VAT group if one of them controls each of the others, or if an individual, partnership or company controls all of them. Only one VAT return is then required and supplies between group members are disregarded for VAT purposes. HMRC may remove companies from VAT groups if they are no longer eligible or if their membership poses a threat to tax revenue. There are provisions to ensure that unfair advantages are not obtained by group treatment, and HMRC have powers to counter VAT avoidance involving group transactions. There are additional eligibility rules for groups with turnover exceeding £10 million, and a company cannot be a member of more than one VAT group at the same time.

Where there is no group registration, VAT has to be added to charges for supplies from one company to the other, such as management charges, and care must be taken to ensure that this is not overlooked.

Basic activities of holding companies, such as holding shares and acquiring subsidiaries, are not regarded under EU law as business activities and any associated input tax cannot be recovered. This only applies, however, to holding companies that neither trade themselves, nor have active trading subsidiaries making taxable supplies outside the VAT group, nor provide genuine management services to separate trading subsidiaries.

Where a business is transferred as a going concern to a partially exempt group, the transfer is treated as a supply to and by the group. The group therefore has to account for output tax, and is only able to recover its allowable proportion of input tax according to the partial exemption rules (see **7.19**). This does not apply if the person who transferred the assets to the group acquired them more than three years previously. Nor does it apply to items covered by the capital goods scheme (see **7.20**).

The group provisions are intended to reduce administrative burdens on businesses, but they also enable groups to improve the overall VAT position by including or excluding companies from the group registration. Where an application is made for a company to leave a VAT group, HMRC may delay the removal of the company from the VAT group registration if VAT avoidance is involved. HMRC guidance on group registration is provided in VAT Notice 700/2.

Transferring a business as a going concern (SI 1995/1268)

[7.41] If a VAT registered trader sells all or part of a business as a going concern, the seller does not normally have to account for VAT on the sale consideration, and the purchaser does not have any input tax to reclaim where the purchaser is a taxable person or becomes a taxable person immediately after the sale. This does not apply to the transfer of land and buildings on which the option to charge VAT has been exercised or to commercial buildings and civil engineering works that are unfinished or less than three years old unless the purchaser has also opted to charge VAT and has so notified HMRC by the date of the transfer. The purchaser must also notify the seller that his option to tax will not be disapplied. (For details of the option to charge VAT, see **32.39**.) If the purchaser is not already registered, the rules for deciding whether he is liable are the same as those outlined at **7.6**, except that the seller's supplies in the previous 12 months are treated as made by the purchaser. The purchaser must notify his liability within 30 days after the transfer, and will be registered from the date of the transfer. If the seller was not, and was not required to be, VAT registered, his turnover would not have to be taken into account by the purchaser in deciding when registration was necessary. For transfers on or after 1 September 2007, as a general rule sellers will normally be required to retain the business records, unless it is essential for VAT compliance purposes for the records to be passed to the purchaser.

The above rules do not apply on a sale of assets, rather than an identifiable part of the business which is capable of separate operation and which the purchaser intends to continue. The sale of a family company is dealt with in **CHAPTER 28**.

HMRC guidance is provided in VAT Notice 700/9. Anti-avoidance rules apply to transfers to partially exempt groups (see **7.40**), and further rules prevent these going concern provisions being used to enable businesses to give goods away without accounting for VAT.

Anti-avoidance

Combating VAT evasion and money laundering (VATA 1994, ss 26AB, 55A, 69B, 77A and Sch 11; SI 2003/3075)

[7.42] HMRC have extensive powers to combat VAT evasion, including the power to require security to be provided by traders reclaiming input tax if the traders deal with businesses in a VAT supply chain that are considered to be involved in tax evasion. In addition there are special rules to counter 'missing trader intra-community' (MTIC) fraud. Under the rules the customer becomes the person liable to register for VAT (if not already registered) and account for and pay the VAT on the supply of specified goods which are commonly used to perpetrate the fraud. This 'reverse charge' procedure has been introduced with effect from 1 June 2007 and applies, with some exclusions, to supplies of mobile phones and computer chips that are made by one VAT-registered business to another and valued at £5,000 and over. FA 2010 extended the primary legislation to cover services, with the stated intention that regulations will be introduced to apply the rules to emissions allowances from 1 November 2010.

The powers of HMRC to inspect goods have been strengthened, and they are able to require businesses to keep records about goods on which they believe VAT may not be paid, subject to a penalty for failure to do so.

[7.43] Businesses that deal in goods and accept the equivalent of €15,000 or more in *cash* for a single transaction (referred to as High Value Dealers — HVDs) are required to register with HMRC and put anti-money laundering systems in place. The registration is renewable annually and an annual fee based on the number of premises from which high value transactions are made. HMRC guidance is available at www.hmrc.gov.uk/mlr. Any breach of the regulations may lead to a financial penalty or criminal proceedings.

VAT avoidance schemes

[7.44] There are special disclosure rules for VAT avoidance schemes (see **45.3**).

8

Council tax and business rates

Introduction

[8.1] This chapter gives an outline of council tax and business rates. Additional points of detail relating to specific areas are dealt with in the appropriate chapters, in particular let property in **CHAPTER 32**.

Council tax was introduced from 1 April 1993 in England, Wales and Scotland, replacing the community charge or 'poll tax', which had replaced domestic rates. Domestic rates are still payable in Northern Ireland. There are some differences in the system in Wales and Scotland and this chapter deals mainly with the system for England.

Council tax in England is based at present on property values in 1991. A revaluation was due to take place in 2007, based on property values in 2005, and subsequent revaluations were to be made at ten-yearly intervals. The 2007 revaluation was deferred, the requirement for ten-yearly revaluations was replaced by a provision for revaluation dates to be set by the Secretary of State and at the time of writing it is unclear when the next revaluation in England will take place. A revaluation did take place in Wales (see **8.2**).

Sir Michael Lyons conducted an inquiry into local government funding and the case for changes, including possible reform of council tax. The Lyons report published in 2007 recommended a revaluation of all domestic properties; the introduction of two additional council tax rate bands at the top and bottom of the present structure; and that the Government should consider assigning a fixed proportion of income tax to local government. The report also recommended introducing a 'new local flexibility' to set a supplement on the national business rate (see **8.10**).

Businesses pay business rates at a uniform level fixed by central government. The uniform business rate, or multiplier, is applied to the rateable value of the property. There are some differences in the business rates provisions for Scotland and Wales, and this chapter briefly summarises the position in England. See **8.10** onwards.

Council tax — the general rules

[8.2] Council tax is payable on a 'dwelling', i.e. a separate unit of living accommodation along with any garden, yard, garage or outbuildings attached to it. Broadly, a self-contained unit within a dwelling is counted as a separate dwelling but where an elderly dependent relative occupies an annexe as his or her main residence then he or she may be exempt from payment. Any part of a property that is wholly used for business purposes is subject to the business rate, with the council tax applying to the 'dwelling' part. Some dwellings are exempt (see **8.3**). Guidance is available at www.voa.gov.uk/council_tax and www.direct.gov.uk/en/homeandcommunity.

Council tax bills may be reduced by one or more of the following:

(a)   Discounts where there is only one occupier (see **8.5**).
(b)   Reduction for disabilities (see **8.6**).
(c)   Council tax benefit and second adult rebate (see **8.7**).

Councils have some flexibility over setting discounts and exemptions, to allow them to reflect local circumstances. This includes giving councils power to reduce discounts for second homes and long-term unfurnished empty properties and most councils have taken the opportunity to reduce such discounts (see **8.5**).

The amount of the bill before any available deductions depends, for properties in England and Scotland, on the estimated value of the property at 1 April 1991 but taking into account any significant alteration to the property before 1 April 1993. Newly built property is similarly valued back to what it would have been worth at 1 April 1991. Properties in Wales were re-valued by reference to values at 1 April 2003.

The bill is calculated according to which of the following valuation bands the property falls in:

Band	England	Scotland	Wales
A	Up to £40,000	Up to £27,000	Up to £44,000
B	£40,001–£52,000	£27,001–£35,000	£44,001–£65,000
C	£52,001–£68,000	£35,001–£45,000	£65,001–£91,000
D	£68,001–£88,000	£45,001–£58,000	£91,001–£123,000
E	£88,001–£120,000	£58,001–£80,000	£123,001–£162,000
F	£120,001–£160,000	£80,001–£106,000	£162,001–£223,000
G	£160,001–£320,000	£106,001–£212,000	£223,001–£324,000

Band	England	Scotland	Wales
H	Over £320,000	Over £212,000	£324,001–£424,000
I			Over £424,000

The council tax bills for the various bands vary according to proportions laid down by law. The full bill for a band H dwelling is twice that for a band D dwelling and three times that for a band A dwelling.

Properties will normally only be re-valued for banding purposes when they are sold or let on lease for seven years or more, even if they have been substantially improved or extended. Such a revaluation takes effect from the date the transaction is completed. There is, however, provision for adjusting values downwards at any time if there is a major change in the area, such as a new sewerage treatment plant being opened nearby, or if part of the property is demolished, or if the property is adapted for someone who is disabled.

It is possible to appeal against a valuation in certain circumstances (see **8.8**). If, because of inaccuracies in the original list, a valuation is wrong, it can be corrected. If the effect of the correction is to *increase* the valuation, the revaluation takes effect only from the day the valuation list is altered. Decreases take effect from the date the valuation list was compiled.

Council tax is calculated on a daily basis and is adjusted appropriately when a change of circumstances affects the bill, such as the property becoming or ceasing to be eligible for exemption or discount. This means that householders need to notify their councils of changes affecting their liability.

Council tax is normally paid by ten monthly instalments, but other payment methods may be offered. If payment is not made on time the right to pay by instalments may be lost and action may be taken for recovery. Collection may then be enforced in various ways, including an attachment of earnings order requiring an employer to deduct the outstanding tax from salary and account for it to the council. If payment is not made at all, the defaulter may be sent to prison.

Exempt dwellings

[8.3] Exemption may be claimed in the following circumstances. The council must be notified if the exemption ceases to apply, otherwise penalties may be imposed:

(a)   Unoccupied property that needs structural alteration/major repair work, or is undergoing such work, or has undergone such work and less than six months have elapsed since the work was substantially completed, but the exemption is limited to a maximum period of 12 months.

(b)   Empty property owned and last used by a charity, exemption applying for up to six months.

(c)   Empty, unfurnished property, for up to six months (ignoring any period of reoccupation for less than six weeks).

(d)   Property left empty by someone in prison (other than for not paying fines or council tax).

(e)   Property left empty by someone now living in hospital or in residential care.

(f)   Property empty following the occupier's death, for up to six months after granting of probate or administration.

(g)   An empty property in which occupation is prohibited by law, e.g. pending compulsory purchase.

(h)   Property left vacant for a minister of religion.

(i)   Property that is empty because the occupier is now living elsewhere to receive care because of old age, disablement, illness, alcohol/drug dependence or mental disorder.

(j)   Property empty because the occupier is resident elsewhere to look after someone needing care as indicated in (i) above.

(k)   Empty property last occupied by a student whose main residence it was but who now lives elsewhere to be near to his place of education.

(l)   Unoccupied mortgaged property that has been repossessed by the lender.

(m)   Students' halls of residence.

(n)   Property wholly occupied by students as their full-time or term-time residence.

(o)   Properties used as accommodation for members of the Armed Forces.

(p)   Properties occupied by Visiting Forces.

(q)   Unoccupied property for which someone is liable only as a Trustee in Bankruptcy.

(r)   A vacant caravan pitch or boat mooring.

(s)   Properties occupied only by people under 18 years of age.

(t)   An annex that cannot be let separately from the main dwelling without breaching planning conditions.

(u)   Properties occupied only by severely mentally impaired people who would otherwise be liable to pay the council tax.

(v)   Properties occupied by diplomats or members of certain international organisations.

(w)   Self-contained annexes and 'granny flats' occupied by dependent relatives.

Who is liable to pay?

[8.4] Each dwelling has only one council tax bill. The person liable is the person who comes first on the following list.

(a)   An owner-occupier, i.e. a resident freeholder.

(b)   A resident leaseholder (including assured tenants under the Housing Act 1988).

(c)   A resident statutory or secure tenant.

(d)   A resident who has a contractual licence to occupy the property, such as someone living in a tied cottage.

(e)   A resident with no legal interest in the property, such as a squatter or someone who has permission to stay.

(f)   The owner (where the dwelling has no residents).

A resident is someone over 18 who lives in the property as his only or main home.

Generally, joint owners or joint tenants are jointly liable for the tax, and couples living together are jointly liable even if only one member of the couple owns or leases the property.

Where there are no residents, the owner is liable. The owner is also liable instead of the residents in the case of the following dwellings:

(a)   Multi-occupied properties such as bed-sits where rent is paid separately for different parts of the property.

(b)   Residential care homes, nursing homes, and some hostels providing a high level of care.

(c)   Dwellings occasionally occupied by the owner whose domestic staff are resident there.

(d)   Monasteries, convents, and dwellings occupied by ministers of religion.

(e)   Property occupied by asylum seekers under statutory arrangements.

Discounts

[8.5] The full amount of council tax is payable if two or more adults live in the dwelling. The bill is reduced by 25% if a person lives alone.

Councils offer a second homes' discount of between 10% and 50% for second homes, holiday homes and job-related accommodation, and they may offer an empty homes discount of up to 50% for dwellings that have been empty and unfurnished for more than six months. Guidance is provided on the relevant local authority's website.

Certain people are not counted in deciding how many residents there are, providing certain conditions are met. These include:

(a)   full-time students, student nurses, apprentices or young people in training;

(b)   severely mentally impaired people;

(c)   hospital patients, or those being looked after in care homes;

(d)   low-paid care workers;

(e)   people with diplomatic privileges or immunities;

(f)   members of visiting forces;

(g)   members of religious communities;.

(h)   people aged 18–19 and either in full time education or between school and further or higher education;

(i)   people staying in certain hostels or night shelters;

(j)   people caring for someone with a disability who is not a spouse, partner or child under 18.

Not being counted as a resident does not alter a person's responsibility for payment. But where, after ignoring those who are not counted, the dwelling is no one's main home, the person liable to pay the tax would get a 50% discount, possibly reduced to 10% as indicated above.

The council must be notified if a discount is no longer applicable (or a smaller discount should apply). Penalties apply if notification is not made.

Reduction for disabilities

[8.6] Homes that provide one of the following special features for a substantially and permanently disabled adult or child who lives in the property qualify for a one-band reduction in the bill if they are in bands B to H. Band A properties qualify for a reduction equal to one ninth of the band D charge. Any discounts and benefits then apply to the reduced amount. The special features are:

(a)   a room other than a bathroom, kitchen or toilet, that is mainly for the use of the disabled person (such as a ground floor bedroom in a two-storey property);

(b)   an extra bathroom or kitchen for the disabled person's use;

(c)   extra floor space for a wheelchair.

To qualify for the reduction, the additional feature need not be specially built, but it must be shown that the disabled person would be severely adversely affected if the feature was not available. A claim should be made each year to the council, who may require additional evidence that the conditions for the reduction are satisfied.

Council tax benefit

[8.7] People on low incomes may claim benefit of up to 100% of the bill, the amount of the benefit depending on their age, income and savings. A 'second adult rebate' of up to 25% is available if a person has a second adult sharing with him (but is not a spouse or partner or paying rent) who is on a low income. Certain changes of circumstances must be notified to the council. Anyone who disagrees with the amount of benefit awarded may appeal to an independent tribunal.

Appeals

Valuation

[8.8] It is possible to appeal against a council tax banding. Appeals are made initially to the local valuation office. The taxpayer then has the option of referring the case to a valuation tribunal once the valuation office has reviewed the banding. Guidance is provided at www.voa.gov.uk/council_tax.

In limited circumstances it is possible to challenge a council tax valuation list entry, e.g. where part of the property has been demolished.

Other grounds for appeal

[8.9] Appeals may also be made on the grounds that:

(a)   a home should not be liable to tax; or
(b)   liability is disputed, either because a person does not consider himself to be the liable person, or because of the calculation of available reductions; or
(c)   a penalty imposed is disputed; or
(d)   a completion notice is disputed identifying the date from which a new building becomes a dwelling, or when structural alterations are completed.

Appeal procedures differ depending on the nature of the appeal.

Business rates

[8.10] Businesses pay a uniform business rate (also called the non-domestic rate) on the rateable value of business premises. Guidance is provided at www.businesslink.gov.uk. Business rates are calculated using the rateable value and the multiplier set by the government. In England the standard multiplier for 2010/11 is 41.4 pence; therefore a business with a rateable value of £10,000 will pay business rates of £4,140 (excluding any discounts or reductions that may be available).

Rateable values are updated every five years, the latest revaluation having been made as at 1 April 2010 (based on rateable values assessed at 1 April 2008). The revaluation is intended to reflect changes in the property market and redistribute the total tax liability for business rates. This means that some rates bills will rise but others will fall, and transitional relief will be available (see 8.11). The valuation office agency has published guidance at www.voa.gov.uk/business_rates/2010_revaluation.htm.

A special business rates relief is available to small businesses (see 8.12). The business rate is collected by individual local councils but it is paid into a national pool and is then distributed on a formula basis to county and district councils. Councils have power to give business rates relief on hardship grounds. They may also give special reductions to businesses in rural areas. For the position of charities, see 43.17.

The Business Rates Supplement Act 2009 creates a new power for 'upper tier' local authorities in England and Wales to levy a local supplement on the business rate, and to retain the funds for investment in economic development in their area. Properties with a rateable value of £50,000 or less, are specified (in regulations) as exempt.

Transitional relief

[8.11] The revaluation at 1 April 2010 increased many rateable values, but decreased others. Transitional arrangements apply for the years up to and including 2014/15, as follows:

	Properties with rateable value of £18,000 or more (£25,500 or more in Greater London)		Properties with rateable value of less than £18,000 (£25,500 in Greater London)	
	Maximum decrease	*Maximum increase*	*Maximum decrease*	*Maximum increase*
	%	%	%	%
2010/11	4.6	12.5	20.0	5.0
2011/12	6.7	17.5	30.0	7.5
2012/13	7.0	20.0	35.0	10.0
2013/14	13.0	25.0	55.0	15.0
2014/15	13.0	25.0	55.0	15.0

There is no transitional relief in Wales and Scotland.

Small business rate relief

[8.12] The small business rate relief is available to all businesses whose rateable value is less than £18,000 (or £25,500 in London). To qualify for the relief businesses must apply to their local authority. The small business rate relief depends on the rateable value of the property, as follows:

(a)   if the rateable value is below £6,000 the rates are calculated using the small business multiplier (40.7p for 2010/11) and then reduced by 50%;

(b)   if the rateable value is from £6,000 to £11,999, the reduction decreases on a sliding scale of 1% for every £120;

(c)   if the rateable value is from £12,000 to £17,999 (£24,499 in London), the rates are calculated using the small business multiplier.

It was announced in the March 2010 Budget (and subsequently confirmed in the June 2010 Emergency Budget) that legislation would be introduced to extend small business relief between 1 October 2010 to 30 September 2011. The proposal is that for this period, eligible ratepayers will receive small business rate relief at 100% (instead of the current 50%) on properties with a rateable value up to £6,000 and a tapering from 100% to 0% for properties up to £12,000.

Miscellaneous points

[8.13] An empty property is exempt from business rates for up to three months (six months for warehouses and industrial property), and rates are payable after the period of exemption has elapsed.

Self-catering holiday accommodation is normally subject to the business rate if available for short-term letting for 140 days or more in a year.

If bed and breakfast accommodation is offered, a person will not be liable to business rates if they intend to offer such accommodation for not more than six people, live in the property at the same time and the property's main use is still as their home.

People in mixed business and private accommodation pay the business rate on the non-domestic part and council tax on the private part (see **8.2**).

9

Administration

Structure

[9.1] UK taxes are administered by the Commissioners for Her Majesty's Revenue and Customs (HMRC), operating through their appointed officers.

In addition to being responsible for income tax, corporation tax, capital gains tax, inheritance tax, VAT and stamp taxes, HMRC deal with national insurance contributions, statutory sick pay and other statutory payments, welfare tax credits and child benefit.

As required under FA 2009, HMRC have published a charter setting out the standards of behaviour and values to which HMRC aspire in dealing with people in the exercise of their functions. This can be found at http://www.hmrc.gov.uk/charter/index.htm.

An increasing amount of HMRC's contact with the taxpayer is taking place online. Consequently the opportunities for face-to-face contact are being reduced, and a number of HMRC offices have been closed.

HMRC's 'workforce change' programme was designed to 'ensure that HMRC gets the right people in the right places with the right skills' and to 'assess the opportunities to reduce the size of our estate'. The department's July 2008 report to Parliament said that 'by centralising more work and workforce we can conduct our business more efficiently and at a lower cost'.

There are numerous telephone helplines, but many people have experienced delays and frustration. Agent priority lines and agent dedicated lines have been set up as part of a programme to improve HMRC's relationship with tax advisers. There has been evidence of ongoing service problems, including delays in repayment of overpaid tax, but online filing services appear to have been improving and very large numbers of self assessment tax returns and PAYE returns are now filed online.

The functions of the independent appeal commissioners were transferred to the tribunals system in April 2009.

Self-assessment: personal tax returns

[9.2] This section deals with personal returns of income and capital gains. The UK operates a self-assessment system, under which the total amount payable comprises not only income tax and capital gains tax (CGT) but also Class 4 national insurance contributions (NICs) for the self-employed and, where relevant, student loan repayments. The provisions for interest, surcharges, penalties and appeals apply to the total amount payable. For employed students the loan repayments are collected through the PAYE system, but for those who self-assess they are included on their returns. See **CHAPTER 23** regarding partnership returns and **9.17** for corporate returns.

Sending in the tax return (TMA 1970, ss 7–9C, 28C)

[9.3] The normal filing date for a paper return is 31 October after the end of the tax year. The normal filing date for a return filed online is 31 January after the end of the tax year. There are automatic penalties for late returns.

Self-assessment tax returns (forms SA 100) are normally sent out in April. If tax is paid under PAYE, coding notices will show the amounts of any underpayments dealt with by coding adjustment.

The tax is calculated automatically for returns filed online. Where a paper return is filed, individuals may calculate their own liability but HMRC will do the calculation so long as the return is filed on time, i.e. by 31 October.

If tax is paid under PAYE and a return (paper or online) is filed by 30 December following the end of the tax year, HMRC will try to adjust the PAYE code to collect an underpayment of up to £2,000 unless it is indicated in the return that the taxpayer prefers to pay the outstanding tax by the 31 January following the end of the tax year.

If pence are included in the return they will not be taken into account. Instead, income and gains should be rounded down and tax paid/tax credits should be rounded up, to the nearest pound. A return containing entries such as 'to be agreed', is incomplete. If the correct figure cannot be established in time a 'best estimate' should be included and it should be clearly marked that a provisional figure has been used. The correct figure should then be notified as soon as possible. It is important to remember that interest is charged on tax paid late.

A penalty may be imposed if HMRC consider that there was insufficient reason to use a provisional figure or they believe an 'unreasonable' one was used. The use of estimated figures may prompt HMRC to open an enquiry into the return.

If a return is not sent in by the due date, HMRC have the power to 'determine' the tax etc. that is owed. There is no right of appeal but their figure will be replaced by the self-assessment figure when it is received.

Corrections, amendments and enquiries (TMA 1970, ss 9ZA–9ZB)

[9.4] HMRC normally have nine months from the date they receive a return to correct obvious errors or omissions, but the taxpayer has the right to reject such a correction within 30 days. The taxpayer will normally have a year from 31 January following the end of the tax year to make amendments to the return, whether it was filed on paper or electronically. For returns issued after 31 October following the end of the tax year the 12-month period runs, broadly, from three months after the date the return was issued.

HMRC may handle minor queries on a return by telephone contact with the taxpayer or his agent. They may open a formal enquiry into the return providing they give the appropriate notice, normally within 12 months from the date the return is filed.

Claims for reliefs, allowances, etc. (TMA 1970, ss 42–43C and Sch 1A)

[9.5] Where a claim is made for capital allowances (see **22.12** to **22.16**), the claim must normally be in the return or an amended return, so the time limits indicated above for the return and amendments apply. Most other claims for reliefs and allowances are made in the same way. For claims that are not included in a return or amended return, a separate claims procedure is laid down, under which HMRC have the same nine-month period after the claim to correct obvious errors and the taxpayer has 12 months from the date of the claim to amend it. Unless another time limit is stipulated in the legislation, the time limit for separate claims is, from 1 April 2010, four years after the end of the tax year to which it relates (prior to 1 April 2010, the time limit was five years after the 31 January following the tax year to which it relates). Where capital losses are incurred, relief may be claimed against capital gains so long as the losses are notified to HMRC within the time limit for claims. There is, however, no time limit during which carried forward capital losses have to be used (see **4.2**).

In certain situations, HMRC may accept a late claim for reliefs, allowances etc if the delay results from events clearly outside the taxpayer's control or any other reasonable cause.

It is possible to provide certain information and make claims by telephone where appropriate. This applies only to individuals (or authorised third parties) and not to partners, trustees or personal representatives. A wider range of services, including the ability to make certain changes to self-assessments, is available to individuals and their agents (HMRC Statement of Practice 1/05).

Backdated claims (TMA 1970, s 42 and Sch 1B)

[9.6] Where relief is claimed for a loss incurred or payment made in one tax year to be set against the income or gains of an earlier tax year, then although the tax saving from the claim is calculated by reference to the tax position of the earlier year, the claim is treated as relating to the later year and is given effect in relation to that later year. Repayment supplement (see **9.42**) is therefore paid only from the balancing payment date for the later tax year (e.g. 31 January 2012 if the later year is 2010/11). This also applies to claims for averaging farming profits (see **31.5** and **31.6**) and carrying back post-cessation receipts (see **21.9**). In these latter two cases, the effect of the claim may be to *increase* the tax etc. payable for an earlier year. Interest on overdue tax etc. (see **9.42**) similarly runs from 31 January following the later tax year.

In calculating the revised tax position for the earlier year, the effect on claims and allowances that were made or could have been made is taken into account. For example, the effect of reducing income may be that age-related married couple's allowance becomes available, or that surplus married couple's allowance is available to transfer to a spouse, or following a loss carryback, the facility to pay personal pension contributions may be restricted, resulting in loss of tax relief on contributions already paid.

Payment of tax (TMA 1970, ss 59A, 59B, 59G, 59H, 70A and Sch 3ZA; SI 1996/1654)

[9.7] The payment dates for tax etc. that is not deducted at source are set out below.

Two equal payments on account (calculated as indicated below) should be made on 31 January in the tax year and 31 July following the end of the tax year, with the balance payable or repayable (taking into account any CGT due) on the following 31 January. Payment may be made by post to the Accounts Office, by bank Giro, by cheque or cash at post offices, by electronic funds transfer through BACS or CHAPS, or via online banking or telephone banking. HMRC recommend that payment is made electronically. If paying by cheque it is essential that either the personal payslip is used or the payer's tax reference number, name and address are given, and it would be sensible to keep a copy of the cheque.

Payments on account need only be made if the amount of income tax etc. due directly to HMRC for the previous year was (a) at least £1,000, and (b) at least 20% of the total tax etc. liability for that year.

[9.8] HMRC issue a self assessment statement based on the tax return but taking account of any amounts owing from earlier years and any payments on account that are outstanding for the current year. Self assessment statements are issued within 45 days of a payment becoming due, every two months if more than £32 is owed, and every month if more than £500 is owed. Taxpayers may also receive a statement if they have overpaid tax, or an underpayment is being collected through their PAYE code, or at the end of an enquiry into their return. Statements can be viewed online (by taxpayers and their agents) if registered with the Self Assessment Online service.

[9.9] Each payment on account for a tax year will normally be equal to half of the net *income tax* etc. liability (CGT is ignored) of the previous tax year (see **9.7**). Where income has fallen, it is possible to make a claim on form SA 303 at any time before the 31 January after the end of the tax year to reduce or eliminate the payments on account. If one or more of the payments has already been paid, the appropriate amount will be refunded with interest from the payment date. On the other hand, if payments are reduced below what they should have been, interest will have to be paid on the shortfall from each payment date and possibly a penalty.

If an amendment is made to a return resulting in extra tax etc. payable, the additional amount is due 30 days after the amendment (although interest on overdue tax etc. runs from the original due date).

[9.10] HMRC operate a 'time to pay' policy, if the taxpayer is unable to pay a tax debt that is due. Under this policy taxpayers may be given the opportunity of clearing tax arrears by instalments, rather than recovery proceedings being instituted for the full amount. This will be particularly likely for those who have not previously been late with their payments. Interest will, however, still be charged on the late payments.

HMRC extended this facility in 2008 to help businesses in the recession. Where a tax debt has not yet become due, the Business Payment Support Service (BPSS) allows businesses in temporary financial difficulty that are unable to pay their tax bills, including income tax, corporation tax, VAT, PAYE and NIC, to spread payment to HMRC over a timetable they can afford. HMRC undertook not to impose additional penalties within a time to pay arrangement but said interest would be charged.

Where a viable business is due to pay tax on the previous year's business profits and is likely to make a trading loss in the current year, those losses could be taken into account when agreeing the level of payments to be made.

The 'managed payment plans' regime, which was due to apply from April 2011, is to be deferred for the time being. (This deferral was announced at the Emergency Budget on 22 June 2010). This regime, when it does operate, will permit taxpayers to enter into a voluntary 'managed payment plan' with HMRC to make payments of income tax, capital gains tax or corporation tax by instalments over a period spanning the normal due date. The instalments paid before and after the due date will be 'balanced' by those to be paid after the due date. Provided the taxpayer pays all of the instalments in accordance with the plan he will be treated as having paid them on the due date and will be protected from interest and penalties.

Surcharges (TMA 1970, s 59C)

[9.11] If a balancing payment for a year is more than 28 days late, then unless reasonable excuse can be shown there will be a surcharge on the late payment of:

(a)   5% of any tax etc. not paid by 28 February.
(b)   A further 5% of any tax etc. still not paid by 31 July.

If additional tax etc. becomes due following an amendment to a return, the additional tax must be paid within 30 days. Surcharges will only arise if the additional amount due is paid more than 28 days after the 30-day period, and the further surcharge only if the payment is not made within a further five months.

The surcharge is in addition to interest on the overdue tax etc (see **9.42**). There is no surcharge, however, if a penalty based on the same amount has been incurred. The surcharge regime does not apply to corporation tax.

Self assessment timetable

[9.12] The key dates for the 2010/11 tax return are as follows:

31 January 2011	2009/10 online returns to be filed. Final payment/repayment for 2009/10, including CGT, plus 1st payment on account for 2010/11 (based on half 2009/10 tax etc. paid directly on all income).
April 2011	2010/11 returns issued.
31 July 2011	2nd payment on account due for 2010/11.
31 October 2011	2010/11 paper returns to be filed.
31 January 2012	2010/11 online returns to be filed. Final payment/repayment for 2010/11, plus 1st payment on account for 2011/12.

Form of self-assessment tax return

[9.13] The 'core return' contains the questions most likely to be relevant. Additional information pages are provided for the less common types of income and tax reliefs etc. Supplementary pages are to be completed for details of income from employment, self-employment, partnerships, property etc. and any capital gains.

HMRC sends a short tax return (four pages) to taxpayers with simple tax affairs including pensioners, some employees, and self-employed taxpayers with turnover below £70,000 (the current VAT registration threshold). Taxpayers that have self-employment income or have income from property below the £70,000 do not need to itemise business expenses or property expenses in their return.

Guidance notes and a tax calculation guide accompany the returns and supplementary pages. HMRC help sheets provide more detailed guidance on particular topics but these are now available online only, at www.hmrc.gov.uk/sa/forms/content.htm.

To file online it is necessary to register with HMRC via www.hmrc.gov.uk/sa. Not all of the supplementary pages can be filed using HMRC's own, free Self Assessment Online service. A wider range of supplementary pages is available using third party software products and HMRC provide a list of third party software companies who have products successfully tested to ensure that their forms and supplementary pages can be filed online. Partnerships and trustees, as well as individuals, may file returns online using third party software.

[9.14] Agents who have registered to use the internet for self-assessment are able to send clients' returns online providing HMRC hold the agent's authorisation form 64–8 for the client. If the form is not held, the client may register with HMRC and provide the appropriate authorisation. Agents must retain a signed hard copy (or electronically signed copy) of completed returns. The online filing system allows attachments to be sent with a return, but it cannot cope with aspects of some returns and it may therefore be necessary to supplement the return with paper information.

[9.15] HMRC have a system of 'post-transaction rulings', under which it may be possible to obtain, before filing a return, a ruling if the tax treatment of a transaction is in doubt because, for example, it was unusual or was entered into in unusual circumstances. It is also possible to ask for any valuations made for CGT to be checked before sending in the return.

A non-statutory clearance service enables businesses to obtain written confirmation of HMRC's view of the tax consequences of a transaction or event, either before or after the event, providing that there is 'material uncertainty' and that the issue is 'commercially significant'.

Additional information

[9.16] The self-assessment return is intended to be comprehensive and most taxpayers are not expected to need to submit accounts and other additional material. If, however, HMRC are not provided with full information and tax is consequently underpaid, they may make a 'discovery assessment'. Any additional material the taxpayer considers relevant may be sent in with the return, but swamping HMRC with information will not provide immunity from an HMRC discovery assessment unless the relevance of the additional material is pointed out.

The return requires details of income, claims for reliefs and allowances and, if relevant, capital gains details, for the year ended 5 April. It is sensible to keep a photocopy of the return in order to keep a full record of the information provided. Remember that even though supporting documentation is not necessarily required with the return, taxpayers may be charged a stiff penalty if they do not keep detailed records relating to their tax affairs for the specified period (see **9.25**). See **9.27** regarding an obligation to notify HMRC if tax is payable and a return form is not received.

Self-assessment: corporation tax returns (TMA 1970, ss 59D, 59E; FA 1998, s 117 and Sch 18; FA 2007, ss 93–97; FA 2009, s 93 and Sch 46)

[9.17] Most of the self-assessment provisions follow those for income tax. The main differences are detailed below:

(a) companies must file a statutory return (CT 600) with supporting accounts and computations within 12 months after the end of the accounting period (or three months after receiving the notice to deliver the return if later). From 1 April 2011 onwards, all companies must submit their tax returns online for any accounting period ending after 31 March 2010. As well as this, companies must file accounts and computations in a set format — Inline eXtensible Business Reporting Language (iXBRL). HMRC provide details of this switchchover at http://www.hmrc.gov.uk/ct/ct-online/file-return/switching.htm and a list of recognised commercial software that is compatible with the Corporation Tax Online service at http://www.hmrc.gov.uk/efiling/ctsoft_dev.htm;

(b) between three and seven weeks after the end of the accounting period the company will receive a notice to deliver a corporation tax return (form CT 603). Prior to 1 July 2010 HMRC also issued hard copies of the return form CT 600 with the CT 603. From 1 July 2010 these are no longer issued in preparation for compulsory online filing for all companies from 1 April 2011 (see (a) above). Where relevant, companies will need to send in supplementary pages, the main ones being loans to close company participators (CT600A), controlled foreign companies (CT600B), and group relief claims and surrenders (CT600C). Where a return is filed online, the supporting accounts and documentation must also be filed online as attachments. If the attachments are not sent, the filing obligation is not satisfied;

(c) companies do not have the option of leaving the tax calculation to HMRC. In addition to self-assessing the tax on its profits, a company is also required to self-assess its liability for tax on close company loans (see **12.14**) and under the controlled foreign companies rules (see **45.15**);

(d) the corporation tax payment date for companies with profits below the upper limit for small profits rate is nine months and one day after the end of the accounting period. Companies with profits above the small profits rate upper limit are required to pay their tax by instalments (see **3.22**);

(e) payments of corporation tax, interest and any flat or fixed rate penalties made after 31 March 2011 must be paid electronically (until that date they can be made as for income tax).

For financial years beginning on or after 21 July 2009, senior accounting officers of certain companies are required to take steps to ensure that the company (and any subsidiaries) establishes and maintains 'appropriate' tax accounting arrangements to enable the company's tax liabilities to be calculated accurately. This measure affects companies and groups, broadly, with a turnover of more than £200 million or a balance sheet total of more than £2 billion.

Corrections, amendments and enquiries

[9.18] HMRC are able to correct obvious errors in the return within nine months, and the company may notify amendments within 12 months after the filing date. HMRC normally have 12 months from the day on which the return was delivered in which to select the return for enquiry. The 12 month period runs from the filing date for groups of companies other than 'small groups', i.e. those with aggregate turnover not more than £6.5 million net, aggregate balance sheet total not more than £3.26 million net and aggregate employees not more than 50. (The enquiry 'window' is extended broadly as for income tax for returns delivered late and amended returns — see **9.31**.) A company may notify amendments to its return within the time limit stated above even when HMRC are enquiring into the return, but the amendments will not take effect until the enquiry is completed. The company and HMRC may jointly refer questions arising during the enquiry to the tribunal. If the return is not selected for enquiry, the self-assessment will stand unless an underpayment of tax is subsequently discovered that arises because the company gave inadequate information or because of its careless or deliberate actions. See **3.25** re returns for companies in liquidation.

Companies may ask HMRC (on form CG34) to check the valuations used to compute their capital gains before sending in their returns. Companies involved in non-arm's length sales (see **45.19**) are required to include any necessary transfer pricing adjustments in their returns.

Claims

[9.19] Claims for capital allowances and group relief must be made in the return or an amended return. If HMRC enquire into the return, the time limit for claims is extended to 30 days after the enquiry is completed (see **22.13** to **22.16** and **26.17**). The procedure for making other claims is the same as for income tax (see **9.5**). Such claims are subject to a time limit of, from 1 April 2010, four years from the end of the accounting period (prior to 1 April 2010, the time limit was six years from the end of the accounting period), unless some other time limit is specified. Where a return is amended following a discovery assessment, provision is made for the company to make additional or amended claims (see **9.35**). See **CHAPTER 26** for further details on loss claims and group relief.

Company law

[9.20] A company's tax return must be accompanied by copies of accounts as prepared in accordance with the Companies Acts (including directors' and auditors' reports). Company law requires companies to file accounts with Companies House not later than six months after the end of the accounting period for a public company, or nine months for a private company. There are automatic penalties for late filing, as set out in guidance note GBA5 available at www.companieshouse.gov.uk.

From summer 2010 (and as part of the introduction of compulsory online filing for tax returns), Companies House will accept company accounts in iXBRL which is the format used for all company tax returns from April 2011 (for accounting periods ending after 31 March 2010).

Self-assessment: inheritance tax returns (IHTA 1984, ss 216–225A, 245–248; SI 2008/605)

Lifetime transfers

[9.21] Most lifetime transfers are 'potentially exempt' from inheritance tax (IHT) but an account of a lifetime transfer on form IHT 100 is required when there is a chargeable event, e.g. a chargeable transfer is made by an individual, or a transferor dies within seven years of making a potentially exempt transfer. This requirement is subject to various exceptions.

A lifetime transfer made by an individual on or after 6 April 2007 is excepted if it meets either of the following conditions:

(a) the value transferred is attributable to cash or quoted stocks and securities, and that value together with the value of chargeable transfers made in the previous seven years does not exceed the IHT threshold; or

(b) the value transferred, together with the value of chargeable transfers made in the previous seven years, does not exceed 80% of the IHT nil rate threshold *and* the value of the value transferred by the current transfer does not exceed the 'net IHT threshold' (i.e. the amount of the threshold less the value of chargeable transfers made in the previous seven years).

Returns are strictly not required until 12 months after the end of the month in which the transfer takes place, but interest on overdue tax runs from earlier dates, so returns should be lodged accordingly (see **CHAPTER 5**).

Transfers on death

[9.22] In the case of death, the return is made in conjunction with the application for a grant of probate (where there is a will) or of administration (where there is no will or where the named executors cannot or will not act).

Guidance on completion of form IHT 400 and the various schedules, and guidance on application for probate, is available at www.hmrc.gov.uk/inheritancetax.

Form IHT 403 is required where the deceased made lifetime transfers. This form requires an annual breakdown of income and expenditure for the seven years before death where the 'normal expenditure out of income' exemption is claimed. It may be prudent for taxpayers makings gifts that may qualify for this exemption to have a copy of form IHT 403 to complete each year, so that in the event of their death within seven years the appropriate evidence is available.

If a deceased's estate is varied (see **5.34**, **35.14** and **35.15**) and the variation results in extra tax being payable, a copy of the variation, together with the additional tax, must be sent to HMRC within six months after the variation.

Anyone liable to pay tax on a potentially exempt transfer that becomes chargeable as a result of the donor's death is required to submit an account. Personal representatives are required to include in their account details of earlier transfers, whether chargeable or potentially exempt at the time, which are required for the calculation of the tax payable at death (see **CHAPTER 5**). It is therefore essential that full records of lifetime gifts are kept.

Excepted estates

[9.23] Personal representatives need not submit an account if the estate is an 'excepted estate'. There are three categories of excepted estate. If a charge arises on an 'alternatively secured pension fund' as a result of the death of the person originally entitled, or of a dependant (see **16.20**), the estate is not an excepted estate even though the other conditions are satisfied. Subject to that proviso, the general rule, where the deceased was domiciled in the UK, is that no account need be delivered where:

(a)   the estate comprises only property passing under the will or intestacy, or by nomination on death, or entitlement to a single interest in possession settlement, or beneficially by survivorship;

(b)   the total gross value of the estate for tax purposes does not exceed the nil rate threshold;

(c)   not more than £100,000 consists of property outside the UK;

(d)   the deceased made no lifetime chargeable transfers (including potentially exempt transfers becoming chargeable on death) except 'specified transfers' e.g. cash, listed shares or an interest in land that did not exceed £150,000;

(e)   not more than £150,000 represents value attributed to settled property.

This is a very brief summary. Detailed guidance is provided in IHT 400 Notes: Guide to completing your Inheritance Tax account.

Where the excepted estates provisions do not apply but certain other conditions are met, a reduced account may be submitted where, because of exemptions, most of the estate is free from IHT.

Personal representatives of estates covered by the procedures for excepted estates may provide the relevant details to a probate registry, such information being treated as provided direct to HMRC. Probate applications in respect of excepted estates must be accompanied by a form IHT 205 (return of estate information) or IHT 207 if the deceased lived abroad.

HMRC 'determinations'

[9.24] HMRC have the power to issue a notice of determination in connection with various IHT matters (for example the value of unquoted shares), against which there is a right of appeal. HMRC also have the power, with the consent of the tribunal, to give notice requiring someone to provide information, documents etc. relevant for IHT purposes. There is no appeal against such a notice. Similar notice (but without the need for the tribunal's consent) may be given to those who are required to deliver an account, against which there is a right of appeal.

Record keeping requirements

Individuals etc (TMA 1970, s 12B)

[9.25] It is not usually necessary to send accounts and supporting documents with the return (see **9.16**) but all records relevant to the return must be kept for a specified period. The period is normally 22 months from the end of the tax year, unless the taxpayer is in business or lets property, in which case the records must be kept for 5 years and 10 months from the end of the tax year (or such shorter period as specified by HMRC). If HMRC have commenced a formal enquiry into a return before the expiry of the time limit, the records must be kept until the enquiry is completed.

Where a claim is made other than in a return (see **9.5**), records relating to the claim must be kept until the day on which any HMRC enquiry into the claim (or amendment to a claim) is completed, or, if there is no such enquiry, until HMRC are no longer able to open such an enquiry (see **9.31**). As far as claims for relief for capital losses are concerned (see **9.5**) this means that the time limit for retaining the records relating to the losses may have expired before the time when the losses are used to reduce a gain.

Records may be kept on computerised systems providing they can be produced in legible form if required.

Companies (FA 1998, s 117 and Sch 18)

[9.26] Companies must keep records relating to information in their returns for six years from the end of the relevant accounting period, or sometimes longer in enquiry cases and where returns are late. Normally the record keeping requirement will be satisfied by the same records that satisfy Companies Act requirements, except for transfer pricing purposes. Records may be kept on computerised systems providing they can be produced in legible form if required.

Provision of information to HMRC

Notification of liability

Individuals (TMA 1970, s 7)

[9.27] HMRC send out tax returns to individuals, trusts and companies when they are aware that tax may be due. Most individuals have their tax dealt with through the PAYE system, and only about nine million out of around 29 million taxpayers receive tax returns. Where taxpayers are no longer required to complete a return they (and their advisers where relevant) will receive a letter from HMRC.

Nevertheless, if a taxpayer does not receive a return but has taxable income or gains on which tax has not been paid and of which HMRC are unaware, the onus is on the taxpayer to tell HMRC and there are penalties for non-compliance (see **9.42**). The time limit for notification of chargeability is 5 October following the end of the tax year, e.g. by 5 October 2011 for 2010/11 income and gains. Different time limits apply for submission of tax returns (see **9.3**).

There is no obligation to notify income where the tax liability has been met by deduction of tax at source. Employees who have a copy P11D from their employers may assume that HMRC know about its contents unless they have reason to believe otherwise, and they are not obliged to notify so long as they are satisfied that the P11D information is correct.

Apart from returns made by employers in respect of earnings of their employees, there are various reporting requirements for others, such as banks and building societies as to interest paid, payers of commissions and royalties, and those who receive profits and income belonging to other people (for example, interest or rent collected by solicitors or other agents).

Companies (FA 1998, s 117 and Sch 18)

[9.28] A company coming within the charge to corporation tax is required to notify HMRC of the date when its first accounting period begins. Notice must be given not later than three months after the beginning of that period. If a company with taxable profits does not receive a return, it must notify HMRC within 12 months after the end of the accounting period that it is chargeable to tax.

HMRC information and inspection powers (FA 2008, s 113 and Sch 36; FA 2009, s 97 and Sch 49)

[9.29] HMRC's investigatory powers have changed significantly in the past few years. FA 2007 made certain powers under the Police and Criminal Evidence Act 1984 available to HMRC officers dealing with direct taxes for the purpose of criminal investigations.

FA 2008 provided HMRC with a common set of information and inspection powers, effective from 1 April 2009, for income tax, capital gains tax, corporation tax and VAT. HMRC said the changes were designed to enable a more flexible approach to be taken to 'compliance checks' to ensure that taxpayers declare the right amount of tax, to make it easier for taxpayers to pay what they owe on time and support HMRC in tackling those who pay late. The most significant change for small businesses was the reform of HMRC's inspection powers, which may result in businesses being visited by HMRC officers with little or no prior warning in some circumstances. The detailed provisions are in FA 2008 Sch 36. With effect from 1 April 2009 an HMRC officer may:

(a)   require, by notice in writing, a person to provide information or to produce a document if it is reasonably required for the purpose of checking that person's tax position (or the tax position of another person whose identity the officer knows), or for the purpose of checking the UK tax position of either a person whose identity the officer does not know or a class of persons whose individual identities the officer does not know; and

(b)   enter a person's 'business premises' and inspect the premises and any business assets and business documents (as defined) on the premises if the inspection is reasonably required for the purpose of checking that person's tax position. He may not enter or inspect any part of the premises that is used solely as a dwelling.

From 1 April 2010, the FA 2008 Sch 36 powers were extended to apply to insurance premium tax, inheritance tax, stamp duty land tax, stamp duty reserve tax, petroleum revenue tax, aggregates levy, climate change levy and landfill tax.

FA 2009 made further changes including the introduction of a power enabling HMRC to issue notices requiring third parties to provide contact details for people in debt to HMRC.

HMRC launched a consultation in July 2009 on proposals to modernise their 'bulk and specialist' information powers, which allow HMRC to obtain information about unnamed taxpayers, either 'in bulk' or as part of a compliance check. One proposal being considered was a power to seek the identities of taxpayers using a disclosable tax avoidance scheme (see **45.2**).

HMRC guidance is available in the department's Compliance Handbook.

Money laundering

[9.30] Regulations to counter money laundering, introduced in 2007, incorporated the provisions of the EC Third Money Laundering Directive. The definition of money laundering includes any process of concealing or disguising the proceeds of *any* criminal offence, including tax evasion.

Accountants and tax advisers, among others, need to have a money laundering reporting officer within their organisation, and to have appropriate systems and staff training programmes. Failing to report to the Serious Organised Crime Agency knowledge or suspicion of money laundering is an offence punishable by imprisonment or an unlimited fine, and HMRC has powers to impose civil penalties for failure to comply with certain requirements set out in the regulations.

A particularly difficult problem is that it is an offence to warn the person concerned that a report is going to be made. Professional legal advisers and accountants, auditors and tax advisers who are members of appropriate professional bodies are, however, exempt from reporting the knowledge or suspicion of money laundering acquired in 'privileged' circumstances. Tax advisers should consider carefully in each case whether the 'privileged reporting exemption' applies.

Accountancy service providers who are not supervised by a designated professional body are required to be registered with HMRC. Guidance is provided at www.hmrc.gov.uk/mlr. The Consultative Committee of Accounting Bodies published guidance (subject to Treasury approval) for accountants and tax advisers in December 2007. That guidance was supplemented by further guidance issued by the professional bodies during 2008, and the leading tax bodies announced in July 2009 that the Treasury had approved the CCAB guidance for tax practitioners. The ICAEW's Tax Faculty and the Chartered Institute of Taxation published supplementary guidance for tax practitioners, to be read as an appendix to the CCAB guidance.

Enquiries, assessments and appeals (TMA 1970, ss 9A–9C, 19A, 28ZA–36, 43A–43C; FA 1998, s 117 and Sch 18; IHTA 1984, s 222)

HMRC enquiries

[9.31] HMRC normally have a period 12 months after the day on which a return is delivered to notify their intention to enquire into the return. If the return is filed late, or an amendment is made to it, this enquiry 'window' extends to the quarter day (31 January, 30 April, 31 July or 31 October) after the first anniversary of the day on which the return or the amendment was filed.

A return may be amended while an enquiry is in progress, although amendments to the amount of tax payable will not take effect until the enquiry is completed. Even then they may be rejected by HMRC or be incorporated in their amendments rather than being dealt with separately. During the enquiry, questions arising may be referred to the tribunal by joint notice from the taxpayer and HMRC. The taxpayer may apply for a direction requiring an HMRC officer to close the enquiry within a specified period.

On completion of the enquiry, HMRC will issue a closure notice and make any necessary amendments and the taxpayer has 30 days in which to lodge any appeal. HMRC have similar powers to enquire into claims made separately from the return.

[9.32] HMRC have the power to require the production of relevant documents in connection with an enquiry, and a penalty may be imposed for failure to do so. For details of HMRC information and inspection powers see **9.29**.

Dealing with an HMRC enquiry will almost certainly involve extra costs, particularly accountancy expenses, which would not normally be allowable in calculating taxable profits (see **20.8**). If the enquiry results in no addition to profits, or an adjustment to profits for the year of review only without a charge to interest or penalties, the additional expenses will be allowed (see HMRC statement of practice SP 16/91).

Postponement of payment of tax

[9.33] Tax etc. still has to be paid on the normal due dates even though an appeal has been lodged, except that in relation to income tax, corporation tax, CGT and stamp duty land tax an application may be made to postpone payment of all or part of the tax etc. The postponement application is separate from the appeal itself and must state the amount of tax etc. which it is considered has been overcharged and the grounds for that belief. The amount to be postponed will then be agreed with the inspector or decided by the tribunal. Any tax etc. not postponed will be due 30 days after the date of the decision as to how much tax etc. may be postponed, or on the normal due date if later.

The appeal itself may be settled by negotiation with the inspector or, failing that, by following the appeal procedure to the tribunal and then if necessary to the courts. Once the appeal has been finally settled, any underpaid tax etc. will be payable within 30 days after the inspector issues a notice of the amount payable. Any overpaid tax etc. will be repaid. Although a postponement application may successfully delay payment of tax, it will not stop interest being charged against the taxpayer on any postponed tax etc. which later proves to be payable (see the due date and interest provisions in **CHAPTERS 2** to **4**).

Appeal procedures

[9.34] Appeals must normally be made within 30 days after the date of issue of an assessment (or HMRC amendment to a self-assessment). An appeal must state the grounds on which it is made. Late appeals may be allowed if HMRC are satisfied that there was a good reason for the delay. If an appeal is not settled between the taxpayer and HMRC it may be referred to an independent tribunal. The tax tribunals system, comprising a First-tier Tribunal and an Upper Tribunal and forming part of the tribunals system administered by the Ministry of Justice, replaced the General and Special Commissioners in April 2009. HMRC guidance on the reform is available at www.hmrc.gov.uk/about/tribunals-reform.htm, and Factsheet HMRC1 sets out what should be done in the event of a disagreement with an HMRC decision.

Most appeals will be heard by the First-tier Tribunal in the first instance, and the Upper Tribunal will hear appeals against decisions of the First-tier Tribunal on a point of law. If either HMRC or the taxpayer is dissatisfied with a tribunal decision on a point of law, further appeal is possible to the High Court, the Court of Appeal and, where leave is granted, the House of Lords.

However a decision to take an appeal to the tribunal on a point of law must be weighed very carefully because of the likely heavy costs involved, particularly if the taxpayer should be successful at the earlier stages and lose before a higher court.

HMRC discovery assessments/determinations

[9.35] HMRC are able to issue an additional assessment for a year within the normal time limits of 5 years 10 months for individuals under self-assessment and six years for companies without alleging that the taxpayer is at fault.

If HMRC do not start an enquiry within the time limit, the tax etc. as calculated will normally stand. However, HMRC may make a 'discovery' assessment in the circumstances set out in TMA 1970, s 29, e.g. where there has been inadequate disclosure or loss of tax due to the taxpayer's careless or deliberate actions. Although the implication is that the innocent taxpayer may regard the year as closed after the 12-month period in **9.31**, this does not sit easily with the fact that in most cases HMRC will not require business accounts and other documents to be sent to them. In order to be sure of finality, it seems that taxpayers will need to make sure that HMRC are given all relevant information relating to their tax affairs, including accounts if appropriate, and draw their attention to any contentious points (see **9.16**).

Under the self-assessment provisions for companies HMRC may also make 'discovery determinations', to which the same provisions apply as to discovery assessments. They may 'discover' that an assessment is inadequate through considering facts already in their hands, such as by comparing gross profit rates from year to year, or through new facts, or even because they change their minds on how something should be interpreted. They have, however, stated that they will not normally reopen an assessment they later believe to be incorrect if they had been given full and accurate information and either the point was specifically agreed or the view implicit in the computation submitted was a tenable one.

Under self-assessment, the taxpayer is protected from further assessment after the HMRC period of enquiry expires (see **9.4** and **9.18**) unless there has been a loss of tax etc due to the taxpayer's careless or deliberate actions, or HMRC have not been supplied with full and accurate information. The protection given to the taxpayer by this provision was seriously undermined by a Court of Appeal case concerning a property valuation relating to a director's benefit in kind. The Court held that a discovery assessment outside the normal enquiry period was possible unless HMRC had been clearly alerted by the taxpayer or his representatives to the insufficiency of the taxpayer's self-assessment. Following that case HMRC issued guidance on their ability to raise discovery assessments and what information should be included in tax returns (SP 1/06). Where a discovery assessment is made, other than one arising from the taxpayer's careless or deliberate actions, provision is made for claims, elections, notices etc. to be made, revoked or varied within one year after the end of the tax year or company accounting period in which the assessment is made.

To reopen years outside the normal time limit, HMRC have to show careless or deliberate actions of the taxpayer. In that event, assessments may be made at any time up to 20 years after the tax year/company accounting period concerned. Under self-assessment for income tax and CGT the time limit is 20 years from the 31 January filing date for the return.

Cases of suspected fraud

[9.36] If HMRC suspect serious fraud, they may undertake a criminal prosecution. In that event, they will proceed under the provisions of the Police and Criminal Evidence Act 1984 (PACE). Prosecutions will be handled by HMRC and the specialist Revenue and Customs Division within the CPS (see **1.3**). Criminal proceedings may be taken under the general provisions for serious fraud and there is a separate criminal offence of fraudulent evasion of income tax.

In the vast majority of cases, investigations are undertaken using civil procedures. The investigation will be handled by HMRC's Special Civil Investigations Office under their code of practice COP 9 (updated in April 2009).

The taxpayer will usually be professionally represented. Interviews between the client and HMRC are conducted using a Civil Investigations of Fraud procedure as set out in COP 9. Such interviews cover both direct and indirect taxes where appropriate. Where the Civil Investigation procedure is used, there will not be a subsequent criminal prosecution for the original tax offence, but a taxpayer may still be prosecuted if he makes materially false statements or provides materially false documents with an intent to deceive during the investigation. HMRC will have provided the taxpayer with a copy of COP 9 before the interview. At the interview they will explain their practice in cases of suspected serious fraud and state that they will accept a money settlement and will not pursue a criminal prosecution if the taxpayer makes a full and complete confession of all tax irregularities. It is up to the taxpayer whether he co-operates with the investigation. If he does not, and evidence of provable fraud is uncovered, the risk of prosecution will have been increased substantially. HMRC will put five formal questions to the taxpayer concerning the accuracy of tax returns relating to direct taxes and, where relevant, four formal questions relating to VAT. The COP 9 procedure gives the taxpayer certainty that he will be able to put his tax affairs in order by making a full disclosure and paying the understated tax, interest and penalties.

Where serious fraud is not suspected, HMRC will usually invite the taxpayer to co-operate in establishing the understated income or gains. Where co-operation is provided, they will then not normally have to resort to their statutory powers to call for documents and to enter and search premises. See **9.30** re problems caused for tax advisers in investigation cases as a result of the money laundering provisions.

Establishing the tax etc. lost

[9.37] In relation to direct taxes, an HMRC investigation will include some or all of the following for the appropriate period, the effect of one on another being considered:

(a)   A full review of the business accounts, often including verification of transactions by third parties such as suppliers.

(b)   A detailed reconstruction of the private affairs, establishing whether increases in private wealth can be substantiated; or a less time-consuming review ensuring that lodgements into non-business bank and building society accounts can be explained.

(c)   A business model based on a sample period, adapted for changing circumstances and compared with the results shown by the business accounts.

(d)   A living expenses review and comparison with available funds to establish the extent to which personal and private expenditure could not have been met out of disclosed income and gains.

At the conclusion of the review, if the need for a revision of profits, income or gains has been established, the calculation of tax underpaid follows automatically.

Where irregularities include an underpayment of VAT, any additional VAT payable will be reflected in the revised profits for income tax or corporation tax.

Alternative to interest and penalty proceedings

[9.38] Instead of formal proceedings being taken for interest and penalties, the taxpayer will usually be invited to make an offer to HMRC in consideration of their not taking such proceedings, (although note that this procedure is to be redrawn, with the penalty structure being formalised as outlined in **9.43** onwards as appropriate).

The amount of the offer will normally be negotiated between HMRC and the taxpayer and will comprise the calculated tax etc. and interest plus a penalty loading, the penalty being reduced principally on three counts:

(a) Whether the initial disclosure was voluntarily made by the taxpayer or induced or partly induced by communication from HMRC.
(b) The size and gravity of the offence.
(c) The degree of co-operation by the taxpayer.

The acceptance of a taxpayer's offer by HMRC creates a binding contract, and if the taxpayer fails to pay, they are able to proceed for the amount due under the contract itself without any reference to the taxation position, although the terms of the contract sometimes allow them to repudiate it if they wish in the case of non- or late payment (HMRC then recommencing negotiations or taking proceedings), and further interest will be charged if payments due under the contract are delayed. This established procedure has been used in the vast majority of cases, and has points both in the taxpayer's and in HMRC's favour, in that the taxpayer may be treated less harshly than if proceedings were taken, and HMRC are spared the trouble of taking those proceedings.

National insurance contributions (SI 2001/1004 regs 87A-87G)

[9.39] Class 4 contributions payable by the self-employed are collected along with income tax through the self-assessment system and are subject to the same provisions in relation to interest on overdue and overpaid amounts, penalties and appeal procedures.

Where employers or employees have a disagreement with HMRC about a national insurance matter that cannot be resolved informally, HMRC will make a formal decision and notify the employer/employee accordingly. An appeal against the decision may be made within 30 days and the appeal will be dealt with under the same procedures as an income tax appeal (as to which see **9.34**). The disputed national insurance liability and interest thereon need not be paid until the appeal is settled, but if the appeal fails the amount payable will attract interest from 14 days after the end of the tax year in which it became due.

Criminal proceedings may be taken for fraudulent evasion of NICs.

Death of taxpayer

[9.40] Death of a taxpayer limits HMRC's right to reopen earlier tax years to the six tax years before that in which he died, and moreover restricts their right to raise new or additional assessments to the three years from 31 January following the tax year in which the death occurs, whatever the reason for the unpaid tax, e.g. by 31 January 2012 for a death in 2007/08 (TMA 1970, s 40). As a result of the Human Rights legislation, however, tax geared penalties are no longer sought from personal representatives in respect of tax evasion by the deceased. HMRC will still seek penalties in these circumstances, but on request they will issue a letter confirming that the penalty will be repaid with interest in the event of an adverse court decision or a change of HMRC view.

Companies and company directors

[9.41] While the liabilities of a company and its directors are entirely separate, their financial affairs will be looked at together if they are suspected of being at fault. Unexplained wealth increases or funding of living expenses will generally be regarded as extractions from the company, and, under his duty to preserve the company's assets, the director must account to the company for the extracted funds. The director does not have to pay income tax on the extracted funds, but is required to account to the company for the extractions, the company's accounts having to be rewritten accordingly and the extractions being subject to tax at corporation tax rates where they represent additional company profits. The company is also accountable for tax at 25% of the extractions unless they are repaid, covered by an amount already standing to the credit of the director or written off (see **12.14**). The tax liability attracts interest and is reckoned in the tax due to HMRC when calculating penalties. The extractions may also affect the income tax payable by the director on the calculated benefit which he has enjoyed from the interest-free use of the company's money.

Interest and penalty regime

Interest (TMA 1970, ss 86–92, 106A; TA 1988, s 824; FA 1998, s 117 and Sch 18)

[9.42] Interest is charged on overdue tax etc. from the date the amount of tax etc. became due, and repayment supplement is payable from the payment dates on tax etc. overpaid (subject to what is said at **9.6**). For further details and an illustration see **2.29** to **2.32**. Where an amendment is made to a return, interest is due on any additional tax etc. payable from the original due date, even though the tax itself is payable 30 days after the amendment. Unpaid surcharges (for income tax purposes, see **9.11**) and penalties (see **9.43**) also attract interest.

In addition to the payment of tax etc. and interest, HMRC have statutory powers to impose penalties when it has been established that tax etc. has been lost through a taxpayer's careless or deliberate actions. For details see **9.43**.

HMRC have power to reduce both interest and penalties. They will rarely reduce interest, but will usually accept a smaller penalty where a settlement is reached with a taxpayer without formal proceedings being taken.

For details of interest payments in relation to the PAYE regime see **10.53**.

Harmonised interest regime (FA 2009, ss 101, 102 and Schs 53 and 54; SI 2010/1878; SI 2010/1879)

[9.42A] HMRC inherited from the former Inland Revenue and Customs & Excise a number of different regimes for interest charged on late payments. Finance Act 2009 created a harmonised interest regime for all taxes and duties administered by HMRC, with the exception of corporation tax and petroleum revenue tax. This regime currently applies only to bank payroll tax (see **3.23**) from 31 August 2010 with further full implementation across all relevant taxes to be staged over a number of years.

Essentially the regime—

(a)   harmonises the formulae used for calculation of interest charged across all taxes and duties for which HMRC are responsible; and

(b)   ensures that the determination of interest rates is based on the official bank rate as announced by the most recent meeting of the Monetary Policy Committee of the Bank of England.

Until the Finance Act 2009 regime is fully implemented, the current interest rate setting regulations have been amended (from 12 August 2009) to harmonise the existing regime along the same lines.

Penalties

[9.43] Over the last few years a unified penalty regime has been introduced (although parts are still to be phased in over the next few years) that essentially applies across all taxes. There will be higher penalties for prolonged and repeated delays, but penalties will not be charged where a time to pay arrangement has been agreed.

FA 2009 provided for HMRC to publish information, including names, relating to deliberate tax defaulters, i.e. people who have been penalised for inaccuracies, failure to notify etc., where the tax lost exceeds £25,000.

Penalties for inaccurate documents (FA 2007, s 97 and Sch 24; FA 2010, s 35 and Sch 10)

[9.44] There is a cross-taxes regime for charging penalties for errors and inaccuracies contained in specified documents (e.g. returns of income and capital gains (including construction industry returns), accounts, allowances claims, PAYE returns, partnership statements; corporation tax returns, statements and accounts; VAT returns and statements; IHT returns and, for all those taxes, any document HMRC are likely to rely on without further enquiry to decide a taxpayer's liability and payments or repayments due).

The regime applies, broadly, for return periods commencing after 31 March 2008 where the return is filed after 31 March 2009 (although for IHT purposes it applies with effect for deaths and other chargeable events occurring on or after 1 April 2009), when a person provides a specified document which contains an inaccuracy that leads to an understatement of tax payable, or a false or inflated statement of a loss, or a false or inflated repayment claim. It also applies where HMRC have issued an assessment and the person assessed did not take reasonable steps to notify them within 30 days that the assessment understated their liability.

The penalties are based on the amount of tax lost and are stepped according to the degree of culpability as follows:

Type of behaviour	Statutory maximum penalty
Careless	30% of tax lost
Deliberate but not concealed	70% of tax lost
Deliberate and concealed	100% of tax lost

An inaccuracy in a document is careless if the taxpayer failed to take reasonable care, deliberate but not concealed if the taxpayer did not make arrangements to conceal a deliberate inaccuracy, or deliberate and concealed if the taxpayer made arrangements to conceal a deliberate inaccuracy. An inaccuracy (that was neither careless nor deliberate at the time the documents were originally submitted) that is discovered after the documents are sent to HMRC will be treated as careless if the taxpayer found out about it later and did not tell HMRC.

The penalties will be reduced if the taxpayer discloses the inaccuracies and cooperates in the investigation of the amount of tax lost. HMRC will also be able to suspend a penalty for a careless inaccuracy for up to two years, subject to specified conditions. They can only do so if this would help the taxpayer to avoid further such penalties. Providing the taxpayer complies with the conditions, the penalty or part of it may be cancelled at the end of the stipulated period.

FA 2010 provided that the level of penalties charged under these provisions could be increased where an income or capital gains tax liability arose on certain undeclared offshore assets. This amendment will come into force on a day to be appointed by Treasury order (although it was indicated at Budget Note BN68 that this will be for tax periods commencing on or after 1 April 2011).

Penalties for failure to notify chargeability (FA 2008, s 123 and Sch 41; FA 2010, s 35 and Sch 10)

[9.45] Specific provisions apply a penalty regime for failing to notify chargeability to tax, liability to register for tax etc. after 1 April 2010, aligned across all relevant taxes and duties. The penalties are based on the amount of tax lost and are stepped according to the degree of culpability, as detailed at **9.44**.

FA 2010 provided that the level of penalties charged under these provisions could be increased where an income or capital gains tax liability arose on certain undeclared offshore assets. This amendment will come into force on a day to be appointed by Treasury order (although it was indicated at Budget Note BN68 that this will be for tax periods commencing on or after 1 April 2011).

Penalties for failure to make returns

Income tax returns (TMA 1970, s 93)

[9.46] The following penalties are charged for late personal returns:

(a) £100 if the return is not delivered by the filing date, plus a further penalty of up to £60 a day if HMRC have applied for and received a direction from the appeals tribunal to charge a daily penalty;

(b) a further £100 if the tribunal has not imposed the daily penalty and the return is not made within six months of the filing date; and

(c) a further penalty, of an amount not exceeding the tax that would have been payable under the return, if the return is not made by the anniversary of the filing date.

The *fixed* late-filing penalties cannot exceed the amount of tax etc. for the year that remains outstanding at the return due date, and no fixed penalty can apply if a repayment is due. If a penalty has already been paid in these circumstances all or the appropriate part of it will be refunded. The daily penalties, however, are not limited to the tax etc. payable. Where more than one return is outstanding the penalty applies to each return.

Corporation tax returns (FA 1998, s 117 and Sch 18)

[9.47] The following penalties are charged for late corporation tax returns:

(a) £100 if the return is up to three months late (£500 for third consecutive late return), £200 if the return is over three months late (£1,000 for third consecutive late return); plus

(b) 10% of tax unpaid 18 months after the end of the accounting period (if the return is submitted 18 to 24 months after the end of the accounting period), 20% of tax unpaid if the return is submitted more than 24 months after the end of the accounting period.

If the return is not sent in by the due date, automatic fixed penalties are payable (although by HMRC concession B46 a penalty will not be charged if the return is received on or before the last business day within seven days after the due date). Note this concession is to be withdrawn on 31 March 2011. This is because, from 1 April 2011, company tax returns for accounting periods ending after 31 March 2010 must be filed online, consequently the concession will have become redundant because the possible causes of late filing it was intended to address can no longer arise.

Tax-related penalties are payable if the return is more than six months late. Where, because of exceptional circumstances, a company cannot produce final figures within the time limit, 'best estimates' may be used without attracting late filing penalties, but the figures must be adjusted as soon as the company is aware that they no longer represent the best estimate, and any late payment of tax will attract interest.

IHT returns

[9.48] If an account is not submitted by the due date, HMRC may impose an initial penalty of £100 plus a further penalty (on a direction by the tribunal) of up to £60 a day until the account is delivered. If an account is delivered late more than six months later but before HMRC have taken proceedings before the tribunal, the penalty is increased to £200. If an account is delivered more than 12 months late, a penalty of up to £3,000 may be charged. The same applies if notification of a variation of a deceased's estate is made more than 12 months late. Fixed penalties (but not daily penalties) cannot exceed the tax chargeable and penalties will not be charged if there is a reasonable excuse for the delay.

Unified penalty regime for failure to make returns (FA 2009, s 106 and Sch 55; FA 2010, s 35 and Sch 10)

[9.49] From a date to be announced by Treasury order the above rules will be replaced by a cross-taxes regime (which currently only applies to the bank payroll tax rules (**3.15**)). Under these provisions, the penalties for late filing of a tax return will range from a fixed penalty of £100, due immediately after the filing date, to a penalty equal to the greater of £300 and 100% of the tax liability where the return has been outstanding for 12 months and the withholding of information is deliberate and concealed.

FA 2010 provided that the level of penalties charged under these provisions could be increased where an income or capital gains tax liability arose on certain undeclared offshore assets. This amendment will come into force on a day to be appointed by Treasury order (although it was indicated at Budget Note BN68 that this will be for tax periods commencing on or after 1 April 2011).

Additionally, as detailed in the June 2010 Emergency Budget, from a date to be announced, a new penalty regime will apply to various indirect taxes where relevant returns are filed late. The taxes covered will include VAT, insurance premium tax, aggregates levy, climate change levy, landfill tax and excise duties. Under these new rules, failure to file a quarterly (or monthly if relevant) return by the filing date will trigger a penalty period of one year and an immediate £100 penalty. The fixed penalty will then escalate by £100 for each subsequent failure within the period, up to a maximum of £400, and the period itself will be extended to the first anniversary of the latest failure. Additional penalties of 5% of the tax on the return will be charged for continuing failure 6 and 12 months after the filing date. Penalties of up to 100% of the tax will be charged where the failure is intended deliberately to withhold information to prevent HMRC correctly assessing the tax.

Penalties for late payment (FA 2009, s 107 and Sch 56; SI 2010/466)

[9.50] From 6 April 2010, penalties will be imposed for late payments of certain amounts due under PAYE and the construction industry scheme, tax charges payable by scheme administrators of registered pensions and payments due under the bank payroll tax regime (**3.15**). The penalties range between 1% and 4% with further penalties of 5% being due of any amounts still unpaid at 6 and 12 months after the due date. This regime will be extended to other taxes from a date to be announced by Treasury order. See also **10.53**.

Additionally, as detailed in the June 2010 Emergency Budget, from a date to be announced, a new penalty regime will apply to various indirect taxes where tax is paid late. The taxes covered include VAT, insurance premium tax, aggregates levy, climate change levy, landfill tax and excise duties. Under these new rules, failure to pay tax due quarterly (or monthly if relevant) will trigger a one year penalty period although no immediate penalty will apply. A second failure in the period will attract a penalty of 2%, a third failure a 3% penalty and further failures a 4% penalty. The penalty period is extended with each failure. Additional penalties of 5% of the tax will be charged for continuing failure 6 and 12 months after the due date.

IHT penalties

[9.51] In addition to the specific penalties mentioned at **9.44** and **9.48**, someone required to deliver an *account* who fails to comply with a HMRC information notice is liable to a penalty of up to £50 plus a daily penalty of up to £30 once the failure has been declared by a court or the tribunal. The penalties for anyone else who fails to comply with an information notice are up to £300 plus up to £60 a day.

Overpayment relief (TMA 1970, ss 30–33 and Sch 1AB; FA 1998 s 117 and Sch 18)

[9.52] If income tax, corporation tax or capital gains tax has been paid and the taxpayer believes that the payment was excessive it is possible may make a claim for overpayment relief (known as error or mistake relief before 1 April 2010) if no other statutory steps are available and the taxpayer has used any available rights of appeal. This claim must be made four years after the end of the tax year or accounting period with effect from 1 April 2010. (Prior to this date the time limit was five years after 31 January following the tax year to which the claim relates, or six years from the end of the relevant accounting period). HMRC are required to give such relief as is 'reasonable and just'. No relief is given if the return was made in accordance with practice generally prevailing at the time when it was made provided that practice is in accordance with the UK's EU treaty obligations.

Official error (TMA 1970, s 43; FA 1998, s 117 and Sch 18; Concessions A19, B41)

[9.53] Unless a specific time limit is stated, the normal time limit for individuals to claim reliefs is four years after the end of the tax year. For companies the time limit is four years after the end of the relevant accounting period. Repayments will, however, be made on claims made outside the time limit where the overpayment was caused by an error by HMRC or another Government department, providing the facts are not in dispute.

Where HMRC discover that they have undercharged income tax or CGT, although they have been given full information at the proper time either by the taxpayer, or by his employer, or (in relation to pensions) by the Department for Works and Pensions, they may, by concession, not collect the underpayment. This will apply only if the taxpayer could reasonably have believed his affairs to be in order.

Equitable liability

[9.54] The time limits for appealing against assessments, and for substituting a taxpayer's own self-assessment for an HMRC determination under the self-assessment provisions, are indicated at **9.34** and **9.35** respectively. If action is not taken within the time limits, the tax assessed or determined becomes payable. Where income tax (including tax due from employers under PAYE) or CGT that has legally become due is higher than it would have been if all the relevant information had been submitted at the proper time, HMRC have been prepared to accept an amount equal to what the correct liability would have been, providing the taxpayer's affairs are brought fully up to date. This practice, known as 'equitable liability', was set out in Tax Bulletin 18 (August 1995).

HMRC announced in April 2009 that this practice was to be withdrawn from April 2010 along with the planned withdrawal of a number of concessions (other concessions being written into legislation). However, the move was criticised and *Taxation* magazine launched a campaign in July 2009 to retain the 'essential elements' of equitable liability. Subsequently, it was announced in the Pre-Budget Report on 9 December 2009, that legislation will be introduced to put this concession on a statutory basis. (A consultation document containing draft legislation to give legislative effect to the 'equitable liability' rules has now been published and comments are sought by 1 October 2010).

Right of set-off (FA 2008, ss 130–133)

[9.55] From 21 July 2008, HMRC have a statutory power to set-off any tax credit owed to a taxpayer against any tax owed by that taxpayer (except in an insolvency situation). Consequently if, for example, a taxpayer has a VAT credit but owes unpaid corporation tax then it will be offset.

Certificates of tax deposit

[9.56] Certificates of tax deposit may be purchased by individuals, partnerships, personal representatives, trustees or companies, subject to an initial deposit of £500, with minimum additions of £250. The certificates may be used to pay any tax except PAYE, VAT, tax deducted from payments to subcontractors and corporation tax, and may also be used to pay Class 4 NICs. Interest accrues daily for a maximum of six years, and provision is made for varying interest rates during the term of the deposit. A lower rate of interest applies if the deposit is withdrawn for cash rather than used to settle tax liabilities. The interest accrued at the time the deposit is used or cashed is charged to tax. Tax deposit certificates are a way of ensuring that liquid resources are earmarked for the payment of tax when due. They also prevent the risk of interest charges when tax is in dispute, because when they are used to pay tax, interest on overdue tax will not be payable unless and to the extent that the deposit was made after the date the tax was due for payment. HMRC guidance and details of interest rates are provided at www.hmrc.gov.uk/payinghmrc/cert-tax-deposit.htm.

Disclosure opportunities

Offshore accounts

[9.57] HMRC announced in July 2009 details of a much-anticipated 'new disclosure opportunity' (NDO) to allow people with unpaid taxes linked to offshore accounts or assets to settle their outstanding liabilities with penalties on favourable terms. People who make a complete and accurate disclosure under the NDO will qualify for a 10% penalty.

A notification of the intention to make a disclosure must be made to HMRC between 1 September 2009 and 4 January 2010 (extended from the initially announced deadline of 30 November 2009). The disclosures can be made:

(a)   on paper by 31 January 2010; or
(b)   electronically by 12 March 2010.

In both cases, full payment (tax, interest and penalties) must be made with the disclosure.

The 10% penalty will apply to those who were not contacted by HMRC under the now closed 'offshore disclosure opportunity' (ODF) in 2007. A 20% penalty will apply to those who were contacted but did not complete the ODF procedure, but wish to disclose under the NDO.

Taxpayers who do not come forward but are found to have unpaid liabilities will face penalties of 'at least 30% rising to 100% of the tax evaded,' and run a risk of criminal prosecution.

Health professionals

[9.58] HMRC announced in January 2010, a disclosure opportunity for health professionals with previously undisclosed UK tax liabilities. Health professionals who disclose are entitled to a reduced penalty, of 10% of the tax due. Liabilities which go back up to 20 years may be disclosed under this scheme. No disclosure is required for years before 2003/04 where the unpaid tax and duty is less than £50. No penalty is due where the unpaid liability is less than £1,000. The scheme consists of two parts: notification and disclosure. Notification of the intention to disclose must have been given to HMRC by 31 March 2010. HMRC will acknowledge the notification and the taxpayer must then make the disclosure and have paid liabilities by 30 June 2010.

Taxpayers who do not come forward but are found to have unpaid liabilities will face penalties of 'at least 30% rising to 100% of the tax evaded,' and run a risk of criminal prosecution.

Tax points

[9.59] Note the following:

- Where a tax repayment is expected, the self-assessment return form enables a charity to be nominated to receive all or part of the repayment directly from HMRC and to indicate that gift aid should apply to the donation. The donation will be regarded as made when the charity receives the payment and it is not possible to treat the gift as made in the tax year to which the return relates. HMRC provide information about the SA Donate scheme at www.hmrc.gov.uk/individuals/giving/tax-return.htm.
- Self-assessment is a difficult exercise even for those with straightforward tax affairs. Remember that individuals *do not have to calculate their own tax*, but a paper return must be submitted by 31 October to avoid a late filing penalty and it would be sensible to ensure that HMRC will calculate the tax in time for tax payments to be made on the due dates.
- Companies must pay their tax and file their tax returns promptly. If they fail to meet the deadlines, they incur automatic interest and penalties. Companies should also be aware of the company law penalties for late filing of accounts.
- It is essential to retain records relating to tax affairs for a stipulated period (see **9.25**). HMRC guidance is available at www.hmrc.gov.uk/sa/record-keeping.htm.
- Where a claim is made to backdate a loss incurred or payment made to an earlier year, the resulting tax etc. adjustment is made for the tax year of loss or payment, so there is no extra benefit in terms of interest on tax overpaid.

- If starting a new business, HMRC will probably need extra information, and they may only be able to get this by making an enquiry into a return. It may therefore be advisable to submit full accounts and explanatory notes (for example the source of monies introduced to start the business) with the self-assessment (see **9.31** to **9.32**).

- The self-employed, with a turnover of less than £70,000 a year, need only show turnover, allowable expenses and net profit on their tax return. They must still have detailed records in case HMRC want to see them.

- It is possible to register to receive bank and building society interest gross. But note this treatment applies only if the person registering expects *no tax liability at all*. Merely being entitled to a repayment of some of the tax paid for the year is not enough. If, having registered, the person finds he is no longer eligible, the bank or building society must be notified straight away, and the tax office informed if tax is or will be due.

- If a taxpayer is aware of irregularities in his tax affairs, a full disclosure to HMRC before they make a challenge will ensure the maximum penalty reduction when an offer in settlement is eventually made. Furthermore, a payment on account of the tax eventually to be accounted for will reduce the interest charge and also possibly any penalty.

- Whilst HMRC will usually settle for a cash sum comprising tax, interest and penalties, they may also take criminal proceedings in cases which they believe amount to provable fraud. They may still seek a civil money penalty on those aspects not brought before the court or where the taxpayer has been acquitted of fraud and they feel able to prove negligence (HMRC codes of practice COP 8 and COP 9).

- HMRC have substantial powers to require banks, lawyers, accountants etc. to provide information and documents that may be relevant in establishing tax liabilities, including cross-border agreements with other countries.

- If business accounts or taxation affairs generally are under investigation, HMRC will issue appropriate leaflets and their Code of Practice. These are no substitute for appropriate professional representation but they do explain taxpayer's rights and are helpful in explaining HMRC procedures.

Employment

10

Employments — taxable income and allowable deductions

Introduction

[10.1] The tax law relating to employment income is contained in the Income Tax (Earnings and Pensions) Act 2003 (ITEPA 2003), as amended by later Finance Acts. ITEPA 2003 deals with employment income (Pts 2–8), pension income (Pt 9) and social security benefits (Pt 10). This chapter discusses employment income and taxable social security benefits. All statutory references are to ITEPA 2003 unless otherwise stated. Pensions are dealt with in **CHAPTER 16**.

Basis of charge (ss 1–13, 682–686)

[10.2] The legislation covers the employment earnings of employees and directors. Tax on such earnings is normally collected by employers through the Pay As You Earn (PAYE) scheme, which also deals with the collection of national insurance contributions (NICs). Class 1 NICs are payable by employees and employers and accounted for by employers along with the tax on the earnings, and Class 1A NICs on employee benefits are payable by employers only and accounted for at the year-end (see **10.52**). Employees' and employers' NICs are discussed in **CHAPTER 13**.

It is often hard to decide whether someone is employed or self-employed — see **CHAPTER 19**. If an employer wrongly treats an employee as self-employed, he is liable for the PAYE and NICs that should have applied, with only limited rights of recovery from the employee of his share. The worker who is classed as employed rather than self-employed will find significant differences in his allowable expenses, the timing of tax payments and the liability for NICs.

Most agency workers are required to be treated as employees. The agency is usually responsible for the operation of PAYE but the client is responsible if he pays the worker direct. Agencies are normally required to deduct PAYE tax and NICs from payments to construction workers supplied by them.

Anti-avoidance

IR35 rules

[10.3] Special rules known as the IR35 rules prevent the avoidance of tax and NICs by operating through a personal service company rather than being employed directly (see **19.6** to **19.14**). All employers have to state on their PAYE annual P35 forms (see **10.51**) whether or not the IR35 rules apply to any worker listed on the return (see **19.14**). Further rules were introduced from 6 April 2007 in relation to 'managed service companies', which were already subject to the IR35 rules but were used to avoid tax and NIC liabilities in different ways. Such companies are now subject to separate rules rather than the IR35 rules. Payments to those working for such companies are treated as employment income if they would not otherwise be so treated, and various other special provisions apply. See **19.15**.

Sale of income from personal occupation (ITA 2007, ss 773–789)

[10.4] This prevents those with high personal earning potential, such as entertainers, avoiding tax by means of contracting their services to a company in which they hold the shares and thereby turning income into capital by later selling the shares at a price reflecting the personal earnings.

Social security benefits (ss 660–676)

[10.5] The tax treatment of social security benefits is complex and the detailed rules are outside the scope of this book. The table below shows which of the main social security benefits are taxable and which are exempt. See the Table of Rates and Allowances for the current amounts payable.

Employment and support allowance replaced incapacity benefit and income support for new claimants from October 2008. HMRC provide guidance on the tax treatment of grants and employment credits under the 'New Deal' programme in their Employment Income Manual at EIM01651. A list of taxable and non-taxable social security benefits can be found at EIM76100–1. A summary is provided below.

SOCIAL SECURITY BENEFITS
TAXABLE:
Bereavement allowance and widowed parent's allowance*   Carer's allowance*   Incapacity benefit* (after first 28 weeks)   Employment and support allowance (if contribution based)   Industrial death benefit paid as pension   Jobseeker's allowance (up to the 'taxable maximum')   Statutory maternity pay, statutory paternity pay and statutory adoption pay   Statutory sick pay   *Excluding any addition for dependent children
EXEMPT:
Attendance allowance   Back to work bonus   Bereavement payment   Child benefit and child's special allowance   Christmas bonus and winter fuel allowances for pensioners   Disability living allowance   Employment and support allowance (if income-related)   Guardian's allowance   Housing benefit and council tax benefit   Incapacity benefit (for first 28 weeks of entitlement)   Incapacity benefit to those receiving the former invalidity benefit at 12 April 1995 for the same incapacity   Income support (except where the claimant is involved in a trade dispute and is claiming in respect of a partner)   Industrial injuries benefit   Maternity allowance   Pension credit   Severe disablement allowance   Tax credits (see **2.33**)   War widow's pension

Benefits payable under an insurance policy taken out to cover periods of sickness or unemployment are exempt from tax. Such policies include mortgage protection policies, permanent health insurance and insurance to meet domestic bills etc. Various conditions must be satisfied, in particular no deduction must have been received for the premiums in calculating taxable income.

Persons liable (Pt 2)

[10.6] Liability to tax on earnings depends on the individual's country of residence, ordinary residence and domicile. Broadly, residence normally requires a person to be physically present in the country at some time in the tax year, ordinary residence means habitual residence and domicile is the country regarded as the individual's permanent home — see **CHAPTER 41**.

An individual who is resident, ordinarily resident and domiciled in the UK is normally charged to tax on world-wide earnings. Non-residents are liable to tax on their UK earnings.

Personal reliefs are available only to UK residents and specified categories of non-resident (see **41.27**). An individual is not entitled to personal reliefs for any tax year for which he claims the remittance basis (see **41.14**). Liability to UK and overseas tax may be varied by double taxation agreements. See **41.16** regarding UK residents working abroad and **41.30** regarding a non-resident's UK earnings.

Taxable earnings (ss 9–13)

[10.7] Pay for income tax purposes includes wages, salaries, commissions, bonuses, tips and certain benefits in kind. To count as pay, earnings must be 'in the nature of a reward for services rendered, past, present or future'. See **CHAPTER 15** for lump sum payments received on taking up or ceasing employment.

Pay for the purpose of Class 1 NICs is broadly the same as pay for income tax. There are, however, still some instances where the treatment differs, and it is essential to study carefully the employers' guides provided by HMRC. Employers' Class 1A NICs are payable on virtually all benefits in kind on which tax is paid by employees earning £8,500 per annum or more and directors (see below), except where the benefits are included in a PAYE settlement agreement and contributions are paid under Class 1B (see **10.55**).

Pay for Class 1 NICs is not reduced by charitable payments under the payroll deduction scheme (see **43.26**), nor by the employee's occupational or personal pension contributions. Employer contributions to employer-financed registered company pension schemes, or to certain other employer-finance schemes, or an employee's registered pension plan, do not count as earnings for either tax or NICs — see **CHAPTERS 16** and **17**.

The NIC treatment of tips depends on how the tips are paid. HMRC booklet E24 'Tips, gratuities, service charges and troncs' deals with the treatment of such items for tax and NICs, VAT and the national minimum wage. The booklet makes it clear that payments made by a tronc master are not liable to NICs providing the money was not originally paid to the employer, and the employer is not deciding the allocation of the payments, directly or indirectly. The 2010 version of the guide is available at www.hmrc.gov.uk/helpsheets/e24.pdf.

If an employer pays a bill that the employee has incurred and is legally liable to pay, this counts as the equivalent of a payment of salary. The employee is charged Class 1 NICs, but not income tax, at the time the employer pays the bill. The employer will show the payment on the year-end form P11D or P9D (see **10.54**), and the tax on it will be included in the amount of tax the employee owes for the year.

Employers must deduct and account for tax and Class 1 NICs under PAYE when they provide pay in certain non-cash forms — see **10.19**.

Tax is charged on the earnings received in the tax year if an employee is resident, ordinarily and domiciled in the UK, no matter what period the earnings relate to. Certain expenses incurred may be deducted in arriving at the taxable earnings — see **10.10**.

Employees earning £8,500 per annum or more and directors — P11D employees (ss 216, 217)

[10.8] Form P11D is the employer's annual return of expenses and benefits (see **10.54**) and a P11D employee is taxed not only on cash pay but also on the cash equivalent of benefits in kind. All directors and employees earning £8,500 a year or more, including benefits, are P11D employees. Full-time directors earning less than £8,500 are not P11D employees unless they own or control more than 5% of the ordinary share capital or, in the case of a 'close company', they are entitled to more than 5% of the assets on a winding up. All part-time directors are P11D employees unless they work for a charity or non-profit making organisation and earn less than £8,500. The legislation used to refer to P11D employees as 'higher-paid' employees.

Lower-paid employees (P9D employees)

[10.9] Employers report taxable benefits and expenses for non-P11D employees at the year end on form P9D (see **10.54**). Non-P11D employees are not normally taxed on benefits unless they can be turned into cash, and the amount treated as pay is the cash which could be obtained. For example, if a non-P11D employee is given a suit which cost the employer £250 but which is valued second-hand at only £30, the employee is taxed only on £30. A non-P11D employee escapes tax on the benefit of use of a car, unless he has the choice of giving up the car for extra wages. In that event, the car could be turned into cash at any time by taking up the offer, so he would be treated as having the extra wages — the rule at **10.34** applies only to P11D employees. Some benefits are chargeable on all employees — see **10.19**.

Benefits provided by an employer, under a contract that the employer has made, must be distinguished from payments by the employer of bills that the employee is legally liable to pay. Such payments do not escape tax or Class 1 NICs — see **10.7**.

Allowable expenses and deductions (ss 229–236, 316A, 333–360A; ITA 2007, s 128; FA 2009, ss 67, 68)

[10.10] In arriving at taxable pay, an employee can deduct expenses that he is obliged to incur and pay as holder of the employment and are incurred wholly, exclusively and necessarily in the performance of the duties of that employment. Relatively few expenses satisfy this stringent rule. Others are specifically allowable by statute or by concession. See **10.41** for the treatment of work-related training costs paid or reimbursed by the employer. HMRC provide guidance on various expenses and benefits at www.hmrc.gov.uk/paye/exb/index.htm

An employee can also deduct qualifying travelling expenses. He is entitled to relief for the full cost he is obliged to incur in travelling in the performance of his duties or travelling to or from a place he has to attend in the performance of his duties, as long as the journey is not ordinary commuting between his home and his permanent workplace or private travel (i.e. travel for a private rather than business purpose).

Site-based employees with no permanent workplace are allowed the cost of travelling to and from home (unless the job at the site is expected to last for more than 24 months, in which case the site counts as a permanent workplace). The 24 month rule does not allow home to work travelling expenses to be claimed by someone whose *employment*, as distinct from temporary place of work, is expected to last 24 months or less. The full cost of meals and accommodation while travelling or staying away on business is allowable as part of the cost of travel. Business travel includes travelling on business from home where the nature of the job requires the employee to carry out his duties at home (but doing work at home for convenience rather than because of the nature of the job does not turn home into a workplace). Where a journey has both a business and a private purpose, the expense will be allowed if the journey is substantially for business purposes. As far as NICs are concerned, they will normally only be payable if the employer makes a payment to the employee that exceeds the cost of a business journey. Payment by the employer of congestion charges in London (or elsewhere) will in the first instance count as an employee benefit where an employee uses his own car, and will be offset by an equivalent allowable expense if incurred on business travel.

In most cases the employer will reimburse allowable expenses, so that expenditure is balanced by the employer's payment. Where this is not the case, the employee needs to claim tax relief himself.

Employee using own transport for business

[10.11] There is a statutory system of tax-free approved mileage allowances for business journeys in an employee's own transport. He is taxable only on any excess over the approved rates. Employers will report any such excess on the year-end form P11D or P9D (see **10.54**). The mileage rates are as follows:

Cars and vans:	First 10,000 miles in tax year	40p per mile
	Each additional mile	25p per mile
Motor cycles		24p per mile
Cycles		20p per mile

If the employer pays less than these amounts, the employee can claim tax relief for the additional amount paid. The rates may be altered by the Treasury by means of regulations, but they have remained unchanged since 2002.

[**10.12**] For NICs, the NICs-free rates for motor cycles and cycles are the same as for tax. For cars and vans, the NICs-free amounts are based on the 40p rate for 10,000 miles regardless of the business miles travelled. The *total* amount paid in the pay period (whether as a rate per mile or regular or one-off lump sum payment) is compared with the NICs-free amount for the number of business miles travelled and Class 1 contributions are payable on any excess. If an employee is paid less than the NICs-free amount there is no relief for the balance.

[**10.13**] If an employee carries fellow employees on business trips, either in his own car or van or an employer's car or van, and receives mileage allowance payments (see **10.11**), the employer may pay up to 5p per mile for each fellow employee free of tax and NICs. The employee cannot claim any relief if the employer does not pay an allowance.

[**10.14**] See **7.5** regarding VAT and fuel for business vehicles.

Other expenses

[**10.15**] Flat rate expenses allowances are available for the upkeep of tools and special clothing in various occupations, although this does not stop an employee claiming relief for the actual cost if that is higher. The flat rate expenses were increased with effect from 2008/09 and the amounts are listed in HMRC's Employment Income Manual at EIM32712. The cost of normal clothing is not allowed even if it costs more than the employee would normally pay and he would not wear the clothes outside work.

If it is *necessary* for an employee to work at home, he may claim the appropriate proportion of the cost of light, heat, telephone calls, etc, but not council tax. Reasonable expenses payments by employers to cover additional household expenses where an employee regularly works at home under homeworking arrangements are exempt from tax. HMRC have stated that up to £3 a week from 6 April 2008 (previously £2 a week) may be paid without supporting evidence of actual costs. They will allow a similar deduction for expenses met by the employee himself. See HMRC's Employment Income Manual at EIM32760–32830 for their views on when relief for homeworking expenses is allowable. See also **10.24** regarding exempt benefits, some of which enable employers to provide those working at home with furniture, supplies etc, without a tax charge, where private use is insignificant. See **30.21**.

An employee away from home overnight on business is exempt from tax and NICs on payment or reimbursement by his employer of incidental personal expenses such as newspapers and telephone calls so long as they do not exceed a VAT inclusive amount of £5 a night (£10 if outside the UK) and certain conditions are met.

Other allowable expenses include contributions to a registered pension scheme (see CHAPTERS 16 and 17), charitable donations under the payroll giving scheme (see 43.26) and most professional subscriptions that are relevant to a job. The cost of business entertaining is not allowed, but the disallowance may fall on the employee or on the employer depending on how payment is made. A deduction cannot be claimed for entertaining expenses paid out of salary or out of a round sum allowance. If an employee receives a specific entertaining allowance from his employer or he is specifically reimbursed for entertaining expenses, he is not taxed on the amount received, but no deduction for it can be claimed by the employer in calculating his taxable profit (see 10.54 for the PAYE treatment).

An employee can claim a deduction in calculating the tax on his earnings for:

(a)   Capital allowances (see CHAPTER 22) if he buys equipment that is necessarily provided for use in his job. The allowances are restricted by reference to any private use, and are not available for expenditure on a car, van, motor cycle or cycle, for which mileage allowances are available instead (see 10.11).

(b)   Interest on money borrowed to finance the purchase of such equipment (restricted by any private use proportion). Relief is given for the tax year of purchase and the three following tax years.

An employee does not have to pay either tax or NICs on any payment by his employer to meet the cost of directors' liability insurance, professional indemnity insurance and work-related uninsured liabilities (provided the main purpose(s) of the payment is not the avoidance of tax). If he meets the cost himself he may treat it as an allowable expense. This treatment is extended to payments made by him or his employer at any time up to six years after the end of the tax year in which the employment ends.

Tax relief for a loss in employment may be available in limited circumstances. HMRC state that the loss must arise directly from the conditions of the employment and the employee must be contractually obliged to suffer a part of the employer's loss, for example a salesperson responsible for bad debts arising from orders taken by him. If the relief is available it may be claimed against the total income of the year of loss or the previous year, or both, and any unused loss may be treated as a loss for capital gains tax purposes (see 25.7). FA 2009 introduced anti-avoidance provisions to deny relief with effect from 12 January 2009 for employment losses derived from arrangements, one of the main purposes of which is the avoidance of tax.

Expenses payments and reimbursed expenses

Dispensations (s 65)

[10.16] The strict application of the rule for allowable expenses would require all expenses payments to employees to be treated as employment income, leaving the employee to claim relief for the allowable part. To avoid a lot of unnecessary work, expenses payments that would not give rise to a tax liability may be the subject of an HMRC dispensation enabling them to be excluded from P11D returns.

Examples of expenses for which a dispensation may be granted are travelling and subsistence allowances on an agreed scale and professional subscriptions. Dispensations are not normally given for round sum allowances and may be denied in respect of a controlling director of a company unless the expenditure is vouched by independent documentation. HMRC provide guidance in the Employment Income Manual at EIM30050.

Removal and relocation expenses (ss 271–289)

[10.17] When an employee moves home because of his job, qualifying removal expenses and benefits are exempt from income tax up to a maximum of £8,000 per move, providing they are incurred, broadly speaking, during the period from the date of the job change to the end of the next following tax year. In order for the expenses and benefits to qualify for relief various conditions must be satisfied. Allowable expenses include expenses of disposing of the old property and buying another, removal expenses, providing replacement domestic goods, travelling and subsistence, and bridging loan expenses (see **30.19**).

Employers do not have to operate PAYE on qualifying expenses payments, even if they exceed £8,000, but PAYE applies to non-qualifying expenses payments. Qualifying expenses payments and benefits in excess of £8,000, and non-qualifying expenses and benefits must be reported on year-end forms P11D and P9D.

Where an employer makes a payment to an employee to compensate him for a fall in value when he sells his home, the payment is fully taxable as earnings. It does not qualify for relief as a relocation expense. See **10.18** re selling the home to the employer or a relocation company and sharing in a later profit.

As far as NICs are concerned, employees are charged Class 1 contributions on all relocation expenses payments that are not eligible for tax relief. No contributions are payable on qualifying removal expenses and benefits up to £8,000. Class 1A employers' contributions are payable on non-eligible relocation benefits and on any excess of qualifying relocation expenses and benefits over £8,000.

Sale of home to relocation company or to employer (TCGA 1992, s 225C)

[10.18] Where there is a guaranteed selling price scheme, the treatment depends on the precise details of the scheme. There will, however, be no taxable benefit where an employee sells his home to the employer or a relocation company at market value and pays his own selling expenses. HMRC guidance is available in the Employment Income Manual at EIM03130.

Where the employee has a right to share in any later profits when the home is sold, he will be exempt from capital gains tax on any additional amount paid to him to the same extent as he was exempt on the original sale, providing the later sale occurs within three years. Part of the original gain may have been chargeable because the home had not always been the main residence, or had been let, etc., in which case the same proportion of the later amount will be chargeable. This rule applied by concession only for disposals before 6 April 2009.

Benefits in kind for all employees — specific charges

[10.19] All employees and directors, no matter how much they earn, pay tax on the provision of living accommodation and non-exempt vouchers (see **10.20** and **10.21**). There is also a tax charge if a loan from the employer is written off by reason of the employee's employment. For P11D employees, this applies even if the employment has ceased — see **12.15**. Loans written off are reported on year-end forms P11D and P9D (see **10.54**). Class 1 NICs are charged at the time of write-off.

Tax has to be accounted for under PAYE where pay is provided in the form of 'readily convertible assets', i.e. stocks and shares (see below), gold bullion, futures or commodities that may be sold on a recognised investment exchange such as the Stock Exchange; assets subject to a fiscal warehousing regime; assets that give rise to cash without any action being taken by the employee; assets in the form of debts owed to the employer that have been assigned to the employee, and assets for which trading arrangements exist or are likely to come into existence. All shares and other securities are within the definition of readily convertible assets unless the employer company is entitled to a deduction for them in calculating corporation tax payable (see **11.1** and **11.3**). The convertible assets provisions apply equally where vouchers and credit tokens are used to provide the assets, and they apply to agency workers and to those working for someone in the UK but employed and paid by someone overseas. Benefits chargeable under the convertible assets provisions are referred to as notional pay. They would have been taxable in any event, but charging tax under PAYE accelerates the payment date for the tax (see **10.48**). Pay in the form of convertible assets is similarly charged to Class 1 NICs.

PAYE also applies where pay is provided in the form of the enhancement of the value of an asset owned by the employee (such as paying premiums to increase the value of an employee-owned life policy).

See **CHAPTER 11** for the detailed provisions dealing with share and securities options and incentives provided by the employer. Where an employee is taxable under ITEPA 2003 when a risk of forfeiture of shares or securities is lifted, or when shares or securities are converted into shares or securities of a different class, PAYE and Class 1 NICs must be applied if the shares or securities are readily convertible assets. PAYE and, for options granted on or after 6 April 1999, Class 1 NICs must also be charged on any gains realised when a share or securities option is exercised (other than under an HMRC approved scheme) or is assigned or released. Unapproved options granted before 6 April 1999 were liable to Class 1 NICs when they were granted.

Living accommodation (ss 97–113, 313–315, 364; FA 2009, s 71)

[10.20] If the employer provides an employee or a member of the employee's family or household with living accommodation, the employee is charged to tax on the amount by which its 'rental value' (see below), or the rent paid by the employer if higher, exceeds any rent the employee pays. FA 2009 introduced provisions to prevent tax avoidance through payment, by the provider of the accommodation, of a lease premium rather than a full market rent. Broadly, the lease premium is to be treated as actual rent paid over the duration of the lease. There is no charge, however, if:

(a)   the employer is an individual and the accommodation is provided in the normal course of his domestic, family or personal relationships; or

(b)   the accommodation is provided by a local authority under its usual terms for non-employees; or

(c)   the employee is a representative occupier, for example, a caretaker; or

(d)   it is customary for employees (e.g. police officers, clergymen) to be provided with living accommodation for the better performance of their duties; or

(e)   the accommodation is provided for security reasons.

Where the accommodation provided by a company falls within (c) or (d) above, a director qualifies for exemption only if he does not have a material interest in the company and either (i) he works full-time for the company or (ii) the company is non-profit-making or established for charitable purposes only.

If an employee is exempt under one of headings (c) to (e), he is also exempt from both tax and NICs on the payment of council tax and water charges by the employer. If he is not exempt, such items paid by the employer count as pay for both tax and Class 1 NICs.

FA 2008 introduced a limited exemption for holiday homes outside the UK. It applies where the property is bought through the taxpayer's own company, for legal or other reasons, and the taxpayer is a director or other officer of the company who would otherwise be liable to tax because the property is available to him. The exemption is treated as having always had effect, and HMRC invited repayment claims from anyone who could show that they had paid tax for years before 2008/09 — see guidance in HMRC Employment Income Manual EIM11374.

The 'rental value' is the rent that would be payable if the property was let to the employee at an annual rent equal to the 'annual value', and the annual value is the rent that might be expected to be charged if the employee paid the council tax and other charges usually paid by a tenant, and the landlord paid for repairs and maintenance. HMRC practice for a UK property is to take the gross rateable value under the old system of rates. For a property outside the UK, HMRC take the amount of rent that could be obtained on the open market.

Where other benefits are provided in connection with the accommodation, an employee is chargeable on their value whether or not he is chargeable on the rental value, but if he is exempt from the charge on letting value under headings (c) to (e) above the charge for other benefits cannot exceed 10% of his net earnings excluding those benefits. Net earnings means earnings after deducting allowable expenses including, where appropriate, contributions to registered pension schemes and capital allowances.

The charge for living accommodation is increased where the accommodation cost more than £75,000. The extra charge over and above the rental value is calculated as follows:

((Cost less £75,000) × appropriate %) less the amount by which any rent the employee pays exceeds the rental value.

The appropriate percentage is the official rate of interest chargeable on beneficial loans, as at the beginning of the tax year. This rate is 4% p.a. from 6 April 2010 (4.75% p.a. for 2009/10). The basic and, where appropriate, additional charges are proportionately reduced if the property is provided for only part of the year, and also to the extent that any part of the property is used exclusively for business. Where the accommodation is provided for more than one employee at the same time, the total benefit charges are restricted to what would have been charged on a single employee.

Vouchers (ss 73–96A, 266–270A)

[10.21] The vouchers rules generally apply to all employees and are wide-ranging.

Cash vouchers and non-cash vouchers exchangeable for readily-convertible assets (see **10.19**) are treated as pay under the PAYE scheme at the time the voucher is provided.

Most other non-cash vouchers are taxable, although not through the PAYE scheme. Where HMRC use their power to exempt minor benefits from tax (see **10.22**), non-cash vouchers in connection with such benefits are also exempt. There is a general provision enabling regulations to be issued to exempt non-cash vouchers that are used to obtain specified exempt benefits.

The employer has to provide HMRC with details of the cost of providing non-exempt vouchers and the cost of goods or services obtained through the provision of employer's credit cards. Tax on the value of the vouchers is usually collected by a PAYE coding adjustment.

Exempt non-cash vouchers include transport vouchers for lower-paid employees of passenger transport bodies, vouchers in connection with a works bus service, or to obtain a parking space for a car, motor cycle or bicycle at or near the workplace, or in connection with cycles or cyclists' safety equipment provided by the employer, vouchers provided by third parties for corporate hospitality, vouchers for incidental overnight expenses within the limits stated at **10.16**, vouchers used in connection with sporting or recreational facilities and childcare vouchers (see **10.25**).

There is still a derisory exemption of 15p per day for meal vouchers, providing they are available to all employees, non-transferable and used for meals only. Any excess over 15p is taxable, details being shown on forms P11D and P9D. No tax arises on free canteen meals that are provided to staff generally as long as they are not provided as part of a salary sacrifice or flexible benefit arrangement from 2011/12 onwards, so the meal voucher rules discriminate against employers who are too small to have their own canteen.

Class 1 NICs are payable on most non-cash vouchers, subject to various exceptions which mainly mirror income tax provisions such as those indicated above and the childcare voucher exemption dealt with in **10.25**. See further HMRC National Insurance Manual NIM02416.

Non-cash vouchers are valued for NICs as for tax purposes, but unlike the tax position, they must be dealt with on a weekly basis rather than at the year end. Vouchers in connection with employer-provided cars and car fuel for such cars are charged under Class 1A rather than Class 1 (see **10.39**).

See **10.55** re accounting for tax and NICs on non-cash vouchers through the taxed award scheme.

Benefits in kind for P11D employees (ss 62–191, 201–220, 237–249, 261–265, 316–325A; FA 2010, ss 58–60)

[10.22] P11D employees are charged to tax on all expenses payments received (unless covered by a dispensation, see **10.16**) and on the cash equivalent of virtually all benefits provided either direct to the employee or to his family or household. Benefits in the form of accommodation, supplies or services used in performing the duties of the employment either on the employer's premises or elsewhere are exempt despite some insignificant private use unless they are motor vehicles, boats, or aircraft, or they involve extension, conversion etc. of living accommodation. This exemption may cover the provision to homeworkers of furniture and equipment, stationery and supplies, providing any private use is insignificant.

The provision of computer equipment is covered under the 'accommodation, supplies and services' exemption outlined above. The use of a computer provided under an arrangement entered into before 6 April 2006 with an annual benefit value up to £500 is exempt, with only an excess being chargeable. See **10.36** regarding telephones.

HMRC have the power to make regulations exempting minor benefits. They have used it, for example, to exempt private use of equipment, services or facilities provided to disabled people (e.g. wheelchairs) to enable them to do their work.

In practice HMRC do not consider an employer's provision of a periodic health screening assessment or medical check-up to give rise to a taxable benefit. This practice was put on a statutory footing in 2007 but the exemption was restricted to cases where the provision was available to all employees on similar terms. FA 2009 removed this restriction and extended the exemption so that it applies to non-cash vouchers and credit tokens provided for such facilities. However, the exemption is restricted to one health-screening assessment and one medical check-up provided by an employer in a tax year.

The charging rules include benefits provided by someone other than the employer, except for corporate hospitality (providing it is not arranged by the employer and is not in return for services rendered by the employee) and gifts costing not more than £250 in total from any one donor. See **10.54** for the year-end requirements for third parties providing benefits.

[10.23] The cash equivalent of a benefit is normally the extra cost to the employer of providing the benefit (including VAT where appropriate, whether recovered or not) less any contribution from the employee. See **10.27** for the calculation of the benefit of use of an asset provided by the employer.

Non-taxable benefits

[10.24] The main benefits that are not chargeable to tax are:

- Free or subsidised meals or light refreshments provided in a staff canteen by the employee's own or another employer, so long as the meals etc. are available to staff generally and are not provided as part of a salary sacrifice or flexible benefit arrangement from 2011/12 onwards. This restriction was introduced in FA 2010 after the Government became aware that some employers and employees had developed remuneration arrangements involving salary sacrifice or flexible benefits to take advantage of the exemption.
- Employer's contributions to a registered occupational or personal pension scheme and the provision of pension information and advice costing not more than £150 per year.
- Directors' liability or professional indemnity insurance etc, subject to anti-avoidance provisions. (see **10.15**).
- Provision of parking facilities for motor vehicles, cycles, motor cycles and vans at or near the workplace.
- Sporting and recreational facilities provided either by the employee's own or another employer.
- Counselling services to redundant employees and welfare counselling services available to employees generally.
- Health screening and medical check-ups (see **10.22**).
- The provision of eye care tests and/or corrective glasses for visual display units.
- Certain childcare provision (see **10.25**).

- Commissions, discounts and cashbacks available to employees on the same basis as to members of the general public (because such benefits do not arise from the employment). To escape tax, cashbacks must be provided under a contract separate from the employment contract and not be given gratuitously.
- Mobile telephones (see **10.36**).
- Employer-provided cycles and cyclist's safety equipment, providing they are available to staff generally and used mainly for journeys between home and work and for business journeys. The provision by the employer of 'qualifying meals' on official cycle to work days is also not taxable.
- Certain works bus services providing the services are used mainly for journeys between home and work, free or subsidised travel on local public stopping bus services used by employees for journeys between home and work, and employer support for other bus services used for such journeys providing employees do not obtain the services on more favourable terms than other passengers. The use of works buses on workdays for trips of up to 10 miles (20 miles return) to local shops or other amenities is also not taxable.
- The benefit of one or more annual staff parties and functions, providing the cost to the employer for each person attending is not more than £150 a year including VAT. If, say, there were three annual functions at £70 each per employee, the exemption would cover two of them and the employee would be taxed on £70.
- Long service awards for those with 20 or more years' service, providing no such award has been made within the previous ten years. The value of the award must not exceed £50 for each year of service. Such awards may be tangible assets or shares in the employer company (or a group company). Cash payments and cash vouchers are excluded.

See also HMRC Helpsheet HS207 for further details.

No taxable benefit arises where benefits such as air miles, points to obtain gifts, etc. are obtained by employees in the same way as members of the public, even though the purchase relates to the business. If, however, employers distributed air miles, etc. under an incentive scheme tax would be charged.

There is no taxable benefit when emergency personnel working for the fire, ambulance and police services have to take their emergency vehicles home when on call.

Employees are not taxed on the provision of medical treatment or insurance that relates to treatment outside the UK when on a business trip. Payments for medical expenses abroad, and insurance against such expenses, also escape NICs.

Scholarships to employees' children are caught unless they are fortuitous awards paid from a trust fund or scheme open to the public at large under which not more than 25% of the total payments relate to employees.

Special rules apply to share option and incentive schemes (see **CHAPTER 11**), the use of cars and vans and the provision of cheap loans (see **10.28** to **10.34**, **10.35** and **10.38**).

Childcare (ss 270A, 318–318D)

[10.25] The benefit of a workplace nursery provided by an employer alone or with other employers, local authorities, etc., but with each employer being partly responsible for finance and management, is exempt from both tax and NICs. This exemption also applies to another employer's staff if they are allowed to use the nursery facility while working at the provider's premises.

The provision by employers of 'qualifying childcare' is also exempt from both tax and NICs to the extent of £55 a week or £243 a month per employee, tax and NICs being charged on any excess over the exempt amount. Qualifying childcare can be contracted for with a local childminder or nursery or provided by childcare vouchers, but there is no exemption if the employer provides cash to cover employees' own childcare expenses. In the case of vouchers, the voucher administration costs are also exempt.

There are very detailed conditions to be complied with for the £55 exemption to apply, but the main requirements are that the scheme must be generally available to all employees, the child must be the employee's child or a child who lives with the employee for whom the employee has parental responsibility, and the childcare must be registered or approved childcare. This does not include care by the employee's spouse or partner, or by a relative either in the child's home or in the relative's home unless the relative also looks after one or more unrelated children. A person is a 'child' until 1 September following his or her 15th birthday (or 16th birthday for a child who is blind or disabled).

It is proposed that from 6 April 2011 the rules will change for an employee who joins an employer-supported childcare scheme involving vouchers or contracted childcare on or after that date. The employer will be required to estimate the employee's likely annual earnings and for those whose expected level of earnings is between the basic and higher rate limits (see **2.5**) the exempt limit will be £28 per week. For those with expected earnings exceeding the higher rate limit the exempt limit will be £22 per week. The exempt limit for those with earnings below the basic rate limit will remain at £55 per week.

HMRC guidance on childcare generally is available at www.hmrc.gov.uk/childcare.

[10.26] The effect of childcare provision on tax credit entitlement needs to be carefully considered because a reduction in the employee's own childcare costs through having the vouchers will affect the childcare element of working tax credit, while additional income up to £25,000 (proposed to be reduced to £10,000 from 6 April 2011) is ignored when making year-end adjustments to the tax credits award (see **2.35**).

Use of employer's assets (ss 205–210)

[10.27] A tax charge normally arises each year if an employee is allowed private use of an asset that belongs to his employer, the amount of the charge usually being the private use proportion of 20% of the cost of the asset plus any expenses, such as a rent or hire charge incurred in connection with the provision of the benefit.

Different rules apply to living accommodation (see **10.20**) and cars and vans (see **10.28** to **10.35**). There is normally no tax charge on cycles and cyclists' safety equipment (see **10.24**). Before 6 April 2006 there was a specific exemption for private use of computers (see **10.22**).

If an asset that has been used or has depreciated is given to the employee, then if it is a car, or a computer made available before 6 April 2006, cycle or cyclists' safety equipment provided as indicated in **10.24**, the employee is charged to tax on its market value. For any other asset, he is charged to tax on the higher of its market value at the date of the transfer to him and the original market value less the benefits already charged to tax (either on him or on others). See Example 1.

Example 1

Television set cost employer £1,000. Used by director for two years, then given to him or any other P11D employee when market value is £100.

Tax will be charged on the following amounts:

For use of asset, 20% × £1,000 =	£200	per annum
On gift of asset, higher of		
(i) £100		
(ii) £1,000 – (2 * £200) = £600	£600	

Motor cars (ss 114–153, 167–172; FA 2010, ss 58–59)

[10.28] The benefit of private use of a car made available by reason of employment is charged to tax according to the price of the car, certain accessories and the 'appropriate percentage' (see below) based on the car's CO_2 emissions figure. An additional charge is made in respect of car fuel provided for private use (see **10.32**). HMRC guidance is available at www.hmrc.gov.uk/cars, which includes an online car benefit calculator.

The price of the car for this purpose is normally the manufacturer's list price including VAT and delivery charges. There are detailed rules to determine when the cost of accessories is to be added to the price of the car. The cost of mobile phones and any equipment provided for use in the performance of the duties, or provided to enable a disabled person to use a car or to enable the car to run on road fuel gas, is excluded.

Where an employee pays towards the initial cost of a car or accessories, a contribution of up to £5,000 is deducted. The appropriate percentage is then applied to the lower of the net figure and an over-riding limit of £80,000. This £80,000 cap is to be abolished from 2011/12.

There is a special rule for classic cars. Cars valued at more than £15,000 and at least fifteen years old at the end of the tax year are taxed according to their open market value (up to the £80,000 ceiling for years prior to 2011/12) if that is more than the price of the car.

If a car is provided for only part of the year (for example, in the year when employment starts or ceases) the charge is proportionately reduced. It is also proportionately reduced if the car is incapable of being used for a period of 30 consecutive days or more. Where a car is replaced during the year, the appropriate proportion of each benefit figure is charged. Employers are required to notify HMRC of certain changes (see **10.51**).

Any contribution an employee makes to his employer for the use of the car is deducted from the car benefit charge. The car benefit charge covers the whole benefit obtained from the use of a car, except the expense of providing a driver, which is charged in addition but may be the subject of a claim for allowable expenses. For example, for employees driving company cars in London no additional taxable benefit arises where the employer pays the congestion charge. Employees using their own cars will, however, only be entitled to relief where the charge is incurred in the course of business travel (see **10.10**).

Calculation of benefit

[10.29] The amount calculated as set out in **10.28** is multiplied by the 'appropriate percentage' (but see below regarding 'discounts') according to the level of the car's carbon dioxide emissions to find the 'cash equivalent' of the benefit. The CO_2 emissions figure is recorded on the vehicle's registration certificate but it can also be found via the 'vehicle enquiry' link at www.tax-disc.direct.gov.uk.

FA 2010 introduced amendments to the calculation of car benefits. Some amendments apply from 2010/11 and others will apply from 2012/13 onwards, see www.hmrc.gov.uk/cars/rule-changes.htm. For cars registered on or after 1 January 1998 the appropriate percentage for 2010/11 is:

*   0% if the car cannot in any circumstances emit CO_2 by being driven,
*   5% for cars with CO_2 emissions of 75 grams per kilometre or less,
*   10% for cars with CO_2 emissions of more than 75 g/km but not more than 120 g/km, and
*   15% (the 'basic percentage') for cars with emissions of more than 120 g/km but not more than 130 g/km.

The 0% and 5% rates apply for five years up to 2014/15, after which they will revert to 9% and 10% respectively, subject to any future announcement by the Government.

The basic percentage is increased by 1% for every 5 g/km above the 130 g/km threshold, up to a maximum of 35%. This 130 g/km threshold will be reduced to 125 g/km for 2011/12.

(Changes in 2012/13 will introduce a 'relevant threshold' of 100 g/km. The rate for emissions of 100 g/km will be 11% and will increase by 1% for every 5 g/km above the 100 g/km threshold, up to the maximum of 35%. The appropriate percentage of 10% will apply to cars with CO_2 emissions of more than 75 g/km but not more than 99 g/km.)

The appropriate percentage is increased by 3% for diesel cars, subject to the overall maximum of 35% (but see **2.8**).

See the TABLE OF RATES AND ALLOWANCES for the appropriate percentages before deduction of the discounts set out below.

The appropriate percentage for cars registered before 1 January 1998, and for cars with no approved carbon dioxide emissions figures, is as follows:

Engine size	Pre–1.1.98 cars	Cars with no approved emissions figures
0–1400cc	15%	15%*
1401–2000cc	22%	25%*
2001cc and over	32%	35%

*plus 3% supplement for diesel cars

The appropriate percentage for cars with no cylinder capacity and no approved emissions figure is 0% for cars which cannot produce CO_2 emissions under any circumstances (see above) and 35% for other cars (or 32% if registered before January 1998).

Disabled drivers of automatic cars who hold a blue badge may use the list price of an equivalent manual car in computing their car benefit.

Discounts

[10.30] The appropriate percentages described above are reduced as follows for 2010/11, as set out in regulations:

- 3% for hybrid cars (i.e. those capable of being propelled by electricity and petrol) registered after 31 December 1997;
- 2% for cars registered after 31 December 1997 and propelled solely by road fuel gas;
- 2% for bi-fuel cars (i.e. those capable of being propelled by petrol and road fuel gas); and
- 2% from 2008/09 for cars registered after 31 December 1997 and capable of being propelled by bioethanol or a mixture of at least 85% bioethanol and unleaded petrol ('E85').

From 6 April 2011 there will no longer be any discounts for alternative fuels following revocation of the regulations.

For 2010/11 and earlier years diesel cars registered after 31 December 1997 and before 1 January 2006 which met a European standard for cleaner cars (which became mandatory on 1 January 2006) are not subject to the diesel supplement. From 6 April 2011 all diesel cars will be subject to the diesel surcharge.

Example 2

Car benefit charges for 2010/11 for car costing £15,000

		£
Petrol car with rounded emissions figure of 190 g/km	27%	4,050
Diesel car with rounded emissions figure of 220 g/km	35%*	5,250

* The diesel supplement is only 2%, to bring the charge up to the maximum 35%

Pool cars and shared private use

[10.31] It is possible to escape tax and Class 1A NICs on the benefit of use of a car if it is a pool car as defined, but the conditions are restrictive. A pool car is one where the private use is merely incidental to the business use, the car is not normally kept overnight at an employee's home, and the car is not ordinarily used by only one employee to the exclusion of other employees.

Where private use of a car is shared, the charge is calculated as if the employee had exclusive use and then reduced on a 'just and reasonable' basis.

Car fuel charge

[10.32] An additional charge is made if, in addition to being provided with a car, an employee is provided with car fuel for private use.

The car fuel scale charge is based on a set figure, fixed at £18,000 for 2010/11 (£16,900 for 2009/10). This figure is multiplied by the 'appropriate percentage' (see **10.29**). The charge is proportionately reduced where an employee stops receiving fuel part way through the year, unless he again receives fuel in the same tax year, in which case the full scale will apply. There is no charge for cars propelled by electricity only.

There is no reduction in the car fuel charge for a contribution to the cost of fuel for private journeys. To escape the fuel charge an employee must reimburse the whole cost of private fuel to the employer, or pay for it himself in the first place. He should keep detailed records of both business and personal mileage to confirm that the amount reimbursed for private mileage is correct, remembering that travel between home and work is regarded as private mileage (see **10.35** relating to the contrasting position for vans).

HMRC publish advisory fuel rates which an employer may use to reimburse the cost of business mileage an employee has incurred or to recoup the cost of private mileage where the employer paid for the fuel. These rates will be accepted as not giving rise to taxable benefits or Class 1 NICs liability but higher rates may be acceptable where, for example, the employer can show that employees need a particular type of car to cover rough terrain.

The advisory fuel rates from 1 June 2010 are as follows:

	Petrol	Diesel	LPG
0–1400cc	12p	11p	8p
1401–2000cc	15p	11p	10p
2001cc and over	21p	16p	14p

Hybrid cars are treated as petrol for this purpose.

The corresponding rates from 1 December 2009 to 31 May 2010 are:

	Petrol	Diesel	LPG
0–1400cc	11p	11p	7p
1401–2000cc	14p	11p	8p
2001cc and over	20p	14p	12p

Earlier rates are set out at www.hmrc.gov.uk/cars/advisory_fuel_archive.htm.

National insurance contributions and VAT

[10.33] The provision of a car for private use and of private fuel for the car also attracts Class 1A employers' (but not employees') NICs — see 10.39. The amounts of the car and fuel benefits for tax purposes are used to determine the Class 1A amounts payable. Employers also have to account for VAT on private fuel provided to both P11D and non-P11D employees whether the car is provided by them or owned by the employee — see 7.5. VAT does not apply to the provision of the car itself, even if the employee makes a payment for private use (unless the employer recovered all of the input VAT on the car, or leases it from a lessor who reclaimed the input VAT on it — see 7.4 — in which case a payment by the employee would attract VAT).

Salary alternative

[10.34] The increasing cost of providing employees with cars and private fuel has led many employers to offer employees extra salary instead. The tax and NICs for a P11D employee are based on what the employee actually gets, either salary or use of a car.

Vans (ss 114–119, 154–164, 168, 169A; FA 2010, s 58)

[10.35] The benefit of private use of a van (i.e. a goods vehicle with a design not exceeding 3,500 kilograms) made available by reason of employment is charged to tax. For tax years 2010/11 to 2014/15 the cash equivalent of the benefit is nil where the van cannot in any circumstances emit CO_2 by being driven, and is £3,000 in any other case.

There is no charge where a van is provided mainly for business use, and private use is restricted to commuting, with any other private use being insignificant. HMRC say insignificant private use would include trips such as an occasional trip to the tip, or to the local shop, but not regular supermarket shopping. See 10.24 for exemption in relation to emergency vehicles.

The taxable benefit is reduced proportionately if the van is not provided for the whole year, or is unavailable for 30 consecutive days or more. The taxable amount is also reduced by any payment by the employee for private use.

Where there is shared use of a van, the charge is calculated as if the employee had exclusive use and then reduced on a 'just and reasonable' basis.

Where the employer provides fuel for private use in a van which does not satisfy the 'mainly for business use' requirements outlined above, there is a separate fuel charge of £550 (£500 for 2009/10), reduced appropriately for shared vans. The provisions in **10.31** regarding pooled and shared cars apply equally to pooled and shared vans, and salary alternative position in **10.34** applies equally to vans.

Mobile telephones, home telephones and internet access (ss 316, 319)

[10.36] The provision to an employee of a single mobile phone, including line rental and private calls paid directly by an employer on that phone, is exempt.

Before 6 April 2006 this exemption covered the provision of phones both to an employee and to his family and household. Where such provision was made, the exemption continues to apply to those particular phones.

Provision of a mobile phone solely for business use is exempt under the general rule discussed at **10.22** (accommodation, supplies or services used in performing the duties of the employment) so long as any private use is not significant.

HMRC previously regarded a personal digital assistant (PDA), such as a Blackberry, as a mobile phone, despite its other functions, including the ability to access the internet and emails. They now regard it as a computer — see **10.22**.

If the employee contracts to pay the bills for the phone, but the bills are paid by the employer, or the employer reimburses the employee, the employee is liable to tax and Class 1 NICs on the amount paid by the employer, less an appropriate deduction for business calls.

[10.37] If an employer pays an employee's home telephone bills, then unless private use is insignificant the employee is taxed on the payments, but he is entitled to a deduction for the proportion relating to the business calls (but not any part of the line rental). Class 1 NICs are payable on the amount paid by the employer for the line rental and private calls.

If the employer is the subscriber rather than the employee, then unless any private use is insignificant the employee is taxed on the cost of the line rental and calls, less any amount made good to the employer, and the employee may claim an expenses deduction for the business calls. The employer is liable for Class 1A NICs on both the line rental and the calls, unless the employee has made good the cost of private calls, or private use is insignificant. If on the other hand there is a clear business need for the telephone to be provided, and the employer has procedures to ensure that private calls are kept to a minimum, the employee may not be taxed either on the line rental or the calls if the cost of the calls is insignificant compared with the total cost. In this event Class 1A contributions would not be due either.

If an employer pays for broadband internet connection in an employee's home solely for work purposes, any private use being insignificant and no breakdown being possible between work and private calls, and the cost of the package is not affected by the private use, the cost of the connection will not be a taxable benefit. If the employee pays for the internet connection and is reimbursed by his employer, it will not usually be possible to identify a separate business element, so that the employee will be taxed on the reimbursement and will not be entitled to any expenses deduction. However, payments made by an employer to reimburse the employee for 'reasonable additional costs' incurred whilst working at home may be exempt from tax. HMRC guidance indicates that such costs would include a broadband subscription where an employee who does not have a broadband connection needs one in order to work from home, but payments to an employee who already subscribes for broadband would not be exempt.

Cheap loans (ss 173–191; FA 2006, s 97)

[10.38] If an employer lends an employee money interest-free, or at a rate of interest below the official rate, the employee is charged to tax on an amount equal to interest at the official rate (see below) less any interest paid.

This does not apply if the loan qualifies for tax relief either in calculating the employee's income (see **2.14**) or as a deduction from business profits or rental income, and the *whole* of the interest would qualify for tax relief. Such wholly qualifying loans are exempt from the charge. If part of the interest on the loan would not qualify for relief, tax is first calculated on the full amount of the loan at the official rate and then reduced by the appropriate tax saving on both the beneficial loan interest and any interest actually paid.

The official rate of interest has been fixed at 4% p.a. from 6 April 2010 (4.75% for 2009/10). The rate is varied by Treasury Order (see 'Official rate of interest — beneficial loans' in the Table of Rates and Allowances). The rate is normally fixed in advance for the whole of the tax year, but may be changed during the year to reflect significant changes in interest rates. For a list of earlier rates see www.hmrc.gov.uk/rates/interest-beneficial.htm

There is no tax charge on loans made to employees on commercial terms by employers who lend or supply goods or services on credit to the general public despite the interest paid being less than the official rate. Nor is there any charge if the total of all non-qualifying beneficial loans to an employee does not exceed £5,000 at any time in the tax year.

If the loan is written off, the employee is charged to tax on the amount written off whether he is still employed or not, with Class 1 NICs also applying (but see **12.15** for controlling directors of close companies).

The above provisions relating to cheap loans apply where on or after 22 March 2006 employers enter into low cost 'alternative finance arrangements' with their employees (such arrangements usually being made to comply with Islamic law prohibiting the payment of interest).

Class 1A NICs (SSCBA 1992, ss 10, 10ZA, 10ZB, 10ZC and Sch 1; SI 2001/1004, Pt 3)

[10.39] Class 1A NICs at 12.8% (proposed to be increased to 13.8% from 6 April 2011) are payable only by employers, not by employees. They are payable on virtually all taxable benefits in kind provided to P11D employees unless the benefits have already been charged to Class 1 contributions, or to Class 1B contributions under a PAYE settlement agreement (see **10.55**). See **10.52** for the way in which Class 1A contributions are accounted for.

The amounts liable to Class 1A are taken from forms P11D (see **10.54**), the relevant P11D boxes being colour coded and marked 1A. Any amounts made good by the employee are taken into account. The total on which contributions are payable is shown on form P11D(b) (see **10.51**) and is then multiplied by the relevant percentage to give the amount payable. Payment is due by 19 July following the end of the tax year.

Benefits covered by a dispensation (see **10.16**) are not shown on forms P11D and are not liable to either tax or Class 1A contributions. If a benefit shown on form P11D is fully offset by a matching deduction for tax purposes (or is covered by the insignificant private use provisions at **10.22**), Class 1A contributions are not payable and the total Class 1A amount shown on form P11D is adjusted accordingly. Where, however, there is both business and private use, Class 1A contributions are payable on the full amount, even though for tax purposes the employee may claim a deduction for the business proportion in his tax return.

Where private fuel is provided for use in an employee's own car from an employer's own pump, or is provided by means of an employer's credit card, garage account or agency card and the garage is told that the fuel is being bought on behalf of the employer, Class 1 contributions are not due but Class 1A contributions are payable. Where private fuel is supplied in other circumstances, Class 1 contributions are payable. See **10.11** for the treatment where a mileage allowance is paid.

Where goods or services are obtained through a company credit card for the personal use of the employee, Class 1 contributions are payable. Where the goods or services are obtained on behalf of the employer, and the supplier is told that that is the case, contributions are not payable unless the goods or services are then transferred to the employee, in which case Class 1A contributions are payable.

Training and education

Scholarship and apprentice schemes

[10.40] Employees on full-time and sandwich courses at universities and colleges lasting one year or more may receive tax-free pay while they are on the course of up to £15,480 for the academic year 2007/08 beginning on 1 September 2007 and subsequent years (HMRC statement of practice 4/86 revised in August 2007). This exemption also applies for NICs.

Work-related training courses (ss 250–260)

[10.41] An employee is not taxed on the payment or reimbursement by his employer of the cost of work-related training, including not only directly job-related training but also training in health and safety and to develop leadership skills appropriate to the employee. As well as the direct costs, the exemption covers learning materials, examination fees and registration of qualifications. Travelling and subsistence expenses are allowed to the same extent as they would be for employment duties. HMRC consider that generally, training cannot be 'work-related' unless the trainee is employed by the employer when the training is undertaken, but they recognise that in some cases the link between the employment and the pre-commencement training will be strong enough that the reimbursement will qualify for exemption.

Retraining costs (s 311)

[10.42] Where a retraining course in the UK for up to two years is made generally available to appropriate employees, the employee is not assessed on the course costs and any incidental travelling expenses paid for by the employer. The employee must have been employed full-time or part-time for at least two years, must leave the employment within two years after the end of the course, and must not be re-employed within two years after leaving.

Summary of main benefits provisions

[10.43]

BENEFIT	AMOUNT CHARGEABLE TO TAX FOR P11D EMPLOYEES*
Use of car	Charge based on 35% of list price, reduced according to the car's carbon dioxide emissions
Car fuel for private motoring	£18,000 × percentage used to calculate benefit of use of car
Parking facilities	Not taxable
Use of van	Charge of £3,000 (but reduced to nil where there are zero CO_2 emissions) where there is unrestricted private use, and £550 for private fuel where the use does not satisfy the 'mainly for business use' requirement. Proportionate charge for shared vans
Living accommodation	Letting value plus 5% of excess cost of property over £75,000 (unless accommodation is job-related)

BENEFIT	AMOUNT CHARGEABLE TO TAX FOR P11D EMPLOYEES*
Provision of services and use of furniture in living accommodation	Cost of services plus 20% p.a. of cost of furniture (but charge cannot exceed 10% of other reckonable earnings from the employment if exempt from living accommodation charge)
Use of other assets (excluding heavy commercial vehicles)	20% of cost
Vouchers other than meal vouchers and childcare vouchers	Full value
Use of employers' credit cards	Cost of personal goods and services obtained
Medical insurance	Cost to employer
Beneficial loans	Interest at official rate (see **10.38**) less any interest paid, but no charge if non-qualifying loans total £5,000 or less.
Loans written off	Amount written off
Creche facilities	Not taxable
Free or subsidised canteen meals	Not taxable if available to all employees (but see **10.24** for anti-avoidance provisions)
Pension provision under approved schemes	Not taxable

*   Non-P11D employees escape tax on benefits except for the following, which are taxed on the same basis as for P11D employees:

    Living accommodation

    Vouchers other than meal vouchers and childcare vouchers

    Use of employers' credit cards

    Loans written off

Example 3

An employee is paid a salary of £30,000 in 2010/11.

He is provided with a two-year old 1500 cc petrol driven company car with a list price of £15,000, and carbon dioxide emissions of 170 g per kilometre. The car is maintained by the employer, including the provision of private petrol and a mobile phone for business and private use.

The employee receives an overnight allowance amounting to £649, in respect of which HMRC has granted a dispensation to his employer.

He pays hotel and meal bills on business trips amounting to £1,540 and spends £500 on entertaining customers. These expenses are reimbursed by his employer. Home telephone bills amounting to £350 are paid by his employer, of which the business use proportion of the calls, as evidenced by the employee's records, amounts to £200.

He receives a round sum expenses allowance of £1,200 out of which allowable expenses of £200 are paid.

The taxable employment income is:

	£	£
Salary		30,000
Charge for use of car (£15,000 × 23%*)		3,450
Car fuel charge (£18,000 × 23%)		4,140
Mobile phone (exempt)		—
Overnight allowance (covered by dispensation)		—
Hotel and meal bills reimbursed		1,540
Entertaining expenses reimbursed		500
Home telephone account paid by employer		350
Round sum expenses allowance		1,200
		41,180
Less: Hotel and meal bills reimbursed	1,540	
Entertaining expenses reimbursed (disallowed in calculating tax on employer's profit)	500	
Proportion of telephone account relating to employment	200	
Other allowable expenses	200	2,440
Employment income		38,740

National insurance. As well as the salary, pay for Class 1 NICs will include the round sum expenses allowance (except to the extent of any identified business expenses).

A private telephone use figure that is supported by the employee's records is accepted for NIC purposes, so that Class 1 contributions in this example will be due only on £150. If there are no such records, pay for Class 1 NICs includes payment of telephone bills, unless the telephone contract is in the employer's name, in which case the employer will be charged Class 1A contributions.

The employer will also pay Class 1A contributions at 12.8% (proposed to be increased to 13.8% from 6 April 2011) on the car and fuel charges of (3,450 + 4,140) = £7,590. Class 1A contributions are not payable on business expenses that are wholly offset by a matching expenses allowance for tax, so there is no liability on the reimbursed hotel and entertaining expenses.

HMRC dispensations are effective for Class 1 and Class 1A NICs as well as for tax, so there will be no NICs on the overnight allowance.

Value added tax. The employer will pay output VAT on the car fuel by reference to a scale rate of £326** per quarter (£276 before 1 May 2010), unless no

> input VAT is being claimed on fuel for any motor vehicle. The input VAT on the mobile phone will be restricted according to the private use proportion, unless the employee pays for the private use, in which case the employer must account for output VAT on the amount received from the employee (see 7.5).
>
> * % charge for car with CO_2 emissions of 170g – see 10.29
>
> ** VAT charge based on CO_2 emissions of 170g — see 7.5

PAYE (ss 682–702; SI 2003/2682)

[10.44] The object of the PAYE system is to require employers to collect and account for tax and NICs on employment income. Employers also have to collect student loan repayments.

Online filing

[10.45] Almost all employers are now required to file their annual PAYE returns (see below regarding 'in-year' information) electronically rather than on paper and there are penalties for non-compliance (see **10.53**). For the few exceptions who are exempt from filing online see www.hmrc.gov.uk/paye/payroll/year-end/paper-filing.htm.

Employers with 50 or more employees are required to send online the 'in-year' forms P45 Part 1 (details of employee leaving work), P45 Part 3 (new employee details) and P46 (employee without a form P45) and similar information relating to pensioners. This requirement will be extended to all employers from April 2011. Again penalties apply for non-compliance (see **10.53**)

Large employers with 250 or more employees are also required to make PAYE payments electronically and penalties are charged for late payment (see **10.53**). HMRC guidance is provided at www.hmrc.gov.uk/payinghmrc/paye.htm.

Operating the PAYE system

[10.46] Detailed guidance on the operation of the PAYE system is available at www.hmrc.gov.uk/paye and in the Employer Helpbook E13, 'Day-to-day payroll'. Newly-registered employers are offered a New Employer pack, which includes the Employer's CD-Rom containing electronic calculators, forms and information.

Employers may use the CD-ROM or tables supplied by HMRC to deduct tax and Class 1 NICs from the weekly or monthly pay (including any statutory sick pay or statutory maternity, paternity or adoption pay).

Employers must make monthly payments (but see below regarding quarterly payments) of the total tax and student loan deductions due, and the total employees' and employer's Class 1 NICs, net of (a) recoveries relating to statutory payments and (b) any NIC rebate in relation to contracted out pension contributions (see **13.12**).

The payments to HMRC must be made within fourteen days after the end of each income tax month ending on the 5th of the month, i.e. by the 19th of each month, or by the 22nd of the month for electronic payments. If the due date falls at the weekend payment must be made by the previous Friday.

Interest is charged on unpaid PAYE amounts for any tax year which remain outstanding after the following 19 (or 22) April (see **10.53**). If during the tax year the cumulative tax paid by an employee exceeds the cumulative amount due, the excess is refunded to him by the employer, who then deducts it from the amount due to HMRC.

Employers who expect their average net monthly PAYE payment to be less than £1,500 may pay quarterly instead of monthly.

Pay records will sometimes need to be kept even though no tax or NICs are payable, for example where the pay is above the NICs lower earnings limit but below the earnings threshold. In such cases year-end forms P14/P60 need to be completed (see **10.51**).

For details on NICs, see **CHAPTER 13**. For details of statutory sick pay and statutory maternity etc. pay, see **CHAPTER 14**.

Code numbers

[10.47] Employers calculate tax using code numbers notified by HMRC on form P9 or using the specified 'emergency' procedure where no code number is received. Once a code number is issued it remains in force from year to year until HMRC notify a change. A change in code number may result from a claim by the employee for further reliefs or allowances.

A code represents the tax allowances an employee is entitled to, such as personal allowances and allowable expenses in employment, less any deduction to collect the tax due on other income such as the state pension, savings interest or employee benefits such as cars or loans, or to collect underpayments arising in earlier years. Allowances may be restricted in order to limit the tax relief given on certain allowances to tax at 10%, and any restriction will vary according to whether the employee is expected to pay basic, higher, or additional rate tax.

The code number is the amount of allowances less the last digit. For example, if allowances total £6,475 the code number is 647. The code effectively spreads the tax allowances evenly over the tax year. This means that if an employee earns some extra pay in a pay period there is no extra tax-free allowance to set against it, so that the whole of the extra suffers tax.

Most codes are three numbers followed by a suffix L, P, Y or T. Code suffix L denotes the basic personal allowance of £6,475. Code P denotes full personal allowance for those aged 65 to 74. Code Y denotes full personal allowance for those aged 75 and over. The code suffixes enable HMRC to implement changes in allowances by telling employers to increase relevant codes by a specified amount. Suffix T means that the code is only to be changed if a specific notification is received from the tax office. A code T may be requested by a taxpayer who does not want his status to be disclosed in this way to his employer.

Some codes have a prefix K instead of a suffix. Prefix K enables tax to be collected during the year where the amount of an employee's taxable benefits or an employed pensioner's state pension exceeds available allowances. The tax deducted under a K code cannot exceed 50% of cash pay (but see **10.48** re notional pay). Other codes are BR, which means basic rate tax applies; NT, which means no tax is to be deducted; and DO, which means that all pay is to be taxed at the higher rate because all allowances, and the basic rate band, are used against other income.

HMRC normally collect an underpayment of less than £2,000 via a PAYE coding adjustment unless the employee asks them not to do so. Coding adjustments may also be made to give effect to reliefs such as losses (see **25.6**).

Payments in non-cash form (notional payments) (s 696)

[10.48] Where employers provide employees with certain assets that are readily convertible into cash (see **10.19**), PAYE and Class 1 NICs must be charged on the amount which, using the employer's best estimate, is likely to be chargeable as employment income, and accounted for in respect of the pay period in which the asset is provided, whether or not the employee has sufficient pay in that period to enable the tax and employee's NICs to be deducted. Any such tax and NI that is not deducted from pay should be made good by the employee within 90 days from the time the asset is provided. If the employee does not do so, the unrecovered amount must be shown as further pay on year-end forms P9D or P11D. The 50% overriding limit on deduction of tax under K codes (see **10.47**) is ignored when dealing with the deductions for notional payments.

Tax tables

[10.49] Tax Table A shows the cumulative free pay based on the tax code for each tax week or month, and it includes the adjustments needed to increase the tax collected from employees with K codes by increasing taxable pay. Table B shows the tax due on taxable pay to date at basic rate of 20% up to the basic rate limit, Table C1 shows the tax due at the higher rate of 40% and Table C2 shows tax due at the additional rate of 50%. Table D is non-cumulative, and is a higher and additional rate tax ready reckoner for use with Table C and for D codes.

Changing jobs or retiring

[10.50] When an employee leaves his job, then unless the employer will be paying a pension, the employer should complete form P45, which is in four parts. He sends the first part to HMRC and gives the employee the other three parts, parts 2 and 3 being for the new employer and part 1A for the employee to retain (he will need it if he has to fill in a tax return, and he needs to retain it in any event as part of his tax records — see **10.56**). The P45 shows the total pay, tax to date in the tax year, the code number in use and whether student loan deductions are to be made. Passing the form to the new employer when the employee starts another job enables the employer to continue to deduct tax on the correct basis. Statutory redundancy pay and certain other amounts received when the employee leaves are not normally treated as pay, but they may be subject to tax under special rules (see **CHAPTER 15**).

If an employee cannot produce form P45 to his new employer, the employer will ask him to complete and sign form P46, indicating whether (A) this is his first job since 6 April and he has not received certain benefits or a pension, or (B) this is now his only job but since 6 April he has had another job or received certain benefits, but he does not receive a state or occupational pension, or (C) he has another job or receives a pension. The P46 procedure enables employers to deduct tax on a cumulative basis straight away for those who tick box A, so that they get the benefit of the personal allowance from the beginning of the tax year. If the employee ticks box B, he will be allocated a single person's allowance, code 647L, on a non-cumulative basis (called week 1 or month 1 basis), which means he will get only one week's (or month's) proportion of the allowance against each week's (month's) pay. If he ticks box C he will pay tax at the basic rate. Form P46 also asks the employee to indicate whether he has a student loan, other than one required to be repaid through his bank or building society account. HMRC will notify revised codes as appropriate after receiving forms P46. If the employee does not sign form P46, the employer will send the form to HMRC and deduct tax from his pay at the basic rate.

Employees seconded to work in the UK must complete form P46 (Expat).

Forms P46 are sent to HMRC unless the employee earns less than the PAYE threshold. Forms P46 for such employees must be retained by the employer, together with details of the employee's name, address and amount of pay. If the employee's earnings equal or exceed the NIC lower earnings limit (£97 a week for 2010/11), a form P11 (deductions working sheet) must be prepared. NI numbers should be shown on forms P46, but if the employee cannot provide the number, or gives an incorrect number, HMRC will notify the correct number to the employer when they get the form. A voluntary NI number tracing service is available where form P46 is not sent in.

If the employee is retiring on pension, the employer will send a retirement statement to HMRC (using either form P46 (Pen) or the employer's own form, the information being similar to that provided on form P45) and give the employee a copy, which he will need if he fills in a tax return. The employer will deduct tax from the pension on a week 1 or month 1 basis (see above) until HMRC tell him what code number to use.

If an employee dies, all four parts of form P45 are sent to HMRC, with 'D' marked in the box at the foot of the form and the employee copy of year-end form P60 (see **10.51**) is scrapped.

Employers' records and returns

[10.51] Employers must keep records of their monthly payments in respect of net income tax and net Class 1 NIC payments (see **10.46**). The totals should be recorded monthly or quarterly either on the employer payment record, form

P32 or in the payslip booklet. Employers are required to keep PAYE records for at least the current tax year and the previous three tax years. However, the self assessment rules require businesses to retain records for longer than this (see for example **9.25**).

Details must be provided to HMRC at the year end for all those who are or have been employed in that year at a rate of pay equal to or exceeding the Class 1 NIC lower earnings limit (£97 for 2010/11), even if no tax or NIC payments have been made because the employee's earnings are below the level at which tax and NICs become payable (£110 for 2010/11). As mentioned in **10.45** most employers must file their end of year returns online. The online filing methods include commercial payroll software, HMRC's Employer CD-Rom, HM-RC's free 'online Return and Forms—PAYE' service via their website, an agent or payroll bureau and Electronic Data Interchange. An employer is not restricted to using just one method. He could, for example, have an agent file the P14s and file the P35 himself using HMRC's free service, see further www.hmrc.gov.uk/paye/payroll/year-end/annual-return.htm#5. HMRC do not accept returns submitted using magnetic media as having been filed online and, therefore, the number of payroll packages that support such means is reducing rapidly. As a result, returns filed via magnetic media will not be accepted from 2010/11 year end onwards.

Form P14 must be submitted online with form P35 by the majority of employers. For those who may continue to file paper year end returns (see **10.45**) the form P14 is in three parts. Two parts are sent to HMRC (one of which is for NIC purposes) and the third is the form P60 which must be given to the employee showing the total pay (including any statutory sick pay and statutory maternity/paternity/adoption pay), student loan deductions and tax and NICs deducted in the year. Forms P60 *must* be provided on paper. P60s relating to former employees are scrapped. Where necessary, employers may issue duplicate P60s (clearly marked as such). Forms P14 also show separate figures for the total statutory sick pay paid in months for which the employer recovered part of it (see **14.12**) and the total statutory maternity etc pay.

The forms to be sent to HMRC at the year end are:

- Two copies of form P14 (or substitutes)
- Form P35 showing for all employees and former employees the total tax, NICs and student loan deductions due, and the amounts recovered by deduction from NIC and tax payments or directly from HMRC in respect of statutory sick pay and statutory maternity etc. pay (see **14.12** and **14.21**). The amounts *paid* in respect of statutory sick pay and statutory maternity etc. pay do not need to be shown
- Forms P11D and P9D for all current and former employees (for details see **10.54**)
- Form P11D(b), which is a combined return for employers' Class 1A contributions and for declaring either that forms P11D are attached for all relevant employees or that no expenses payments or benefits have been provided.

See **10.45** above regarding compulsory online filing.

The deadline for sending in forms P14 and P35 is 19 May, and the deadline for forms P11D, P11D(b) and P9D is 6 July. Those who were in employment at the end of the tax year must be given year-end form P60 by 31 May after the tax year, and also a copy of form P11D or P9D as appropriate by 6 July. Copies for employees who left after 5 April may be sent to the last known address. Employers may consider it appropriate to provide copy P11Ds and P9Ds to employees who left *during* the tax year, but they are not *required* to do so unless the employee makes a written request (within three years after the end of that year).

Employers have to give HMRC details of new and changed arrangements for the provision of cars and car fuel to employees on form P46 (Car). The form must be submitted within 28 days after each quarter to 5 July, 5 October, 5 January and 5 April. The requirement to complete this form if the employer replaced one car with another was removed from 6 April 2009.

National insurance contributions

[10.52] Employers' Class 1A NICs (see 10.39) are calculated annually from the P11D entries, the boxes on the P11D relevant for Class 1A contributions being colour coded. The total of the amounts liable to Class 1A contributions is recorded on form P11D(b) as indicated above and multiplied by the appropriate percentage (12.8% for 2010/11 but proposed to be increased to 13.8% from 6 April 2011), and the payment is sent to HMRC Accounts Office using a special Class 1A payslip. The due date for payment is 19 July after the relevant tax year, i.e. by 19 July 2011 for 2010/11. For payments made electronically the payment date is 22 July. When a business ceases, Class 1A contributions are due within 14 days after the end of the income tax month in which the last payment of earnings is made. If a business changes hands, the employer before the change must similarly pay over Class 1A contributions for any employee not continuing with the new owner within 14 days after the end of the final month. The liability for payment of the Class 1A contributions for continuing employees falls on the successor.

Interest and penalties

[10.53] As stated at 10.46, interest is charged if PAYE and NICs for any year to 5 April are paid late. Except for Class 1A payments, interest runs from 19 April following the end of the tax year or 22 April for electronic payments (which is a month earlier than the due date for submitting the year-end forms P14 and P35). For Class 1A, interest runs from the due date of payment, i.e. from 19 July 2011 for the 2010/11 payment (or 22 July for electronic payments). For recent rates of interest, see the Table of Rates and Allowances.

From 6 April 2010 late payment penalties also apply to the monthly, quarterly and annual PAYE periods. The penalties range between 1% and 4% with further penalties of 5% being due if the payment continues to be late. Employers must notify HMRC either using their PAYE payslip booklet, by phoning, or via an online form if no payment is due for a particular PAYE period. HMRC provide guidance at www.hmrc.gov.uk/paye/problems-inspections/late-payments.htm.

Automatic penalties are payable by employers who do not send in end of year forms P14 and P35 by 19 May or who send in incorrect returns. By concession a penalty will not be charged if the end of year forms are received on or before the last business day within seven days of the filing date but this concession will be withdrawn on 31 March 2011. The penalty payable for late filing is £100 for every 50 employees (or part of 50) for each month or part month the return is late. For example, an employer with 110 employees who does not send in his 2010/11 return until 10 September 2011 (between three and four months late) would be liable to a penalty of £300 × 4 = £1,200. Additional penalties are payable if the failure continues beyond 12 months.

Penalties may be charged if an employer sends part or all of the year end form P35 on paper or magnetic media when it was required to be filed online. The penalty applies whether or not the return is filed on time and even if a subsequent return is filed online. The amount of the penalty depends on the number of P14s included in the return and is up to a maximum of £3,000.

Penalties may also be charged if employers (currently those with 50 or more employees) fail to file their in-year forms (P45 and P46) online. The penalty ranges from £100 up to a maximum of £3,000 depending on the number of forms that should have been filed online. The first penalties will be issued for the quarter ended 5 April 2010.

Penalties are also charged for late filing of forms P11D and P9D (see **10.54**). For *each form*, there is an initial penalty of up to £300 plus up to £60 a day if the failure continues.

The monthly penalties of £100 per 50 employees for late P14s and P35s also apply to late P11D(b) Class 1A NICs returns (due date 6 July as indicated above, although the form states that penalties will be charged if it is not submitted by 19 July).

See **9.44** regarding penalties for errors in relation to PAYE and P11D/P9D returns.

Forms P11D and P9D

[10.54] Employees who complete self assessment tax returns must include details of expenses payments and benefits from their employers. Employers are therefore required to provide all current employees (and former employees if they so request) with copies of forms P11D or P9D as appropriate (see **10.51**).

Forms P9D show taxable benefits and expenses payments for those earning less than £8,500. The main items are expenses payments totalling more than £25 for the year (other than those wholly for business purposes), payment of an employee's bills, gifts (at second-hand value), non-cash vouchers (including the excess of meal vouchers over 15p a day), and living accommodation.

Forms P11D show the cash equivalents of benefits for employees earning £8,500 per annum or more and directors (see **10.8**). HMRC provide optional working sheets for working out the cash equivalents for living accommodation, cars and fuel, vans, mileage allowance payments and passenger payments, beneficial loans and relocation expenses. Employers do not take into account any reduction an employee is entitled to for the business proportion of an expense. These reductions are dealt with by employees on their tax returns. Employers' Class 1A contributions are based on the P11D figures, and employers therefore have to pay full contributions on benefits where there is mixed business/private use (see **10.39**). This has the effect of costing the employer 12.8% (proposed to be increased to 13.8% from 6 April 2011) on a business expense, albeit reduced by the income tax or corporation tax relief on that amount.

P11Ds and P9Ds do not have to show amounts covered by a dispensation (see **10.16**) or by a PAYE settlement agreement (see **10.55**), and employees similarly need not show such amounts in their own tax returns. It is sensible for employers to make sure employees know what items are covered in this way and the Class 1A liability makes it important for employers themselves to ensure that dispensations are obtained if appropriate.

Where employees receive a specific amount for entertaining expenses, employers must state on P11Ds or P9Ds whether the expense has been disallowed in calculating tax on their business profits. In that event, the employee is able to offset the expenses payment received by an equivalent expenses claim (see **10.15**).

An employer must include in P11Ds and P9Ds any benefits he has arranged for a third party to provide (for example, where another group company provides cars or medical insurance). The onus of providing the information falls on the third party rather than the employer if the employer has not arranged for the third party to provide the benefits, and the third party must provide the information to the employee by 6 July after the end of the tax year. The rules for benefits provided directly by third parties do not apply to gifts costing not more than £250 per year or to corporate hospitality. Third parties do not need to send details of the taxable benefits to HMRC unless they receive a return requiring them to do so. Class 1A contributions are payable on taxable third party benefits, including non-cash vouchers (see **10.39**). See **10.55** re the liability for paying the Class 1A contributions.

PAYE settlement agreements and taxed award schemes

[10.55] Employers may enter into a PAYE settlement agreement (PSA) with HMRC, under which they make a single annual payment covering the tax and NICs on certain benefits and possibly expenses payments. Items covered by the PSA are not shown on year-end forms P35, P14, P11D and P9D and employees are not subject to tax or NICs on them. The scheme covers items which are either minor or occasional, or are made in circumstances when it would be impracticable to apply PAYE (e.g. on shared benefits). Details are in HMRC Statement of Practice SP 5/96. PAYE settlements frequently include payments for those who had been treated as self-employed and are reclassified as employees.

As far as NICs are concerned, employers pay a special class of contributions, Class 1B, at 12.8% (proposed to be increased to 13.8% from 6 April 2011) on the benefits etc. taxed under the PSA plus the tax thereon, to the extent that there would have been an NIC liability under Class 1 or Class 1A. Both the tax payment under the PSA and the Class 1B contributions thereon are payable by 19 October after the end of the tax year to which the payment relates. For payments made electronically the payment date is 22 October. Interest is charged from the due date if the payment is made late.

Employers and third parties who operate formal incentive award schemes are able to enter into arrangements known as taxed award schemes (TAS), which work in a similar way to PSAs. Employers operating such schemes directly (but not third parties) may use a PSA instead if they wish. Employers have to account for Class 1 or Class 1A NICs as the case may be on non-cash vouchers or other benefits provided to employees, where the vouchers/benefits are provided directly or where the employers arranged for them to be provided by a third party. They also have to pay Class 1 contributions on the tax paid under a TAS. Where non-cash vouchers or other benefits are provided by a third party (whether under a TAS or not), Class 1A rather than Class 1 contributions are payable. Where the employer has not arranged for the awards to be provided, third parties must pay the Class 1A contributions on the award, and if they also pay the associated tax, they are liable for the Class 1A contributions on the tax payment. Third parties may use the TAS accounting arrangements to make payment. Guidance is provided in HMRC's Employment Income Manual at EIM11235.

Employees' records and self-assessment

[10.56] All taxpayers are required to keep records relating to their tax liabilities (see 9.25). Most employees will not need to fill in tax returns, because their tax will usually be dealt with through the PAYE system (see 9.27), but they should still keep records for the statutory period in case there is any query. Employees need to keep records for 22 months from the end of the tax year, unless they are also self-employed or receive rental income, in which case the period is 5 years 10 months (or such earlier date as may be specified in writing by HMRC). In both cases, if HMRC are conducting an enquiry into the taxpayer's affairs (see 9.31), the period is extended until the enquiry is completed.

The main records employees need to keep are year-end certificates P60 and forms P11D or P9D, forms P45 when they change jobs or Form P46 (Pen) if they retire on pension, and records, receipts and vouchers to support expenses claims. They should also keep any other records that relate to their employment income, such as coding notices, information relating to employee share schemes, information re earnings abroad (and proof of any foreign tax deducted), etc.

Tax points

[10.57] Note the following:

- Smaller employers in particular face an onerous burden in dealing with obligations to deduct and account for tax, NICs and student loan repayments. Payroll software can alleviate the problem, but there are severe penalties for getting things wrong so businesses need to be sure that their systems can cope. Almost all employers are required to file their year-end PAYE returns online with effect for the 2009/10 returns, and larger employers are required to file some in-year information online (see **10.45**).

- The imposition of employers' Class 1A NICs on taxable benefits in kind has removed the main advantage of paying such benefits. A significant tax and NIC advantage in respect of non-P11D employees, and an employee's NIC saving for P11D employees earning less than the upper earnings limit of £844 a week (but proposed to be reduced from 6 April 2011, see **13.2**), may be available. Even where there is no such saving, it may be possible to provide benefits for less than the employee would have paid himself, by use of in-house services, staff discounts, etc.
- Employers pay Class 1A NICs on benefits even if the employee claims an equivalent deduction as a business expense in his tax return. Employers should in those circumstances seek a dispensation so that the item is not reckoned as a benefit in the first place.
- Where tips are received, great care needs to be taken in relation to the PAYE, NIC and national minimum wage treatment as set out in HMRC leaflet E24.
- Watch the 'pecuniary liability' trap. Tax (and NICs) may be avoided for non-P11D employees on certain payments providing the *employer* is legally responsible for paying them, for example, heat and light in employer-provided living accommodation and home telephones. Payment by an employer of an *employee's* debt counts as pay for *all* employees and must be reported on year-end forms P11D and P9D. Class 1 NICs are payable at the time of the payment.
- Travelling expenses from home to a permanent workplace are not deductible in calculating taxable earnings unless the nature of the employee's job requires him to carry out his duties at home. Area representatives and those holding part-time employments, such as consultants and tribunal members, should seek to establish that their place of employment is at their home or other workbase, making their travelling expenses from that base deductible.
- HMRC have introduced a new framework for compliance checks which apply to some taxes including PAYE from 1 April 2009. Details can be found at www.hmrc.gov.uk/about/new-compliance-checks.htm.
- HMRC test payroll software packages and award a payroll standard kitemark to those that meet the PAYE requirements.
- HMRC offer to help small businesses in various ways with PAYE problems, including offering workshops and presentations, see www.hmrc.gov.uk/payeonline/help-with-filing.htm and www.hmrc.gov.uk/bst/index.htm.
- Employers will find it costly if they do not comply with the requirements of the PAYE scheme. To give two examples, failing to apply the P46 procedure properly for new employees who do not produce form P45 could make the employer liable to pay the tax that should have been deducted from the amount paid; if forms P11D and P9D are not properly completed and sent in promptly for each current or former employee, employers face severe penalties.

- Forms P11D are increasingly subject to close scrutiny and testing by HMRC as to their accuracy, for example through visits to business premises, knowledge of directors' personal circumstances and a close inspection of the position as regards loans to directors. Care should therefore be taken to ensure that all sections of the form are correctly completed, and in particular that all expenses of the employee met by the employer are declared (except those covered by a dispensation or PAYE settlement agreement), a claim being made by the employee in his annual tax return for a corresponding deduction if the expenses are allowable for tax.

- The definition of 'earnings at the rate of £8,500 per annum' includes certain car expenses met by the employer as well as the car and car fuel charges. This brings some employees whose salary is less than £8,500 into the P11D reporting net.

- The total cost in tax, NICs and VAT of the provision of private car fuel to employees has risen dramatically and in many cases it will be cheaper, as well as far more straightforward in terms of reporting requirements, to pay the employee extra wages to compensate him for buying his own private fuel.

- Remember that an employee's contribution towards the cost of a car (maximum £5,000) and payments for the private use of a car both reduce the car benefit charge, but payments by the employee for car fuel are not taken into account unless they cover the whole cost of private use.

- If a car is provided for a relative of a P11D employee, the benefit will be charged on the car user rather than the P11D employee if the car user is also an employee and the duties of the employment are such that the car is required in the performance of those duties (e.g. where the employee is a commercial traveller) and would be provided to any employee in equivalent circumstances.

- If an employee is required to use his own vehicle, motor cycle or bicycle in employment, mileage allowances based on HMRC approved mileage rates (see **10.11**) may be received from the employer free of both tax and NICs. If he pays his own running expenses, he can claim the approved rates for the business miles. If the employer pays him a mileage allowance below the approved rates he can claim an allowance for the shortfall for tax but not NIC purposes.

- If an employer arranges for his employees earning less than £8,500 per annum to eat at a local café which sends the bill to the employer, the employee avoids tax on the provision of the meals. This will not work for P11D employees unless the café can provide a private room, which then effectively becomes the works canteen.

- There is no tax on an interest-free loan to a P11D employee to buy a season ticket unless the total loans at a nil or beneficial interest rate that are outstanding in that tax year from the employee exceed £5,000.

- An employee is charged to tax on benefits arising from employment even though the employer is not the payer. The most common example is tips. Another example is where one of the employer's suppliers pays for the employee to have a foreign holiday as a sales achievement reward. Such a supplier may operate a 'taxed award scheme' under which he accounts for the tax. The employee must be provided with relevant details of all third party benefits to enable him to complete his tax return, but he is responsible for the entries on the return.

- Third party benefits to employees in the form of corporate hospitality, such as entrance to and entertainment at sporting and cultural events, and non-cash gifts to an employee from a third party costing not more than £250 in a tax year, are exempt providing the benefits and/or gifts are not procured by the employer and are not related to services performed or to be performed in the employment.
- HMRC frequently reviews the list of professional subscriptions which are allowable in computing the taxable pay of an employee. An employee should therefore check if his own subscription has not so far been allowed.
- If an employee *occasionally* works very late, he is not charged to tax if his employer pays for his transport home. Those who regularly work late get no such exemption, although exemption applies if the employer pays for the transport home because of a temporary breakdown in regular home to work car sharing arrangements.
- 'Payment' for PAYE purposes can be triggered much earlier than when money changes hands, especially as regards directors.
- Under self-assessment, an individual needs to keep records relating to his tax affairs — see **10.56**. HMRC provide guidance at www.hmrc.gov.uk/sa/record-keeping.htm.

11

Employee share options and awards

Background

[11.1] Tax law provides various incentives to encourage employees and directors to participate in their employing companies. HMRC guidance recognises that studies have shown that 'when the interests of employees are aligned with those of their employer through shareholdings in the employer company, there is a correlation with increased company productivity'. Four statutory arrangements are designed to 'encourage employees to hold shares in their employer'.

However, stringent and lengthy anti-avoidance provisions exist to block arrangements designed to reward employees without attracting the appropriate amount of tax and national insurance contributions (NICs). The Government gave notice on 2 December 2004 that any such arrangements would be closed down, with retrospective effect to that date if necessary, and they introduced such legislation in FA 2006 in relation to securities options (see **11.4** and **11.7**). There have been many changes in this area but most have not affected the approved schemes set out in legislation. These are:

* SAYE linked share option schemes ('Sharesave') — see **11.10**
* Company share option plans (CSOPs) — see **11.12**
* Enterprise management incentive (EMI) share option schemes — see **11.13**
* Share incentive plans (SIPs) — see **11.19**

Statutory references in this chapter are to the Income Tax (Earnings and Pensions) Act 2003 (ITEPA 2003) unless otherwise stated. HMRC guidance is available at www.hmrc.gov.uk/shareschemes and in HMRC's Employment-Related Securities Manual and Employee Share Schemes User Manual.

The legislation applies to employment-related 'securities'. Employment-related means, broadly, acquired in connection with an employment. Securities include shares, debentures, loan stock and other securities issued by companies, and a wide range of other financial instruments including options, futures, contracts for differences and rights under contracts of insurance.

Reporting requirements (ss 421J–421L; FA 2007, Sch 26)

[11.2] There is a general requirement to report certain events relating to shares and securities obtained by reason of an employment. Form 42 is provided at www.hmrc.gov.uk/shareschemes/ann-app-schemes.htm for this purpose, and comprehensive guidance notes are also provided. The information must be submitted to HMRC's Employee Shares and Securities Unit before 7 July following the tax year in which the event occurred, and there are penalties for non-compliance. Following the introduction of online filing of forms 42, paper copies of the form will no longer be issued. Companies will instead receive a notice to file the form and they must then file online, or through the HMRC issued Employer CD-Rom, or send a paper copy which can be downloaded from the HMRC website.

The reportable events include:

- a person's acquisition or deemed acquisition of securities, or an interest in securities or a securities option, where the acquisition is pursuant to a right or opportunity available by reason of his employment or another person's employment;
- a 'chargeable event' in relation to restricted securities, restricted interests in securities, convertible securities or interests in convertible securities;
- the doing of anything that artificially enhances the market value of the securities and gives rise to a tax charge on 'non-commercial increases';
- an event which discharges a 'notional loan' that arose where, for example, securities were acquired for less than market value;
- a disposal of securities for more than market value in certain circumstances;
- the receipt of a benefit from securities or interest in securities giving rise to taxable employment income;
- the assignment or release of an employment-related securities option in certain circumstances; and
- the receipt of a benefit in money or money's worth in connection with an employment-related securities option.

There are, however, a large number of exceptions from the reporting requirements. These include transfers of shares in the normal course of family or personal relationships, share for share exchanges, and rights and bonus issues.

Form 42 is not used for most events relating to approved schemes. For example, form 34 is used to report the grant or exercise of options under SAYE-related share option schemes; form 35 is used to report the grant or exercise of options under a company share option plan; form 39 records the award of shares to an employee under a share incentive plan; and the grant of options within specified limits under an enterprise management incentives (EMI) scheme is reported on form EMI40 (but the grant of an option outside the limits would be reportable on form 42).

PAYE tax and NICs

[11.3] Employers are required to operate PAYE, and account for tax and Class 1 NICs, when shares etc. that are 'readily convertible assets' (see 10.19) are acquired by a person (not necessarily the employee) and the right or opportunity to make the acquisition is available by reason of an employment of that person or any other person outside the terms of an approved scheme.

Shares etc. are readily convertible assets if they may be sold on the Stock Exchange or arrangements exist or are likely to exist for them to be traded. These provisions apply to shares etc. acquired directly and through the exercise of unapproved options that were granted on or after 27 November 1996. They also apply where tax is charged when a share or securities option is assigned or released (see 11.7), or a chargeable event occurs under the anti-avoidance provisions outlined in 11.6.

Where shares etc. acquired in such circumstances are not readily convertible assets, neither Class 1 nor Class 1A NICs are payable, but tax is chargeable through the self-assessment system (see 11.34). From 10 July 2003, however, shares etc. that would not otherwise be readily convertible assets are automatically treated as such (except for the purposes of the share incentive plan rules at 11.27) if no corporation tax deduction is available under the provisions at 11.32. Where the chargeable event takes the form of a receipt of money, or of an asset which is a readily convertible asset, PAYE etc. applies regardless of whether or not the scheme shares are themselves readily convertible assets (ss 698, 700). Where the tax treatment of readily convertible assets is retrospectively amended (as it was in FA 2006 in relation to securities options — see 11.7), the deemed payment date for PAYE purposes will be the date the relevant Act is passed, except in relation to PAYE arising from the FA 2006 provisions, for which the deemed payment date was 6 April 2007. Detailed and complex provisions apply as to the way in which the payments are treated, including re-allocating the payments to the appropriate tax year and providing revised PAYE forms.

In the case of share options granted on or after 6 April 1999 that relate to shares that are readily convertible assets, NICs are payable when the options are exercised. Because of the unpredictable timing and amount of a company's liability to pay employer's secondary contributions on unapproved options, employees and employers may make formal joint elections to HMRC for the employees to pay the employers' secondary NICs when the option is exercised. Such elections need HMRC approval. Alternatively the employer and employee may make an agreement for the contributions to be paid by the employee. In this event the formal liability remains with the employer. In either case, any amount paid by the employee will reduce the amount chargeable as employment income in respect of the option for tax purposes (but not for NICs). It will not affect the corporation tax deduction allowable to the company (see **11.32**), nor the allowable cost of the shares for capital gains tax (CGT), but see **11.8**. The same provisions have applied since September 2004 in relation to chargeable events in respect of restricted securities and convertible securities (see **11.6**).

Other provisions

[11.4] The Employee Share Ownership Trusts provisions enabled companies to set up trusts that have more flexibility than approved schemes, although without their tax benefits. Such trusts could be run in conjunction with approved schemes. Companies may transfer shares held in such trusts at certain dates into an approved share incentive plan trust without adverse tax consequences.

Subject to certain restrictions, employers can get tax relief for the costs of setting up approved share option schemes and approved share incentive plans, and see the relief at **11.32** for the cost of providing shares for employee share schemes. For capital gains tax (CGT) purposes, on the grant of an option under an approved or unapproved scheme, the employer is treated as receiving the amount, if any, paid by the employee for the option (rather than market value, which usually applies to non-arm's length transactions — see **4.23**), so no tax charge on chargeable gains arises.

Shares acquired under SAYE linked share option schemes, approved share incentive plans or approved profit sharing schemes may be transferred free of CGT into an Individual Savings Account up to the annual limit for ISA investments (see **36.24**) even if they are unquoted. There is no similar provision in relation to enterprise management incentive share options, but favourable CGT treatment applies to such options. Shares acquired under SAYE schemes, share incentive plans or profit sharing schemes may be transferred into personal pension schemes and tax relief obtained thereon (see **17.12**).

Special rules apply where employees of universities and other research institutions acquire shares in 'spinout' companies formed to develop intellectual property (IP) that the employees helped to create. The value of the IP will not be taken into account at the time it is transferred to the spinout company, thus removing a potential tax and NIC charge at that time, and various other provisions in this chapter are disapplied.

Share awards outside approved schemes

Issue of shares for less than market value (ss 446Q–446W)

[11.5] If shares are issued at a price equal to the current market value, with the price being paid by agreed instalments, no charge will arise under the general charging provisions since full market value is being paid, and this will apply even though the market value has increased by the time the shares are paid for. Any growth in value of the shares is liable only to CGT.

A director or an employee who acquires shares other than under the approved schemes and does not pay the full price for shares immediately is, however, regarded as having received an interest-free loan equal to the deferred instalments, on which tax is charged at the beneficial loans interest rate (see the Table of Rates and Allowances) unless the total of all beneficial loans outstanding from that director or employee in the tax year, including the deferred instalments, does not exceed £5,000 (see **10.38**). The loan is regarded as being repaid as and when the instalments are paid. Any amount written off is taxed as employment income at that time; any amount so taxed is taken into account for CGT purposes when the shares are disposed of.

The notional loan provisions do not apply if, on or after 2 December 2004, something affecting the shares has been done as part of a scheme to avoid tax and/or NICs. Instead the amount that would have been treated as a loan is treated as employment income in the tax year when the acquisition takes place.

Anti-avoidance rules

[11.6] There are wide ranging anti-avoidance provisions in relation to employment-related shares and securities. They do not apply in relation to shares that comply with the provisions of approved schemes, but enterprise management incentive schemes (see **11.13**) are not regarded as approved schemes for this purpose. The provisions apply to advantages gained not just by the employee but by 'associated persons'. 'Associated persons' include the person who acquired the shares (if not the employee), persons connected with the employee (or with the person who acquired the shares) and members of the same household as the employee (or person who acquired the shares). (The definition of 'connected' is broadly the same as in **4.23**.) There are exemptions from some of the provisions where the shares are acquired under a public offer, or are shares in an employee-controlled company or where the event in question affects all the company's shares of the same class and the majority of them are held by outside shareholders; these exceptions apply in respect of restricted shares, convertible shares and post-acquisition benefits.

The anti-avoidance provisions under which tax and NIC charges may arise fall under the following headings:

- Restricted securities (ss 422–432)
- Convertible securities (ss 435–444)
- Securities with artificially depressed market value (ss 446A–446J)
- Securities with artificially enhanced market value (ss 446K–446P)
- Securities acquired for less than market value (ss 446Q–446W — see **11.5**)
- Securities disposed of for more than market value (ss 446X–446Z)
- Post-acquisition benefits from securities (ss 447–450)

If the securities concerned are readily convertible assets, the amounts chargeable will be liable to PAYE tax and Class 1 NICs (see **11.3**).

Exercise, assignment, release etc. of option (ss 420, 471–484, TCGA 1992, ss 119A, 120, 144, 144ZA–144ZD)

[11.7] Where a director or employee is granted an option to acquire shares or securities (referred to as shares etc. in what follows) by reason of employment (whether his own or someone else's), there are various circumstances in which a tax charge can arise. However, favourable tax treatment is given for options under approved schemes (see **11.10** to **11.18**). Securities options such as call options are excluded from the tax charging provisions unless they were acquired on or after 2 December 2004 for the purpose of avoiding tax or national insurance.

Where the option is granted other than under an approved scheme, an income tax charge arises when the option is *exercised* on the difference between the open market value at that time and the cost of the shares. If the shares are readily convertible assets, the tax will be collected through PAYE, and Class 1 NICs will also be payable, although the employee may agree to pay the employer's secondary Class 1 NICs (see **11.3**).

For both approved schemes and other options, where a right to acquire shares etc. is assigned or released, an income tax charge arises on the amount received. The same applies where the option holder realises a gain or benefit by allowing the option to lapse, or granting someone else an option over the shares etc. The same comments apply as above if the shares etc. are readily convertible assets.

These tax charges apply on the exercise, assignment or release of the option by any associated person and not just by the employee (i.e. the person by reason of whose employment the option was granted). 'Associated persons' include the person to whom the option was granted (if not the employee), persons connected with the employee (or with the grantee) and members of the same household as the employee (or grantee).

A tax charge also arises on the amount or market value of any benefit received, in money or money's worth, by the employee (or an associated person) in connection with the option, which might include, for example, sums received for varying the option or as compensation for its cancellation.

Whatever the reason for a tax charge, any amount paid for the option itself and expenses incurred in connection with the exercise, assignment, release or receipt of benefit are deductible in determining the taxable amount.

[11.8] For CGT, the amount taxed as income on exercise of an unapproved employee shares etc. option often counts as part of the cost of acquisition of the shares etc. (as does anything paid for the option itself). However, HMRC have changed their view in relation to shares acquired on the exercise of an option before 10 April 2003. In computing the capital gain or loss no deduction should be made of any amount chargeable to income tax on the exercise of the option. See HMRC Briefs 30/2009 and 60/2009 for full details.

Grant of option (s 475)

[11.9] No income tax liability arises on the *grant* of an option, unless exceptionally the option is granted at a discount under a company share option plan scheme (see **11.12**). (The cost figure taken into account for CGT is, however, subject to anti-avoidance provisions.) Where a discount is charged to tax on the grant of an option it is deducted from the amount chargeable when the option is exercised.

SAYE linked share option schemes (ss 516–519, Sch 3; TCGA 1992, Sch 7D; ITTOIA 2005, Pt 6 Ch 4)

[11.10] These HMRC-approved schemes enable an employer company to grant to employees and directors an option to acquire shares in the company in the future at today's price, the shares eventually being paid for out of the proceeds of a linked Save as you Earn (SAYE) scheme. No income tax charge arises on the grant of the option, and there is no charge on the difference between cost and market value of the shares when the option is exercised. HMRC guidance is provided in the Employee Share Schemes User Manual at ESSUM 30100. FA 2009 introduced changes to simplify administration of SAYE share option schemes and to ease certain practical difficulties concerning invitations sent to employees shortly before a change in bonus rates.

Contributions of between £5 and £250 per month are paid for up to five years, and are normally deducted from pay, under an SAYE contract with a bank or building society. The employee/director will normally be able to exercise the option after three years, five years or seven years, when the SAYE contract ends. The contributions will be of an amount that will secure as nearly as possible, when interest is added, the repayment of a sum equal to the exercise price. Interest and bonuses added to contributions are tax-free.

Various conditions must be met. In particular the scheme must be available to all full-time directors and all employees with a stipulated length of service which cannot be set at more than five years, and all members of the scheme must participate on similar terms. Part-time employees must be included, but part-time directors may be excluded.

An individual cannot participate if he has a material interest (or has had one at any time in the previous 12 months) in either a close company (see **3.26**) whose shares may be acquired as a result of exercising the options or a close company controlling the company whose shares may be acquired. A material interest is defined, broadly, as owning or controlling (alone or together with certain associates) more than 25% of the ordinary share capital or rights to more than 25% of the assets in a winding up.

The shares to be acquired must be ordinary shares in the company that established the scheme or a company which controls it. If the employing company or the part of its business in which the employee works is sold or otherwise leaves the group operating the scheme, the scheme may provide for the employee to exercise the option within six months after that event, but if this results in the employee exercising the option within three years of joining the scheme, any gain arising is charged to income tax and NICs (see **11.3**).

An employee who has been transferred to an associated company which is not participating in the scheme may nonetheless be permitted by the scheme rules to exercise his option within six months after his savings contract matures. If an employee dies before completing the contract, the option may be exercised within 12 months after the date of death. If an employee leaves through injury, disability, redundancy or retirement, the option may be exercised within the following six months. An option held by an employee leaving for any other reason must lapse, unless he had held it for at least three years, in which case he may be permitted to exercise it within six months after leaving.

Regardless of the treatment of the option, the SAYE contract itself may be continued by an employee after he leaves, by arrangement with the savings body, so that the benefit of receiving tax-free interest and bonuses at the end of the contract (see below) is retained. Contributions will then be paid direct to the savings body.

The price at which the option may be exercised must not normally be less than 80% of the market value of the shares at the time the option is granted. The employee does not get tax relief for the SAYE contributions but he gets the benefit of tax-free interest and bonuses at the end of the contract, and when the shares are taken up there is no income tax charge on the excess of the market value over the price paid. If the shares are not taken up, the employee retains the proceeds of the SAYE contract together with the tax-free interest and bonuses.

The scheme must not stipulate a minimum monthly contribution higher than £10 and it must not have features that discourage eligible employees from participating. Companies may require scheme shares to be sold if an employee or director leaves the company, thus helping family companies who wish to ensure that their control is not diluted, and scheme rights can be exchanged for equivalent rights in a company taking over the employer company.

Capital gains tax

[11.11] The CGT base cost of the shares is the price paid by the employee so that when they are disposed of, the benefit of acquiring them at less than their market value is then partly lost, because the gain is charged to tax (except for the benefit of any unused annual exemption). The employee has, however, had the benefit of the SAYE tax-free interest and bonuses. See **11.31** for the special CGT rules for identifying share disposals with acquisitions. If the opportunity is taken to transfer the shares into an Individual Savings Account (ISA) within 90 days of exercise of the option and within the annual ISA limits (see **36.24**), the capital gain on the transfer to the ISA is tax-free.

Company Share Option Plan (CSOP) schemes (ss 521–526, Sch 4; TCGA 1992, Sch 7D; FA 2010, s 39)

[11.12] Options under company share option plans must not be granted at a discount (i.e. at an option price below the current market value of the shares) and the total market value of shares that may be acquired under the option and any other approved options held by the employee under the company share option plan must not exceed £30,000. Providing the scheme complies with these and other conditions, there is no tax charge when options are granted. If, exceptionally, an option *is* granted at a discount, the discount is taxed as employment income for the tax year in which the option is granted, though the amount taxed is deductible in computing any amount that falls to be taxed subsequently, for example on exercise of the option after the scheme has had its approval withdrawn, or in determining the amount of any interest-free loan under **11.5**. HMRC guidance is provided in the Employee Share Schemes User Manual at ESSUM 40100.

There is no income tax charge when the option is exercised, providing it is exercised between three and ten years after it was granted. There is also no income tax charge if the option is exercised within three years after it was granted but within six months of the employment coming to an end because of injury, disability, redundancy or retirement. Where the income tax exemption applies, tax (i.e. CGT) is payable only at the time of disposal of the shares. The total amount paid for the shares, including any discount charged to income tax when the option was granted and any amount paid for the option itself, is deducted from the proceeds in calculating any capital gain. See **11.31** for the special CGT rules for identifying share disposals with acquisitions. If options are exercised in breach of the stipulated time limits or at a time when the scheme is not an approved scheme, they are taxable in the same way as unapproved options, with PAYE tax and NICs applying if the shares are readily convertible assets (see **11.7**). PAYE also applies if the option is exercised more than ten years after it was granted.

Both full-time and part-time employees may be included in a scheme, but only full-time directors are eligible. HMRC guidance indicates that 'full-time' is taken to mean a working week of at least 25 hours excluding meal breaks. In contrast to SAYE linked share option schemes at **11.10**, there is no requirement that the scheme be made available to all directors and employees who are eligible.

An individual cannot participate if he has a material interest (or has had one at any time in the previous 12 months) in either a close company (see **3.26**) whose shares may be acquired as a result of exercising the options or a close company controlling the company whose shares may be acquired. A material interest is defined, broadly, as owning or controlling (alone or together with certain associates) more than 25% of the ordinary share capital or rights to more than 25% of the assets in a winding up.

The shares to be acquired must be ordinary shares in the company that established the scheme or a company which controls it. FA 2010 introduced anti-avoidance provisions to prevent the exemption for options over shares in an unlisted company which is under the control of a listed company. There is a transitional period of six months during which the scheme rules can be amended in order to prevent withdrawal of HMRC approval of the scheme. However, the change affects all options granted on or after 24 March 2010 including any granted in the transitional period. Schemes may provide that participants must exercise their options when their employment ends but may also provide for options to be exchanged for equivalent options in a company taking over the employer company. The scheme may provide for options to be exercised within one year after the employee's death.

Enterprise management incentive share options (ss 527–541, Sch 5; TCGA 1992, Sch 7D)

[11.13] Small, higher-risk companies may offer their employees enterprise management incentive (EMI) share options, subject to a limit of £3 million on the total value of shares in respect of which there are unexercised share options. Providing the scheme rules are complied with, there will normally be no income tax or employers' and employees' NICs to pay on the exercise of the option. There is no requirement for the scheme to be registered, but notice must be given when options are granted (see **11.16**). HMRC guidance is provided at www.hmrc.gov.uk/shareschemes/emi-new-guidance.htm.

For an option to be a qualifying EMI option, the company must be a qualifying company (see **11.14**), the employee must be an eligible employee (**11.15**), and certain conditions must be satisfied in relation to the option itself (**11.16**).

Qualifying companies

[11.14] For a company to be a qualifying company, the following conditions must be satisfied. The company may be either quoted and unquoted:

(a)   The company must not be a 51% subsidiary, or otherwise controlled by another company and persons connected with that company.

(b)   If the company has subsidiaries, they must be 51% owned, except for property managing subsidiaries, which must be 90% owned.

(c)   The company's (or if relevant, the group's) gross assets must not exceed £30 million.

(d)   For options granted by a 'single company' on or after 21 July 2008, the company must have fewer than 250 'full-time equivalent employees'. The number is calculated by taking the number of full-time employees and adding 'just and reasonable' fractions for other employees. Directors (but not employees on maternity or paternity leave, or students on vocational training) are counted as employees for this purpose. In the case of a parent company, employees of both the parent and its subsidiaries count towards the limit. HMRC regard 'full-time' for this purpose as a standard working week, excluding lunch breaks and overtime, of at least 35 hours.

(e)   Broadly, the company or group must carry on one or more qualifying trades wholly or mainly in the UK, on a commercial basis and with a view to profit, although this rule is proposed to be relaxed so that a company is only required to have a permanent establishment in the UK. Qualifying trades exclude:

dealing in land, commodities, futures, shares, securities or other financial instruments;

dealing in goods other than in an ordinary trade of wholesale or retail distribution;

banking, insurance, money-lending, debt-factoring, hire-purchase financing or other financial activities;

leasing or receiving royalties or licence fees (with certain exclusions);

legal and accountancy services;

property development;

farming or market gardening, woodlands, forestry activities and timber production;

hotels, nursing homes or residential care homes; and

shipbuilding, producing coal, or producing steel (in relation to options granted on or after 21 July 2008).

Eligible employees

[**11.15**] The employee must be employed by either the company whose shares are the subject of the option or that company's qualifying subsidiary. He must be required to work, on average, at least 25 hours a week or, if less, 75% of his working time (which includes time spent in both employment and self-employment). He and his associates must not have a 'material interest' in the company. A material interest is defined, broadly, as owning or controlling more than 30% of the ordinary share capital or, where the company is a close company, rights to more than 30% of the assets in a winding-up.

Qualifying options

[**11.16**] Various other requirements must be met in relation to the option itself. The principal additional requirements are:

(i)   The option must be granted for commercial reasons to recruit or retain an employee and not for tax avoidance purposes.

(ii)   An employee may not hold unexercised options (including any CSOP options — see **11.14**) in respect of shares with a total value of more than £120,000 (from 6 April 2008) at the time the options were granted. Any excess share options are not qualifying options. In addition, if an employee has been granted *EMI* options with a total value of £120,000 (from 6 April 2008), then whether or not the options have been exercised or released, any further options granted within three years after the date of the grant of the last qualifying EMI option are not qualifying options.

(iii)   The total value of shares in respect of which there are unexercised qualifying EMI options must not exceed £3 million.

(iv)   The shares that may be acquired under the option must be fully paid, irredeemable ordinary shares, and the option must be capable of being exercised within ten years from the date it is granted and must be non-transferable.

The company must give notice of the option to HMRC within 92 days after it is granted, together with such supporting information as HMRC require and also a declaration from the relevant employee that he meets the 'working time' requirement (see **11.15**). HMRC provide form EMI1 for this purpose and have the right to correct obvious errors in the notice within nine months, and to enquire into an option within 12 months after the 92 day period. The enquiry may be made to the company or, in relation to whether the 'working time' requirement is met, to the relevant employee. If at the conclusion of an enquiry, HMRC decide that the qualifying option requirements have not been met, the company and the relevant employee have the right to appeal against the decision.

Income tax and NICs

[11.17] There is no charge to tax or NICs when the option is granted. Providing the option is exercised within ten years after it was granted, there is also not normally a tax charge when it is exercised except to the extent that the market value when the option was granted (or when it was exercised if lower) exceeds the amount paid for the shares. There are, however, detailed provisions about disqualifying events. Where tax is charged on the exercise of the option, Class 1 NICs would be payable if the shares were readily convertible assets (see **11.3**). The anti-avoidance rules at **11.6** apply to shares acquired under qualifying options as they do to shares acquired under unapproved schemes.

Capital gains tax

[11.18] The excess of any sale proceeds for the shares over the sum of the amount paid for them plus, in certain circumstances, any amount charged to income tax (see **11.17**) is charged to CGT. However, HMRC have changed their view in relation to shares acquired on the exercise of an option before 10 April 2003. In computing the capital gain or loss no deduction should be made of any amount chargeable to income tax on the exercise of the option. See HMRC Briefs 30/2009 and 60/2009 for full details. See **11.31** for the special CGT rules for identifying share disposals with acquisitions.

Share incentive plans (ss 488–515, Sch 2; ITTOIA 2005, ss 392–396, 405–408, 770; TCGA 1992, Sch 7D; FA 2010, s 42)

[11.19] Companies may set up a share incentive plan or SIP (previously referred to as an all-employee share ownership plan), under which employees may allocate part of their salary to acquire shares in their employer company (known as partnership shares) without paying tax or NICs, nor will employers' NICs be payable. Employers may also award free shares to employees, including extra free shares (matching shares) for employees who have partnership shares.

SIPs are operated through a trust and the trustees hold the shares for the employees until they are taken out of the plan or sold. A parent company may have a group SIP for itself and its subsidiaries. The legislation is lengthy and complex, and what follows is only an outline. HMRC guidance for employers and advisers is provided at www.hmrc.gov.uk/shareschemes/sip_employers.htm.

General rules

[11.20] HMRC approval is required for the SIP and provision is made for approval to be withdrawn if a 'disqualifying event' occurs, such as the SIP being operated in a way that does not comply with the legislation. The company may appeal within 30 days against the refusal of HMRC approval or the withdrawal of approval.

The SIP must be available to all eligible employees and must not contain features which would discourage eligible employees from participating. Employees must be entitled to participate on the same terms (but taking into account remuneration, length of service and hours worked), and the SIP must not have features likely to have the effect of conferring benefits wholly or mainly on directors and employees on higher levels of remuneration. The SIP must not contain arrangements for loans to any of the employees. Shares must be withdrawn from a SIP when an employee leaves the employment. The SIP may provide for employees to lose their free or matching shares if they leave within three years, and for employees who leave to be required to sell their shares.

Eligible employees

[11.21] Eligible employees must be employees of the company or a group company and, if so provided by the SIP, must have been an employee throughout a qualifying period of (broadly) not more than 18 months. An employee within a group satisfies the qualifying period conditions even though he has worked for more than one group company during the period. An individual cannot participate if he has a material interest (or has had one at any time in the previous 12 months) in either a close company whose shares may be awarded under the SIP or a company controlling that close company. A material interest is defined, broadly, as owning or controlling (alone or together with certain associates) more than 25% of the ordinary share capital or rights to more than 25% of the assets in a winding up. An employee cannot participate *simultaneously* in two or more awards of shares under different SIPs established by the same company or a connected company. *Successive* participation in two or more awards in the same tax year is permitted but the limits on free shares, partnership shares and reinvested dividends (see **11.23**, **11.24** and **11.26**) apply as if all such SIPs were a single SIP.

Eligible shares

[11.22] There are detailed requirements for shares to be eligible shares, the main points being that the shares must be in a quoted company (or its subsidiary) or an unquoted company not controlled by another company, and the SIP shares must be fully paid, non-redeemable ordinary shares. They may, however, be non-voting shares. Shares in a 'service company', i.e. one whose main business is the provision of its employees' services to a person or persons having control of the company, or to an associated company, are prohibited.

Free shares

[11.23] The company can award free shares in any tax year valued at up to £3,000 per employee at the time of the award. SIPs may provide for the awards to be linked to performance, statutory rules being laid down for such performance allowances. Details of the relevant performance targets must be provided to employees. Free shares must normally be kept in the SIP for a stipulated period, which may not be less than three years nor more than five years.

Partnership shares

[11.24] Employees may authorise employers to deduct part of their salary to acquire partnership shares, such deductions reducing the pay for tax and NIC (but not pension) purposes. The maximum permitted deduction is £1,500 in any tax year, or 10% of salary if less. The minimum stipulated deduction on any occasion cannot exceed £10. Earnings of a kind specified in the SIP, e.g. bonuses or overtime payments, may be excluded from 'salary' in applying the 10% rule. The amount deducted will be held by the SIP trustees until used to acquire partnership shares. The SIP may stipulate a maximum number of partnership shares that may be purchased. Employees may stop and restart deductions to the SIP on giving written notice to the company, or may give notice to withdraw from the SIP, in which case any money held will be refunded. Any money refunded will be liable to tax and NICs. Partnership shares may be withdrawn from the SIP at any time (but see **11.27** for the tax position).

Matching shares

[11.25] A SIP may provide for employees who acquire partnership shares to be awarded matching shares at the same time, on the basis of not more than two matching shares for one partnership share. The same holding period requirements apply as for other free shares.

Reinvestment of cash dividends and rights shares

[11.26] SIPs may either provide that dividends on SIP shares be reinvested in further SIP shares or that they be paid over to employees. The total value of reinvested dividends cannot exceed £1,500 per employee in any tax year. Reinvested dividends are free of income tax (but do not carry a tax credit) providing that the shares acquired are held in the SIP for three years.

Trustees must normally act on an employee's instructions in relation to rights issues. This may include selling some of the rights shares in order to raise funds to acquire the remainder. No CGT is payable on the proceeds of such rights sales. Rights shares acquired in this way are treated as having been acquired when the SIP shares were acquired. If rights shares are acquired using funds other than from such rights sales, they are not SIP shares.

Income tax and capital gains tax

[11.27] There is no charge to income tax or NICs at the time when SIP shares (including dividend shares) are awarded, nor will there be a charge on any free, partnership or matching shares held in a SIP for five years. If such shares are held for between three and five years, income tax (and Class 1 NICs if the shares are readily convertible assets — see **11.3**) will be charged on the initial value of the shares, or their value at the time of withdrawal if lower. If the tax charge is based on the initial value of the shares, it will be reduced by any tax charged on capital receipts (see below). Where the shares are held for less than three years, tax (and Class 1 NICs if the shares are readily convertible assets) will be payable on their value at the time when they cease to be held in the SIP. Where the shares are readily convertible assets, the tax and NICs will be collected from employers under PAYE. The employee's PAYE amount must be paid over to the employer either by the employee or the trustees (who are empowered to dispose of an employee's SIP shares for this purpose). Tax payable in respect of shares that are not readily convertible assets will be payable through the self-assessment system (see **11.34**).

If dividend shares are held in a SIP for less than three years, an amount equal to the reinvested dividends is chargeable to tax and is deemed to carry a tax credit at the rate in force at the time of withdrawal. Any dividend upper rate or dividend additional rate tax is reduced by the tax on any capital receipts (see below).

The charges on SIP shares do not apply if the employee leaves through injury, disability, redundancy, or retirement (at a specified age not less than 50), nor on the employee's death.

PAYE tax and Class 1 NICs will be charged on capital receipts (sale of rights etc.) re SIP shares acquired fewer than five years earlier (three years for dividend shares). This does not apply where the trustees sell some rights shares to raise funds to buy the remainder (see **11.26**).

If shares are kept in a SIP until they are sold, employees will not be liable to CGT. If employees take them out of the SIP and sell later, there will be a chargeable gain equal to the increase in value after the shares were withdrawn from the SIP.

Shares withdrawn from a SIP may be transferred free of CGT into an Individual Savings Account or ISA (see **36.28**) within 90 days from the date they cease to be SIP shares.

Capital gains tax roll-over relief (TCGA 1992, s 236A, Sch 7C)

[11.28] A special roll-over relief is available in relation to unquoted companies, which is particularly relevant where family members and family trusts wish to transfer shares to employees. The relief applies where existing shareholders (other than companies) transfer ownership of shares they hold in the company to an approved SIP that holds (either immediately or within twelve months after the transfer) 10% of the company's shares. Gains arising on the shares transferred may be treated as reducing the acquisition cost of replacement chargeable assets acquired within six months after the disposal (unless the replacement assets are shares on which enterprise investment scheme income tax relief is given (see **29.17**) and subject to some special provisions relating to dwelling houses).

Shares held in existing qualifying employee share ownership trusts

[11.29] Shares could be transferred into a SIP from a qualifying share ownership trust or QUEST without the trust or company suffering a tax charge. Such shares must be used as either free or matching shares under the plan rules. Corporation tax deductions for QUESTs no longer apply and notes on the qualifying conditions for such trusts are in earlier editions of this book.

Corporation tax (CTA 2009, ss 983–998; FA 2010, s 42)

[11.30] In computing its taxable profits, the company is entitled to deduct the costs of setting up and running the SIP. It is also entitled to deduct the market value of free or matching shares at the time they are acquired by the trustees, and the excess of the market value of partnership shares on acquisition by the trustees over the employees' contributions, such deductions being made in the accounting period in which the shares are awarded. Subject to the deduction for running expenses, no deduction is allowed for any expenses in providing dividend shares.

An earlier corporation tax deduction for the provision of SIP shares may be claimed where the company makes a contribution to the SIP trustees to enable them to acquire the company's shares, providing that the shares are not acquired from a company, and that at the end of twelve months from the date of purchasing shares with the money contributed, the trustees hold at least 10% of the company's total ordinary share capital. Where that condition is satisfied, the deduction is given in the accounting period in which the twelve-month anniversary falls, and no deduction is then given when the shares are awarded to employees. There are further detailed conditions, including a requirement for at least 30% of the shares acquired with the contribution to be transferred to employees within five years, and all the shares to be transferred within ten years.

FA 2010 introduced anti-avoidance provisions to prevent a corporation tax deduction if one of the main purposes of the company making the payment is to obtain the deduction.

Capital gains tax treatment of shares (TCGA 1992, Sch 7D para 4)

[11.31] Where a shareholder makes several acquisitions of shares of the same class in a company, special rules apply to a disposal on or after 6 April 2008 to identify which shares were disposed of (see CHAPTER 38). The shares are pooled together and shares disposed of are matched with the shares comprised in the pool — subject to prior rules for shares bought and sold on the same day or within the following thirty days. SIP shares are treated as being of a separate class while they are retained by the trustees. This means that any disposals of shares owned by the employee outside the SIP are not matched with SIP shares.

Corporation tax relief for cost of shares provided (CTA 2009, Pt 12)

[11.32] A corporation tax deduction is given for the cost of providing shares for employee share schemes where the employees are taxable in respect of the shares they acquire or would be taxable if the scheme were not an approved scheme. The deduction is normally based on the market value of the shares, at the time they are awarded or the share option is exercised (whichever is applicable), less any contribution made by the employee towards them. (Payment by the employee of the company's secondary NICs is not taken into account — see **11.3**.) The deductions allowed for shares provided under share incentive plans (see **11.30**) take priority over this relief. This relief relates only to the cost of providing shares; it does not displace reliefs for costs of setting up or administering schemes. The shares themselves must be fully-paid, non-redeemable, ordinary shares in a quoted company, a subsidiary of a quoted company or an unquoted company not under the control of another company.

The relief is generally given for the accounting period in which the employee acquires the shares, subject to special rules for restricted shares and convertible shares.

Employee share plans will often relate to a group of companies. HMRC provide guidance relating to the transfer pricing issues (including those relating to UK–UK transactions) that may arise on such group plans. The guidance, updated in December 2005, is available via www.hmrc.gov.uk/international/transfer-pricing.htm.

Priority share allocations for employees (ss 542–548)

[11.33] When shares are offered to the public, a priority allocation is often made to employees and directors. Where there is no price advantage, the general rule is that right to shares in priority to other persons is not a taxable benefit, so long as the shares that may be allocated do not exceed 10% of those being offered, all directors and employees entitled to an allocation are entitled on similar terms (albeit at different levels), and those entitled are not restricted wholly or mainly to persons who are directors or whose remuneration exceeds a particular level. This treatment still applies where the offer to employees is strictly not part of the public offer, as a result of the employees' offer being restricted to shares in one or more companies and the public offer being a package of shares in a wider range of companies.

Where employees get shares at a discount compared with the price paid by the public, the discount is chargeable to income tax. The employee's base cost for CGT is the amount paid plus the amount of the discount.

Self-assessment — employees' responsibilities

[11.34] Employees who do not get tax returns must notify HMRC by 5 October after the end of the year if they have income or gains that have not been fully taxed (see **9.27**).

HMRC provide detailed guidance, in the additional information notes to the self assessment tax return, as to which items should be returned in respect of shares and options. These include amounts arising from both approved and unapproved schemes, and amounts that may have been taxed under PAYE.

Employers tick a box on forms P11D if there are taxable benefits relating to shares, but do not give details of taxable amounts, so the employee needs to obtain the relevant information himself. Since employers are required to report details to HMRC (see **11.2**), they should be able to provide the appropriate figures.

Tax points

[11.35] Note the following:

- There is no clearance procedure under any of the anti-avoidance rules at **11.6**. To the extent that charges to tax, and possibly NICs, arise under these rules other than on an acquisition or disposal, employment-related shares and securities are particularly vulnerable to uncertainty.
- In the case of unquoted companies, the value of shares has to be agreed when appropriate with HMRC's valuation division.
- Group employees may participate in schemes through their parent company.
- If an employee acquires shares under an approved share option scheme and immediately disposes of them, the gain will be subject to CGT (unless covered by reliefs or exemptions). Gains on shares acquired under SAYE-linked options (and also gains on approved share incentive plan shares) can be sheltered to the extent that shares valued at up to the annual limit are transferred into an ISA (see **36.28**).
- Employers face penalties if they fail to provide to HMRC the returns and information required under the provisions outlined in this chapter.

- An approved SAYE share option scheme or share incentive plan cannot apply to a subsidiary company unless the parent is a non-close company listed on the Stock Exchange. For a company share option plan the subsidiary cannot be an unlisted company under the control of a listed company (see **11.12**).

- Unquoted companies may see disadvantages to approved share incentive plans, because they cannot choose which employees may participate, there may not be a ready market for the shares if the employee wants to sell, an immediate market valuation is not available and the effect on existing shareholders must be considered. A condition can, however, be imposed that employees must sell their shares when the employment ends.

- Where an employee has a tax liability in connection with share schemes, he should make sure he includes the appropriate entries on his tax return (see **11.34**).

12

Directors of small and family companies

Directors and shareholders

[12.1] In family companies, directors and shareholders are usually the same people, and they can benefit from the company in various ways, e.g. the payment of remuneration, the provision of benefits or the distribution of profits through dividends.

The freedom to use company profits in the most tax-efficient manner has been challenged by HMRC in some circumstances under the 'settlements' legislation (see **12.10**). Special rules now apply to personal service companies and managed service companies (see **19.6** and **19.15**), and the material in this chapter is not relevant for such companies that are caught by those rules.

When considering to what extent, and in what form, to withdraw profits, the treatment for tax and national insurance contributions (NICs) is an important factor (and companies need to be aware of the comparative tax and NIC cost of paying remuneration and dividends at different profit levels). There are other considerations, in particular the effect on pensions. Remuneration and benefits are earned income in the hands of the shareholder, whereas dividends are unearned income. Only earned income is taken into account in calculating the maximum tax relievable contributions to a registered pension scheme.

Therefore, taking a low salary means that tax-efficient pension contributions are correspondingly restricted (although it is possible to contribute up to £3,600 a year to a personal pension scheme regardless of earnings level). See CHAPTERS **16** and **17**.

The national minimum wage (NMW) also needs to be taken into account. Family members who are employees of the company must be paid, from October 2010, at least £5.93 per hour for those aged 21 and over, £4.92 for those aged between 18 and 20, and £3.64 for 16 and 17-year-olds. The previous rates, in force from October 2009, were £5.80, £4.83 and £3.57 respectively (with the qualifying age for the higher rate being 22 years and over, as opposed to 21 years). HMRC guidance indicates that an exemption for work done by certain family members does not apply to a business carried on by a company.

HMRC enforce the NMW on behalf of the Department for Business, Innovation and Skills (BIS). The former Inland Revenue provided detailed guidance on the NMW and directors in Tax Bulletin 50 (December 2000), in the form of an article prepared by the Tax Faculty of the Institute of Chartered Accountants in England and Wales. The text was agreed before publication by the former Inland Revenue and the Department of Trade and Industry.

That guidance indicated that a director who does not have an 'explicit' employment contract is highly unlikely to be subject to the NMW legislation. Where such a contract (which need not be in writing) exists, however, the legislation is likely to apply — even if the company is making losses — on the basis that a worker/employer relationship has been created. HMRC indicated that where there is no express employment contract it is not normally necessary to pay the NMW to directors of new businesses; loss-making family companies; group companies; dormant companies; trade associations; companies where the director works out of a sense of public duty rather than for payment; or flat management companies.

In all cases it should be remembered that dividend income from shares jointly owned by spouses/civil partners is split according to the actual ownership (see **33.6**).

Taking profits as pay

[12.2] For 2010/11, profit taken as pay costs the company 12.8% Class 1 NICs on pay in excess of £110 a week, but the contributions are deducted in arriving at taxable profits for corporation tax purposes. Class 1 or Class 1A NICs are also payable on virtually all taxable benefits in kind (see **CHAPTER 10**). Employees do not have to pay NICs on the first £110 a week, but those earning £97 or more have their rights to state benefits protected. From 6 April 2010, the rate of employees' contributions on earnings between £110 and £844 per week is 11% and employees must also pay contributions at 1% on all earnings above £844 a week.

The additional cost of the employer's 12.8% NICs on pay above £110 per week for the year to 31 March 2011, after deducting tax relief at the various rates of corporation tax (see **3.12– 3.14**), is as follows.

Company's tax rate	Net cost of NI
21% (on profits up to £300,000)	10.11%
29.75% (marginal small profits rate on profits between £300,000 and £1,500,000)	8.99%

28%   (on profits of £1,500,000 and over)   9.22%

Taking profits as dividends

[12.3] When profits are taken as dividends, the dividends are not deducted in calculating taxable profits, but the company's tax is effectively offset to the extent of the tax credits passed on to the shareholders. Tax credits are $^1/_9$ of the cash dividend, representing a tax rate of 10% on the gross (i.e. tax-credit inclusive) amount. Basic rate taxpayers have no further tax to pay. Higher rate taxpayers with taxable income below £150,000 have to pay a further 22.5% of the gross amount. Higher rate taxpayers with taxable income above £150,000 have to pay a further 32.5% of the gross amount (see **2.5** and **2.11**). Non-taxpayers, on the other hand, cannot claim a refund of the tax credits.

Comparative tax rates for pay and dividends

[12.4] For 2010/11, the effective tax rate on a given amount of profits paid as salary or dividend to a higher rate director/shareholder is as follows.

Liable to tax at 40% and already paying maximum NICs at the 11% rate

(a) Salary payment (not affected by company's tax rate, since taxable profits are reduced by the payment)

	£	£
Available profit		100.00
Employer's NI on salary (12.8% of 88.65)		11.35
Gross salary		88.65
Tax @ 40%	35.46	
Employee's NI @ 1%	0.88	36.34
Net income		52.31
Effective tax rate		47.69%

(b) Dividend payment

Company's tax rate	21%	29.75%	28%
Available profit	100.00	100.00	100.00
Corporation tax	21.00	29.75	28.00
Cash dividend	79.00	70.25	72.00
Tax credit $^1/_9$	8.78	7.81	8.00
Shareholder's gross income	87.78	78.06	80.00
Tax @ 32.5%	28.53	25.37	26.00
Net income	59.25	52.69	54.00
Effective tax rate	40.75%	47.31%	46.00

Liable to tax at 50% and already paying maximum NICs at the 11% rate

(a) Salary payment (not affected by company's tax rate, since taxable profits are reduced by the payment)

	£	£
Available profit		100.00
Employer's NI on salary (12.8% of 88.65)		11.35
Gross salary		88.65
Tax @ 50%	44.33	
Employee's NI @ 1%	0.88	45.21
Net income		43.44
Effective tax rate		56.56%

(b) Dividend payment

Company's tax rate	21%	29.75%	28%
Available profit	100.00	100.00	100.00
Corporation tax	21.00	29.75	28.00
Cash dividend	79.00	70.25	72.00
Tax credit $^1/_9$	8.78	7.81	8.00
Shareholder's gross income	87.78	78.06	80.00
Tax @ 42.5%	37.31	33.18	34.00
Net income	50.47	44.88	46.00
Effective tax rate	49.53%	55.12%	54.00%

Dividends for such director/shareholders are therefore more tax-effective than salary where the company pays corporation tax at the small profits rate, and marginally more tax-effective for companies paying at the full rate or the small profits marginal rate. Where the dividend straddles different tax rate bands, detailed calculations need to be done to decide the most tax-effective position.

The position is different for director/shareholders taxable at less than 40%. For 2010/11 employees' NICs are payable at 11% on weekly earnings between £110 and £844 and at 1% on additional earnings. For those whose income does not exceed £844 (a week), taking dividends rather than pay can give a substantial NIC saving.

Example 1

Company paying tax at the small profits rate uses profits of £25,000 in the year to 31 March 2011 to make a payment to a director/shareholder who has no other income. Director does not have an explicit contract of employment (see **12.1**). His personal allowance for 2010/11 is £6,475.

If profit is taken as	salary only £	salary and dividend £
Company's tax position on the payment is:		
Profits	25,000	25,000
Salary	(22,812)	(6,475)
Employer's NICs	(2,188)	(97)
Taxable profits	—	18,428
Corporation tax at 21%		(3,870)
Cash dividend		14,558
Tax credit $1/_9$		1,617
Director's dividend income		16,175
Director's tax position:		
Salary	22,812	6,475
Dividend, including tax credit	—	16,175
	22,812	22,650
Personal allowance	(6,475)	(6,475)
Taxable income	16,337	16,175
Tax payable (£16,337 @ 20%)	3,267	
(dividends £16,175 @ 10%)		1,617
Tax credit on dividend		(1,617)
Tax payable		—
Disposable income:		
Salary	22,812	6,475
Employee's NICs	(1,881)	(84)
Dividend	—	14,558
Tax	(3,267)	—
	17,664	20,949
Saving through paying dividend		£3,285

The saving through paying the dividend is made up as follows:

Extra income available as dividend through saving in employer's NICs		2,091
Less 21% corporation tax (i.e reduced tax relief for employer's NICs)	439	1,652
On the balance of taxable profits, i.e. 18,428 − 2,091 = 16,337:		
Company pays corporation tax 16,337 @ 21%		3,431

Director saves income tax 16,337 @ 20%	3,267	(164)
Reduction in employee's NICs		1,797
		£3,285

The salary in the second alternative has been fixed at the personal allowance of £6,475. Fixing the salary at the Class 1 NIC earnings threshold of £5,715 would remove the liability to employers' and employees' NICs (even though rights to social security benefits would be protected because the salary was in excess of the lower earnings limit of £97 a week, see **13.2**). However, some personal allowances would be wasted.

Retention of profits within the company or payment as remuneration or dividends

[12.5] Retaining profits within the company will increase the net assets and hence the value of the shares if a subsequent sale is based wholly or partly on the underlying assets. Having already suffered corporation tax, the retained profits will thus swell the value of the shares and the potential gain chargeable to capital gains tax (CGT).

Paying remuneration or dividends may, therefore, ultimately reduce the shareholders' chargeable gains, but this must be weighed against the immediate tax cost of drawing profits, the 18% flat rate of CGT (or 28% depending upon the individual's tax circumstances, see **4.2**) and the availability of entrepreneurs' relief and other CGT reliefs (see **4.22**). Reducing taxable profit by means of a permissible contribution to a pension fund from which the director will benefit will sometimes be an attractive alternative (see **12.8**).

Effect on earlier years (CTA 2010, ss 37–44; FA 2009, s 23, Sch 6)

[12.6] A decision on whether to pay remuneration or leave profits to be charged to corporation tax should not be taken by reference to the current year in isolation. The payment of remuneration may convert a trading profit into a trading loss, which, after being set against any non-trading profits of the current year, may be carried back against the profits of the previous year, both from the trade and from other sources. See CHAPTER 26 for details including a temporary extension to this provision for trading losses incurred in accounting periods ending after 23 November 2008 and before 24 November 2010.

Looking into the future

[12.7] If all current-year profits are used to pay remuneration, there will be nothing against which to carry back any future trading losses. Expected future performance, including any imminent capital expenditure which will attract capital allowances, should therefore be taken into account in considering whether to take steps to reduce or eliminate taxable profits for the current year.

Pensions

[12.8] The pensions regime, implemented in April 2006, applies to both occupational and personal schemes. It provides a single tax relief regime for pension savings. Tax relief is available on contributions when they are put into a scheme, although from 6 April 2011 tax relief on such contributions will be restricted to relief at the basic rate for individuals whose income is £150,000 or more. 'Anti-forestalling' rules are designed to prevent people potentially affected from forestalling this change by increasing their pension savings in excess of their normal regular pattern (see **16.13** and **17.18**).

The company may have its own pension scheme, either through an insurance company or self-administered. Provided that the possible benefits under the scheme are within the parameters laid down by the legislation, the company's contributions are not taxable on the director. The contributions will be allowed in calculating the taxable profit providing they are *wholly and exclusively for the purposes of the trade*. In deciding whether this rule is breached in small and family companies, HMRC consider the overall remuneration package of directors and family members. HMRC guidance is available in the Business Income Manual at BIM 46001.

A director may pay premiums himself under a personal pension plan but employees' pension contributions do not reduce earnings for employers' and employees' NICs. The company could itself contribute to the director's pension plan within the available limits, and neither tax nor NICs would be payable on the amount contributed by the company. Again this is subject to the caveat that the company's contributions must satisfy the 'wholly and exclusively' rule.

Since the income and gains of both company and personal pension funds are usually exempt from tax (but the tax credits on dividend income cannot be reclaimed), paying permissible pension contributions rather than taking salary and investing it privately will normally be a more tax-efficient method of saving for the future, although of course the pension benefits available will depend on the performance of the pension investments and on the changing legislation, with the pension funds themselves often being unavailable for many years to come. For the detailed provisions on pensions, see CHAPTERS 16 and 17.

Limits on allowable remuneration and waiver of remuneration (IHTA 1984, s 14)

[12.9] Remuneration, like any other trading expense, must be incurred wholly and exclusively for the purposes of the trade (see CHAPTER 20). If it is regarded as excessive in relation to the duties, part may not be allowed as a deduction in calculating company profits. This should be borne in mind when considering payments of remuneration, either by way of cash or as benefits in kind, to members of a director's or shareholder's family. On the other hand, the national minimum wage legislation may prevent wages being paid at too low a level (see **12.1**).

Employing a spouse or civil partner and children in the family company may be useful, particularly if they are not otherwise using their personal allowance, but the work done must be of sufficient quantity and quality to justify the amount paid. If children are under 16 the regulations as to permitted hours of work must also be complied with, which vary according to local bye-laws. Payments by a farmer to his very young children have been held to be 'pocket money' and disallowed in calculating the taxable profits of the farm.

A higher rate taxpayer might consider (subject to the minimum wage legislation) waiving entitlement to remuneration to assist, for example, in a difficult period of trading. See **12.10**, however, regarding the possible application of the settlements rules and the possibility of legislation being enacted to counter 'income shifting'. No inheritance tax liability arises from such a waiver providing certain conditions are met. The waiver might enable the company to pay higher remuneration to other directors or family members (provided always that it is justifiable under the 'wholly and exclusively' rule) or to increase its profits available for dividends. Dividends cannot, however, be used to generate tax refunds for non-taxpayers because the tax credit attached to a dividend is not repayable.

'Income shifting' and the settlements rules (ITTOIA 2005, ss 624–627)

[12.10] The rules relating to 'settlements' prevent someone gaining a tax advantage by arranging to divert his/her income to family or friends taxable at a lower or nil rate. An outright gift of income-producing property (such as shares in the case of a family company) is outside these provisions unless, for example, (a) the gift does not carry a right to the whole of the income, or (b) the property given is wholly or substantially a right to income.

HMRC increased their use of these rules in recent years to attack some tax planning arrangements in family companies and partnerships. They gave detailed guidance and illustrations setting out their interpretation of the rules, including how they affect family companies. The illustrations included a main earner drawing a low salary from a family company so that there were higher profits out of which to pay dividends to family or friends. Many professional advisers disagreed with HMRC's detailed guidance. In July 2007 the House of

Lords decided the long-running 'Arctic Systems' case in favour of the taxpayers, on the basis that, while there was a settlement, an exemption for outright gifts between spouses applied.

The Government announced immediately after the House of Lords decision its intention to make changes to the legislation in order to counter 'income shifting'. It intended to introduce new rules with effect from 2008/09 but decided to defer implementation to provide more time for consultation in the light of criticism of its proposals. It announced in the 2008 pre-budget report that given the current 'economic challenges' it was deferring action on income shifting and would not bring forward legislation at Finance Bill 2009. The Government would instead keep the issue under review. However, it reiterated that it firmly believes that 'it is unfair to allow a minority of individuals to benefit financially from shifting part of their income to someone else who is subject to a lower rate of tax'.

It is essential to look very carefully at any arrangements that are being considered, or are already in existence, and to take appropriate professional advice which should take account of HMRC's views as set out in their Trusts, Settlements and Estates Manual at TSEM 4000.

Employee benefits provided by the company

[12.11] P11D employees, i.e. directors and employees with earnings of £8,500 or more per annum, are charged to tax on the cash equivalent of benefits provided either for them or for their family or household. Directors are caught by these provisions even if they earn less than £8,500, unless they own no more than 5% of the ordinary share capital (including shares owned by close family and certain other people) and either work full-time or work for a charitable or non-profit-making body.

NICs are also payable on virtually all taxable benefits, either Class 1 contributions payable by both employer and employee or Class 1A contributions by the employer only depending on the benefit. In most cases, therefore, it will usually be equally tax/NICs efficient, and far more straightforward, to provide cash pay rather than benefits. See **CHAPTER 10** for details.

If benefits are to be provided, care must be taken to distinguish benefits provided by the company in the form of payments made on behalf of the director/employee for which the director/employee is legally responsible. Such payments are treated as pay for *all* employees (see **10.7**), for both tax and NICs.

Gifts of company assets (CTA 2010, s 1064; IHTA 1984, s 94)

[12.12] Gifts of company assets to directors and employees are covered by the benefits rules mentioned above and explained in detail in CHAPTER 10. If a close company (see **3.26**) gives an asset to a shareholder who is not a director or employee, the cost is treated as a dividend and the total of the cost of the asset and the related tax credit is included in the shareholder's taxable income.

If a close company makes a transfer of value for inheritance tax purposes (see CHAPTER 5) that value may be apportioned among the 'participators' (as defined, to include shareholder and others) according to their interests in the company and treated as a transfer made by them for inheritance tax purposes. There is no apportionment, however, of any amount that is treated as the participator's income.

Loans from the company (TMA 1970, s 109; CTA 2010, ss 455–459; ICTA 1988, s 826(4); ITEPA 2003, ss 173–191, 223; ITTOIA 2005, ss 415–421)

[12.13] P11D employees who overdraw their current accounts with the company or who receive specific loans from the company, either interest-free or at a beneficial rate, are treated as having received remuneration equivalent to interest at the 'official rate' (see **10.38**) on the amount overdrawn or lent, less any amount paid to the company towards the benefit they have received. This does not apply if the whole of the interest on the loans qualifies for tax relief, nor if the total non-qualifying loans outstanding in a tax year do not exceed £5,000. The loans provisions apply to loans made to a spouse, civil partner or relatives of the director or employee, as well as to the director/employee himself. Where a director or employee receives an advance for expenses necessarily incurred in performing his duties, or for incidental overnight expenses (see **10.15**), the advance is not treated as a loan provided that:

(a) the maximum amount advanced at any one time does not exceed £1,000,
(b) the advances are spent within six months, and
(c) the director or employee accounts to the company at regular intervals for the expenditure.

Tax effect on company

[12.14] As well as the tax charge on the director or employee on interest-free or cheap loans, there are tax implications for the company if it is a close company in which the director or employee is a 'participator' or associate of a participator (see **3.26**), and these provisions do not depend on whether any interest is charged. 'Participators' are not confined to shareholders but the rest of this chapter refers to shareholders only. Loans and advances to shareholders give rise to a tax liability on the company, unless the loan is made in the ordinary course of the company's trade, or the loan does not exceed £15,000 and is made to a full-time working director or employee who does not own more than 5% of the ordinary share capital. Where a loan does not fall within the above exceptions, the company has to notify HMRC not later than 12 months after the end of the accounting period in which the loan is made, and must pay tax at 25% on the amount of the loan or overdrawn account balance.

The due date for payment of the tax is nine months after the end of the accounting period in which the loan is made (i.e. the same as the due date for the corporation tax of that period). (For companies required to pay tax by instalments under corporation tax self-assessment (see **3.22**) the tax on such a loan is to be taken into account in the instalment payments.) Under corporation tax self-assessment, companies show the tax on loans as part of the total tax due, but may claim an offsetting deduction if the loan has been repaid or if it has been released or written off. Where the loan is repaid after the tax falls due and has been paid by the company, the tax paid may be reclaimed. The tax repayment is due nine months after the end of the accounting period in which the loan is repaid, and will be increased by interest from that nine months date if relevant.

Example 2

A close company with an accounting year end of 31 December makes an interest-free loan of £20,000 to a director/shareholder on 10 January 2009. The company is not liable to pay its corporation tax by instalments. The director repays the loan on:

(a)   10 September 2010

Since this is before 1 October 2010, when the company is due to pay its corporation tax for the year to 31 December 2009, the company will not have to pay tax at 25% of the loan, as the tax due is off set by the tax repayable.

(b)   10 October 2010

Since the loan has not been repaid by 1 October 2010 the company must pay tax on that date at 25%, i.e. £5,000, and cannot claim repayment of the tax until 30 September 2011.

The director/shareholder will in any event be taxed under the benefits rules on interest on the loan at the official rate from 10 January 2009 to the repayment date.

The Companies Act 2006 changed the law on loans to directors with effect from October 2007. Such loans are permitted with shareholder consent.

Loans written off or released

[12.15] If a loan or overdrawing is written off or released by the company, the tax treatment is different for loans made to shareholders by close companies and for other loans.

If a loan by a close company to a shareholder is written off, the amount written off is not an allowable expense in calculating corporation tax, although the company can recover the 25% tax it paid when the loan was made (see **12.14**). Loans written off by non-close companies are allowable in calculating corporation tax under the 'loan relationships' rules (see **26.5**), except for loans between companies where one controls the other or both are under common control.

The write-off of loans does not affect the shareholder unless he is a higher rate taxpayer. Higher rate taxpayers are taxed as if the amount written off was income net of the dividend ordinary rate of 10%. Tax is therefore chargeable at the excess of the dividend upper rate of 32.5% (or, where applicable, the dividend additional rate of 42.5% (see **2.5**)) over 10%. A loan of £10,000 will thus be regarded as income of £11,111, on which an extra 22.5% tax is payable, amounting to £2,500 (or, if the additional dividend rate applies an extra 32.5% tax will be payable, amounting to £3,611).

If the borrower is not a shareholder, but the loan was obtained by reason of his employment, whether or not it is at a rate of interest below the 'official rate', the borrower is treated as having received an equivalent amount of remuneration at the time of the write-off. For a P11D employee this applies even after he has left, but not if the loan is written off on death.

The NICs position on loans written off is unclear. HMRC's National Insurance Manual says that the write-off of a loan to an employee becomes earnings and is liable to Class 1 NICs. The manual makes no distinction for an employee who is also a shareholder, although the tax treatment is different, as indicated above.

Liabilities in connection with directors' remuneration

[12.16] Remuneration is regarded as paid not only when it forms part of the payroll but also when it is credited to the director's current account with the company, and the liability of the company to account for PAYE and NICs arises at that time. The credit to the current account should therefore be made net of employee's tax and NICs. Drawings from the account can be made without any further liability once PAYE and NIC have been accounted for to HMRC. If a company pays remuneration to a director and bears the PAYE itself, the amount that should have been borne by the director is treated as extra remuneration and charged to tax and NIC accordingly.

Where a director receives payments in advance or on account of future remuneration this has to be treated as pay for tax and NICs purposes at the time of the advance, unless the advances are covered by a credit balance on the director's loan account or are on account of expenses as indicated at **12.13**.

An advance payment of remuneration is not the same as a loan. The income tax treatment of loans is stated at **12.13**. NICs are not payable unless a director's account becomes overdrawn *and* the director's earnings are normally paid into that account (see **13.11**).

Directors' NICs cannot be reduced by paying remuneration at uneven rates and irregular intervals, because of the rules for calculating earnings limits. The detailed provisions are in **CHAPTER 13**.

If employers fail to deduct and account for PAYE and NICs when due, they may incur interest and/or penalties. Directors may also be personally liable to pay the tax on their remuneration if they knew of the failure to deduct or account for tax.

Tax points

[12.17] Note the following:

- Always look at the combined company/director/shareholder position in considering the most appropriate way of dealing with available profits, and consider past years and the following year as well as the current year.
- Make effective use of company or personal pension funds, which should grow faster than individual investments because of their available tax exemptions. Remember, in the case of company pension funds, that in calculating corporation tax, relief is only given in the accounting period when the contribution is paid to the pension scheme, so that it is not possible to reduce taxable profits of one year by making a payment in the next year and relating it back. It is therefore essential to anticipate the profit level if a pension contribution is to be used as a way of reducing corporation tax for a particular accounting period.
- When considering dividend payments, remember that they may affect the valuation of shareholdings.
- Dividend income on shares in family companies held jointly by spouses or civil partners in unequal proportions is split according to their actual ownership rather than being split equally.
- In considering the payment of a dividend instead of remuneration, remember to take into account the national minimum wage rules, which are enforced by HMRC. The legislation does not regard family companies as a special case, although directors who do not have an explicit employment contract are unlikely to be covered by the rules.
- The existing 'settlements' rules may prevent a person from gaining a tax advantage by diverting income to others whose income is taxable at a lower rate. Bear in mind also the possibility that specific rules may be introduced to counter 'income shifting' (see **12.10**).
- Tax or NICs is not charged on pension contributions paid by an employer to an approved company scheme or an approved personal pension scheme. Employee contributions either to a company or private scheme reduce income for income tax purposes, but not for employees' NICs.
- Director/shareholders taking a sizeable dividend from a company might consider taking advantage of the 100% initial allowance available for investment in a commercial building in an enterprise zone (see **22.52** to

22.56), subject of course to commercial considerations. To retain the tax allowance, however, they would have to leave the money invested for at least seven years.

- Remuneration is regarded as paid when it is credited to an account with the company in the name of a director. The fact that it is not drawn by him but left to his credit in the company (in other words, available for drawing) does not prevent the appropriate tax and NICs being payable at the time the remuneration is credited. The director's account should be credited only with the net amount after tax and NICs. If the gross amount is credited, whether or not it is drawn out, and the company fails to account to HMRC for the tax and NICs, the director may be personally liable for the failure under the PAYE regulations.

- Interest is charged on tax and NICs that remain unpaid 14 days after the end of the tax year (or 17 days for electronic payments), e.g. from 19 (or 22) April 2011 for 2010/11.

- If the company has failed to pay over the PAYE tax and NICs on pay within 14 days (or 17 days for electronic payments) after the end of the tax year, HMRC may look to the individual for payment plus interest if they were aware of the company's failure to comply with the PAYE regulations. Additionally, they may be held personally liable as a director for *any* unpaid NICs due from the company if the non-payment is due to their fraud or negligence.

- If, before a director is credited with additional remuneration, his current account with the company is overdrawn, HMRC will invariably contend that the date on which the additional remuneration can be regarded as credited is that on which the accounts are signed (or the date when a clear entitlement to the remuneration was established — for example a properly evidenced directors'/shareholders' meeting) rather than the end of the accounting year for which the additional remuneration was paid. This can significantly affect the tax charge on the director in respect of beneficial loan interest (see **10.38**) and can also affect the liability of the company to pay tax under the provisions for loans to directors (see **12.14**).

- If it is intended to pay additional remuneration to a director after the end of the accounting period, a board minute to that effect should be in place before the end of the accounting period. Otherwise HMRC may argue that the remuneration cannot be charged in calculating the taxable profit of the accounting period to which the remuneration relates. If the minute is precise as to the amount, it may also enable the credit to a director's loan account to be made at an earlier date than the date of adoption of the accounts for the period (see previous bullet point).

- Where HMRC discover that a director's private expenses have been paid by a company and not shown as benefits on form P11D, they will usually seek to treat the payments as loans to the director. Such payments, including any VAT, must be reimbursed to the company by the director or charged against money owed by the company to the director. They are neither allowable as an expense in calculating the company taxable profit nor assessable as income on the director.

- HMRC's National Insurance Contributions Office take the view that if payment of a director's personal bills by his company is not covered by a credit balance on the director's account, and his earnings are normally paid into that account, NICs are due on the amount paid (see **12.16**).
- Even though a director is taxable on his remuneration, the amount of the remuneration must be commensurate with the director's duties for it to be allowable in calculating the company's taxable profits.

13

National insurance contributions — employees and employers

Introduction

[13.1] A large part of the cost of the social security system is funded from national insurance contributions (NICs) based on the present day earnings of employed and self-employed workers. The main provisions are found in the Social Security Contributions and Benefits Act 1992 (SSCBA 1992) and statutory instruments. Great Britain excludes Northern Ireland, which has its own system of social security law, but arrangements provide effectively for a single system of social security in the UK so that, in general, references in this chapter to Great Britain may be read as references to the UK.

NICs for self-employed people are discussed in **CHAPTER 24**. See also **9.39** for interest, penalties and appeals relating to NICs.

The amount of NICs payable and the rules for collecting it depend upon which 'class' of contribution is payable (see **13.2**), and the contribution rates are shown in the Table of Rates and Allowances. HMRC's National Insurance Contributions Office (NICO), see www.hmrc.gov.uk/nic, deals with NICs but the Department for Work and Pensions is responsible for social security benefits. See **CHAPTER 10** for employment aspects of NICs and collection of contributions through the PAYE system.

Contributions

[13.2] Unless they are 'contracted out' (see **13.12** and **16.5**), employees and their employers pay Class 1 NICs towards the State Second Pension (S2P) system, which replaced the State Earnings Related Pension Scheme (SERPS) in

2002. The contributions are based on a percentage of earnings. Payments made by employees are 'primary' contributions and employer contributions are 'secondary' contributions. Employees' primary contributions are payable at two rates, a 'main primary percentage' of 11% (but proposed to be increased to 12% from 6 April 2011), applicable to earnings up to the upper earnings limit (£844 a week for 2010/11, but proposed to be reduced from 6 April 2011 in line with the basic rate tax limit after the September 2010 retail price index figure is known), and an 'additional primary percentage' of 1% (proposed to be increased to 2% from 6 April 2011) applies to all earnings above that level.

Neither employers nor employees pay tax or NICs on pay up to an 'earnings threshold' (£110 a week for 2010/11 but proposed to be increased from 6 April 2011 by £570 per year for employees and by £21 per week above indexation for employers). Employees have their rights to state pensions and other contributory benefits protected by reference to a lower pay figure. They are treated as paying notional NICs between the 'lower earnings limit' (£97 a week for 2010/11) and the earnings threshold.

A separate category of contributions, Class 1A, is payable annually by employers (not employees) on taxable benefits provided to P11D employees that are not chargeable to Class 1 or Class 1B contributions — see **10.39**. Class 1B contributions are payable only by those employers who enter into a PAYE Settlement Agreement with HMRC and are payable at the same time as the tax due under that arrangement (see **10.55**).

Class 1 contributions are collected through the PAYE system. Class 1A contributions are paid separately to HMRC — for details, see **CHAPTER 10**. The self-employed pay Class 2 and Class 4 contributions (see **CHAPTER 24**). Voluntary Class 3 contributions may be paid by those who would otherwise not pay enough contributions to earn a full pension (see **13.5** to **13.7**). Employees and the self-employed cease to pay contributions when they reach pensionable age, but employers must continue to pay secondary Class 1 contributions and Class 1A and 1B contributions (see **13.15**).

It is sometimes difficult to decide whether someone is employed or self-employed but it is important to get it right — see **19.1** for the NIC implications.

There are penalties for the late payment of PAYE/NIC by employers (see **CHAPTER 9**).

Pensions

[13.3] Occupational and personal pension schemes, including stakeholder pensions, are dealt with in **CHAPTER 16** and **CHAPTER 17** respectively. People with no earnings may pay pension contributions up to £3,600 a year and obtain tax relief — for details see **17.10**.

The state pension scheme provides a basic state pension, currently £97.65 a week, and an earnings-related 'second pension' or 'additional pension'. From 6 April 2011 it is proposed that the basic state pension will be uprated by earnings, prices or 2.5%, whichever is the highest. The growing cost of the state scheme has been causing concern, while at the same time it has been recognised that many pensioners are existing on very low incomes. Provisions are already in force to equalise pensionable ages for men and women, and the pensionable age for a person born after 5 April 1978 will be 68. The current provisions are as follows:

- a man born before 6 April 1959 attains pensionable age at age 65;
- a woman born before 6 April 1950 attains pensionable age at age 60;
- a woman born between 6 April 1950 and 5 April 1955 attains pensionable age on a date (between age 60 and age 65) set out in Pensions Act 1995, Sch 4 (as substituted by Pensions Act 2007);
- a woman born after 5 April 1955 but before 6 April 1959 attains pensionable age at age 65;
- a person born between 6 April 1959 and 5 April 1978 attains pensionable age on a date (between ages 65 and 68) set out in Pensions Act 1995, Sch 4; and
- a person born after 5 April 1978 attains pensionable age at age 68.

The effect of the Pensions Act 2007 reform is a gradual rise in the state pension age for men and women to 68 between 2024 and 2046, increasing the number of years in which they will be required to pay NICs. However, the Government is to make a further review of the state pension age to determine when it will rise to 66. It will also consider future increases in the state pension age. The Government provides a state pension age calculator at http://pensions.direct.gov.uk/en/state-pension-age-calculator/home.asp.

[13.4] Further reform of the UK's pension system has been enacted following the publication of two white papers, 'Security in retirement: towards a new pensions system' (May 2006) and 'Personal Accounts: a new way to save' (December 2006). The key measures include:

- reducing from 2010 the number of qualifying years needed to receive a full basic state pension to 30 years, linking cost of living increases to earnings, and changing the contribution conditions;
- introducing NIC credits for the State Second Pension from 2010 for those with long-term disabilities and people with caring responsibilities; and
- provisions for eligible workers who are not already in a good quality workplace scheme to be enrolled automatically, from 2012, into their employer's pension scheme or a new 'personal account scheme'. Mandatory employers' contributions and tax relief will be added to employees' contributions to workplace pension schemes. The scheme is called the National Employment Savings Trust (NEST) and it is proposed that it will be registered with HMRC for tax purposes. The Government published a 68-page booklet entitled 'State Pensions Your Guide' in November 2009 which can be downloaded from www.direct.gov.uk.

See www.dwp.gov.uk/policy/pensions-reform for more information on these reforms, including details of NEST. A further review of the state pension age was announced in the June 2010 Emergency Budget. The Government has also been considering the alignment of the income tax and NIC systems. Clearly these proposals represent long term planning and there is no certainty that they will be implemented. In the meantime the following provisions apply.

There are various provisions to give equality of treatment to spouses and civil partners. A spouse or civil partner may get a basic state pension based on the NIC record of the other spouse or partner, and a spouse or civil partner may claim an increase for a dependent spouse or partner. Those of pensionable age may earn a higher pension by deferring it, and when they do take benefits they may take a lump sum instead of extra pension (see **16.4**).

[13.5] The present rules provide, broadly, that in order to get a full basic state pension an individual must have paid or have been credited with Class 1, 2 or 3 NICs, on an amount equal to 52 times the lower earnings limit (see **13.1**) in a number of 'qualifying years' in working life between age 16 and pensionable age (as set out in SSCBA 1992, Sch 3 as amended by Pensions Act 2007). From 6 April 2010 the number of qualifying years depends on age and is different for men and women. For example, men born before 6 April 1945 usually need 44 qualifying years. Women born before 6 April 1950 usually need 39 qualifying years. However, men born after 5 April 1945 and women born after 5 April 1950 only need 30 qualifying years (see **13.4**).

For the purpose of the basic pension, an individual may be credited with contributions when they are registered as unemployed or receiving jobseeker's allowance, or unable to work through incapacity or disability, or because they receive carer's allowance for looking after someone who is disabled, or if they receive working tax credit, disabled person's tax credit, maternity allowance, statutory maternity pay, statutory adoption pay or statutory sick pay, or if they are on certain training courses, on jury service, wrongly imprisoned, or accompanying a spouse or civil partner who is a member of HM forces on assignment outside the UK. An unemployed man aged 60 to 64 who meets certain residence requirements will automatically get credits whether or not he is ill or on the unemployment register. Credits will usually be given to those aged 16 to 18 who would otherwise not have paid enough NICs, and also for certain periods of full-time training lasting up to twelve months, but not for longer courses such as university degree courses. Those who stay at home to look after children or sick or elderly people used to get Home Responsibilities Protection (HRP), which reduced the number of years needed to qualify for full pension. From 6 April 2010 they get national insurance credits. If HRP has been built up before 6 April 2010, up to 22 of those years will automatically be converted into credits, see further www.hmrc.gov.uk/ni/intro/credits.htm#1.

[13.6] An individual who does not earn enough, either as an employee or in self-employment, to achieve the required level of Class 1 or 2 contributions, may pay voluntary Class 3 contributions (£12.05 per week for 2010/11) to help to qualify for the basic retirement pension and, for those under pensionable age, bereavement benefits. He can check with HMRC's NICO to see whether his contribution record is good enough to earn a full pension. Guidance notes and an application form are provided at www.hmrc.gov.uk/nic/ca5603.pdf.

The general rule is that Class 3 contributions can be paid up to six years after the year to which they relate (but sometimes at a higher rate). There were extended time limits in some earlier tax years and special rules apply to people who reach state pension age between 6 April 2008 and 5 April 2015. HMRC normally notify people annually if their contribution record is inadequate. The Pensions Act 2008 introduced new rules which allow some people to buy up to six additional years of Class 3 contributions. Guidance is provided at www.thepensionservice.gov.uk/state-pension/basic/faqs.asp and www.hmrc.gov.uk/ni/volcontr/whentop-up.htm.

However, a proposed reduction in the number of qualifying years for the basic state pension from 2010 (see **13.4**) may mean that some people will already have enough contributory years without paying voluntary contributions. Those who may be affected can apply for a pension forecast at www.direct-.gov.uk. The Government announced that refunds may be claimed if Class 3 contributions paid after 24 May 2006 but before 26 July 2007 would not have been paid if the payer had been aware of the Government's intentions.

[13.7] Certain married women pay reduced contributions (see **13.14**), in which case they are not entitled to contribution credits and cannot pay Class 3 contributions. They may be entitled to a basic state pension based on their husband's or civil partner's NICs record when they reach pensionable age and the husband or civil partner claims the state pension. The same applies to other married women who have not paid enough full rate contributions to earn a higher pension in their own right, and this treatment was extended to husbands and civil partners who have an insufficient contribution record.

Alternatively, an increase of up to £58.80 a week may be payable in respect of a dependent adult. Guidance is available at www.direct.gov.uk.

[13.8] The State Second Pension Scheme (S2P) replaced the State Earnings Related Pension Scheme (SERPS) in 2002. Until 5 April 2009 the amount of the accrued pension depended broadly on the Class 1 NICs paid on earnings between the NIC lower and upper earnings limits in each tax year. With effect from 6 April 2009 the upper earnings limit is replaced by an upper accrual point (UAP) for the purpose of capping entitlement to the state second pension. The UAP is fixed at £770 a week, while the upper earnings limit for contributions payable in 2010/11 is £844 (but is proposed to be reduced from 6 April 2011, see **13.2**). Freezing the UAP in cash terms will erode earnings-related accruals. An explanatory note to the National Insurance Contributions Act 2008 said: 'The [UAP] was to be brought in along with a flat rate accrual amount of around £1.50 a week that would replace accruals on earnings between the lower earnings limit and the low earnings threshold. Taken together, it was expected . . . that these two measures would deliver entitlement to the state second pension on a completely flat rate basis by around 2030.'

[13.9] A person whose husband, wife or civil partner has died may be able to inherit additional pension from him or her. The pension entitlement of widows and widowers can be complex. Guidance is available at www.direct.gov.uk. The Department for Work and Pensions provides a detailed guide NP46 on the state pension for professional advisers.

Persons liable to pay Class 1 contributions (SSCBA 1992, ss 2, 6(1))

[13.10] 'Employed earners' and their employers are required to pay Class 1 NICs unless they are exempt (see below). An 'employed earner' is a person who is gainfully employed in Great Britain (either under a contract of service or in an office) with earnings that are chargeable to tax as employment income (see **CHAPTER 10**). See **19.1** regarding the importance of distinguishing between employment and self-employment.

Certain people are specifically brought within the liability to pay Class 1 NICs, including office cleaners, some agency workers, a spouse or civil partner working in the other spouse's/partner's business (other than in a partnership), ministers of religion paid chiefly by way of stipend or salary, and certain lecturers and teachers.

Certain employees are exempt from payment of Class 1 contributions as indicated below. The exemptions also apply to employers' contributions, except for employees in category (a) below who are over State pension age.

(a)   People aged under 16 or over pensionable age.
(b)   People whose earnings are below the weekly lower earnings limit (£97.00 for 2010/11).
(c)   A wife employed by her husband for a non-business purpose and vice versa.
(d)   People employed for a non-business purpose by a close relative in the home where they both live.
(e)   Returning and counting officers and people employed by them in connection with an election or referendum.
(f)   Certain employees of international organisations and visiting armed forces.

Special rules apply to those who go to work abroad — see **41.39** to **41.43**.

Earnings (SSCBA 1992, ss 3, 4)

[13.11] Class 1 contributions are calculated on gross pay, which is broadly the same as pay for income tax under PAYE and includes certain benefits in kind (see **10.7**), but is before deducting employees' contributions to registered pension schemes and any charitable gifts under the payroll giving scheme. The employers' guides supplied by HMRC need to be studied carefully to identify other differences between pay for tax and NIC purposes.

Expenses payments to employees count as pay except to the extent that they are for proper business expenses, for which receipts or records must be available. Reimbursement of an employee's parking expenses, for example, must be for recorded business-related journeys. Where HMRC have granted a dispensation allowing expenses payments to be ignored for tax purposes, the same treatment applies for NICs, and the exemptions (see **10.15**) for incidental personal expenses and payments for directors' liability insurance also apply.

Virtually all benefits in kind that do not attract Class 1 NICs attract a liability for employers' Class 1A contributions, but only where they are provided to P11D employees. There is no Class 1A charge on the employee (see **CHAPTER 10**, in particular **10.39**).

Class 1 contributions are not payable on benefits unless they have been made specifically chargeable (see below), so as well as non-P11D employees, P11D employees earning less than £844 a week will still get a significant advantage from receiving certain benefits rather than cash pay (the saving to those earning above £844 a week in 2010/11 being 1% rather than 11%), but it is proposed that these rates and thresholds will change from 6 April 2011 (see **13.2**).

It is, however, important to distinguish benefits from payments by the employer for which the employee is legally responsible. The key question is who made the contract. If it is the employee, NICs are payable (subject to deduction of any identifiable business proportion). If it is the employer, the payment is a benefit and is not liable to Class 1 NICs unless it is for one of the specifically chargeable items. For example, if an employer contracts to buy an employee a television set, or groceries, Class 1 NICs are not payable (but the employer would have a Class 1A liability if the employee is a P11D employee). If the employee contracts to make the purchases and the bill is paid by the employer, Class 1 NICs are payable. HMRC's guidance for employers provides detailed information and careful study is recommended. See for example www.hmrc.gov.uk/paye/exb/a-z/a/index.htm.

Payment of a director's bills where the payment is charged to the director's account with the company does not count as pay unless the account becomes overdrawn, and even then, only if the director's earnings are normally credited to the account.

Pay for Class 1 NICs specifically includes benefits that are in the form of 'readily convertible assets' (see **10.19**). Readily convertible shares and share options (other than under HMRC approved schemes) come within these provisions (see **11.3** for details). Class 1 NICs are also payable on virtually all non-cash vouchers, the exceptions being broadly those that are exempt for income tax (see **10.21**).

Contracted-out employees

[13.12] The state retirement pensions comprise a basic flat-rate pension and an additional pension related to earnings (see **13.3**).

Employees who are members of occupational pension schemes may be 'contracted-out' of S2P by their employers (see **16.5**). Benefits accrued under contracted-out schemes may be either salary-related (COSR schemes) or related to the amount contributed, i.e. money purchase (COMP schemes). Contracted-out employees are still eligible for the basic state pension but they obtain their additional pension from their employer's scheme.

To help meet the cost of setting up and running a separate pension scheme, contracted-out employers and their employees are entitled to a rebate of Class 1 NICs on earnings between the lower and upper earnings limits (£97 and

£844 a week respectively for 2010/11). The rebate payable through the PAYE scheme is 1.6% for employees, for both COSR and COMP schemes. For employers the rebate is 3.7% for COSR schemes and 1.4% for COMP schemes. Employees in COMP schemes are entitled to a further age-related rebate, which is paid by HMRC (see below regarding this and the effect of the new 'upper accrual point'). The treatment of the PAYE rebates is complicated, because the rebates are given on the band of earnings between £97 and the earnings threshold of £110, on which neither employers nor employees pay contributions. Where an employee's rebate exceeds the contributions payable by him, the balance reduces the employer's liability. See Examples 1 and 2 (but note that the rates and thresholds are proposed to change from 6 April 2011, see **13.2**).

Example 1

If an employer had a COSR scheme in 2010/11 and an employee's weekly earnings were exactly £120, the position would be:

		£
Employee	First £110	—
	Remaining £10 @ (11 – 1.6 =) 9.4%	0.94
	Rebate on (110 – 97 =) £13 @ 1.6%	(0.21)
	Contributions payable	0.73
Employer	First £110	—
	Remaining £10 @ (12.8 – 3.7 =) 9.1%	0.91
	Rebate on (110 – 97 =) £13 @ 3.7%	(0.48)
	Contributions payable	0.43

The total employee's/employer's contributions payable would be (73p + 43p =) £1.16.

Example 2

Facts as in Example 1 but employee's earnings were (a) £111 or (b) £99.

The position would be:

(a)

		£
Employee	First £110	—
	Remaining £1 @ (11 – 1.6 =) 9.4%	0.09
	Rebate on (110 – 97 =) £13 @ 1.6% = (0.21) of which amount allocated to employee is	(0.09)
	Contributions payable	nil
Employer	First £110	—
	Remaining £1 @ (12.8 – 3.7 =) 9.1%	0.09

Rebate on (110 – 97 =) £13 @ 3.7%		(0.48)
Balance of employee's rebate		(0.12)
		(0.51)

The total employee's/employer's contributions payable would be nil and the employer would be entitled to deduct 51p from his overall NIC liability.

(b)		£
Employee	Contributions payable on £99	nil
	Rebate on (99 – 97 =) £2 @ 1.6% = 3p allocated to employer	
Employer	On £99	—
	Rebate on (99 – 97 =) £2 @ 3.7%	(0.07)
	Employee's rebate	(0.03)
		(0.10)

The total employee's/employer's contributions payable would be nil and the employer would be entitled to deduct 10p from his overall NIC liability.

Employees may also contract out of S2P by entering into personal pension arrangements, to which their employers may or may not contribute (see **CHAPTER 17**). Both employer and employee continue to pay full NICs, and the contracting-out rebate is paid by HMRC into the personal pension scheme.

The Class 1 contributions rebate is age-related for both personal pension plans and contracted-out money purchase schemes (but not salary related schemes). The relevant percentages were set out in the Social Security (Reduced Rates of Class 1 Contributions, Rebates and Minimum Contributions) Order 2006 (SI 2006/1009) and the position has been complicated further by the introduction in 2009/10 of the upper accrual point (see **13.8**). HMRC guidance is provided in booklet E13, available at www.hmrc.gov.uk/employers/working_out.htm.

Contribution rates (SSCBA 1992, ss 1, 5, 8, 9)

[13.13] National insurance rates for 2009/10 and 2010/11 are shown in the **TABLE OF RATES AND ALLOWANCES** but they are proposed to change from 6 April 2011 (see **13.2**). Only the lower earnings limit changed in 2010/11. All other thresholds and rates remained the same.

Employers' NICs are deductible in arriving at their taxable profits but tax on employees' earnings is calculated on the gross pay before deducting NICs.

For 2010/11 employers pay Class 1 secondary contributions at 12.8% on the whole of the excess of an employee's pay above the earnings threshold of £110 a week. For employees there is a lower earnings limit of £97 a week and employees earning at or above that level must be brought within the PAYE system and a P11 working sheet completed for them. No contributions are, however, payable unless earnings exceed the earnings threshold of £110 a week. Employees who are not contracted out pay Class 1 primary contributions at the main primary percentage of 11% on earnings between £110 and £844 a week and at the additional primary percentage of 1% on earnings above £844 a week.

The rate of Class 1A contributions payable by employers on most taxable benefits in kind provided for P11D employees and directors (see **13.2**) is 12.8%.

See **13.12** re rebates of contributions for contracted-out employees and see **13.14** for the reduced rate of employees' contributions payable by certain married women and widows.

Employee contributions

Reduced rate for certain married women and widows

[13.14] Women who were married or widowed as at 6 April 1977 had the option before 12 May 1977 to choose to pay Class 1 contributions at a reduced rate. If they are still entitled to pay the reduced contributions, the certificate of election must be handed over to the employer to enable him to deduct contributions at the correct rate. The reduced rate for 2010/11, which applies once earnings exceed £110 a week and is the same for both contracted-out and non-contracted-out employees, is 4.85% on earnings between £110 and £844 per week and 1% on earnings above £844 a week. If a married woman is self-employed, the election makes her exempt from paying Class 2 contributions, but not Class 4 contributions (see **CHAPTER 24**). Note that the NIC rates and thresholds are proposed to change from 6 April 2011, see **13.2**.

Although substantial amounts may be paid in reduced rate contributions, they do not entitle the payer to any contributory state benefits (but statutory sick pay and statutory maternity or adoption pay are payable where appropriate). Many married women and widows considered that they were inadequately informed about the effects of not building up a contribution record of their own, but the Government did not accept that any compensation should be paid. A woman without a contribution record of her own may claim retirement pension or bereavement benefits based on the contribution record of her husband (see **13.7**).

An election to pay reduced rate contributions is effective until it is cancelled or revoked. A woman loses the right to pay reduced rate contributions:

(a)   if she is divorced, in which case the right is lost immediately after the decree absolute, or has the marriage annulled, or

(b)   if she becomes widowed and is not entitled to widow's benefit, in which case the right is not lost until the end of the tax year in which the husband dies, or the end of the following tax year if he dies between 1 October and 5 April, or

(c) if she pays no reduced rate Class 1 contributions and has no earnings from self-employment for two consecutive tax years.

An election can be revoked in writing at any time and the revocation will, in most instances, take effect from the beginning of the following week. If the election is revoked, the wife will start earning a pension, including earnings-related pension, in her own right, and she will also be entitled to claim maternity allowance, jobseeker's allowance and employment and support allowance if appropriate. Those who are considering revoking may apply for a pension forecast (see **13.6**) to assist them in their decision. Women earning between the lower earnings limit of £97 and the earnings threshold of £110 a week would benefit from revoking the election, because they would become entitled to contributory benefits even though they would not have to pay any contributions (see **13.1**). If their earnings increased to above the earnings threshold, however, they would pay 11% rather than 4.85% on the excess.

People over pensionable age

[13.15] No contributions are payable by an employee who is over pensionable age (see **13.3**), although the employer is still liable for secondary contributions where earnings exceed the earnings threshold, such contributions always being at non-contracted-out rates.

Employees who are not liable to pay contributions should apply for a certificate of age exception. This should be given to the employer as authority for Class 1 contributions not to be deducted from earnings.

More than one employment

[13.16] A person who has more than one employment is liable to pay primary Class 1 NICs in respect of each job. There is, however, a prescribed annual maximum contribution. The rates and thresholds used here relate to 2010/11 but they are proposed to change from 6 April 2011, see **13.2**.

The calculation of the maximum used to be straightforward, but now that contributions at 1% are chargeable on all earnings above the upper earnings limit (£43,875 for 2010/11), the calculation can be complex and has several stages. Detailed guidance on the calculation of the annual maximum is available in HMRC's National Insurance Manual at NIM01160.

If the contributions paid for 2010/11 exceed the maximum a refund may be claimed of the excess from NICO so long as that excess is greater than 1/15th of a Class 1 contribution at the main 11% rate on earnings at the upper earnings limit (i.e. £5.38 for 2010/11).

To avoid having to pay contributions in all employments throughout the year and being refunded any excess after the end of the year, an employee may apply to defer some of his contributions. Application for deferment is made on form CA72A and HMRC have produced guidance notes to accompany the form. If deferment is granted the employee will remain liable to pay Class 1 NICs at the rate of 1% on all earnings above the earnings threshold of £110 a week in the 'deferred' employment.

Deferment has no effect on employers' contributions, which are payable at 12.8% in each employment on the earnings over the earnings threshold. Employees who have (or are considering having) an appropriate personal pension plan into which HMRC pay minimum contributions (see **17.15**) should note that HMRC take account only of employments in which full contributions are paid when paying minimum contributions, so deferring contributions in those employments would affect the pension entitlement.

Where a person has more than one job with the same employer, earnings from those employments must be added together and contributions calculated on the total. Where a person has jobs with different employers who 'carry on business in association with each other', all earnings from 'associated' employers must be added together for the purpose of calculating contributions.

These rules will not be enforced if it is not reasonably practicable to do so. See HMRC's National Insurance Manual at NIM10000 onwards for HMRC's views on these provisions, in particular NIM10009 for their interpretation of 'not reasonably practicable'.

Income from self-employment

[13.17] The position of the employee who also has income from self-employment is dealt with in **CHAPTER 24**.

Company directors

[13.18] Directors sometimes receive a salary under a service contract and also fees for holding the office of director. They are often paid in irregular amounts at irregular time intervals, for example a fixed monthly salary together with a bonus after the year end, once the results of the company are known. To ensure that this does not lead to manipulation of liability to pay NICs, directors in employment at the beginning of a tax year have an annual earnings period coinciding with the tax year. Those appointed during a tax year have an earnings period equal to the number of weeks from the date of appointment to the end of the tax year. No Class 1 contributions are due unless and until the director's earnings reach the annual earnings threshold (£5,715 for 2010/11, but see **13.2** regarding proposed changes from 6 April 2011) or a pro-rata limit for directors appointed during a tax year (using the appropriate multiple of the weekly limit).

For directors who earn regular amounts, the annual earnings period causes an unnecessary distortion in their NIC payments, but it is possible for contributions to be paid as if the special rules did not apply. The director still has an annual earnings liability, however, so that those seeking to manipulate the rules are still prevented from doing so.

All earnings paid to a director during an earnings period must be included in that earnings period (irrespective of the period to which they relate). Earnings include fees, bonuses, salary, payments made in anticipation of future earnings, and payments made to a director which were earned while he was still an employee.

If a director resigns, all payments made to him between the date of resignation and the end of the tax year that relate to his period of directorship must be linked to his other 'directorship earnings' of that tax year. If any such earnings are paid in a later tax year, they are not added to any other earnings of the year in which payment is made. Instead, they are considered independently on an annual earnings basis, and Class 1 NICs accounted for accordingly.

Many directors have payments in anticipation of future earnings, e.g. a payment on account of a bonus to be declared when the company's results are known. Liability for Class 1 contributions arises when the payments are made. The advance bonus payments are added to all other earnings of the annual earnings period. When the bonus is determined, any balance will become liable to Class 1 contributions in that tax year. A bonus is deemed to be paid whether it is placed in an account on which the director can draw or left in the company, unless exceptionally it is not placed at the director's disposal.

To the extent that a director makes drawings against a credit balance on his director's loan account, no Class 1 liability will arise as these drawings simply reduce the balance of the loan account. If the loan account has been built up from undrawn remuneration, the Class 1 liability will have arisen at the time the remuneration was credited to it.

See **12.17** re a director's personal liability for both his own NICs and other contributions due from the company if he has been carelessly or deliberately inaccurate.

Employers' NIC holiday

[13.19] There are proposals to introduce a scheme involving an employers' NIC holiday to help new businesses in targeted areas of the UK. During a three year qualifying period new businesses starting up in certain areas will not have to pay the first £5,000 of employers' Class 1 NICs due in the first 12 months of employment in respect of each of the first ten employees hired in the first year of business, giving a potential saving of £50,000. The scheme is intended to start no later than 6 September 2010, and any new business set up from 22 June 2010 may benefit from the scheme. The areas are: Scotland, Wales, Northern Ireland, the North East, Yorkshire and the Humber, the North West, the East Midlands, the West Midlands, and the South West. Various restrictions apply.

Tax points

[13.20] Note the following. The rates and thresholds used relate to 2010/11, but see **13.2** regarding proposed changes from 6 April 2011:

- Employees earning between £97 and £110 a week satisfy the contribution conditions for contributory social security benefits even though no contributions are payable.

- If an employee has several employments, he can get back NICs in excess of the annual maximum. Refunds are not, however, available in respect of employers' contributions.
- If a wife or husband or civil partner pays maximum contributions at the 11% rate in a separate job and also does some work in the family business run by their spouse or civil partner, employers' national insurance on the earnings from the family business cannot be reclaimed, so it may be more sensible to pay the spouse or civil partner less than the earnings threshold of £110 a week. Remember, however, that earnings of either spouse or civil partner as an *employee* of the family business must be justified if relief for tax is to be given in calculating the business profits. On the other hand, remember that the national minimum wage legislation may apply (see **12.1**).
- Except for company directors, who have an annual earnings period coinciding with the tax year, or for the remainder of the tax year in which they are appointed, NICs are not calculated on a cumulative basis. If average earnings will not exceed the earnings threshold of £110, try to ensure that the actual earnings in any week do not do so, otherwise both the employee and the employer will be liable to pay NICs for that particular week even though on a cumulative basis the threshold may not have been reached.
- If an employee has more than one job and earns more than £844 a week from one of them, he should consider applying for deferment. Even if he does not earn more than £844 a week from one job, but his *total* earnings exceed that amount, it may be better to apply for deferment rather than wait for a refund after the year end. The effect of deferment is that NICs will be payable at 1% rather than 11% on earnings above £110 a week in all jobs other than the main job.
- Dividends paid to shareholders do not attract NICs at present. It may be appropriate for shareholders/directors to receive dividends rather than additional remuneration (not forgetting the national minimum wage and personal/managed service company legislation, the comments in **12.10** about the 'settlements' rules). It is important to ensure that dividends are properly documented so that they cannot be challenged as pay. Changes to the tax and NIC rules may follow a review of small business taxation.
  The NIC aspect must not be looked at in isolation. Many other factors are important, e.g. the level of remuneration for company or personal pension purposes, and the effect of a dividend policy on other shareholders. See **CHAPTER 12** for illustrations.
- If a wife has been paying the reduced married woman's rate of NICs, she should watch the circumstances in which she has to revert to the full rate, for example a divorce (see **13.14**). If she underpays, even by mistake, she will probably have to make up the difference. But no NICs at all are payable from pensionable age.
- Where a spouse/civil partner works in the business of the other spouse/partner, then even though the recipient is paid as a self-employed individual issuing invoices to the paying spouse/partner and after

appropriate charging and accounting for VAT, for NIC purposes the paying spouse/partner is regarded as an employer, with Class 1 NICs being payable.

- If an individual has not satisfied the contribution conditions for a year to be classed as a qualifying year, his State pension may be affected (see **13.3**). Class 3 voluntary contributions can be paid to maintain the contribution record. But see **13.4** regarding the changes enabling a full pension to be earned after 30 years' contributions.

- If an employer pays an employee's debt, it counts as pay for Class 1 NICs and for income tax. Where possible, make sure the contract is made by the employer. In that case, Class 1 NICs will not be payable unless the payment relates to a specifically chargeable item. If the employee is a P11D employee the employer will be liable to Class 1A NICs.

- Records are needed to prove business use in certain areas, such as for mileage allowances to those who use their own cars (see **10.12** re business mileage rates), and for contributions towards an employee's telephone bill, unless, in the case of telephones, there is an agreed business proportion for tax, which will also be accepted for NIC purposes.

- Where Class 1A NICs are payable on a benefit with mixed business/private use, the employer has to pay contributions on the full amount, without any offset for the business proportion.

14

Statutory sick pay and statutory maternity etc pay

Background

[14.1] This chapter deals with the main provisions relating to statutory payments for sickness, maternity, paternity and adoption. More detailed information is available in HMRC guidance for employers, the department's Statutory Payments Manual and other published material. Various rules applying to leave periods, as distinct from paid absences, are dealt with only briefly here.

The main provisions relating to statutory sick pay (SSP) and statutory maternity, paternity and adoption pay (SMP, SPP, SAP) are in the Social Security Contributions and Benefits Act 1992 as amended. Much of the detail is contained in regulations.

Most employees are entitled to receive SSP from their employers for up to 28 weeks of sickness absence. Employers are, however, entitled to opt out of the SSP scheme if they pay wages or sick pay at or above the SSP rates (see **14.13**). SSP is paid at a single flat rate.

Employers are also required to pay SMP, SPP and SAP where the relevant conditions are satisfied (although they will be able to claim reimbursement of most or all of it).

SMP, SPP and SAP are paid at two rates, the higher rate being dependent on the employee's earnings and the standard rate being a fixed amount.

SSP, SMP, SPP and SAP all count as pay for income tax and national insurance contributions (NICs).

Employers are entitled to recover SSP if and to the extent that it exceeds a stipulated monthly threshold (see **14.12**). Employers are able to recover 92% of SMP/SPP/SAP, unless they qualify for Small Employers' Relief, in which case they can recover 100% of the SMP etc. plus a further 4.5% to compensate for the NICs on the SMP etc (see **14.21**).

Employers who fail to comply with the statutory requirements are liable to various penalties.

Statutory Sick Pay (SSP)

Employees entitled to receive SSP

[14.2] The definition of an employee is the same as that of an 'employed earner' for Class 1 NICs (see **13.10**), except that there is no age restriction for SSP (the lower age limit of 16 and upper age limit of 65 do not apply). An employee is entitled to SSP unless he falls into one of the excluded groups (see **14.3**). Married women and widows paying reduced rate Class 1 contributions are also entitled to SSP.

An employee is entitled to SSP for each job he has, so that if an individual is employed by two different employers he will be paid SSP by each employer when off work through illness.

When an employee is being paid SSP he is not entitled to Employment and Support Allowance (formerly incapacity benefit). Employees who are not entitled to SSP and those who have exhausted their SSP entitlement may claim Employment and Support Allowance.

Employees excluded from SSP

[14.3] Employees who fall into certain categories at the beginning of a 'period of incapacity for work' (see **14.6**) are not entitled to SSP. These include:

(a) Those whose average weekly earnings* (usually calculated over the previous eight weeks) are below the lower earnings limit for NICs (£97 for 2010/11 — see **CHAPTER 13**).

(b) Those who have claimed certain state benefits in the period before falling ill. An employee who has received one of these benefits will receive a letter from the Department for Work and Pensions (known as a 'linking letter') notifying the employer of the period of exclusion.

(c) 'Welfare to work' beneficiaries (i.e. certain people previously entitled to benefits because they were incapable of work) who are sick within 104 weeks of starting/returning to work.

(d) A person who has not begun work under his contract.

(e) Those who become ill while they are away from work because of a trade dispute, unless the employee can prove that he is not participating in, or directly interested in, the dispute.

(f) A woman who is pregnant or has just given birth, and becomes sick during her 'disqualifying period' (see **14.4**).

(g) Those who have received 28 weeks' SSP and the new period of sickness 'links' to the last one.

(h) Those who fall ill while in prison or in legal custody.

(i) Those who are outside the UK, if their employer is not liable to pay secondary Class 1 NICs on their employees' earnings.

* If an employee's average weekly earnings would otherwise be too low to qualify for SSP, but would qualify if the employer included an amount for expenses or benefits subject to a PAYE settlement agreement (where Class 1B NICs are paid by the employer, see **10.55**), then the employer must recalculate the earnings including the amount on which Class 1B contributions are payable.

Agency workers are not excluded from SSP. (It used to be the case that if the contract with the employment agency was for a specified period not exceeding three calendar months, agency workers did not qualify for SSP. This restriction was removed with effect from October 2008).

An employer who cannot pay SSP because the employee is excluded is required to complete form SSP 1 and give it immediately to the employee, who may be able to claim state benefits.

Pregnancy

[14.4] Statutory sick pay cannot be paid during a disqualifying period. For those entitled to statutory maternity pay or maternity allowance, the disqualifying period starts with the day the employee is first entitled to that payment and normally runs for 39 weeks.

For those not entitled to either of those payments and not already getting SSP, the disqualifying period runs for 18 weeks, normally starting on the earlier of the Sunday of the week in which the baby is born and the Sunday of the week the employee is first off sick with a pregnancy-related illness on or after the start of the fourth week before the baby is due. The starting date rules are sometimes slightly different if the baby is born early.

If SSP is already being paid to a pregnant woman not entitled to SMP or maternity allowance, the disqualifying period starts with the earlier of the day after the birth and the day after the first day she becomes sick with a pregnancy-related illness on or after the start of the fourth week before the baby is due.

Qualifying conditions for SSP

[14.5] For SSP to be payable two qualifying conditions must be met:

(a)   there must be a 'period of incapacity for work'; and
(b)   there must be one or more 'qualifying days'.

Period of incapacity for work

[14.6] A period of incapacity for work (PIW) is a period of four or more consecutive days of incapacity for work, counting rest days and holidays as well as normal working days. Night shift workers falling ill during a shift being treated as working only on the day on which the shift began.

A person who is not incapable of work may be deemed to be incapable if a medical practitioner advises that he or she should not work for a precautionary reason, or he or she is a carrier of (or has been in contact with) a contagious disease.

HMRC guidance states that any changes to the SSP scheme in the event of a pandemic alert being declared by the Government would be notified via HMRC's web pages and the Employer Helpline, and more general information would be provided via the Department for Work and Pensions' website, TV and radio.

If two PIWs are separated by 56 days or less, they are treated as one single PIW (called a linked PIW).

Example 1

An employee is incapable of work through illness from Friday 3 December 2010 to Tuesday 7 December 2010 inclusive and from Sunday 23 January 2011 to Thursday 17 February 2011 inclusive. The two PIWs are separated by 46 days and are therefore treated as a linked PIW.

Tables to help employers work out whether PIWs link are included in the SSP Tables issued by HMRC.

Qualifying days

[14.7] SSP is payable only in respect of 'qualifying days'. These are days of the week agreed between the employer and employee and will normally be those days on which the employee is required to work. Employer and employee may, however, come to other arrangements if they wish but qualifying days cannot be defined by reference to the days when the employee is sick. There is an overriding rule that there must be at least one qualifying day each week even if the employee is not required to work during that week.

SSP is not payable for the first three qualifying days in any PIW not linked to an earlier PIW. These are 'waiting days'.

Example 2

An employee with qualifying days Monday to Friday each week, who had not been ill during the previous two months, was ill on the bracketed days in the table below and returned to work on the 31st of the month.

M	T	W	Th	F	Sa	Su
	1	2	(3)	(4)	(5)	(6)
7	8	9	10	11	12	13
14	15	16	17	18	19	20
(21)	(22)	(23)	(24)	(25)	26	(27)
(28)	(29)	(30)	31			

There are three PIWs, from the 3rd to the 6th, from the 21st to the 25th, and from the 27th to the 30th.

In the first, there are two qualifying days which count as waiting days, and no SSP is payable.

> In the second, which begins not more than 56 days after the end of the first and is therefore linked with it, the 21st is the third waiting day and SSP is payable for the other four qualifying days.
>
> The third begins not more than 56 days after the end of the second and is therefore linked with it. As there are three waiting days in the (earlier) linked PIWs, SSP is payable for each of the three qualifying days in the third PIW.

Amount of SSP

[14.8] Providing the employee's average weekly earnings are at or above the national insurance lower earnings limit (£97 for 2010/11), SSP is payable on a daily basis at a flat weekly rate of £79.15 (from 6 April 2009).

The daily rate of SSP is the weekly rate divided by the number of qualifying days in the week (beginning with Sunday). For example, an employee who has five qualifying days in a week will receive SSP at a daily rate of £15.83 (£79.15 ÷ 5). HMRC provide a daily rates table for this purpose.

SSP will usually be paid on the employee's normal pay day. Wages paid to an employee can be offset against any SSP due for the same day. If the wages are less than the SSP due, the employer must make up the payment to the appropriate rate of SSP.

When SSP ends

[14.9] SSP ends with whichever of the following first occurs:

(a)   the period of incapacity (PIW) ends and the employee returns to work;
(b)   the employee reaches his maximum entitlement to SSP;
(c)   the employee's linked PIW has run for three years (which could only happen in exceptional circumstances where there were a large number of very short, four-day illnesses);
(d)   the employee's contract of employment ends;
(e)   the employee is taken into legal custody;
(f)   a pregnant woman's disqualifying period begins (see **14.4**).

The maximum period for which the employer is liable to pay SSP is normally 28 weeks. Where, however, a new employee commences a PIW within eight weeks of the day when a PIW with a previous employer ended, the weeks of SSP shown on the leaver's statement provided by the previous employer (see **14.10**) are taken into account to determine the new employer's maximum SSP liability. The previous period of sickness does not, however, affect the new employer's calculations in any other way and is not treated as a linked PIW.

Where entitlement to SSP ends while the employee is still sick, the employee will be able to claim Employment and Support Allowance (formerly incapacity benefit). To facilitate the change-over, the employer must issue change-over form SSP1 to the employee at the beginning of the 23rd week of SSP (or, if sooner, two weeks before the employee's entitlement to SSP is due to end). If the employee's entitlement ends unexpectedly (e.g. through being taken into legal custody), the change-over form must be issued immediately. Form SSP1 must also be issued at the start of the pregnancy disqualification period.

Leaver's statements

[14.10] If an employee has a PIW which ends not more than 56 days before his employment ceases, and SSP was payable for one week or more, a leaver's statement SSP1(L) (or the employer's own version of the form) must be issued if requested by the employee, showing the number of weeks' SSP payable (rounded to whole weeks, counting more than three odd days of payment as a week, and ignoring three odd days or less). The statement must be issued not later than the seventh day after the day the employee asks for it or, if that is impracticable, on the first pay day in the following tax month.

Notification and evidence for SSP

[14.11] The payment of SSP is triggered by the employee notifying his employer that he is unfit for work. An employer can draw up his own procedure for notification subject to the following limitations:

(a)   reasonable steps must be taken to notify employees of the procedures;
(b)   it is not legal to insist that notification:
    (i)   is made by the employee in person, or
    (ii)   is made by a particular time of day, or
    (iii)   is made more than once weekly for the same illness, or
    (iv)   is made on a form provided by the employer or on a medical certificate, or
    (v)   is given earlier than the first qualifying day; and
(c)   where the employee is a new employee with a leaving statement from his former employer, the statement must be accepted if it is produced not later than the seventh day after his first qualifying day of sickness.

If no notification procedures have been drawn up, the employee should inform his employer in writing by the seventh day after his first qualifying day of absence. If an employee fails to notify within the laid-down time limits, an employer may withhold SSP until the date of notification, but late notification may be accepted if there was good cause for delay.

Having been notified by an employee of his illness, the employer must satisfy himself that the illness is genuine before paying SSP. Employers usually obtain 'self-certificates' for the first week of illness and medical notes for longer absences. (The employer cannot insist on a medical certificate for the first seven days of a period of incapacity.)

An employer may withhold SSP when notification is late, and he may refuse to pay SSP if he feels that the employee is not in fact sick. In both these instances the employer, if required by the employee, must provide written reasons for withholding or refusing to pay SSP. An employee who disagrees with his employer's actions has the right to appeal for an official decision.

Recovery of SSP by employer

[14.12] Employers may recover that part of the SSP paid in a tax month that exceeds 13% of their combined employer/employee NICs in that tax month (not including any Class 1A or Class 1B contributions but after deducting any contracted-out contributions rebate due (see **13.12**)).

Example 3

Total employer/employee NICs for October are £4,000. 13% thereof is £520. SSP would be recovered as follows:

SSP paid in month	£520 or less	£600	£1,000
SSP recovered	Nil	£80	£480

SSP is recovered from amounts due to be paid over to HMRC's Accounts Office in respect of national insurance and PAYE tax payable, and if it exceeds those amounts, the employer can either carry the excess forward or apply to the Accounts Office for a refund.

Opting out of SSP

[14.13] Employers may opt out of the SSP scheme if they pay wages or sick pay above the SSP rates. They do not need to apply to do so, and may, if they wish, opt out for some but not all employees or periods of sickness. They must keep records of all dates of employee sickness lasting four or more consecutive days, and all payments of earnings or occupational sick pay.

Statutory Maternity Pay (SMP)

Employees entitled to SMP

[14.14] To be entitled to statutory maternity pay (SMP), an employee must satisfy the qualifying conditions (see **14.15**). Those who do not qualify for SMP may be able to claim maternity allowance from the Department for Work and Pensions instead. SMP is usually paid for 39 weeks even if the employee does not return after the baby has been born. HMRC provide detailed guidance in booklet E15, Employer Helpbook for Statutory Maternity Pay.

Married women paying reduced NICs and widows getting a state widow's benefit are entitled to SMP if they satisfy the qualifying conditions. SSP and SMP cannot be paid at the same time, and SSP must cease on the last day before the maternity pay period (see **14.17**) starts, even if for some reason the employee is not entitled to SMP.

Employed women are entitled to a total of 52 weeks maternity leave, comprising 26 weeks of 'ordinary maternity leave' and 26 weeks of 'additional maternity leave'.

Qualifying conditions for SMP

[14.15] To qualify for SMP an employee must have been continuously employed (normally by the same employer) for at least 26 weeks into the 15th week (the qualifying week) before the baby is due. The employee's average weekly earnings in the eight weeks ending with the qualifying week must be not less than the lower earnings limit for NICs at the end of that week (currently £97). The employee must still be pregnant at the 11th week before the expected date of birth. There are special rules for premature births. If an employee satisfies the qualifying rules with more than one employer she can receive SMP from each employer.

If Class 1B NICs have been paid in respect of the employee, the earnings on which they are considered to have been paid must be included in calculating average weekly earnings if the employee would otherwise fail to qualify for SMP, in the same way as for SSP (see **14.3**). In that event they must also be taken into account to calculate the higher rate of SMP (see **14.18**).

As a result of a decision of the European Court of Justice, if a woman is awarded a pay rise that is backdated to cover any part of the period from the start of the eight weeks ending with the qualifying week to the end of a woman's maternity leave (either ordinary or additional leave), she may claim for her average weekly earnings to be recalculated taking into account the pay rise and for any additional SMP arising to be paid to her. Arrears of SMP are not, however, payable for any period earlier than six years before the date of the claim. Where an employee has left, the time limit for a claim is six months after her leaving date.

Employees excluded from SMP

[14.16] An employee is not entitled to SMP if:

(a)   she is not employed during the qualifying week (see **14.15**);
(b)   she has not been continuously employed for 26 weeks;
(c)   the earnings rule (see **14.15**) is not satisfied;
(d)   she has not given notice at an acceptable time of the date she is stopping work;
(e)   medical evidence of her expected confinement date is not provided;
(f)   she is in legal custody at any time in the first week of her maternity pay period.

An employee who is outside the European Economic Area is not eligible for SMP unless the employer is liable to pay Class 1 NICs (see **41.39** and **41.40**).

If an employee is not entitled to SMP at the start of the maternity pay period, she is not entitled to it at all (subject to what is said in **14.15** about backdated pay rises).

An employee who is not entitled to SMP must be given form SMP1 immediately, together with any maternity certificate she has provided. These forms will need to be produced to the Department for Work and Pensions if she claims maternity allowance.

Payment of SMP

[14.17] SMP is payable for a maximum of 39 weeks, called the maternity pay period, starting normally at the same time as the maternity leave period. The employee may work for up to ten 'keeping in touch' days without affecting her SMP (or statutory adoption pay (see **14.20**)) entitlement. She may also continue to work or start work for another employer while on maternity leave before the baby is born without affecting her entitlement. The employer will no longer be liable to pay SMP if, after the baby is born, the employee starts work for a new employer or returns to work for another employer who did not employ her in the qualifying week. SMP will also cease if the employee is taken into legal custody.

Amount of SMP

[14.18] SMP is paid at the rate of 90% of the employee's average weekly earnings for the first six weeks and then at the lower of the standard rate (£124.88 for 2010/11) and 90% of average weekly earnings for the remainder of the period.

Statutory Paternity Pay (SPP)

[14.19] Statutory paternity pay (SPP) may be claimed by the baby's biological father, a partner/husband other than the biological father, or a female partner in a same sex couple. See **14.20** for SPP for adoptive parents.

The same rule applies as for SMP for the SPP claimant to have a continuous period of employment of at least 26 weeks into the 15th week before the baby is due, and for SPP the claimant must continue to work for that employer until the baby is born. As with SMP, the claimant's averaged weekly earnings in the eight weeks before the 15th week before the baby is due must be at least £97.

The SPP claimant may choose to take either one or two (consecutive) whole weeks' leave within the eight weeks after the baby's birth (or for babies born more than 15 weeks before the original due date, within the period from the date of birth to the end of eight weeks from the Sunday of the week the baby was originally due). The employee must normally give 28 days' notice of the date he intends to take leave. The weekly amount of SPP payable is the lower of £124.88 and 90% of average weekly earnings.

The employee must tell his employer by the end of the 15th week before the baby is due (or as soon as reasonably practicable) that he is going to take paternity leave, and he must notify the employer of the date the baby is born. Employers must give SPP claimants a form SC3 (*Becoming a parent*) which explains the terms and conditions for SPP, and includes a tear-off slip for the employee to provide relevant information, including a 'declaration of family commitment' that the employee will be responsible for the child's upbringing and will take time off work to support the mother or care for the child. SPP cannot be paid unless the declaration is provided. If the employee does not qualify for SPP the employer must give him a form SPP1.

An employee cannot get SPP and SSP at the same time.

Statutory Adoption Pay (SAP) and Statutory Paternity Pay (SPP) for adoptive parents

[14.20] Providing the relevant conditions are satisfied, SAP may be claimed by male or female employees adopting a child aged up to 18. SPP may be claimed by anyone (male or female) who is the partner of someone adopting a child on their own or is adopting a child with their partner. Adopting couples must choose which will claim SAP and which will claim SPP.

The same rules broadly apply for both SMP and SAP, adapted appropriately by reference to the time when a child is matched for adoption (i.e. the adoption agency has decided that the person is suitable to adopt that child) and when a child is placed for adoption with the adoptive parents. The SAP period must start from the date of the child's placement, or from a fixed date up to 14 days before the expected date of placement. The SPP rules are similarly adapted to cover adoptive parents. The SPP period must start not earlier than the date of the child's placement and must be completed within eight weeks of the placement. The employer must give the employee form SC4 (*Becoming an adoptive parent*), which contains a tear-off slip for the employee to provide relevant information, including a 'declaration of family commitment'. If the employee does not qualify for SPP the employer must give him form SPP 1. The weekly rates of both SAP and SPP are the lower of £124.88 and 90% of average weekly earnings.

Employees must give employers notice, 28 days before the adoption pay period starts or as soon as is reasonably practicable, of the date the child is placed with them for adoption, supported by a certificate from the adoption agency confirming the date they were told that they had been matched with a child. For SPP, the employee must provide a declaration of family commitment (see **14.19**) and information on the dates when the parental leave is to be taken.

Recovery of SMP, SPP and SAP by employer

[14.21] Employers other than 'small employers' are able to recover 92% of the gross amount of SMP/SPP/SAP paid in any month.

Small employers can recover all the SMP etc. paid, plus an extra 4.5% of the amount paid to compensate for the employer's Class 1 contributions on the payments. Small employers are those whose total annual employer/employee NICs (excluding Class 1A and Class 1B contributions but after deducting any contracted-out contributions rebate due (see **13.12**)) are £45,000 or less. The annual contributions taken into account for small employers are those for the tax year *before* that in which the SMP 'qualifying week' (see **14.15**) starts, or in adoption cases, the tax year before that in which the adoptive parents were told by the adoption agency that they had been matched with a child.

The employer recovers the amount he is entitled to in the same way as for SSP (see **14.12**), i.e. by deducting it from the total payments he makes to HMRC's Accounts Office in respect of tax and NICs. If the employer calculates that he has insufficient money to cover all the payments he needs to make, he can apply to the Accounts Office for an advance payment. This request may be sent by email if the employer wishes.

Employer's records

[14.22] Employer's records are particularly important, as the information required to be kept may have to be made available to HMRC. Employers may use record sheets SSP2, SMP2, SPP2 and SAP2 available from HMRC offices, if they wish. The form the records take is up to the employer, but the following must be kept:

For SSP

[14.23] Records for SSP:

(a)   records of dates of employees' PIWs;
(b)   all payments of SSP made during a PIW.

For SMP, SPP and SAP

[14.24] Records for SMP, SPP and SAP:

(a)   records of payment dates and amount paid;
(b)   the date the pay period began;
(c)   for SMP and SAP, records of any weeks in maternity or adoption pay period when payment wasn't made, with reasons, and for SPP, records of any unpaid SPP with reasons;
(d)   for SMP, maternity certificates (forms MAT B1) or other medical evidence, and copies of certificates returned to employees, for example when liability has ended;
(e)   for SPP, the declaration of family commitment (or a copy);
(f)   for SAP, the evidence your employee gave you from the adoption agency (or a copy).

For all statutory payments

[14.25] Records must also be kept of the monthly amounts paid, and certain details need to be included on the end of year returns of pay, tax and national insurance (see **10.51**). Records must be kept for a minimum of three years after the end of the tax year to which they relate. In addition to the records outlined above, HMRC recommends that certain other records are also retained for further reference. For details see the various HMRC guides.

15

Golden handcuffs and golden handshakes

Introduction

[15.1] A 'golden handcuff' or 'golden hello' is the popular term for a lump sum payment received on taking up an employment, and a 'golden handshake' is the term for a lump sum payment received when you leave an employment.

Lump sum payments on taking up employment (ITEPA 2003, ss 62, 225, 226)

[15.2] Where a lump sum payment is made to a prospective employee, it will be taxed as advance pay for future services unless it represents compensation for some right or asset given up on taking up the employment. It is difficult to show that a payment does represent compensation, and professional advice should be sought for payments received in this category.

Sometimes a lump sum is paid in return for agreeing to restrict conduct or activities in some way, for example agreeing not to leave to join a competitor within a certain period of time. Any such special payments are treated as pay, both for tax and for national insurance contributions (NICs). If an employee makes such an agreement in return for a non-cash benefit, the value of the benefit still counts as pay for both tax and NICs.

Lump sum termination payments and benefits (ITEPA 2003, ss 225, 226, 309, 393–416)

[15.3] Lump sum payments received on termination of employment are taxed depending upon the exact nature of the payment. HMRC set out a step by step process (at EIM12810) that must be followed to establish whether a payment is taxable or not, as follows:

(a)   First of all, establish whether the rules in relation to receipts from non-approved and employer-financed retirement benefits schemes apply. Ex-gratia payments made when employment is terminated by the employee's retirement (other than premature retirement through redundancy or disability) or death (other than as the result of an accident, see **15.5**) are fully taxable under the employment income rules as benefits under an employer-financed retirement benefit scheme that is not a registered pension scheme (see **16.36**). Guidance on this is at EIM15010 onwards;

(b)   If (a) above does not apply it is necessary to consider (in order) whether:

   (i)   the payments are already taxable under the normal rules for earnings from employment. A payment will be taxable as employment income if it is a payment for services rendered, i.e. it is really deferred pay. Pay in lieu of notice or compensation for loss of office are chargeable to both tax and NICs in the normal way if they are provided for in the employee's terms and conditions of employment, and this may be the case even if the payment is discretionary, for example the employment contract provides for four weeks' notice to be given, or, at the employer's discretion, pay in lieu of notice. HMRC's views are set out in their Tax Bulletin 63 (February 2003) and the Employment Income Manual at EIM12976;

   (ii)   the payments are for a restrictive covenant, and therefore taxable. HMRC may seek to tax them as payments made in return for a restrictive undertaking (see **15.2**), if they are paid in return for an agreement by the employee to restrict his future conduct or activities. This will not normally apply where the only undertaking by the employee is that he will not pursue an action against the employer concerning the termination of his employment (unless a specific sum was attributed to the undertaking, which would be very unusual);

   (iii)   the payment is made in connection with termination and therefore fall within the special rules that provide an exemption for the first £30,000 (see **15.4**). To be within these special rules, payments must be by way of compensation because the employer has *broken* the employment contract, or be purely ex gratia payments that are not part of the employer's established practice. A statutory redundancy payment under the Employment Rights Act 1996 is exempt from income tax, but does reduce the overall £30,000 limit. Redundancy pay over and above the statutory amount will also be treated as a termination payment within the special rules so long as, broadly speaking, it is paid because the job has ceased to exist rather than as a payment for services rendered by the employee.

In the case of an ex gratia payment, it will be more difficult to demonstrate to HMRC that it was made because of the termination of employment rather than for services rendered. Note that lump sum payments from an approved or registered retirement benefits scheme are exempt from tax.

For either compensation or ex gratia payments, the following circumstances may give rise to further complications:

(a) Where the employee is also a shareholder, it may be difficult to show that the payment is not a distribution, for which no deduction would be given in calculating the employer's trading profit (see **CHAPTER 3**).

(b) Where the payment is made at the same time as a change in voting control, a clear distinction must be demonstrated between the payment and the share transactions if the payment is not to be regarded as part of the capital transaction.

(c) If the employee continues with the employer in a new capacity, either as an employee or perhaps under a consultancy agreement, it becomes that much harder to show the payment was not for services rendered or to be rendered in the future.

Taxation of lump sum termination payments and benefits

[15.4] Provided that the payment and/or benefit is not caught as taxable earnings, a distribution or as part of a capital transaction, it will be taxed according to the special rules for termination payments. Under these rules (subject to what is said below about wholly exempt payments), the first £30,000 is exempt and only the balance is taxable as earnings. Non-cash benefits are valued using the cash equivalents that apply in calculating employment income (see **CHAPTER 10**) unless, exceptionally, the 'money's worth' value is higher. This would apply where, for example, a house is transferred as part of the termination package and its value has increased since the employer acquired it. Various benefits that would normally escape tax in a continuing employment are also excluded from the taxable termination payment. Statutory redundancy payments are not taxable as earnings (see **15.3**) but are subject to the special rules for termination payments and will, therefore, use part of the £30,000 exemption.

The taxable amount is treated as income of the tax year in which it is received or (for non-cash benefits) enjoyed. This makes it easier to deal with cash amounts payable by instalments and continuing benefits. Where the continuing benefit is a beneficial loan, then unless the taxable amount is covered by the £30,000 exemption, the notional interest charged to tax is treated as interest paid by the employee, so that tax relief is given if appropriate (see **10.38**). Employers deduct tax under PAYE on cash payments (see **15.7**), and employees account for higher rate tax on such payments, and the whole of the tax on non-cash benefits, in their self-assessments.

Exemptions

[15.5] Some payments are completely exempt from tax, for example those on accidental death in service, in respect of disability or where the service has been predominantly abroad. Where service abroad does not qualify for complete exemption, there is a proportionate reduction of the taxable amount according to the time spent abroad.

Lump sums received under registered pension schemes are exempt. They may be boosted by agreed special contributions from the employer to the fund prior to the termination of employment so long as the various limits are not exceeded (see **CHAPTER 16**). In view of HMRC's position on ex gratia payments (see **15.3**), this route provides an alternative where there is a registered pension scheme.

The £30,000 exemption applies after all other available exemptions, but it is taken into account before giving proportionate relief for foreign service that is not completely exempt.

Calculation of tax payable

[15.6] Tax on the chargeable amount is calculated by treating it as the top slice of taxable income (except for life policy gains (see **40.9**). This is different to the normal rules, where dividend income, followed by savings income is treated as the top slice (see **2.5**). This may reduce the tax payable.

Example 1

An individual's taxable income in 2010/11, after reliefs and allowances, comprises non-savings income of £22,600, dividend income of £10,000 (inclusive of tax credits) and £12,000 in respect of a taxable lump sum. The comparison of the tax position if the normal rules treating dividend income as the top slice of income applied with the special rules for dealing with lump sums is as follows:

	£		£	£
If no special rules applied				
Non-savings income including lump sum	34,600	@ 20%	6,920	
Dividends (part)	2,800	@ 10%	280	
	37,400			
Dividends (balance)	7,200	@ 32.5%	2,340	
	44,600			9,540
Lump sum of £12,000 treated as top slice of income				
Non-savings income other than lump sum	22,600	@ 20%	4,520	
Dividends	10,000	@ 10%	1,000	

	32,600		
Lump sum (part)	4,800	@ 20%	960
	37,400		
Lump sum (balance)	7,200	@ 40%	2,880
	44,600		9,360
Reduction in tax through treating lump sum as top slice of income			180

> The reduction of £180 represents a saving of tax at 22.5% on £7,200 of the dividends = £1,620, less an additional 20% tax on £7,200 (the part now taxed at 40%) of the lump sum = £1,440.

PAYE and reporting requirements

[15.7] If the termination settlement is made before the employee leaves, the employer must deduct and account for PAYE tax on the excess of chargeable termination payments over £30,000 and also on ex gratia sums on retirement or death for which approval has not yet been granted (tax being refunded as and when approval is received). Cash payments will be shown on tax deduction sheets and forms P45. If payments are made after the employee has left and been issued with form P45, tax must be deducted under PAYE at the basic rate. Any higher rate tax due will then be collected directly from the employee on 31 January after the end of the relevant tax year, along with the tax on any non-cash benefits. Although this may give a cash flow advantage at the time, it may result in increased payments on account for the following year (see **9.9**), because tax paid directly affects payments on account, whereas tax under PAYE does not.

Unless the package is wholly cash, or the total value of the package including benefits is estimated not to exceed £30,000, the employer must provide details of the termination package to HMRC not later than 6 July following the end of the tax year in which the termination package was awarded (copies being provided to employees to enable them to complete their tax returns). The details should cover the total value of the package, the amounts of cash and the nature of the benefits to be provided and their cash equivalents, indicating which, if any, amounts and benefits are to be provided in later years. No further report needs to be submitted unless, exceptionally, there is a subsequent variation increasing the value of the package by more than £10,000, in which case a report must be sent to HMRC by 6 July following the tax year of variation. If a report is not submitted because a package is originally estimated to have a value not exceeding £30,000, but the package is subsequently changed so that it exceeds that amount, a report and employee copy must be provided by 6 July following the tax year in which the change occurs. There are penalties for non-compliance (see **CHAPTER 9**).

Calculating the employer's profits (CTA 2009, ss 76–81; ITTOIA 2005, s 79)

[15.8] To be deducted in arriving at taxable profits, expenses must be wholly and exclusively for the purposes of the trade. Apart from statutory redundancy payments, which are specifically allowable, there is no special rule for termination payments, but it will usually be easier to show that they meet the 'wholly and exclusively' requirement when they are compensation rather than ex gratia payments, and when the trade is continuing rather than when it is not (but see below regarding permanent discontinuance of a trade).

It may be particularly difficult for the employer to obtain a deduction where the payment is ex gratia and is associated with a sale of the shares or a change in voting control, or where it is an abnormally high payment to a director with a material interest in the company.

Where a trade is permanently discontinued, it is specifically provided that an additional payment up to three times any amount paid under the statutory redundancy pay provisions is allowable as a deduction in computing the employer's profits. Any payments in excess of this amount are disallowed unless they are made to an employee on cessation under a pre-existing contractual or statutory obligation (not ex gratia amounts).

Counselling services for redundant employees (ITEPA 2003, s 310)

[15.9] The provision of counselling services by employers for redundant employees, or payment by the employer of an employee's costs for such counselling is specifically exempt from tax for employees, and the cost is fully allowed to employers.

Expenses incurred in obtaining a lump sum payment

[15.10] Some employees may incur expenses, for example fees to advisers, in obtaining a lump sum payment. These will not reduce the taxable part of the lump sum as they will not have been wholly, exclusively and necessarily incurred in the performance of the duties of the employment. By concession, where an employer pays an employee's legal costs in obtaining a compensation payment, HMRC will not treat the payment as a taxable benefit if it is made direct to the employee's solicitor following an out of court settlement, or if it is made to the employee under a court order (HMRC concession A81).

Tax points

[15.11] Note the following:

- An ex gratia payment to a director or shareholder of a close company is especially vulnerable to HMRC attack, on either or both of the following grounds:

(a)   it is not a deductible trading expense;

(b)   it is a distribution of profits.

- If an ex gratia payment by a close company is not allowed in calculating profits, HMRC may contend that each shareholder has made a proportionate transfer of value for inheritance tax. There is a specific exclusion where the payment is allowed in computing profits.

- Ex gratia payments may be taxed as non-exempt 'retirement benefits' (see **15.3**). Such a charge takes precedence over a charge under the rules for termination payments.

- If an employee who receives a termination settlement is allowed to keep a company car as part of the package, the market value of the car will be taken into account for the purpose of the exempt £30,000 unless it is regarded as a reward for past services, in which case the full market value would be chargeable as pay. An alternative is to increase the lump sum and give the employee the opportunity to buy the car at market value. If the lump sum was taxable as an unapproved retirement benefit (see **15.3**), the value of the car would similarly be taxable.

- If one or more termination payments are paid after an employee has left and been given his P45, tax only has to be deducted at the basic rate. The employee will then pay any higher rate tax due on 31 January after the end of the tax year. Under self-assessment, however, this may lead to increased payments on account for the following year (see **15.7**).

- Unless the former employee obtains new sources of income to replace his salary, the tax cost of a termination payment may be lower if the termination occurs shortly after 6 April rather than before, because all or part of the payment may fall within the basic rate band, whereas it might have attracted 40% or 50% tax if it was received in addition to a full year's salary.

- It is essential that proper documentation and board minutes are available so that the nature of payments can be demonstrated to HMRC.

- The tax reliefs for lump sum payments are only available to employees and not to those working under a contract for services, whose earnings are taxed as trading income (see **19.1**). If, exceptionally, employment income is included by agreement with HMRC in the calculation of self-employed profits, e.g. directors' fees where the directorship is held in a professional capacity and the fees are included as income of the professional practice, this in itself will not prevent a lump sum qualifying for the reliefs outlined in this chapter.

- A termination payment may affect the former employee's entitlement to social security benefits if he is then unemployed, but the employee will be entitled to unemployment credits for the period covered by the compensation payment so that his NIC record is not affected.

Pensions

16

Pension provision

Background

[16.1] State pensions are recognised as providing an inadequate income in old age, even though employees' state pensions are boosted by an earnings-related addition. Rights to the earnings-related addition used to be built up under the State Earnings Related Pension Scheme (SERPS). SERPS was replaced in 2002 by the State Second Pension Scheme (S2P) which provides better benefit levels than under SERPS for lower earners. S2P aims to provide a flat rate benefit for those on low incomes and to encourage middle and high income earners to make independent provision and contract out by providing substantial national insurance rebates. The Government will introduce further new state pension provisions in 2012. Under these provisions, S2P would be gradually turned into a flat-rate weekly top-up to the basic state pension. For details of the latest proposals see **13.4**.

For those who wish to contribute to pensions other than under the state pension scheme, there are two main types of scheme — occupational schemes for employees who have an employer offering such a scheme, and personal pension schemes (which include stakeholder schemes), to which employers may or may not contribute. Occupational pension schemes may either be 'defined benefit' schemes, i.e. final salary schemes, or 'defined contribution' schemes, i.e. money purchase schemes. Some employers have offered inducement payments to employees in final salary schemes to obtain their agreement to a reduction in benefits or a transfer to a money purchase scheme. HMRC announced in January 2007 a change in their view of the law. They previously took the view that such payments made to the scheme member escaped liability in some circumstances, but they now consider that the payments are employment income liable to tax and Class 1 national insurance contributions (NICs).

Contributions to personal pension schemes may be made by non-earners, as well as the employed and self-employed. Personal pension schemes are dealt with in CHAPTER 17.

Those in money purchase occupational schemes and personal pension schemes (including stakeholder schemes) receive regular illustrations of what their benefits might be in present-day prices, so that people have a more realistic idea about the value of their pension funds and what options are available to them. The illustration may incorporate state pension information supplied by the Department for Work and Pensions if the pension provider and employee so wish.

Tax treatment of state pensions

[16.2] State retirement and widows' pensions are taxable under the provisions of the Income Tax (Earnings and Pensions) Act 2003 (see **10.1**). The amount chargeable is the pension accruing in the tax year. Wounds and disability pensions, war widows' pensions, lump sums payable under the armed forces early departure scheme and illness or injury benefits under an armed and reserve forces compensation scheme are exempt from tax. Tax on state pensions is collected through PAYE deductions (via a coding adjustment) from earnings or other pensions with any balance normally being included in the self-assessment.

[16.3] Taxable state pensions are earned by the payment of NICs. For employees, the entitlement is built up under the S2P scheme and is earnings related (see **13.2** and **16.1**). For the self-employed, the pension is at a flat rate and there is no earnings-related addition (see **24.1**). As indicated in **16.1**, employers may arrange for their employees to be contracted out of the state scheme, an equivalent or better pension being paid instead from the employer's scheme (see **16.5**). The Government intends to reintroduce the link between annual state pension increases and average earnings from 6 April 2011. When they do so, money purchase schemes will no longer be able to contract out of S2P (see **13.4**).

Deferring state pensions

[16.4] Incentives are provided for those who defer taking their state pension. Extra state pension may be earned at 1% for every five weeks deferral (10.4% for each year), or alternatively for a minimum deferral period of 12 months a taxable lump sum may be paid, based on the pension that would have been earned in the period of deferral plus compound interest. Guidance is provided at www.direct.gov.uk.

Taxable lump sums will be *treated* as income and taxed at the top rate applicable to the recipient's other sources of income, but will not count as part of their total income, so that entitlement to age relief and marginal tax rates will not be affected.

Contracting out of the State Second Pension Scheme (S2P) (FA 2004, ss 202, 233)

[16.5] At present employers may arrange for their employees to be contracted out of S2P (thus entitling both employers and employees to pay lower national insurance contributions) if they operate either a salary-related scheme (COSR) or a money purchase scheme (COMPS) (but see **16.3** re the Government's planned changes). Contracting out rebates do not count towards the pension annual allowance.

Rebates of national insurance contributions for salary-related schemes are currently 3.7% for employers and 1.6% for employees (see **13.12**). Employers with money purchase schemes must make minimum payments into the scheme equal to the combined employer/employee rebates of 3% — employee 1.6%, employer 1.4%. HMRC top up the payment by age-related rebates up to a maximum combined figure of 7.4% at age 49 or over for 2010/11 (see **13.12**). Employers may run combined salary-related/money purchase schemes (COMBS) (although a single member cannot be in both at the same time).

Many employers, particularly family companies, remain contracted in to the state scheme and provide their own pension scheme in addition. The employee then gets full benefits under the state scheme (and pays full contributions) plus the additional benefits provided by his employer's scheme.

Employees in a contracted-in scheme are able to contract out of S2P independently while remaining in their employer's scheme, either by making a free-standing additional voluntary contribution (AVC – see **16.27**) or through a separate personal pension plan (see **17.16**). The rebates in such separate personal pension plans are calculated by applying different rebate percentages to bands of earnings so as to provide low earners with increased benefits (see **13.12**). This weighting does not apply to the rebates for contributions to money purchase schemes, including free-standing AVCs, which are flat percentages depending on age as indicated above.

New regime for pension schemes from 6 April 2006 (FA 2004, ss 149–284 and Schs 28–36)

[16.6] From 6 April 2006 the previous tax provisions relating to occupational and personal pension schemes were replaced by a single scheme for all tax-privileged pension savings. As originally enacted in FA 2004, the new provisions opened up pension planning opportunities that the Government considered unacceptable and changes have been made in Finance Acts 2006, 2007 and 2008. Measures in FA 2008 are designed to tighten the rules on the spreading of tax relief for abnormally large contributions made by employers; prevent the inheritance of tax-privileged pension savings; and to ensure that the regime works as intended.

Paragraphs **16.7** to **16.22** of this chapter deal with the overall position, and the remainder covers matters specifically relevant to occupational schemes. **CHAPTER 17** deals with additional points relating to personal pension schemes.

[16.7] The previous complex requirements for obtaining approval for schemes were replaced by a simpler process of scheme registration. Schemes that were approved schemes before 6 April 2006 automatically became registered schemes on that day. Individuals may contribute to as many schemes as they wish. There is no longer any provision for carrying contributions back or forward. The minimum pension age is 55 from 6 April 2010, earlier retirement still being permitted on ill health grounds (see **16.25**). The latest age for taking benefits remains 75.

[16.8] Within the original new scheme provisions, it was possible to obtain tax relief on pension contributions used to fund life assurance policies. This is not possible for occupational scheme contributions paid on or after 1 August 2007, unless the insurer received the application for the policy before 29 March 2007 and the policy was taken out before 1 August 2007. The relief for employers' contributions is not affected. For personal pension contributions the relief was withdrawn from 6 April 2007, unless the policy was taken out before 1 August 2007 and the insurer received the application before 14 December 2006 (or 13 April 2007 in some circumstances).

Key features of new scheme (FA 2004, ss 196–200, 214–238)

[16.9] The new regime has two key features:

- A single 'standard lifetime allowance' on the total amount of pension savings that can benefit from tax relief, which was set at £1.5 million for 2006/07, rising to £1.6 million for 2007/08, £1.65 million for 2008/09, £1.75 million for 2009/10 and £1.8 million for 2010/11 up to and including 2015/16. If benefits are withdrawn in excess of the allowance, tax will be charged on the excess as indicated at **16.16**.
- An annual allowance for maximum 'pension inputs', i.e. annual contributions paid to money purchase schemes and/or annual increases in accrued benefits under defined benefit (final salary) schemes (calculated using a special formula). The allowance for 2010/11 is £255,000 (for 2009/10 it was £245,000). It was set at £215,000 for 2006/07, to increase by £10,000 a year for each of the next four years, and it was intended that it would remain at the 2010/11 level of £255,000 up to and including 2015/16. If pension inputs exceed the annual allowance, the scheme member will pay tax at 40% on the excess.

The annual allowance could be significantly reduced in future years. The Labour Government introduced a restriction on pensions tax relief from 6 April 2011 (see **16.13**), and whilst the coalition Government agreed to continue with these provisions for the time being, it believes the approach could have unwelcome consequences for pension saving. It will, therefore, review alternative approaches, one of which might be to reduce the annual allowance to between £30,000 and £45,000. See further **16.13**.

[16.10] For employers, the new scheme provisions apply to all contributions paid in accounting periods ending on or after 6 April 2006. In order to be deductible from profits, employers' contributions to registered schemes must be wholly and exclusively for the purposes of the trade. Where that condition is satisfied, the contributions are then normally allowed in the accounting period in which they are paid.

If there is an increase of over 210% in the contributions of an accounting period compared with the previous period, and the higher amount is at least £500,000 more than 110% of the lower amount, the contributions are spread over two to four years depending on the amount of the contribution. Provisions in FA 2008 are designed to ensure that spreading applies to contributions made indirectly in the same way as they apply to contributions made directly by the employer.

Scheme investments (FA 2004, ss 174A, 185A–185I, 273ZA and Sch 29A)

[16.11] Pension providers are normally able to invest in all types of investment. Restrictions apply, however, to 'investment-regulated pension schemes', broadly those where one or more members can direct, influence or advise on the investments the scheme makes. The main examples are Self-Invested Personal Pension Schemes (SIPPS — see **17.19**) and Small Self-Administered Schemes (SSAS — see **16.37**).

The restrictions apply to investments in 'prohibited assets', namely residential property and assets such as fine wines, classic cars, art and antiques. The rules apply both to direct investment and also indirect investment where it has been used to get round the new rules (such as a SIPP holding all the shares in a company that owns residential property). The rules do not apply to genuine commercial investment, such as investment in a Real Estate Investment Trust unless the holding is 10% or more (see **32.32** onwards).

If such assets are purchased, the purchase will be subject to the unauthorised payments charge (see **16.18**), so that the member will be charged to tax at up to 55% on the value of the prohibited asset and the scheme administrator will be liable to the scheme sanction charge of 15%. If the value of the prohibited asset exceeds 25% of the value of the pension scheme's assets, the scheme may be deregistered, which would lead to a 40% tax charge on the value of the scheme's assets.

Anti-avoidance provisions

[16.12] As indicated in **16.11**, the new provisions have been amended from the outset to remove the tax advantages for 'investment-regulated pension schemes' of investing in residential property and assets such as fine wines, classic cars, art and antiques.

They also prevent pension funds being artificially boosted by recycling tax-free lump sums (see **16.19**).

Contributions (FA 2004, ss 188–190; FA 2007, s 68 and Sch 18; FA 2009, s 72 and Sch 35; FA 2010, ss 23, 48 and Sch 2; F(No.2)A 2010, s 5; SI 2010/429)

[16.13] There is no limit on the contributions that may be made by or on behalf of an individual, but tax relief will only be given on contributions up to the higher of 100% of relevant earnings and £3,600 gross, and is further restricted to the annual allowance (see **16.9**) and the high income excess relief charge from 6 April 2011, including the anti-forestalling provisions applying from 22 April 2009 (see below). Relief is not available for contributions paid after the individual has reached age 75. From 6 April 2007 (subject to transitional provisions), relief is not available for life assurance contributions. Contributions may be made not only by scheme members and employers but also by anyone else on their behalf — spouse, civil partner, parents, grandparents etc. The scheme member will get tax relief on such contributions within the permitted limits. Donors would need to consider the inheritance tax implications (see **CHAPTERS 33** and **34**). See **16.10** in relation to employer contributions. Tax will be charged at 40% as indicated in **16.9** if total 'pension inputs' exceed the annual allowance. The actual relief obtained will therefore be the relief on the contributions less any tax charged on excess pension inputs. The amount of relief on the contributions paid before 6 April 2011 depends on the individual's marginal tax rate(s). Before this date, someone who has sufficient earned income (after allowances) taxable at 40% will save tax on the contribution at 40%. At the other extreme, someone whose income is covered by available allowances will get no tax relief at all. See **2.40** for possible additional savings where tax credits are received.

Tax relief on pension contributions made by persons with gross income of £150,000 or more and relevant income of not less than £130,000 will be restricted to the basic rate of tax (currently 20%) from 6 April 2011, except where the individual has gross income between £150,000 and £180,000 in which case tax relief is tapered from their marginal rate of tax to the basic rate. 'Gross income' comprises income before deduction or relief for pension contributions and charitable donations, but for employees includes the value of any pension benefit funded by their employers. 'Relevant income' is calculated in the same way as gross income but for employees does not include the value of any pension benefits funded by the employer and includes, instead, taxable employment income the employee agreed to give up under a salary sacrifice or flexible remuneration arrangement after 22 April 2009 (see **17.14**). This means only employees with relevant income of £130,000 or more will need to establish the value of the pension funded by their employer to determine whether their gross income is £150,000 or more and that the restriction applies.

The relief is clawed back by imposing the high income excess relief charge on an individual's total pension savings amount at an appropriate percentage, so that the total relief for pension contributions does not exceed 20%. The 'total pension savings amount' is the aggregate of pension savings amounts for each pension arrangement the taxpayer has. For money purchase arrangements the pension savings amount is broadly the total of employee and employer pension contributions. For defined benefit schemes it is broadly calculated by reference to the increase in the value of any pension and lump sum during the year and by reference to the taxpayer's age. The appropriate percentage will vary depending on the rate at which the individual received tax relief on the pension contributions. It can therefore be 0%, 20% or 30% and, where an individual's gross income is between £150,000 and £180,000, is reduced by 1% for every £1,000 that the individual's gross income is less than £180,000 (but to no less than 0%). The charge will be collected through the individual's self-assessment.

Example 1

An individual has gross income of £200,000 and makes a £60,000 personal pension contribution. He receives tax relief on £50,000 of the contribution (the amount above the higher rate limit of £150,000) at 50%, and 40% tax relief on the balance of £10,000 of the contribution. Total tax relief is therefore £29,000. A restriction of 20% is applied to the £10,000 receiving 40% relief and a restriction of 30% is applied to the remaining £50,000 receiving 50% relief. The restriction thus totals £17,000 with relief of £12,000 being given (£60,000 at 20%).

Example 2

An individual with gross income of £165,000 makes a pension contribution of £10,000. As gross income is £15,000 less than £180,000, the high income excess relief appropriate percentage is reduced by 15% (1% for every £1,000) to 15%. The high income excess relief charge is therefore £10,000 at 15% = £1,500.

FA 2009 introduced anti-forestalling provisions (subsequently amended by FA 2010) to prevent individuals who will potentially be affected by the restriction increasing their pension savings in excess of their normal regular pattern. The provisions have effect for affected contributions paid under money purchase schemes on or after 22 April 2009, or in respect of affected increases in the rights of individual members under final salary schemes on or after 22 April 2009. They will not apply to individuals with income of less than £130,000 for the tax year and for both of the preceding two tax years, or to individuals with income of £130,000 or more in any of those years who continue with their existing pattern of regular pension savings and who do not make any additional pension savings. The income threshold introduced in FA 2009 was £150,000 but this was reduced to £130,000 in FA 2010 following the introduction of different definitions of 'gross income' and 'relevant income' in relation to the pensions high income excess relief charge (see above). An individual whose relevant income is less than £150,000 in 2009/10 is nonetheless treated as a high-income individual in that year if his relevant income in either of the two preceding tax years was £130,000 or more.

Individuals who do increase their pension savings on or after 22 April 2009 over and above their normal pattern of regular pension savings will only be affected by the provisions if their total pension savings in that year are over £20,000. Broadly, the tax charge (the special annual allowance charge) will only apply to the additional savings, regardless of who makes the contributions, and will have the effect of restricting tax relief on those savings to the basic rate. For those individuals who had relevant income below £150,000 in 2009/10 certain pension input amounts made before 9 December 2009 do not give rise to the charge. Individuals can request a refund of pension contributions paid in 2009/10 which may otherwise create a liability to the charge.

A late amendment to the anti-forestalling charge during the passage of the Finance Bill 2009 provided that, if irregular contributions have been made over the past three years, the special annual allowance used in calculating this tax charge will be increased to the average of those contributions, subject to an upper limit of £30,000. Further amendments were made by the Special Annual Allowance Charge (Protected Pension Input Amounts) Order SI 2010/429. The amendments provide protection against the charge where there is a change in pension provider on or after 22 April 2009, for contributions which the individual or his employer was contractually committed to at 22 April 2009 but which had not commenced at that date, and certain lump sum contributions made on 22 April 2009.

HMRC have produced guidance on the high income excess relief charge which will be incorporated in the HMRC Registered Pension Schemes Manual.

The current Government believes an alternative approach to the high income excess relief charge involving the reform of existing allowances, principally a significantly reduced annual allowance (see **16.9**), might be a better way of meeting the objective of restricting the generosity of pensions tax relief. It has therefore introduced legislation to bring in powers to repeal the high income excess relief charge at any time before 31 December 2010.

Drawing benefits (ITEPA 2003, ss 636A–636C; FA 2004, ss 160–169, 218–220; F(No.2)A 2010, s 6 and Sch 3)

[16.14] Before changes introduced by F(No.2)A 2010, pension income had to be taken from a fund before age 75 by way of a scheme pension, purchase of an annuity, or drawing income directly from the pension fund as an unsecured pension, or after age 75 by drawing income directly from a fund as an 'alternatively secured pension' (see **16.20**). However, legislation has been introduced to increase to 77 the age by which members of a money purchase scheme have to buy an annuity or otherwise secure a pension income. This change applies to individuals who have not reached age 75 before 22 June 2010. The Government announced in the June 2010 Emergency Budget that it will end from April 2011 the existing rules that create an effective obligation to purchase an annuity by age 75. This will enable individuals to make more flexible use of their pension savings. It has launched a consultation on the details of these changes. See HMRC guidance at www.hmrc.gov.uk/pensionschemes/technical-note.pdf. The adjustment to age 77 enables individuals to defer their decision on what to do with their pension savings until after the new rules are finalised. Payment of a pension or annuity may be guaranteed for ten years. Previously this provision also applied to alternatively secured pensions, but it no longer applies to such pensions for deaths on or after 6 April 2007.

[16.15] All schemes (including additional voluntary contribution schemes) are able to offer a tax-free lump sum of up to 25% of the fund, subject to an overriding maximum of 25% of the lifetime allowance (which may be an increased amount under the transitional provisions — see **16.21**). The tax-free lump sum must be paid before the scheme member reaches age 77 (but see **16.14** for full details).

[16.16] Occupational schemes may offer flexible retirement, enabling employees to draw benefits while continuing to work for the employer.

The lifetime allowance is considered at any time when benefits are withdrawn. On the first withdrawal of benefits, if the funds being used exceed the lifetime allowance, the excess will be taxed at 25% to the extent that it is used to buy a pension (the pension itself then being taxed at 40% for a higher rate taxpayer or 50% for an additional rate taxpayer) and at 55% where it is taken as a lump sum. On a later withdrawal, the *percentage* of the lifetime allowance used up when the first withdrawal was made is taken into account to calculate the lifetime limit remaining available at the time of the second withdrawal, and so on for further withdrawals. For example, say benefits were taken in 2006/07 amounting to £750,000, i.e. 50% of the 2006/07 lifetime allowance of £1.5 million. If further benefits were to be taken in 2008/09, the part of the lifetime allowance already used would be 50% of the *2008/09* limit of £1,650,000, i.e. £825,000. This would leave £825,000 of the lifetime allowance still available, rather than (£1,650,000 – £750,000 =) £900,000.

[16.17] Individuals aged between 60 and 77 (but see **16.14** for full details) with total pension savings not exceeding 1% of the lifetime allowance (£18,000 for 2010/11), will be able to take the whole amount as a lump sum if their pension provider agrees. If their pension savings are in more than one pension plan, all providers must agree and all lump sums must be taken within twelve months. A quarter of the lump sum will be tax-free and the remainder taxed as income.

Unauthorised payments (FA 2004, ss 208–213, 239–242)

[16.18] If a registered scheme makes unauthorised payments, there is a charge of up to 55% on the scheme member, and a scheme sanction charge of 40% (usually reduced to 15%) on the scheme administrator. There is also a de-registration charge of 40% on the scheme administrator if a scheme's registration is withdrawn.

Recycling lump sums (FA 2004, Sch 29)

[16.19] There are anti-avoidance provisions to prevent pension funds being boosted by pre-planned recycling of lump sums. The provisions affect lump sums paid on or after 6 April 2006, but HMRC state that they could apply where the contributions were paid in 2004/05 or 2005/06. The provisions do not apply where no more than 30% of the lump sum is recycled, nor do they apply to the recycling of total lump sums received within 12 months that do not exceed 1% of the lifetime allowance (£18,000 for 2010/11). Where the provisions do apply, the lump sum(s) will be treated as an unauthorised pension payment, liable to tax at up to 55%, and the administrator of the pension scheme will be subject to a scheme sanction charge of between 15% and 40%, depending on the amount of the payment (see **16.18**).

The recycling provisions do not affect tax relief for the pension contributions, which may be claimed under the normal rules.

Alternatively secured pensions (FA 2004, ss 165, 167, 172B, 172BA, 181A and Sch 28; IHTA 1984, ss 151A–151C; F(No.2)A 2010, s 6 and Sch 3)

[16.20] Someone in a money purchase scheme who does not wish to buy an annuity at age 77 (but see **16.14** for full details), possibly because of religious objections to risk pooling, may take his pension by way of income withdrawal from the pension fund (referred to as an 'alternatively secured pension' — ASP). The Government considered, however, that these provisions were being used in circumstances where they were not intended to apply, and introduced provisions both in FA 2006 and FA 2007 to limit significantly the way in which ASP funds may be used.

For alternatively secured pension years beginning on or after 6 April 2007, a minimum income must be drawn of 55% of the comparable annuity that would be payable to a 77-year old. If this is not done, the scheme administrators will normally be liable to a 40% tax charge on the shortfall. Annual withdrawals must not exceed 90% (previously 70%) of the annuity available to someone aged 77. When the person dies, there is provision for annual payments to be made to dependants. The balance of the fund remaining on the death of the member or last dependant will either be gifted to a charity nominated by the member or dependant, or by the scheme administrator where there is no such nomination. For deaths before 6 April 2007 it was also possible for the balance of a fund to be transferred to another member of the scheme nominated by the member or dependant, or in the absence of such a nomination, selected by the scheme administrator. For deaths on or after 6 April 2007, however, any such transfers are no longer authorised payments and if they are made they will suffer an unauthorised payments charge (as to which see **16.18**). For inheritance tax purposes, this income tax charge will be taken into account in arriving at the value of the deceased's estate.

The amount of ASP funds left over when a scheme member dies will be treated as part of the member's estate for inheritance tax purposes, unless the funds are paid to charity. Where the funds are used to provide pension benefits for the scheme member's spouse, civil partner or person financially dependent on the scheme member when he dies, any inheritance tax charge on the left-over ASP funds will not be made until the entitlement to such benefits ceases. The inheritance tax payable will be calculated using the inheritance tax rates in force at that time, if lower than those applicable at the date of the member's death.

Transitional provisions

[16.21] Transitional provisions protect pre-6 April 2006 pension rights and rights to lump sums. In respect of the lifetime allowance, there are two main options:

- Primary protection applicable to the excess value over £1.5 million. The pension scheme member had to notify HMRC that there was such an excess by 5 April 2009, and each year's lifetime allowance will then be enhanced to the extent of that excess value. For example someone with funds totalling £1.8 million at 6 April 2006 has an excess of £0.3 million, i.e. 20%, and their lifetime allowance for each year would be 120% of the standard amount. This protection does not extend to funds which at 6 April 2006 are surplus under the old rules. Thus if the funds of £1.8 million were themselves £150,000 over the previously calculated permitted limit, the primary protection would only apply to £1.65 million, with the remaining £150,000 being taxed under **16.16** if withdrawn and the lifetime allowance becoming 110% of the standard amount.

- Enhanced protection available to those who ceased membership of approved schemes before 6 April 2006 and do not resume membership of any registered scheme. All benefits becoming payable after 5 April 2006 will normally be exempt from the lifetime allowance charge, providing the member notified HMRC by 5 April 2009 that enhanced protection was being claimed and thereafter all the relevant conditions are satisfied.

Separate transitional provisions apply for a member of an occupational scheme who is entitled under the pre April 2006 rules to a tax-free lump sum but has not opted for primary or enhanced protection. If the member's lump sum entitlement gave an amount in excess of 25% of the lifetime allowance at 6 April 2006 (£375,000), for example because it was based on average earnings, this entitlement can be preserved, and increased in line with the lifetime limit increases stated in **16.9**. This provision only applies where all pensions payable under the scheme from 6 April 2006 become payable on the same date.

Employees who had the right to draw pensions earlier than the retirement age of 55 which applies from 6 April 2010 may have that right protected, and there is special protection for employees who are members of pre-6 April 2006 schemes with lower normal retirement ages, such as athletes. The available lifetime allowance for these protected groups will, however, be reduced. The Government intends to introduce regulations to remove an unintentional unauthorised payments tax charge where an individual aged 50 or over, but under 55, transfers his pension payment to another pension provider.

Unregistered schemes

[16.22] A scheme that is not registered under the new provisions is not subject to any restrictions but is not entitled to any tax advantages (see **16.36**). Transitional protection applies to pension rights accrued within non-registered schemes at 6 April 2006.

Membership of employers' schemes

[16.23] Employees cannot be compelled to be members of their employers' schemes, and may instead (or as well) take out personal pension plans (see CHAPTER 17) or rely on the state pension scheme. Subject to various conditions, pension rights from an existing occupational scheme may be transferred to a personal pension plan and it is normally possible to transfer back from a personal pension plan to an employer's scheme if the scheme agrees or to a free-standing additional voluntary contribution scheme (FSAVCS, as to which see **16.27**).

Taxation advantages of registered schemes

[16.24] The advantages are as follows:

(a) The employer's contributions reduce taxable business profits providing they are wholly and exclusively for the purposes of the business.

(b) The employer's contributions are not treated as a taxable employee benefit, nor do they count as the employee's earnings for national insurance contributions (NICs).

(c) Relief for an employee's own contributions is given under the 'net pay scheme', so that the contributions reduce taxable earnings. (They do not, however, reduce pay for NICs.)

(d) A tax-free lump sum can be paid to the employee when benefits are taken.

(e) Provision can be made for a lump sum to be paid if an employee dies before taking benefits (see **16.31**).

(f) The investment income and capital gains of the fund are not taxed (although tax credits on dividends cannot be reclaimed).

Retirement age

[16.25] Normal retirement age may be any age between 60 and 77 (but see **16.14** for full details). (For schemes approved before 25 July 1991, the normal retirement age is 55 for women and 60 for men, with an upper limit for both of 70.) Early retirement may presently be allowed from age 55 (or earlier for those in certain occupations, such as athletes). See **16.21** for transitional provisions.

Providing the scheme rules so provide, ill-health retirement will be permitted at any age. For someone whose life expectancy is less than one year, full commutation will be possible and the commuted amount below the lifetime allowance (£1.8 million for 2010/11) will be tax-free.

Maximum contributions

[16.26] As indicated in **16.13**, the employee contributions qualifying for tax relief depend on an employee's earnings, which means the employment income on which he is chargeable to tax, including benefits and also amounts taxable as earnings under the rules relating to lump sum termination payments (see CHAPTER 15) and the acquisition and disposal of shares and share options (see CHAPTER 11).

Employers' contributions are required to be wholly and exclusively for the purposes of the business. Relief may be restricted in some circumstances where the registered scheme is linked to an unregistered 'employer-financed retirement benefits scheme'. The employers' contributions are deductible only in the accounting period in which they are paid, and not when provision is made in the accounts. There is provision for irregular contributions to be spread in certain circumstances (see **16.10**).

The overall 'pension inputs' in each tax year are subject to the annual allowance (£255,000 for 2010/11 — see **16.9**).

Additional voluntary contributions (AVCs)

[16.27] The benefits available to an employee depend on the funds available in the employer's scheme. An employee wishing to increase his potential pension may pay additional voluntary contributions (AVCs) to the employer's scheme, or to a scheme of his choice to which only he makes contributions (free-standing AVCs). Free-standing AVCs are paid net of basic rate tax and HMRC pays the tax to the pension scheme. Relief at the higher rate of tax, where appropriate, is claimed in the employee's tax return, but see **16.13** for details of restrictions on relief.

From 6 April 2006, all AVC schemes may allow lump sum benefits of 25% of the fund to be taken. Benefits may also be taken by income drawdown rather than all at once (see **16.29**).

Before 6 April 2006 some free-standing AVCs had to be refunded on retirement or earlier death if the combined benefits from occupational and free-standing schemes were excessive, tax being deducted from such refunds at 32%. From 6 April 2006 total benefits are restricted only by the lifetime limit (see **16.9**) and there are no special rules for AVCs.

A free-standing AVC may be used to enable an employee to contract out of S2P individually, even though his employer's scheme is contracted in. The AVC is boosted by the contracting-out rebate, which is equal to a percentage of earnings between the national insurance lower and upper earnings levels. The percentage depends on the employee's age and earnings. With free-standing AVCs, the employee does not get the benefit of an addition for tax relief on the payment by HMRC in respect of his share of the contracting-out rebate. If an employee wishes to contract out of S2P while remaining in his employer's scheme, it is therefore more sensible to do so by means of a personal pension plan, where HMRC payment for the employee's rebate is grossed up for tax relief (see **17.15**).

Sharing pension rights on divorce or dissolution of civil partnership

[16.28] There are provisions to enable a share in pension rights to be transferred on divorce or dissolution of civil partnership. The provisions cover all pension rights, i.e. under occupational and personal schemes (including stakeholder pensions) and S2P. It is not compulsory for a couple to share pensions, but all schemes (whenever they were approved) are regarded as including pension sharing provisions. Although the legislation overrides the provisions of existing schemes in this respect, such schemes are expected to change their rules to incorporate pension sharing as and when they make other (non-trivial) amendments. Where the pension is shared, the spouse or civil partner in a pension scheme will get reduced pension rights (a 'pension debit') and rights will be allocated to the other spouse (a 'pension credit'). The transferred pension credit rights may be held in the same scheme or transferred to another scheme. The benefits available to the ex-spouse/partner will broadly follow those available to the scheme member. The scheme member's pension debit will be taken into account in determining his entitlement under the scheme, deducted from his benefits on retirement, or on leaving pensionable service if earlier. The debit will count in the calculation of maximum benefits.

Deferring pension benefits

[16.29] Pension fund trustees may allow a member of a money purchase occupational scheme to defer taking an annuity on all or part of the pension benefits until at latest age 77 (but see **16.14** for full details). Up to that point part of the fund can be earmarked for benefits (called crystallisation) without affecting the flexibility within the remainder of the fund, enabling the member to take a tax-free lump sum of 25% of the crystallised amount. Thus someone with a fund of £1 million could crystallise, say, £200,000, which would entitle him to a tax-free lump sum of 25%, i.e. £50,000, and to the income attributable to the remaining £150,000. The full entitlement to the income does not have to be drawn. The pension taken could be between 0% and 120% of the maximum annuity that could have been purchased with the crystallised fund. A member could continue to crystallise benefits in tranches until the whole of the fund had been crystallised, but this would only usually be appropriate for someone with a significant fund.

If the member dies, the crystallised part of the fund can be used to pay income benefits to survivors, or the fund itself less a tax deduction of 35% could be paid to the survivors. See **16.31** for the treatment of the uncrystallised part of the fund. The opportunity to take the 25% tax-free cash is lost if not done by age 77 (but see **16.14** for full details). If an annuity is not purchased by that age, and the income payments continue under the rules for an 'alternatively secured pension', then on death the fund is dealt with as indicated at **16.20**.

The above provisions could apply to money purchase AVC arrangements, including free-standing AVCs. They are not appropriate for contracted-out money purchase schemes because of social security rules.

Provision for dependants (FA 2004, ss 167, 168 and Schs 28, 29; IHTA 1984, s 12; SI 2009/1989)

[16.30] Provision for dependants may be made for death both before and after taking benefits. A dependant is defined as:

(a) a spouse or civil partner;
(b) a former spouse or civil partner if the scheme rules so provide;
(c) a child who is under 23;
(d) a child over 23 who is dependent because of physical or mental impairment;
(e) for pensions arising before 1 July 2008 a child over 23 who is financially dependent on the scheme member before his death, or where the financial relationship with the member at his date of death was one of mutual dependence; and
(f) someone else who, in the scheme administrator's opinion, is dependent on the member.

Death before taking benefits

[16.31] When a scheme member dies before having crystallised his whole fund (and before age 77, but see **16.14** for full details), the pre 6 April 2006 restrictions on the amount of a lump sum no longer apply, and payments are restricted only by the lifetime allowance (see **16.9**). For a salary related scheme, a dependants' pension and/or lump sum may be paid. For a money purchase scheme, the scheme rules may provide for the whole amount of the fund to be paid, subject only to the lifetime allowance.

As far as inheritance tax is concerned, there is no charge on the uncrystallised part of the fund so long as a scheme member has not failed to exercise a right with the intention of benefiting someone else. Thus there will be no inheritance tax charge where a scheme member chooses to defer taking benefits, resulting in enhanced death benefits being paid to beneficiaries, unless the member knew at the time of deferral that he was likely to die within two years. Even in these circumstances, there is no inheritance tax charge where the beneficiary is a dependant or a charity.

Death after taking benefits

[16.32] Provision may be made for an employee's pension or annuity to continue for ten years after benefits commence despite earlier death. Separate pensions for dependants can also be provided, subject to the normal limits.

Changing employment (FA 2004, s 205)

[16.33] When an employee changes employment, then providing he has been in the pension scheme for at least two years, he may either have a preserved pension which will become payable on retirement, or a transfer payment to a new scheme (if the scheme will accept it) or to an insurance company or to a personal pension plan. Where there is a preserved pension under a final salary scheme, it must normally be increased each year in line with the increase in retail prices. For contracted-out final salary schemes, the employer must ensure that the preserved pension must at least equal the guaranteed minimum pension under the state scheme for the period to 5 April 1997 and the statutory standard thereafter (see **16.5**).

From April 2006, tax is deducted from short service refunds at 20% on payments up to £10,800 and 40% on any excess over that amount. The refund is not, however, treated as income for tax purposes. Where employees leave after three months but within the stipulated period, they must be offered a cash transfer sum (which will include the value of employers' contributions as well as their own) to take to another occupational or personal pension scheme, or to use to buy an annuity, as an alternative to a refund of contributions.

Pension scheme surpluses (FA 2004, ss 177, 207)

[16.34] There used to be special rules requiring pension scheme surpluses to be reduced once they reached a certain value. From 6 April 2006 this no longer applies. Where on an actuarial valuation, a scheme has a surplus, an 'authorised surplus payment' may be made by the scheme administrator to the sponsoring company. The administrator must deduct tax at 35% from the payment and account for it to HMRC.

Misuse of contributions by employer and scheme insolvency

[16.35] The risk for an employee of his contributions being misused is significantly reduced by a compensation scheme. Where an occupational pension scheme's funds have been misappropriated and the employer is insolvent, compensation may be payable from the Pension Protection Fund to cover 90% of the loss or to bring the fund up to 90% funding. The compensation scheme is paid for by a levy on occupational schemes.

The Pension Protection Fund also protects the pension rights of employees in final salary schemes whose employers have become insolvent without funds having been misappropriated. Again, compensation from the Fund is partly financed by a levy on occupational schemes. The levies are based on an assessment of the risk exposure of the particular scheme and the scheme's size. The levy payments are deductible in calculating the taxable profits of the employer. If a scheme cannot be rescued, and cannot secure benefits at least equal to the compensation payable from the Pension Protection Fund, the Fund will pay compensation at broadly 100% (but with limited inflation protection) to existing pensioners, and will pay pensions at normal pension age to employees at broadly 90% of their existing accrued rights (again with limited inflation protection and with an overall cap).

For schemes wound up between 1 January 1997 and 5 April 2005 the Pension Protection Fund function was performed by the Financial Assistance Scheme (FAS). Provisions were introduced in FA 2009 which mean that in future the FAS will make payments similar to those made by a registered pension scheme and such payments will accordingly be given broadly the same tax treatment as if they had been made by such a scheme. This means that the individual will not be disadvantaged by incurring charges to income tax that would otherwise arise because the payment is received from a body that is not a registered pension scheme. Similar provisions have been introduced where an insurer qualifies for assistance from the Financial Services Compensation Scheme (FSCS). There will be broadly the same tax treatment for the resulting payments or transfers as if the FSCS had not intervened.

Unregistered pension schemes (ITEPA 2003, ss 393–400; FA 2004, ss 245–249)

[16.36] Before 6 April 2006, there were two types of unapproved schemes, funded schemes (FURBS) and unfunded schemes (UURBS), detailed provisions of which are in earlier editions of this book. There are transitional provisions in relation to tax-free lump sum rights at 6 April 2006.

Under FA 2004, UK unregistered schemes are termed 'employer-financed retirement benefit schemes'. Under the rules for such schemes, employers will not receive tax relief for pension contributions until benefits are paid out of the fund (and employees will not be taxed on the benefit of the employers' contributions), income and gains in the fund will be taxed at the 50% trust rate (applying from 2010/11, previously 40%) (42.5% for dividends, previously 32.5%), and employees will be taxed on any cash or non-cash benefits from the fund at their marginal tax rates, the benefits being treated as earned income. Benefits already taxed as pension income are excluded, as are certain other 'excluded benefits', such as those paid on ill-health or disablement of an employee during service. Further benefits may be excluded by statutory instrument, and this has been done in relation to certain benefits provided to retired employees, which mirror exemptions for various minor benefits provided to employees. The employers' contributions and accrued funds will not have any effect on employees' annual allowance and lifetime allowance limits.

Self-administered pension schemes (SI 1991/1614; FA 2004 Sch 29A)

[16.37] A self-administered pension scheme is one where the contributions remain under the control of trustees appointed by the company, as distinct from being paid to a pensions provider such as a life assurance company. It was previously necessary for one of the trustees to be an independent person approved by HMRC, known as a pensioner trustee. This is no longer necessary from 6 April 2006. The limits on contributions and benefits are the same as for other registered schemes, but the benefits are dependent on the funds within the scheme, so to that exte

17

Personal pension schemes

Introduction (FA 2004, ss 149–284 and Schs 28–36; FA 2009, s 72 and Sch 35; FA 2010, ss 23, 48 and Sch 2; F(No.2)A 2010, s 6 and Sch 3)

[17.1] There are two types of scheme for those making pension arrangements in addition to or instead of employers' (occupational) schemes — personal pension schemes and, for arrangements made before 1 July 1988, retirement annuity contracts. Personal pension schemes incorporate stakeholder pension schemes — see **17.2**. The separate rules for occupational, personal pension and retirement annuity schemes were replaced from 6 April 2006 by a single regime covering all tax-privileged pension schemes. These provisions are dealt with in **16.6** to **16.22**. The requirement for schemes to have tax approval was replaced by a simpler requirement for them to be registered. All schemes that had HMRC approval at 5 April 2006 are treated as registered, unless they notified HMRC by that date that they did not wish to be registered. The Financial Services Authority regulates the operation of personal pension schemes, including self-invested personal pension schemes or SIPPs.

Those without earnings may pay up to £3,600 a year into a pension fund. All personal pension contributions are paid net of basic rate tax, which is particularly beneficial to non-taxpayers (see **17.10**). It is now possible for retirement annuity premiums to be paid net of basic rate tax as well so long as the insurance company agrees. Otherwise retirement annuity premiums continue to be paid gross. In other respects, most of the rules are the same for both types of scheme.

Personal pension schemes may allow members to direct where their funds are to be invested, subject to restrictions for 'investment-regulated pension schemes' — see **16.11**. These are particularly relevant to SIPPs — see **17.19**). As indicated in CHAPTER 16, members of personal pension schemes (including stakeholder schemes) receive regular illustrations of what their future pension might be in present-day prices, so that they have a more realistic idea about the value of their pension funds and the options open to them. The illustration may incorporate state pension information supplied by the Department of Work and Pensions if the pension provider and pension fund member so wish.

Stakeholder pensions

[17.2] A stakeholder pension is a private pension that must meet certain standards laid down by government in relation to charges, flexibility and provision of information. Annual charges cannot exceed a specified percentage of the member's fund, members must be able to transfer into or out of the scheme without charge, minimum contributions cannot exceed £20, and the scheme must be run by trustees or by scheme managers authorised by the Financial Services Authority. For those joining stakeholder schemes on or after 6 April 2005, the maximum annual charge is 1.5% of the fund's value, reducing to 1% after the first ten years. For those who joined before that date the maximum annual charge was and continues to be 1%.

If an employer does not either (i) have an occupational pension scheme open to all employees within one year of starting work, or (ii) provide employees with access to a personal pension scheme satisfying various conditions (in particular that the employer contributes an amount equal to at least 3% of the employee's earnings), he must offer access to a registered stakeholder pension scheme if he has five or more employees, of whom at least one meets the conditions to be provided with such access. Employees need not be provided with access if they have been employed for less than three months, or if they have earned less than the national insurance lower earnings limit (£97 a week for 2010/11) for one or more weeks within the last three months, or if they are ineligible to join a stakeholder scheme because they do not normally live in the UK.

Giving access means that the employer must choose a stakeholder scheme, consult with employees, formally designate the chosen scheme, give details of the scheme provider to employees and give the scheme provider access to the employees. Employers are not required to contribute to the scheme. If employees joining a scheme so wish, the employer must deduct the contributions from pay and pay them over to the scheme provider by the 19th of the following month. As with all personal pensions, contributions are paid net of basic rate tax (see **17.1**). Employers must keep detailed records of payments and must notify any changes to the scheme provider. Employers who fail to comply with the requirements of the stakeholder pension provisions are liable to fines of up to £50,000. As indicated in **17.1**, the tax treatment of stakeholder pension schemes is incorporated within the personal pension scheme provisions.

Tax relief and payment of contributions (FA 2004, ss 188–195A, 213A–P; FA 2010, s 23 and Sch 2)

[17.3] Personal pension contributions may be paid by someone aged under 75 who is resident in the UK and was resident both at some time during the previous five tax years and when he became a member of the pension scheme. Those who meet these requirements (or someone else on their behalf — see **16.13**) may make unlimited contributions to registered pension schemes, but tax relief for all contributions in a tax year, including occupational pension scheme contributions, is given only on the higher of 100% of relevant UK earnings and £3,600 gross (£2,880 net for 2010/11), and is further restricted to the annual allowance (£255,000 for 2010/11 — see **16.9**) and the high income excess relief charge which applies from 6 April 2011, including the anti-forestalling provisions which apply from 22 April 2009. Broadly tax relief on pension contributions made by individuals with gross income of £150,000 or more and relevant income of not less than £130,000 will be restricted to the basic rate of tax (see **16.13** which explains the restrictions and the anti-forestalling provisions in detail). The Government is reviewing tax relief on pensions, see the comments in **16.9** and **16.13**.

The pension contributions are accumulated in a fund free of income tax and capital gains tax (although tax credits on dividends cannot be reclaimed). Pension scheme administrators will ensure that applicants are eligible to join the scheme. Legal guardians must complete application forms for those under 18.

Personal pension contributions can be paid to a life assurance company, friendly society, bank, building society, unit trust, or personal pension scheme trust established by employers and others. Retirement annuity premiums have to be paid to an insurance company. In both cases, the retirement benefits themselves are purchased from an authorised insurance company with the fund monies at retirement, and the 'best buy' available at that time can be selected. It is also possible to have a self-invested scheme — see **17.19**.

See **16.23** re transferring personal pension plan funds on entering or leaving pensionable employment.

Mis-sold personal pensions (FA 1996, s 148)

[17.4] It would not normally be beneficial for those eligible to be in an occupational scheme to which both they and their employer contribute to opt out of the employer's scheme and take out a personal pension plan funded by their own contributions. However, many people were wrongly advised to do so in the late 1980s and early 1990s. Compensation received for 'bad investment advice' (as defined) all or some of which was given between 29 April 1988 and 30 June 1994 is exempt from tax.

Permissible benefits

[17.5] The pension benefits must commence not later than age 77 (but see **16.14** for full details) nor earlier than age 55 (from 6 April 2010), except in cases of ill health or where the occupation is one in which earlier retirement is customary, for example dancers and athletes for whom HMRC may approve a scheme with an earlier retirement date.

[17.6] A taxpayer may have several different pension funds, which gives him flexibility as to when and in what manner to take benefits. Once benefits are taken from a fund, no further contributions may be made to that fund (although the fund will continue to build up tax-free). See **16.14** to **16.16** and **16.20** for the ways in which benefits may be taken. If a lump sum is to be taken, this must be done before age 77 (but see **16.14** for full details). The pension options for those in a money purchase arrangement are purchase of an annuity or income withdrawal (or 'drawdown'). Income withdrawal cannot continue beyond age 77 (but see **16.14** for full details) and at that time either an annuity or an 'alternatively secured pension' must be taken (see **16.20**). Payment of an annuity may be guaranteed for ten years. This also applied to an alternatively secured pension up to 5 April 2007 but a guarantee may not be provided for such pensions after that date.

[17.7] The position where a taxpayer with a personal pension fund dies before taking benefits is the same as for an employer's money purchase scheme as outlined in **16.31**. The funds may be paid to the personal representatives or to any other person. Alternatively, the contract may provide for the death benefits to be held in trust, with the monies payable at the trustees' discretion. If paid to the personal representatives, the sum refunded will form part of the estate for inheritance tax purposes, but tax will not be payable to the extent that the estate is left to the surviving spouse or civil partner. Inheritance tax will also usually be avoided where the proceeds are held by the trustees of the fund for nominees, but where someone delays taking benefits with the deliberate intention of benefiting someone else, a charge to inheritance tax may arise as with an occupational scheme (see **16.31**).

[17.8] Where a taxpayer with a personal pension fund dies after taking benefits and before age 77 (but see **16.14** for full details), then pensions may be payable to dependants (as defined in **16.30**) and possibly lump sums. If a pension protection lump sum death benefit, or an annuity protection lump sum benefit, or an income withdrawal lump sum benefit, is paid, tax will be deducted by the scheme administrator or insurance company at 35% (subject to transitional provisions where a guarantee period started before 6 April 2006). Tax is not chargeable on uncrystallised funds (except to the extent that they exceed the lifetime allowance — see **16.9**).

[17.9] Some people take the income withdrawal option for their benefits because annuity rates are low. Although flexible income withdrawal may appear attractive, annuity rates might not improve, and sufficient of the fund needs to be left invested to retain a wide spread of investments to reduce risk. Many advisers consider that income withdrawal or drawdown (see **17.6**) is suitable only for those with pension funds of at least £100,000 or, in some circumstances, about £250,000. The same considerations apply to alternatively secured pensions, which are income withdrawal pensions for those taking benefits at age 77 (but see **16.14** for full details) or over. Restrictions apply to such pensions from 6 April 2007 (see **16.20**).

Allowable contributions

[17.10] As indicated in **17.3**, personal pension contributions of up to £3,600 a year may be paid by non-earners, and indeed non-taxpayers, as well as those with UK earnings. Since basic rate relief is deducted and retained when paying the contribution (except for some retirement annuity premiums — see **17.18**), this means that someone can establish a pension fund of £3,600 by making a payment of £2,880 (i.e. £3,600 less 20%). Anyone over the personal pension retirement age of 55 could in fact take benefits immediately, either by way of an annuity based on £3,600, or by way of a lump sum of £900 (see **17.6** and **16.15**) (reducing the net outlay to £1,980) and an annuity based on £2,700. For a 40% taxpayer the net cost of establishing a fund of £3,600 is £2,160.

[17.11] Higher contributions may be paid according to the individual's UK earnings. For a self-employed person, relevant earnings means his taxable profits, after deducting capital allowances, losses set against the profits and any excess of business charges (such as patent royalties paid) over general investment income. If a loss is set against income other than relevant earnings (see **CHAPTER 25**), later relevant earnings must be reduced by the amount of the loss. For an employee, relevant earnings include not only cash pay but also the cash equivalent of benefits, as reduced by expenses allowable against those earnings, and any other amounts treated as earnings.

[17.12] A scheme may provide for personal pension contributions to be made not only in cash but by way of transfer of shares received under approved SAYE share option schemes, share incentive plans and approved profit sharing schemes (as to which see **CHAPTER 11**). Such transfers must be made within 90 days of exercising the SAYE option or of shares being appropriated to the employee, and will be treated as contributions equal to the market value of the shares at the date of the transfer to the scheme. Tax relief will then be given on the contributions in the same way as for cash contributions.

[17.13] Employees making personal pension plan arrangements may elect to contract out of the State Second Pension (S2P — previously the State Earnings Related Pension Scheme or SERPS), still, however, contributing for a basic retirement pension (see **17.15**). It is also possible for an employee in a contracted-in pension scheme to remain in the scheme but contract out of S2P independently through a personal pension plan. See **17.16**.

[17.14] As indicated in **10.7**, neither employers' nor employees' national insurance contributions (NICs) are payable on personal pension contributions paid by employers. This means that if the employee agreed to a salary sacrifice, and the employer made a pension contribution boosted by the employer's NIC saving, the pension contribution would be higher than would result from an employee payment (see Example 1). Care must be taken with salary sacrifice arrangements to ensure that they are effective, and HMRC provide guidance in their Employment Income Manual at EIM42750 and also on their website at www.hmrc.gov.uk/paye/payroll/special-pay/salary-sacrifice.htm and www.hmrc.gov.uk/specialist/salary_sacrifice.htm. The potential pay must be given up before being received and the legal outcome must be that the employee is entitled to lower cash remuneration and a benefit. Other effects of reducing the employee's earnings must not be ignored (in particular the effect on state pension entitlement under S2P — see **13.3**). See also **16.13** regarding the effect of a salary sacrifice arrangement on the calculation of relevant income for the high income excess relief charge.

Example 1

If a basic rate taxpayer earning £25,000 a year makes a personal pension contribution of £1,000 gross, £800 net in 2010/11, the amount of salary required to cover the contribution would be:

		£
Salary		1,159
Tax @ 20%	232	
NI @ 11%	127	359
Net salary to cover contribution		800

If he made a salary sacrifice arrangement and agreed to receive a salary of (25,000 − 1,159 =) £23,841 plus a non-taxable benefit in the form of a pension contribution paid by his employer, the employer could contribute £1,159 plus the employer's NIC saving of £148 (12.8% × £1,159) giving £1,307. The employee's net pay would be £800 lower, leaving him in the same position he was before (having paid the pension contribution), but the gross pension contribution paid into the fund would increase by £307.

Contracting out of the State Second Pension (S2P) by employees not in an employer's scheme (SI 2001/1354; SI 2004/263; SI 2006/1009; SI 2009/3094)

[17.15] Employees not in an occupational scheme may contract out of S2P by taking out a personal pension plan that satisfies conditions laid down in the legislation, referred to as an appropriate personal pension plan (APP) or appropriate personal pension stakeholder pension (APPSHP). The contribution under the plan is paid net of basic rate tax and HMRC pay the tax into the plan. The employee and his employer continue to pay full NICs, but HMRC pay into the plan the contracting-out rebate. Contracting out rebates do not count towards the pension annual allowance. The calculation of age-related contracting-out rebates for appropriate personal pension plans (but not money purchase plans or salary related schemes) is made by applying different percentages to earnings in up to three bands (see **13.12** for further details). Since personal pension plans qualify for tax relief whereas NICs do not, HMRC also pay in tax relief on the gross equivalent of the employee's share of the rebate. The contracting-out rebate and the tax relief on the rebate are known as 'minimum contributions'. The pension fund relating to the minimum contributions is known as 'protected rights'. See Example 2.

Example 2

Employee aged 33 in non-pensionable employment who earns £32,500 a year contracts out of S2P by contributing £1,300 per year to an appropriate personal pension plan.

The earnings on which the contracting-out rebate is paid for 2010/11 are £32,500 less £5,044 (equivalent to £97 per week) lower earnings limit, i.e. £27,456*. The overall rate of rebate for 2010/11 at age 33 for someone earning £32,500 is 12.2% on earnings between £5,044 and £14,100 and 3.05% on earnings between £14,101 and £32,500, of which the employee's share is 1.6%.

The annual investment in the plan in 2010/11 is as follows:

	£
Employee pays £1,300 less 20% tax (£260.00)	1,040.00
HMRC pays in the tax relief of	260.00
plus contracting-out rebate:	
Employer's contribution at 12.2% × £14,100–£5,044	1,104.83
Employer's contribution at 3.05% × £32,500–£14,100	561.20
Tax relief on gross equivalent of employee's contribution of 1.6%:	
on £1,104.83 x 1.6/12.2 x 20/80	36.22
on £561.20 x 1.6/3.05 x 20/80	73.60
	£3,075.85

Had the employee earned between £5,044 and £14,100 a year, the employer/employee rebate percentage would have been 12.2%, and it would have been calculated as if the annual earnings were exactly £14,100.

For years before 2010/11 the rebate percentages were based on earnings within three bands. However, from 6 April 2010 the S2P will accrue at only two different rates, one between the lower earnings limit and low earnings threshold and the other between the low earnings threshold and the upper accrual point. Therefore rebates will also only reflect the two rates of accrual.

*The contracting-out rebate is based on earnings between £97 and the weekly pay, even though NICs are payable only on earnings above £110 a week. See **13.2** for details of proposed changes to NIC rates and thresholds from 6 April 2011.

The protected rights part of the pension funded by HMRC contracting-out payment could previously only be paid from State pension age. It could not be commuted for a lump sum and it had to include provision for index-linking and for pensions for surviving spouses or civil partners. From 6 April 2006 all these restrictions have been removed except the requirement to provide for benefits for surviving spouses/civil partners, and the benefits payable are subject only to the overall lifetime limit (see **16.9**). The earliest date that benefits may be taken is the minimum pension age stated in **17.5**.

Contracting out of S2P and remaining in an employer's scheme

[17.16] An employee who is in an occupational scheme that is contracted in to S2P may remain in the employer's scheme but opt out of S2P by means of an individual personal pension plan. The way that this is done is that the employee and employer continue to pay full NICs, and the payment into the personal pension plan is made solely by HMRC, who contribute the same amount as indicated in Example 2 for employees not in a pension scheme, i.e. the age-related rebate percentage by reference to the employee's earnings between the low earnings threshold and upper accrual point plus tax relief on the employee's share of the contracting-out rebate.

Funding the contributions

[17.17] Two often expressed objections to personal pension provision are, first, the cost and, second, the fact that you cannot use the fund until you reach minimum pension age.

With the limit for tax allowable contributions now being 100% of earnings (subject to the annual allowance), a windfall such as a legacy could be used to pay a substantial amount into the fund and thus catch up on earlier years where significant funding was not possible.

Although it is not possible for a lender to take a charge on a personal pension fund, several pension providers have arrangements under which a lender will make an appropriate loan to a taxpayer with a sufficiently large accumulated fund, or who is paying regular contributions to a fund, usually in the latter case based on a multiple of regular contributions and the age of the taxpayer. The terms of the loan are usually that interest is payable year by year but capital repayments are taken from the eventual tax-free lump sum on retirement. Whether security for the borrowing is required often depends upon the trade or profession carried on by the taxpayer.

The loan could itself be used to fund contributions to the scheme, so that a significant part of the maximum allowable contribution might be funded from a loan made at the same time from the fund itself.

Tax relief is not available on the interest paid to the lender unless the borrowing is for a qualifying purpose, such as the relief for the acquisition of a business property or a partnership share (see CHAPTER 2). There will thus not be any relief for interest paid on a loan used to pay pension scheme contributions.

Way in which relief is given

[17.18] As indicated in **17.1**, retirement annuity premiums may now be paid net of basic rate tax if the insurance company agrees, in which case relief is given in the same way as for personal pension contributions. Where they are paid gross, relief is given to the self-employed by deduction in the payer's self-assessment and to employees by coding adjustment. The premiums are deducted from earnings in calculating the tax liability.

Personal pension contributions are paid net of basic rate tax, and the pension provider reclaims the tax from HMRC. This enables both taxpayers and non-taxpayers to get basic rate tax relief on their payments. Higher rate relief must be claimed and will be given in the taxpayer's self-assessment or by coding adjustment for employees. The extra higher rate relief is given by extending the basic rate limit in the tax computation by the gross amount of the contribution. Strictly the extra higher rate relief only applies where *income* attracts higher rate tax, but by HMRC concession A101 it also applies in relation to capital gains taxed at the higher rate (for example in years before 2008/09). Where an employee contracts out of S2P, however, there is no higher rate relief on the part of HMRC contribution that relates to the employee's contracting-out rebate. See **17.3** regarding the restriction of tax relief on contributions applying from 6 April 2011 with related anti-forestalling provisions applying from 22 April 2009.

Example 3 shows the difference in treatment for personal pension contributions and retirement annuity premiums that are paid gross.

Example 3

Self-employed taxpayer entitled only to the single personal allowance has income in 2010/11 comprising earnings of £40,000 and interest of £6,000 gross. He paid a pension premium, the gross amount of which was £1,000. The treatment of the premium if it is either a retirement annuity premium paid gross or a personal pension contribution is as follows:

	Retirement annuity premium £	Personal pension contribution £
Earnings	40,000	40,000
Less: Retirement annuity premium	(1,000)	
	39,000	
Savings income	6,000	6,000
	45,000	46,000
Personal allowance	(6,475)	(6,475)
Taxable income	38,525	39,525

Tax thereon:

Basic rate	37,400	@ 20%	7,480	38,400*	@ 20%	7,680
(balance)	1,125	@ 40%	450	1,125	@ 40%	450
	38,525			39,525		
						8,130
Less: Basic rate tax retained 1,000 @ 20%						(200)
						7,930

*Basic rate limit increased by personal pension contribution.

Where personal pension contributions are made in the form of shares (see **17.12**), the market value of the shares is treated as an amount net of basic rate tax, so that with basic rate tax at 20%, shares to the value of £800 would be treated as a gross contribution of £1,000.

Self-invested personal pension schemes (FA 2004, ss 174A, 182–185I, 273ZA and Sch 29A)

[17.19] Self-invested personal pension schemes (SIPPs) are schemes which allow members to direct where their funds are to be invested. Before 6 April 2006 there were specific provisions in relation to SIPPs, which required them to provide details of investments and borrowing transactions to HMRC, and restricted the scheme's borrowing powers and investments involving the member of the SIPP.

The original intention of the FA 2004 pension provisions was that all schemes would have the same powers in relation to investments and borrowing powers. Because of the widespread promotion of SIPPs as vehicles for purchasing residential property and valuable assets, such as art and antiques, special provisions now apply to 'investment-regulated pension schemes', which are those where members are able to influence the scheme's investments. Such schemes cannot invest in 'prohibited assets' (see **16.11**).

In addition to the restrictions on investments, SIPPs are affected by a change in borrowing powers for registered schemes. Before 6 April 2006 schemes could borrow up to 75% of the value of scheme property. From 6 April 2006 the maximum borrowing is 50% of the total fund value, with any value added tax within the cost of the property purchased being included in calculating the maximum borrowing.

Despite the changed rules, SIPPs still give investors greater control over where their money is invested and how and when benefits are taken. They are, however, most likely to be beneficial for those with substantial funds. From 6 April 2007 they are regulated by the Financial Services Authority (see **17.1**).

Payment of pensions (ITEPA 2003, s 683)

[17.20] Annuities under a personal pension plan are taxed through the PAYE scheme in the same way as occupational pensions, with tax being charged at the appropriate rate and coding adjustments being made where some or all of the available allowances have been used against other income, such as State pensions (see CHAPTER 10).

From 6 April 2007 annuities under a retirement annuity contract are paid through the PAYE scheme in the same way as personal pension plan annuities. Previously, retirement annuities were normally paid net of basic rate tax, with any under- or overpayment of tax being dealt with in the taxpayer's self-assessment (or, for repayments, by a separate repayment claim — see 2.32). Non-taxpayers were able to ask their pension provider for form R89 which enabled payments to be made gross.

Tax points

[17.21] Note the following:

- Contributions to personal pension plans before 6 April 2011 attract tax relief at the top rate in the majority of cases making them a highly tax-efficient means of providing for the future (see 17.3 for proposed changes to tax relief for high-earners, including anti-forestalling provisions applying from 22 April 2009). The available pension at retirement will, however, be determined by the investment performance of the funds into which the pension contributions are paid.
- Commission may be received on personal pension contributions. The pension contribution will be treated as the net amount paid if the commission is deducted from the contribution or a discounted premium is paid. If the contribution is paid gross and the commission received separately, tax relief will be given on the gross amount.
- Most people are entitled to pay a personal pension contribution of up to £3,600 a year whether or not they have any earnings. Basic rate tax relief is retained out of the contribution whether or not the payer is a taxpayer. If contributions are paid for the payer's children (of whatever age), it must be remembered that they cannot take benefits until at earliest age 55. Retired people under 75 can similarly get the tax saving from paying net contributions and can take the benefits immediately — but although this buys an annuity at a low cost the individual needs to live long enough to reap the benefit.
- Some building societies and other lenders will allow the borrower to pay only interest during the period of a loan, with an undertaking that the loan itself will be repaid from the tax-free lump sum from a pension fund on retirement.
- The purchase of an annuity with a personal pension fund can be delayed until at latest age 77 (but see 16.14 for full details), which may be useful when annuity rates are at a low level. There is, of course, the risk that the annuity rates may have fallen even further at the time when the individual wants to buy the annuity. The flexible rules from 6 April

2006 give the opportunity of having various different funds, and taking benefits in various ways. Income withdrawal up to age 77 (but see **16.14** for full details) enables an individual to leave as much of his fund invested as he wishes, but he needs to have a substantial fund for this to be appropriate.

• Trading losses set off against other income (see **CHAPTER 25**) must even so be taken into account by reducing the next available profits from the trade in order to establish earnings for the purpose of calculating maximum pension contributions.

• Contributions to a personal pension will reduce reckonable income for working and child tax credits (see **2.40**).

Trading activities

18

Sole trader, partnership or company?

Tax and non-tax considerations

[18.1] The alternatives when a person starts in business or needs to consider a change in how to operate are to become a sole trader, to form a partnership with others or to form a limited liability company. All relevant factors need to be considered when making a decision. A sole trader is liable for the debts of the business to the full extent of his personal assets, and can in the extreme be made bankrupt. The same applies to partners, unless they have formed a limited liability partnership, which enables them to restrict their liability, broadly, to the capital contributed (see **23.27**). A company shareholder's liability is normally limited to the amount, if any, unpaid on his shares. Protection of private assets is usually one of the main reasons for trading through a company (and this is also a reason for forming limited liability partnerships). However, lenders, landlords and sometimes suppliers often require directors to give a personal guarantee in respect of the company's obligation, which reduces significantly the benefit of limited liability. There are also major compliance requirements for a company under the Companies Acts, including the need to produce accounts in statutory form, which must be sent promptly to Companies House (see **9.20**). In general, companies whose turnover is £6.5 million or less need not, however, have their accounts audited unless their gross assets exceed £3.26 million. Limited liability partnerships have similar reporting obligations to companies.

The general commercial and family considerations must be weighed alongside the comparative tax positions when choosing what form the business is to take. It has never been sensible to allow the tax system to dominate this important decision. Furthermore, the basic rate of income tax (20% for 2010/11) is currently lower than the small profits rate of corporation tax (21% for the financial year ending 31 March 2011 although it is proposed to be reduced to 20% from 1 April 2011). The increase in the small profits rate (known as the small companies' rate before the introduction of CTA 2010) in

FA 2008 was designed to dissuade sole traders and partners from incorporating their businesses in order to benefit from lower effective tax rates on profits either retained or paid out as dividends, but there are still savings to be made, as illustrated in Example 2 at **18.8**. However, the possibility of significant changes to small business taxation should always be considered — see **18.7**.

Comparative tax/NIC position for the unincorporated trader and the company director

[18.2] There are so many variables to take into account in comparing the tax/national insurance position for the unincorporated trader and the company director that it is impossible to draw hard and fast conclusions, and detailed calculations need to be made in every case. Simplified assumptions and comments on some of the variables are made in the illustrations which follow, which are based on the tax and national insurance rates for 2010/11. Note that there are proposed changes from 6 April 2011 to NIC rates and thresholds (see **13.2** and chapter 24) and to the personal allowance and basic rate limit (see chapter 2).

[18.3] A sole trader or partner will pay combined income tax and national insurance contributions (NICs) for 2010/11 at 41% on all profits (after personal allowances) in excess of the basic rate limit of £37,400, whether he leaves those profits in the business or withdraws them. The £37,400 threshold is available to each member of a married couple or civil partners working in partnership. A controlling director/shareholder of a company can decide how much profit to take in the form of remuneration or dividends (on which income tax will be paid) and how much to leave to be taxed at corporation tax rates. The net of tax remuneration or dividend need not be withdrawn from the company — it can be left to credit on loan account.

[18.4] Special rules apply, however, to personal service companies and managed service companies, and certain partnerships. Where the company acts as an intermediary providing the services of a director/employee to clients, and the arrangements are such that he would have been an employee of the client if he had contracted directly with the client, the intermediary company is deemed to make a salary payment on the last day of the tax year equal to the difference between the amount received from the client (less certain deductions) and the amount actually paid out as remuneration to the director/employee (see **19.6**). Personal service companies are therefore unable to allocate profits to remuneration or dividends as they see fit. Special rules also apply for managed service companies, under which any payments to those working for such a company are treated as employment income (see **19.15**).

[18.5] For those not caught by the personal service company or managed service company rules, NICs are one of the most significant factors in comparing the liabilities under the respective formats. Sole traders and partners pay much lower NICs than the combined employee/employer contributions for a company director.

In a partnership of husband and wife or civil partners both have to pay Class 4 NICs. They also both have to pay Class 2 contributions unless, in the case of a married couple, the wife elected not to do so on or before 11 May 1977 and holds a certificate of exemption. NICs are not an allowable deduction in arriving at business profits for tax purposes. The Class 1 NICs on remuneration paid by a company depend on the earnings (see **13.13**). If in 2010/11 remuneration is taken at £844 a week (the upper limit for employees' contributions at the 11% rate), i.e. £43,875 over the year, the combined employer's and employee's contributions would be £9,083. The employer's share (£4,885) is, however, allowable as a deduction in calculating the profits of the company which are liable to corporation tax (reducing the total figure to £8,057 if corporation tax is at 21%). The national insurance cost for a sole trader with profits of £43,875 is:

Class 2 contributions 52 × £2.40		125
Class 4 contributions 8% × (43,875 − 5,715)	3,053	£3,178

The extra national insurance cost of operating through a company at that profit level would therefore be (8,057 − 3,178 =) £4,879.

[18.6] The overall comparative tax position is significantly affected by whether profits are withdrawn as salary or dividends. Dividends are not subject to NICs. The shareholder pays no extra tax on the dividend unless his taxable income exceeds the basic rate limit (£37,400 for 2010/11). If it does exceed that limit he pays tax at only 25% of the cash dividend (32½% of the tax credit inclusive amount) on dividends above that level but up to £150,000. If taxable income exceeds £150,000 he pays tax at 36% of the cash dividend (42½% of the tax credit inclusive amount).

[18.7] Various other points should be borne in mind. To obtain a deduction in calculating taxable profits, earnings as a director or employee are required to be 'wholly and exclusively for the purposes of the trade', so particularly where a spouse or civil partner does not work full-time in a business, the earnings may be challenged by HMRC as excessive in calculating the taxable profit of the company. There is no such requirement for a spouse or civil partner who is an active partner in a business partnership rather than a company, albeit working less than full-time, although artificial arrangements will not work (see **23.25**).

Furthermore, HMRC have used the 'settlements' rules to challenge some commonly used tax planning measures in family companies under the rules for 'settlements'. Although outright gifts between spouses and civil partners are not normally within the settlements rules, this exception does not apply if the gift is wholly or substantially a right to income. A gift of ordinary shares from one spouse to another has traditionally been considered by tax advisers to be outside this exception, because ordinary shares carry other rights in addition to income rights, for example rights to a share of the assets if the company is wound up. This would obviously be particularly relevant if the couple separated. HMRC considered, however, that in some circumstances gifts of ordinary shares were caught as settlements. In July 2007 the House of Lords decided a case in favour of the taxpayers on the basis that, while there was a settlement, an exemption for outright gifts between spouses applied. The Government subsequently expressed an intention to introduce new legislation to counter 'income shifting'. However in the 2008 pre-budget report it announced that given the 'economic challenges' prevailing at the time it would instead keep the matter under review (see **12.10**). Professional bodies called for a review of small business taxation rather than the introduction of complex legislation to deal with this single issue. In the meantime, there is a degree of uncertainty which makes it difficult for small businesses to plan their tax affairs.

In view of the complexity of this issue anyone who is considering such tax planning measures should take professional advice. Other relevant factors are that some benefits, in particular jobseeker's allowance and the State Second Pension, are not available to the self-employed, and the rate of inheritance tax business property relief for assets owned personally may be reduced when operating through a company (see **5.40**).

[18.8] The profit level at which the retentions after tax and national insurance will be less operating through a company than as a sole trader or partner is not a static figure but one which will vary according to whether there are other sources of income, how much remuneration is paid by the company, and whether any dividends and pension contributions are paid. Example 1 shows that in 2010/11, if an individual with no other income is paid a salary of £43,875 by a company to leave him with taxable income equal to the basic rate threshold of £37,400, the profit level at which the tax burden using the company format equates with that of an individual trader is £68,271. (If pension contributions were being paid, this would need to be taken into account in the calculations.) The turning point would be at a lower profit level on a salary of less than £43,875 and a higher level on a salary above £43,875 (and would in any event be double for a business of husband and wife or civil partners). There could, however, be further tax liabilities on the company retentions at a later date, but these may never materialise, through changes in tax rates, exemptions, etc., and in the meantime cash will have been conserved in the company. Example 2 illustrates that the company format can be more tax-effective even at much lower profit levels if most of the profits are extracted by way of dividend. The other disadvantages of incorporation would, however, probably outweigh the tax/national insurance advantage at that profit level.

Example 1

Business profits before tax and national insurance are £68,271 and there are no other sources of income. A sole trader is liable to income tax on the full amount. If a company director was paid a salary of £43,875 during 2010/11 (which after the personal allowance of £6,475 leaves income of £37,400 to use the basic rate band), the comparative position is:

			Trader	Company director
Profits/remuneration			68,271	43,875
Personal allowance			6,475	6,475
Taxable income			61,796	37,400
Tax thereon:	37,400	@ 20%	7,480	7,480
	24,396	@ 40%	9,758	
			17,238	7,480
Class 2 NI (flat rate)			125	Employee's NI** 4,198
Class 4 NI*			3,297	
Total personal tax and NI			20,660	11,678
Company's tax and NI:				
Profits				68,271
Less: Director's remuneration				(43,875)
Company's NI thereon				(4,884†) 4,884
Taxable profits				19,512
Tax thereon @ 21%				4,098 4,098
Retained profits				15,414
Total tax and NI liabilities			20,660	20,660
Drawn or undrawn profits			47,611	47,611
			68,271	68,271
				£
*	On (43,875 – 5,715) @ 8%		3,053	
	On (68,271 – 43,875) @ 1%		244	3,297
**	On (43,875 – 5,715) @ 11%			4,198
†	On (43,875 – 5,715) @ 12.8%			4,884

Each extra £1 of profit would cost the sole trader 41p in tax and national insurance and the company 21p (see **3.14**).

Possible further tax liabilities if company retentions of £15,414 are paid out:

If distributed as dividends, income tax of (32.5 – 10)% on £17,127 (i.e. £15,414 plus tax credit £1,713)   £3,853

If taxed as capital gains, 18% on £15,414 (or 10%, i.e. £1,541 if entrepreneurs' relief available) Note, however, for gains realised on or after 23 June 2010, the capital gains tax rate could be 28%, depending on the individual's personal tax position (see 4.2).   £2,774

Example 2

Say total profits are £25,000 and there are no other sources of income. The comparative position for a sole trader compared with a company director who is paid a salary of £7,500 and receives the balance after corporation tax as a dividend is as follows:

	Trader			Company director
	£			£
Profits/remuneration	25,000			7,500
Personal allowance	6,475			6,475
Taxable income	18,525			1,025
Tax thereon:	18,525 @ 20%	3,705	1,025 @ 20%	205
Class 2 NI (flat rate)		125	Employee's NI	
Class 4 NI (25,000 – 5,715 = 19,285 @ 8%)		1,543	(1,785 @ 11%)	196
Total personal tax and NI		5,373		401
Company's tax and NI:				
Profits			25,000	
Less: Director's remuneration			(7,500)	
Company's NI thereon (1,785 @ 12.8%)			(228)	228
Taxable profits			17,272	
Tax thereon @ 21%			(3,627)	3,627
Dividend (tax covered by tax credit)			13,645	
		5,373		4,256

Saving through operating as company	<u>1,117</u>

Paying tax on the profits (TMA 1970, ss 59A, 59B, 59D, 59E)

[18.9] Directors' remuneration is subject to tax and national insurance under the PAYE scheme immediately it is paid or credited to the director's account, with corporation tax on any profits left in the company being payable nine months after the end of the accounting period.

An unincorporated business makes tax payments on account half-yearly on 31 January in the tax year and 31 July following the tax year. The payments on account are based on the total income (not just the business profits) of the previous tax year, with an adjustment to the correct figure, including any tax due on capital gains, on the 31 January following the tax year. The extent to which the unincorporated business will be better off than the company from a cash flow point of view will depend on whether directors' remuneration has been taken (and if so, how much and when), and whether the tax payments on account are significantly less than the full amount due. See Example 3.

Example 3

Say accounts of a business that started in 2000 were made up for the year to 31 December 2010. The profits of that year would be part of the total income of 2010/11 and tax on that total income would be payable provisionally in two equal instalments on 31 January 2011 and 31 July 2011, based on the previous year's income. The actual tax liability on the income plus capital gains of 2010/11 would be notified by 31 January 2012 for returns filed online (see 9.3), and a balancing payment or repayment would be made accordingly. The first provisional payment for 2011/12 would also be due on 31 January 2012.

If the business had been a company, tax on the profits of the year to 31 December 2010 (after paying directors' remuneration) would have been due on 1 October 2011, with PAYE tax and national insurance being payable at the time when any remuneration was paid. For income tax purposes, the additional tax on dividends for higher rate taxpayers is payable as part of the balancing payment when the dividends are received for the first time, but is then taken into account in arriving at payments on account for subsequent years.

There is an additional flexibility open to unincorporated businesses. By choosing an accounting date early in the tax year, say 30 April, they may benefit from lower tax rates and higher thresholds in the year of assessment compared with those in force when most of the profits were earned (although the rates can of course go up as well as down). The possible advantage of an accounting date early in the tax year may, however, be counterbalanced by the rules for taxing profits when the business ceases. For the detailed rules on how profits are charged to tax, see **CHAPTER 21**.

Losses (ITA 2007, Pt 4; CTA 2010, Pt 4; TCGA 1992, s 253; FA 2009, s 23, Sch 6)

[18.10] If a new business is expected to make losses in its early years, it is essential to bear in mind the different loss reliefs available to individuals and to companies. (These are dealt with more fully in **CHAPTERS 25** and **26**.)

Individuals can claim generous reliefs for trading losses in a new business. Losses in any of the first four tax years of a new business may be carried back to set against *any* income of the previous three tax years, earliest first. The tax liability of the earlier years is recalculated accordingly to establish the tax saving. Effect is, however, given to the saving in the tax year in which the loss is incurred rather than the tax year in which the loss has been set off, so the tax saving is not boosted by a corresponding payment of interest on overpaid tax. For losses in later years (or instead of a carry-back claim for opening year losses) a claim may be made to set them against the total income of the tax year in which the loss is sustained or the previous tax year, and tax will be discharged or repaid. FA 2009 introduced a temporary extension of the carry back of a limited amount of trade losses incurred in 2008/09 and 2009/10. Broadly the carry back is extended from the one year entitlement to a period of three years (see **25.6**). The losses may have been boosted, or indeed created, by capital allowances. In some circumstances, trading losses may be set against capital gains. Unrelieved trading losses may always be carried forward to set against future trading profits of the same trade.

If a new company makes trading losses, they may only be set against any current profits of the company, such as bank interest or chargeable gains, or carried forward against the company's later *trading* profits. Trading losses of an established trading company may be set against the profits from other sources, if any, in the same accounting year, then against the total profits of the previous year, with any balance being carried forward against trading profits. FA 2009 introduced a temporary extension of the carry back of a limited amount of trade losses incurred in accounting periods ending after 23 November 2008 and before 24 November 2010. Broadly the carry back is extended from the one year entitlement to a period of three years (see **26.4**). The relief for established companies is thus similar to that for established unincorporated businesses.

Funds introduced to a limited company to support losses, either as share capital or on loan, do not qualify for any immediate relief (but see **2.14** as regards relief for interest payable on any borrowing to enable the funds to be introduced). There are two relieving measures for shares and loans, but they are only available when shares are disposed of or when money lent becomes irrecoverable. The provisions are as follows:

(a)   An individual can set a capital loss on the disposal of shares that he had *subscribed for* in an unquoted trading company against any of his income in the same way as a trading loss, as an alternative to setting the capital loss against capital gains.

(b)   The loss of money loaned to the company (or paid to cover a bank guarantee) may be deducted against the lender's capital gains.

To get the first relief, the shares must be disposed of or they need to have become virtually worthless, probably because the business has failed. The second relief is also only likely to be available because the company is in financial difficulties. The distinction between the shares relief being given against income and the loan relief only against capital gains is important, because relief against income gives more flexibility and the opportunity for early relief. These two relieving measures are available both to working directors and to others providing funds to a company.

Pensions

[**18.11**] Self-employed persons are currently entitled to relief at the top rate of tax on contributions to a personal pension scheme, providing it is a registered scheme. However, tax relief on pension contributions made by individuals broadly with gross income of £150,000 or more will be restricted from 6 April 2011, with anti-forestalling provisions applying from 22 April 2009 (see **16.13** for the full details).

Company directors/employees in non-pensionable employment can also take advantage of the personal pension provisions, but it is often preferable for a family company to operate its own pension scheme. Providing the scheme is a registered scheme, there is not normally any restriction on contributions other than the annual limit under the new provisions, and the general requirement that any payment by a business must be wholly and exclusively for business purposes. In certain circumstances employers' contributions may have to be spread forward rather than all being deducted in a single accounting period. There are some special provisions where there is both a registered scheme and an unregistered employer-financed scheme. Unless these special rules apply, the company's contributions reduce the company's taxable profits when the benefits are paid and are not charged either to tax or national insurance on the employee, and the individual's contributions, if any, are allowed in calculating tax on his earnings from the company (although not deducted from pay in calculating employers' and employees' NICs). The same restrictions on the individual's tax relief as described in the above paragraph in relation to personal pension contributions will also apply to company pension contributions from 6 April 2011, with the anti-forestalling provisions applying broadly after 22 April 2009 (see **16.13**).

Capital gains

[**18.12**] Where realised chargeable gains are not covered by available reliefs, the first £10,100 of the total gains in 2010/11 is exempt from capital gains tax (CGT) for individuals (£10,100 each for husband and wife and civil partners), tax being charged at a flat rate (of either 18% or 28%, depending upon the individual's personal tax position , see **4.2**) unless entrepreneurs' relief is available to bring the effective rate down to 10%. Companies are not entitled to any exemption and pay corporation tax on the full amount of their chargeable gains (but, unlike individuals, companies remain entitled to an indexation allowance to compensate for inflation). The rate of tax on a company's gains for the year to 31 March 2011 could therefore be anything between the small companies' corporation tax rate of 21% and the marginal rate of 29.75% on profits between £300,000 and £1,500,000. This means that the effect of gains being realised within a company depends on the company's tax rate and the way in which the gains are passed to the shareholder. The corporation tax rates are set to be reduced from April 2011 (see **3.11**) The possible effect if the gains are passed on as a dividend is shown in Example 4.

If the gains are retained within the company until the shareholder disposes of his shares or the company is liquidated, the shareholder will be liable to CGT on the increase in value of his shareholding, and since the gain made by the company will have borne corporation tax when it was made this would effectively give a double tax charge. Reliefs may, however, be available at the time the shares are disposed of (see below).

Example 4

Company makes a gain of £10,000 in year to 31 March 2010, which is passed on to shareholders as a dividend.

Rate of tax on profits

	21%	Marginal rate of 29.75%*	28%
	£	£	£
Company's capital gain	10,000	10,000	10,000
Corporation tax	(2,100)	(2,975)	(2,800)
Leaving for cash dividend	7,900	7,025	7,200
Tax credit on dividend at $^1/_9$	878	781	800
Shareholder's income	8,778	7,806	8,000
Maximum income tax @ 42.5%	3,731	3,318	3,400
Leaving shareholder with net cash of	5,047	4,488	4,600
Combined company and personal tax	4,953	5,512	5,400
i.e.	49.53%	55.12%	54%

* For details of the marginal rate on profits between £300,000 and £1,500,000 see **3.14**.

Whether or not a business is incorporated, the increase in the value of its chargeable assets may lead to chargeable gains in the future, and in the case of a company there is the possibility of further personal chargeable gains where the share value is increased by profit retentions. There is no CGT liability on death. Legatees effectively take over the assets of the deceased at their market value at the date of death and thus get a tax-free uplift in base cost where values of shares or personally owned business assets have risen.

There are important reliefs which lessen the CGT impact, and these reliefs are available to sole traders, partners and company shareholders.

Entrepreneurs' relief is available on a disposal after 5 April 2008 of all or part of a business, or shares in a 'personal' trading company, where certain conditions are satisfied for at least a year preceding the disposal. This relief reduces the effective rate of CGT from 18% or 28% to 10% (see **29.2**).

Hold-over relief is available if gifts of certain business assets are made (see **4.24**). Gifts are generally treated as disposals at open market value, which may give rise to chargeable gains. The donor and the donee may, however, jointly claim to treat the gain as reducing the donee's cost in the event of a future disposal, and thus avoid an immediate tax charge on the donor.

Roll-over relief is available to defer CGT liability where business assets are replaced. It is not available for disposals of shares, but may be claimed in relation to certain disposals of assets used by a company in which the disponer is a shareholder (see **29.11** and **29.16**).

A further relief is available under the enterprise investment scheme where gains (whether arising through the business or otherwise) are reinvested by subscribing for ordinary shares in a qualifying unquoted trading company (see **29.21**). Tax on the reinvested gains is deferred until the new shares are disposed of.

See **CHAPTERS 4** and **29** for discussion of these reliefs.

Inheritance tax (IHTA 1984, ss 103–114)

[18.13] There is usually no inheritance tax to pay on gifts of all or part of a business in lifetime or on death, whether it is operated by an individual or through a company. Business property relief is available at 100% on transfers of all or part of an individual's business and on transfers out of unquoted shareholdings (providing the company carries on a qualifying business — see **5.40** — and providing any lifetime gifts of such property, or qualifying replacement property, are still retained by the donee when the donor dies). Shares traded on the NASDAQ are treated as quoted shares. Shares on the Alternative Investment Market, the EU junior markets and NASDAQ Europe are treated as unquoted shares. The rate of inheritance tax business property relief on assets owned outside a partnership or company but used within the business is only 50% and in the case of a company the relief is only available to a controlling director. For details, see **CHAPTER 5**.

To pass on a business gradually to other members of the family, the company format has the edge in terms of flexibility, since it is easier to transfer shares than to transfer a part of an unincorporated business.

Raising finance and attracting high calibre employees

[18.14] The enterprise investment scheme gives a qualifying company an advantage over an unincorporated business in attracting funds from outside investors. Individuals may obtain income tax relief at 20% on up to £500,000 invested for at least five years in shares of qualifying unquoted trading companies, and gains on disposal of the shares are exempt from tax. Similar provisions apply to investments in venture capital trusts, which are quoted companies that invest in unquoted companies. The rate of income tax relief on venture capital trust investments is 30%. The enterprise investment scheme also enables chargeable gains that are matched by equivalent investments in scheme shares to be deferred until the scheme shares are sold. (This deferred relief used to be available for gains reinvested in venture capital trust scheme shares, but it does not apply in relation to such shares if they are issued after 5 April 2004.) Smaller, high risk companies have a further advantage over unincorporated businesses in the form of 'enterprise management incentives'. Under the enterprise management incentives provisions, qualifying companies may provide employees with share options worth up to £120,000 per employee (up to an overall maximum of £3 million), but FA 2008 introduced a new limit by reference to the number of employees. In addition, corporate venturing relief gave corporation tax relief at 20% to companies who subscribed for shares in smaller, high risk companies but the relief does not apply to shares issued after 31 March 2010. The detailed provisions on these schemes are in CHAPTER 11 for enterprise management incentives and CHAPTER 29 for the other schemes.

Changing from one format to another

[18.15] It is a simple matter for an unincorporated business to change from a sole trader to a partnership or vice versa (see CHAPTER 23). Where an unincorporated business is to be incorporated, careful planning is necessary to ensure the best tax position and to minimise the disadvantages — see CHAPTER 27. Unfortunately there are no special tax provisions to help companies who wish to disincorporate. If the company has accumulated trading losses, these cannot be transferred to the shareholders. If the shareholders take the company's assets into personal ownership in order to use them in a new unincorporated business, the disposal by the company will be an open market value disposal for the purpose of calculating a taxable gain, and where there are trading losses, any capital gains can only be reduced by current and not by brought forward losses. Corporation tax will then be payable on any remaining gains. The consequences of either paying out gains as dividends or as capital distributions in a liquidation are illustrated in CHAPTER 28. If the company's disposal of any of the assets should yield a capital loss, no relief would be available unless the company had gains in the same accounting period against which to set it, and if the disposal was to the shareholders, they would be acquiring the assets at a lower CGT base cost than was paid by the company.

Tax points

[18.16] Note the following:

- Don't let the tax tail wag the commercial dog. Consider *all* aspects of alternative business forms.
- The loss rules for individuals, particularly the three year carry-back of new business losses, make an unincorporated start an attractive proposition where there is heavy initial expenditure, particularly on revenue items but also on capital items which attract tax allowances. The business can later be converted to a company if appropriate.
- To get income tax relief on a capital loss where shares in an unquoted trading company are disposed of, the shares must have been issued *to the disponer* by the company. Shares acquired by transfer from a previous shareholder do not qualify.
- The possible double tax charge where a company first sells chargeable assets at a profit, thus paying corporation tax on the profit and also increasing the value of its shares, can be avoided by shareholder/directors retaining personal ownership of assets such as freeholds or leaseholds and allowing the company to use them. But inheritance tax business property relief at 50% is only available on those assets where a shareholder *controls* the company, whereas the 50% reduction is available to any partner who personally owns assets which are used by the partnership.
- Entrepreneurs' relief is available on a disposal of shares only if the company is a personal company. This means, broadly, that the disponer must have a stake of at least 5% in the company. There is no similar requirement for partners in a partnership, so that partners with very small interests may be eligible for the relief.
- The differing rates of income tax and capital gains tax should be borne in mind. Income tax deductions cannot be set against capital gains. But a dividend from a company, even if payable out of a capital profit, counts as income in the hands of the shareholder, enabling available deductions to be set off and saving tax at higher rates accordingly, although dividend tax credits cannot be repaid.

19

Starting up a new small or part-time business

Is it self-employment?

[19.1] It is essential to establish at the outset whether a person is working as an employee or is self-employed. Alternatively, he may be neither employed nor self-employed but receiving sums taxable under the 'miscellaneous income' provisions (for example receiving payments for writing the occasional article, but not often enough to be regarded as an author carrying on a trade or profession). Exceptionally, the activity may not be taxable at all.

The distinction between employment and self-employment is important in deciding whether PAYE tax and employees' national insurance contributions (NICs) should be deducted from payments (and employers' NICs paid); what expenses may be deducted in working out the income chargeable to tax; and whether there is a need to account for VAT. If a taxpayer operates through a personal service company the tax legislation looks through the legal structure to ensure that those in 'disguised employment' pay the same tax and NICs as someone employed directly (see **19.6**) and there are similar provisions for those working for a 'managed service company' (see **19.15**).

[19.2] One important distinction between employment and self-employment is whether a payment is made under a contract of *service* and is thus employment income subject to PAYE, or made under a contract *for services* entitling payment against an invoice or fee note, the payment being included in the self-employed accounts. But the decision is not clear-cut. Employment status is a matter of general (not tax) law and depends on the overall circumstances rather than just the form of the contract.

HMRC leaflets ES/FS1 (for workers) and ES/FS2 (for employers) outline the main points to be considered. These leaflets replaced the earlier guidance contained in booklet IR56, a guide to employment status, in 2008. HMRC also have an online 'Employment Status Indicator' tool which can be used in 'all but the most complex of cases', such as directors, agency workers and anyone providing services through an intermediary.

Factors pointing to employment are that the person needs to carry out the work personally; he has to take orders as to how, where and when to do it, and work set hours; and be paid a regular salary or wage and be paid for overtime, sickness and holidays.

Factors pointing to self-employment are that the person risks his own capital and bears any losses; he controls whether, how, when and where to do the work; provides his own equipment; is free to employ others to do the work; is required to bear the cost of correcting anything that goes wrong; and regularly works for a number of different people.

None of these factors is conclusive — indeed many of them will be irrelevant in particular cases — and all the circumstances have to be taken into account. The tax and NIC rules are not always the same, and the tax and NIC treatment is not conclusive for VAT.

HMRC have provided separate guidance for contractors in the construction industry, where special rules apply — see **CHAPTER 44**. There are also special rules for agency workers, divers, office cleaners, lecturers and teachers, and entertainers. HMRC guidance is available at www.hmrc.gov.uk/employment-status.

A person can challenge a ruling by HMRC that he is an employee, and some taxpayers have had some success, but this can be costly and time consuming.

If a taxpayer engages a worker it is the taxpayer's responsibility to determine his or her employment status. See **10.2** regarding the re-classification of workers as employees.

[19.3] Someone who occasionally buys and sells may contend that his activities are not a trade but remain a hobby, a collector's activity or an investment, such as collecting and restoring antique furniture, sometimes selling the occasional piece at a profit. Buying and selling on eBay has almost become a national pastime — but in many cases those doing so are almost certainly trading. HMRC published an online guide at www.hmrc.gov.uk/guidance/selling which also examines the tax position in relation to income from sales via classified advertisements and car boot sales. Self-assessment tax returns tell taxpayers to contact their tax office if they are unsure whether they are carrying on a business or not. If they do not do so, and HMRC subsequently enquire into their tax position, they could be faced with interest and penalties for non-disclosure. It may be HMRC rather than the taxpayer who take the view that an activity is a hobby, particularly where there are losses, because to accept that it is a commercial activity would open the way for loss reliefs against other income. Each case depends on the facts, with appropriate rights of appeal if HMRC do not see it in the same way as the taxpayer.

[19.4] Depending on the scale of the activities, there may be VAT consequences as well. In a case relating to eBay trading heard before the VAT Tribunal in 2006, the Tribunal agreed with the taxpayer's contention that the early eBay transactions were largely out of a collection of antiques bought over the years, and that VAT registration was only relevant from the date the taxpayer accepted as being the start of a business. See **7.22** regarding VAT and second-hand goods.

Registering for tax, national insurance and VAT

[19.5] Once a person has established self-employment he has responsibilities in relation to tax, national insurance and possibly VAT. HMRC's leaflet SE1 — Are you thinking of working for yourself? — sets out the basic requirements for those who have started, or are thinking of starting, in business, and he can telephone a helpline for the newly self-employed on 0845 915 4515 for guidance. More detailed information is provided in leaflet SE2 — Giving your business the best start with tax — available at www.hmrc.gov.uk/startingup.

A person may register for tax and NICs by telephoning the helpline, or completing form CWF1 which is in leaflet SE1, or by registering online via www.hmrc.gov.uk/selfemployed.

See **9.39** regarding penalties for failure to register for Class 2 NICs. A person needs to register even if he is going to claim deferment of Class 2 contributions because he is both employed and self-employed and he already pays Class 1 contributions (see **24.11**).

HMRC advice teams run free workshops and presentations at locations throughout the country (see www.hmrc.gov.uk/startingup). Help on PAYE matters for new employers is available at www.hmrc.gov.uk/paye. HMRC now manage the Government's Business Link website at www.businesslink.gov.uk which provides information and support on a wide range of topics including tax and VAT, employment, health and safety, sales and marketing, and sources of finance. It also has guidance on Government and other rules and regulations for setting up a business.

Personal service companies (ITEPA 2003, ss 48–61; SI 2000/727)

[19.6] Special rules known as the IR35 rules prevent people paying substantially less tax and national insurance by operating through an intermediary, such as a personal service company or partnership, than they would have to pay if they were employed directly. New rules to counter avoidance through the use of 'managed service companies' were introduced in 2007 (see **19.15** onwards).

The personal service companies rules apply where a worker provides services under a contract between a client and an intermediary company or partnership that meets certain conditions, and the income would have been treated as employment income if the worker had contracted directly with the client. The rules apply whether the client is a business or a private individual, so that they apply to domestic workers such as nannies provided by a service company. The existing tests to differentiate employment from self-employment outlined at **19.1** above still apply.

HMRC provide guidance at www.hmrc.gov.uk/ir35 and in their Employment Status Manual. The status tests set out in the manual were, however, criticised by the judge in a judicial review of the IR35 rules, although the judge found that the rules were not a breach of the human rights legislation and European law, and following an appeal on the European issue the Court of Appeal also found that European law was not contravened. Many IR35 cases have come before the appeal commissioners but each depended on the particular circumstances and no clear guidelines have emerged. Careful drafting of the contract is essential and professional advice is recommended. The Government announced in the June 2010 Emergency Budget that it remains committed to a review of IR35 and small business tax.

[19.7] A company is within the IR35 provisions if the worker (alone or together with his associates) has a material interest in the company (i.e. broadly, he owns or controls more than 5% of the ordinary share capital or has rights to more than 5% of any distributions from the company), or he receives or could receive payments or benefits which are not salary but which could reasonably be taken to represent payment for services provided to clients. A partnership is within the provisions if the worker (alone or together with relatives) is entitled to 60% or more of the partnership profits, or where most of the partnership profits come from work for a single client, or where a partner's profit share is based on his income from relevant contracts.

[19.8] Where the rules apply and the intermediary is a company, the company operates PAYE and accounts for tax and Class 1 NICs on the worker's earnings during the tax year in the normal way, and pays Class 1A NICs on any benefits provided. At the end of the year, the excess of the amount of cash and non-cash benefits that the company has received from clients for the worker's services (net of VAT and net of allowable expenses, see **19.9**, paid by the company) over the amount the company has paid to the worker as earnings plus non-cash benefits (including mileage allowance payments for use of the worker's own car and 5p per mile passenger payments if relevant — see **10.11** and **10.12**) is treated as pay on 5 April and liable to PAYE tax and Class 1 NICs accordingly. This means that the extra tax and NICs are payable by 19 April after the year-end and interest will be charged on underpayments from that date (but see **19.14** regarding an HMRC concession).

This deemed employment payment is included in the worker's year-end earnings certificate P60 and will be shown on his self-assessment return. (It is not, however, included in income for tax credits purposes.) All employers have to state on their PAYE annual P35 forms whether the IR35 rules apply to any employee listed on the return and if so, whether a deemed employment payment has been included on the form.

[19.9] The intermediary's allowable expenses broadly comprise a flat rate allowance of 5% of the net of VAT payment for the relevant contracts, expenses paid by the intermediary (or by the worker and reimbursed by the intermediary) that would have been allowable to an employee of the client (including travelling expenses from home to the client's premises plus subsistence expenses, providing the job for the client is expected to and does last less than 24 months), capital allowances that could have been claimed by the worker, employer pension contributions, and the amount of Class 1 and Class 1A employer's NICs paid by the company in respect of the worker's earnings. Allowable expenses include mileage allowances, on the same basis as if the worker had been employed direct by the client and had used his own car for the client's business (see **10.11**).

[19.10] The excess amount arrived at is treated as inclusive of employer's Class 1 NICs, which are then deducted to arrive at the deemed employment payment. See Example 1.

Example 1

During 2010/11 the client pays £50,000 to the company for the worker's services. The contract is caught by the IR35 rules. The company pays the worker's salary of £18,000 through PAYE and provides taxable benefits of £2,000. It also pays pension contributions of £4,000. The deemed employment payment is:

		£	£
Total from client			50,000
Less:	5% × 50,000	2,500	
	Pension contributions	4,000	
	Employer's NIC on £20,000 (Class 1 £1,572, Class 1A £256)	1,828	8,328
			41,672
Less:	Salary actually paid and benefits provided		20,000
Excess amount			21,672
Less:	Employer's Class 1 NIC therein (12.8/112.8)		2,459
			19,213

The company is deemed to pay the worker £19,213 on 5 April 2011 and must account for PAYE tax and NIC thereon by 19 April 2011. See **13.2** regarding proposed changes to NIC rates and thresholds from 6 April 2011.

[19.11] Similar provisions apply where the intermediary is a partnership receiving gross payment under a contract. The worker is deemed to receive employment income on 5 April, and liable to tax and national insurance accordingly, and such income will be excluded from the worker's share of the partnership profits (although small amounts of employment income may be left as part of partnership profits).

[19.12] The deemed employment payment and the intermediary's national insurance contributions thereon are allowable deductions in computing the intermediary's profits of the accounting period in which the deemed payment is treated as made for corporation tax purposes or, if earlier, the accounting period in which the trade ceases.

[19.13] It is important to realise that later payments of salary by reference to the deemed employment payment at 5 April *cannot* be made free of tax and NICs. Actual salary payments reduce the deemed payment of the tax year in which they are *paid*. The only way to avoid double taxation on the deemed payment is to pay a dividend. The company may make a claim to regard the dividend as reduced by the deemed payment (net of tax and employee's NICs). This relief applies to dividends paid to the worker before dividends paid to anyone else, and to dividends paid in the same tax year as the deemed payment before dividends paid in later years. When the relief is claimed, the company's distributions will be reduced accordingly. The amount of the worker's dividend income and associated dividend tax credits would be similarly reduced. (The dividend received would, however, count as income for tax credits.)

[19.14] The time frame for paying the tax and NICs due on deemed employment payments (see **19.8**) is very short. By concession, HMRC will accept a provisional payment on account of the tax and NICs due on the deemed employment payment if the employer is unable to calculate the amount by 19 April. The employer should inform HMRC in a note accompanying the form P35 that the amount paid on 19 April, and reflected in the end of year forms sent in by 19 May, is provisional. No penalties will be charged so long as the employer files supplementary forms P35 and P14 and pays any balance of tax and NICs due by the following 31 January, but interest will be payable. For companies filing form P35 online, the same treatment will apply if the company ticks box 6 on the form. Unpaid amounts may be collected direct from the worker if the company does not pay.

One final twist is that the deemed employment payment is not wages for the purposes of the national minimum wage, so that actual pay (excluding benefits other than accommodation) must be sufficient to meet the minimum wage requirements (see **12.1**).

Managed service companies (ITEPA 2003, ss 61A–61J, 688A; ITTOIA 2005, s 164A)

[19.15] New rules were introduced from 6 April 2007 to counter tax avoidance by the use of managed service companies (MSCs). Following the introduction of the new provisions, MSCs appeared unlikely to be commercially viable.

The definition of MSC covers both companies and partnerships. MSCs are similar to personal service companies (as to which see **19.6** onwards), but are usually provided by an outside business that controls the administration and financial management. The personal service company rules do not apply to those within the scope of the new legislation. The MSC provisions apply where the business consists wholly or mainly of providing the services of an individual to another person, the individual receives most or all of the payment for his services, he receives a greater amount (net of tax and national insurance) than he would have received as employment income, and an MSC provider is 'involved' with the MSC. An MSC provider is someone who is in business to promote the use of companies to provide the services of individuals. The MSC provider is involved with the MSC if it benefits financially, or influences the provision of the individual's services or the way they are paid for, or influences or controls the company's finances or activities, or undertakes to make good any tax loss.

[19.16] The MSC rules require payments for services provided through such companies that are not already treated as employment income to be treated as a deemed employment payment by the MSC. The deemed employment payment is arrived at by deducting expenses that would have been allowable, and also employers' NICs that would have been payable. Tax will not be charged if there would have been no tax liability in a direct worker/client relationship by reason of the worker being resident, ordinarily resident or domiciled abroad, or the client being resident or ordinarily resident abroad, or the services being provided outside the UK. Where the worker is UK resident and provides the services in the UK, the MSC is treated as having a UK place of business whether it actually has one or not.

[19.17] If a company that is treated as making a deemed employment payment pays a dividend in the same or following tax year, it may claim to reduce the amount of the dividend for tax purposes by the deemed employment payment.

[19.18] Where HMRC consider that an amount of PAYE is due that has not been paid, they can recover it from a director, office-holder or associate of the MSC, the MSC provider, or someone who has been actively involved in providing the worker's services (excluding those providing legal or accountancy advice in their professional capacity).

[19.19] In computing its own profits, the MSC may deduct the deemed employment payment and employers' NICs thereon paid by the MSC. The deduction cannot, however, create a loss.

Computation of taxable profits

[19.20] CHAPTER 20 examines the detailed rules for calculating profits and CHAPTER 22 deals with capital allowances for the purchase of buildings, equipment, etc. A newly-established business is often run from home, perhaps using an existing car for any business travelling that is required. A claim can be made for the business proportion of car expenses, and also the business proportion of capital allowances on the value of the car at the time it was first used for business (or the purchase price if less). A deduction can also be claimed for business use of home telephone. Where the business is run from home, expenses of part of the home can be allowed against taxable profits if they are wholly and exclusively for the business, so that a proportion of, for example, the light and heat can be charged for the part of the residence used for the business, such as a study/office, surgery, workshop, etc. The business will be liable to pay business rates on that part of the property, as well as paying the council tax on the rest of the property (see **8.2**). If paid, business rates are allowable in calculating taxable profits. Where business rates are not paid, an appropriate proportion of the council tax can be treated as a business expense according to the business use of the home.

Under self-assessment details of the business income and expenses have to be shown under specified headings in the tax return. If turnover was below £68,000 for 2009/10 the 'short' self employment pages designed for more straightforward businesses may be completed in most cases. Alternatively, if other circumstances permit, the short tax return (SA200) may be completed.

This does not mean that the detailed information should not be kept. Keeping records is often not a strong point for many small businesses, but under self-assessment it is vital that adequate records relating to business expenses (and indeed other tax liabilities — see **9.25**) are kept, and that, if challenged, the way in which the allowable part of mixed expenses has been calculated can be justified.

If no part of the home is used wholly and exclusively for the business, capital gains tax (CGT) private residence relief (see **30.3**) will not be affected. If part of the property is so used, that part will be outside the CGT owner-occupier exemption. Any gain need not be charged to tax immediately if the property is sold and the business is continued from a new residence, because a roll-over relief claim may be made for the gain to be regarded as reducing the cost for CGT of the business part of the new residence, although it would not be necessary to make that claim if the chargeable gain was covered by the annual CGT exemption. See Example 2.

Example 2

House bought June 1995 for £60,000, sold June 2010 for £220,000.

Used to June 2005 wholly as residence then 1/6th for self-employment for remainder of period

Total gain (220,000 – 60,000)	£160,000
Chargeable gain: Business use 1/6th for 5 years out of 15: $^1/_6 \times$ $^5/_{15} \times$ £160,000	£8,889

The chargeable gain is covered by the 2010/11 annual exemption of £10,100 unless the exemption is already used against other gains.

Employing staff (CTA 2009, ss 1288–1289; ITTOIA 2005, ss 36–37, 865)

[19.21] If a business employs staff, it will need to operate the PAYE scheme (see **CHAPTER 10**). It must also make sure it complies with the national minimum wage legislation, which requires payment of hourly rates (from October 2010) of at least £5.93 for those aged 21 and over, £4.92 for those aged between 18 and 20 and £3.64 for 16 and 17-year-olds (see **12.1** for the previous rates). Before October 2010, the main rate applied to those aged over 22. An apprentice minimum wage of £2.50 per hour will also be introduced from October 2010. This will apply to apprentices under 19 and those aged 19 or over who are in the first year of their apprenticeship. There is also an exception for family members who live at home and work in the family business (but not if the business is a company). HMRC is responsible for enforcing the legislation (see **12.1**). If a business employs five or more people, it may need to offer access to a stakeholder pension scheme (see **17.2**).

As far as PAYE is concerned, HMRC will supply all the necessary documentation (and see **19.5** regarding getting help from HMRC). It is important to make sure that PAYE is operated properly, particularly where casual or part-time employees are taken on. Even if someone is paid less than the tax and national insurance threshold, tax must still be deducted if they have significant other earnings. Form P46 must be completed for any employee who does not produce form P45 (the leaving certificate provided by the previous employer). In a new small business, the first employees are very often members of the family and the PAYE rules apply equally to them. In addition, the salary payments must be both justified and paid. If HMRC open an enquiry into a self-assessment return (which they may well do for someone who has just started in business), they will be unwilling to accept that an amount drawn for housekeeping or personal use includes family wages. They will also be better able to challenge the validity of the expense if it is left as an amount owing rather than having actually been paid. Payments of wages must in any case be made within nine months after the end of the accounting period if they are to be allowed in calculating the taxable profits of that period rather than a later period.

If family wages can be justified for the work done, they enable personal allowances (see **2.15**) to be used if they have not already been set against other income. For 2010/11, neither employers nor employees are liable for NICs on pay up to £110 a week. Employees earning more than £97 a week (i.e. the NIC lower earnings limit), but no more than £110 a week, would have their rights to benefits protected but would not be liable to pay NICs (see **13.1**). See also **13.2** regarding the proposed changes in NIC rates and thresholds from 6 April 2011.

How are profits charged to tax?

[19.22] The first profits of a sole trade or partnership usually form the basis of the first two years' tax bills (see **21.4**). A part-time start may therefore help to reduce the tax burden for those years so long as the transition from the part-time activity to full-time self-employment cannot be argued by HMRC as the start of an entirely new trade. Linking a slow start with a 30 April year end may be particularly helpful (see Example 3), although the initial and ongoing advantage where profits are rising needs to be set against the possible disadvantage of a higher taxable profit when the business ceases (see **21.5**).

Example 3

Trader starts business on a part-time basis on 1 May 2008 and makes up accounts to 30 April 2009, showing a profit for the first year of £12,000. He then devotes all his time to the business and makes a profit of £30,000 in the year to 30 April 2010. The tax position on those profits is as follows:

2008/09	1.5.08 – 5.4.09	$^{11}/_{12} \times$ £12,000	£11,000
2009/10	1.5.08 – 30.4.09		£12,000
2010/11	1.5.09 – 30.4.10		£30,000

Although £11,000 of the £12,000 profit is taxed twice, a deduction of £11,000 will be made from taxable profits, in the form of overlap relief, when the business ceases or possibly on a change of accounting date.

The effect of choosing a 30 April year end is that the profits taxable in the current year were largely earned in the previous year. The actual profit in 2009/10 was $^{1}/_{12}$ of £12,000 and $^{11}/_{12}$ of £30,000 = £28,500, whereas the taxable profit is £12,000.

Loss relief

[19.23] If a person makes losses in the first four tax years of a new sole trade or partnership business, they may be treated as reducing any income of the previous three tax years, earliest first, or set off against any other income and chargeable gains of the tax year of the loss. HMRC will then either make a tax refund or an equivalent amount of tax owed will be discharged. If a loss is carried back, the tax saving from the claim is calculated according to the tax position in the earlier year, but it is still regarded as a claim relating to the loss year, so that interest on the repayment will only be available from the 31 January following the tax year in which the loss occurred (see **CHAPTER 9**). See **CHAPTER 25** for details of this relief.

Pension provision

[19.24] Earnings from a small business can support a personal pension contribution, both in respect of the self-employed earnings and for the family employees. It does not matter that the self-employed taxpayer or family employee is also in separate pensionable employment. Tax relief can be obtained on the greater of £3,600 or the amount of earnings. Tax relief for more substantial contributions is limited by reference to annual and lifetime allowances, and restrictions for higher rate taxpayers were introduced in FA 2009. See CHAPTERS **16** and **17** for details.

VAT registration

[19.25] A business must register for VAT at the end of any month if turnover in the previous twelve months exceeded £70,000 (from 1 April 2010, previously £68,000). A business is required to notify HMRC and will then be registered unless it can show that turnover will not exceed £68,000 (previously £66,000) in the coming twelve months. If a business expects turnover in the next 30 days to exceed £70,000, it must register immediately. These limits must be monitored carefully because there are severe penalties for not complying with the rules. Even if turnover is below the limit a business may wish to register voluntarily in order to recover input VAT on purchases. But this will not be an advantage unless most customers are VAT registered. There is a special VAT flat-rate scheme for small businesses. See CHAPTER **7**.

National insurance contributions

[19.26] For the tax year 2010/11, a self-employed person pays Class 2 contributions of £2.40 a week, and also Class 4 contributions at 8% on profits between £5,715 and £43,875 and 1% on profits above that level. It is proposed from 6 April 2011 that 9% will be payable on profits between the lower and upper profits limits, with 2% payable on profits above the upper limit. It is also proposed to increase the lower profits limit by £570 per year and reduce the upper profits limit in line with the basic rate limit to a figure to be announced after the September 2010 retail price index figure is known. The detailed provisions are in CHAPTER **24**. Note particularly the provisions for deferring contributions if a person is both employed and self-employed. Neither deferment nor a refund affect the liability of the employer to pay employers' contributions.

If self-employed earnings were below £5,075 in 2009/10 and circumstances have not materially changed, or earnings are expected to be below £5,075 in 2010/11, an application can be made for a certificate of exception from Class 2 contributions (see CHAPTER **24**). This will, however, affect the contribution record for social security benefit purposes, particularly retirement pension. Since Class 2 contributions are presently only £2.40 a week it may be worth paying them to maintain the right to benefits. See **9.42** regarding the penalty for failure to register as self-employed within three months of starting business.

Occasional earnings not treated as from self-employment

[19.27] If a person is not treated as self-employed, occasional earnings are taxed according to the amount earned in the tax year, with a deduction for justifiable expenses. The tax should be accounted for in the self-assessment along with the tax on other income. If the person is also an employee, HMRC will sometimes, for convenience, offset small amounts of occasional earnings against tax allowances when arriving at the PAYE code number.

Any losses can be set off against certain other categories of miscellaneous income (see **2.28**), but it is unlikely that there will be any, in which case the losses are carried forward to reduce any future occasional earnings or other miscellaneous income.

Tax points

[19.28] Note the following:

- When a new business starts, there will be a tax liability for the tax year in which the business starts, unless the profit is covered by reliefs and allowances. If a tax return is not issued, the taxpayer must let HMRC know that he has taxable profits by 5 October following the tax year (see **9.27**), otherwise he will be liable to an income tax penalty. Unless he expects profits to be below the national insurance exemption level he will need to arrange to pay Class 2 NICs (quarterly or by direct debit — see **24.2**).
- Losses incurred in the early years of a business may be set against income of the three previous tax years (see **25.3**).
- If turnover was below £68,000 the 'short' self employment pages of the 2009/10 tax return, or the short tax return, can usually be completed — see **19.20**.
- A business should not take people on without making sure of their employment status. If a mistake is made there are only limited rights to recover underpaid tax and NICs from the worker, and interest and penalties may have to be paid as well.
- A useful test on the self-employed status is whether there is a risk of loss as well as gain, normally implying self-employment; and whether the worker has to carry out corrective work without payment.
- The rules for personal service companies bring enormous practical problems for those affected. HMRC provide detailed guidance at www.hmrc.gov.uk/ir35. A deemed payment under the IR35 rules is generally treated in the same way as actual pay, so that it counts as earnings in calculating the maximum permissible pension contributions but not in reckoning income for tax credits. On the other hand, a dividend paid out of profits represented by the deemed payment *is* reckoned in calculating income for tax credits.
- A business should not forget to register for VAT if appropriate. A check must be made at the end of every *month* to make sure that the annual turnover limit has not been exceeded. See **19.25** and CHAPTER 7.

- If a spouse or civil partner works in the business, then even if he or she is paid as a self-employed person issuing invoices (and charging and accounting for VAT if appropriate), for national insurance purposes they are regarded as employed, and Class 1 contributions are payable.

20

How are business profits calculated?

Background (ITTOIA 2005, Part 2; ITA 2007, s 989; CTA 2009, s 1119, Pt 3)

[20.1] Taxable profits from trades, professions and vocations are broadly calculated in the same way. It is usually obvious that a trade is being carried on, but the charge on trading profits is extended beyond what would normally be regarded as trading and can cover occasional transactions and those to which an investment motive cannot be attributed, where the circumstances point to a trading intention.

Important indicators of possible trading, when there is any doubt, are the nature of the asset itself (e.g. if it is income producing, or something to get enjoyment from owning, that would indicate investment rather than trading); the reason for acquiring it; how long it is owned; whether it was worked on to make it more saleable; the reason for selling; and how often such transactions were undertaken.

General rules for computing trading profits (FA 2005, ss 80–83 and Sch 4; ITTOIA 2005, ss 25, 33, 34; ITA 2007, s 997; CTA 2009, Pt 3 Chs 3–5; CTA 2010, ss 624–5, 996, 1127)

[20.2] Whether the business is that of an individual trader, a partnership or a company, profits are calculated in accordance with generally accepted accounting practice so as to give a true and fair view. They are then subject to adjustment as required by tax legislation, for example the prohibition of relief for capital nature (see **20.10**).

The two most important rules for expenses are first that they must be wholly and exclusively for the purposes of the trade, and second, that they must be of a revenue (not capital) nature.

There are special 'transfer pricing' rules for businesses that are connected with one another, in particular companies in the same group, to require an arm's length price to be used on transactions between them. These are dealt with briefly in **45.19**.

In recent years, different rules have been introduced for companies compared with unincorporated businesses in relation to the tax treatment of certain expenditure. The main areas are the treatment of 'loan relationships' (see **3.5** and **26.5**), intangible assets, including goodwill (see **20.30** to **20.36**), cleaning up contaminated or derelict land (see **20.37**), and various reliefs related to research and development (see **29.38** to **29.41**). The amount deductible from profits for tax purposes under the contaminated or derelict land and research and development provisions is greater than the amount of the expenditure, and loss-making companies may claim a cash payment in respect of the appropriate part of their unrelieved losses.

Alternative finance arrangements (FA 2007, s 53; ITA 2007, Pt 10A; CTA 2009, ss 501–521)

[20.3] There are various finance arrangements, in particular those designed to meet the requirements of Islamic law, that do not involve paying or receiving interest but have a similar effect. The legislation broadly equates the tax treatment of such payments and receipts with the treatment of interest. They are therefore brought into account for individuals and partnerships as trading expenses or trading receipts and for companies under the loan relationships rules outlined in **3.5**. The range of alternative finance arrangements covered by the legislation may be extended by statutory instrument.

'Wholly and exclusively' (ITTOIA 2005, s 34; CTA 2009, s 54)

[20.4] A sole trader or partner cannot deduct an expense that is incurred for both business and private purposes, such as clothing bought primarily for business but also for private purposes. Part of a mixed expense may, however, be incurred wholly and exclusively for the purposes of the trade and thus be deductible in calculating profits, such as the business element of line rental and call charges for business telephone calls from a home telephone. The same applies to mixed business and living accommodation, where again it may be possible accurately to separate the business and private areas (see **19.20**). Where meals are taken while working away from the place of business, the cost is not generally regarded as wholly and exclusively for business. HMRC accept, however, that those who travel regularly in their work, and those who make occasional business journeys outside the normal pattern, are entitled to claim for reasonable expenses incurred. Where one or more nights need to be spent away from home, reasonable costs of overnight accommodation and subsistence are allowed.

[20.5] Sole traders or partners may have some car mileage which is wholly and exclusively for business, some which is purely for private purposes, and some may be partly both. Where expenditure is for the sole purpose of the business, any incidental private benefit would be ignored. But if trips are undertaken both for business and private purposes, strictly no claim can be made for a deduction for any part of the expenses, even though the business derives benefit from the trip. Providing the trip has a genuine business purpose, however, in practice a claim is allowed for an expenses deduction based on the time spent on business. See Example 1.

Example 1

A trader's recorded mileage in a twelve-month period of account was as follows:

Purely business journeys	5,000
Purely private journeys	4,000
Home to business	2,000
Journeys for combined business/private purposes	1,000
	7,000
	12,000

Allowable business proportion is 5/12ths. In addition, a deduction could usually be claimed for an appropriate proportion of the expenses for the mixed purpose journeys.

Allowable car expenses are strictly required to be worked out by taking the business mileage proportion of the actual expenses incurred. If turnover is below the VAT threshold (£70,000 from 1 April 2010, previously £68,000), however, HMRC authorised mileage rates may be used (see the Table of Rates and Allowances and **10.11**) instead. In that event a claim cannot be made for capital allowances as well, but (in contrast to the rules for employees) a claim may also be made for relief for the business proportion of interest on a loan to buy the car.

[20.6] In the case of a company, there can be no private use by the company itself. Where a company or unincorporated employer incurs expenses that benefit employees or directors, the usual treatment is that the expenses are allowed in calculating the taxable profits of the employer, but are treated as taxable earnings of the employee or director (see **CHAPTER 10**). Sometimes, directors' fees, wages paid or the cost of benefits provided to members of the family who do not work full-time may not be allowed in full if the payment is considered excessive in relation to the work done, because it would then not be regarded as wholly and exclusively for the business. It is also particularly important where a business employs family members that payment of wages is properly made (see **19.21**).

In the case of family and similar companies, a distinction must be drawn between company expenditure which benefits a shareholder who is a director and the payment by the company of the personal debts of the shareholder/director, for example school fees, private entertaining, or expenses of a private residence. A payment for personal debts should be treated as a payment of salary, and declared on form P11D (see **10.7**), and Class 1 national insurance contributions (NICs) should be accounted for at the time of the payment. If HMRC discover that the payment has not been properly dealt with, they will normally treat the amount as a loan which the shareholder/director must repay to the company and it is then neither an allowable business expense nor taxed as a benefit on the shareholder/director. The loan has tax consequences both for the company and the director, and possible NIC consequences — see **12.13** to **12.16**.

In family companies, loans to directors and employees may sometimes be written off. For non-controlling shareholder directors and employees, the amount written off is treated as taxable pay and is allowed as a deduction in calculating the taxable profits of the company, subject to what is said above about remuneration that is excessive for the work done. If the director or employee is a controlling shareholder, special rules apply to prevent the company obtaining a deduction for the write-off, and to treat it as dividend income of the shareholder net of 10% tax, the shareholder then being liable to pay the extra tax due if he is a higher rate or additional rate taxpayer. See **12.15**.

[20.7] Where an employer takes out insurance against loss of profits arising from the death, accident or illness of a key employee, the premiums will usually be allowable in calculating trading profits and any policy proceeds treated as a trading receipt. If in the event of accident or illness the benefits of the policy were passed on to the employee, they would be taxed either as normal pay if the employee had a contractual right to them or as sick pay.

[20.8] Any accountancy expenses that relate to calculating the tax on profits rather than calculating the profits themselves are incurred in the capacity of taxpayer rather than trader, so they are not strictly deductible in calculating taxable profits. In practice such expenses are allowed, except where they arise as a result of an HMRC enquiry into an individual's tax affairs. Even then, they will be allowed if adjustments arising from the enquiry are made to the current year only and they do not arise through careless or deliberate actions.

[20.9] The costs of preparing a trader's tax return or calculating capital gains are not allowable, but if such matters are straightforward these costs are likely to be fairly low. Where a business is run through a company, and the company's accountants deal with the directors' tax returns, it is preferable for the work for the directors to be billed to them directly. If, in that event, the bill is actually paid by the company, then unless the amount has been charged to the director's loan account the company would be settling the director's personal liability and the director should be charged to tax and Class 1 NICs through the PAYE system on the amount paid. If the company has contracted with the accountant for dealing with directors' tax returns, the fees, including VAT, should be treated as a benefit in kind to the directors (as to which see

CHAPTER 10). The company would be allowed a deduction for the amount paid in calculating its taxable profits, so long as the total remuneration falls within the wholly and exclusively rule (see **20.4** above).

Capital or revenue (ITTOIA 2005, s 33; CTA 2009, s 53)

[20.10] Revenue expenditure is an allowable expense in calculating taxable profit unless specifically prohibited, such as business entertaining expenses (see **20.14**).

A capital expense cannot be deducted in calculating profits, although many items of capital expenditure may attract capital allowances (see **CHAPTER 22**). The usual definition of a capital expense is one made 'not only once and for all, but with a view to bringing into existence an asset or an advantage for the enduring benefit of the trade'. One person's stock in trade will be another person's fixed assets. Business premises are clearly a capital item, but if a business builds and sells factories, the factories will be trading stock and the cost will be taken into account in calculating profit. Cars used by traders and employees are capital items, but cars held for sale by a motor dealer are trading stock. Normally, repair expenditure is revenue expenditure and is allowable in calculating profits, but if a trader buys a capital asset that cannot be used in the business until it is renovated, the cost of renovating it is part of the capital cost. The distinction is often hard to draw, and has led to many disputes between the taxpayer and HMRC which have had to be settled by the courts.

Similar considerations apply in deciding whether a particular item is reckonable as trading income or as a capital profit.

As indicated at **20.2**, the categorisation of expenditure as capital or revenue now differs in certain respects for companies and unincorporated businesses, and generally accepted accounting principles are used to arrive at profits for tax purposes except to the extent that they conflict with tax law.

Provisions for future liabilities

[20.11] Provisions for future liabilities are normally allowable for tax purposes, so long as they do not conflict with the tax legislation as interpreted by the courts and they follow accepted accounting practice.

The accepted accounting treatment changed following the issue by the Accounting Standards Board of accounting standard FRS 12, which deals with 'Provisions, Contingent Liabilities and Contingent Assets'. The standard requires a provision to be made if, at the balance sheet date, a *present* obligation exists as a result of a *past* event and a *reliable estimate* can be made of the expenditure which will probably be required to meet the obligation. HMRC's Business Income Manual has guidance on the application of FRS 12 at BIM46515. With some exceptions for smaller businesses, the standard needs to be followed for tax purposes, so that appropriate tax adjustments must be made.

Any reductions of earlier provisions that have been allowed in calculating taxable profits increase the taxable profit of the period in which the adjustment is made.

Allowable and non-allowable expenses

[20.12] The principles outlined above provide a broad guide to what expenses are allowed, and points of detail relating to certain expenses are covered below. Some specific examples are listed in **20.28**, including items specifically allowed or disallowed by the tax legislation.

Payment of remuneration (ITTOIA 2005, ss 36, 37; CTA 2009, ss 1288, 1289)

[20.13] Directors' and employees' pay may only be taken into account as an expense of the accounting period to which it relates if it is paid during or within nine months after the end of the period. If the payment is provided in the accounts rather than having been paid in the accounting period, there must be sufficient evidence of the liability (e.g. a board minute) for it to be included as an expense in the accounts (see **20.11**). Otherwise it may only be deducted in the accounting period in which it is paid.

Business entertaining (ITTOIA 2005, ss 45–47; CTA 2009, ss 1298–1300)

[20.14] The cost of business entertaining and business gifts (apart from the £50 gifts exemption noted in **20.28**) is not allowable. Expenditure on entertaining staff (and their guests) is normally allowable, unless it is incidental to entertaining those with whom the employer does business, but there will be a benefits charge on P11D employees (subject to the exception noted at **10.24**).

The VAT position is slightly different. Input VAT on business entertaining is not recoverable, but where proprietors or employees act as hosts at meals with clients, etc. while away from work on business, input VAT other than that relating to the clients is recoverable (unless business entertainment was the main purpose of the trip). As far as staff entertainment is concerned, the proportion of input VAT relating to *guests* at a staff function is not recoverable, but you can recover the proportion relating to staff. In the same way as for income tax, there is a £50 gifts exemption (see **7.3**).

Any unrecovered input VAT on entertaining expenditure is not allowable when calculating taxable profit.

Bad and doubtful debts (ITTOIA 2005, ss 35, 97; CTA 2009, ss 55, 94, 358–361, 479, 481, 970)

[20.15] Normal trading bad debts and specific provisions for bad debts may be deducted from profits for tax purposes. In accordance with the principles outlined above, however, a *general* provision for bad debts cannot be allowed in calculating taxable profits. Any specific debts written off or provided for that are subsequently recovered must be included in profits for tax purposes.

A creditor may treat a debt as bad if he has released the debt as part of a statutory insolvency arrangement. The debtor in a voluntary arrangement will not have to bring into his trading profit debts that have been released in this way but debts released other than under such arrangements must be brought in as trading receipts.

For companies, bad debts that do not relate to ordinary trading transactions are dealt with under the loan relationships rules — see **26.5** to **26.7**. However, where a company is released from a trade debt on or after 22 April 2009, the release is also taxed under the loan relationship rules. This ensures that if the debtor and the creditor are connected there is no charge on the debtor and no tax relief for the creditor. There are provisions to impose a taxable profit on a debtor when a written-down debt to an unconnected company is acquired by a company connected to the debtor. There is an exemption to the charge for corporate rescues where the debtor is in financial difficulties. FA 2010 introduced provisions to ensure the exemption only applies to genuine corporate rescues. See also **12.15** re losses on loans to close company directors, employees and shareholders.

Interest paid (TMA 1970, ss 86, 87, 87A, 90; TA 1988, ss 787, 826, 826A; ITTOIA 2005, s 29; ITA 2007, Pt 8 Ch 1, Pt 15; CTA 2009, s 443, Pt 5)

[20.16] Interest paid on business borrowings must be wholly and exclusively for the purposes of the business in order to be allowable as a deduction.

Companies pay interest in full in a wide range of circumstances. Other interest paid by companies is paid net of income tax at 20%, and the company pays over to HMRC the income tax it has deducted (see **3.21**). Interest relating to the trade is deducted from the company's trading profits. All other interest is taken into account in arriving at the profit or loss on the company's non-trading loan relationships. See **3.5** for details.

Individuals normally pay interest in full and deduct interest relating to the trade as a trading expense. Partners may obtain tax relief for interest on a loan used for lending money or introducing capital to a partnership by deducting the interest from their total income (see **2.14** and **23.12**). So may those who introduce funds into their family company (see **2.14**).

Where interest is paid on borrowing to acquire a property that is partly private and partly business, the interest has to be split to arrive at the part that is allowable as a business expense and the part that is for the living accommodation. This will depend on the respective values of the parts of the property. Where part of the property is sometimes but not always used exclusively for business, the period of business use will also be taken into account.

Since interest on home loans does not qualify for tax relief, individuals should consider business borrowings instead, or if they are partners, borrowing money individually to lend to the firm (see **2.14**), rather than leaving undrawn profits in the business in order to boost the business capital. Capital can also be withdrawn (except to the extent that it represents asset revaluations), leaving the business to obtain funding from partners' loans or from other sources. If, however, withdrawing funds leads to a proprietor's capital/current account with the business becoming overdrawn, interest on business borrowings that had enabled the drawings to be made would not be wholly and exclusively for the trade. And partners must not withdraw their capital *after* making loans to the business, because to that extent they would be regarded as merely withdrawing what was introduced, with tax relief for interest on the loans being restricted accordingly.

There are some anti-avoidance provisions affecting both individuals and companies, and professional advice is essential.

Where interest arises on overdue or overpaid tax, the treatment is different for individuals and companies. For an individual, interest paid on overdue tax is not allowed in calculating profits and interest received on overpaid tax is not taxable. For a company, interest on overdue and overpaid tax is taken into account in computing profits and losses on the company's loan relationships (see **3.5**).

Leasing of cars (ITTOIA 2005, ss 48–50B; CTA 2009, ss 56–58B)

[20.17] Broadly, for expenses incurred on a hire agreement under which the hire period begins on or after 6 April 2009 for income tax, or on or after 1 April 2009 for corporation tax, the restriction on deductible hiring costs is at a flat rate of 15% for cars with CO_2 emissions of more than 160g/km. (If there is a subsequent rebate of rentals, the amount brought in as a taxable receipt is reduced in the same proportion.) A further restriction will apply where the sole trader or partner uses the car privately. The hire period begins on the first day that the car is required to be made available for use under the agreement. This restriction does not apply to motor cycles. There is no restriction on the deductible hiring costs for all cars which were first registered before 1 March 2001, regardless of their CO_2 emissions, cars registered after that date with CO_2 emissions of 160g/km or less, electric cars, and 'qualifying hire cars'. 'Qualifying hire car' for this purpose is generally a car hired under a hire-purchase agreement where there is either no option to purchase or there is an option to purchase at a maximum of 1% of the retail price, or a car leased under a long funding lease.

Where the hire agreement is entered into on or before 8 December 2008 and the hire period begins on or after 6 April 2009 but before 6 April 2010 for income tax, or on or after 1 April 2009 but before 1 April 2010 for corporation tax, the hirer can elect for the new rules not to apply (see below for the old rules). The irrevocable election must be made by the first anniversary of the normal time limit for amending a return for the tax year in which the relevant chargeable period ends for income tax, or within two years of the end of the relevant chargeable period for corporation tax. The relevant chargeable period is the first chargeable period for capital allowances purposes in which any expenditure is incurred under the agreement. Therefore for income tax purposes, where a sole trader incurs this expenditure in his accounts for the year ended 31 December 2008, the election must be made by 31 January 2011.

The restriction on the deductible hiring costs does not apply where, broadly, the car is hired by the taxpayer for a period of not more than 45 consecutive days, or where the taxpayer hires the car out to a customer for a period of more than 45 consecutive days. Further provisions detail how these periods should be calculated and what happens where two or more persons in a chain of leases are connected.

For expenses incurred on a hire agreement under which the hire period began before 6 April 2009 for income tax or 1 April 2009 for corporation tax the restriction of deductible hiring expenses was based on the retail price of the car (including motor cycles) when new. A deduction was made from profit of the proportion of the total hire charge that £12,000 plus the retail price bore to twice the retail price, and for cars used by sole traders and partners, the allowable amount had to be further restricted by the private proportion. (If there was a subsequent rebate of rentals, the amount brought in as a taxable receipt was reduced in the same proportion.) See Example 2. Lease contracts may either be operating leases (contract hire), under which the lease rental covers repair and maintenance as well as the provision of the car, or finance leases, under which only the car is provided and repair and maintenance costs are borne by the lessee (see **20.18**). Where a car was acquired on contract hire, if the contract hire company split the lease rental between the amount paid for the car and the repair and maintenance charge, the £12,000 restriction would only apply to the car hire payment.

Example 2

Car with retail value of £30,000 leased on 1 May 2008 for £9,000 a year.

Allowable hire charge:

$$9,000 \times \frac{12,000 + 30,000}{60,000} = £6,300$$

The £6,300 will be further restricted if the car is used privately by a sole trader or partner.

No tax relief is available for the remaining £2,700.

The above restriction on allowable hire charges did not apply to the hiring of an electric car, or car with low CO_2 emissions, providing the car was first registered on or after 17 April 2002 and the hire began before 1 April 2008. It did not apply to a 'qualifying hire car', generally a car hired under a hire-purchase agreement where there is no option to purchase, or a car or motor cycle used for a trade of hire to members of the public where certain conditions are met.

See **20.23** for the VAT position on leased cars.

Finance leases of plant and machinery (FA 1997, s 82 and Sch 12; FA 2006, s 81 and Schs 8, 9)

[20.18] Although for accounting purposes a trader is treated as owning plant and machinery acquired under a finance lease, it is in law owned by the lessor. The tax treatment used to follow the legal position, so that the lessor was entitled to the capital allowances and the lease rental payments were a revenue expense allowable in calculating profit, restricted as indicated in **20.17** for a car costing more than £12,000 where expenditure was incurred broadly before 2009/10. This treatment still continues for leases of up to five years (or seven years in some circumstances). For longer leases (referred to as long funding leases) finalised on or after 1 April 2006 (subject to certain transitional provisions), the tax treatment is aligned with the accounting treatment. Lessors cannot claim capital allowances on the cost of the leased asset, and all the rentals received are taken into account in calculating profits. Lessees may claim capital allowances as they would have been able to if they had bought the asset, and may deduct as an expense the part of the rentals on which capital allowances are not available (effectively the finance charge).

There were already special provisions to prevent exploitation of the tax treatment and to align it more closely with the recognised accounting treatment. Extensive new provisions were introduced by FA 2006. For a note on the position for capital allowances see **22.5**.

Goods and services for private purposes (ITTOIA 2005, ss 172A–F; CTA 2009, ss 156–161)

[20.19] Goods taken from stock for private purposes are reckoned for tax purposes broadly at the amount which they would have realised if sold in the open market at the time they were appropriated. Services are valued at cost, so no notional profit has to be included for services provided free of charge to, say, a relative. Where business is carried on through a limited company, the directors are charged on goods and services taken for their own use under the benefits rules (see **CHAPTER 10**) and the cost is allowed in calculating the company profits, unless some of the directors' total remuneration including benefits is considered not to be wholly and exclusively for the trade (see **12.9**).

Stock and work in progress — valuation (ITTOIA 2005, ss 173–186; CTA 2009, Pt 3 Ch 11)

[20.20] Stock is valued at the lower of cost or realisable value, opening and closing stock being brought into the accounts in determining profit. Work in progress is similarly brought into account, and an appropriate addition for direct or indirect overheads must be included in its value.

It is the view of both the Consultative Committee of Accountancy Bodies (in CCAB Guidance on UITF 40 which can be found in HMRC Business Income Manual BIM74270) and the ICAEW (in Taxguide 8/06) that the value of a proprietor's or working partner's time in an unincorporated business is not a contributory part of cost and should not be included in the value of work in progress. However, the value of work in progress must be distinguished from revenue for which there is a right to receive payment but which has not yet been billed. This must be fully brought in.

This is unlikely to have a significant effect where meaningful charges for work carried out have been made as the work has progressed, nor is it appropriate where the rewards are contingent on a later stage being completed. Put simply, the accounts should recognise unbilled revenue, albeit not within work in progress, if the work has been completed to a stage where the full anticipated amount is expected to be received. How it is described will depend upon personal preference, and how it is valued, upon the particular circumstances of the project, but when it first needs to be recognised in the accounts a one-off tax charge will arise (see **20.21**), with future revenue being brought in more quickly. Tax on the one-off charge can be spread forward over three tax years, or sometimes longer. HMRC have advised the professional bodies that they may wish to understand the basis on which work in progress has been calculated but they would not expect to dwell on it except where it did not appear to be calculated on a reasonable and consistent basis.

New barristers need not bring in work in progress for their first seven years of business. They must include it thereafter, but they may spread the amount brought in (called the catching-up charge) over ten years, with the flexibility of increasing the amount of the charge in any of the earlier tax years, an appropriate reduction then being made in later years.

When a trade ceases (other than because of the death of a sole trader), stock is valued at the price received, if sold to an unconnected UK trader. Where the stock is transferred with other assets, the total price is apportioned between the assets on a just and reasonable basis. If the UK trader is connected with the vendor (e.g. through a family link, or as companies in the same group), then the stock is valued at an arm's length price. If, however, that value is greater than both the actual sale price and the cost of the stock, the two parties may make a claim to use the higher of cost and sale price instead of arm's length value. Stock that is disposed of other than by being sold to a UK trader, for example taken by a trader for his personal use, is valued at open market value.

Where a business ceases because of the death of a sole proprietor, the closing stock and work in progress is valued at the lower of cost and market value. Its acquisition value for executors or beneficiaries is, however, its market value at the date of death, both for capital gains purposes and for income tax purposes if they carry on the business.

Change in basis of computing profits (FA 2002, ss 65–66; ITTOIA 2005, ss 25–27, 226–240; FA 2006, s 102 and Sch 15; CTA 2009, s 46, Pt 3 Ch 14)

[20.21] Where a valid basis of accounting is changed such that income is not included or expenditure is included more than once, then in calculating taxable profits the excluded income is brought in as a one-off tax charge and the double counted expenditure is reckoned only once. Such changes might occur because of the adoption of generally accepted accounting practice or court decisions.

Where completed, unbilled work is brought into accounts for the first time, its value at the beginning as well as at the end of that accounting period is brought in, so that the profits of the year are stated on a consistent basis. The inclusion of the value at the start of the accounting period without a corresponding amount being included in the accounts at the immediately preceding year-end would mean that the 'uplift' would not be charged to tax but for the one-off tax charge.

The one-off charge is reckoned for tax purposes on the first day of the accounting period in which the change occurs. The effect of reckoning an uplift within profits is spread forward in certain circumstances.

The legislation does not cover a change from an invalid basis to a valid basis of accounting, for example where by reference to accepted methods of valuation work-in-progress has been inadequately valued. In such cases, the tax consequences of having adopted an invalid basis have to be corrected, often with interest and penalties being incurred.

Value added tax

[20.22] If a business is VAT registered, VAT is not normally taken into account either as part of turnover or part of expenses. VAT is collected on supplies of goods and services, and any VAT that anyone has charged the business is recouped, subject to an adjustment where there is non-business use, with the balance being paid to or recovered from HMRC. Where there is non-business use, the input VAT is normally apportioned. Alternatively input VAT may be claimed in full and output VAT on non-business use accounted for over the economic life of the asset. HMRC did not permit the use of this second alternative for land and buildings, but as the result of a decision of the European Court they had to change their view. They did, however, reduce the period over which the VAT must be accounted for. For details of the revised treatment see **32.37**. Once again from 1 January 2011 this method will not apply, and full input tax recovery will not be available, on the purchase of land and property. Instead input tax will be restricted to the business use proportion. The capital goods scheme (see **7.20**) will be amended accordingly. In addition this method is not available where the non-business use is not private use, for example the use by a charity for non-commercial purposes. Where an asset on which input VAT was restricted is sold, output VAT is not charged on the non-business proportion of the sale proceeds.

[20.23] These general rules are subject to various specific provisions. VAT on business entertaining expenditure (subject to what is said in **20.14**) and on the purchase of cars cannot be recovered from HMRC unless, in the case of cars, they are used *wholly* for business purposes, e.g. by private taxi firms, self-drive hire firms, driving schools and leasing companies — see **7.4**. The unrecovered VAT on entertaining cannot be allowed in calculating taxable profit either, because business entertaining itself is not so allowed (subject to what is said in **20.14**). But disallowed VAT on cars forms part of the cost for capital allowances (see **CHAPTER 22**). Where assets are acquired on lease, the VAT included in the leasing charges is normally recoverable, but if there is any private use of a leased car on which the lessor recovered the input VAT, the lessee may only recover 50% of the input VAT on the leasing charges. The balance, restricted by the actual private use proportion, would then form part of the lease charges deducted from profits. (There would be no 50% restriction on any input VAT relating to a charge for repairs and maintenance if the charge was made in a separate contract as mentioned in **20.17.**) Private car fuel is subject to a VAT scale charge (see **7.5**). Unlike the provisions for income tax and NICs, the VAT scale charge applies to private fuel provided for any employees, no matter what they earn, and no matter whether the car is provided by the employer or belongs to the employee. The VAT accounted for to HMRC on the fuel may be included as part of the travelling expenses allowed in calculating profit, except any relating to private use by a sole trader or partner, which will be disallowed along with the private expenditure itself (see **20.5**). There is no disallowance of the input VAT on car repair and maintenance expenditure, providing there is some business use (see **7.5**). It is HMRC's view that amounts of VAT originally wrongly declared which are refunded following a repayment claim are trade receipts. See HMRC Brief 14/2009 for full details.

[20.24] If a business is not registered for VAT, any VAT suffered on business expenditure (other than on business entertaining expenses, which are wholly disallowed) forms part of expenditure in calculating taxable profits. It will either qualify for capital allowances as part of the cost of a capital item or it will be an expense in arriving at the profit. The same applies where, although the business is VAT registered, some of the supplies made are exempt from VAT. The business may then not be able to recover all the input VAT from HMRC, and the non-deductible amount is taken into account as part of expenditure for income tax or corporation tax.

[20.25] If a business has joined the VAT flat-rate scheme (see **7.23**), the accounts will normally show turnover and expenses inclusive of output and input VAT. The amount of flat-rate VAT paid, calculated on the turnover inclusive of output VAT, may either be deducted from the turnover figure or treated as an expense. Under the scheme, input VAT may be recovered on capital items with a VAT-inclusive value of more than £2,000. Any such input VAT would be recovered by set-off against the flat-rate VAT payable to HMRC. It would not reduce the flat-rate VAT charged as an expense in the accounts, but would instead be deducted from the cost of the capital item. Where input VAT on capital items is not recovered, it forms part of the cost of the asset for capital allowances purposes.

National insurance contributions

[20.26] The employers' class 1 NICs paid on employees' wages, Class 1A NICs on the provision of taxable benefits to P11D employees and Class 1B NICs under a PAYE Settlement Agreement (see **10.55**) are allowable in calculating the taxable profit. No deduction is allowed for a sole trader's or partner's own Class 2 and Class 4 NICs.

Foster carers etc (ITTOIA 2005, ss 803–828, Sch 2 Pt 10)

[20.27] A special tax exemption is available to foster carers whose gross receipts do not exceed an individual limit. The limit is a fixed amount of £10,000 a year plus an additional amount per child (£200 a week for a child under eleven and £250 a week for a child aged eleven or older). Where the limit is exceeded, foster carers may either compute their profits in the normal way or they may make a written election to treat their taxable profits as being the excess over their individual limit. Such an election must be made by the first anniversary of the normal self assessment filing date for the relevant tax year (e.g. 31 January 2013 for 2010/11).

Where foster carers choose to treat their profits in the normal way they may claim capital allowances for capital expenditure. The legislation currently has some technical anomalies in the way the special capital allowances rules for foster carers are applied. It is proposed to amend this legislation to correct the anomalies.

It is also proposed that shared lives carers, including adult placement carers, staying put carers and certain kinship carers who provide care for up to three people and share their home with them, will be allowed to claim broadly the same income tax relief as foster carers, as outlined above, from 6 April 2010. It will be known as qualifying care relief. This will include the ability to claim capital allowances.

A non-statutory tax relief is available to adult placement carers, who look after vulnerable adults who are placed with them by local authorities or charities. Those who care for up to three adults may calculate their profits on a fixed expenses basis, with no taxable profit arising within the stipulated limit. It is proposed that for 2010/11 these simplified arrangements may continue to be used but that from 2011/12 onwards they will be abolished and the relief for shared lives carers should be claimed instead.

Up to 5 April 2010 special guardians and kinship carers could use the simplified arrangements for adult placement carers to compute their taxable profits. From 6 April 2010 it is proposed that qualifying guardians will be exempt from income tax on any qualifying payments they receive. Kinship carers who provide care to a child who has not been placed with them under a residence order will not qualify for the exemption but can claim qualifying care relief as outlined above.

Both foster carers and adult placement carers are liable to Class 2 and Class 4 NICs where appropriate, although no Class 2 NICs are payable if the profits are exempt, or fall within the small earnings exception. Carers may wish to pay Class 2 NICs in any event to maintain their right to various benefits, including employment and support allowance and state pension (the amount payable for 2010/11 being only £2.40 a week). HMRC's help sheet HS236 deals with both the tax and NIC position for carers.

Examples of allowable and non-allowable expenditure
[20.28]

Allowable expenditure

Accountancy expenses (see **20.8**)

Advertising

Bad debts written off and provision for specific bad debts (see **20.15**)

Business travel

Car hire (see **20.17**)

Contributions to local enterprise organisations etc. (see **29.37**)

Cost of raising loan finance (excluding stamp duty), for example debentures (not share capital)

Cost of staff temporarily seconded to charities and educational establishments

Counselling services for redundant employees

Employer's Class 1 NICs on employees' wages, Class 1A NICs on the provision of taxable benefits to P11D employees and Class 1B NICs under a PAYE settlement agreement (see **20.26**)

Gifts of medical supplies and equipment from a company's trading stock for humanitarian purposes

Gifts of trading stock to educational establishments, charities or registered amateur sports clubs

Interest on business borrowings (see **20.16**)

Legal expenses on debt recovery, trade disputes, defending trade rights, employees' service agreements and, by concession, renewing a short lease (i.e. 50 years or less)

Non-recoverable VAT relating to allowable expenses, for example where turnover is below VAT threshold, or VAT partial exemption applies (see **20.22**)

Premium for grant of lease for 50 years or less, but limited to the amount taxed on the landlord as extra rent (see **CHAPTER 32**), spread over the term of the lease

Rent and rates of business premises

Repairs

Qualifying research and development expenditure (see **29.38** to **29.41**), and certain sums paid to research and development associations

Staff wages, benefits in kind and pension scheme contributions (see **20.13**)

Non-allowable expenditure

Business entertaining expenses including the VAT thereon (except on a reasonable scale when entertaining staff) (see **20.14**)

Charitable subscriptions, and charitable donations unless exceptionally the donation satisfies the wholly and exclusively rule (but see CHAPTER 43 re gift aid donations)

Cost of improvements, extensions, additions to premises and equipment

Depreciation (capital allowances are available on certain assets — see CHAPTER 22)

Donations to political parties

Expenses of private living accommodation (unless assessable on directors or employees as a benefit)

Fines and any legal expenses connected therewith

Gifts to customers, except gifts with a conspicuous advertisement that cost not more than £50 per person per year and are not food, drink, tobacco or gift vouchers

Illegal payments such as bribes (including payments overseas that would be illegal in the UK)

Legal expenses on forming a company, drawing up partnership agreement, acquiring assets such as leases

Payments made in response to threats, menaces, blackmail and other forms of extortion

Profit shares in the form of interest on partners' capital

Self-employed NICs

Taxation (but see above as regards VAT)

Non-trading income and capital profits

[20.29] Any non-trading income of sole traders and partners included in the business accounts is charged to tax under the appropriate heading rather than as part of the business profits, for example, interest as savings and investment income and rent as property income. Small amounts of rental income may be included in the trading income if they are from subletting a part of business premises that is temporarily surplus to requirements. Under self-assessment, tax on all sources of income (and capital gains) is calculated as a single figure. It is still necessary to keep different sources of income separate, however, particularly because of the treatment of losses. In the case of a partnership, non-trading income has to be shown separately from the trading profit in the partnership return, and partners show their shares of trading income and non-trading income in their personal returns (see CHAPTER 23).

A company's non-trading income is excluded in calculating the trading profit, but the company is chargeable to corporation tax on all its sources of income plus its chargeable gains, tax being payable by self-assessment. See CHAPTERS 9 and 21.

Capital profits of sole traders and partners are liable to capital gains tax, subject to any available reliefs and to the annual exemption (see CHAPTER 4).

Treatment for companies of intangible fixed assets (CTA 2009, Pt 8)

[20.30] From 1 April 2002 separate rules apply for companies in relation to the tax treatment of goodwill, intellectual property (which includes patents, trade marks, copyrights, know-how, licences etc.) and other intangible assets (intangible assets being as defined for accounting purposes). Goodwill for these purposes includes 'internally-generated' goodwill. The rules generally apply to expenditure on the creation, acquisition or enhancement of intangible fixed assets on or after 1 April 2002, to abortive expenditure on the assets, and to expenditure on their preservation and maintenance. Certain intangible assets are excluded, for example rights over land, financial assets and rights in companies. Computer software treated as part of the cost of the related hardware is excluded except to the extent of any royalties payable in respect of the software. The company may *elect* to exclude capital expenditure on computer software, enabling capital allowances to be claimed instead (see **22.22**). Where a company reclassifies an asset as an intangible asset, and capital allowances had been given on it when it was treated as a tangible asset, the asset is not dealt with under the intangible assets rules despite the reclassification.

Expenditure on research and development is excluded from the rules so as to preserve the special research and development tax reliefs (see **29.38** to **29.41**). Profits from the exploitation of research and development are, however, brought into account, and in calculating gains on realisation of assets, expenditure on research and development is excluded from the allowable cost.

There are extensive anti-avoidance provisions to prevent the rules being manipulated.

[20.31] Gains and losses on intangible fixed assets are brought into account in calculating a company's income. There are rules similar to those for loan relationships (see **3.5**) for bringing such amounts into account. Amounts relating to a trade are brought into account in calculating trading income, amounts relating to a property in calculating property business income, and non-trading amounts are taxed as non-trading income. If there is a non-trading loss, the company may claim, not later than two years after the end of the accounting period, to set it against the total profits of the same period. Any loss not relieved in that way and not surrendered under the group relief provisions (see **26.12** onwards) will be carried forward to set against later non-trading profits.

[20.32] The cost of intangible fixed assets will in most cases be depreciated for tax purposes according to the amounts charged in the accounts. This will often be by way of straight line depreciation over the asset's useful life. The company may, however, make an irrevocable election, not later than two years after the end of the accounting period in which the asset was acquired or created, to claim allowances at a fixed rate of 4% per annum, which would be beneficial for assets with an indefinite life and long-life assets. Payments for the use of intangible assets, such as royalties, are also within the special rules whether they relate to assets acquired before or after 1 April 2002. Gains and losses when intangible fixed assets are disposed of are brought into account in calculating income, although companies may claim a special roll-over relief where the proceeds for the assets are reinvested in new intangible fixed assets that are capitalised in the accounts. This roll-over relief follows the same rules as the capital gains relief, i.e. the proceeds must be reinvested within one year before and three years after the date of disposal.

[20.33] Where a company changes its accounting policy, for example because it has changed from using UK generally accepted accounting practice to using international accounting standards, an adjustment must be made where the closing and opening values of intangible assets are different, unless the company has elected to claim 4% fixed rate allowances as indicated above.

[20.34] Apart from the royalty treatment indicated above, assets acquired or created before 1 April 2002 are still subject to the previous rules. (Internally generated goodwill is treated as created before 1 April 2002 if the business was carried on at any time before that date by the company or a related party, as to which see below.) When such assets are disposed of on or after 1 April 2002, they qualify for the roll-over relief referred to above.

[20.35] Special provisions apply to 75% groups. Assets may be transferred from one group company to another on a no loss/no gain basis, subject to a degrouping charge (as in **3.29**) if the acquiring company leaves the group within six years. The intangible fixed asset roll-over relief provisions apply where one group company makes a qualifying disposal and another acquires a qualifying replacement, and the same provisions apply as in **3.29** to allow a degrouping charge to be reallocated to another group company and for the company chargeable in respect of the degrouping gain to claim the intangible assets roll-over relief against replacement assets where appropriate.

[20.36] There are special provisions dealing with company reconstructions and also for transfers between related parties, which are normally treated as taking place at market value. The definition of related parties is complex, but is broadly as follows. Companies are related where one controls the other or the same person controls both or both companies are members of the same group. A person is related to a company if the company is a close company and the person is a participator or associate of a participator in the company or in another company that has a major interest in the company (see **3.26** re close companies). A company's acquisitions of intangible assets on or after 1 April 2002 from a related party will only be within the post-April 2002 provisions if the asset was within the provisions in the hands of the related party, or the related party acquired the asset on or after 1 April 2002 from an unrelated party, or the asset was created on or after 1 April 2002 by the related party or someone else. Even so, on disposal by the company, such assets no longer qualify for the capital gains roll-over relief.

Tax relief for companies for cleaning up contaminated or derelict land (CTA 2009, Pt 14)

[20.37] A special relief may be claimed by companies that acquire contaminated or derelict land (excluding nuclear sites) for the purposes of a trade or property business. The relief is equal to 150% of qualifying expenditure incurred on cleaning up the contaminated land ('land remediation expenditure'). The expenditure must be additional to normal site preparation. If the deduction results in a trading or property business loss, then to the extent that the loss is not relieved against profits of the company (or where relevant, a group company), the company may claim a 'land remediation tax credit' equal to 16% of the amount of the deduction (i.e. 24% of the corresponding expenditure), or 16% of the unrelieved loss if lower. Losses available to be carried forward are reduced accordingly. The claim for the tax credit must be made in the company's tax return or an amended return. The tax credit will be paid to the company by HMRC (subject to set off against any outstanding tax liabilities). It does not count as income for tax purposes.

Films (ITA 2007, s 115; CTA 2009, Pt 15)

[20.38] Over recent years there have been many changes to the tax treatment of films, partly to encourage the British film industry, but mainly to block various tax avoidance practices involving films, particularly those involving film partnerships. FA 2006 replaced most of the previous provisions with new legislation and this has been rewritten in CTA 2009. The film partnership anti-avoidance provisions remain and a new anti-avoidance provision was introduced from 10 March 2006 to restrict the relief for interest available to a partner in such a partnership (see **25.13**).

For British films that commence principal photography on or after 1 January 2007, where qualifying UK expenditure is at least 25% of the production expenditure, a 'film tax relief' is available to film production companies (not to partnerships). The activities relating to each film will normally be treated as a separate trade. The relief takes the form of an additional deduction in computing the company's trading profits. Where qualifying production expenditure does not exceed £20 million the deduction is 100%. If the qualifying expenditure exceeds £20 million the deduction is 80%. If a loss arises, the loss can be surrendered for a tax credit at the rate of 25% or 20% respectively of the qualifying expenditure (or the loss if less), or carried forward against future income. The deduction or tax credit will not be given if arrangements have been entered into specifically to obtain the deductions or credits. Provisions were introduced in FA 2007 to enable a company to elect to be treated as not qualifying as a film production company, so that its film production activities will be taxed under the normal corporation tax rules. It is proposed to introduce legislation to correct an anomaly restricting the amount of tax credit claimable where films are produced over more than one accounting period. It will apply for accounting periods ending on or after 9 December 2009.

The previous reliefs for production expenditure apply only to films that were completed before 1 January 2007. The previous reliefs for acquisition expenditure apply only to films acquired before 1 October 2007.

Profits averaging for authors and creative artists (ITTOIA 2005, ss 221–225)

[20.39] Special averaging provisions are available for authors and creative artists that follow the same rules as those that apply to farmers (see **31.5** and **31.6**). Claims may be made by individuals and partners to average the profits of two consecutive tax years if the profits of the lower year are less than 70% of the profits of the higher year or are nil, with marginal relief if the profits are more than 70% but less than 75%. The time limit for averaging claims is the first anniversary of the normal self-assessment filing date for the second of the tax years, e.g. 31 January 2013 for a claim to average 2009/10 and 2010/11. The effect of the claim on Class 4 NICs needs to be taken into account. Where all or part of the higher profits were above the Class 4 upper limit, thus attracting NICs at only 1%, the averaging claim may bring profits below that limit, attracting NICs at 8% instead. See chapter 24 for proposed changes to Class 4 NIC rates and thresholds from 6 April 2011.

Tax points

[20.40] Note the following:

- Try to avoid mixing business and private expenditure. Businesses should make sure they do not cloud a genuine business expense with a private element.
- Wholesalers or retailers should use their business connections to make private purchases at lower cost, rather than taking goods out of their own stock and suffering tax on a figure equivalent to the profit that would have been made if the goods had been sold to a customer.
- Since any expense for the benefit of staff is normally allowable in computing profits, it is sometimes more appropriate to provide acceptable benefits than to pay higher salaries. The employee will usually be taxable on the benefit but may prefer the tax charge to having to fund the purchase himself. As far as NICs are concerned, Class 1 NICs are payable on some benefits by both P11D employees and lower-paid employees, and also by employers (see **CHAPTER 10**). Other benefits are chargeable to Class 1A NICs, which apply only for P11D employees, and are payable only by employers. There is therefore an 11% NIC saving on benefits within the Class 1A category for employees paying NICs at the main rate, and a 1% saving for employees earning above the upper earnings limit of £43,875. See chapter 13 for proposed changes to NIC rates and thresholds from 6 April 2011.
- If a deduction is claimed that is not commercially justifiable, interest may have to be paid on tax underpaid as a result, and possibly a penalty as well. This is very important when considering the 'wholly and exclusively' business element of a mixed expense, such as accommodation and motor expenses. An inaccurate claim and/or providing insufficient information to HMRC may be costly in the long run.

- Wages payments to a spouse or civil partner must not only be commercially justifiable for the participation of the spouse or partner in the business but must be properly made and the payment entered in the business records. If HMRC enquire into a tax return, they will usually challenge the charge if it has not been separately paid, but has instead been regarded as included in the amount drawn by the trader or for housekeeping, with an accounting entry being made to create the wages charge.

- Similar considerations apply where mature children are able genuinely to participate in the business, for example in farming, retail and wholesale trades.

- Remember that wages paid after the end of an accounting period must be paid within nine months if they are to be deducted from the profits of that period, otherwise they will be deducted from profits in the period of payment.

- If bonuses to employees are to be paid after the end of an accounting period, they will only be allowable in calculating the profits of that accounting period if there is adequate evidence before the end of the period of the obligation to pay the bonus.

- Although expenses incurred by a company from which a director or employee derives a personal benefit are allowable in computing trading profit and taxed as earnings of the director or employee, this must be distinguished from using company funds to meet the private expenditure of a director/employee who is a shareholder and not treating the amount as pay. This will usually be treated as a loan from the company, which will have tax and sometimes NIC consequences both for the director and the company — see **12.17**.

- Where part of the home is used for business, the trader will usually pay business rates. If not, the appropriate part of the council tax can be claimed as a business expense — see **19.20**.

- If a trader pays congestion charges incurred by him or his employees while travelling on business in Central London (or elsewhere), they are allowable against profit. For employees who have private use of company cars, the taxable benefit covers congestion charge payments (see **10.28**).

- All business records relating to tax affairs must be kept for broadly at least 5 years 10 months after the end of the tax year. However, from 1 April 2009 HMRC have the power to reduce the period for which records must be retained by stating this in writing. Penalties of up to £3,000 per tax year apply if they are not kept. See **9.25**. HMRC guidance is available at www.hmrc.gov.uk/startingup/keeprecs.htm.

- The value to be included for uncompleted work will always be debatable. While circumstances will differ in each business, the following is a practical way of looking at it.

Was it possible to send a bill?	'Yes'
Was a bill sent?	'No'

The full amount of the bill which could have been sent must be included in the accounts under 'debtors'.

For work in hand at an accounting date for which a bill could not properly be sent, the value should be based on the cost of the work to the business or the recoverable amount if less.

- Although there are provisions to spread tax payments forward where there is a one-off charge to tax because of a change in accounting basis, the effect of the tax charge for one year on the payment on account for the next year reduces the benefit of the spreading.

21

How are business profits charged to tax?

Companies	**21.1**
Individuals	**21.2**
Pre-trading expenditure	**21.8**
Post-cessation receipts	**21.9**
Post-cessation expenses	**21.10**
Tax points	**21.11**

Companies (TMA 1970, ss 59D, 59DA, 59E; CTA 2009, ss 5–12; FA 1998, s 117 and Sch 18)

[21.1] Although taxable business profits for individuals and companies are calculated on similar lines, the way company profits are taxed is much more straightforward. A company's trading profits are taxed with its other profits, such as interest, rents and chargeable gains, by reference to chargeable accounting periods (see **3.9**). A chargeable accounting period can be as short as the company wishes but cannot exceed twelve months. If a company makes up an account for say fifteen months it is split into two chargeable accounting periods for tax purposes, the first of twelve months and the second of three months. Capital allowances (which are available on certain assets, notably plant and machinery and industrial buildings — see **CHAPTER 22**) are then deducted in arriving at the trading profits. The capital allowances are not calculated for the fifteen-month period and divided pro rata. They are calculated for the separate periods of twelve and three months according to the events of those periods.

Companies self-assess their profits and they are required to file their returns with supporting accounts and computations within twelve months after the end of the accounting period. Assessments will not normally be issued by HMRC except in cases of fraudulent or negligent conduct. For details, see **9.17** to **9.19**.

Example 1

A company makes trading profits of £150,000 in the 15 months to 30 June 2010. The profits are charged to tax as follows:

	12 months to 31.3.2010 £	3 months to 30.6.2010 £
12/15, 3/15	120,000	30,000
Less capital allowances (say)	10,000	8,000
	£110,000	£22,000

Tax payable:	£
1.4.2009 – 31.3.2010, £110,000 @ 21%	23,100
1.4.2010 – 30.6.2010, £22,000 @ 21%	4,620

The due date for payment of corporation tax is nine months and one day after the end of the chargeable accounting period, i.e. 1 January 2011 for the twelve-month account and 1 April 2011 for the three-month account in Example 1. Under corporation tax self-assessment, large companies have to pay corporation tax by quarterly instalments (see **3.22**). Interest is charged on tax paid late (see **3.24**).

Individuals (ITTOIA 2005, ss 196–220)

Basis of assessment

[21.2] The general rule is that income tax is charged on the income of the tax year. For business profits this does not mean that accounts have to be made up for the tax year itself, because businesses are free to choose their annual accounting date. Apart from special rules for the opening years and when the accounting date is changed, the taxable profits of a tax year are taken to be those of the accounting year ending in the tax year.

There is no stipulation as to the length of the first accounting period, or indeed of subsequent accounting periods. The consequences of having a first accounting period shorter or longer than twelve months are dealt with in **21.4** and the change of accounting date rules are dealt with in **21.7**. If accounts are not available at the time when the tax for the relevant tax year is due for payment, tax must be paid on an estimated basis, and interest will be charged from the original due date on any underpayment (or allowed on any overpayment) when the correct figures are known.

Capital allowances

[21.3] Capital allowances are treated as a trading expense and balancing charges as a trading receipt of the accounting period. If the accounting period is shorter or longer than twelve months, the annual writing-down allowances are reduced or increased proportionately. The detailed provisions are in CHAPTER 22.

Taxable profits in the early years

[21.4] In their first tax year, new businesses are taxed on their profit from the start date to the end of the tax year. The second year's charge is normally based on the profits of the accounting year ended in the second tax year. Part of that profit has usually already been taxed in the first year, and this is called the 'overlap profit' (see Example 2). Overlap profits can also occur on a change of accounting date. Relief for overlap profits is given when the business ceases or on a change of accounting date (see **21.5**).

Businesses that were in existence at 5 April 1994 may also have 'transitional overlap profits', which arose when the rules for taxing business profits and some other income changed from the 'previous year basis' to the current year basis. The transitional overlap profits normally cover the period between the annual accounting date in 1996/97 and 5 April 1997, that period also having been included in the taxable profits for 1997/98. For example, a pre-6 April 1994 business that makes up accounts to 30 June would have a transitional overlap period from 1 July 1996 to 5 April 1997. The detailed transitional provisions are covered in earlier editions of this book.

Example 2

Business started 1 January 2010 and made up its first accounts for 12 months to 31 December 2010, then annually to 31 December.

The taxable profits are:

2009/10	1.1.10 – 5.4.10	3/12 × 1st year's profits
2010/11	1.1.10 – 31.12.10	1st year's profits
2011/12	1.1.11 – 31.12.11	2nd year's profits
Overlap profits are:		3/12 × 1st year's profits

Where profits need to be apportioned, the apportionment may be made in days, months, or months and fractions of months providing the chosen method is used consistently. If a business makes up accounts to 31 March, the year to 31 March is treated as being equivalent to the tax year itself (unless the trader elects otherwise), so that for such a business starting on say 1 April 2010 the result of the first five days would be treated as nil, giving a nil profit for 2009/10. The profit of the first twelve months to 31 March 2011 would be taxed in 2010/11 and there would be no overlap profits and no overlap relief. Similarly, if a business changes its accounting date to 31 March, relief for all overlap profits is given at that time.

If the first accounts are made up to a date in the second tax year, but for a period of less than twelve months, the charge for the second tax year is based on the profits of the first twelve months.

Example 3

Business started 1 January 2010 and made up its first accounts for 9 months to 30 September 2010, then annually to 30 September. The taxable profits are:

2009/10	1.1.10 – 5.4.10	3/9 × 1st year's profits
2010/11	1.1.10 – 31.12.10	Profits of 1st 9 months plus 3/12 × profits of yr to 30.9.11
2011/12	1.10.10 – 30.9.11	
Overlap profits are:		3/9 × 1st year's profits plus 3/12 × profits of yr to 30.9.11

If accounts are made up to a date in the second tax year, and are for twelve months or more, the charge for the second tax year is based on the profits of twelve months to the accounting date (see Example 4 and also Example 2 at **23.3** re the admission of a new partner).

Example 4

Business started 1 October 2009 and made up its first accounts for 15 months to 31 December 2010, then annually to 31 December.

The taxable profits are arrived at as follows:

2009/10	1.10.09 – 5.4.10	6/15 × 1st year's profits
2010/11	1.1.10 – 31.12.10	12/15 × 1st year's profits
2011/12	1.1.11 – 31.12.11	
Profits of 1st 15 months have therefore been used to charge tax for 18 months, so overlap profits are:		3/15 × 1st year's profits

---

If the first accounts are made up for more than twelve months and no accounting period ends in the second tax year, the charge for the second tax year is based on the profits of the tax year itself, and the charge for the third tax year is based on twelve months to the accounting date.

Example 5

Business started 1 January 2010 and made up its first accounts for 16 months to 30 April 2011, then annually to 30 April.

The taxable profits are arrived at as follows:

2009/10	1.1.10 – 5.4.10	3/16 × 1st year's profits
2010/11	6.4.10 – 5.4.11	12/16 × 1st year's profits
2011/12	1.5.10 – 30.4.11	12/16 × 1st year's profits
Profits of first 16 months have therefore been used to charge tax for 27 months, so overlap profits are:		11/16 × 1st year's profits

---

Taxable profits when business ceases

[21.5] When a business ceases, it is taxed on its profits from the end of the basis period for the previous tax year to the date of cessation (unless it ceases in its second tax year, in which case it is taxed in that final year on the profits from 6 April to the date of cessation). See Example 6. Depending on the dates to which accounts are made up, there may be two accounts that together form the basis for the final taxable profit (see Example 7).

Overlap profits and overlap relief

[21.6] The effect of the rules for overlaps is that the business is taxed over its life on the profits made. There is, however, no provision for any inflation-proofing of overlap profits. A record needs to be kept not only of the amount of overlap profits but also the length of the overlapping period. If an overlapping period shows a loss, it must be recorded as an overlap of nil for the appropriate period (relief for the loss being available separately). This is important because overlap relief is given either when the business ceases, as in Examples 6 and 7, or partly or wholly at the time of an earlier change of accounting date to the extent that more than twelve months' profit would otherwise be chargeable in one year (see Examples 8 and 9 at **21.7**).

Example 6

Business started 1 January 2006 and makes up accounts annually to 31 December. It ceased on 30 June 2010. Profits after capital allowances were as follows:

		£
Year to 31 December	2006	24,000
	2007	30,000
	2008	28,000
	2009	34,000
6 months to 30 June	2010	20,000
		136,000

The profits are charged to tax as follows:

			£
2005/06	1.1.06 – 5.4.06 $^3/_{12}$ × £24,000		6,000
2006/07	1.1.06 – 31.12.06		24,000
	(Overlap profit £6,000)		
2007/08	1.1.07 – 31.12.07		30,000
2008/09	1.1.08 – 31.12.08		28,000
2009/10	1.1.09 – 31.12.09		34,000
2010/11	1.1.10 – 30.6.10	20,000	
	Less overlap profit	6,000	14,000
			136,000

Thus the business is taxed over its life on the profits earned.

Example 7

Facts as in Example 6 but business ceases three months earlier, on 31 March 2010, i.e. in the tax year 2009/10. The accounts for the three months ending on that date show profits of £10,000, so that the total profits are £126,000.

The taxable profits from 2005/06 to 2008/09 are the same as in Example 6, totalling £88,000. The final taxable profit for 2009/10 is as follows:

1.1.09 – 31.12.09	34,000
1.1.10 – 31.3.10	10,000

	44,000	
Less overlap profit	6,000	£38,000

Total taxable profits are therefore equal to the profits earned, i.e. (88,000 + 38,000 =) £126,000.

Change of accounting date

[21.7] Notice of a change of accounting date has to be given to HMRC by 31 January following the tax year of change. The fact that HMRC do not recognise a change unless notice is given means that formal accounts may be made up to an intermediate date for commercial reasons, say when a partner leaves, without the annual accounting date being altered. The rules also provide that a change of date will not be recognised if the first accounting period to the new date exceeds 18 months. This does not mean that accounts cannot be prepared for longer than 18 months, but tax has to be computed according to the old date (apportioning results as necessary) until the rules can be satisfied.

Example 8

Accounts were made up for 12 months to 30 June 2008, then for the 21 months to the new accounting date of 31 March 2010 and annually thereafter. Taxable profits will be calculated as follows:

2008/09	12 months to 30 June 2008
2009/10	12 months to 30 June 2009 (i.e. $^{12}/_{21}$ × accounts to 31 March 2010)
2010/11	21 months to 31 March 2011 (i.e. $^{9}/_{21}$ × accounts to 31 March 2010 and 12 months to 31 March 2011)
	Less relief for all previous overlap profits*

* The full amount of available overlap relief is given if the accounting date is changed to 31 March — see above.

Example 9

Business starts on 1 January 2010 and makes a loss in the year to 31 December 2010, profits arising thereafter. There is no taxable profit in 2009/10 or 2010/11, but the overlap period is from 1 January 2010 to 5 April 2010, i.e. (to the nearest month) three months, the overlap profit being nil. If the accounting date was later changed to 30 June, this would give a further overlap of six months. The combined overlap period would be *nine months*, with an overlap profit of nil plus a six months' proportion of the profit at the time of the later overlap.

If the accounting date was subsequently changed again to, say, 30 September, 15 months' profit would be charged at that time, less a deduction for a

> three months' proportion of the overlap profit, but this would amount to 3/9ths, not 3/6ths.

The rules for dealing with the change broadly ensure that twelve months' profit is charged in each tax year, except the first year and the last year. If accounts are made up to a date earlier in the tax year than the previous date, profits of *twelve* months to the new date will be charged, but this will result in overlap profits for which relief will be due later. The overlap profits and period to which they relate will be combined with any earlier overlap profits (including any transitional overlap profits on the change from previous year to current year basis) and overlap period to give a single figure for a single period. If accounts are made up to a date *later* in the tax year, more than twelve months' profits will be charged in the year of change, but a proportion of the available overlap relief will be deducted, according to how many more than twelve months' profits are being taxed. If the earlier overlap period(s) showed a loss rather than a profit, however, there would be no overlap relief due (relief for the loss having been given separately), so that the charge on more than twelve months' profit would stand. The *length* of the total overlap period is not affected by the fact that one or more earlier overlap periods showed a loss (see **21.6**). This is particularly important when calculating how much relief may be given when more than twelve months' profit would otherwise be charged in one year.

Even where losses are not involved, the overlap profit may have been seriously eroded by inflation, so that the amount deductible when more than twelve months' profits would otherwise be charged, or on cessation, may be of much less real value than the profits currently being charged to tax.

Example 10

Say a business started on 1 January 2006, making up accounts to December, and the overlap profit for the 3 months to 5 April 2006 amounted to £6,000. If the business continued with a 31 December year end until 31 December 2014, making profits in that year of £96,000, and then made up a 9-month account to 30 September 2015, the assessment for 2015/16 would be based on the profits of 12 months to 30 September 2015, so that $^3/_{12}$ths of the profits of the year to 31 December 2014, i.e. £24,000, would be taxed twice. That amount would be an additional overlap profit, which would be combined with the earlier overlap profit of £6,000, giving total overlap profits of £30,000 for six months. Overlap relief for that amount would be given either on cessation or in an earlier year to the extent that more than 12 months' profit would otherwise be taxed.

Alternatively, say that instead of making up accounts to 30 September 2015, the business made up a 14-month account to 28 February 2016, showing a profit of £112,000. The profits of the year to 31 December 2014 would be taxed in 2014/15. The profits of the 14 months to 28 February 2016 would be taxed in 2015/16, reduced by two months' overlap relief, i.e. $^2/_3$ of £6,000 = £4,000 (although two months at the then profit rate represents profits of £16,000). The balance of the overlap relief of £2,000 would be

> given on cessation or when tax was again being charged for a period
> exceeding 12 months.

Changes of accounting date are not permitted more than once in every five years unless HMRC are satisfied that the change is for commercial reasons. In the absence of HMRC approval, the taxable profits are calculated using the previous accounting date, with the figures being apportioned on a time basis.

Pre-trading expenditure (CTA 2009, ss 61, 210, 330, 456–463; ITTOIA 2005, s 57)

[21.8] Some expenditure, for example rent, rates and interest, may be incurred before trading actually starts. So long as it is a normal trading expense and is incurred not more than seven years before the trade starts, it may be treated as an expense of the first trading period. These provisions apply to sole traders and partners and also apply to companies, except in relation to interest paid. Pre-trading interest paid by a company is brought into the calculation of the company's *non-trading* profit or loss at the time of payment (see **3.5**). If this results in a loss (a non-trading deficit), it is deducted from the taxable profits of that period, or carried back against loan relationship profits of the previous twelve months, or carried forward against later non-trading profits. The company may, however, make a claim, within two years after the end of the period in which the deduction was taken into account, to treat the interest as an expense of the first *trading* period instead, and it will be deducted in that period providing the trade starts within seven years after the end of the period in which the non-trading deduction was originally taken into account.

Post-cessation receipts (CTA 2009, ss 188–200; ITTOIA 2005, ss 241–257, 349–356)

[21.9] Income may arise after a business has ceased which has not been included in the final accounts. Any such income is charged to tax separately from profits of the trade but is still treated as trading income. The chargeable amount may be reduced by any expenses, capital allowances or losses that could have been set against the income if it had been received before the business ceased. The taxable amount is treated as income of the tax year or company accounting period in which it is received. If the taxable amount is received within six years after cessation, the taxpayer or company can elect to have it treated as arising in the tax year or accounting period when trading ceased. For income tax purposes the carry-back election must be made within one year after the 31 January following the tax year in which the income was received. For corporation tax purposes the election must be made within two years of the end of the accounting period in which the income is received. In general, the amount of tax payable on the additional income will be calculated by reference to the tax position of the earlier year, but it will be treated as additional tax payable for the tax year in which the amounts were received.

Post-cessation expenses (ITTOIA 2005, ss 250, 255; ITA 2007, ss 96–101)

[21.10] Certain expenditure incurred by sole traders or partners in the seven years after a trade or profession has ceased that has not been provided for in the final accounts and cannot be set against any post-cessation receipts may be set against the total income and capital gains of the tax year in which it is incurred. This applies to professional indemnity premiums, the cost of remedying defective work plus any related damages and legal expenses, bad debts and debt recovery costs. For the relief to apply, a claim must be made within one year after the 31 January following the tax year in which the expenditure was incurred.

Tax points

[21.11] Note the following:

- Choosing an accounting date early in the tax year in an unincorporated business gives more time for planning the funding of tax payments. It also means that tax is being paid each year on profits that were largely earned in the previous year, giving an obvious advantage if profits are rising. When the business ceases, however, the final tax bill may be particularly high, because the profits then being earned may be very much higher than the early overlap profits for which relief is given on cessation.

- This chapter contains examples of claims which are available to taxpayers. There is always a time limit involved, which depends on the type of claim being made. The legislation should be checked for the time limit whenever a claim is available. From 1 April 2010 the general time limit under income tax self-assessment is four years after the end of the tax year where no other time limit is specified. This is subject to certain transitional provisions for individuals, trustees or partners who are not within self-assessment for the period concerned. In these cases the four-year claims period comes into effect for claims submitted on or after 1 April 2012 (see **25.10**).

- The time limit for notifying liability to income tax or capital gains tax if no tax return has been received is six months from the end of the tax year, e.g. by 5 October 2011 for someone who started a new business between 6 April 2010 and 5 April 2011 (see **9.27**). The taxpayer may have to complete his self-assessment on an estimated basis and amend it later, because the information may not be available in time (see the next tax point). There are penalties for late notification of liability, and also penalties for late returns, together with interest and surcharges on late payments (see **9.11**, **9.46** and **9.43**). A new penalties regime, discussed in CHAPTER 9 applies where the obligation to notify arises on or after 1 April 2010. This new regime also applies to the obligation to notify liability to pay Class 2 NIC (see **9.39**). A new penalties regime for late returns and late payment was introduced by FA 2009 and will be phased in over a number of years (see CHAPTER 9).

- New unincorporated businesses may often incur interest charges on underpaid tax under self-assessment, because interest runs from the 31 January online filing date for the return (or three months after the return is issued, if later) on what the tax finally turns out to be. If a business commences on say on 1 January 2009 and makes up accounts to 31 December 2009, tax (and Class 4 NICs) was due on 31 January 2010 (i.e. the return filing date) on the profit from 1 January to 5 April 2009. It is unlikely that the December 2009 accounts had been completed by that date. If the tax and Class 4 NICs due was underestimated, interest would run on the underpayment from 31 January 2010 (although the tax and national insurance payment itself would not have been due until 30 days after the filing of an amendment to the return).

22

Capital allowances

Background

[22.1] Capital expenditure cannot be deducted in calculating income for tax purposes, but capital allowances may be claimed instead. The law is contained in the Capital Allowances Act 2001 as amended by subsequent legislation. Significant changes to the capital allowances system were introduced in Finance Acts 2007 and 2008, with further amendments being made in FA 2009 and FA 2010.

A 100% annual investment allowance is available for 2008/09 and 2009/10 for the first £50,000 of expenditure on plant and machinery excluding cars. This is increased to the first £100,000 of expenditure from 2010/11 (see **22.24**) although it is proposed to be reduced to £25,000 from April 2012.

A temporary first year allowance at 40% on expenditure on most plant and machinery applied for 2009/10 only (see **22.25**).

The main rate of writing down allowance for expenditure on plant and machinery is 20% but certain expenditure is allocated to a 'special rate pool' for which writing down allowances are given at 10%. It is proposed to reduce the main rate to 18% and the special rate to 8% for chargeable periods ending on or after 1 April 2012 for corporation tax and 6 April 2012 for income tax.

Industrial buildings allowances and agricultural buildings allowances are being phased out and will be withdrawn completely by April 2011, the Government having decided that they now provide a 'poorly focused subsidy'.

A first-year tax credit is available where a company has incurred a loss attributable to enhanced capital allowances for expenditure on 'green' plant and machinery. The loss is surrendered in exchange for a cash payment, instead of being carried forward and set against future profits.

The calculation of capital allowances on business cars was reformed in 2009/10. The rate at which capital allowances can be claimed is now determined by the carbon dioxide emissions of the car rather than the cost (see **22.23**).

[22.2] The most important allowances presently available are those in respect of expenditure on:

- Plant and machinery
- Industrial buildings
- Agricultural buildings (see CHAPTER 31)
- Hotels
- Buildings in enterprise zones, other than dwelling houses
- Patents
- Know-how
- Research and development
- Mineral extraction

These allowances are available to sole traders, partnerships and companies, except that for companies, capital allowances are no longer claimed on patents and know-how acquired on or after 1 April 2002. Relief for such acquisitions is given by a deduction in computing income under the 'intangible assets' rules (see **20.30**). See also **22.22** re computer software.

Capital allowances at 100% are available in respect of expenditure on renovating or converting space above qualifying shops and commercial premises to provide flats for rent (see **32.15**) and expenditure on renovating business premises in designated disadvantaged areas (see **32.16**).

Plant and machinery allowances are available not only to businesses but also to employees who have to provide plant and machinery for use in their employment (see **10.15**), and to those who let property and/or equipment, in respect of fixtures, fittings, etc. (see **22.40**). An example of qualifying expenditure on plant and machinery by an employee might be a musical instrument purchased by an employee of an orchestra. As well as claiming allowances on fixtures, landlords of let property may claim industrial and agricultural buildings allowances (but see **22.42** regarding the withdrawal of those allowances) when qualifying buildings are let.

If an asset is used partly for private purposes by sole traders or partners, or by employees claiming allowances for their own plant and machinery, allowances are given only on the appropriate business fraction. There is no restriction where company assets are used privately by directors or employees, but the director/employee is taxed on the benefit obtained.

Expenditure qualifying for relief (CAA 2001, ss 13A, 34A, 38A–51, 57–59, 67–70YJ, 219, 290, 291, 532–543)

[22.3] Capital allowances are available when expenditure is incurred on a qualifying asset, even if the expenditure is funded by means of a loan or bank overdraft. Interest on such funding is, however, allowed as a business expense and not as part of the cost of the asset. Where an industrial building is let at a premium on a long lease (more than 50 years), the landlord and tenant may elect for the premium to be treated as the purchase price for the building, so that industrial buildings allowances may be claimed by the tenant. If the tenant himself incurs capital expenditure on a qualifying building, he is entitled to allowances on that expenditure.

[22.4] When an asset is purchased under a hire-purchase agreement, the expenditure is regarded as incurred as soon as the asset comes into use, even though the asset is not strictly owned until the option-to-purchase payment is made. The hire-purchase charges are not part of the cost but are allowed as a business expense, spread appropriately over the term of the agreement.

[22.5] Where plant and machinery is acquired on a finance lease, then although for accounting purposes the assets are treated as owned by the lessee, they belong in law to the lessor and it has previously been normally the lessor who received the capital allowances. With the exception of leases of less than 5 years (and some other longer leases), since 1 April 2006 the tax treatment has been aligned with the accounting treatment (see **20.18**). Where capital allowances remain available, finance lessors are normally entitled only to writing-down allowances (see **22.24** for exceptions), and the allowances are restricted on a time basis according to when in the accounting period the plant and machinery was acquired. For the treatment of the lease payments see **20.18**. There are already extensive anti-avoidance provisions in relation to finance leases, and to sale and leaseback or lease and leaseback transactions and these have been extended further by FA 2010. These anti-avoidance provisions are not dealt with in this Guide.

[22.6] Subsidies or contributions from third parties must be deducted from the allowable cost of the asset. Where the qualifying expenditure on an asset has been reduced by such a contribution or subsidy, the third party may claim allowances on the amount contributed, even though strictly he does not have an interest in the asset, so long as certain conditions are met.

[22.7] Where VAT has been paid and cannot be recovered, for example on motor cars or, in the case of other asset purchases, because of the partial exemption rules or because the trader is not VAT registered, it forms part of the allowable expenditure for capital allowances. HMRC guidance is provided in Statement of Practice B1. Capital allowances computations have to be adjusted where input VAT on buildings and computers is later adjusted under the capital goods scheme (see **22.19**).

Chargeable periods (CAA 2001, s 6)

Corporation tax

[22.8] For a company, capital allowances are treated as an expense of the trade and deducted in calculating the trading profits. The chargeable period by reference to which capital allowances are given and balancing charges are made is the company's chargeable accounting period, so that where a period of account exceeds twelve months, it is split into a twelve-month chargeable accounting period or periods and the remaining period, and relief for capital expenditure is first available according to the chargeable period in which the expenditure is incurred. Writing down allowances are proportionately reduced for accounting periods of less than twelve months.

Income tax

[22.9] For individuals, capital allowances are treated as trading expenses (and balancing charges are treated as trading receipts) of the period of account. This is normally the period for which accounts are drawn up. If the period of account is longer or shorter than twelve months, writing-down allowances are increased or reduced accordingly. Where the £3,000 maximum allowance for cars costing more than £12,000 applies in the transitional period where the car was purchased before 2009/10 (see **22.23**), that allowance is similarly increased or reduced.

If a period of account exceeds eighteen months, however, capital allowances are calculated as if it was one or more periods of account of twelve months plus a period of account covering the remainder of the period. The aggregate allowances for the separate periods are then treated as a trading expense of the whole period. This prevents undue advantage being gained as a result of the long account. See Example 2 at **22.34**.

Chargeable periods for non-trading individuals

[22.10] For employees and landlords who are individuals, the chargeable period is the income tax year itself.

Date expenditure is incurred (CAA 2001, s 5)

[22.11] This is generally the date on which the obligation to pay becomes unconditional (i.e. normally the invoice date), but if any part of the payment is not due until more than four months after that date, that part of the expenditure is regarded as incurred on the due date of payment. The due date of payment is also substituted where the unconditional obligation to pay has been brought forward to obtain allowances earlier. It sometimes happens that, under large construction contracts, the purchaser becomes the owner at an earlier date than the time when the obligation to pay becomes unconditional, e.g. on presentation of an architect's certificate. Where, in those circumstances, ownership passes in one chargeable period, but the obligation becomes unconditional in the first month of the next, the expenditure is regarded as incurred in the earlier period.

Way in which capital allowances are given (CAA 2001, ss 3, 247–262, 352, 353, 432, 450, 463, 478–480; ITA 2007, ss 118–120; FA 1998 Sch 18 Pt IX; FA 2010, s 25)

[22.12] As indicated at **22.8** and **22.9**, the allowances claimed are treated as trading expenses of the period of account for sole traders and partners, and as expenses of the chargeable accounting period for trading companies, so they may form part of a loss or turn a profit into a loss. For the reliefs available for trading losses see **CHAPTER 25** for individuals and **CHAPTER 26** for companies.

Allowances claimed by individual or corporate property investors are deducted as an expense in arriving at the profit of the letting business — see **32.11** onwards.

If the letting business makes a loss then an individual investor may claim to set an amount equal to the capital allowances included in the loss against any income of the same tax year or of the following tax year. See Example 7 at **22.52**. The time limit for such a claim is one year from 31 January following the tax year in which the loss arises. Any loss not relieved in this way is carried forward against future income from the letting business (see **32.7**). This is subject to anti-avoidance provisions which prevent relief for losses attributable to the annual investment allowance (AIA) which arise in connection with certain tax avoidance arrangements (see **22.24**).

A corporate investor cannot make a separate claim relating to capital allowances included in a loss on a letting business, but more generous relief for a loss on a letting business is available to a corporate investor than an individual investor (see **32.9**).

Claims

[22.13] Both individuals and companies must make a specific claim for capital allowances in a tax return or amended return.

[22.14] For companies, the normal time limit for making or amending claims is two years after the end of the accounting period, but if HMRC enquire into the return the time limit is extended to 30 days after the time when the profits or losses of the period are finally settled. If the effect of a claim following an enquiry is to reduce the allowances available for a later period for which a return has been submitted, the company has 30 days from the settlement of the enquiry to make any necessary amendments to the return, failing which amendments will be made by HMRC. If HMRC make an assessment under their 'discovery' powers (see **9.35**), then providing the company had not made careless or deliberate inaccuracies, further claims may be made within one year from the end of the accounting period in which the assessment is made. See **CHAPTER 9** for further details.

HMRC's view is that, once a business has chosen to claim one type of capital allowance rather than another, that choice may not be reversed in respect of expenditure incurred in a closed year under the 'error or mistake' provisions (replaced by overpayment relief from 1 April 2010, see **9.52**). This is particularly relevant following the gradual withdrawal of industrial and agricultural buildings allowances (IBAs and ABAs). Taxpayers would not be able to substitute claims for plant and machinery capital allowances for expenditure on certain building fixtures for part of their previous IBA or ABA claims in closed years. Full details can be found in HMRC Brief 12/2009.

[22.15] For individuals, capital allowances are subject to the same time limits as for other entries in returns, i.e. the time limit for a capital allowances claim is the same as the time limit for filing the return. Any amendment must normally be made within twelve months after the 31 January filing date for the return, although special rules apply to fixtures (see **22.40**). If HMRC enquire into the return, amendments may be made up to 30 days after the settlement of the enquiry, providing the original return was submitted within the time limit. If HMRC make an assessment under their 'discovery' powers (see **9.35**), then providing the taxpayer had not made careless or deliberate inaccuracies, further claims may be made within one year from the end of the tax year in which the assessment is made. See **CHAPTER 9** for further details.

[22.16] A taxpayer may claim less than the full allowances available if so wished. This may enable him to make better use of other available reliefs and allowances (see Tax points at **22.61**).

Balancing allowances and charges (CAA 2001, ss 55, 56, 60–64, 314, 417, 418, 441–445, 457, 458, 471, 472; FA 2007, s 36)

[22.17] The capital allowances legislation provides that when an asset is sold, a 'balancing allowance' is given for any amount by which the sale proceeds fall short of the unrelieved expenditure on the asset. If the proceeds exceed the unrelieved expenditure, the excess is included in taxable income by means of a 'balancing charge'. If the proceeds exceed the original cost, however, the excess over cost is dealt with under the capital gains rules (see **22.41**), except for sales of know-how where special rules apply (see **22.58**).

No balancing adjustments are to be made in respect of industrial buildings as defined in **22.43** (except enterprise zone buildings) or agricultural buildings (as to which see **31.10** onwards) for balancing events on or after 21 March 2007 (subject to certain transitional provisions), see **22.42** and **31.10**.

For plant and machinery, balancing allowances and charges are normally dealt with on a 'pool' basis for most assets (see **22.30** onwards).

There are provisions to prevent businesses obtaining increased allowances on disposal of certain assets, in particular industrial and agricultural buildings and certain flat conversions, as a result of a tax avoidance scheme. These are dealt with briefly in **22.50**, **31.13** and **32.15**. FA 2009 introduced a revised formula for calculating the disposal proceeds to be brought into account by the lessee under a long funding lease in order to counter tax avoidance.

Connected persons, etc. (CAA 2001, ss 61, 265–268, 567–570, 573, 575; CTA 2010, Pt 22 Chapter 1)

[22.18] If an asset is withdrawn from a business for personal use or sold to a connected person for use other than in a business, the amount to be included as sales proceeds is usually the open market value. (The definition of 'connected person' is broadly the same as that for capital gains tax — see **4.23** — although it is slightly wider.)

On a sale of plant and machinery between connected persons, open market value is not used for the seller if the buyer's expenditure is taken into account for capital allowances (so that, for example, intra-group transfers are taken into account at the price paid).

On a sale of assets other than plant and machinery, open market value is used, except that providing the sale was not made to obtain a tax advantage, a joint claim may be made by seller and buyer, within two years after the sale, for the sale to be treated as made at written-down value. This is largely irrelevant in respect of sales after 20 March 2007 because of the withdrawal of balancing allowances/charges on industrial buildings.

Where the transfer of an asset to a connected person takes place at the time when the business itself is transferred, the assets are treated as being sold at open market value. But the predecessor and successor may make a joint election, within two years from the date of the transfer, for it to be treated as made at the tax written-down value, so there will be no balancing adjustment on the predecessor and the successor will take over the claims for allowances from that point. The most common example of the application of these rules is when a business is transferred to a company (see **27.2**). Such an election cannot be made for corporation tax purposes where the transferor and transferee are both carrying on a business of leasing plant and machinery.

Special rules apply where a trade is transferred from one company to another, and at some time within one year before the transfer and two years after the transfer, the same persons own three-quarters or more of the trade (see **26.18**). These rules enable the predecessor's capital allowances computations to continue. First year allowances on plant and machinery are claimed by whoever incurred the expenditure and balancing adjustments are made on the company carrying on the trade at the time of the disposal. Writing-down allowances are split on a time basis.

FA 2010 introduced measures to prevent tax avoidance through the transfer of an entitlement to benefit from capital allowances on plant and machinery where the tax written down value exceeds its balance sheet value. Broadly the legislation is designed to prevent a company or group acquiring a company, or an increased share in a company, or a partnership, or a trade, for the purpose of accessing the capital allowances and claiming relief for those allowances against its existing profits. It does not prevent relief being given after the change of ownership transaction, but the relief can only reduce the same profits and to the same extent that they could have been reduced before the change.

Interaction with VAT capital goods scheme (CAA 2001, ss 234–246, 345–351, 446–449, 546–551)

[22.19] Input VAT adjustments under the VAT capital goods scheme (see **7.20**) are reflected in capital allowances computations. Changes to VAT paid in respect of an industrial building are added to or deducted from the unrelieved expenditure on the building and writing-down allowances recalculated over the remainder of the building's tax life. This will no longer be relevant once writing-down allowances are withdrawn (see **22.42**). Similarly, adjustments for VAT on computers are made in the plant and machinery main pool or short-life asset pool in the period in which the VAT adjustment is made. Where the original expenditure qualified for the first year allowance on plant and machinery (see **22.24** onwards), any additional VAT liability is treated as additional expenditure qualifying for extra initial or first-year allowance, the extra allowance being given in the adjustment period.

Plant and machinery

What is plant and machinery? (CAA 2001, ss 21–33, 71)

[22.20] There is no overall definition of plant and machinery in the legislation, although there are certain items that are specifically stated to be within the definition, for example thermal insulation in industrial buildings, and expenditure on safety at sports grounds. Allowances for expenditure on adding thermal insulation to a building were extended in FA 2008 to include insulation of both industrial and commercial buildings used for any 'qualifying activity'.

In addition the legislation explicitly lists certain expenditure on buildings and structures that cannot be treated as plant or machinery, and lists other items of expenditure which are not affected by the exclusions and which will in general be accepted by HMRC as plant and machinery. Most of these items derive from court decisions.

[22.21] Deciding what 'machinery' is does not pose much of a problem, but the question of what is and is not plant has come before the courts many times. The main problem lies in distinguishing the 'apparatus' *with* which a business is carried on from the 'setting' *in* which it is carried on. Items forming part of the setting do not qualify for allowances unless they do so as part of the building itself and not as plant, for example where it is an industrial building, or unless the business is one in which atmosphere, or ambience, is important, but, even so, allowances for plant are not available on expenditure on an asset which becomes part of the premises, such as shop fronts, flooring and suspended ceilings. (Although initial expenditure on a shop front is disallowed, the cost of a subsequent replacement is allowed as a revenue expense against the profit, but excluding any improvement element.) Lifts and central heating systems are treated as plant, while basic electricity and plumbing systems are not. Specific lighting to create atmosphere in a hotel and special lighting in fast food restaurants have been held to be plant. A tenant who incurs expenditure on items that become landlord's fixtures can nonetheless claim allowances — see **22.40**.

[22.22] Expenditure on computer hardware is capital expenditure on plant and machinery. Allowances will usually be claimed under the 'short-life assets' rules (see **22.35**). Unless it is developed 'in house', computer software is usually licensed for lifetime to a particular user or users rather than being purchased outright. Despite the fact that a licence to use software is an intangible asset, it is specifically provided that capital expenditure on licensed software and electronically transmitted software qualifies for plant and machinery allowances. Where computer software is treated as part of the cost of the related hardware, it is not affected by the rules for companies relating to intangible assets (see **20.30**) and it remains within the capital allowances regime. Where it is not so treated, it will be dealt with under the intangible assets provisions unless the company elects, within two years after the end of the accounting period in which the expenditure was incurred, for the capital allowances provisions to apply. Such an election is irrevocable.

If licensed software is acquired on rental, the rentals are deducted from profit over the life of the software. Where a lump sum is paid, HMRC normally take the view that the cost of software with an expected life of less than two years may be treated as a revenue expense and deducted from profit. Otherwise, subject to what is said above about the intangible assets provisions for companies, it will usually be treated as capital expenditure for which plant and machinery allowances may be claimed (first year allowances thus being available for 2009/10 — see **22.25**, and short-life asset treatment being used if appropriate — see **22.35**). The treatment of in-house software is broadly similar, being either treated as capital or revenue depending on the expected period of use.

The cost of developing a website is regarded by HMRC as capital expenditure, with updating costs being revenue expenditure. The expenditure should qualify for allowances as computer software. Subsequent expenditure on updating the site will normally qualify as revenue expenditure, unless the whole site is completely rewritten. The cost of acquiring a domain name is incurred on an intangible asset, so capital allowances would not be available, but the expenditure would be dealt with for companies under the intangible assets rules (see **20.30**).

Capital allowances on cars (CAA 2001, ss 104A, 104AA, 104E, 208A, 268A–268D)

[22.23] Before 2009/10 the capital allowances treatment of cars required any car costing £12,000 or more (other than a low emission car) to be kept separate, with allowances being calculated for each such car. This method was considered by businesses as outdated and onerous to comply with. Following consultations the rules were reformed in FA 2009.

In keeping with the Government's environmental objectives the allowances are now based on the car's carbon dioxide emissions rather than cost. First year allowances continue to be available until 31 March 2013 on cars with very low carbon dioxide emissions (see **22.27**) but expenditure on other cars is allocated to one of the two plant and machinery pools. Expenditure on cars with CO_2 emissions exceeding 160g/km will be allocated to the special rate pool (see **22.30**) on which the writing down allowance is 10%. Expenditure on cars with emissions of 160g/km or less are allocated to the main rate pool (see **22.32**) on which the writing down allowance is 20%. However, see **22.1** regarding proposed reductions in the rate of allowances from April 2012. All cars registered before 1 March 2001, and cars which are electrically propelled, are also 'main rate cars'. Cars do not include motor cycles.

Cars that are used partly for private use will continue to be allocated to a single asset pool (see **22.36**) to enable the private use adjustment to be made, but the rate of writing down allowance will still depend on the car's CO_2 emissions.

These new rules apply to expenditure on cars incurred on or after 6 April 2009 for income tax or on or after 1 April 2009 for corporation tax, or to expenditure incurred under an agreement for the provision of a car entered into after 8 December 2008 where the car is not required to be made available before 6 August 2009 for income tax and 1 August 2009 for corporation tax. Expenditure incurred before these dates will continue to be subject to the old rules (see **22.37**) for a transitional period of broadly five years. Any expenditure remaining in the single asset pool, and which relates to cars with no private use, will be transferred to the main capital allowances pool at the beginning of the first chargeable period to commence on or after 6 April 2014 for income tax or on or after 1 April 2014 for corporation tax.

Various provisions prevent the artificial generation of balancing allowances in certain circumstances.

Allowances presently available (CAA 2001, ss 39, 45A–46, 52, 55, 56, Sch A1; FA 2008, ss 71–83; FA 2009, s 24; FA 2010, s 5)

[22.24] FA 2008 introduced a new *annual investment allowance* (AIA) of up to £50,000 for investment in plant and machinery, subsequently increased to £100,000 by FA 2010, but now proposed to be reduced to £25,000 from April 2012. The AIA provides a 100% allowance for the first £100,000 of investment in plant and machinery (excluding cars but including long-life assets and integral features), irrespective of the size of the business. The new allowance does not replace the existing first year allowances for specific types of expenditure.

The £100,000 cap is increased or reduced where the chargeable period is more or less than a year. Qualifying expenditure in excess of the limit enters either the 'main pool' or the new 'special rate' pool and is eligible for either a writing down allowance at 20% or 10% or a first year allowance (see below). However, see **22.1** regarding proposed reductions in the rate of allowances from April 2012.

The AIA is available for expenditure incurred on or after 6 April 2008 for income tax and on or after 1 April 2008 for corporation tax and the increased limit of £100,000 applies to expenditure incurred on or after 6 April 2010 for income tax and on or after 1 April 2010 for corporation tax. There are rules to fix the maximum allowance where a chargeable period straddles the relevant date of the introduction of the allowance or of the increase in the limit (see Example 3 in **22.34**). A claim may be limited to part of the qualifying expenditure.

A partnership of which all the members are individuals is eligible for a single AIA of up to £100,000. A single company is also entitled to one AIA. A group of companies is entitled to only one AIA, which can be shared between the companies. Special rules apply where two or more groups of companies are under common control.

The effect of the restriction in CAA 2001, s 51E is that where two or more companies are under common control but do not form a group, each company is entitled to an AIA of up to £100,000 unless:

- the companies are engaged in similar activities (determined by reference to turnover and the NACE classification system, guidance on which is available at www.statistics.gov.uk);
- the companies share the same premises at the end of the relevant chargeable period of one or both of the companies.

Anti-avoidance provisions introduced in FA 2010 prevent relief against general income for a loss from a UK or overseas property business which is attributable to the AIA and arises from relevant tax avoidance arrangements (see **22.12**).

The allowances otherwise available for investment in plant and machinery are writing-down allowances and, in some circumstances, first year allowances. There are also balancing allowances and balancing charges which arise when the business ceases or sometimes when a particular asset is disposed of. *Writing-down allowances* are given at 20% per annum on expenditure in the main pool (on the reducing balance method) from 6 April 2008 for income tax and 1 April 2008 for corporation tax. Expenditure on certain assets is now allocated to a 'special rate pool' which attracts writing down allowances at 10% only (see **22.30**). However, see **22.1** regarding proposed reductions in the rate of allowances from April 2012.

The main rate of writing down allowance was 25% per annum for earlier chargeable periods. A 'hybrid rate' applies where a chargeable period spans 6 April (or 1 April). Broadly, the 25% rate is applied to the proportion of the period falling before the relevant date and the 20% rate is applied to the proportion of the period falling after it. HMRC have provided a ready reckoner to calculate this hybrid rate. It can be found at www.hmrc.gov.uk/capital_allowances/read-reck-intro.htm.

For companies, the writing-down allowance is reduced proportionately in respect of accounting periods of less than twelve months. For individuals, the writing-down allowance is proportionately reduced or increased if the period of account is less than or more than twelve months, and there are special rules if it exceeds 18 months (see **22.9** and Example 2 at **22.34**).

First year allowances are available in the circumstances indicated below, the allowances being instead of the first year's writing-down allowance. Any available first year allowance (FYA) may be claimed in full regardless of the length of the chargeable period. FYAs cannot be claimed for the chargeable period in which the trade is permanently discontinued. Nor can they be claimed on transactions between connected persons (as to which see **22.18**), or on plant and machinery used for other purposes before being brought into the trade or obtained as a gift, or where obtaining capital allowances is the main benefit of the transaction. Subject to what is said below, FYAs are not available for expenditure on plant and machinery for leasing or letting on hire, cars (except certain low emission cars), taxis, sea-going ships and railway assets.

FA 2009 introduced a temporary first year allowance at 40% for expenditure incurred on most plant and machinery on or after 6 April 2009 but before 6 April 2010 for income tax and on or after 1 April 2009 but before 1 April 2010 for corporation tax (see **22.25**).

FA 2008 introduced a new *first-year tax credit* to provide a cash flow benefit where a loss-making company buys 'green' plant and machinery. The credit is available where a company has incurred a loss attributable to enhanced capital allowances for such expenditure. The loss is effectively surrendered in exchange for a cash payment, instead of being carried forward and set against future profits.

There is a wide range of assets on which FYAs are presently available, the allowance under some headings being restricted to expenditure within a specified period. The headings are as follows and the detailed rules are summarised below:

- Expenditure on most plant and machinery for 2009/10 only (see **22.25**)
- Expenditure on energy-saving equipment* (see **22.26**)
- Expenditure on low CO_2 emissions cars* — extended to 31 March 2013 (see **22.27**)
- Expenditure on natural gas/hydrogen refuelling equipment* — extended to 31 March 2013 (see **22.27**)
- Expenditure on environmentally beneficial plant or machinery (see **22.28**)

* Expenditure incurred on or after 17 April 2002 on such plant and machinery for leasing qualifies despite the general exclusion stated above for plant and machinery for leasing.

[22.25] FA 2009 introduced a temporary FYA at 40%, for expenditure incurred on or after 6 April 2009 but before 6 April 2010 for income tax and on or after 1 April 2009 but before 1 April 2010 for corporation tax, on most plant and machinery other than long-life assets, assets leased or let on hire, cars (including taxis but not motor cycles), sea-going ships, railway assets and certain assets on which expenditure is referred to as 'special rate' expenditure (see **22.30**). The restriction on leased assets does not prevent property lessors from claiming the FYA on expenditure on background plant and machinery for a building, provided it is not special rate expenditure. Any pre-commencement expenditure incurred before 6 April 2009 for income tax or 1 April 2009 for corporation tax, where the business commenced after these dates, does not qualify for FYAs.

It is proposed to introduce a 100% FYA for expenditure on new, unused zero-emission goods vehicles for five years from April 2010. A zero-emission goods vehicle is one which cannot under any circumstances produce CO_2 emissions when driven and is of a design primarily suited to the conveyance of goods or burden. Certain exclusions, including the exclusion of expenditure on assets for leasing, will apply.

Previously FYAs at the rate of 40% were available for expenditure incurred by small or medium-sized businesses on new or second-hand plant and machinery (other than long-life plant and machinery). For *small* businesses, the rate was increased to 50% for expenditure incurred in 2006/07 and 2007/08 by individuals and in the financial years to 31 March 2007 and 2008 by companies. These particular FYAs were withdrawn from 6 April 2008 for income tax and 1 April 2008 for corporation tax.

Businesses qualified as small/medium-sized for this purpose if they satisfied two of the following conditions (taking into account other companies in the same group, or for unincorporated businesses, other businesses carried on by the same sole trader or partnership):

* Turnover not more than £22.8 million
* Assets not more than £11.4 million
* Not more than 250 employees

The conditions for businesses to qualify as small were that, taking into account other companies in the same group, or for unincorporated businesses, other businesses carried on by the same sole trader or partnership, two of the following conditions were satisfied, i.e. the turnover was not more than £5.6 million, the assets total was not more than £2.8 million, and there were not more than 50 employees.

[22.26] 100% FYAs are available for expenditure on new plant and machinery within stipulated categories (heat and power systems, lighting, refrigeration etc.) that have been certified as meeting energy efficiency criteria. Businesses such as energy service companies may claim the allowance on such equipment provided and operated on a client's business premises under an energy management contract if the company and the client make a joint election. The FYA for such expenditure is also available to leasing businesses.

[22.27] 100% FYAs may be claimed for expenditure incurred on new electric cars and cars with low CO_2 emissions (i.e. not more than 110g/km, reduced from 120g/km in FA 2008 subject to transitional rules). FA 2008 extended this allowance, which was due to expire on 31 March 2008, for a further five years to 31 March 2013. 'Car' in this case includes a taxi but does not include a motor cycle. 100% FYAs may also be claimed for expenditure between the same dates on new plant and machinery for refuelling stations used to refuel vehicles with natural gas or hydrogen fuel. These FYAs are available to leasing businesses.

[22.28] 100% FYAs are available for certain expenditure on environmentally beneficial plant and machinery (other than long-life plant and machinery). The allowances apply to expenditure on designated plant and machinery to save energy, reduce water use, or improve water quality. The qualifying technologies and products are detailed in the energy and water technology criteria lists available at www.eca.gov.uk. The list of qualifying categories is updated, usually annually, by Treasury Order.

[22.29] With effect from 1 April 2008 it is possible for FYAs on both energy-saving plant and machinery (see **22.26**) and environmentally beneficial plant and machinery (see **22.28**) to be converted into a repayable tax credit where they give rise to a loss. The relief applies to companies only and broadly the company may claim a first-year tax credit equal to 19% of the loss, subject to an upper limit and certain other restrictions.

Pooling expenditure (CAA 2001, ss 53, 54, 57–59)

[22.30] Subject to certain exceptions, qualifying expenditure on plant and machinery is pooled for the purpose of calculating writing-down allowances, balancing allowances and balancing charges.

With effect, broadly, from April 2008, 'special rate expenditure' must be allocated to a new 'special rate pool' for which the rate of writing down allowance is 10% (rather than the rate of 20% applicable to the main pool). However, see **22.1** regarding proposed reductions in the rate of allowances from April 2012.

'Special rate expenditure' is expenditure incurred on or after 6 April 2008 (for income tax) or 1 April 2008 (for corporation tax) on thermal insulation, integral features, or long-life assets (see **22.38**). Expenditure before the relevant date on long-life assets is also to be included if it was allocated to a pool in a chargeable period starting on or after that date.

Expenditure incurred broadly on or after 6 April 2009 for income tax or on or after 1 April 2009 for corporation tax on a car that is not a 'main rate car' (see **22.23**) is also included in the special rate pool.

[22.31] *Single asset pools* are required for:

- Short life assets (at the taxpayer's option, any asset that is expected to be disposed of within five years — see **22.35**).
- Any asset with part private use by a sole trader or partner (see **22.36**).
- For expenditure incurred broadly before 6 April 2009 for income tax or before 1 April 2009 for corporation tax (see **22.23** for exceptions to these dates) on cars costing over £12,000 (see **22.37**). 'Cars' were defined for this purpose as all motor vehicles (including motor cycles) except those primarily suited for carrying goods, those not commonly

used as private vehicles and unsuitable to be so used, those let on a short lease (i.e. where the car is normally hired to the same person for less than 30 consecutive days and for less than 90 days in any twelve months), those let to someone receiving mobility allowance or disability living allowance, and electric and low CO_2 emissions cars qualifying for 100% FYA (see 22.27).

Class pools are required for:

- Long-life assets (see 22.38) — but these are now allocated to a special rate pool, see 22.30.
- Assets for foreign leasing (see 22.39).

[22.32] The writing-down allowance at the rate of 20% (however, see 22.1 regarding proposed reductions in the rate of allowances from April 2012) per annum (reducing balance method) is calculated on the unrelieved expenditure brought forward from the previous period, plus expenditure in the period (excluding expenditure on which FYA has been claimed, unless the asset has been disposed of in the same period, in which case any unallowed expenditure is included), less any sales proceeds (up to, but not exceeding, the original cost — see 22.41). If the proceeds exceed the pool balance, a balancing charge is made. Any available FYA is calculated separately and the remainder of the expenditure is then included in the pool balance carried forward (unless already included as indicated above). See example 1. Where a FYA is available, it will sometimes be possible to avoid a balancing charge by not claiming the allowance on all or part of the qualifying expenditure and including the expenditure in the pool instead.

Where a person incurs AIA qualifying expenditure and an AIA is made in respect of that expenditure, the expenditure is added to the pool and the balance in the pool is reduced by the amount of the AIA. This ensures that the rules on allocating disposal proceeds work correctly on a subsequent disposal of any asset on which the AIA was claimed.

FA 2008 introduced a 'small pools' writing down allowance, available for the main pool and the special rate pool only (i.e. not for any single asset pool). Where the pool balance is £1,000 or less the taxpayer may claim all or part of that balance as a writing down allowance. This is a simplification measure removing the need for businesses to carry forward small balances and calculating the writing down allowance each year.

[22.33] A balancing allowance will not arise on the main pool, except on a cessation of trade where the total sales proceeds are less than the pool balance. The same applies to long-life asset pools (see 22.38). See 22.39 for assets for foreign leasing. For single asset pools, a balancing allowance or charge is made when the asset is disposed of. If the single asset is disposed of in the period in which it is acquired for less than cost, there will be a balancing allowance on the shortfall. If it is disposed of in that period for more than cost the excess will not be brought into account for capital allowances at all and the capital profit will be dealt with under the capital gains tax legislation (the gain being exempt if the asset is a car).

[22.34] The general rules, and the way in which a balancing charge may be avoided by not claiming FYA, are illustrated in Example 1. See also Example 2, which illustrates the special rules mentioned in **22.9** for income tax accounting periods that exceed 18 months.

Example 1

A trader has the following transactions in 'main pool' plant in the years ended 31 December 2008 and 2009, plant purchases qualifying for the FYA (see 20.25) where appropriate:

		£
April 2008	Arm's length purchase of low CO_2 emission car	10,000
June 2008	Proceeds of sales	3,000
August 2008	Purchase from associated business	5,000
January 2009	Proceeds of sales	7,500
March 2009	Purchase of plant and machinery for which full AIA claimed	50,000
May 2009	Arm's length purchase of plant and machinery	10,000
December 2009	Arm's length purchase of main rate car	7,000

The main pool balance brought forward at 1 January 2008 is £8,000.

The allowances are calculated as follows:

	£	£
Year to 31 December 2008		
Pool balance brought forward		8,000
Additions not qualifying for FYA:		
August 2008 from connected person (not based on market value since dealt with as a sale in the computations of the associated business — see 22.18)		5,000
		13,000
Less sales proceeds June 2008		(3,000)
		10,000
Writing-down allowance 21.32% hybrid rate (see 22.24) (reduces taxable profit)		(2,132)
		7,868
Additions April 2008 qualifying for FYA	10,000	
FYA 100% (reduces taxable profit)	(10,000)	
Balance allocated to main pool		—
		7,868
Year to 31 December 2009		
Additions not qualifying for FYA		7,000

Sales proceeds January 2009		(7,500)
		7,368
Writing-down allowance 20% (reduces taxable profit)		(1,474)
		5,894
Additions qualifying for FYA:		
May 2009	10,000	
FYA 40% (reduces taxable profit)	(4,000)	
Balance allocated to main pool		6,000
Pool balance carried forward		£11,894

If the sale proceeds in January 2009 had been, say, £17,000, they would have exceeded the pool balance of £14,868 by £2,132. The balancing charge of that amount that would have arisen could have been avoided by not claiming FYA on £2,132 of the May 2009 expenditure, as follows:

	£	£
Year to 31 December 2009		
Balance brought forward		7,868
Additions not qualifying for FYA		7,000
Additions on which FYA not claimed		2,132
		17,000
Sale proceeds		(17,000)
Additions on which FYA claimed:		
May 2009 (remaining expenditure)	7,868	
FYA 40%	(3,147)	
Balance allocated to main pool		4,721
Pool balance carried forward		£4,721

Thus taxable profits would be reduced by FYAs of £3,147 instead of being reduced by FYAs of £4,000 and increased by a balancing charge of £2,132. The net immediate benefit of not claiming full FYAs would be an additional allowance of £1,279, although the balance carried forward would be correspondingly reduced.

Example 2

A trader's 22–month account is made up from 1 January 2008 to 31 October 2009. Main pool balance brought forward is £100,000. The only addition was a new low CO_2 emission car qualifying for 100% FYA that cost £10,000 in March 2009. The allowances will be calculated as follows:

	£	£
Year to 31.12.2008		
Pool balance brought forward		100,000
WDA 21.32% hybrid rate (see 22.24)		21,320
		78,680
10 mths to 31.10.2009		
WDA 20% x 10/12		13,113
		65,567
Additions qualifying for FYA	10,000	
FYA 100%	(10,000)	
Balance allocated to main pool		—
Written down value carried forward		65,567
Total allowances for period treated as trading expense (21,320 + 13,113 + 10,000)		£44,433

Example 3

The maximum AIA entitlement of a company with a 12-month accounting period ending on 31 December 2010 is calculated as follows:

Period 1 January 2010 to 31 March 2010	3/12 x 50,000 =	12,500
Period 1 April 2010 to 31 December 2010	9/12 x 100,000 =	75,000
Maximum entitlement		£87,500

Note that for the period 1 January 2010 to 31 March 2010 only a maximum of £50,000 of the company's expenditure would be covered, being the limit before the increase in FA 2010. Therefore if the company incurred qualifying expenditure of £60,000 in February 2010 and no other expenditure for the remainder of the accounting period, the maximum AIA would be £50,000.

Short-life assets (CAA 2001, ss 83–89)

[22.35] Some assets have a very short life and depreciate very quickly. Pooling them within the main pool would not give relief for their cost over their life span because when they are disposed of, any unrelieved expenditure remains in the pool to be written off over future years (unless the business has ceased, when a pool balancing adjustment is made — see **22.32** and **22.33**). An election may be made to have the capital allowances on specified items of plant and machinery calculated separately in single asset pools under the 'short-life assets' provisions. A balancing allowance or charge will then arise if the asset is disposed of within four years from the end of the accounting period in which it is acquired. If the asset is still held at the end of that period, the tax written-down value is transferred into the main pool. Cars (including hire cars other than those hired to someone receiving mobility allowance or disability living allowance) and any assets which would not in any event have been included in the main pool of expenditure cannot be dealt with under the short-life assets rules. 'Special rate expenditure' (see **22.30**) is also excluded. Where a car hired to someone receiving mobility allowance or disability living allowance is treated as a short life asset and is still held four years from the end of the accounting period in which it was acquired, the tax written down value will be transferred to one of the two plant and machinery pools, depending on the level of CO_2 emissions (see **22.23**).

The election for this treatment is irrevocable, and must be made within two years after the end of the accounting period in which the expenditure is incurred for companies and within one year after the 31 January following the tax year in which the period of account in which the expenditure was incurred ends for individuals. HMRC have issued guidelines (Statement of Practice SP 1/86) on practical aspects of the short-life assets rules, including provisions for grouping classes of assets where individual treatment is impossible or impracticable.

Assets with part private use (CAA 2001, ss 205–208)

[22.36] Any business asset that is privately used by a sole proprietor or by a partner in a business is dealt with in a separate single asset pool. Allowances and charges for each privately-used asset are calculated in the normal way, but the available allowance or charge is restricted to the business proportion. An individual balancing adjustment is made when the asset is disposed of.

This does not apply to assets used by directors of family companies. The use of company assets for private purposes by directors or employees does not affect the company's capital allowances position, but results in a benefits charge on the director/employee (see **CHAPTER 10**).

Cars costing more than £12,000 (CAA 2001, ss 74–77)

[22.37] For expenditure incurred broadly before 2009/10 (but see **22.23** for full details) each car (as defined at **22.31**), other than a low emission car, that costs more than £12,000 when acquired is dealt with in a separate single asset pool, and the available writing-down allowance is £3,000 per annum or 20% (however, see **22.1** regarding proposed reductions in the rate of allowances from April 2012) of the unrelieved balance, whichever is less. If such a car is used privately by a sole trader or partner the available amount is further restricted by the private proportion. When the car is sold a balancing allowance or charge arises. See **20.17** for the treatment of a car with a value of more than £12,000 that is leased instead of bought. Any expenditure remaining in the single asset pool at the beginning of the first chargeable period to commence on or after 6 April 2014 for income tax or on or after 1 April 2014 for corporation tax, which does not relate to cars with private use, will be transferred to the main capital allowances pool.

Long-life plant and machinery (CAA 2001, ss 90–103; FA 2008, s 83)

[22.38] Plant and machinery first bought new since 26 November 1996 with an expected working life of 25 years or more has normally qualified for writing-down allowances at only 6% per annum (on the reducing balance) throughout its life rather than 20% per annum (or 25% before 6 April 2008) (total expenditure on such assets being included in a separate 'class pool').

The 6% rate of writing down allowance was increased to 10% from 6 April 2008 (for income tax) or 1 April 2008 (for companies) and any balance of unrelieved expenditure in the long-life asset class pool is now to be allocated (subject to transitional rules) to the new 10% 'special rate pool' (see **22.30**). However, see **22.1** regarding proposed reductions in the rate of allowances from April 2012.

The long-life asset provisions do not apply to cars (including hire cars), taxis, motor cycles or to certain ships or railway assets bought before the end of 2010, or to assets used in a dwelling-house, retail shop, showroom, hotel or office. Nor do they apply where total expenditure on such long-life assets does not exceed £100,000 a year (divided pro rata for associated companies). Most of the plant and machinery affected by these rules would alternatively qualify for industrial buildings allowances and businesses may choose which allowances to claim. Those who have chosen industrial buildings allowances will now be denied relief for any unrelieved balance of their expenditure when the allowances cease in 2011 (see **22.1**).

The reduced rate of writing-down allowance does not apply to second-hand assets if the pre–26 November 1996 rules applied to the vendor.

When all or any of the long-life assets are disposed of, a balancing charge will arise if the total proceeds exceed the pool balance brought forward. If the total proceeds are less than the pool balance, writing-down allowances will continue to be given on the remaining expenditure. A balancing allowance will not arise until the trade ceases, even if all the assets are disposed of before that time.

Assets for overseas leasing (CAA 2001, ss 107, 109)

[22.39] Assets leased to non-UK residents who do not use them for a UK trade are kept in a separate class pool, normally attracting writing-down allowances at 10%, balancing charges where the total sales proceeds exceed the tax written-down value of all such assets, and a balancing allowance where the tax written-down value exceeds the total proceeds in the final chargeable period (i.e. the period after which there can be no more disposal receipts). In some circumstances, no allowances at all are available.

Fixtures (CAA 2001, ss 70A–70YJ, 172–204)

[22.40] Complex rules apply in relation to plant and machinery allowances on fixtures. Those who let property can claim the allowances on expenditure incurred on fixtures and fittings (subject to what is said below). Where a business tenant incurs the expenditure, and the fixtures become the land-lord's property in law, the tenant can nonetheless claim allowances. Where fixtures are provided by equipment lessors, the lessee (who may be the owner or tenant of the property) and the equipment lessor may elect for the equipment lessor to claim the allowances.

From (broadly) 1 April 2006, these provisions do not apply to 'long funding leases'. A long funding lease is essentially a financing transaction. Under the long funding lease provisions, the lessee is normally allowed to claim the allowances (thus equating the position with someone who borrows to buy an asset rather than leasing it). Again this is subject to complex rules.

See **22.26** re elections by energy service companies and their clients to enable the companies to claim 100% FYAs on energy saving plant and machinery. See that section also for the entitlement of equipment lessors to claim 100% FYAs on certain assets.

Allowances cannot be claimed on fixtures leased to non-taxpayers, such as charities, unless the lessor has an interest in the relevant land. Nor can they be claimed by equipment lessors or landlords on fixtures in dwelling-houses. An exception was made for expenditure incurred by equipment lessors between 28 July 2000 and 31 December 2007 on boilers, radiators, heat exchangers and heating controls installed in low income homes under the Government's Affordable Warmth Programme. Where capital allowances are not available, landlords will usually be able to claim a wear and tear allowance instead under the provisions of HMRC concession B47 (see **32.13**).

Allowances are not available on any amount in excess of the original cost of the fixtures when new. Vendors and purchasers may make a joint election (within two years of the date of the contract) fixing how much of the purchase price of a building relates to fixtures, the agreed amount being limited, however, to the vendor's original cost. Where a claim in a return becomes incorrect, for example because of such an election, the claimant must notify an amendment to the return within three months after becoming aware of that fact.

There are anti-avoidance provisions to prevent allowances on fixtures being artificially accelerated. From 2008/09 the rate of writing-down allowance on certain 'integral features' of a building is 10%. However, see **22.1** regarding proposed reductions in the rate of allowances from April 2012. 'Integral features' include electrical (including lighting) systems; cold water systems; space or water heating systems; powered systems of ventilation; air cooling or air purification (and any floor or ceiling comprised in such systems); lifts, escalators and moving walkways; and external solar shading. Expenditure on such items is allocated to the new 'special rate pool' (see **22.30**).

Effect of capital allowances on capital gains tax computation (TCGA 1992, ss 41, 55(3))

[22.41] Capital allowances are not deducted from cost in computing a capital gain, but are taken into account in computing a capital loss. There will only be a gain if an asset is sold for more than cost, and in that event any capital allowances given will be withdrawn by the cost being taken out of the capital allowances computation and will not therefore affect the computation of the gain. There will not normally be a capital loss, since any amount by which the sale proceeds for an asset fall short of the written-down value will be taken into account in the capital allowances computation.

For plant and machinery that is moveable rather than fixed, there is no chargeable gain if it is sold for £6,000 or less. Where the proceeds exceed £6,000, the chargeable gain cannot exceed 5/3rds of the excess of the proceeds over £6,000 (see **39.3**). If plant and machinery is fixed rather than moveable, gains are not exempt but they may be deferred if the item is replaced (see **29.11** onwards). See Example 4.

Example 4

Plant which cost a trader £50,000 in December 2004 was sold in September 2009 for £65,000. Incidental costs of sale were £1,000.

Since the plant was sold for more than cost, the capital allowances would be fully withdrawn by deducting £50,000 from the pool balance. There would be a capital gain of (65,000 − 50,000 − 1,000 =) £14,000.

If the plant was fixed plant, the gain would be eligible for roll-over relief.

If the plant was instead sold for £40,000 in September 2009, with incidental costs of sale the same at £1,000, part of the capital allowances would be withdrawn by way of a balancing charge. However, a total of £10,000 capital allowances previously given will not be withdrawn. The capital gains computation on disposal will then be:

	£	£
Proceeds	40,000	
Incidental costs of sale	(1,000)	
		39,000
Allowable expenditure		
Original cost	50,000	
Capital allowances given	(10,000)	
		40,000
Allowable loss		(£1,000)

Effectively the allowable loss is restricted to the incidental costs of sale.

See CHAPTER 4 for detailed capital gains tax provisions.

Industrial buildings

Changes to allowances for industrial buildings (FA 2007, s 36; FA 2008, ss 84–87 and Sch 27)

[22.42] Writing down allowances for industrial buildings and agricultural buildings (see CHAPTER 31) are being gradually phased out and will be withdrawn completely by April 2011. The effective rate of the writing down allowance for a chargeable period of a year is reduced (for income tax) from 4% to 3% for 2008/09, 2% for 2009/10, 1% for 2010/11 and nil after 5 April 2011. For corporation tax, the rates will change on 1 April rather than 6 April. Time apportionment rules will apply where a chargeable period straddles any of the relevant dates.

FA 2007 provided for the abolition of balancing allowances and balancing charges on most relevant events occurring on or after 21 March 2007, subject to a transitional rule in cases where a written contract was made before 21 March 2007. The purchaser will get writing down allowances based on the residue of unallowed expenditure at the time of purchase, i.e. he will take over allowances at the rate claimed by the seller. See **22.47** onwards. Balancing adjustments were retained for enterprise zone expenditure (see **22.52**).

Previously, industrial buildings allowances were given at 4% per annum on a straight line basis and balancing adjustments were made on the disposal of a qualifying building.

Buildings qualifying for relief (CAA 2001, ss 271, 274, 277, 283)

[22.43] Industrial buildings allowances in respect of qualifying construction expenditure are presently available under four headings: buildings in use for a qualifying trade, qualifying hotels, qualifying sports pavilions, and commercial buildings and structures in enterprise zones. Qualifying hotels are dealt with in **22.51** and enterprise zone buildings in **22.52**. A sports pavilion qualifies for the allowances if it is provided by a person carrying on *any* trade for the welfare of employees.

As far as qualifying trades are concerned, the most common examples are manufacturing or processing goods or materials. Businesses which provide services such as transport, water, sewerage or electricity are also within the definition. Buildings used to store goods and materials before and after manufacture or processing are included. Offices, shops, hotels, wholesale warehouses and buildings used as retail shops (including repair shops), and buildings used for ancillary purposes, are not qualifying trades (but see **22.51** below re qualifying hotels). HMRC treat a vehicle repair workshop as an industrial building if it is completely separate from the vehicle sales area, does not have a reception, and public access is discouraged. Allowances would be restricted to the extent that vehicles for resale were repaired in the workshop. Where part of a building is outside the definition (for example offices in a factory), the whole building qualifies for allowances providing the expenditure on the non-industrial part does not exceed 25% of the total cost. This applies only where the non-industrial part is housed within the same building, not where it is a separate building. Where a building is in an enterprise zone, there is no restriction on the use to which it may be put (except that a private dwelling does not qualify) and much more generous allowances are available (see **22.52**).

Allowances for new buildings and additional capital expenditure on existing buildings (CAA 2001, ss 272, 285, 292–297, 309–313; FA 2007, s 36)

[22.44] Industrial buildings allowances will not be available for expenditure incurred on or after 6 April 2011 (for income tax) or 1 April 2011 (for corporation tax). See **22.42** for rate of writing down allowance and the reductions that apply from April 2008.

Writing-down allowances are available for the chargeable period in which the building is brought into use. Allowances are given on the cost of construction and no allowances are available for the cost of the land, although site preparation works qualify. Where a building is bought from the builder, allowances are available on the amount paid (again excluding an amount for the land). Where additional capital expenditure is incurred on an existing qualifying building, the additional expenditure qualifies for allowances as if it were a separate building. This enables a tenant to get allowances on any capital expenditure he incurs on a qualifying building, and it is specifically provided that if any repair expenditure on a qualifying building does not qualify as a business expense for tax purposes, it is treated as qualifying capital expenditure. Furthermore, expenditure on items that become part of the building does not qualify for plant and machinery allowances and counts instead as part of the building expenditure — see **22.21**.

[22.45] In earlier years, initial allowances were available at various rates from time to time in addition to writing-down allowances, the allowances being given in the chargeable period related to the incurring of the expenditure. The allowances have not been available since 31 March 1986.

[22.46] A claim need not be made for all of the writing-down allowance (or initial allowance when available). Before FA 2007 the effect of claiming reduced amounts would have been to extend the writing-down period beyond the building's normal tax life of 25 or 50 years, unless the building was disposed of in the meantime. This no longer applies, as indicated in **22.42**.

Example 5

A factory built in Spring 2006 was bought from the builder for £500,000 (excluding land) in October 2006 by a trader making up accounts to 31 December. The building was brought into use immediately. The annual writing-down allowance at 4% is £20,000. Unless there was a change of accounting date, or the building was sold, the trader would have expected to get allowances of that amount from 2006/07 to 2030/31. Following FA 2007 and FA 2008 the allowances are reduced from 2008/09 and will cease altogether after 2010/11.

> Had the building not been brought into use until say February 2007, in the accounting period to 31 December 2007, the first writing-down allowance would have been given in 2007/08.

Where a building was sold before the expenditure had been fully relieved, there was previously a balancing adjustment between the seller and the buyer, and the buyer was entitled to writing-down allowances over the remainder of the building's tax life. Balancing adjustments are no longer made for events on and after 21 March 2007, except for certain transitional provisions (see **22.42** and **22.47**).

Sale of the building (CAA 2001, ss 314–331, 354; FA 2007, s 36)

[22.47] Before FA 2007, there was a balancing adjustment on the seller when a building was sold (unless the building was sold after the end of its tax life — see below) and a possible claim for relief by the purchaser (but see **22.50** re anti-avoidance provisions).

Whilst there were rules to deal with periods of non-industrial use, the basic adjustment was to give the seller a balancing allowance to make up any shortfall between the unrelieved expenditure and the sale proceeds, or to make a balancing charge to withdraw excess allowances if the sale proceeds exceeded the unrelieved expenditure. If a building was disposed of after the trade had ceased, any balancing allowance was treated as if it were an expense of a property letting business, so the treatment for such businesses in **22.12** would apply. A balancing charge was similarly treated as a letting income, but it might have been reduced by any amounts that could have been set against it if it had been received before the trade ceased, in the same way as for post-cessation receipts (as to which see **21.9**).

[22.48] Providing the purchaser used the building for a qualifying trade, allowances were available on the part of the original building cost remaining unrelieved after the balancing adjustment on the seller. This amount was relieved by way of equal annual allowances over the remainder of the 'tax life' of the building. No matter how much the purchaser paid for the building, the maximum amount on which relief could be claimed was the original building cost, which might have been incurred many years earlier and bear little relation to current prices. No relief was available for the cost of the land whether relating to new or used buildings. The tax life of industrial buildings was 25 years from the date the building was first used for expenditure on or after 6 November 1962 and 50 years for expenditure before that date. If a building's tax life had already expired, there was no balancing adjustment for the seller and the purchaser could not claim any allowances at all, unless additional capital expenditure on the building had been incurred at a later date, in which case that expenditure would have been treated as if it related to a separate building with its own tax life (see **22.44**). Despite the fact that once a building's tax life had expired, the seller did not lose the capital allowances claimed, the full cost of the building was (and still is) taken into account in the computation of a capital gain on disposal. Capital allowances are still taken into account in computing a capital loss.

As indicated in **22.46**, balancing adjustments will not be made for disposals on or after 21 March 2007, unless the transitional provisions apply (see **22.42**). Example 5 illustrates the treatment of a sale in February 2007, with the balancing adjustment being made but the later allowances being reduced and then withdrawn. Example 6 illustrates the position as in Example 5, but with the sale taking place on 31 March 2007.

Example 6

The construction costs of an industrial building in April 1994 were £400,000, the land cost being £50,000. Annual allowances of £16,000 for 12 years, totalling £192,000 in all, have been claimed.

The building (including £100,000 for the land) is sold on 28 February 2007 for:

(a) £280,000   (b) £450,000   (c) £960,000

The vendor's position is:	(a)	(b)	(c)
	£	£	£
Sale proceeds	280,000	450,000	960,000
Land included	100,000	100,000	100,000
Building proceeds	180,000	350,000	860,000
Building cost	400,000	400,000	400,000
Cost of owning building	220,000	50,000	Nil
Allowances already given	192,000	192,000	192,000
Balancing allowance/(charge)	£28,000	£(142,000)	£(192,000)

In the case of (c) there would also be a capital gain:

Proceeds (land and buildings)	960,000
Cost (land and buildings)	450,000
Chargeable gain (before any available indexation allowance and taper relief)	£510,000

The purchaser would get reliefs as follows:

	(a)	(b)	(c)
Cost to him (building only)	£180,000	£350,000	£860,000
Restrict to original cost if less than purchase price			£400,000
Annual allowance ¹/₁₃th*	£13,846	£26,923	£30,769

(*13 years of 25-year life remaining, ignoring fractions of year for illustration.)

The annual allowance for 2007/08 would be at the calculated amount, but it would then be reduced by one quarter of that amount for each of 2008/09, 2009/10 and 2010/11, no further allowances being available thereafter.

If the building had been built in 1975, there would have been no balancing adjustment for the seller and no allowances to the buyer, because it would be over 25 years old. The capital allowances given would not be deducted from the cost to calculate the capital gain.

If the building had been built in March 1960, there would still be three years remaining out of the original writing-down life of 50 years (for expenditure incurred before 6 November 1962), but the allowances would relate to any unallowed balance of the 1960 building cost, and would then be reduced by one quarter for each of the second and third of those three years.

Example 7

Facts as in Example 5, but the sale of the building took place on 31 March 2007.

Since the sale is after 20 March 2007, there would be no balancing adjustments. The purchasers (or anyone purchasing from them) would in each case receive writing down allowances at the rate of £16,000 for 2007/08, £12,000 for 2008/09, £8,000 for 2009/10, £4,000 for 2010/11, and nil thereafter. The computation of the capital gain in part (c) of Example 6 would remain the same.

[**22.49**] Where plant and machinery is purchased with a building, the purchase price needs to be apportioned and plant and machinery allowances can then be claimed on the appropriate part of the purchase price. This is particularly important now that industrial buildings allowances are being withdrawn. There is no restriction of plant and machinery allowances to the original cost of the items, except for fixtures (see **22.40**).

[**22.50**] Anti-avoidance provisions have applied to certain sales of buildings within the industrial buildings definition (see **22.43**). Where the sale price had been artificially depressed as a result of a tax avoidance scheme, the seller was not entitled to a balancing allowance, but the buyer's allowances were calculated as if the balancing allowance had been made. These provisions are not relevant from 21 March 2007, unless the transitional provisions in **22.42** apply.

Hotels (CAA 2001, s 279)

[**22.51**] Relief is presently available for construction costs in respect of a qualifying hotel or hotel extension. The hotel or extension must be of a permanent nature, be open for at least four months between April and October, and when open must have at least ten letting bedrooms offering sleeping accommodation. It must provide services of breakfast, evening meal, making beds and cleaning rooms. The relief works in the same way as that for industrial buildings, so that balancing adjustments will not be made from 21 March 2007 (unless the transitional provisions apply) and writing down allowances are reduced from 2008/09 and will be withdrawn completely from April 2011 (see **22.42** and **22.44** onwards). Allowances will not be withdrawn if the hotel is in an enterprise zone. Enterprise zone hotels qualify for the allowances described in **22.52** onwards, with no restriction on months of opening or number of bedrooms, etc.

Buildings in enterprise zones (CAA 2001, ss 298–313, 327–331)

[22.52] When an area has been designated as an Enterprise Zone by the Secretary of State, expenditure incurred or contracted for within ten years after the creation of the zone on any buildings other than dwelling houses qualifies for industrial buildings allowances at a special rate (also known as enterprise zone allowances or EZAs). An initial allowance of up to 100% (or whatever lower amount is claimed) is available. If part of a building is used as a dwelling, the whole expenditure still qualifies, providing the expenditure on that part does not exceed 25% of the total building cost. Any expenditure on which initial allowance is not claimed qualifies for writing-down allowances of 25% of cost (straight line method) until it is written off in full. See **22.12** for the way in which an investor may get relief for the allowances he claims, which is illustrated in Example 7 below. Where fixed plant or machinery is an integral part of the building, it can be treated as part of the building for the purposes of claiming EZAs.

EZAs are to be withdrawn from April 2011 along with other industrial buildings allowances (see **22.42**) but EZAs are not being phased out. Where the initial allowance is not claimed in full and the 25% writing down allowance is available for a period straddling the abolition date, the writing down allowance will be time apportioned.

Balancing charges in relation to EZAs, however, were not abolished with effect from March 2007. They are being retained for a limited period, and a charge may still arise where a business disposes of a building within seven years of first use.

> ### Example 8
>
> In September 2006, i.e. in the tax year 2006/07, a single man purchased a workshop in an enterprise zone from a developer for £72,000 (including land £6,000), the first letting taking place in the following tax year, i.e. 2007/08. He had rent income from another property of £10,000 in 2006/07 and he had other income of £46,000. His total income in 2007/08 was £65,000 and is expected to continue at that level. The allowance he can claim in 2006/07 is any amount up to a maximum of 100% of £66,000. The amount claimed can be set against just his rent income of that year and later years, or alternatively the loss created by the claim may be set against his total income of either 2006/07 or 2007/08 or both years, any unrelieved balance then being set only against rental income in later years. If he claimed the maximum of £66,000, however, and claimed relief for the resulting loss

against his income of 2006/07 he would waste his personal allowance in that year and there would be an unrelieved balance of £10,000 carried forward to 2007/08. He could instead claim allowances as follows.

Initial allowance	18,000
Which will be set against rent income of 2006/07	10,000
	8,000
Loss relief which may be claimed against other 2006/07 income of £46,000	8,000
Leaving taxable income (just below basic rate threshold after personal allowance) of (56,000 – 10,000 – 8,000)	£38,000

The unrelieved expenditure would be £48,000 (£66,000 – £18,000) and this could be relieved as follows:

2007/08 (25% × £66,000)	16,500
2008/09 (25% × £66,000)	16,500
2009/10 (the remainder)	15,000
	£48,000

If he wanted to eliminate his taxable income in 2006/07 he could instead claim initial allowance of £50,965 for that year and a writing-down allowance covering the remaining expenditure in the next year, the effect on his taxable income after making loss claims where appropriate being as follows.

	2006/07	2007/08	2008/09
Total income	56,000	65,000	65,000
Initial allowance	50,965		
Writing-down allowance		15,035	—
Leaving taxable income (before personal allowance) of	£5,035	£49,965	£65,000

This would save starting and basic rate tax in 2006/07 at the expense of additional higher rate tax in 2008/09 and 2009/10.

Balancing allowances or charges continue to apply (see above) on the disposal of buildings on which EZAs have been claimed, using the same rules as applied for industrial buildings before 21 March 2007 (see **22.47** and Example 5), and treating the life of the building as being 25 years. This means that if the building is sold in the early years, the seller will usually lose all or a large part of the benefit of the 100% allowances. Furthermore, if a lease is granted for a capital sum within seven years after the date of the contract to acquire the interest in the building, the receipt of the capital sum triggers a balancing charge on the lessor (or if he has not claimed the maximum allowance, a reduction in the unrelieved expenditure qualifying for writing-down allowances). This treatment does not apply to leases granted after more than seven years unless the lessor has a guaranteed exit arrangement, in which case a balancing charge is made on the granting of a lease at *any* time within the building's 25-year life. If the lease is for 50 years or less, the amount already charged as additional rent (see **32.18**) is excluded from the capital sum in calculating the balancing charge. If the lease is for more than 50 years, these special rules do not apply if the landlord and tenant have *elected* to treat the capital sum as sale proceeds so that the tenant may claim allowances (see **22.3**).

Purchase within two years after first use

[22.53] Someone who acquires an enterprise zone building within two years after it is first used is treated as if he had acquired an unused building, so that he can claim the 100% initial allowance or 25% writing-down allowance as indicated above. As far as any subsequent second-hand purchaser is concerned, the position is the same as for purchasers outside the first two years (see **22.54**), but the 25-year life of the building dates from the date of first use by the person who acquired it within the first two years of use.

Purchase more than two years after first use

[22.54] Where the first disposal of an enterprise zone building occurs more than two years after it is first used, the purchaser cannot claim the 100% or 25% enterprise zone allowances. He gets writing-down allowances only, normally on the lower of the price paid by him and the original construction cost. The writing-down allowance is calculated by spreading the unrelieved expenditure over the balance of the building's 25-year life which is unexpired at the date of purchase. Where, however, a building is transferred between connected persons (say husband and wife or civil partners), they may make a claim to treat the transfer as being at written-down value (see **22.18**), so that the benefit to the vendor of the higher enterprise zone building allowances is not lost as a result of the transfer.

Limits on enterprise zone allowances

[22.55] Where part of the expenditure on a building was incurred neither within the ten-year life of the enterprise zone, nor under a contract entered into within the ten-year period, that part of the expenditure qualifies only for the normal level of buildings allowances (i.e. for industrial buildings or hotels, which are, however, being withdrawn by April 2011), or not at all if it is a non-qualifying building.

Enterprise zone allowances cannot be claimed on expenditure incurred more than 20 years after the site was included in the enterprise zone, no matter when the contract was entered into.

Way in which allowances are given

[22.56] Enterprise zone allowances may be claimed both by traders and investors. See **22.12** to **22.16**.

Patents (CAA 2001, ss 464–483; CTA 2009, ss 911–923; ITTOIA 2005, ss 587–599)

[22.57] Expenditure incurred in devising and patenting an invention (or an abortive attempt to do so) is allowable as a business expense (and qualifies for the research and development reliefs —see **29.38** to **29.41**). Where, however, patent rights are purchased, capital allowances are available to individuals as follows. These provisions also apply to companies in respect of expenditure incurred *before* 1 April 2002. For expenditure incurred on or after that date, patents are dealt with for corporation tax under the 'Intangible assets' provisions outlined at **20.30** onwards.

The capital allowances available are writing-down allowances at 25% on the reducing balance method, with all expenditure on patent rights being pooled.

Balancing charges arise in the usual way, and a balancing allowance is given on any unallowed expenditure if the last of the rights come to an end without subsequently being revived or on the permanent discontinuance of the trade.

Although a balancing charge can never exceed the allowances given, there are specific provisions to charge a capital profit on patent rights as income rather than as a capital gain. The profit is not dealt with as part of the business profits but is charged to income tax separately over six years in equal instalments, commencing with the tax year in which it is received, unless the taxpayer elects to have the whole sum charged in the year of receipt.

Patents allowances granted to non-traders can only be set against income from the patent rights and not against any other income.

Know-how (CAA 2001, ss 452–463; CTA 2009 ss 908–910; ITTOIA 2005, ss 583–586)

[22.58] 'Know-how' is defined as any industrial information or techniques which are likely to assist in a manufacturing process, or the working of a mine, or the carrying out of agricultural, forestry or fishing operations. Revenue expenditure on creating know-how related to a trade is allowable as a business expense (and qualifies for the research and development reliefs — see **29.38** to **29.41**).

For companies, know-how is dealt with in respect of expenditure incurred on or after 1 April 2002 under the 'Intangible assets' provisions outlined at **20.30** onwards. In respect of company expenditure before that date, and expenditure by individuals, the treatment is as follows.

Capital expenditure on the acquisition of know-how for use in a trade qualifies for an annual writing-down allowance of 25% on the reducing balance method. Any additional expenditure is added to the unrelieved balance and any sale proceeds are deducted from it before calculating the writing-down allowance. If the sale proceeds exceed the tax written-down value, a balancing charge is made and this is not restricted to the allowances given, so that the balancing charge will include any excess of the proceeds over the original cost.

If know-how is sold as part of a business, the payment is regarded as being for goodwill and thus dealt with under the capital gains rules, unless both seller and buyer elect within two years of the disposal for it to be treated as a sale of know-how.

If the trade ceases during the writing-down period but the know-how is not sold, relief for the unallowed expenditure is given at the time of cessation by way of a balancing allowance.

Research and development (CAA 2001, ss 437–451; ITA 2007, s 1006; CTA 2009 ss 1039–1142; CTA 2010, s 1138)

[22.59] The term 'research and development' has been substituted for the earlier term 'scientific research' in the capital allowances legislation. Subject to any express provisions to the contrary, research and development means activities that would be treated as such in accordance with generally accepted accounting practice. Detailed guidelines are published by the Department of Trade and Industry.

Capital allowances are available at 100% on capital expenditure on research and development. The allowance need not be claimed in full. Expenditure on land and dwelling houses does not generally qualify for relief. On disposal, a balancing charge is made equal to the amount by which the disposal value (i.e. sale proceeds, compensation for destruction etc.) exceeds the allowance given, or the allowance claimed if less. If there is a capital profit it is dealt with under the capital gains rules.

If the sale takes place in the same chargeable period as that in which the expenditure is incurred, then if the proceeds are less than the expenditure the allowance is equal to the shortfall, and if the proceeds exceed the expenditure no allowance is given and the excess is dealt with under the capital gains rules.

Revenue expenditure on research and development is allowed in full as a business expense, as are certain amounts paid to research and development associations etc. Special reliefs apply to revenue expenditure on research and development by companies (see **29.39** and **29.40**).

Mineral extraction (CAA 2001, ss 394–436)

[22.60] Expenditure on mineral extraction qualifies for writing-down allowances on a reducing balance basis at the following rates:

	Rate
Acquisition of a mineral asset (mineral deposits, land comprising mineral deposits, etc.)	10%
Other qualifying expenditure	25%

A balancing charge is made if sales proceeds exceed tax written-down value. A balancing allowance is given in the chargeable period when the mineral extraction trade ceases, or when particular mineral deposits cease to be worked, and in the case of pre-trading expenditure, when trading commences or exploration is abandoned before then.

Tax points

[22.61] Note the following. The rates referred to are those applying for 2010/11. However, see **22.1** regarding proposed reductions in the rate of allowances and in the annual investment allowance from April 2012:

- HMRC guidance indicates that if a trader incurs capital expenditure in excess of £100,000 he may allocate the new 100% annual investment allowance between different types of expenditure as he sees fit. For example, he may allocate it first against expenditure on integral features that would otherwise qualify for the lower 'special rate' of 10%.
- A specific claim for capital allowances must be made by individuals, partnerships and companies, so it is important to ensure that the appropriate entries are made on the tax return.
- If claiming the maximum capital allowances on plant and machinery means wasting personal allowances, a trader can reduce his capital allowances claim, or not claim allowances at all — see **22.16**. He will then get writing-down allowances on an increased amount in future years.
- Both individuals and companies can revise capital allowances claims within the period allowed for making returns or amendments to returns, but see **22.13** regarding the inability to change the choice of allowances claimed in closed years.
- Companies will benefit by not taking allowances where they want to leave profits high enough to take advantage of reliefs which are only available in the current period, such as group relief for losses or double tax relief. The amount on which writing-down allowances will be available in later years is increased accordingly, except in relation to industrial buildings allowances, which will be withdrawn completely by April 2011. However see **22.18** regarding the restriction on the transfer of entitlement to plant and machinery allowances in certain circumstances.
- Allowances available on capital expenditure incurred on commencing trading as a sole trader or in partnership may contribute to a trading loss, which may be carried back against the income of earlier years (see **CHAPTER 25**).
- Whereas only a maximum 20% writing-down allowance is available on purchased cars (and only 10% in some cases), if a car is leased instead, the whole of the leasing charge can be set against profit, subject to disallowance of any private element and the restriction on the allowable hire charge where applicable— see **20.17**.

- When a group of assets, such as goodwill, plant and machinery and trade premises are bought or sold, some will be subject to capital allowances at different rates and some will not qualify for allowances at all, with the tax treatment of goodwill depending upon the status of the buyer and seller (see **20.30** onwards). It is essential that the price apportionment is realistic and is agreed with the other party at the time of purchase or sale in order to avoid complications when tax returns are submitted. See also **22.40** for the special provisions relating to fixtures.

- If there is doubt as to whether a contract for the purchase of plant or machinery is a hire-purchase contract or a leasing contract, it is advisable to check with the finance company as to the nature of the payments to them to ensure the correct treatment in accounts/tax computations.

- Writing-down allowances at 20% on the reducing balance method will write off about 87% of the expenditure in nine years. The option to keep short-life assets out of the plant and machinery main pool enables a trader to shorten this time to five years or less if the assets are sold or scrapped within that period.

- For companies, expenditure on patents and know-how from 1 April 2002 is dealt with under the 'Intangible assets' rules (see **20.30** onwards) rather than by way of capital allowances. In general the cost will be written off over the economic life of the assets, which will not normally be as generous as the capital allowances regime.

- If a trader takes over a business from someone with whom he is connected, the election to continue the predecessor's capital allowances computation has to be made within two years after the change (see **22.18**).

- Following the announcement of the withdrawal of industrial buildings allowances from April 2011, a trader should make sure he maximises his allowances claims for plant and machinery within an industrial building.

- If a trader wants to invest in an enterprise zone building but the cost is too high, he can participate on a co-ownership basis or through an enterprise zone property trust.

- The allowances for buildings in enterprise zones are available for any commercial buildings and not just industrial buildings — see **22.52**.

- Capital allowances for hotels may in appropriate circumstances be claimed for construction expenditure on holiday parks and caravan parks. It is essential to look at all the required conditions carefully to ensure that the particular buildings and services offered meet the requirements of the legislation. If the park qualifies, writing down allowances at 4% per annum will be available as indicated in **22.51** (but only until their withdrawal in April 2011).

23

Partnerships

Nature of partnership

[23.1] Partnership is defined in the Partnership Act 1890 as 'the relation which subsists between persons carrying on a business in common with a view of profit'. An ordinary partnership is not a separate legal entity except in Scotland. A limited liability partnership, however, is a corporate body with a separate legal personality and limits the liability of the partners for the firm's debts (see **23.27**). In the Tax Acts persons carrying on a trade in partnership are referred to collectively as a 'firm'.

Self assessment (ITTOIA 2005, ss 846–863; TCGA 1992, s 59)

[23.2] A partnership is required to send in a partnership tax return and the individual partners must show their partnership income and gains in their personal returns (see **23.5** to **23.10**).

Partners are separately liable for their own tax on all sources of income and HMRC cannot proceed against other partners if a partner fails to pay. Partners would, however, be affected by the irresponsible conduct of their fellow partners which caused partnership profits to be understated, in that they would be liable for tax on any consequent increase in their profit shares even though the normal time limit for an HMRC challenge to their self-assessments had expired (see **9.35**).

Although partners do not have joint liability for tax on the partnership trading profits, partnership profits still have to be agreed globally, no partner being able to agree an adjustment to his share of profits independently of the others. It is only the liability for the tax that is separated.

Sharing profits and losses

[23.3] The trading profits of the accounting period, as adjusted for tax purposes, are divided between the partners according to the sharing arrangements in the period. Each partner's share of the profit is then treated as arising to him individually, and the basis period rules (see **21.2**) for opening and closing years and for overlap relief depend on when he joins and leaves the firm (see Examples 1 and 2). Losses are similarly shared on an accounting period basis and treated as arising to the partners individually, loss relief claims being made accordingly.

Example 1

A, B and C, who have been in business for many years, shared profits equally in the year ended 30 November 2009. From 1 December 2009 they amended the profit-sharing ratio to 2:1:1.

The profits for tax purposes will be shared in the same way as the accounts profits, the profit of the year to 30 November 2009 (taxable in 2009/10) being shared equally and that of the year to 30 November 2010 (taxable in 2010/11) being shared 2:1:1.

Example 2

D and E commenced in partnership on 1 January 2008, making up accounts annually to 31 December and sharing profits equally. F joined them as an equal partner on 1 July 2009 and E left the partnership on 28 February 2010. Profits and their division between the partners for the first three years are as follows:

Year ended	Prof-its	D	E	F
	£	£	£	£
31.12.08	40,000	20,000	20,000	
31.12.09	60,000	25,000	25,000	10,000
31.12.10	90,000	42,500	5,000	42,500

Total profits for period	87,500	50,000	52,500

Assessments and overlap profits available for relief are:

	D £	E £	F £
2007/08			
1.1.08 – 5.4.08	5,000	5,000	
2008/09			
1.1.08 – 31.12.08	20,000	20,000	
Overlap profits	(5,000)	(5,000)	
2009/10			
1.1.09 – 31.12.09	25,000		
1.1.09 – 28.2.10 (25,000 + 5,000)		30,000	
Less overlap relief		(5,000)	
		25,000	
1.7.09 – 5.4.10:			
To 31.12.09	10,000		
To 5.4.10 $^3/_{12}$ × £42,500	10,625		20,625
2010/11			
1.1.10 – 31.12.10	42,500		42,500
Overlap profits			(10,625)
Profits assessed over 4 tax years and overlap profits available for relief			
Total assessable profits	92,500	50,000	63,125
Overlap profits	(5,000)	—	(10,625)
Tax adjusted accounts profits	87,500	50,000	52,500

A change in partners is not regarded as a cessation of the partnership unless none of the old partners continues after the change.

Non-trading income

[23.4] Partnership non-trading income is shared for tax purposes according to the sharing arrangements in the accounting period. If the income is received net of tax (or, in the case of dividends, accompanied by a tax credit), the partners' shares for the relevant accounting periods are then allocated to the appropriate tax year, those amounts being shown in the partnership tax return (see **23.5**) and each partner shows his income for the tax year in his personal tax return. If the income is untaxed income, it is treated as if it arose from a separate trade that commenced when the partner joined the firm and taxed according to the same periods as the trading income, so that normally the taxable amount for each partner will be his profit share in the accounting year ending in the tax year. There may be overlap relief on commencement and possibly on a change of accounting date. The overlap relief for non-trading income will be allowed to the extent that more than twelve months' income would otherwise be charged in one year as a result of a change of accounting date, and otherwise in the tax year in which a partner ceases to be a partner (even if the source of income ceased earlier). The deduction will be given against the untaxed non-trading income of the relevant tax year. If it exceeds that untaxed income it will be relieved against other income of that tax year.

Self-assessment tax returns (TMA 1970, ss 12AA–12AE, 28B, 30B, 31, Sch 1AB)

[23.5] A partnership tax return, form SA 800, must be sent to HMRC each year, incorporating a statement showing the name, address and tax reference of each partner, and each partner's share of profits, losses, taxed interest and any tax deducted from income. There is a short version of the partnership statement for partnerships with only trading profits and taxed interest (or alternative finance receipts) and a full version for partnerships with other types of income and/or capital gains. HMRC provide guidance notes with the return.

[23.6] Standardised accounts information must normally be shown in the partnership return by completing the relevant boxes. Where turnover is below £68,000 (previously £30,000), however, only the turnover, expenses (including capital allowances) and net profit needs to be shown. If turnover is above £15 million, accounts and computations must be submitted but only certain boxes need to be completed. Otherwise, accounts need not be sent in unless HMRC ask for them, although it is advisable to submit them to make sure HMRC have full information (see **9.16**).

The return includes details of income other than from the trade and of disposals of partnership chargeable assets. The details provided normally relate to the accounting year ended in the tax year. Details of *taxed* income, partnership charges, such as an annuity to a retired partner (see **23.16**), and disposals of chargeable assets are, however, shown for the tax year itself rather than for the accounting year ended in the tax year, so that the partners will have the information they need to complete their own returns. HMRC's notes on partnership savings, investment and other income states that the taxed income shown in the accounts of the relevant accounting periods should be apportioned to arrive at the figures for the tax year. The return will not include calculations of tax payable, because these will be in each partner's separate return.

[23.7] The partnership return must presently be submitted by the 31 January following the tax year if the return is filed online, i.e. by 31 January 2011 for 2009/10. However, the normal filing date for paper returns is now 31 October after the end of the tax year, i.e. 31 October 2010 for the 2009/10 return. Different dates apply to partnerships with corporate partners or if the notice requiring the partnership to make the return is given after 31 July 2010. Details are given in the guidance notes.

There are automatic penalties for late returns, chargeable on the partners rather than the partnership. There is an initial automatic penalty of £100 and further penalties for continued delay. See **9.43** for the new regime which will be implemented in due course. The provisions for amending returns and for HMRC enquiries into them are the same as for individual returns (see **9.4** and **9.31** to **9.32**). If HMRC enquire into a partnership return, this automatically means that the enquiry extends to partners' personal returns, since the personal returns must reflect any changes to the partnership return. An enquiry into a personal return relating to non-partnership matters does not affect the other partners.

[23.8] Before 1 April 2010 error or mistake relief could be claimed where there was an error or mistake in a partnership statement. From 1 April 2010 error or mistake relief claims can no longer be made. They are replaced by overpayment relief claims which may be made no later than four years after the end of the tax year to which the claim relates. See HMRC Self Assessment Claims Manual SACM12000 and **CHAPTER 9**.

[23.9] Each partner's personal return will include his share of the partnership income and charges as shown in the partnership statement, and capital gains on his share of partnership assets. Any expenses paid personally by partners and capital allowances on partners' own cars must be included in the *partnership* return. They cannot be separately claimed in the personal return, where a corresponding adjustment should be made, in the partnership pages, to the partnership net profit figure with a note being made in the 'any other information' section.

[23.10] Class 4 national insurance contributions are included in a partner's personal return. The partnership pages include provision for a partner to indicate that he is excepted from contributions or that contributions have been deferred. Where deferment applies, Class 4 contributions remain payable at 1% on the excess of the total profits over the specified lower limit, £5,715 for 2010/11. Contributions at the 1% rate will therefore be included in returns. However, see **CHAPTER 24** regarding proposed changes to Class 4 NIC rates and thresholds from 6 April 2011.

Work in progress and changes in accounting practice (ITTOIA 2005, ss 25–27, 227–240; FA 2006, s 102 and Sch 15)

[23.11] HMRC used to accept that work in progress did not need to be included in the accounts of established professional practices. If it was not included, then in order to comply with a requirement for the accounting basis to show a 'true and fair view', work in progress had to be brought in and treated as income arising on the first day of the first accounting period beginning *after* 6 April 1999. Tax was payable on the amount of the adjustment, known as the 'catching-up charge', over a maximum of ten years, normally starting in 1999/00, but exceptionally in 2000/01. The detailed rules are in earlier editions of this book. The catching-up charge is limited to $1/_{10}$th of the taxable profit before deducting capital allowances in the first nine years, with the balance taxable in the tenth year. The charge is made on partners according to their profit shares in the accounting year before the anniversary of the date on which work in progress was brought in. This means that partners leaving the partnership during the ten-year period will escape tax and partners joining will pay tax on part of the charge, adjustments to avoid the obvious inequity normally being made between partners within the arrangements for admission and departure.

If the business ceases, the charge continues for the remainder of the ten year period with the subsequent annual charges split between the former partners according to the profit sharing arrangements of the period prior to the cessation.

An election may be made to pay tax on all or part of the charge earlier, for example if there are allowable losses which could be set off, but it must be made by all who were partners in the relevant twelve-month period, unless the partnership has ceased, in which case it is made by each former partner separately.

The amount charged to tax counts as earnings for the purposes of calculating personal pension contributions. It does not, however, attract Class 4 national insurance contributions.

Similar problems arose following a change of accounting practice for periods ending on or after 22 June 2005 in relation to revenue recognition in service contracts — in particular, concerning the stage at which completed unbilled work needs to be taken into account. In this case there are provisions for spreading forward the tax charge arising for three years, or sometimes longer (see **20.20** and **20.21**).

The accounting aspects of work in progress are particularly important in the interests of consistency and fairness between the parties when firms merge, often with resulting tax consequences.

This whole area is extremely complex and professional advice is essential.

Introducing funds to a partnership (ITA 2007, ss 383, 398–399, 406)

[23.12] If a partner who is neither a partner in an investment LLP (see **23.27**) nor a limited partner (see **23.34**) borrows to introduce funds to a partnership, either as capital or on loan, interest on the borrowing is allowable as a deduction from his total income at his top tax rate (see **2.14**). If, however, a partner then withdraws all or part of his capital, the introduced funds will be treated as repaid up to the amount of the withdrawal, restricting or eliminating the amount on which interest relief is available whether or not any part of the personal loan has been repaid. This provision does not apply if the partner withdraws his capital *before* introducing new funds. The partnership would, however, need to be able to bridge the gap between the withdrawal of the existing funds and the introduction of the new. See **20.16**.

If borrowings are made by the partnership itself, the interest is allowed as a business expense except to the extent that the borrowing enables a partner to overdraw his personal account.

Consultancy

[23.13] An outgoing partner may perform consultancy services for the partnership. He is taxed on the income either as employment income, if he is an employee of the partnership, or as trading or professional income, if the payments to him are in his capacity of self-employed consultant (see **19.2**). The payments are an allowable deduction in calculating the taxable profits of the partnership so long as they satisfy the 'wholly and exclusively' rule (see **CHAPTER 20**).

Trading losses (ITA 2007, Pt 4; FA 2009, s 23 and Sch 6; FA 2010, s 24 and Sch 3)

[23.14] CHAPTER 25 deals with the calculation of the available loss reliefs and ways in which relief may be given. Relief for partnership trading losses may be claimed by each partner quite independently of the others. Thus one partner may decide to carry forward his share of the loss, another to set his against other income of the same tax year, another to set it against any income of the previous tax year, another to carry back against the income of the previous three tax years in the early years of his being a partner, and so on.

The carry-back loss rules for the first four years of a new trade only apply to a new partner, not to the continuing partners. There is an anti-avoidance provision blocking carry-back claims by a new partner if he is joining his spouse or civil partner in a continuing business.

A temporary extension of the loss carry back provisions means broadly that continuing partners may carry back a limited amount of loss incurred in 2008/09 and 2009/10 to set against trade profits of the previous three years.

There are special anti-avoidance provisions in relation to partnership losses — see **25.13**.

Partnership assets (TCGA 1992, ss 59, 286; HMRC Statements of Practice D12 (10/2002), 1/79 and 1/89)

[23.15] When partners join or leave a partnership, this usually involves a change in the persons who are entitled to share in the partnership assets. There is no capital gains tax (CGT) consequence if an incoming partner introduces cash which is credited to his capital account. Nor is there normally any CGT consequence when an outgoing partner withdraws his capital account. In the first instance, an incoming partner is paying in a sum which remains to his credit in his capital account, whilst in the second instance, an outgoing partner is only withdrawing what belongs to him.

If, however, before an outgoing partner withdraws his capital account, that capital account has been credited with a surplus on revaluation of partnership assets (e.g. premises or goodwill), his leaving the partnership crystallises a chargeable gain in respect of the excess on revaluation, and whether or not the capital is withdrawn or left on loan to the partnership, there is a charge to CGT.

This charge will arise not only when a person ceases to be a partner, but whenever a partner's capital account includes a revaluation of chargeable assets and his entitlement to share in the assets is reduced. He is treated as having disposed of a proportion of the chargeable assets equivalent to the drop in his entitlement. The change will usually correspond with the change in the profit-sharing ratio, except where income and capital profits are shared differently, when the capital ratio will apply.

A payment by an incoming partner to the existing partners for a share in the chargeable assets such as goodwill or premises constitutes a disposal by the existing partners for CGT, and a cost for CGT to the incoming partner. The same applies where there is a payment, whether in cash or through an accounting adjustment, on a variation of profit-sharing arrangements without a change in partners. It makes no difference whether the amount is left in the partnership (by a credit to the capital account of those disposing) or is withdrawn by them, or indeed is dealt with outside the partnership itself. The test is whether a partner receives consideration for reducing his share in the partnership. Conversely, if he does not receive consideration, whilst there is still a disposal in the sense that his partnership share is less than it was, then, unless the partners have a family connection, the market value of the assets is not substituted for the purpose of calculating and charging the gain that could have been made, and thus no chargeable gain arises.

Example 3

X and Y are in partnership. Z is admitted as a partner in July 2010, sharing equally in both capital and income. He introduces £45,000 as capital which

---

is credited to his capital account. The £45,000 is neither a CGT base cost for Z nor a disposal by X and Y. The partnership assets include premises worth £180,000, which cost £63,000 when acquired in 1990.

Consider the following alternatives:

(**1**) Before Z's admission, X and Y revalue the premises up to £180,000 by crediting each of their capital accounts with £58,500.

On Z's admission they each make a chargeable gain of:

		£
Value of premises reflected in their capital account (½ each)		90,000
Share of premises retained after Z's admission ($^1/_3$ each)		60,000
Disposal proceeds		30,000
Less cost:		
Cost was ½ each × £63,000	31,500	
Cost is now $^1/_3$ each × £63,000	21,000	
Cost of part disposed of		10,500
Gain		£19,500

The £19,500 gain is the $^1/_3$rd of the increase in value of £58,500 which has been realised by the reduction in the partnership share from $^3/_6$ths to $^2/_6$ths. The other $^2/_3$rds which remains unrealised is not charged to tax until realisation.

The cost of Z's share in the premises is £60,000 ($^1/_3$ × £180,000), equivalent to the disposal proceeds of X and Y.

(**2**) The premises are not revalued on the admission of Z.

There is then no deemed gain by X and Y, and the cost for CGT purposes for each of X and Y is $^1/_3$ × £63,000 = £21,000. Z's cost will be £21,000.

(**3**) Z privately pays £60,000 (£30,000 each) to X and Y, for a $^1/_3$rd share in the partnership premises.

X and Y are treated as receiving £30,000 each as in (1).

The capital gains cost for future disposals in the case of (1) and (3) is:

	X	Y	Z
	£	£	£
Original cost	31,500	31,500	—
On introduction of Z	(10,500)	(10,500)	21,000
Gains on which X and Y are assessable			39,000
	21,000	21,000	60,000

Annuities to outgoing partners (HMRC Statements of Practice D12 (10/2002) and 1/79)

[23.16] An outgoing partner may be paid an annuity by the continuing partners when he retires. He will not be charged to CGT on the capitalised value of the annuity so long as it is regarded as reasonable recognition for past services to the partnership. For this purpose, the average of the partner's best three years' assessable profit shares out of the last seven is calculated and the annuity is considered reasonable if it does not exceed the fraction of that average amount obtained from the following table:

Years of service	Fraction
1–5	1/60 per year
6	8/60
7	16/60
8	24/60
9	32/60
10	2/3

The paying partners can deduct their share of the annuity in calculating their taxable income. They deduct basic rate income tax when making the payment and claim relief at the higher rate where appropriate by an adjustment in their personal tax returns. The annuity forms part of the recipient's taxable income. Since it is received net of basic rate tax, the recipient may have further tax to pay or tax to reclaim depending on his tax position.

An annuity paid by the continuing partners must be distinguished from a sum paid by them to an insurance company with which to purchase an annuity for the outgoing partner. The cost of such annuity counts as proceeds of the disposal of the outgoing partner's share.

Capital gains tax reliefs

Replacement of business assets (TCGA 1992, ss 152–157)

[23.17] Roll-over relief for the replacement of business assets (see **29.11** onwards) is available where an asset owned personally by a partner and used in the partnership is disposed of and replaced. This is not affected by the payment of rent by the partnership.

Partner acquiring asset from the partnership (Statement of Practice D12 (10/2002))

[23.18] When a partner acquires an asset from the partnership, he is not regarded as disposing of his fractional share in it.

Death of a partner

[23.19] Where a partner dies in service:

(a)   any gains arising on the disposal of his share in partnership assets by reason of the death are exempt from CGT, like gains on any other chargeable asset held at death;

(b)   the annuity dealt with in **23.16** may be paid to his spouse, civil partner or dependants.

Inheritance tax

[23.20] Inheritance tax is examined in CHAPTER 5. The amount of a deceased partner's capital account, plus his share of any increase in the value of partnership assets, qualifies for the 100% business property relief unless the surviving partners are obliged to acquire his partnership share, in which case it is regarded as an entitlement under a contract for sale and not therefore eligible for relief. Relief is not lost where there is an option, as opposed to an obligation, for the share to be acquired by the surviving partners.

The amount on which the 100% relief is available may be restricted if the partnership assets include any not required for the trade (for example excessive cash balances). The rate of business property relief for assets owned personally and used by the partnership is 50%.

Although the option to pay tax by ten annual instalments applies to the transfer of a partnership share, the instalment option is irrelevant for such transfers where the 100% relief is fully available. The instalment option is still relevant for transfers of land owned by an individual partner and used in the business, the rate of business property relief for such land being 50%. Interest is, however, charged on the full amount of tax outstanding rather than just on overdue instalments.

[23.21] A gift of an interest in a partnership, including the whole or part of the partner's capital account, will qualify for business property relief so long as it is made whilst the donor is a partner and the partnership assets all qualify for relief because of their use in the trade. A gift of the balance on the capital account after ceasing to be a partner will not qualify for business property relief since the amount will have become a partnership creditor rather than part of the business capital.

Value added tax

[23.22] HMRC need to be notified of a change of partner within 30 days, but not of a change in profit-sharing arrangements. The registration number will normally continue. A retiring partner remains liable for VAT due from the partnership until the date on which HMRC are notified of his retirement. See **23.31** re limited liability partnerships and CHAPTER 7 regarding VAT generally.

National insurance

[23.23] See **24.9** for the national insurance position of partners generally and **23.33** regarding sleeping partners.

Stamp duty and stamp duty land tax

[23.24] There is no stamp duty on a partnership agreement, nor does stamp duty normally apply on the document effecting the division of assets when a partnership is dissolved.

The treatment of transfers of interests in a partnership for stamp duty and stamp duty land tax is dealt with in **6.22** and **6.23**. Stamp duty does not arise where an incoming partner merely introduces capital to his own capital or current account. See **23.29** re limited liability partnerships. See **45.25** re anti-avoidance provisions.

Partnerships of spouses and civil partners (ITTOIA 2005, ss 622–627)

[23.25] Many married couples or civil partners form business partnerships because of the practical and commercial advantages such a partnership can bring. The effect on their respective tax and national insurance positions will be an important factor.

The national insurance cost of employing a spouse or civil partner is usually greater than if the spouse/civil partner were a partner. The tax advantages of being a business partner must be weighed against a partner's legal liability, which includes the possibility of being made bankrupt if the partnership cannot pay its debts.

Taking a spouse or civil partner into a business partnership may be regarded as an appropriate way of maximising the benefit of personal reliefs and basic rate bands, but the partnership must be genuine, with the spouse's/civil partner's share being appropriate to his or her contribution to the business, otherwise there is the risk of the partnership arrangement being treated under the provisions of ITTOIA 2005, ss 625 and 626 as a settlement, in which case the income would remain that of the other spouse/civil partner for tax purposes.

HMRC have contended in recent years that certain gifts between spouses were caught by the settlements legislation and were not effective for tax purposes. In July 2007 the House of Lords decided the 'Arctic Systems' case in favour of the taxpayer, a director and shareholder in a family company, on the basis that while there was a settlement an exemption for outright gifts between spouses applied. The Government subsequently consulted on proposed legislation to counter 'income shifting' but announced in the 2008 pre–budget report that, given the 'economic challenges' prevailing at the time, it would instead keep the matter under review (see **12.10** and **18.7**). This is a difficult area and there is a good deal of uncertainty. Those who feel they may be affected should consider taking professional advice.

Corporate partners (CTA 2009, ss 486A–486E, Pt 17)

[23.26] A company may be a partner with individuals. In this case the profit share of the company for the relevant accounting period is liable to corporation tax, whilst the share applicable to the partners who are individuals is charged to income tax. There are, however, differences in the way profits are calculated for companies and individuals, so separate corporation tax and income tax calculations must be made.

Where a money debt is owed to or by the partnership, the corporate partner computes loan relationship debits and credits on its share, and brings the result into its corporation tax computation.

Anti-avoidance provisions were introduced from 17 March 2004 and applied to amounts received by corporate partners. These were aimed at schemes where income is allocated to non-UK partners and capital to UK company partners. A UK company partner was charged to corporation tax on any amount that it realises as capital where the capital represents partnership profits on which the company would have been charged to corporation tax if the partnership profits had been allocated in proportion to shares of partnership capital. There were provisions to ensure that any amounts chargeable under these provisions will not also be taxed as capital gains. These provisions were replaced from 22 April 2009 by the disguised interest provisions which are part of numerous loan relationship anti-avoidance provisions not dealt with in this book.

Limited liability partnerships (ITA 2007, ss 107–109, 399, 1004; ITTOIA 2005, s 863; TCGA 1992, ss 59A, 156A, 169A; IHTA 1984, s 267A; FA 2003, s 65; SSCBA 1992, s 15; CTA 2009, s 1273; CTA 2010, ss 55–61; SP D12 (10/2002))

[23.27] Partners may register as a 'limited liability partnership' (LLP) under the Limited Liability Partnerships Act 2000. An LLP is a corporate entity and the liability of the partners is limited to the capital contributed, although partners in LLPs are liable in the same way as company directors for fraudulent trading and there are provisions to protect creditors. LLPs have to file annual accounts and an annual return with Companies House. An LLP partner may be either a company or an individual. Corporate partners are liable to corporation tax on their profit shares, with individual partners being generally treated for tax and national insurance purposes in the same way as partners in any other partnership. The actions of an LLP are regarded for tax purposes as those of its members. The transfer of an existing partnership to an

LLP will normally be on a tax neutral basis. If the LLP goes into formal liquidation, however, it is treated as a company rather than a partnership for capital gains purposes. Any gains held over by partners under the business assets or gifts roll-over provisions will be treated as realised by those partners at the start of the formal liquidation and will be chargeable on them accordingly.

[23.28] Certain reliefs for a trade loss incurred by a partner in an LLP cannot exceed the amount of the partner's contribution to the firm. There are anti-avoidance provisions in relation to partnership losses, which apply both to ordinary partnerships and LLPs — see **25.13**.

[23.29] Stamp duty or stamp duty land tax is not charged on property transferred to an LLP within one year after its incorporation if the partners' shares remain unchanged. The exemptions do not strictly apply if partners join or leave at the time the LLP is formed, but a charge can be avoided if the change takes place immediately before or after incorporation (providing evidence is available to that effect). See **6.22** and **6.23** for the general stamp duty/stamp duty land tax provisions for partnerships, which apply equally to LLPs.

[23.30] Inheritance tax business and agricultural property reliefs are available for shares in appropriate partnership assets (see **CHAPTER 5**).

[23.31] For VAT purposes, an LLP will be registered as a separate entity. While there will be a VAT liability on the transfer of assets if an existing partnership becomes an LLP, this will be subject to the rules for transfers of going concerns (see **7.41**). The partnership's VAT number may be transferred to the LLP.

Miscellaneous

[23.32] A *salaried partner* must be distinguished from a partner who is allocated a salary as part of the profit-sharing arrangement. Senior employees are often described as partners in professional firms whilst retaining their salaried employee status. They remain liable to income tax as employees, receiving a salary for the duties of their employment, with national insurance being payable appropriately.

There is a further distinction where a partner is on a fixed share of profit, not because he is a salaried partner but his profit share being certain rather than depending on results. So long as the circumstances do not imply an employment, such a partner pays tax and national insurance as a self-employed person.

[23.33] The profit share of a *sleeping partner* does not rank as relevant earnings and cannot, therefore, support a pension contribution higher than the £3,600 a year limit (see **17.1**). On the other hand a sleeping partner is not liable either to Class 2 or Class 4 national insurance contributions, since he is not 'gainfully employed' for Class 2 and does not have earned income for Class 4. Relief for losses incurred by non-active partners is restricted (see **25.13**).

[23.34] A partnership may include a *limited partner* under the Limited Partnership Act 1907, whose liability is limited to the amount of the partner's agreed capital contribution. The limited partner, who may be either an individual or a company, cannot take part in the management of the partnership, although he is not barred from taking part in a non-managerial capacity. If the profit share of a limited partner ranks as unearned income, it cannot be used to support a pension premium higher than the £3,600 limit available to all UK residents under 75 (see **17.1**). Certain reliefs available to a limited partner cannot exceed the amount of the partner's contribution to the firm. There are restrictions to reliefs for trading losses against income other than trading income from the partnership (see **25.6**, **26.2** and **26.12**).

[23.35] Partnership itself, and matters arising, need not be governed by *formal written agreement*. In the absence of such agreement, sometimes indeed despite it, HMRC will require other evidence of partnership, for example the name of, and operating arrangements for, bank accounts, VAT registration, names on stationery, contracts, licences, etc.

The overseas aspect of partnerships is dealt with in **CHAPTER 41**.

Anti-avoidance provisions

[23.36] See **45.13** regarding the restriction of loss relief for leasing partnerships.

See **25.13** for restrictions on partnership losses in relation to non-active partners.

See **6.5** regarding avoidance in relation to stamp duty.

There are also anti-avoidance provisions designed to prevent a company from using a partnership to transfer losses and other reliefs from one company to another person where profits or losses are sold by one partner to another.

Tax points

[23.37] Note the following:

- HMRC accept that the overhead content of work in progress is likely to be minimal for professional firms of up to four partners and can normally be ignored in calculating the work in progress figure. Work in progress must, however, be distinguished from unbilled revenue (see **20.20**).
- Since, in the case of spreading, the work in progress and change of accounting practice catching-up charges are allocated to partners by reference to their profit shares in the ensuing years, financial arrangements on the retirement and admission of partners will have to seek to match the tax burden with the benefit.
- A merger of two or more firms is strictly a cessation of each firm and the commencement of one new firm. The converse applies where one firm splits into two or more new firms. In both cases it may not be clear

whether the rules for partnership changes apply. HMRC's views are explained in Statement of Practice SP 9/86. This area is one where professional advice and consultation with HMRC is essential.

- Calculate annuities to retiring partners within the allowable CGT limits (see **4.21**), leaving them taxable only as income in the hands of the recipient and allowable for income tax to the payers. An inflation-linked increase to an annuity which is initially within the allowable limits does not affect the capital gains exemption.

- A pension payment by continuing partners to a retired partner, whilst assessable as income on the recipient, is not regarded by HMRC as deductible in calculating the partnership taxable profits, since it is regarded as a payment to the outgoing partner to acquire his partnership share. The annuity arrangements in the previous tax point are a more tax-efficient way of providing income to a retired partner.

- Under self-assessment, partners are responsible for paying their own tax, and the half-yearly instalments due on 31 January and 31 July are on account of a partner's total income tax liability, not just his partnership share — see **9.7** to **9.10**. In some circumstances it is prudent for partnerships to retain part of a partner's profit to meet the tax liability on partnership income, releasing it to HMRC as part of each partner's personal liability on the due dates. Many partnerships find it best to adopt this procedure.

- If there is a choice of borrowing to buy a home and borrowing to introduce funds to a partnership (other than as a limited partner or partner in an investment LLP), interest on the partnership borrowing will save tax at the highest rate, whereas that on the home loan will not save tax at all.

- If one spouse or civil partner takes the other into a business partnership as an active partner, it should not be forgotten that the new partner has to pay Class 2 national insurance contributions. Penalties apply for failure to notify liability to pay Class 2 national insurance contributions, see **9.39**.

- A capital gain may arise where partners sell partnership assets (e.g. land and buildings) to raise funds to pay out a retiring partner. Rather than pay tax on that gain, the partners will be able to deduct it from the cost of acquisition of the outgoing partner's share of any of the remaining business assets of the partnership that qualify for roll-over relief. An alternative to paying out the retiring partner's share in land and buildings might be for him to retain that share as a co-owner with his former partners. There will not have been a disposal of his share in these circumstances, since he retains what he had before, albeit it will no longer be a qualifying asset for inheritance tax business property relief.

- Income and capital profit-sharing ratios need not always be the same. Established partners can retain the right to the whole of the future increase in value of partnership premises, to the exclusion of incoming partners, by excluding the incoming partners from the capital profit-sharing ratio.

Any running expenses of those premises, including interest on borrowing, remain allowable in calculating trading profit, which is divided in the income-sharing ratio.

24

National insurance contributions for the self-employed

Background

[24.1] HMRC are responsible for national insurance contributions (NICs) and the department's National Insurance Contributions Office (NICO) handles administration and collection of contributions — see www.hmrc.gov.uk/nic. However, the Department for Work and Pensions administers state benefits including contributory benefits. The main legislation relating to NICs is found in the Social Security Contributions and Benefits Act 1992 (SSCBA 1992) and statutory instruments.

A self-employed person over the age of 16 must, unless specifically exempted, pay both Class 2 and Class 4 contributions. Class 2 contributions are payable at a flat weekly rate and entitle the contributor to short-term employment and support allowance, maternity allowance, state pension and bereavement benefits. Class 4 contributions are payable on all business profits in excess of a specified limit that are chargeable to income tax as trading income (see **2.7** and **CHAPTERS 18** to **29**). They carry no entitlement to benefits of any kind.

National insurance credits are awarded in some circumstances in order to maintain or enhance a person's contribution or earnings record for the purpose of state benefits (see **13.5**).

The Government has been considering the alignment of the income tax and NIC systems, and is introducing significant changes to state pension provision including the new National Employment Savings Trust (NEST, formerly called the National Pension Savings Scheme), which is due to be launched in 2012. These changes will mainly affect employees, but the self-employed and non-workers will be able to participate in the new scheme – see **13.4**.

HMRC conducted a consultation exercise in 2008 on the scope for improving the collection of NICs from the self employed. The intention is to align the payment dates of Class 2 contributions with those for self assessment liabilities.

See **9.39** for interest, penalties and criminal proceedings in relation to NICs.

Class 2 contributions

Payment (SSCBA 1992, s 11; SI 2001/1004)

[24.2] If a person becomes self-employed, he must notify HMRC that he is liable to pay Class 2 contributions — even if he is going to apply for deferment because he pays maximum Class 1 contributions as an employee at the main primary rate (see **24.11**). If notification is not made by 31 January following the tax year in which self-employment commenced he may be liable for a penalty (see **9.45**) unless he can show that trading profits are below the small earnings exception limit (see **24.4**).

Arrangements must also be made to pay Class 2 contributions, unless he is not liable to pay (see **24.3** and **24.4**). The weekly rate for 2010/11 is £2.40. Payment is made either by monthly direct debit or quarterly in arrear. If payment is made quarterly, HMRC will send a bill and payment is due within 28 days. Late payment of Class 2 contributions may affect entitlement to benefits, and a higher rate than the rate which applied on the due date may be payable.

Exempt persons

[24.3] Class 2 contributions are payable by 'self-employed earners', which means those who are 'gainfully employed' other than as employees. The Class 2 net is wider than Class 4, because it includes a 'business', whereas Class 4 only covers a trade, profession or vocation.

The following people are not liable to pay Class 2 contributions:

(a)   persons under 16;
(b)   persons over pensionable age. This is 65 for a man and 60 for a woman born before 6 April 1950. It is 65 for a woman born after 5 April 1955, and there is a sliding scale to determine pensionable age for women born between 6 April 1950 and 5 April 1955 (see **13.3**);
(c)   married women who chose on or before 11 May 1977 to pay reduced rate Class 1 contributions or to pay no Class 2 contributions (provided that this election has not been automatically revoked by divorce or possibly revoked by widowhood — see **13.14**);
(d)   someone with small earnings who obtains a certificate of exception or is told by NICO that a certificate is not needed (see **24.4**);
(e)   someone who, for a full week, is
        (i)   incapable of work, or
        (ii)   in legal custody or prison, or
        (iii)   receiving incapacity benefit, employment and support allowance or maternity allowance;
(f)   someone who, for any day in a particular week, receives carer's allowance or unemployability supplement; and

(g)   volunteer development workers.

In the case of (e) and (f), the exemption is applicable only to the particular week concerned.

Special rules apply to those who go to work abroad — see **41.39** to **41.43**.

Small earnings

[24.4] Class 2 contributions are not payable if earnings are small, but since the amount payable is presently only £2.40 a week, then unless there are also earnings on which Class 1 contributions are paid it is probably sensible to pay Class 2 contributions and maintain the contribution record for social security benefits, particularly the state retirement pension. The contribution record could alternatively be maintained by paying Class 3 voluntary contributions (see **13.6**), but these are now at a much higher rate than Class 2, being £12.05 a week for 2010/11.

If an application for a certificate of exception for a tax year is made it needs to be shown that:

(i)   earnings for that tax year are expected to be less than a specified limit; or

(ii)   earnings for the previous tax year were less than the limit specified for that year and circumstances have not materially altered.

In this context 'earnings' are net earnings from self employment as shown in the profit and loss account as opposed to taxable earnings, but excluding income under the New Deal scheme. If employed earnings on which Class 1 contributions have been paid are included in the accounts, these are excluded. Full details are given in the HMRC National Insurance Manual. Where an accounting period overlaps 5 April, earnings are strictly apportioned on a time basis between tax years but in considering (ii) above, it is thought that HMRC will normally take the accounts year ended in the previous tax year.

The small earnings exception limits are:

2008/09	£4,825
2009/10	£5,075
2010/11	£5,075

An application for a certificate of exception may be made on form CF10, available on HMRC's website. The exception cannot be backdated more than 13 weeks (but see below regarding refunds). A certificate issued on registration for self-employment expires at the end of that tax year, but later certificates last for three years. NICO automatically invites existing holders to apply for renewal.

If a person paid contributions but could have claimed exception, he may apply for a refund (but as already indicated, consideration should be given to the impact on the contribution record before going ahead with a claim). A refund of contributions paid for 2009/10 must be claimed before 31 January 2011.

More than one self-employment

[24.5] People who are self-employed have to pay only one weekly Class 2 contribution no matter how many self-employed occupations they may have. For the purposes of entitlement to a certificate of exception on the grounds of small earnings, self-employed earnings from all sources are added together.

Class 4 contributions

Payment (SSCBA 1992, ss 15–17 and Sch 2; SI 2001/1004)

[24.6] Class 4 contributions are payable at a main percentage rate of 8% on trading income chargeable to income tax (see **CHAPTER 19**) which fall between specified upper and lower limits, and at the additional percentage rate of 1% on profits above the upper limit. The lower and upper limits for 2009/10 and 2010/11 are:

2009/10	£5,715 and £43,875
2010/11	£5,715 and £43,875

It is proposed that from 6 April 2011 the main percentage rate will be increased to 9% and the additional percentage rate will be increased to 2%. In addition the lower profits limit will increase by £570 per year and the upper profits limit will be reduced in line with the basic rate limit to an amount that will be established after the September 2010 retail price index figure is known.

If a person has more than one self-employment, all the profits are added together when calculating the Class 4 liability.

In general, 'profits' are computed in the same way for Class 4 contributions as for income tax but certain special rules apply. For example, trading losses allowed under ITA 2007, ss 64 and 72 (see **CHAPTER 25**) against non-trading income and capital gains for tax purposes are set only against trading income for Class 4 NICs. Unused losses may be carried forward against future profits for calculating Class 4 contributions.

Class 4 contributions are collected along with income tax under self-assessment, so that the half-yearly payments on account made on 31 January and 31 July include Class 4 contributions based on the previous year's figures, with any balancing adjustment shown in the tax return and payable or repayable on the following 31 January. Provision is made in returns for the taxpayer to indicate that he is exempt from Class 4 contributions (see **24.7**), in which case no contributions are shown, or that deferment applies (see **24.11**), in which case contributions are payable at the 1% rate on all profits above the lower profits limit (but see above regarding the proposed increase in this percentage).

Exempt persons

[24.7] The following people are not liable to pay Class 4 contributions:

(a)   persons under 16 at the beginning of the tax year who hold a certificate of exception;

(b)   persons over pensionable age (see **24.3**(b)) at the beginning of the tax year;

(c)   those who are not resident in the UK for income tax purposes;

(d)   trustees and executors who are chargeable to income tax on income they receive on behalf of other people (e.g. incapacitated persons);

(e)   'sleeping partners' who supply capital and take a share of the profits but take no active part in running the business;

(f)   divers and diving supervisors working in connection with exploration and exploitation activities on the Continental shelf or in UK territorial waters;

(g)   certain self-employed earners who pay income tax on their trading income but are liable to pay Class 1 NICs on that income.

Late payment or overpayment of contributions

[24.8] The income tax rules for charging interest (see **2.29** to **2.31**) apply if Class 4 contributions are paid late and the related penalties are applied in the event of a taxpayer's careless or deliberate actions (see **9.42**). The income tax provisions for interest on overpaid tax also apply where contributions are refunded.

Partnerships

[24.9] Each active partner is liable to both Class 2 and Class 4 contributions (unless a wife is exempt from Class 2 contributions — see **24.10**), and the Class 4 profit limits apply separately to each partner's profit share.

A partner's Class 4 contributions are entered in the partner's personal return. Where a partner carries on a further trade or trades, the profits of all such businesses are considered together when calculating his overall Class 4 liability.

Married women

[24.10] Women who were married or widowed before 6 April 1977 could elect on or before 11 May 1977 not to pay full national insurance contributions. If the election has been made, Class 1 contributions as an employee are paid at a reduced rate. Class 2 self-employed contributions do not have to be paid, however, Class 4 contributions must be paid.

The right to pay no Class 2 and reduced rate Class 1 contributions is lost in some circumstances. See **13.14**.

Self-employed and employed in the same tax year

[24.11] If a person is both self-employed and an employee, he is liable to pay Class 1, 2 and 4 contributions, and if he has more than one employment is liable to Class 1 contributions in each employment. There is, however, a maximum figure above which contributions will be refunded.

Before 6 April 2003 the maximum was worked out in a straightforward way and was the same for all taxpayers. Now that contributions at 1% are chargeable on all earnings/profits above the upper earnings/profits limit (£43,875 for 2010/11), the calculation can be very complicated and has up to nine stages. Detailed guidance on the calculation of the annual maximum is available in HMRC's National Insurance Manual at NIM24030 and NIM24150. If contributions for 2010/11 exceed the maximum, a refund of the excess may be claimed from NICO so long as the excess is greater than 1/15th of a Class 1 contribution at the main 11% rate on earnings at the upper earnings limit — i.e. £5.38 for 2010/11. See **13.2** and **24.6** regarding the proposed changes in NIC rates and thresholds from 6 April 2011.

If contributions for a tax year are expected to exceed the maximum, application should be made to defer payment of contributions. Application for deferment of Class 2 and 4 contributions must be made on form CA72B. Where deferment is granted, Class 4 contributions remain payable for that tax year at 1% on all profits above the lower profits limit of £5,715 for 2010/11. Confirmation of deferment is made on form CA2703. Application for deferment of Class 1 contributions should be made on form CA72A. The employer will receive notification of deferment on form CA2700. Deferment only applies for a particular tax year. A new deferment application needs to be made where appropriate for each tax year. Guidance notes are issued with both forms CA72A and CA72B.

If a person feels he has overpaid contributions he may apply to NICO for a refund. This could happen, for example, if he has several businesses and the profits of those businesses have been totalled incorrectly in arriving at the overall Class 4 liability, or if he has paid Class 1 contributions that have not been taken into account in calculating the Class 4 liability. If the error affects tax as well as NICs, however, repayment will normally be made by adjusting the self assessment.

Tax points

[24.12] Note the following:

- Make sure to notify HMRC of any weeks for which a Class 2 contribution is not due, for example when receiving employment and support allowance, so that an adjustment can be made.
- If a person is both employed and self-employed, he should make sure he claims deferment if eligible. This is better than waiting till after the year end for a refund.

- Remember that trading losses set off against non-trading income for income tax purposes are carried forward against trading profits for Class 4 contributions purposes. There is a worksheet in the tax return guide to make the appropriate adjustment to the profits.
- Make sure to notify HMRC as soon as self-employment commences — see **9.39** regarding penalties. If a spouse or civil partner is taken into partnership a liability to Class 2 contributions, together with a potential penalty, will almost certainly arise.
- A married woman who has elected not to pay Class 2 contributions should watch the circumstances in which contributions become payable, for example following widowhood or divorce.

25

Losses of sole traders and partners

Introduction

[25.1] Losses may arise in a trade, profession or vocation carried on in the UK or abroad, or in a business of property letting. Capital losses may arise on the disposal of chargeable assets. Losses relating to rented property may normally be relieved only against rental income, and are dealt with in CHAPTER 32. Relief for losses relating to businesses controlled abroad is restricted to profits from the same source (see CHAPTER 41). Capital losses are normally set against capital gains of the same tax year, with any balance carried forward against later gains (see CHAPTER 4), although capital losses on certain unquoted shares may be set against income (see 38.22). Other aspects relating to capital losses are dealt with in context in other chapters. The remainder of this chapter deals with losses of UK trades. The rules for trading losses apply equally to professions or vocations.

Calculation of losses and reliefs available

Calculation of loss (ITA 2007, s 61)

[25.2] Losses for sole traders and partners are calculated using the same basis periods as those used for calculating profits. So a loss of the year to 31 August 2010 would be regarded as a loss of 2010/11 in the same way as a profit of that year would be taxed in 2010/11. The loss basis period could be longer than twelve months if the accounting date has been changed (see 21.7), subject to the rules mentioned below for overlapping basis periods. Furthermore, a basis period of more than twelve months would result in the loss being increased by an appropriate proportion of available overlap relief (see Example 1).

Example 1

Trader started business on 1 July 2006, making up his accounts to 30 June annually, and made profits each year until the year to 30 June 2009. He then made up a 15-month account to 30 September 2010 showing a loss. The position is as follows:

Basis periods

2006/07	1.7.06 – 5.4.07
2007/08	1.7.06 – 30.6.07 (overlap profits 9 mths to 5.4.07)
2008/09	1.7.07 – 30.6.08
2009/10	1.7.08 – 30.6.09
2010/11	1.7.09 – 30.9.10 (loss)

Relief may be claimed for the 2010/11 loss of the 15 months to 30 September 2010, augmented by overlap relief of 3/9ths of the overlap profits.

The basis period rules apply on cessation as they do in a continuing business. Any available overlap relief is taken into account in computing the result of the final accounting period. If a business that had made up accounts annually to 30 June ceased trading on 30 April 2010, making a loss in the final ten months, the loss of that ten months would be treated as a 2010/11 loss and would be increased by any available overlap relief (but see **25.9** re terminal loss claims). Where a loss would be taken into account in two successive tax years (for example, in the first trading period of a new business or on a change of accounting date), it is only taken into account in the first year. See Example 2.

Example 2

Trader starts in business on 1 August 2008 and makes a loss of £24,000 in the year to 31 July 2009 and a profit of £15,000 in the year to 31 July 2010. The assessments for 2008/09 and 2009/10 are therefore Nil.

8/12ths of the loss, i.e. £16,000, is treated as the loss of 2008/09 and 4/12ths, i.e. £8,000, as the loss of 2009/10. The profit of £15,000 is assessed in 2010/11.

Loss reliefs available

[25.3] There are various ways in which relief for trading losses may be claimed by sole traders and partners (see **23.14** for general comments on partnership losses and **25.12** and **25.13** for anti-avoidance provisions for new partners in general partnerships, limited partners and partners in limited liability partnerships). The losses may be relieved as follows:

(a) Carry forward against later profits of *same trade* (ITA 2007, s 83).

(b) Set against *general* income of tax year of loss and/or the previous tax year (ITA 2007, s 64). The claim for either year may, if the taxpayer wishes, be extended to include set-off against capital gains (ITA 2007, s 71 and TCGA 1992, s 261B).

(c) In a new trade, carry back against *general* income of previous three tax years, earliest first (ITA 2007, s 72).

(d) When a loss occurs on ceasing to trade, set against *trading* income of final tax year, then carry back against *trading* income of previous three tax years, latest first (ITA 2007, ss 89, 90).

(e) Carry back against profits of same trade of the previous three years where loss incurred in 2008/09 and 2009/10 (FA 2009, s 23, Sch 6).

Loss claims are taken into account to the maximum possible extent against the relevant income (i.e. *general* income under ITA 2007, ss 64 and 72 and *trading* income for ITA 2007, ss 83 and 89, and FA 2009, s 23, Sch 6). Since the set-off is made *before* deducting personal allowances, in many cases personal allowances will be wasted. Relief for losses under (b) and (c) above is commonly known as 'sideways relief'.

Capital allowances

[25.4] Capital allowances are treated as trading expenses, and therefore form part of the trading result. There is some flexibility, however, because the capital allowances claim can be reduced to whatever amount is required (see **22.16** and **22.61**). There are anti-avoidance provisions regarding losses arising in respect of first year allowances or the annual investment allowance (see **25.13**).

Loss carried forward (ITA 2007, s 83)

[25.5] The most straightforward way of obtaining relief for a loss is by carrying it forward to reduce later income of the same trade, so that in Example 1 the total available losses, including the overlap relief, would be carried forward to reduce trading profits of 2011/12 and later years. In Example 2 the total losses of £24,000 would eliminate the 2010/11 assessment of £15,000 leaving £9,000 still to carry forward. The set-off can only be made against profits of the *same* trade, so that a change in activity will cause relief to be denied. See **25.10** for time limits for claims.

There are obvious disadvantages in carrying forward a loss. The trade may cease, or its nature change, before the loss is fully relieved. There is also a considerable delay before the loss results in a cash saving by reducing or eliminating a tax bill.

Loss set against other income (ITA 2007, ss 64–70, 74ZA), temporary extension of carry back against trade profits (FA 2009, s 23, Sch 6) and restriction on sideways relief (FA 2010, s 24, Sch 3)

[25.6] Earlier relief may be obtained by setting off the loss against any other income of the tax year in which the loss is incurred or of the previous tax year, or, if the loss is large enough, of both tax years (subject to anti-avoidance provisions for new partners in general partnerships, limited partners and partners in limited liability partnerships — see **25.12** and **25.13**). If claims are to be made for both available years, the taxpayer must decide which claim comes first. If there are losses in successive years, and both a current year loss and a carried back loss are to be relieved in the same tax year, the earlier year's loss is set off first. If there were other sources of income, section 64 claims could be made for the 2010/11 loss in Example 1 against the income of 2010/11 and/or 2009/10. Section 64 claims could be made in Example 2 for the 2008/09 loss of £16,000 in 2008/09 and/or 2007/08, and for the 2009/10 loss of £8,000 in 2009/10 and/or 2008/09. If, however, the taxpayer claimed against 2008/09 income in respect of both the 2008/09 loss and the 2009/10 loss, the 2008/09 loss would be set off first. This assumes no claims are made under FA 2009, s 23, Sch 6 (see below). See **25.8** re the claims possible in Example 2 under section 72.

A temporary extension of the carry back of trade losses was introduced for such losses incurred in 2008/09 and 2009/10. The trade loss carry back is extended from the current one year entitlement to a period of three years with losses being carried back against later years first. The person may make a claim for relief under these provisions if one of two conditions is met. The first condition is that a claim is made under ITA 2007, s 64 for the loss. The second condition is that the total income in both the year of loss and the preceding tax year is either nil or does not include any income from which a deduction could be made under an ITA 2007, s 64 claim. The amount of trading loss that can be carried back to the preceding tax year remains unlimited. However, the deductible amount that may be carried back to the two earlier tax years is subject to a £50,000 limit for each tax year of loss and can be set against profits from the *same trade* only. Therefore, where a person makes a loss in the tax year 2008/09 and claims relief under ITA 2007, s 64 for the tax year 2007/08 (whether or not the claim is for 2007/08 only or for both 2007/08 and 2008/09) the amount of the available 2008/09 loss not relieved against general income under s 64 for 2007/08 (and 2008/09 if claimed) is deducted firstly from the profits of the trade for 2006/07 with any balance being deducted from profits of the trade for 2005/06. However, the total amount that may be deducted for 2005/06 and 2006/07 cannot exceed £50,000. Where no s 64 claim is made for relief in 2007/08 the available 2008/09 loss is deducted firstly from the profits of the trade for 2007/08 with any unrelieved amount being deducted from such profits for 2006/07 and, if relevant, 2005/06. The total amount which may be deducted for 2005/06 and 2006/07 is limited to £50,000.

Example 3

Trader makes a trade loss of £130,000 in 2009/10. He has other income in the year of £10,000.

His trade profits and other income for earlier years were:

	Trade profit	Other income
	£	£
2008/09	40,000	5,000
2007/08	30,000	5,000
2006/07	25,000	5,000

He claims relief against general income for the tax years 2009/10 and 2008/09. This reduces the loss to £75,000. He can claim a maximum of £50,000 relief against trade profits under FA 2009, Sch 6 for 2007/08 and 2006/07. This extinguishes the £30,000 trade profit in 2007/08 and reduces the 2006/07 trade profit to £5,000. The total loss utilised is £105,000 (10,000 + 40,000 + 5,000 + 30,000 + 20,000). The balance of £25,000 may be carried forward.

See **25.10** for time limits for claims.

A claim under ITA 2007, s 64 or FA 2009, s 23, Sch 6 cannot be made for losses incurred in 'hobby' trades as distinct from commercial activities. A claim is also specifically prohibited for the sixth year of a consecutive run of farming and market gardening losses, reckoned before capital allowances (ITA 2007, s 67, see **31.4**).

Anti-avoidance rules introduced in FA 2008 are designed to prevent relief against income (and, where appropriate, capital gains — see **25.7**) being obtained where an individual carries on a trade other than in partnership but in a 'non-active capacity' — see **25.15**. Further anti-avoidance provisions were introduced by FA 2010 to prevent sideways relief being given to a person for losses from a trade where the loss arises from tax avoidance arrangements. The legislation is specifically targeted at persons who enter into tax avoidance arrangements with a main purpose of obtaining a tax reduction by way of sideways relief. The restriction applies to losses arising as a result of such arrangements entered into on or after 21 October 2009. The loss may still be carried forward against future profits of the same trade.

Extending s 64 claim to capital gains (ITA 2007, s 71; TCGA 1992, s 261B)

[25.7] A section 64 claim (see **25.6**) may be extended to include set-off against capital gains, in either or both of the tax year of loss and the previous tax year. The claim against income of the year must be made first (personal allowances therefore being wasted, except where married couple's age allowance is transferred (see **2.18**)) and the loss available to set against capital gains is also reduced by any other loss relief claimed, for example under section 64 in the previous year or by carry-back under section 72 in a new business (see **25.8**). From 2004/05, the maximum amount of capital gains available to relieve the trading loss is the amount of the capital gains after deducting any capital losses of the relevant year and unrelieved capital losses brought forward from earlier years but before deducting the annual exemption. The amount available for relief is the lower of the available loss and the available amount of capital gains. The available amount is treated as an allowable capital loss of the relevant year and is therefore set off against capital gains in *priority* to brought forward capital losses. Depending on the levels of gains and losses, the claim may mean wasting all or part of the annual exemption.

Example 4

Married trader makes loss of £70,000 in year to 31 December 2010, and claims section 64 relief for 2010/11 against his other income for that year of £10,000, and against his capital gains. His capital gains of the year (net of capital losses of the year) were £65,000 on disposals made before 23 June 2010. There were no capital losses brought forward and no claim is made under FA 2009, s 23, Sch 6 for carry back of losses.

The section 64 claim against income utilises £10,000 of the loss, and wastes personal allowances (although if he is entitled to married couple's age allowance, the allowance may be transferred to his wife). The unrelieved trading loss is therefore £60,000, which is lower than the available capital gains of £65,000.

After setting off the loss of £60,000 this leaves gains of £5,000, reduced to Nil by the annual exemption which is £10,100. Therefore, £5,100 of the annual exemption is wasted.

If the claim against capital gains had not been made, there would have been an unrelieved trading loss to carry forward of £60,000 and the capital gains tax payable would be:

	£
Gains	65,000
Annual exemption	10,100
Amount chargeable to tax	54,900
Tax thereon @ 18%	£9,882

The effective rate of relief on the loss of £60,000 is therefore 16.47% rather than 18% because part of the annual exemption is wasted. If gains in 2010/11 arose on or after 23 June 2010 they could be chargeable at 28% depending on the individual's personal tax position. See **4.2** regarding the differing capital gains tax rates applying from 23 June 2010.

Where there are capital losses brought forward that already reduce gains to the exempt level, the trading loss claim would give no immediate tax saving and it would be a question of whether it would be preferable to have unrelieved trading losses carried forward or unrelieved capital losses carried forward.

New trades — carry-back of losses (ITA 2007, s 72)

[25.8] Where a loss occurs in any of the first four tax years of a new sole trade, or of a new partner's membership of a partnership, relief may be claimed against that person's general income of the three previous tax years, *earliest* first (subject to anti-avoidance provisions for new partners in general partnerships, limited partners and partners in limited liability partnerships — see **25.12** and **25.13**). A section 72 claim is a single claim and the loss must be set off to the maximum possible extent against the income of all three years. See Example 4. There is no set-off against capital gains in those previous three years. As with section 64 (see **25.6**), this carry-back claim cannot be made unless the trade is carried on commercially. Where a loss is large enough, a section 64 claim may be preceded or followed by a section 72 claim. See **25.10** for time limit for claims.

Example 5

In Example 2 at 25.2, the trader incurred losses of £16,000 and £8,000 respectively in his first and second tax years of trading, 2008/09 and 2009/10.

As an alternative to claiming relief under section 64 (or in addition to a section 64 claim, depending on the level of other income) relief could be claimed under section 72 as follows:

2008/09 loss of £16,000
Against total income of 2005/06, then 2006/07, then 2007/08.

2009/10 loss of £8,000
Against total income of 2006/07, then 2007/08, then 2008/09.

Any losses not relieved under either section 64 or section 72 would be carried forward under section 83 (see 25.5).

Because of the way losses are calculated where basis periods overlap (see Example 2 at **25.2**), choosing an accounting date early in the tax year may restrict the section 72 claims available. See Example 6.

Example 6

New business started 1 May 2008. If there are losses in the early years and accounts are made up annually to 31 March, section 72 claims will be possible in respect of losses made in the 11 months to 31 March 2009, and the years to 31 March 2010, 2011 and 2012. If accounts are made up annually to 30 April, section 72 claims will only be possible in respect of the loss of the year to 30 April 2009 (the claim being split as to 11/12ths in

---

> 2008/09 and 1/12th in 2009/10), and the years to 30 April 2010 and 2011.

Although the tax saving from section 72 claims is *calculated* by reference to the tax position of the carry-back years, repayment supplement runs from 31 January following the loss year (see **25.11**).

Loss on cessation of trade (terminal loss) (ITA 2007, ss 89, 90; CAA 2001, s 354)

[25.9] Losses towards the end of a business clearly cannot be carried forward against future profits. A claim may be made to set the loss of the last twelve months of trading (called a terminal loss) against the *trading* income (after capital allowances) of the tax year in which the business ceases, then the three tax years prior to that tax year, *latest* first. The terminal loss is calculated in two parts, splitting the last twelve months at the tax year end, i.e. at 5 April. If the *result* of either part is a profit, it is treated as nil in the calculation. Profits must, however, be taken into account in arriving at the figures for each part, as shown in Example 7. The full amount of any available overlap relief is included in the terminal loss. The tax saving flowing from carrying back the loss is calculated by reference to the tax position of the earlier years, but it is given effect in relation to the loss year, with a consequent reduction in the amount of repayment supplement payable (see **25.11**).

Where there is other income, a section 64 claim (see **25.6**) may be made in addition to (or instead of) the terminal loss claim. Unlike the terminal loss calculation, a loss of the final tax year for section 64 is on an accounting period basis, as shown in Example 6. Where both claims are made, the taxpayer may choose which claim is to be dealt with first.

Example 7

Trade ceases 30 September 2009.

Previous accounts have been to 31 December, recent results up to the cessation being:

Year to 31 December 2006	Profit £17,500
Year to 31 December 2007	Profit £12,000
Year to 31 December 2008	Profit £7,200
Period to 30 September 2009	Loss £27,000

Overlap relief brought forward is £3,000.

Assessments will be (see **CHAPTER 21**):

	£
2006/07 (year to 31.12.2006)	17,500
2007/08 (year to 31.12.2007)	12,000

	£
2008/09 (year to 31.12.2008)	7,200
2009/10 (9 months to 30.9.2009)	—

Terminal loss of year to 30 September 2009:

		£	£
1.10.08 to 5.4.09			
First 3 months	Profit	1,800	
Next 3 months	Loss	(9,000)	(7,200)
6.4.09 to 30.9.09	Loss	(18,000)	
Overlap relief (in full)		(3,000)	(21,000)
			(28,200)

Since there is no trading income in 2009/10, the terminal loss may be carried back and set off against trading assessments as follows:

2008/09		7,200
2007/08		12,000
2006/07	(balance, reducing assessment to £8,500)	9,000
		28,200

If there had been insufficient trading income to obtain relief for the terminal loss (or as an alternative to a terminal loss claim), a section 64 claim could be made to set the 2009/10 loss against *any* income or chargeable gains of that year and/or 2008/09. The 2009/10 loss for a section 64 claim is the full £27,000 loss to 30 September 2009 plus the overlap relief of £3,000, totalling £30,000, less any terminal loss relief claimed.

Where an industrial building, qualifying hotel or building in an enterprise zone is sold after the cessation of a trade and a balancing charge arises, unrelieved trading losses, expenses and capital allowances may be carried forward to set against the balancing charge. Balancing charges will not normally arise on industrial buildings and hotels after 20 March 2008, except where they are in enterprise zones (see **22.42**).

Time limits for claims

[25.10]

ITA 2007, s 64	Set off against income and gains of same tax year or previous tax year	Within one year from 31 January after the end of the tax year in which the loss occurs
ITA 2007, s 72	Set off new business losses against income for three previous tax years, taking earlier before later years	Within one year from 31 January after the end of the tax year in which the loss occurs
ITA 2007, s 83	Carry forward indefinitely against future profits of same trade	Within four years from the end of the tax year in which the loss occurs
ITA 2007, ss 89, 90	Carry-back of terminal losses	Within four years from the end of the tax year in which the business ceases
FA 2009, s 23, Sch 6	Temporary extension of loss carry back to previous three years	Within one year from 31 January after the end of the tax year in which the loss occurs

Repayment supplement (TMA 1970, Sch 1B para 2; TA 1988, s 824)

[25.11] A loss claim will either prevent tax being payable or cause tax already paid to be repaid. Repayment supplement runs from the date of an overpayment, but the rate of interest is significantly lower than that charged on unpaid tax and currently it is 0.5% compared with 3%. Furthermore, where a loss is carried back and set against the income of an earlier tax year, then although the tax saving is calculated by reference to the tax position of the earlier year, the adjustment is made by reducing the tax liability of the loss year (see **9.6**) and supplement runs from the 31 January payment date for that year. This significantly affects the benefit of carrying back new business losses for up to three years (see **25.8**).

Losses of limited partners and partners in limited liability partnerships (ITA 2007, ss 102–116; CTA 2009, ss 55–61, 1273; CTA 2010, ss 55–61)

[25.12] Some partnerships have 'limited partners', whose liability for partnership debts is limited to a fixed capital contribution (see **23.34**). These limited partners may be either individuals or companies. A loss claim by such partners in any year against income other than income from the trade cannot exceed the total of the limited partner's net capital contribution plus undrawn profits to the end of that year and the amount the partner is liable to contribute on a winding up, less loss relief already given against non-trading income. The loss claims referred to are those under ITA 2007, sections 64 and 72 for individuals, and under CTA 2010 section 37 or the group relief provisions in Part 5 for companies (see **26.3** and **26.14**). See **25.13** for revised provisions for individuals relating to the definition of capital contribution and recovery of excess loss relief. There is no restriction on the right of limited partners to carry forward their unused losses against later profits from the same trade.

Similar rules apply in relation to partners in limited liability partnerships (LLPs — see **23.27** to **23.31**). Undrawn profits cannot, however, be included in a partner's subscribed capital unless such profits are unconditionally treated as part of the partner's capital. Losses unrelieved in one tax year against income other than from the trade because of the restriction are available for relief against non-trading income in subsequent years, similarly restricted by reference to the subscribed capital of the later year. Anti-avoidance provisions apply to losses of individual partners in LLPs in the first four tax years (see **25.13**). These rules operate for those years instead of the provisions in this section.

Anti-avoidance provisions

Partnership losses, an individual's losses and partnership interest payments (ITA 2007, ss 75–79, 102–116, 399, 790–809)

[25.13] There are anti-avoidance rules to prevent manipulation by individuals of the tax reliefs for partnership losses. They affect 'non-active partners', i.e. those who do not spend at least ten hours a week personally engaged in the activities of a trade whose activities are carried on on a commercial basis and with a view to realising profits. The 'commercial basis' condition was added in Finance Act 2008, which introduced similar rules for individuals (see **25.14**).

The rules apply to losses arising in the first four tax years in which the partner carried on the trade. They prevent such partners in general partnerships and limited liability partnerships (LLPs) claiming relief for losses against non-trading income and capital gains (see **25.6 TO 25.8**) to a greater extent than the amount of their capital contribution and profit share. The amount of a partner's capital contribution will exclude amounts contributed on or after 2 March 2007 where a main purpose of the contribution was to obtain tax relief for a loss against non-trading income and/or capital gains. Furthermore, for losses arising on or after that date, there is an annual limit of £25,000 on the amount of trading losses for which non-active partners will be able to claim relief against other income/gains (subject to an exclusion for certain film-related expenditure). The anti-avoidance provisions also impose an 'exit charge' where such partners share in large early losses in trades that acquire a licence which entails significant expenditure before any income arises, obtain relief for the losses against their other income or gains, and then dispose of their share of the benefit of the income from the licence without attracting an income tax charge.

From 2 December 2004 loss relief given against non-trading income may be recovered by an excess relief charge to the extent that the individual's capital contribution falls below the amount of loss relief claimed. This applies to limited partners (as to which see **25.12**) as well as general partners, and for limited partners the provisions are not restricted to the first four tax years in which the individual is a partner.

A separate anti-avoidance provision relates solely to film partnerships, affecting interest accruing on or after 10 March 2006. Relief for interest on a loan to buy into a film partnership is restricted to 40% of the interest paid where the loan is secured on an investment in another partnership in which the borrower's right to share in income is disproportionately low compared with his capital contribution to that investment partnership. See **20.38** for the general taxation provisions relating to films.

Where an individual incurs expenditure on the provision of plant or machinery for leasing in the course of a trade, capital allowances on the expenditure can only be included in the loss computation for sideways relief if, broadly, the trade has been carried by the individual for a continuous period of at least six months beginning or ending in the period of loss, and the claimant devotes substantially the whole of his time to the trade throughout that period.

Sideways relief (including relief under FA 2009, Sch 6) is denied where the loss arises in respect of first year allowances or annual investment allowance granted to an individual where the plant or machinery concerned was used for leasing in the course of a qualifying activity carried on by the individual and he was carrying on that activity in partnership with a company or arrangements had been or were later made for him to do so.

Such relief is also denied in respect of the allowances, broadly, where they are made in connection with relevant qualifying activities or assets and arrangements have been made where the main benefit is to reduce tax liabilities.

Loss relief for non-active traders (ITA 2007, ss 74A, 74C–D; FA 2009, s 23, Sch 6)

[25.14] Finance Act 2008 introduced provisions to prevent section 64 relief against income (see **25.6**) and capital gains (**25.7**) being obtained where an individual carries on a trade other than in partnership but in a 'non-active capacity'. FA 2009 extended the restriction to FA 2009, s 23, Sch 6 losses (see **25.6**).

Having implemented similar anti-avoidance measures in relation to partners (see **25.13**) the government said it had seen evidence of schemes to enable individuals to generate such losses in order to obtain tax relief.

The new rules apply, broadly, from 12 March 2008 and limit to £25,000 the amount of relief that can be claimed against general income or capital gains for losses arising from a trade carried on in a non-active capacity. They also provide that no relief is given where a loss arises from 'tax avoidance arrangements'.

An individual carries on a trade in a non-active capacity for this purpose if he does not spend at least ten hours a week personally engaged in the activities of a trade whose activities are carried on on a commercial basis and with a view to realising profits.

National insurance

[25.15] Losses reduce the profit for Class 4 national insurance as well as for income tax. If a claim is made for income tax relief for the loss against non-trading income or against capital gains, the loss can still be set against future trading income for Class 4 national insurance purposes.

Where a loss claim results in Class 4 contributions being refunded, the refund attracts repayment supplement.

Tax points

[25.16] Note the following:

- When considering how to claim relief for losses, the key questions are how much tax will be saved, when it will be saved and how much tax-free repayment supplement will be received. Watch the effect of changes in tax rates and allowances in the various years. HMRC have issued Helpsheet 227 for 2009/10 to provide guidance to traders on how to utilise their losses.
- More than one claim will frequently be possible and a trader's tax position may be different according to the order in which claims are taken into account. A trader may generally stipulate which claims take priority.
- Claiming carry-back relief under section 72, instead of current year relief under section 64, for a first year loss leaves other income of the loss year available for a possible carry-back claim under section 72 for a loss in later years.
- Loss relief against general income is restricted to those losses incurred in a demonstrably commercial trade and this may be difficult to prove. This is particularly so in the case of a new trade, so that a viable business plan is often essential to support a carry-back claim under section 72.
- A loss in the opening years carried back under section 72, in preference to a claim under section 64, must be fully relieved under section 72 before the balance of available losses can be relieved under section 64. It is not possible to carry back sufficient of the loss to relieve income of the third year back and then not to proceed against the income of the second year back and then the first. The carry-back facility must be exhausted if claimed at all, before a section 64 loss claim is made in respect of the balance remaining unrelieved. A claim under FA 2009, s 23, Sch 6 in conjunction with a s 64 claim could be considered but the loss can only be set against income from the same trade for the second and third year back (see **25.6**).

If there is a loss in the next year of trading this forms an entirely new claim. Relief for that loss can be claimed under section 64 in preference to section 72 but, if a section 72 claim is embarked upon first, again the carry-back facility must be exhausted in respect of that particular loss before the balance can be relieved under section 64.

- There are time limits both for making claims and for amending them (see **9.5** and **25.10**). Claims do not have to be agreed by HMRC within the time limits, but HMRC may challenge the validity of the claims if they open an enquiry (see **9.32**).

26

Company losses

Introduction

[26.1] Companies may incur losses in their trades, in the course of letting property, in relation to investment income if expenses exceed the income, and in their capital transactions. In some cases the losses will relate to activities outside the UK. The overseas aspect is dealt with in CHAPTER 41. The treatment of losses on rented property is dealt with in CHAPTER 32. The treatment of non-trading losses on intangible assets is dealt with in **20.30** onwards. The treatment of capital losses is dealt with in CHAPTER 4 and in context in various other chapters (including CHAPTER 3 in relation to capital losses within a group of companies and CHAPTER 45 in relation to various anti-avoidance provisions on capital losses). The loss of money lent is regarded as an income loss rather than a capital loss. Such losses are dealt with in this chapter at **26.5**.

Reliefs available for trading losses

[26.2] Trading losses of companies are calculated in the same way as trading profits. The following options are available for obtaining relief for such losses:

(a)   set-off against current profits from other sources (CTA 2010, s 37(3)(*a*));
(b)   carry-back against earlier profits from all sources (CTA 2010, s 37(3)(*b*); FA 2009, s 23, Sch 6);
(c)   carry-forward against future trading profits (CTA 2010, s 45).

Additionally, where a company is in a group, trading losses may be surrendered from one company to one or more other companies within the group, provided the necessary conditions are satisfied (see **26.12**).

Set-off against current profits (CTA 2010, s 37(3)(a))

[26.3] A trading loss of a company can be set against any profits of the same chargeable accounting period, thus reducing or eliminating the corporation tax bill. Profits for this purpose includes not only all sources of income (including dividends, although most will be exempt from corporation tax) but also capital gains (see **3.1**). A claim against current profits in respect of a non-trading deficit relating to loans takes priority over this claim (see **26.7**). See **26.8** for the treatment of qualifying charitable donations.

Carry-back against previous profits and carry-forward (CTA 2010, ss 37(3)(b), 45; FA 2009, s 23, Sch 6)

[26.4] After a trading loss has been set against all profits of the current period, any balance may be carried back and set against the total profits of accounting periods falling wholly or partly within the previous 12 months (but in certain situations, this carry back is extended to three years), so long as the trade was carried on in the earlier period. If the loss period is less than 12 months this does not restrict the carry-back period.

The carry back is extended to three years in the following situations:

(a) on the cessation of trade. In such situations, the three year carry back applies to losses of accounting periods falling wholly or partly within the last 12 months of trading. Where an accounting period falls only partly within the last 12 months, the carry-back period for the part of the loss within the last 12 months is three years, the normal 12 month carry-back applying to the remainder of the loss. As far as the carry-back period is concerned, results are similarly apportioned as necessary where an accounting period falls only partly within the 12-month or three-year period. (Note, from 21 May 2009, legislation was introduced to counter a scheme notified to HMRC which engineered a deemed cessation of trading to allow a company to obtain terminal loss relief in circumstances 'not intended by Parliament');

(b) for trading losses incurred in accounting periods ending after 23 November 2008 and before 24 November 2010 (with losses being carried back against later years first). The amount of trading losses that can be carried back to the preceding year is unlimited. However, there is a limit on the amount of unused losses which can be carried back to the earlier two years. It is limited to a maximum of £50,000 incurred in accounting periods ending after 23 November 2008 and before 24 November 2009 and a maximum of £50,000 incurred in accounting periods ending after 23 November 2009 and before 24 November 2010. It does not matter how many accounting periods fall within each of these periods. Where the accounting period in which the loss is made is less than 12 months the amount of loss that can be carried back is limited to a proportion of the £50,000 limit.

Example 1

A company has trading losses of £190,000 in the 12 month accounting period to 30 September 2009 and further trading losses of £100,000 in the next 12 month accounting period to 30 September 2010. It has been profitable in all earlier accounting periods. The company can offset this loss as follows:

Accounting period	Profit/(loss)	Commentary
Year ending 30 Sept 2010	(£100,000)	£50,000 can be carried back to 2007 leaving £50,000 loss to be carried forward to future accounting periods
Year ending 30 Sept 2009	(£190,000)	£120,000 can be carried back (£70,000 to 2008 (unlimited carry back) and £50,000 to 2007 (capped carry back)) leaving a loss of £70,000 to be carried forward to future accounting periods
Year ending 30 Sept 2008	£70,000	£70,000 loss from 2009 available to offset £70,000 profit
Year ending 30 Sept 2007	£100,000	£50,000 capped loss from 2009 and £50,000 capped loss from 2010 available to relieve £100,000 profit

---

As with the claim against current profits, the set-off in the carry-back period is not limited to trading profits and is made against profits of any description. If in the period of set-off there is a non-trading deficit relating to loans for which relief is claimed against the profits of that period, that claim takes priority over the claim to set off carried back trading losses (see **26.7**). See **26.8** for the treatment of qualifying charitable donations.

Any loss not relieved against current or previous profits may be carried forward for set-off against future trading profits of the same trade, without time limit on its use unless there is a change of ownership to which the anti-avoidance provisions outlined at **26.19** apply. Although any carried-forward losses cannot normally be relieved after a trade ceases, where a building is sold after the cessation and a balancing charge is made to withdraw excess capital allowances, unrelieved trading losses may be set against that balancing charge (see **22.47**). Balancing charges will not normally arise on industrial buildings and hotels after 20 March 2007, except where they are in enterprise zones (see **22.42**).

Claims to set off losses against current and previous profits of any description are only permitted if the company carries on business on a commercial basis with a view to the realisation of profit (and see **31.4** for additional restrictions for farming companies). There is no commercial basis restriction for carrying losses forward, since the permitted set-off is only against trading profits of that same trade.

Losses relating to loans and derivative contracts (CTA 2010, s 99; CTA 2009, Pt 5 Ch 16, s 574)

[26.5] Losses arising out of loan relationships (see **3.5**) and/or derivative contracts (see **3.7**) for the purposes of the trade are taken into account in arriving at the trading result and relieved accordingly (see **26.2**).

For non-trading loan relationships/derivative contracts interest, expenses and profits and losses on disposal are aggregated. If there is an overall profit it is charged to corporation tax. If there is a loss, i.e. a 'non-trading deficit', relief for *all or part of the loss* may be claimed as follows:

(a) by way of group relief (see **26.16**);
(b) against any other profits (including capital gains) of the deficit period;
(c) against any loan relationship/derivative contract profits of the previous 12 months.

[26.6] Any part of the deficit for which relief is not claimed under (*a*) to (*c*) above is carried forward automatically and set against the *total* non-trading profits of later accounting periods. A claim may, however, be made for all or part of any carried forward amount not to be set against the non-trading profits of the next accounting period. This enables all or part of the carried forward deficit effectively to 'leapfrog' the period in which it would otherwise be set off which could in appropriate cases avoid loss of double tax relief in that period, such relief being available only to the extent that there are chargeable profits.

Relief may not be claimed for loans written off if the borrower and lender are 'connected persons'. A person (including another company) is connected with a company if the person holds shares, voting power or other rights that enable that person to control the company. See **12.15** for detailed notes on writing off loans to controlling shareholders.

Priority of reliefs

[26.7] Relief against the other profits of the same accounting period under **26.5**(b) is given *after* relief for brought forward trading losses but *before* relief for current or carried back trading losses (see **26.3, 26.4**) or for carried back non-trading deficits under **26.5**(c).

Carry-back relief for any accounting period under **26.5**(c) is given against the profits of the period of set-off *after*:

(a) relief for a deficit incurred in an earlier period,

(b)   relief claimed against the profits of the set-off period under **26.5**(b),

(c)   group relief under **26.5**(a),

(d)   current or carry-back relief for trading losses (see **26.3**, **26.4**).

Qualifying charitable donations (CTA 2010, ss 189–217)

[26.8] Having arrived at the company's total profits (both income and capital), qualifying charitable donations (referred to as charges on income prior to the rewrite to CTA 2010) are deducted to arrive at the profits chargeable to corporation tax. For details of what constitutes a qualifying charitable donation see CHAPTER 43.

Qualifying charitable donations may be deducted not just from trading profits but from total profits, including capital gains. If, however, there are insufficient profits to cover available reliefs, both current and carried back trading losses and/or non-trading deficits take priority over qualifying charitable donations. If there are insufficient profits remaining to cover the qualifying charitable donations, they may not be carried forward for relief against later profits. They may, however, be the subject of a group relief claim (see **26.16**).

Effect of carry-back of losses on tax paid

[26.9] Carry-back loss claims result in corporation tax already paid being repaid, or in tax otherwise due not having to be paid. This means that it may (depending upon the company's profit levels) be possible to obtain loss relief at differing rates: the small profits rate, the marginal small profits rate and the main rate (see **3.11**). Details of the various rates for earlier years are in previous editions of this book.

Interest calculations (TA 1988, ss 825, 826)

[26.10] Repayments attract interest from nine months after the end of the relevant period or, if later, from the actual date of payment of tax for that period (see **3.24**) (although the interest rate is significantly lower than the rate charged on overdue tax). The latest available interest rates are set out in the Table of Rates and Allowances.

For calculating interest on repayments resulting from current and carried back losses, a repayment is normally treated as relating to the *loss* period, but a repayment relating to an accounting period falling *wholly* in the 12 months before the loss period is treated as relating to that accounting period.

Example 2

A company has the following results up to the date it ceased to trade on 31 March 2010.

Year ended 31 March	2008	2009	2010
	£	£	£
Trading profit (loss)	50,000	20,000	(40,500)
Investment income	3,000	3,000	3,000
Chargeable gains	4,000	2,500	2,000
Total profits	57,000	25,500	5,000
If loss relief is claimed:			
Profits	57,000	25,500	5,000
Less loss	(10,000)	(25,500)	(5,000)
Total profits	47,000	—	—

Any tax repayment for the year to 31 March 2009 resulting from carrying the loss back 12 months will attract interest from the corporation tax payment date for that year, i.e. from 1 January 2010. The repayment for the year to 31 March 2008 will attract interest from 1 January 2011 (the payment date for corporation tax for the *loss* year to 31 March 2010).

Time limits for claims
[26.11]

CTA 2010, s 37; CTA 2009, s 459(1)	Set off trading losses or non-trading deficits against profits of same accounting period and previous accounting periods	Within two years after the end of the accounting period of loss or deficit, or such further period as HMRC allow
CTA 2010, s 45	Carry forward trading losses against later trading profits from same trade	No claim is required. Losses are entered on the corporation tax return and any unrelieved amounts are carried forward automatically
CTA 2009, s 457	Carry forward non-trading deficit against total non-trading profits of later accounting periods	No claim is required
CTA 2009, s 458	Non-trading deficit not to be set off against total non-trading profits of next accounting period	Within two years after the end of that next accounting period

See HMRC Statement of Practice 5/01 in relation to the circumstances in which they may admit late claims.

Group relief for losses etc. (CTA 2010, ss 97–188)

Trading losses

[26.12] In a group consisting of a holding company and its 75% subsidiaries, trading losses may be surrendered from one company to one or more other companies within the group, provided the necessary conditions are satisfied. This enables the company to which the loss has been surrendered to reduce its taxable profits by the surrendered amount. (Note, this 75% link for group relief purposes is defined very much more restrictively than simply 75% of ordinary share capital, to prevent companies taking advantage of the provisions by means of an artificial group relationship (CTA 2010 s 151).

Example 3

A Ltd: Profit of
£100,000
|
B Ltd: Loss of £60,000

Under the group relief provisions, it is possible to surrender the loss of £60,000 from B to A reducing A's taxable profit and its corporation tax liability.

Example 4

A Ltd: Loss of
£100,000
|
B Ltd: Profit of £60,000

The group relief claim here will be a maximum of £60,000. A Ltd will have the remaining loss of £40,000 which it may be able to set off in the current year, carry back, or carry forward. Losses that are unutilised (through either group relief, carry back or current year offset) can only be carried forward in the company that originally sustained them.

The loss available to be surrendered must relate to an accounting period of the loss-making company that corresponds with that of the claimant company. This will not pose any difficulty when accounts within the group are prepared to the same date, but where accounts are prepared to different dates, part of the loss period will correspond with part of one accounting period of the claimant company and the remainder with part of the next accounting period. The loss available for relief and the profits against which it may be set must be apportioned as indicated below. Relief is also proportionately restricted if the parent/subsidiary relationship does not exist throughout the accounting period, usually on a time basis, but by reference to what is just and reasonable where a time basis would give an unreasonable result.

[26.13] The set-off rules are quite flexible, and broadly the loss-making company may surrender any part of its trading loss (without first claiming other reliefs available), up to a maximum of the available total profits of the claimant company or companies for the corresponding period. The rules enable the loss to be divided among several group companies in order to obtain the maximum loss relief. A claimant company cannot, however, claim more *in total* than an amount equal to its profits of the period that overlaps with the accounting periods of surrendering companies, and a loss company cannot surrender more *in total* to fellow group companies than its loss in the overlapping period(s).

Example 5

Alpha Ltd owns all the shares in Beta Ltd; both companies make up accounts to 30 September. On 1 January 2010 Alpha Ltd acquires all the shares of Gamma Ltd which makes up its accounts to 31 March.

Beta Ltd has a trading loss for the year to 30 September 2010 and Gamma Ltd claims group relief for its accounting period ending 31 March 2010 in respect of that loss.

The period common to the accounting periods of Gamma Ltd and Beta Ltd is 1 October 2009 to 31 March 2010, but as Gamma Ltd was not a member of the Alpha Ltd group until 1 January 2010, the overlapping accounting period will be restricted to 1 January 2010 to 31 March 2010.

Example 6

A company with a loss in the year to 30 June 2010 had two fellow group companies making up accounts to 31 December. The *total* surrender to the two companies for their year to 31 December 2009 can not exceed 6/12ths of the loss, leaving the loss of the second half of the year to be surrendered against a maximum of 6/12ths of the profits of each of the companies for the year to 31 December 2010. The profits of the claimant company available for relief are profits from all sources, including capital gains, but after deducting qualifying charitable donations.

A significant factor in deciding the optimum loss claim is the rate of tax saving. Other things being equal, it will be best to surrender the loss if possible against profits being charged at the small profits marginal rate (or indeed not to surrender it at all if the company's own profits are charged at that rate).

Example 7

Company A has been the wholly owned subsidiary of Company B for many years. There are no other subsidiaries. Small profits rate marginal relief limits are therefore reduced for each company to £150,000 and £750,000. Both companies prepare accounts to 31 March, and for the year to 31 March 2010 results are as follows:

Company A has a trading loss of	£80,000
and other profits of	£10,000
Company B has total profits of	£205,000

In the year to 31 March 2009, Company A had total profits of £170,000. Company A's profits for the year to 31 March 2011 will be between £100,000 and £150,000.

Company A may claim its own available loss reliefs and not surrender any part of the loss to Company B; or it may surrender the full £80,000 and pay tax on its own profits of £170,000 in 2009 and £10,000 in 2010; or it may surrender any amount up to £80,000, as the companies wish, and claim its own loss reliefs on the balance.

Rates of tax at which relief is available for the loss:	On Company A's profits	On Company B's profits
Year to 31 March 2010	21% on £10,000	29.75% on £55,000 21% on £25,000
Year to 31 March 2009	29.75% on £20,000 21% on next £50,000	No relief available
Year to 31 March 2011	21%	

The most tax-efficient claim is to surrender £50,000 of the loss to Company B, achieving a 29.75% tax saving thereon against Company B's profits, and to claim relief for £30,000 against Company A's own profits, giving relief on £10,000 at 21% in the year to 31 March 2010 and £20,000 at 29.75% in the year to 31 March 2009. Therefore tax on £70,000 of the loss can be saved on the loss at the marginal small profits rate.

Where a loss would otherwise be unrelieved, it might be appropriate for a profit-making company in a group to disclaim some of the allowances on its plant and machinery, to give it a higher profit against which to make a group relief claim (see **22.16** and **22.61**). The profit-making company would then have a higher pool balance carried forward on which to claim capital allowances in the future, whereas if it has insufficient current profit to cover the loss available for surrender, the surrendered loss has to be restricted.

[26.14] The group relief provisions are also available in certain circumstances to a consortium of companies that owns at least 75% of the ordinary share capital of a trading company or of a holding company with 90% trading subsidiaries, with the consortium members each owning at least 5% of that ordinary share capital. Losses in proportion to the consortium member's interest in the consortium-owned company can be surrendered both from the trading companies to the consortium companies and from the consortium companies to the trading companies. The consortium members interest is the lower of its percentage shareholding in the company, its percentage entitlement to any profits available for distribution from the company or its percentage entitlement of any assets of the company on a winding up. A fourth test is to be added based on the proportion of voting rights and the extent of control the member holds in the consortium. The relevant legislation for this test will be introduced later in 2010 and will apply for accounting periods beginning on or after the date the legislation is published.

[26.15] To satisfy the requirements for group or consortium relief, it was previously necessary for claiming and surrendering companies to be either resident in the UK or carrying on a trade in the UK through a permanent establishment. Following a decision of the European Court of Justice, the rules were changed from 1 April 2006 to permit loss-making group companies resident (or with a permanent establishment) in another state in the European Economic Area to surrender losses to UK group companies if they would otherwise be unrelievable. This applies only in very limited circumstances and is subject to anti-avoidance provisions to prevent abuse of the rules (see **41.46**).

Group relief for other unrelieved amounts

[26.16] In addition to trading losses, group relief may also be claimed in respect of:

(a) excess qualifying charitable donations (see **26.8**);
(b) property business losses (see **32.9**);
(c) excess management expenses of companies with investment business;
(d) non-trading losses on intangible assets (see **20.31**); and
(e) all or part of a non-trading deficit relating to loans or derivative contracts (see **26.5**).

The amounts in (a) to (d) that are eligible for group relief can only be surrendered to the extent that they exceed the company's profits of the surrender period. For (e), as with trading losses, a company may surrender a non-trading deficit relating to loans or derivative contracts without claiming other reliefs available.

Procedure for group relief claims (FA 1998, Sch 18 Pt VIII; SI 1999/2975)

[26.17] Companies may make, vary and withdraw group relief claims up to the latest of one year from the filing date for the claimant company's return (see **9.19**), 30 days after the completion of an HMRC enquiry into the return, 30 days after the notice of HMRC amendments to the return following an enquiry, and 30 days after the final determination of an appeal against such an amendment. Each group company makes initial claims for specified amounts of group relief and shows amounts available for group relief surrenders on its own individual corporation tax return or amended return. Claims must show the name and tax district reference number of the surrendering company and be accompanied by a copy of the surrendering company's consent. The surrendering company will send the notice of consent to its own tax district. Where a group has non-resident company members, group relief claims must identify non-resident claimant or surrendering companies and any non-resident companies through which common group or consortium membership is established. Where original claims are to be varied, the original claim must be withdrawn and replaced by a new claim. Groups dealt with mainly within one tax district may enter into simplified arrangements under which group companies may authorise one company to amend returns on behalf of all group companies in relation to making and withdrawing claims and surrenders of group relief.

Company reconstructions without change of ownership (CTA 2010, ss 938–957)

[26.18] Where a trade is transferred from one company to another and, at some time within one year before and two years after the transfer, the same persons own three-quarters or more of the trade, it is treated as transferred to the successor company rather than being discontinued. This prevents the predecessor carrying trading losses back under the terminal loss rules, and enables the successor to take over the unrelieved losses of the predecessor (subject to special rules restricting the available loss where the successor does not take over all the predecessor's assets and liabilities). The successor also takes over the predecessor's capital allowances computations (see **22.18**).

Anti-avoidance provisions

[26.19] The group relief provisions are flexible and of great benefit to many companies. However, the rules are tightly controlled to prevent abuse of the regime (as mentioned, where appropriate, in the relevant commentary). In addition there are several specific provisions that broadly deal with the position on a change in ownership of a company, as detailed below.

Losses incurred before a change in ownership cannot be relieved under the rules that normally apply to trading losses if either:

(a)   within a period of three years there is both a major change in the nature or conduct of a trade carried on by a company and a change in its ownership; or

(b)   after the scale of activities in a trade carried on by a company has become negligible and before any considerable revival, there is a change in ownership (CTA 2010, ss 673–676).

The provisions prevent losses incurred before the change of ownership being carried forward, and prevent losses in an accounting period *after* the change of ownership from being carried back to an accounting period *before* the change. HMRC Statement of Practice SP 10/91 gives their views on the meaning of a 'major change in the nature or conduct of a trade'.

Where there is a change in ownership of a company with investment business, there are provisions to prevent the company carrying forward unrelieved management expenses, non-trading deficits on loans and derivative contracts, and non-trading losses on intangible fixed assets (CTA 2010, ss 677–691). There are similar provisions preventing losses being carried forward on a change in ownership of a company carrying on a property business (CTA 2010, ss 704–705).

Group relief is not available for a part of an accounting period in which arrangements exist whereby the loss-making company could cease to be a member of the group (CTA 2010, s 154).

See **45.10** for anti-avoidance provisions relating to capital loss buying and capital gains buying by groups.

Tax points

[26.20] Note the following:

- When considering loss claims, always look at the amount of tax saved. There are three relevant tax rates, the full rate, the small profits rate and the marginal rate. The full rate is presently 28% and the small profits rate is 21%. The marginal rate varies as the rates change (see **3.12, 3.13**).
- Group relief for losses is not available if there is less than a 75% link between holding and subsidiary companies.
- If two or more companies are controlled by the same individual(s), group relief is not available. But unused trading losses are still available against the future profits of a trade if that trade is transferred from one company to another under the same control (see **26.18**).
- Anti-avoidance provisions may restrict or deny group relief. For example, an arrangement made part-way through an accounting period to sell a loss-making subsidiary will prevent group relief being claimed for the remainder of the accounting period even though the parent/subsidiary relationship exists throughout.
- Exceptional revenue expenditure, such as extraordinary repairs, or establishing or boosting a company pension scheme within permissible limits, may result in a normally profitable trade incurring a loss. When a company is planning such expenditure or considering when, or indeed whether, it should be incurred, the carry-back of losses against earlier profits, resulting in tax not having to be paid, or being repaid, is an important consideration.

27

Transfer of business to limited company

Choice of date

[27.1] When the trade of an individual or partnership is transferred to a company the trade has ceased for income tax purposes, so that the closing year rules dealt with in CHAPTER 21 apply.

Under the income tax rules, except where accounts are prepared to 31 March, there will be an amount of overlap relief to be deducted from the profits of the final trading period (unless the overlap period showed a loss). The amount to be deducted will not be affected by the choice of cessation date. The timing of the cessation still needs to be considered in the light of expected income in the years affected, for example the deduction of the overlap profit may reduce higher rate tax, or possibly create a loss to be relieved against other income of the current tax year or carried back against earlier income. The effect of capital allowances also needs to be considered — see **27.2**.

Capital allowances (CAA 2001, ss 265–268, 567–570)

[27.2] Normally the cessation of trade would involve a balancing allowance or charge by reference to the proceeds of disposal to the company of plant and equipment.

The sole trader or partners and the company may usually, however, jointly elect within two years after the transfer date for the assets to be treated as transferred at the tax written-down value (see **22.18**) even though the justifiably higher market value is used for accounting purposes. The company gets writing-down allowances (but not first year allowances) on the price it pays or the tax written-down value as the case may be (see **22.24**).

In neither case is there a writing-down allowance in the tax period up to cessation, consequently either increasing the written-down value carried into the company or affecting the amount of the balancing allowance or charge.

Open market value has been used in the case of industrial buildings unless an election to transfer at the tax written-down value was made. For transfers on or after 21 March 2007 (subject to certain transitional provisions), there will be no balancing adjustments on the transfer of industrial buildings (except for buildings in enterprise zones), and the company will take over the writing down allowances of the sole trader or partners (see **22.42**).

Trading stock (ITTOIA 2005, ss 173–181)

[27.3] While the legislation requires the transfer of stock to be at market value, the sole trader/partners and the company can normally elect for the greater of the cost or the price paid by the company to be used instead if that would give a lower figure. The election must be made within one year from 31 January after the end of the tax year in which the cessation occurred.

Unused trading losses (ITA 2007, s 86)

[27.4] If there are unused trading losses, these cannot be carried forward to a company as such, but they may be relieved against income received by the trader or partners from the company, either in the form of directors' fees or dividends, so long as the business is exchanged for shares and the shares are still retained at the time the loss is set off. Other available loss claims may be made first, e.g. under ITA 2007, s 64 against income of the year of loss or the previous year, or terminal loss relief for a loss of the last twelve months against the trading income of the previous three years (see **CHAPTER 25**), and the relief against income from the company would then be available on the balance of unrelieved losses.

Capital gains tax (TCGA 1992, ss 17, 18, 162, 162A, 286; F(No.2)A 2010, s 2 and Sch 1)

[27.5] When the transfer takes place, the general rule is that those assets chargeable to capital gains tax (CGT) which have been transferred are treated as being disposed of to the company at their open market value. Current assets (stock, debtors, etc.) are not chargeable assets. Plant and equipment, even though covered by an election to transfer at the tax written-down value for capital allowances purposes, may be a chargeable asset for CGT and thus treated as transferred at market value. Moveable plant and equipment is chargeable unless valued at £6,000 or less for each item (see **CHAPTER 39**), but it will not normally be valued at more than cost, so that CGT will not usually apply, leaving the most likely assets on which a liability may arise as freehold or leasehold premises, fixed plant and machinery and goodwill. Although goodwill acquired by a company on or after 1 April 2002 is normally dealt with under the rules for intangible assets rather than the capital gains rules, this does not apply in most cases to acquisitions from a related party, which would include a transfer on incorporation (see **20.36**). Such goodwill would accordingly still be a chargeable asset for capital gains in the hands of the company.

[27.6] An obvious way of avoiding the charge on premises is for the proprietor or partners to retain ownership and to allow the company to use the property either at a rent or free of charge. This also saves the stamp duty land tax that would have been incurred on the transfer (see **27.12**). There is no stamp duty charge on any assets transferred to the company except marketable securities.

Whether goodwill exists and if so at what value is always arguable. It depends upon many factors, such as the type of business, its location and profitability. Where it does attach to the business which is transferred, the only way of not reckoning its value on a transfer of the business is if the sole trader/partners continue to own it whilst licensing the company to carry on the trade, but unless this is commercially practicable, sensible and properly done, the goodwill will follow the trade in appropriate circumstances. The valuation of goodwill depends not only on the size of the profits but also on the extent to which the profits depend on the skills of the proprietor or partners, the nature of the trade and many other factors.

The CGT effect of the incorporation of a business in 2010/11 is considered in Example 1.

Example 1

The net assets of a trader at the time of incorporation of his business in July 2010 were:

	£
Freehold premises at current market value	204,000
Goodwill at current market value	120,000
Plant and equipment (cost £320,000)	140,000
Net current assets other than cash	256,000
Cash and bank balances	80,000
	£800,000

The premises had been acquired for £120,000 and the trade newly commenced in 1989.

The potential chargeable gains on incorporation are:

		£
Freehold premises — market value	204,000	
Less: Cost	120,000	84,000
Goodwill — market value	120,000	

Less:	Cost	Nil	120,000
Chargeable gains			£204,000

The gain on the premises could be avoided by the trader retaining ownership, but a gain on the goodwill would arise on the transfer of the trade, unless it was possible to retain it while licensing the company to use it.

Provided that the trader has owned the business for one year entrepreneurs' relief will be available to reduce the rate of CGT on a disposal — see **29.2** to **29.10** for full details of the relief. See also HMRC guidance in tax return Helpsheet (for 2009/10) HS275. The annual CGT exemption of £10,100 may also be available.

	£
Chargeable gains as above	204,000
Less:	
Annual exemption	(10,100)
Gain taxable @ the lower rate of capital gains tax for entrepreneurs' relief of 10%	£193,900
Tax payable	£19,390

Note that if the disposal had been made before 23 June 2010 the calculation of entrepreneurs' relief would be as follows:

	£
Chargeable gains as above	204,000
Less:	
Entrepreneurs' relief (4/9 x 204,000)	(90,667)
	113,333
Annual exemption	(10,100)
Gain taxable @ 18%	£103,233
Tax payable	£18,582

The calculation before 23 June 2010 gives a lower amount of tax payable. There was an anomaly in the calculation under the old rules which meant that the annual exemption and losses (other than 'relevant losses', see **29.9**) received relief at 18% even if the whole gain would otherwise be taxable at the effective 10% rate. The amendments in F(No.2)A 2010, Sch 1 have removed this anomaly so that relief is only received at the prevailing rate of 10%. However, for 2010/11 where the gain is taxable at more than one rate the annual exemption and allowable losses can be applied in a way that produces the lowest possible tax charge. Therefore, where an individual has gains both before and after 23 June 2010 which would otherwise qualify for entrepreneurs' relief, the exemption and losses should be applied to the gains arising before 23 June 2010. This is subject to any existing legislation that limits the way in which certain losses may be set off.

[27.7] Prior to the introduction of entrepreneurs' relief there were two main alternatives for reducing or eliminating an immediate CGT charge on incorporation. These alternatives remain under the new regime but the interaction of reliefs needs to be considered.

One alternative is the roll-over relief provided by TCGA 1992, s 162, known as incorporation relief. This requires *all* the assets (except cash) to be transferred to the company, and defers gains only to the extent that the consideration is received in the form of shares in the company. HMRC guidance (for 2009/10) is available in tax return Helpsheet HS276.

The second alternative is a combination of retaining some assets in personal ownership and making a claim under the business gift relief provisions of TCGA 1992, s 165 (outlined at **4.24** to **4.26**) to limit the gains on other chargeable assets (notably goodwill) to the amount actually received, the company then being treated as acquiring those assets at market value less the gains not chargeable on the transferor. Under this alternative, any consideration received from the company for the assets that are transferred need not be in the form of shares, and a credit may be made to a loan account or cash taken instead. HMRC guidance (for 2009/10) is available in tax return Helpsheet HS295.

Another possible alternative if the company is a qualifying unquoted trading company is CGT deferral relief under the enterprise investment scheme (see **27.10**).

Incorporation relief (TCGA 1992, ss 162, 162A)

[27.8] For section 162 incorporation relief (see **27.7**) to apply in Example 1, all assets other than the £80,000 cash would have to be transferred.

The chargeable gains on the disposal of the business are calculated and they are treated as reducing the CGT base cost of the shares received in exchange for the business. The lower base cost for the shares will of course increase the potential CGT liability on their future disposal.

The whole of the gain of £204,000 accruing on the incorporation is rolled over against the acquisition cost of the shares and no chargeable gain arises at that time. There would therefore be no 'relevant gain' for the purposes of TCGA 1992, s 169N(1) and a claim for entrepreneurs' relief would not appear to be appropriate (see HMRC Capital Gains Manual CG64136 which refers to business asset roll-over relief under TCGA 1992, s 152, but which applies to a 'provision which rolls (that) gain, or a proportion of it, over against the acquisition cost of a replacement asset').

On a subsequent disposal of the shares entrepreneurs' relief (see **CHAPTER 29**), enterprise investment scheme deferral relief and gift relief may be available. There is no CGT if the shares are still held on death. See Example 2.

Example 2

In consideration of the transfer of the trade in 2010/11 in Example 1, the trader receives 700,000 shares of £1 each, fully paid, in the new company, transferring all assets except the cash of £80,000.

The base cost of the shares will be:

700,000 shares (£800,000 assets – £80,000 cash)	720,000
Less gains otherwise arising on premises and goodwill	204,000
Cost of 700,000 shares for CGT purposes	£516,000

The difference between the £700,000 par value of the shares and the £720,000 assets value in Example 2 represents a share premium. It is almost inevitable that the par value will not correspond with the asset values since those values cannot be precisely determined before the transfer date.

If the transfer is made only partly for shares, and partly for cash or credit to a loan account, then only proportionate relief is given. See Example 3.

Example 3

Suppose the consideration of £720,000 in Example 2 was satisfied as to £480,000 shares and £240,000 cash. Only two-thirds of the chargeable gains of £204,000, i.e. £136,000, can be deducted from the base cost of the shares.

		Shares	Cash
Consideration		480,000	240,000
Gains	£204,000	136,000	£68,000
Cost of shares for CGT purposes		£344,000	

The chargeable gain remaining is £68,000. Provided the trader had owned the business for a year entrepreneurs' relief would be available. See 29.2 to 29.10 for full details of the relief. When entrepreneurs' relief was introduced by FA 2008 there was some uncertainty as to the order of set off of reliefs (see, for example Tolley's Practical Tax Newsletter Vol 29 No 13, dated 20 June 2008). However, HMRC's view, as expressed in their Capital Gains Tax Manual at CG64136 (which refers to business asset roll over relief under TCGA 1992 s 152, but which applies to a 'provision which rolls (that) gain, or a proportion of it, over against the acquisition cost of a replacement asset') appears to support a claim to entrepreneurs' relief in respect of the amount of the gain that remains chargeable. The annual CGT exemption may also be available.

Chargeable gain as above	68,000
Less:	
Annual exemption	(10,100)
Gain taxable @ the lower rate of capital gains tax for entrepreneurs' relief of 10%	£57,900

See Example 1 in 27.6 for details of the calculation where the disposal is made before 23 June 2010.

Obtaining the maximum deferral of gains under section 162 therefore requires the consideration for the shares to be locked in as share capital. If the consideration is provided through leaving money on loan account, tax will not be deferred, but the money can later be withdrawn at no personal tax cost.

The section 162 relief is given automatically without the need for a claim, although if the transferor has acquired business assets for use in another trade and wants to claim the business assets roll-over relief under section 152 instead (see **29.11** onwards), that roll-over relief claim takes priority over section 162. Otherwise section 162 must be applied even if gains would be covered by, say, the annual exemption. To avoid the problem, the appropriate part of the consideration resulting in chargeable gains equal to available exemptions could be left on loan account, so that a gain would be immediately realised, as shown in Example 3. Using the figures in that example, if £35,647 of the consideration of £720,000 was in cash, the proportionate part of the gain relating to the cash consideration would be £10,100 which is the amount of the annual exemption for 2010/11.

Where assets that are being transferred to the company are depreciating assets against which gains have been held over under the business assets roll-over provisions (see **29.11** onwards), the disposal to the company *triggers* the deferred gains, but the deferred gains do not actually arise on the transfer, so relief for them is not available under section 162.

The taxpayer may *elect* for section 162 relief not to apply, so that gains that would otherwise have been deferred are chargeable in respect of the transfer to the company, with any later gains being chargeable when the shares are disposed of. The time limit for the election is two years from 31 January following the tax year of transfer, unless all the shares are disposed of by the end of the tax year following the tax year of transfer, in which case the time limit is one year from 31 January following the tax year of transfer. This enables taxpayers to obtain section 162 relief initially and then make the election later if appropriate. The availability of entrepreneurs' relief may affect the calculations.

Example 4

Say the trader in Example 1 had transferred all the assets except cash to the company in July 2010 with full s 162 relief, so that his shares had a base value of £720,000 less gains £204,000 = £516,000 as in Example 2. On 1 March 2011 he accepted an offer of £800,000 for the shares.

Without the election the gain of £284,000 on disposal of the shares (£800,000 − £516,000) would have been fully chargeable, subject to the annual exemption if available. No entrepreneurs' relief is available as the shares have not been held for at least a year. The trader may, however, *elect* for incorporation relief not to apply, the time limit for the election being 31 January 2013. His chargeable gains for 2010/11 would then be £204,000 (as in Example 1) plus £80,000 (£800,000 − £720,000) on disposal of the shares, making £284,000 in total. The gain of £204,000 would be taxable at the lower 10% rate applicable to gains qualifying for entrepreneurs' relief and the remaining £80,000 gain would be taxable at a flat rate (of either 18% or 28% depending on the individual's personal tax

---

position (see **4.2**) but in determining which rate should apply to individuals, gains qualifying for entrepreneurs' relief are set against any unused basic rate band before non-qualifying gains). The gains could be reduced by the annual exemption if available. See **27.6** regarding the allocation of the annual exemption in 2010/11.

To summarise, section 162 relief on incorporation results in total chargeable gains of £284,000 (nil plus £284,000) which do not qualify for entrepreneurs' relief. If relief is disclaimed, the total gains are still £284,000 but £204,000 of the gains qualify for entrepreneurs' relief and are therefore taxable at the lower capital gains tax rate of 10%. If the trader had held the shares for at least a year and the other criteria set out in **29.4** were met, entrepreneurs' relief would have been available on the disposal of shares. Also, it must be borne in mind that there is a £5 million lifetime limit for entrepreneurs' relief applying from 23 June 2010 (£1 million for disposals before 6 April 2010 and £2m for disposals from 6 April 2010 to 22 June 2010) and in some cases it may be considered wiser to roll over the gain where possible (i.e. not elect to disapply the relief) in order to maximise the relief available on future disposals.

Where a business is owned by partners, each partner has a separate right to elect or not in relation to his partnership share.

Gifts of business assets (TCGA 1992, s 165)

[27.9] If, in Example 1, the premises were retained in personal ownership, saving CGT and stamp duty land tax, this would leave the gain on the goodwill to be considered. The business gift relief enables the whole of the gain on goodwill to be deferred providing any consideration received does not exceed the CGT base cost of the goodwill. In Example 1, that cost was nil, so that the full gain on the goodwill could be deferred only if nothing was charged for it. Goodwill will have a CGT cost either if it was purchased or if it had a value at 31 March 1982. As indicated in **27.5**, in the hands of the company the goodwill will normally be a chargeable asset for capital gains rather than being within the rules for intangible assets. If, however, the goodwill of the unincorporated business arose after 31 March 2002, either because the business started after that date or the goodwill was purchased after that date from an unrelated third party, it should be possible for the acquiring company to obtain tax relief on its writing off within acceptable accounting principles. This aspect is therefore likely to become more important in the future.

The disadvantage of charging consideration only equal to the CGT base cost is that the transferor is credited in the accounts of the company with that amount, not with the greater market value at the time of transfer, and that lower value will be the company's acquisition cost.

The chargeable asset could be transferred at a figure in excess of CGT base cost, but less than market value, any exemptions being set off against the gains arising by reference to the transfer price. This has the advantage of more cash being received on the transfer or a higher credit to a loan account, and in either case a higher base value for the asset in company ownership. The business assets gift relief eliminates the chargeable gain on the difference between market value and the value used for the transfer. See Example 5.

Example 5

Say the trader in Example 1 had retained the premises in personal ownership and transferred the goodwill to the company for £50,000, claiming gift relief under s 165. As the gift relief eliminates the chargeable gain on the difference between the market value and the value used for the transfer the position would be:

	£
Trader:	
Goodwill — market value	120,000
Less: Business gift relief	70,000
Chargeable gain	50,000*

It is HMRC's view that entrepreneurs' relief is available on the trader's disposal, see HMRC Capital Gains Manual CG64137 and the gain would therefore be taxable at the lower capital gains tax rate of 10%.

Company:	
Goodwill at market value	120,000
Less: Rolled over gain	70,000
Acquisition cost	50,000

Deferring gains under the enterprise investment scheme (EIS) (TCGA 1992, s 150C and Sch 5B)

[27.10] The disadvantage of the section 162 roll-over relief is that all assets must be transferred to the company, whereas it may be preferred to retain premises in personal ownership. The disadvantage of the business gift relief is the reduced value at which the company is regarded as acquiring the gifted assets. Both disadvantages can possibly be eliminated if the company is a qualifying unquoted trading company for EIS purposes by claiming EIS deferral relief instead (see **29.21**), although the rules are extremely complex and it is not certain that the incorporation of the business can be structured in such a way as to enable the relief to be claimed. If the relief is available, an individual would only need to transfer such assets as he wished, and they would be transferred at full market value. Money need only be locked into share capital to the extent necessary to cover the gains arising on the transfer values. If the EIS option is being considered, professional advice is essential.

Value added tax (VATA 1994, s 49; SI 1995/1268, para 5; SI 1995/2518, paras 5, 6)

[27.11] On the transfer of a business to a company, VAT will not normally arise on the assets transferred and the company will take over the VAT position of the transferor as regards deductible input VAT and liability to account for output VAT (see **7.41**). This VAT-free treatment does not apply to transfers of land and buildings in respect of which the transferor has opted to charge VAT (see **32.39**), or of commercial buildings that are either unfinished or less than three years old, unless the transferee company gives written notification before the transfer that it has opted to charge VAT on future transactions in connection with the land and buildings. In that case any VAT charged by the transferor would be recovered as input VAT by the transferee, leaving HMRC in a neutral position, and VAT is not therefore chargeable on the transfer. Otherwise, VAT must be charged. A claim may be made by the trader or partners and the company for the existing VAT registration number to be transferred to the company. It is essential to contact the appropriate VAT office in good time to obtain the necessary forms and ensure that the various requirements are complied with. HMRC guidance is available in Notice 700/9 (April 2008).

Stamp duty and stamp duty land tax

[27.12] Stamp duty applies only to instruments relating to stocks and shares and marketable securities (and also transfers of interests in partnerships to the extent of the value of any such instruments included in the partnership transfer, but this is not relevant to the incorporation of a business). Stamp duty will not therefore be payable on the transfer agreement unless and to the extent that such assets are included. Land transactions are charged to stamp duty land tax (SDLT). The detailed provisions on both stamp duty and stamp duty land tax are in **CHAPTER 6**.

On the transfer of a business, SDLT will only be payable if the business premises are transferred. In that event, then since the person transferring the business is connected with the company, SDLT will be charged on the open market value of the premises, regardless of the transfer value (see **6.8**). The value on which SDLT is charged includes any VAT on the transaction. Since SDLT is a self-assessed tax, it is up to the taxpayer to calculate the amount of SDLT due. If SDLT was paid on the basis that the transfer of going concern rules applied (see **27.11**) and this turned out not to be the case, the additional SDLT would be payable plus interest from the date of the transaction.

Inheritance tax

[27.13] There will not usually be any direct inheritance tax implications on the incorporation of a business, but three situations need watching.

The first is the effect on the availability of business property relief where partners form a company. If assets such as premises are owned within the partnership, they form part of the partnership share and 100% business property relief is available. A partner who personally owns assets such as premises used in the business is entitled to business property relief at the rate of 50%. Relief at the 50% rate for personally-owned assets is available to a shareholder only if he is a controlling shareholder, and no relief is available at all for such assets owned by minority shareholders. Shares of husband and wife or civil partners are related property and the available rate of relief is determined by their joint holdings. Where the assets are reflected in the value of the shareholdings, business property relief will apply to the value of the shares (see **5.40**).

The second situation arises where assets have been transferred using the CGT provisions for gifts to the company of business assets (TCGA 1992, s 165). Gifts to a company are not potentially exempt transfers for inheritance tax. They may be covered by the 100% business property relief, but if not, the amount of the transfer of value is the amount by which the sole trader's or partner's estate has fallen in value. In measuring that fall in value, the value of the shares acquired in the company (enhanced by the ownership within the company of the gifted assets) will be taken into account. The result may be that there is no transfer of value. Alternatively, there may be an argument that there is no transfer of value because the incorporation was a commercial transaction not intended to confer gratuitous benefit (see **5.3**).

If there is a transfer of value, no tax may be payable, because of annual exemptions and the nil rate threshold. If tax is payable, the tax may be paid by instalments if the company as donee pays the tax.

Thirdly, what was previously a sole trader's or partner's capital/current account which attracted business property relief will, unless converted into appropriate shares or securities, no longer qualify because it will be an ordinary debt due from the company.

See **CHAPTER 5** for further information on inheritance tax.

Issuing shares to directors (ITEPA 2003, ss 421B, 421J–421L)

[27.14] On the incorporation of the business, the sole trader or partners will usually become directors, and shares in the company will be issued to them (or transferred from the formation agent if the company is bought 'off the shelf'). In most cases the issue of shares in these circumstances will not need to be reported to HMRC as being by reason of the directors' employment or prospective employment. HMRC simplified and shortened form 42, and issued a detailed guidance note in July 2007, listing events that do not need to be reported, and also events that may not need to be reported (see **CHAPTER 11**). In the event that a form 42 is required, there are penalties for failing to comply with the reporting requirements.

Care should be taken to ensure that shares are issued or transferred at market value, to avoid a potential tax liability on a benefit in kind.

National insurance

[27.15] If a sole trader or partner becomes a director and/or employee in the company, national insurance contributions on earnings from the company are payable by both the employer and the employee. The burden is significantly higher than the maximum self-employed contributions under Classes 2 and 4. See CHAPTER 18 for further details.

Business rates

[27.16] The incorporation of a business means a change of occupier for rating purposes.

Tax points

[27.17] Note the following:

- Where a trader is seeking roll-over relief under TCGA 1992, s 162 on the transfer of a business, he should minimise the amount locked up in share capital by not transferring cash. If the cash is needed to assist the liquidity of the company, it can always be introduced on director's loan account.
- Roll-over relief on the replacement of business assets under TCGA 1992, s 152 can be claimed on premises owned personally and used in the owner's personal trading company — see **29.16**. A personal company is one in which the individual owns at least 5% of the voting rights.
- The payment of rent by the company for property owned personally by the former sole trader or partners does not affect business property relief for inheritance tax (but the size of the shareholding does).
- It is not possible to get the best of all worlds on incorporation of a business. Maximising the capital gains deferral can only be done at extra cost in terms of stamp duty land tax (where applicable) and with the disadvantage of locking funds into share capital. Retaining premises saves stamp duty land tax, and using gift relief on those assets that are transferred enables the funding of the company by making loans to it, but the loan account is credited with a lower figure in respect of the gifted assets and that value becomes the company's base value for capital gains. This could also significantly reduce the indexation allowance when the company disposes of the assets.
- When considering how much of the proceeds for the transfer of the business should be locked in as share capital, do not forget that funds may need to be drawn for the payment of taxation relating to the former sole trade or partnership. Unless there are sufficient funds on loan account, it will not be possible to withdraw the required funds from the company without incurring a further tax liability on remuneration or dividends.

- It may be possible to reduce the problems of locking in share capital by using redeemable shares, which can be redeemed gradually as and when the company has funds and possibly using the annual CGT exemption to avoid a tax charge on the shareholder. There are, however, anti-avoidance provisions, and also a clearance procedure, and professional advice is essential.
- If, when a sole trader or partners transfer a business to a company, shares are issued to other family members, HMRC may seek to use the settlements provisions of ITTOIA 2005, s 625 to tax the income from dividends on the former sole trader/partners rather than the shareholding family members.
- The lack of writing-down allowances in the last tax period before incorporation may cost tax relief at 40% or 50% compared with a much lower rate of relief in the first accounting period of the company.
- It is worth considering transferring chargeable assets, such as goodwill, at their full value, with a corresponding credit to a loan account. This will increase the CGT payable at the time (subject to available reliefs), but will provide a greater facility to draw off the loan account at no future personal tax cost.
- Care should be taken not to overstate the value of goodwill. To do so will risk HMRC seeking to reduce the credit to the loan account, perhaps resulting in its becoming overdrawn, leading to a liability for the company under CTA 2010, s 455 (loans to participators), or the amount being regarded as a distribution of company profits. The valuation is particularly tricky, and might even be arguably nil, where it depends upon individual qualities of the former sole trader or partners.
- The private use of motor cars used in a sole trade or partnership will have been dealt with by excluding part of the running costs and capital allowances from the allowable business costs for tax purposes. If the cars are acquired by the company, the private use will then be reckoned under the employee benefits rules. The resulting tax and national insurance costs need to be considered when deciding if the cars should be transferred, or retained in personal ownership, with an appropriate business mileage claim being made. If cars previously included in the business assets up to the time of transfer are retained in personal ownership, all the assets will not have been transferred, denying section 162 roll-over relief.

28

Selling the family company

Background

[28.1] There are two ways in which a business run via a family company may be sold. The shares can be sold, or the company assets can be sold and then either the company can be liquidated or kept and dividends drawn from it. The most difficult aspect of the sale negotiations is usually reconciling the interests of the vendors and the purchasers.

The vendors will often prefer to sell the shares rather than the assets to avoid the 'double' capital gains tax (CGT) charge which will arise on the assets sale and then on the distribution to shareholders if the company is wound up. The purchaser may prefer to buy assets in order to be able to attract tax-efficient investment for their purchase through the enterprise investment scheme (see **29.17** to **29.24**), to claim tax allowances on purchases of equipment, plant and goodwill, or capital gains roll-over relief on earlier disposals, through the purchase of appropriate assets. Buying assets is sometimes more straightforward than a share purchase, with consequently lower costs. Stamp duty is charged on share transactions and stamp duty land tax on the acquisition of land and buildings, but the stamp duty land tax rates are much higher. The vendors may intend staying in business, so that a sale of assets by a trading company, with the company then acquiring replacement assets, may give an opportunity for capital gains roll-over relief. If the vendors plan to invest in another company, then providing their investment would qualify for enterprise investment scheme deferral relief (see **29.21**), all or any part of the gains on the disposal of the shares in the existing company (and any other gains they may have) may be held over to the extent that shares are subscribed for in the new company. (The relief is not available where the acquisition is of shares already in existence.) The gain is not deducted from the cost of the new shares and the tax payable crystallises when they are disposed of unless further relief is then available.

Buying a company carries certain risks that are not associated with a straightforward purchase of assets. Known and 'latent' liabilities and obligations of the company will remain as company liabilities following a sale of the shares, making it most important that extreme care is taken for commercial and taxation purposes (often referred to as due diligence). The purchaser will clearly require indemnities and warranties from the vendors, but the vendors will want to limit these as much as possible, and in any event the purchaser would have the inconvenience of trying to enforce them.

The outcome of the negotiations, including the adjustments each party agrees to in order to resolve points of difference, will depend on the future intentions of the vendor, the relative bargaining strength of each party and how keen vendor and purchaser are to conclude the transaction.

Selling shares or assets

[28.2] Part of the sale consideration may relate not to tangible assets but to the growth prospects or the entrepreneurial flair of those involved with the company, and where goodwill is a substantial factor, the valuation placed on it will be an important part of the negotiations, providing flexibility in agreeing a price.

The tax cost of selling the shares can be significantly less than that of selling the assets followed by a liquidation. See Example 1 for a straight comparison of a share sale and an assets sale based on the same values.

Example 1

Trading company was formed in 1987 and 1,000 £1 shares were issued at par. Balance sheet of company immediately prior to intended sale at the end of April 2010 was:

	£		£
Share capital	1,000	Net current assets	50,000
Accumulated profits	99,000	Premises at cost	50,000
	£100,000		£100,000

A sale is now proposed on the basis of the goodwill and premises being worth £350,000.

If the shares are sold:

Assets per balance sheet	100,000
Increase in value of premises and goodwill (350,000 − 50,000)	300,000
Sale proceeds for shares	400,000
Cost	1,000
Chargeable gain*	£399,000

CGT @ 18% (ignoring any set-offs and exemptions)*   £71,820

* If the conditions for entrepreneurs' relief (see **29.2**) are met on the sale of shares, the gain of £399,000 will be reduced by $^4/_9$ths, leaving £221,667 taxable at 18%. The CGT of £39,900 is 10% of the gain of £399,000. See Example 1 at **27.6** for calculations of entrepreneurs' relief for disposals on or after 23 June 2010, and see **4.2** for the differing capital gains tax rates applying from that date.

If assets are sold and company is liquidated:

Assets per balance sheet		100,000
Increase in value of premises and goodwill	300,000	
Less provision for corporation tax on sale (£300,000 less, say, £60,000 for indexation to April 2010 on cost of premises)		
Gain £240,000 @ say 28%**	67,200	232,800
Amount distributed to shareholders on liquidation (ignoring liquidation costs)		332,800
Cost of shares (no indexation allowance)		1,000
Chargeable gain***		£331,800
CGT @ 18% (ignoring any set-offs and exemptions)***		£59,724

** The illustrative rate of 28% would probably be somewhere between 21% and the small profits marginal rate depending on the profits for the accounting period in which the disposal took place. See **3.11** regarding the changes in corporation tax rates applying from April 2011.

*** If the conditions for entrepreneurs' relief (see **29.2**) are met on the distribution, the gain of £331,800 will be reduced by $^4/_9$ths, leaving £184,333 taxable at 18%. The CGT of £33,180 is 10% of the gain of £331,800. See Example 1 at **27.6** for calculations of entrepreneurs' relief for disposals on or after 23 June 2010, and see **4.2** for the differing capital gains tax rates applying from that date.

Amounts received by shareholders (assuming no entrepreneurs' relief):

	Proceeds	CGT	Net
	£	£	£
On sale of shares	400,000	71,820	328,180
On liquidation	332,800	59,724	273,076
Extra cost of liquidation route			£55,104

Knowing the tax advantage of the share sale to the vendor, coupled with the potential tax liability if the company in its new ownership sells its premises and goodwill (which still have a cost of £50,000 even though the share sale is based on a value of £350,000), the purchaser may well seek a reduction in price if this route is to be followed.

Other factors

[28.3] The disadvantages of selling assets may be mitigated if the company has current (as distinct from brought-forward) trading losses which may be set off against the gains on the assets.

If it is intended that the company shall continue trading in some new venture rather than be wound up, it may be possible to roll-over or hold-over the gains by the purchase of new assets. Alternatively, if the new trade commences before the old trade ceases, trading losses may arise in that new trade against which the gains may be set under the normal rules for set-off of trading losses.

Goodwill (FA 2002, s 84 and Sch 29)

[28.4] Where a company buys goodwill from an unrelated party, or from a related party that commenced business after 31 March 2002, it can claim tax relief over a period on the price paid (see **20.30** to **20.36**). The purchase of goodwill is also exempt from stamp duty. See **28.11** for the stamp duty land tax position.

The purchaser in Example 1 might therefore be reluctant to buy the shares, but as illustrated the vendor is seriously disadvantaged if the company has first to sell its assets and then distribute its available cash. This might provide a bargaining opportunity under which the purchaser pays somewhat more for goodwill, the real cost, however, being reduced by the forthcoming tax relief, whilst the vendor accepts that his company must sell assets and pay the appropriate corporation tax, while his share proceeds will be higher because of the increased amount his company has received for goodwill.

Payments in compensation for loss of office

[28.5] Compensation and ex gratia payments are dealt with in detail in **CHAPTER 15**. There are two aspects, first whether the director/shareholder will be exempt from tax on the first £30,000 of the payment, and second whether the payment will be deductible as an expense in calculating taxable profits.

As far as the individual is concerned, in order for the £30,000 exemption to apply, the company must be able to demonstrate that any payments are wholly unassociated with a sale of the individual's shares in the company and moreover do not represent an income dividend. Ex gratia payments may also be challenged as being benefits under an employer-financed scheme that is not a registered pension scheme (see **15.3**).

As far as the company is concerned, the company must show that the payments are wholly and exclusively for the purposes of the trade, which is more difficult if the payment is ex gratia rather than compensation for loss of office. Where the company's trade ceases following a sale of the assets, an ex gratia or compensation payment cannot satisfy the 'wholly and exclusively' rule because there is no longer any trade. The part of the company's payment that can be set against the company's trading profits in those circumstances is limited to the amount of statutory redundancy pay to which the director is entitled plus a sum equal to three times that amount, unless the payment is made under a pre-existing contractual or statutory obligation (see **15.8**). Where a compensation or ex gratia payment is made prior to a sale of the shares, the company's trade continuing, this restriction in calculating taxable profits will not apply.

Whether there is a sale of the shares or an assets sale followed by a liquidation, the compensation payment will reduce the value of the company's assets, and thus the amount of disposal proceeds on which the shareholder's CGT liability will be calculated.

Payments into a pension scheme

[28.6] Prior to selling the shares, the cash resources of the company, and thus, effectively, the eventual sale proceeds, may also be reduced by an appropriate pension scheme contribution, the benefits of which may be taken partly as a tax-free lump sum and partly as a pension. Again, the trading profits prior to the sale are reduced, with a corresponding saving in corporation tax. This is of course only acceptable if the amount of the contribution and effect on the value of the fund is within the stipulated limits. Company pension schemes are dealt with in **CHAPTER 16**.

Sale of a trading subsidiary

[28.7] Where a single trading company (or member of a trading group) is selling a trading subsidiary (or holding company of a trading group), then so long as the shareholding in the company which is being sold exceeds 10% and has been owned for a continuous period of twelve months within the preceding two years, the shares can be sold by the parent company to another trading company or group holding company without a charge to corporation tax on the capital gain arising (see **3.31**).

Whilst this relieves the selling company of the corporation tax on its gain, there is still no tax relief to the purchaser because assets have not been purchased, so there is still some inconsistency between the aims of buyer and seller.

Selling on the basis of receiving shares in the purchasing company (TCGA 1992, ss 126–139, 279A–279D)

[28.8] Where, as consideration for the sale of their shares, the vending shareholders receive shares in the company making the acquisition, then each vending shareholder is normally treated as not having made a disposal of the 'old shares', but as having acquired the 'new shares' for the same amount and on the same date as the 'old shares' (known as 'paper for paper' exchanges).

Where the consideration is part shares/part cash, that part received in cash is liable to CGT, whilst the 'new shares' again stand in the shoes of the old. See Example 2.

Example 2

Shares cost £10,000. As a result of an acquisition of the entire share capital by another company, the shareholder receives cash of £40,000 and shares in the acquiring company valued at £60,000. The capital gains position is:

		Cash £	Shares £
Cost of £10,000, divided in proportion to the proceeds		4,000	6,000
Proceeds:			
Cash	40,000	40,000	
New shares	60,000		
Total consideration	100,000		
Chargeable gain (subject to available exemptions)		£36,000	
Cost of 'new shares'			£6,000

[28.9] In such paper for paper exchanges it is possible that the disposal of the original shares at the time of the exchange would result in a gain that could qualify for entrepreneurs' relief, whereas the gain on the later disposal of the new holding may not qualify, for example because the company may no longer be the individual's personal company following the exchange (see **29.4**). In such circumstances, and provided that all the relevant criteria are met, it will be possible to make an election to claim entrepreneurs' relief as if the exchange involved a disposal of the original shares, thus crystallising a gain against which entrepreneurs' relief may be claimed. The time limit for the election is one year from 31 January following the tax year in which the exchange takes place. HMRC have confirmed that where there is a share for share exchange, the twelve month ownership requirement for entrepreneurs' relief does 'in principle' include the holding period of the original shares.

Where part of the consideration depends upon future performance, say the issue of further shares or securities if a profit target is met, the value of the right to receive further shares or securities (known as an earn-out right) is normally treated as part of the disposal proceeds at the time the original shares are sold. Where the vendor is employed in the business and is to continue in employment in some capacity for a period after the sale, it must be clear that the earn-out right is not linked in any way to the future employment, otherwise the value of shares issued under the earn-out would be charged to tax and national insurance as employment earnings rather than being dealt with under the capital gains rules. Where the capital gains rules apply, the value of the right is treated as a security, so that any capital gains are rolled over until the further shares or securities are sold. The taxpayer may elect for this treatment not to apply, making the value of the earn-out right itself liable to CGT.

[28.10] The roll-over treatment does not apply if the future consideration is to be cash. In that event, the whole of the value of the right to future consideration is liable to CGT at the time of the sale, with a further liability on the difference between that value and the amount of consideration actually received, or the proceeds of selling the right. Where cash is to be received, then if the proceeds of deferred unascertainable consideration or of selling the right to receive it are less than the estimated value brought in for the right, and the disposal occurred in a tax year later than that when the original gain arose on the undeferred consideration, the taxpayer may elect for the loss to be carried back to that earlier tax year. The time limit for a carry back claim is the first anniversary of the 31 January following the tax year of the loss.

Stamp duty and stamp duty land tax

[28.11] Where there is a sale of shares, stamp duty is normally payable by the purchaser at ½% on the consideration for the sale. Where there is a sale of assets, stamp duty is only payable on stocks, shares and marketable securities, but stamp duty land tax (SDLT) is payable on land transactions, the rate of tax being 1%, 3%, 4%, or 5% depending on the sale proceeds (see **6.9**). As far as goodwill is concerned, where it is regarded as attributable to the land (referred to as inherent goodwill), it is included in the amount on which SDLT is payable. Goodwill that is 'personal' goodwill does not attract SDLT. If HMRC raise an enquiry into the SDLT return, they may well challenge the part of the consideration that has been apportioned to personal goodwill.

The value on which SDLT is payable includes any VAT on the sale. It may not be known when a business is sold whether the VAT 'going concern' treatment will apply (see **28.12**). If VAT is excluded from the amount on which SDLT is paid, and the 'going concern' basis proves not to be available, the appropriate amount of additional SDLT would be payable, plus interest from the date of the sale.

Value added tax (VATA 1994, ss 49, 94 and Sch 9 Group 5; SI 1995/1268, para 5; SI 1995/2518)

[28.12] Where the family company is sold by means of a share sale, the sale does not attract value added tax (VAT) because the shares are not sold in the course of business but by an individual as an investment.

Where all or part of the business is sold as a going concern by one taxable person to another, no VAT is charged by the vendor and the purchaser has no input VAT to reclaim on the amount paid (subject to what is said at **27.11** for land and buildings). The going concern treatment only applies, however, where the assets acquired are such that they represent a business which is capable of independent operation (see **7.41**).

Where the 'going concern' concept does not apply, VAT must be charged on all taxable supplies, and any related input VAT suffered by the seller is recoverable. Taxable supplies include goodwill, trading stock, plant and machinery, and motor vehicles (except that cars on which input VAT was not recovered when they were acquired will only be chargeable to the extent, if any, that the disposal proceeds exceed original cost). Business premises on which the seller has exercised his option to tax are also included, and the seller can therefore recover any VAT relating to the costs of sale, for example on legal and professional fees. The disposal of book debts, and of business premises over three years old on which the option to tax has not been taken, is an exempt supply and does not attract VAT. For partially exempt businesses there are some complex rules as to how the sale of the business is treated.

It is important to ensure that the purchase agreement provides for the addition of VAT and that the purchase consideration is allocated over the various assets acquired. If VAT is not mentioned in the purchase agreement, the price is deemed to be VAT-inclusive.

Tax points

[28.13] Note the following:

- Because there are so many pitfalls and problems when selling or buying a family company, it is essential to get expert professional advice.
- When a company ceases to trade, this denotes the end of a chargeable accounting period, and if there are current trading losses these cannot be relieved against chargeable gains arising after the cessation. But gains are deemed to be made on the contract date, not on completion, so if the company enters into the contract for sale of the chargeable assets while it is still trading, the right to set off current trading losses against chargeable gains in that trading period will be preserved.
- Compensation for loss of office and ex gratia payments upon cessation of employment can only be expected to escape HMRC challenge if they are genuine payments for breach of contract or reasonable ex gratia amounts bearing in mind years of service, etc. and even so, ex gratia payments may not qualify for the £30,000 exemption (see **28.5** and **CHAPTER 15**).
- When shares are being sold in a family company with significant retained profits, HMRC may argue in some circumstances that the increased share value as a result of the retained profits represents not a capital gain but sums that could have been paid out as income, and that they are chargeable as such. Consideration should therefore be given to whether HMRC clearance should be obtained for the proposed sale.
- When buying the shares in a company, the purchaser should look particularly for any potential capital gains liabilities which will be inherited, such as the crystallisation after ten years of gains on depreciating business assets which have been held over because the company acquired new qualifying assets, or, if the company being purchased is leaving a group, the crystallisation of gains on assets acquired by it from another group company within the previous six

years. Moreover, the accounts value of the company assets may be greater than the tax value because earlier gains have been deducted under the roll-over relief provisions from the tax cost of the assets now held or the assets have been revalued for accounts purposes. Thus a chargeable gain may arise on the company even though the item is sold for no more than its value in the accounts. Taxation due diligence is essential.

- If a company with unused trading losses is purchased, the losses cannot be used when the company returns to profitability if the change of ownership takes place within a period of three years during which there is also a major change in the nature or conduct of the business. There is also a restriction on availability of trading losses where the company being acquired has succeeded to the trade of another company without taking over that other company's liabilities (see **26.19**).

- Whether shares or assets are purchased, the purchaser will take over the predecessor company's Class 1A national insurance liability for that part of the tax year before the succession. Again, taxation due diligence is essential.

- The purchase consideration may partly depend on the company's future profit performance, sometimes referred to as an 'earn out', and when it is received it may be partly in cash and partly in the form of shares or securities in the purchasing company. The CGT position is complicated and professional advisers have to look very carefully at this aspect, if possible obtaining the views of HMRC when they apply for clearance on the share sale.

- The carryback to an earlier tax year of a loss arising in relation to deferred unascertainable consideration is not limited to where the original disposal was of shares. It could equally apply to a disposal of goodwill by a sole trader or partners, where further consideration depended upon profit performance, or where the proceeds of land depended on planning consents.

- A private company may avoid the costs of putting a company into formal liquidation by distributing the assets and then having the company struck off the companies register as a defunct company. Although strictly the distribution of assets in these circumstances is an income distribution on which the shareholders would be liable for income tax, HMRC will usually agree to treat it as if it were a capital distribution in a formal liquidation (and, therefore, subject to CGT) providing there is a commercial objective for the dissolution as distinct from an attempt to obtain a tax advantage (concession C16). It is essential to get HMRC's formal approval, which will require certain undertakings on behalf of the company and by the shareholders. Care is needed where there are non-distributable reserves.

- Corporation tax payable on current year profits by the company being sold will reduce the net assets and usually in consequence the price to be received by the vending shareholders. The rate of corporation tax depends upon the number of associated companies at any time in the accounting period, which will inevitably be increased if the share purchase is by a company or group. Ensure that there is a clause in the purchase/sale agreement saying that any additional corporation tax because of an increase in rate occasioned by the new grouping is not to be deducted in calculating the net assets to be taken into account in fixing the selling price of the shares.

29

Encouraging business investment and enterprise

Background

[29.1] This chapter deals with various schemes that encourage investment in new and expanding companies and other measures to promote business enterprise, efficiency and innovation. It gives only an outline of the provisions and professional advice is recommended.

CHAPTER 11 at **11.13** onwards deals with the enterprise management incentive share option scheme that is available to small, higher risk companies. See also **3.31** regarding the exemption for company gains on substantial shareholdings and **20.30** onwards regarding the corporation tax regime for intellectual property, goodwill and other intangible assets.

Entrepreneurs' relief (TCGA 1992 ss 169H–S; FA 2010, s 4; F(No.2)A 2010, s 2 and Sch 1)

[29.2] Entrepreneurs' relief was introduced following the major reform of the capital gains tax (CGT) regime in FA 2008. It was the outcome of discussions with business groups who had protested against the abolition, for disposals after 6 April 2008, of taper relief (which had reduced to 10% the effective CGT rate on business assets for many higher rate taxpayers) and indexation allowance (see **4.1**).

[29.3] Entrepreneurs' relief is available for 'qualifying business disposals' taking place after 5 April 2008. The effect of the relief is to reduce the effective rate of CGT from 18% or 28% (see **4.2**) to 10%. The following disposals are qualifying business disposals:

(a) a material disposal of business assets, e.g. the disposal of all or part of a business — see **29.4**;

(b) a disposal of trust business assets where there is a qualifying beneficiary of the trust — see **29.5**; and

(c) a disposal associated with a relevant material disposal, e.g. the disposal of a business property used by a company where that disposal is associated with a disposal of shares in the company — see **29.6**.

Where the disposal is not one of shares or securities (see **29.4**) relief under each of these three headings is restricted to the disposal of 'relevant business assets' (see **29.7**).

For disposals before 6 April 2010 there is a lifetime limit of £1m of gains in respect of qualifying business disposals, but this was increased to £2m for disposals on or after 6 April 2010 and increased again to £5m for disposals on or after 23 June 2010. This latter increase was to lessen the impact of the increase in the capital gains tax rate for higher rate taxpayers to 28% (see **4.2**). In the case of the first increased limit on 6 April 2010, where the individual makes qualifying gains above the £1m limit before 6 April 2010, no additional relief is available for that excess. However, if he makes further qualifying gains after 5 April 2010 relief can be claimed on up to a further £1m of the additional gains, giving relief on accumulated qualifying gains up to the new limit of £2m. The same applies in respect of the increase in the limit to £5m on 23 June 2010. No additional relief will be allowed in respect of any excess of qualifying gains made before 23 June 2010 above the previous limit applying at the time of disposal. In view of the fact that differing rates of capital gains tax apply from 23 June 2010 (see **4.2**), in determining at what rate an individual should be charged to capital gains tax on any other gains, the gains qualifying for entrepreneurs' relief on disposals on or after 23 June 2010 are set against any unused basic rate band before non-qualifying gains.

There was an anomaly in the entrepreneurs' relief calculation for disposals made before 23 June 2010 which meant that the annual exemption and losses (other than 'relevant losses', see **29.9**) received relief at 18% even if the whole gain would otherwise be taxable at the effective 10% rate (see Example 1 at **27.6**). The amendments in F(No.2)A 2010, Sch 1 have removed this anomaly so that relief is only received at the prevailing rate of 10%. However, for 2010/11 where the gain is taxable at more than one rate the annual exemption and allowable losses can be applied in a way that produces the lowest possible tax charge. Therefore, where an individual has gains both before and after 23 June 2010 which would otherwise qualify for entrepreneurs' relief, the exemption and losses should be applied to the gains arising before 23 June 2010. This is subject to any existing legislation that limits the way in which certain losses may be set off.

Entrepreneurs' relief is based broadly on retirement relief, which was abolished in 2003, but there are some significant differences. There is no age limit, for example. In addition the conditions for the new relief are not identical to those which determined whether an asset was a business asset for taper relief purposes.

Material disposal of business assets

[29.4] Relief is available if an individual makes a disposal of business assets and that disposal is a material disposal. A disposal of business assets is either:

(a)   a disposal of the whole or part of a business that the individual has owned for at least a year;

(b)   a disposal of assets that were in use for the business when the business ceased, providing that the individual owned the business for at least a year up to the date of cessation and the disposal takes place within three years of that date; or

(c)   a disposal of shares or securities of a company (see below).

With regard to (c), for a period of one year up to the date of the disposal the company must be the individual's personal company and it must be either a trading company or the holding company of a trading group. The individual must be an officer or employee of the company or of another group company. Alternatively, relief is available if these conditions are met for at least a year up to the date when the company ceases to be a trading company or a member of a trading group, and the individual disposes of the shares within three years of that date. HMRC have confirmed that where there is a share for share exchange (see **28.8**) the twelve month ownership requirement does 'in principle' include the holding period of the original shares.

A partner in a partnership is treated for these purposes as though he is carrying on the business on his own account, so that for example a disposal of an interest in the partnership's assets is treated as a disposal of the whole of a part of the partnership's business.

Disposal of trust business assets

[29.5] There is a disposal of trust business assets where the trustees dispose of settlement business assets, i.e. assets forming part of the settled property that are either shares or securities of a company or assets used (or previously used) for a business. There must be an individual who is a qualifying beneficiary (B), (i.e. an individual who has an interest in possession in either the whole of the settled property or a part of it that includes the business assets), and a further condition must be met.

The further condition in the case of a disposal of shares or securities is that, for a period of one year ending not earlier than three years before the disposal, the company is B's personal company and is either a trading company or the holding company of a trading group, and B is an officer or employee of the company or of another group company.

The further condition in the case of other assets is that the assets are used for the business carried on by B for a period of one year ending not earlier than three years before the disposal, and B ceases to carry on the business either on or within three years before the date of the disposal.

Disposal associated with material disposal

[29.6] There is a disposal associated with a relevant material disposal if:

(a) an individual makes a material disposal of business assets (see **29.4**) which is the disposal of either:
  (i) an interest in the assets of a partnership; or
  (ii) the shares or securities of a company;

(b) the individual makes the disposal — i.e. the 'associated' disposal — as part of his withdrawal from participation in the business of the partnership or the company; and

(c) the assets disposed of are in use for the business for a period of one year up to the earlier of the date of the material disposal and the date of cessation of the business.

Relief is restricted where, on the associated disposal, the assets disposed of are in use for the business for only part of the period of ownership; or only part of the assets are in such use; or the individual is concerned in carrying on the business for only part of the period of such use; or the availability of the assets is dependent on the payment of rent (see **29.10**).

Relevant business assets

[29.7] Relief is restricted to the disposal of 'relevant business assets' where the disposal is not one of shares or securities. Relevant business assets include goodwill but exclude shares and securities and other assets held as investments. Generally, an asset is a relevant business asset if it is:

(a) in the case of a material disposal of business assets (see **29.4**), used for the purposes of the business carried on by the individual or a partnership of which he is a member;

(b) in the case of a disposal of trust business assets (see **29.5**), used for the purposes of the business carried on by the qualifying beneficiary or a partnership of which he is a member; or

(c) in the case of a disposal associated with a relevant material disposal (see **29.6**), used for the purposes of a business carried on by the partnership or the company.

Claims

[29.8] Entrepreneur's relief must be claimed on or before the first anniversary of 31 January following the tax year in which the disposal is made. For example, relief must be claimed by 31 January 2013 in respect of a qualifying business disposal made on 1 September 2010. A claim relating to a disposal of trust assets is to be made jointly by the trustees and the qualifying beneficiary.

Operation of the relief

[29.9] The operation of the relief differs depending on whether the qualifying business disposal is before or after 23 June 2010 (see Example 1 in **27.6**). For such disposals before 23 June 2010, the 'relevant gains' and 'relevant losses' arising are aggregated, and the losses are deducted from the gains. Relief is available only if the resulting amount is a positive amount, and is given by reducing that amount by 4/9ths.

The lifetime limit (£1m for disposals before 6 April 2010, £2m for disposals on or after 6 April 2010 but before 23 June 2010) mentioned in **29.3** is applied where the aggregate of the resulting amount (A) and the corresponding amount in respect of earlier qualifying business disposals (B) exceeds the limit applying. The 4/9ths reduction is applied only to so much of A as (when added to B) does not exceed the limit. The amount remaining after deduction of entrepreneurs' relief is the taxpayer's chargeable gain. The chargeable gain is then taxable at 18% which results in an effective tax rate of 10%. A chargeable gain may be deferred if the taxpayer makes a qualifying investment under the enterprise investment scheme (see **29.17**).

For qualifying business disposals on or after 23 June 2010 when there are differing capital gains tax rates (see **4.2**) the previous operation of the relief would not give an effective rate of 10%. Therefore for such disposals the 'relevant gains' and 'relevant losses' are still aggregated as before and the resulting amount is a chargeable gain taxed at a rate of 10%, provided that the gain together with any previous gains that benefited from entrepreneurs' relief do not exceed £5m (the limit applying from 23 June 2010). The 10% rate only applies to gains which do not exceed the £5m limit, any balance being taxed at either 18% or 28% depending on the circumstances (see **4.2** for individuals, **42.5** for personal representatives, and **42.18** for trustees). In determining which rate should apply to individuals, gains qualifying for entrepreneurs' relief are set against any unused basic rate band before non-qualifying gains. For 2010/11 where gains are taxable at more than one rate the annual exemption and allowable losses may be applied in a way that produces the lowest possible tax charge, subject to any existing legislation which limits the way certain losses may be set off.

There are specific rules dealing with reorganisation of share capital (see **28.9**), and relief is available where gains that have been deferred prior to 6 April 2008 become chargeable because of an event occurring on or after that date (see **29.21** to **29.23**).

Definitions

[29.10] The legislation sets out several important definitions for the purpose of the relief, including:

A business — a trade, profession or vocation conducted on a commercial basis and with a view to the realisation of profits;

Personal company — a company in which the individual holds at least 5% of the ordinary share capital and can exercise at least 5% of the voting rights.

Rent — includes any form of consideration given for the use of the asset.

Trade — defined as in ITA 2007, s 989, i.e. 'trade' includes any venture in the nature of trade, but the commercial letting of furnished holiday accommodation is treated as a trade for the purpose of entrepreneurs' relief.

Roll-over/hold-over relief on replacement of business assets and compulsorily purchased land (TCGA 1992, ss 152–159, 175, 247)

[29.11] Where there is a chargeable gain on the disposal of a qualifying business asset and the proceeds (or deemed proceeds if the asset is given away) are matched by the acquisition of another qualifying business asset within the period commencing one year before and ending three years after the disposal, a claim may be made for the gain to be deferred. HMRC have discretion to extend the time limit. The replacement asset need not be used in the same trade where one person carries on two or more trades either successively or at the same time. For holding companies and their 75% subsidiaries, the disposal and acquisition need not be made by the same group company. But an asset acquired intra-group on a no loss/no gain basis cannot be treated as a qualifying acquisition. A group company that is chargeable on a deferred gain when it leaves a group may claim roll-over relief in appropriate circumstances (see **3.29**).

Qualifying assets

[29.12] The relief applies to land and buildings, fixed plant and machinery, ships, aircraft, hovercraft, satellites, space stations and spacecraft including launch vehicles, goodwill, milk and fish quota, farmers' payment entitlements under the single payment scheme and Lloyd's syndicate rights. The replacement asset does not have to be in the same category as the asset disposed of, providing both are qualifying assets, and the proceeds of a single disposal could be applied in acquiring several qualifying assets or vice versa. For companies, disposals of goodwill and fish and agricultural quotas on or after 1 April 2002 and of farmers' single payment entitlements are dealt with under the intangible assets rules (see **20.30** to **20.36**) rather than the CGT rules. (There was an exception for replacement assets acquired before 1 April 2002 and within twelve months prior to the disposal, for which the company had a choice whether to claim capital gains roll-over relief or the intangible assets roll-over relief.) Disposals of other qualifying assets by companies on or after 1 April 2002 cannot be rolled over against acquisitions of goodwill and quotas on or after that date (unless the acquisitions are from related parties and are thus not within the company rules for intangible assets). The rules for individuals remain unchanged.

If only part of the sale proceeds is used to acquire replacement assets within the roll-over period, the remaining part of the gain is chargeable immediately, treating the gain as the last part of the proceeds to be used.

See **4.15** for the treatment of disposals after 5 April 1988 (but, for taxpayers other than companies, before 6 April 2008) that are affected by deferred gains on assets acquired before 31 March 1982. See CHAPTER **31** for further details in relation to farming assets. See CHAPTER **41** for the overseas aspect of roll-over/hold-over relief.

Roll-over relief

[29.13] If the replacement asset has a predictable life of more than 60 years (e.g. freehold land or, for individuals, goodwill or farmers' single payment entitlements), the gain may be rolled over and treated as reducing the cost of the replacement asset.

If a gain has been rolled over in this way against a replacement asset acquired before 31 March 1982, the effect of using 31 March 1982 value as the cost of such an asset is that the rolled over gain escapes tax altogether.

Hold-over relief for depreciating assets

[29.14] If the replacement is a depreciating asset with a life of 60 years or less (which in fact applies to most of the business assets qualifying for relief), the gain does not reduce the CGT cost of the replacement but it is held over for a maximum of ten years. The held over gain becomes chargeable when the replacement asset is sold or ceases to be used in a business carried on by the taxpayer, or, at latest, ten years after acquisition of the replacement asset (see Example 1). The gain will not crystallise at that point, however, if at or before that time a non-depreciating asset has been acquired against which a claim is made for the gain to be rolled over instead.

Example 1

Qualifying business asset that cost £200,000 before 6 April 1998 was sold by a sole trader on 1 May 2010 for £300,000, giving rise to a gain of £100,000. Qualifying replacement asset (freehold land) acquired within roll-over period for:

£360,000   Full gain reinvested, therefore CGT cost of replacement reduced to £260,000. No entrepreneurs' relief is due when the whole of the gain accruing upon the disposal of the old asset is rolled over against the acquisition cost of the new asset. There is no chargeable gain at that time and therefore there is no 'relevant gain' for the purposes of TCGA 1992, s 169N(1) (see HMRC Capital Gains Manual CG64136). Entrepreneurs' relief may be available on a subsequent disposal of the replacement asset if the relevant criteria are met (see 29.3).

£290,000	£10,000 of the proceeds (and hence the gain) not reinvested, so gain of £10,000 chargeable immediately (unless other qualifying assets acquired within roll-over period) but entrepreneurs' relief* of £4,444 (4/9 x £10,000) will reduce that £10,000 gain to £5,556 (see CG64136 as above). £90,000 of gain deducted from £290,000 cost of replacement, reducing CGT cost to £200,000.
£198,000	No part of gain reinvested therefore full £100,000 chargeable less £44,444 entrepreneurs' relief* (4/9 x £100,000) (unless other qualifying assets acquired within roll-over period).

*If the asset was sold on or after 23 June 2010, the operation of entrepreneurs' relief would apply in a different way (see 29.9). If the replacement had been a depreciating asset, there would be no change in the gains immediately chargeable. The CGT cost of the replacement asset would, however, not be reduced. Instead that part of the gain that was reinvested would be deferred for up to ten years (see above).

Both rolled-over and held-over gains escape tax completely on the taxpayer's death.

Claims

[29.15] Roll-over/hold-over relief claims must give full details of assets disposed of and acquired, including dates and amounts (and where two group companies are involved, they must make a joint claim). For companies, the time limit for the original roll-over or hold-over claim is four years from the end of the accounting period to which the claim relates. The time limit for individuals is four years from the end of the tax year to which the claim relates. The claim will normally be sent in with the tax return. There is a form for individuals to make the claim in HMRC Helpsheet HS290.

Where the replacement asset(s) have not been acquired by the due date for the return, a provisional claim may be made with the return for the tax year or company accounting period in which the disposal took place, and the relief is then given as for an actual claim. The provisional claim will be superseded by an actual claim, or will be withdrawn, or will cease to have effect:

(a)   for an individual, three years from 31 January following the tax year of disposal (e.g. for a disposal in 2010/11 provisional relief would no longer apply after 31 January 2015), or

(b)   for a company, on the fourth anniversary of the last day of the accounting period of disposal.

All necessary adjustments will then be made, including interest on underpaid tax from the date the tax would have been payable if no provisional claim had been made. Where a hold-over claim is being replaced by a roll-over claim as a result of the later acquisition of a non-depreciating asset (which could in fact be up to thirteen years after the disposal giving rise to the gain that had been held over), it is thought that the claim to switch from hold-over to roll-over relief would need to be sent in with the return for the year in which the non-depreciating asset was acquired.

The strict rules for roll-over relief are relaxed by various HMRC concessions, notably D16 and D22–D26. There are anti-avoidance provisions to counter abuse of the concessions (see **4.29**).

Personally owned assets and investment property

[29.16] Roll-over relief is also available where an asset owned personally and used in the owner's trading or professional partnership or personal trading company is disposed of and replaced. A 'personal trading company' is one in which the individual owns 5% or more of the voting rights. The receipt of rent from the partnership or trading company does not affect the availability of the relief.

Apart from that exception, roll-over relief is only available on investment property in two instances. If the property is the subject of compulsory purchase (or compulsory acquisition by a lessee), the relief is available provided that the replacement is not a CGT exempt dwelling-house — see **32.30**. (Companies in a 75% group can claim this relief if one company makes a disposal under a compulsory purchase order and another acquires the replacement.) The relief is also available on property let as furnished holiday accommodation (see **CHAPTER 32**).

Enterprise investment scheme

Income tax relief (ITA 2007, Pt 5)

[29.17] Income tax relief at 20% is given where a 'qualifying investor' subscribes for shares in a company, and both the shares and the company meet several requirements. The relief is subject to detailed anti-avoidance provisions. HMRC guidance on the enterprise investment scheme (EIS) is available at www.hmrc.gov.uk/eis.

The subscription must normally be wholly in cash and be fully paid up at the time of issue. The shares must be issued to raise money for a qualifying business activity (see below). For shares issued before 22 April 2009 at least 80% of the money raised had to be used for a qualifying business activity within 12 months after the shares were issued or, if later, within 12 months after the commencement of the trade, with the remainder being required to be used within the following 12 months. For shares issued on or after 22 April 2009 the requirement is that all the money must be used within two years of the date of issue, or commencement of the trade if later. Various terms used in the legislation are defined broadly as follows.

A 'qualifying investor' is one who is not 'connected' with the company in a specified period. This rule mainly excludes someone who is or has been an employee or director, or who controls more than 30% of the company's capital or voting power (the rights of associates being counted), or is able to secure that the company's affairs are conducted in accordance with his wishes.

Someone who was not connected with the company before the shares were issued may, however, become a paid director without affecting his entitlement to relief. Non-resident investors are eligible but should bear in mind that EIS reliefs are reliefs against UK tax.

The shares must meet several requirements. They must be new ordinary shares that are not redeemable for at least three years. The arrangements surrounding the issue of shares must not provide for a 'pre-arranged exit'; the shares must be for genuine commercial reasons and not as part of a tax avoidance scheme; and there is an exclusion for shares linked to certain loans.

For shares issued after 18 July 2007 the annual amount raised by an issuing company through risk capital schemes, including the EIS, must not exceed £2 million. The company must be a 'qualifying company' in relation to the shares. Broadly, it must exist wholly for the purpose of carrying on one or more qualifying trades or be the parent company of a group whose business does not consist wholly or substantially in carrying on 'non-qualifying' activities. The issuing company or a qualifying 90% subsidiary must carry on the qualifying business activity. HMRC consider that relief is not available where the activity is carried on by the company in partnership or by a limited liability partnership of which the company is a member. They will apply this interpretation broadly to shares issued after 8 December 2009 but see HMRC Brief 77/2009 for full details. The issuing company must be an unquoted company (shares on the Alternative Investment Market and the PLUS Quoted or PLUS Traded Markets being regarded as unquoted), and it must be neither a subsidiary of, nor under the control of, another company. It is proposed that relief will not be available if it is reasonable to assume that the company would be treated as an 'enterprise in difficulty' for the purposes of the European Commission's Rescuing and Restructuring Guidelines.

For shares issued after 5 April 2006 the total gross assets of the company (and, where relevant, other companies in the same group) must not exceed £7 million immediately before the issue of the shares, nor £8 million immediately afterwards. For shares issued after 18 July 2007 the issuing company (or, where, relevant, the group) must have fewer than 50 full-time employees.

Any subsidiary of the qualifying company must be its 'qualifying subsidiary', i.e. broadly a 51% subsidiary, and any 'property managing subsidiary' must be a 'qualifying 90% subsidiary'.

A qualifying business activity may be carried on by either the issuing company or a qualifying 90% subsidiary, and is defined broadly as (a) carrying on, or preparing to carry on, a qualifying trade (see below), or (b) carrying on research and development meeting certain conditions. A qualifying business activity is one that is carried on wholly or mainly in the UK. It is proposed that the requirement will be that the company issuing the shares must simply have a permanent establishment in the UK.

A qualifying trade is a trade that is conducted on a commercial basis and with a view to the realisation of profits and does not at any time in a specified period consist wholly or substantially in carrying on excluded activities. Dealing in land or shares, banking, insurance, leasing, providing legal or accountancy services, property development and farming are among the many excluded activities (ITA 2007, ss 192–199).

HMRC's Small Company Enterprise Centre operates an 'advance assurance scheme' that allows a company to submit its plans before the shares are issued and seek advice on whether the proposed issue is likely to qualify for EIS reliefs.

Claims for relief cannot be made until a certificate has been received from the company, issued on the authority of an HMRC officer, stating that the relevant conditions have been satisfied. Providing the certificates are received in time, claims may be included in tax returns, or amendments to returns. Otherwise claims are made on the form incorporated in the certificate from the company. The overall time limit for claiming the relief is five years from the 31 January following the tax year in which the shares are issued. If any of the requirements for a 'qualifying individual' are breached during a 'relevant period' — broadly three years after the issue of the shares, the relief will be withdrawn.

Amount of relief

[29.18] From 6 April 2008 the maximum amount on which an individual can claim income tax relief in a tax year is £500,000.

This annual limit is available to each spouse or partner in a marriage or civil partnership. Relief is given in the tax year when the shares are subscribed for, but for shares issued before 22 April 2009 one-half of the amount subscribed before 6 October in any tax year can be carried back for relief in the previous tax year, up to a maximum carry-back of £50,000. For shares issued in 2009/10 or subsequent years the only restriction on carry back relief is the overriding investment limit for any year. Both the date restriction of 6 October and the limit restriction of £50,000 are removed. Although the tax saving from the carry-back claim is calculated by reference to the tax position of the earlier year, it reduces the tax liability of the tax year in which the shares are subscribed for, so that any interest on overpaid tax will run only from 31 January after the end of that tax year — see **9.6**. The claim for carry-back must be made at the same time as the claim for relief, and the carry-back cannot increase the relief for a tax year to more than £500,000. The minimum subscription by an individual to one company is £500 except where the investment is made through an investment fund approved by HMRC.

Income tax relief is given at 20% of the qualifying amount in calculating the individual's income tax liability for the year. The tax saved cannot, however, exceed the tax payable on the investor's income. For shares issued after 5 April 2007 investors may restrict a claim in respect of a single issue of shares in order to obtain income tax relief on only some of the shares.

Withdrawal of relief

[29.19] The shares must be held for a minimum of (broadly) three years, otherwise the relief is withdrawn completely if the disposal is not at arm's length, and the tax saving is lost on the amount received for an arm's length bargain. Relief is not withdrawn when a shareholder dies.

Relief is also withdrawn if the individual receives value from the company within, broadly, one year before or three years after the issue of the shares. 'Value' is exhaustively defined and includes the repayment of loans that had been made to the company before the shares were issued, the provision of benefits, and purchase of assets for less than market value. It does not, however, include dividends that do not exceed a normal return on the investment, and receipts of insignificant value are ignored. The repayment of loans made before the shares were issued does not constitute value received unless the repayment is made in connection with any arrangements for the acquisition of the shares.

An amount received in respect of an option to sell EIS shares will cause the loss of an appropriate amount of relief, but an arrangement to sell them (say to the controlling shareholders) after the qualifying period will not.

Where relief is to be withdrawn, HMRC will issue an assessment outside the self-assessment system. Although tax on such assessments is payable within thirty days after they are issued, interest runs from an earlier date, depending on the event that triggered the withdrawal.

Capital gains tax reliefs

CGT exemption (TCGA 1992, ss 150A, 150B)

[29.20] There is no charge to CGT if shares for which EIS income tax relief has been given are disposed of at a profit after a retention period of (broadly) three years, although deferred gains may become chargeable under the deferral relief provisions outlined below. There is no exemption for disposals within the retention period (and EIS income tax relief will be withdrawn as indicated above). Gains may, however, be deferred if reinvested in new EIS shares (see **29.21**). If the disposal results in a loss, relief is available for the loss whether the disposal is within or outside the retention period, but in calculating a loss, the allowable cost is reduced by the EIS income tax relief that has not been withdrawn (see Example 2). A loss can be relieved either against chargeable gains (including deferred gains triggered by the disposal), or against income (under the provisions outlined at **38.22**).

	£
Example 2	
Cost of shares acquired under EIS	10,000
Income tax relief at 20%	2,000
Net cost of investment	8,000
Disposed of six years later for	6,500
Cost net of EIS relief	8,000
Loss available for relief	£1,500

The normal CGT identification and pooling rules do not apply to EIS shares. Where shares have been acquired at different times, disposals are identified with shares acquired earlier rather than later. Where shares were acquired on the same day, disposals are identified first with shares to which neither EIS income tax relief nor capital gains deferral relief (see **29.21** to **29.23**) is attributable, then with shares to which deferral relief but not income tax relief is attributable, then with shares to which income tax relief but not deferral relief is attributable, and finally shares to which both reliefs are attributable.

CGT deferral relief (TCGA 1992, ss 150C, 150D and Schs 5B, 5BA; F(No.2)A 2010, s 2 and Sch 1)

[29.21] A claim may be made for all or any part of a chargeable gain on the disposal of *any* asset (or a gain arising on a chargeable event under the EIS or venture capital trust provisions or following the withdrawal of 'reinvestment relief') to be deferred to the extent that it is matched by a qualifying subscription for EIS shares within one year before and three years after the disposal. HMRC may extend these time limits in some circumstances.

There are several conditions and anti-avoidance rules attached to deferral relief, and professional advice is recommended before proceeding with an investment. The relief is only available if the investor is resident and ordinarily resident in the UK. The subscription for the shares must be wholly in cash, the issue must not be part of arrangements to avoid tax, and the shares must be issued to raise money for a qualifying business activity. The money raised must be used for that purpose within two years. Relief is not available where there are guaranteed exit etc. arrangements. For shares issued after 18 July 2007 the annual amount raised by an issuing company through risk capital schemes including the EIS must not exceed £2 million.

Gains may be deferred whether or not income tax relief was available on the EIS shares. Entrepreneurs' relief may be claimed in respect of the gain if the relevant conditions are met (see **29.2**), so that on qualifying business disposals before 23 June 2010 the gain is reduced by 4/9ths and the reduced gain may then be deferred against an investment in EIS shares. The operation of entrepreneurs' relief is different for disposals on or after 23 June 2010 (see **29.9**), and from that date an individual may choose between claiming entrepreneurs' relief and paying tax on the gain at 10%, or deferring the gain under the EIS rules and paying tax later when the gain comes into charge at the appropriate rate of 18% or 28% (see **4.2**). If the gain exceeds the £5m limit for entrepreneurs' relief it will be possible to claim the relief on the gain up to that limit and to defer the remainder under the EIS rules.

[29.22] The deferred gain (as distinct from the gain on the EIS shares, which is dealt with at **29.20**) becomes chargeable on any of a number of specified events occurring within a certain period (normally three years). These events include disposal of the shares (other than to a spouse or civil partner living with him during the tax year); the investor becoming non-resident; and the shares ceasing to be eligible shares (for example, where the company ceases to be a qualifying company). The deferred gain is not triggered if the investor (or a spouse or civil partner to whom the shares have been transferred) dies.

Where the gain is triggered, it may be further deferred by another EIS investment if the conditions are satisfied.

Example 3

In May 2010 an investor buys shares in a qualifying EIS company from an existing shareholder for £40,000. On 1 January 2011 he subscribes £90,000 for further shares, so that his total investment in the tax year is £130,000.

He will get 20% income tax relief on the £90,000 subscribed for new shares. No relief is available for the purchased shares.

Gains realised up to three years before (or 12 months after) an EIS subscription can be deferred into the EIS shares. Therefore gains of up to £90,000 can be so deferred if they are realised between 1 January 2008 (i.e. three years before the subscription) and 1 January 2012 (i.e. 12 months after the subscription).

[29.23] Where a charge to CGT in respect of all or part of a gain arising to an investor before 6 April 2008 has been deferred and all or part of it comes into charge on the occasion of a 'chargeable event' on or after 6 April 2008, entrepreneurs' relief may be claimed at the time of the 'first relevant chargeable event' in respect of the whole of the deferred gain that attaches to the shares held by the investor immediately before that event. The gain attached to any shares transferred to a spouse or civil partner, and not held by the investor at the time of that event will not be eligible for the relief. The entrepreneurs' relief can only be claimed in respect of the deferred gain if the 'relevant disposal' (broadly the disposal on which the original gain arose) would have been a 'material disposal of business assets' if entrepreneurs' relief were in force at the time of that disposal (for further details see HMRC Capital Gains Manual CG64170, which gives an example).

If the 'first chargeable event' takes place before 23 June 2010 the whole of the deferred gain that had not come into charge before 6 April 2008 is reduced by 4/9ths. If the 'first relevant chargeable event' takes place on or after 23 June 2010 entrepreneurs' relief is given by charging the deferred gain to capital gains tax at 10% (following a change in the operation of the relief, see **29.9**). However, where the 'first relevant chargeable event' takes place between 6 April 2008 and 22 June 2010, any part of the deferred gain that qualified for entrepreneurs' relief and did not come into charge before 23 June 2010 will have been reduced by 4/9ths (see the example in HMRC Capital Gains Manual CG64170), so when that reduced gain comes into charge on or after 23 June 2010 it will be charged at either 18% or 28% as appropriate (see **4.2** for individuals, **42.5** for personal representatives, and **42.18** for trustees).

Withdrawal of investment after relevant period

[29.24] Potential investors may see a disadvantage in their being locked in as minority shareholders. The company may, however, build up reserves by retaining profits, and use the reserves to purchase its own shares after five years, using the rules described in **29.32**. The rules regarding 'pre-arranged exits' (see **29.17**) and a possible trap where value is received by other investors must be borne in mind.

Venture capital trusts (ITA 2007, Pt 6; TCGA 1992, ss 151A, 151B and Sch 5C; ITTOIA 2005, ss 709–712)

[29.25] Those who wish to support new and expanding companies but are unwilling to invest directly in unquoted shares may obtain tax relief for investment through venture capital trusts (VCTs) that is similar in many respects to that available under the EIS (see **29.17**). HMRC guidance on VCTs is available at www.hmrc.gov.uk/guidance/vct.htm. Individual investors aged 18 or over are entitled to two income tax reliefs and relief from capital gains as set out below.

VCTs are quoted companies holding at least 70% of their investments in shares or securities they have subscribed for in qualifying unquoted companies trading wholly or mainly in the UK, although it is proposed that this latter requirement be replaced by one stipulating that the company must simply have a permanent establishment in the UK. At present shares making up the VCT's ordinary share capital must be included in the official UK list, but it is proposed that this will be replaced with a requirement that the shares be admitted for trading on any EU regulated market. From 6 April 2007 disposals of shares held for at least six months will not be taken into account for the six months after disposal when considering the 70% rule. At least 30% of such holdings must be in 'eligible' shares (broadly ordinary non-redeemable shares which carry no preferential right to dividends or to the company's assets in a winding up), and no single holding may be more than 15% of total investments. It is proposed that the 30% limit be increased to 70% but the definition of 'eligible' shares will be changed to include shares which may carry certain preferential rights to dividends. Furthermore, loans or securities that are guaranteed are excluded and at least 10% of the total investment in any company must be ordinary, non-preferential shares. It is also proposed to exclude shares if it is reasonable to assume that the company would be treated as an 'enterprise in difficulty' for the purposes of the European Commission's Rescue and Restructuring Guidelines.

For shares and securities issued before 22 April 2009 80% of the money invested in a company by the VCT had to be used for the purposes of the company's trade within 12 months. The remainder must have been used within a further 12 months. For shares and securities issued on or after 22 April 2009 all of the money must be used within two years. Companies on the Alternative Investment Market (AIM) count as qualifying unquoted companies providing they are carrying on a qualifying trade. The VCT must not retain more than 15% of its income from shares and securities and must satisfy the gross assets test (see below).

VCTs are exempt from tax on their capital gains. There are anti-avoidance provisions to prevent the exemption being exploited by means of intra-group transfers, or by transferring a company's business to a VCT or to a company that later becomes a VCT.

There are regulations that enable VCTs to retain their tax approval when they merge and also treat VCTs as being approved while they are being wound up. Investors do not therefore lose their tax reliefs in these circumstances.

The main exclusions from the definition of qualifying trading company are the same as for the EIS (see **29.17**). For shares issued after 5 April 2006 the total gross assets of the investee company (and, where relevant, other companies in the same group) must not exceed £7 million immediately before the VCT acquired the holding, or £8 million immediately afterwards.

For shares issued to the VCT on or after 6 April 2007 (subject to a transitional rule) the issuing company (or, where, relevant, the group) must have fewer than 50 full-time employees, and the annual amount raised by an issuing company through risk capital schemes, including VCTs, must not exceed £2 million.

Income tax reliefs

[29.26] When new ordinary shares are *subscribed for*, income tax relief may be claimed on up to £200,000 of the amount subscribed each tax year. The rate of relief is 30% for shares issued after 5 April 2006. Claims may be made in tax returns. The tax saved cannot exceed the tax payable on the investor's income.

The relief will be withdrawn to the extent that any of the shares are disposed of (other than to the holder's spouse or civil partner, or after the holder's death) within five years (three years for shares issued before 6 April 2006). If the disposal is at arm's length and at a loss, relief is withdrawn in the proportion that the consideration received on disposal bears to the amount subscribed. A disposal not at arm's length results in the withdrawal of relief that was obtained for the shares disposed of.

Where shares are acquired from a spouse or civil partner, the acquiring spouse/civil partner is treated as if he or she had subscribed for the shares. The relief will also be withdrawn if the VCT loses its qualifying status within the five (or three) year period. Where relief is to be withdrawn, HMRC will issue an assessment outside the self-assessment system, tax being payable within thirty days after the assessment is issued. Unlike the EIS position (see **29.19**), there are no special provisions for interest on overdue tax where VCT relief is withdrawn, and it would appear that interest would run from 31 January following the end of the tax year for which the relief was given.

Dividends from ordinary shares in VCTs are exempt from tax to the extent that not more than £200,000 in total of shares in VCTs are *acquired* each year, whether the shares were acquired by subscription or by purchase from another shareholder. Dividend tax credits are, however, not repayable.

The reliefs are not available if avoiding tax is a main purpose of acquiring the shares.

Capital gains tax position

CGT exemption

[29.27] Gains arising on the disposal of VCT shares that were acquired by subscription or purchase up to the £200,000 limit in any year are exempt from CGT (and any losses are not allowable). There is no minimum period for which the shares must be held. Disposals are matched with acquisitions according to the rules outlined in **29.29**. Where gains are chargeable, they may be deferred if reinvested in new EIS shares (see **29.21**).

Example 4

Say the facts were the same as in Example 3, except that the purchase of and subscription for shares related to a VCT instead of an EIS company.

The position regarding the income tax relief would be the same except that the income tax relief on the £90,000 subscribed for new shares would be given at the rate of 30%. In addition, dividends on both the shares bought for £40,000 and the £90,000 of shares subscribed for would be exempt from income tax. The CGT exemption would apply to the same amount.

It would not, however, be possible to defer capital gains by reference to the investment in the VCT shares (see **29.28**).

CGT deferral relief

[29.28] Deferral relief is not available for gains reinvested in VCT shares issued on or after 6 April 2004. This relief enabled all or any part of gains on the disposal of *any* assets by someone resident or ordinarily resident in the UK to be deferred to the extent that they were reinvested, within one year before or one year after the disposal, in VCT shares on which income tax relief was given and which (where relevant) were still held at the time of the disposal.

The *deferred* gains (not the gains on the VCT shares themselves) become chargeable if the VCT shares are disposed of (other than to a spouse or civil partner), or the investor (or spouse/civil partner who has acquired the shares) becomes non-resident within three years after acquiring the shares, or the VCT loses its approval, or the income tax relief is otherwise withdrawn. The deferred gain is not triggered by the death of the investor (or spouse/civil partner to whom the shares have been transferred). Where deferred gains are triggered, they may again be deferred if further reinvested in new EIS shares (see **29.22**) if the conditions are satisfied. The same provisions regarding entrepreneurs' relief apply as for EIS shares as illustrated in **29.23**, except that the gain deferred would have arisen before 6 April 2004 when the VCT deferral relief was withdrawn.

CGT rules for matching disposals with acquisitions

[29.29] Any disposals of shares in a VCT are identified first with shares acquired before the trust became a VCT. To decide whether other disposals relate to shares acquired in excess of the £200,000 limit in any year (£100,000 for shares acquired before 6 April 2004), disposals are identified with shares acquired earlier rather than those acquired later. Where shares are acquired on the same day, shares acquired in excess of the £200,000 (or £100,000) limit are treated as disposed of before qualifying shares. Any shares not identified with other shares under these rules qualify for the VCT capital gains exemption on disposal, and they are not subject to the normal CGT rules for matching disposals with acquisitions.

Corporate venturing scheme (FA 2000, s 63 and Sch 15)

[29.30] The corporate venturing scheme (CVS) is available to companies in respect of qualifying shares issued on or after 1 April 2000 and before 1 April 2010. The scheme is intended to encourage companies to invest in small higher risk trading companies (defined broadly as for EIS and VCT — see **29.17**) and to form wider corporate venturing relationships. Financial companies that invest by way of business are not eligible to claim the relief.

For shares issued before 22 April 2009 80% of the money invested in the small company had to be used for the purposes of the company's trade within 12 months. The remainder had to be used within a further 12 months. For shares issued on or after 22 April 2009 all the money must be used within two years. The small company must be an unquoted company that is not a 51% subsidiary of another company and is not controlled by another company. At least 20% of the small company's shares must be owned by independent individuals. Its gross assets must not exceed £7 million immediately before, and £8 million immediately after, the shares are issued.

For shares issued on or after 19 July 2007 the issuing company (or, where relevant, the group) must have fewer than 50 full-time employees, and the annual amount raised by an issuing company through risk capital schemes, including the CVS, must not exceed £2 million.

Investing companies are entitled to 20% corporation tax relief on cash subscriptions for new ordinary shares of a qualifying unquoted small company providing the investing company has received from the small company a certificate of compliance that the requirements for investment relief are met. Small companies may obtain advance clearance that their shares will qualify. The relief is given against the corporation tax payable for the accounting period in which the shares are issued. The relief will be withdrawn if the company disposes of the shares within three years, or in certain other circumstances.

When the shares are disposed of, then whether or not the corporation tax relief is withdrawn as a result, tax on any capital gain arising may be deferred to the extent that the gain is reinvested in another CVS holding within one year before or three years after the disposal. If capital losses arise on disposals, then as an alternative to relief against capital gains, relief may be claimed for the amount of the loss (net of the corporation tax relief obtained) against the CVS company's income of the current or previous accounting period. Entrepreneurs' relief may be available (see HMRC Capital Gains Manual CG64095).

Relief is not available if the CVS company, alone or with connected persons, controls the small company. Connected persons include the CVS company's directors but not its employees. The CVS company's holding must not exceed 30%. There is no minimum investment requirement.

Relief is not lost if the small company becomes quoted during the three year qualifying period providing there were no prior arrangements to do so. Nor is it lost if the small company is wound up for genuine commercial reasons.

Community investment tax relief (FA 2002, s 57, Sch 16)

[29.31] Investments made by individuals and companies in a community development finance institution (CDFI) qualify for tax relief of 5% per annum of the amount of the investment for a period of five years, so that the total relief is 25%. For an individual, the five-year period commences in the tax year in which the investment is made. For a company the relief applies to the accounting period in which the investment is made and the accounting periods in which the next four anniversaries of the investment date fall. The relief is set against the amount of tax payable (but is not repayable if it exceeds that amount). The aim of the relief is to encourage private investment in businesses and social enterprises in disadvantaged communities (referred to as Enterprise Areas) via accredited CDFIs. Investments may be by way of loans or subscription for shares or securities, and CDFIs will supply investors with a tax relief certificate. Claims for relief cannot be made earlier than the end of the tax year or company accounting period in which the investment is made. In the case of loans, the amount of the investment is calculated in each of the five years following the investment date according to the average balance in that year (or, for the third, fourth and fifth years, the average capital balance for the period of six months starting 18 months after the investment date if less).

As with all such schemes, there are detailed conditions that must be complied with, and if the CDFI loses its accreditation in the five years after the investment date, investors will lose the right to claim further relief. The relief will be restricted, or in some circumstances withdrawn completely, if the investor disposes of all or part of the investment or receives value within the five years after the investment date.

Purchase by company of its own shares (CTA 2010, ss 1033–1048)

[29.32] Where an unquoted trading company or the unquoted holding company of a trading group buys back its own shares (or redeems them or makes a payment for them in a reduction of capital) in order to benefit a trade, the transaction is not treated as a distribution, and thus liable to income tax in the hands of the vending shareholder, but as a disposal on which the vending shareholder is liable to CGT. This does not apply if there is an arrangement the main purpose of which is to get undistributed profits into the hands of the shareholders without incurring the tax liabilities on a distribution.

The main requirements are that the shareholder must be UK-resident, he must normally have owned the shares for at least five years, and he must either dispose of his entire holding or the holding must be 'substantially reduced'.

A company may apply to HMRC for a clearance that the proposed purchase will not be treated as a distribution.

Any legal costs and other expenditure incurred by a company in purchasing its own shares are not allowable against the company's profits.

Where the purchase of its own shares by a company is *not* covered by the above provisions, the purchase is treated as a distribution on which income tax is payable.

It used to be common, where CGT reliefs were not available, for a purchase of own shares to be deliberately structured so as to breach the conditions for CGT treatment because the effective tax rate on net dividend distributions for higher rate taxpayers was 25% compared with up to 40% CGT. However, the position may be different now that the effective tax rate on net dividend distributions can be as high as 36% (see **18.6**), there is a maximum CGT rate of 28% (see **4.2**) and entrepreneurs' relief (see **29.11**) may be available to reduce the effective rate to only 10%. Comparative calculations are therefore advisable.

Buy back from trustees (ITA 2007, s 482)

[29.33] There is a special treatment for shareholders who are trustees if a company makes distributions in the form of payments on the redemption, repayment or repurchase of its own shares, or on the purchase of rights to buy its own shares. The trustees are taxed on the tax-credit inclusive amount of such distributions at the dividend trust rate of 32.5%. This does not apply where trust income is treated as belonging to the settlor, or where the trust is a unit trust, charitable trust, or pension trust.

Management buyouts

[29.34] The provisions enabling a company to purchase its own shares could assist a management buyout team to acquire the company for which they work, in that only shares remaining after those bought in by the company need then be acquired by them.

If only part of a trade is to be acquired, the existing company could transfer the requisite assets into a subsidiary company using the reconstruction provisions of CTA 2010, Pt 22 (see **26.18**), the buyout team then buying the shares in the subsidiary.

Alternatively, if the buyout team form an entirely new company and purchase assets from their employing company, capital allowances will be available where appropriate and the new company may be able to raise some of the funds it needs through the enterprise investment scheme, or by attracting investments from venture capital trusts (see **29.25**).

Demergers (CTA 2010, ss 1073–1099; TCGA 1992, s 192)

[29.35] The aim of the demerger legislation is to remove various tax obstacles to demergers, so that businesses grouped inefficiently under a single company umbrella may be run more dynamically and effectively by being allowed to pursue their separate ways under independent management. The detailed provisions are very complex, the following being an outline.

A company is not treated as having made a distribution for corporation tax purposes (and the members are not treated as having received income) where the company transfers to its members the shares of a 75% subsidiary, or transfers a trade to a new company in exchange for that new company issuing shares to some or all of the transferor company's shareholders.

In order for these provisions to apply, all the companies must be UK-resident trading companies, the transfer must be made to benefit some or all of the trading activities, and the transfer must not be made for tax avoidance reasons.

A qualifying distribution by the holding company of shares in subsidiaries to its members is also not treated as a capital distribution for CGT purposes, and the capital gains charge when a company leaves a group on assets acquired within the previous six years from other group companies (see **45.26**) does not apply.

There are detailed anti-avoidance provisions, and there is also provision to apply for HMRC clearance of proposed transactions.

Enterprise zones

[29.36] Certain areas in which the Government particularly wanted to encourage investment were designated as enterprise zones, and those who set up business within an enterprise zone have received relief from business rates and entitlement to 100% tax relief for expenditure on new buildings for use in the trade. The Government has now decided to withdraw enterprise zone allowances from April 2011 along with the phasing out of other allowances for industrial and agricultural buildings (see **22.52**).

Contributions to local enterprise organisations etc. (IT-TOIA 2005, ss 82–86; CTA 2009, ss 82–86)

[29.37] Businesses may claim a deduction from their profits for contributions they make to local enterprise agencies, the Young People's Learning Agency (YPLA), Skills Funding Agency (SFA), Education and Learning Wales (ELWa), Scottish local enterprise companies, business link organisations and urban regeneration companies.

Local enterprise agencies are bodies approved by the Secretary of State that promote local industrial and commercial activity and enterprise, particularly in forming and developing small businesses. YPLA, SFA and ELWa are mainly concerned with Government training programmes. Scottish local enterprise companies provide a similar function but cover economic development and environmental functions as well as training. Business link organisations are authorised by the Department of Trade and Industry to use the 'Business Links' service mark and provide a single point of access for local enterprise agencies, chambers of commerce and local authorities. Urban regeneration companies are independent bodies that coordinate the regeneration of a designated regeneration area. Urban regeneration companies have to be designated as such by the Treasury.

Revenue expenditure on research and development (CTA 2010, s 1138; FA 1998, Sch 18 Pt 9A; FA 2004, s 53; ITTOIA 2005, ss 87, 88; SI 2004/712; CTA 2009, s 87 and Pt 13)

[29.38] Tax relief is available, in the form of a deduction in computing trading income, for revenue expenditure on research and development (R&D) related to the trade. R&D is defined as activities falling to be treated as research and development in accordance with generally accepted accounting practice, but the definition is modified by Treasury regulations.

Companies whose qualifying expenditure is £10,000 or more may claim an enhanced deduction, the rate depending on whether they are small/medium-sized or large companies (see **29.39** and **29.40**). Claims must be made in the company's tax return. Capital expenditure on research and development qualifies for 100% capital allowances (see **22.59**).

For accounting periods beginning on or after 1 January 2005, companies that treat R&D for accounts purposes as part of the cost of an intangible asset rather than as revenue expenditure may nonetheless still claim R&D tax reliefs.

FA 2008 introduced provisions to deny relief for R&D expenditure where the company is not a going concern, and to limit the 'total R&D aid' in respect of a research and development project to 7.5 million euros.

It is proposed that for any R&D expenditure incurred by a small/medium-sized company in an accounting period ending on or after 9 December 2009, it will not be a requirement that any intellectual property deriving from that R&D will be vested in the company.

Expenditure by small and medium-sized companies (CTA 2009, Pt 13)

[29.39] From 1 August 2008 small and medium-sized companies as defined can claim R&D tax relief for 175% (previously 150%) of their qualifying revenue expenditure on research and development, providing it amounts to not less than £10,000, or pro rata amount for an account of less than 12 months. Expenditure on R&D work subcontracted to them by large companies (see **29.40**) is included in deciding whether the £10,000 threshold has been reached. Relief at 175% of the expenditure gives companies liable to pay the small profits rate (formerly the small companies' rate) of 21% a tax saving equal to 36.75% of the R&D expenditure. Any intellectual property (know-how, patents, trade marks etc.) created as a result of the R&D must be vested in the company (alone or with others). See **3.11** regarding the change in corporation tax rates applying from 6 April 2011.

Companies carrying on R&D before they start to trade may treat the R&D relief as a trading loss. Where a company has an unrelieved trading loss (excluding brought forward or carried back losses), it may surrender the R&D tax relief (or the unrelieved loss if lower) in exchange for a tax credit equal to 14% of the surrendered amount (from 1 August 2008, previously 16%). The credit cannot, however, exceed the company's PAYE tax and NIC liabilities for payment periods ending in the relevant accounting period. The tax credit will be paid to the company, or used to discharge outstanding corporation tax liabilities.

From 1 August 2008 small and medium-sized companies are broadly defined as those with fewer than 500 employees, having a turnover of not more than €100 million and/or assets of not more than €86 million. Previously all three thresholds were half of these amounts.

Small and medium-sized companies who do subcontract R&D work for large companies may claim relief in respect of their expenditure on such work as indicated in **29.40**, in addition to the relief outlined above for other R&D expenditure. There is no provision for companies to be able to claim a tax credit for this relief where they have trading losses.

Expenditure by large companies etc (CTA 2009, Pt 13)

[29.40] Large companies (i.e. those not within the definition of small and medium-sized companies in **29.39**) may claim R&D relief of 130% (125% for expenditure incurred before 1 April 2008) of their qualifying revenue expenditure on research and development, providing it amounts to not less than £10,000, or pro rata amount for an account of less than 12 months. Qualifying expenditure includes direct R&D expenditure, expenditure subcontracted by the company to an individual, partnership, university, charity or other qualifying body, and contributions to individuals, partnerships and qualifying bodies for independent R&D which is relevant to the company. There is no provision for large companies to surrender R&D relief for a tax credit payment.

Where a large company subcontracts work to a small or medium-sized company, the small/medium-sized company may claim R&D relief of 130% (125% for expenditure incurred before 1 April 2008) of the qualifying expenditure, providing its total R&D expenditure, including that undertaken independently (see **29.39**) is not less than £10,000, reduced pro rata for an account of less than 12 months.

Expenditure on vaccines research

[29.41] Small/medium-sized and large companies (see **29.39** and **29.40**) may claim an extra 40% relief (from 1 August 2008, previously 50%) for their qualifying expenditure on research and development related to vaccines and medicines for TB and malaria, HIV and AIDS. This is subject to a £10,000 threshold as indicated in **29.39** and **29.40**. The relief is also available for contributions to charities, universities and scientific research organisations for funding independent research related to a trade carried on by the company.

The same provisions apply as under **29.39** for small/medium-sized companies to treat the relief in respect of pre-trading vaccines research expenditure as a trading loss and for surrendering losses in exchange for a tax credit payment of 14% of the surrendered amount. The time limit for making claims also applies.

Tax points

[29.42] Note the following:

- The detailed conditions and anti-avoidance rules in relation to most of the provisions dealt with in this chapter are too extensive to deal with in detail, but should be looked at carefully by interested companies and investors.
- Although qualifying companies or fund managers will issue certificates to individuals investing under the enterprise investment scheme, each individual must make a specific claim for income tax relief within the time limit indicated at **29.17**. Capital gains deferral relief for reinvestment in EIS shares must also be claimed within the same time limit.
- When gains are reinvested by subscribing within the appropriate limits for EIS shares, 20% income tax relief can be obtained on the shares and any CGT liability deferred. Although deferral is not the same as an exemption, further deferral may be possible when the deferred gains are triggered. The gains may eventually become chargeable if they are triggered before death.
- Although gains deferred under the EIS provisions may become chargeable as indicated above, gains on the disposal of the shares themselves up to the relevant holding limits are exempt, providing that they were subscribed for and held for the three year period.

- EIS income tax relief is not available to individuals connected with the company, but the connected persons rules do not apply to the EIS deferral relief enabling a deferment of tax on capital gains up to the amount invested.
- Shares in companies on the Alternative Investment Market (AIM), the PLUS Quoted or PLUS Traded Markets are treated as unquoted, so EIS relief is available providing the company is a qualifying company. The limit on the company's assets of £7 million immediately before the issue of the shares and £8 million immediately afterwards will, however, exclude many of these companies.
- HMRC will not usually give a clearance under the demerger provisions where companies in the same ownership are first merged and then demerged so that each company ends up in the ownership of independent people.
- Several specialist R&D tax credit units have been set up around the country to deal with all R&D tax credit claims except those dealt with by the Large Business Service. See HMRC Corporate Intangibles Research & Development Manual CIRD80350 for details.

Land and buildings

30

The family home

Background

[30.1] There are various tax aspects to consider in relation to the family home. Apart from inheritance tax (IHT) considerations, the most important are the capital gains tax (CGT) aspects, but consideration also needs to be given to the income tax position when rental income is received for the property or it is used for employment or business. The relevant provisions in relation to council tax and business rates must also be borne in mind. Stamp duty land tax is an increasingly important factor. See **6.9** for the rates of stamp duty land tax on residential property and **6.19** for the exemption from (or reduction of) stamp duty land tax on a new 'zero-carbon' home.

The main CGT provisions are dealt with in this chapter. See also **33.15** for the CGT provisions in relation to the family home on separation or divorce, or dissolution of a civil partnership, and **33.19** for points in relation to cohabiting couples.

Older people may be considering raising money from their homes by some sort of equity release plan. These are dealt with in **34.11**.

As far as IHT is concerned, the large increases in property values that have taken place over recent years, coupled with the minimal increases in the IHT nil rate band, have left many people with significant IHT problems in relation to the family home. This aspect is dealt with in **35.6**.

Leasehold reform

[30.2] As a result of the Commonhold and Leasehold Reform Act 2002, those acquiring property in new developments are able to buy the freehold of their individual flats and become members of a 'commonhold association' that is responsible for the management and upkeep of the common parts of the property. Commonhold land is registered with the Land Registry. Leaseholders of existing developments may convert to commonhold if all leaseholders agree.

There were already arrangements to enable leaseholders to acquire the freehold of their flats through a nominee purchaser. The rules relating to such acquisitions have been simplified and leaseholders are able to acquire the freehold of their units through an RTE (Right to Enfranchisement) company. The rate of stamp duty land tax on the consideration for the acquisition of the freeholds is arrived at by dividing the total amount payable by the number of flats and the rate on that fractional amount is applied to the total consideration. Whether or not the leaseholders form an RTE, they may take over the management of the common parts of the development through an RTM (Right to Manage) company.

For those participating in commonhold associations or RTM/RTE companies, various tax points need to be borne in mind, particularly where some tenants buy and some do not. Someone has to be responsible for dealing with the tax on any income, such as interest on the maintenance fund, and there are also CGT considerations. Professional advice is essential.

Capital gains tax private residence relief (TCGA 1992, ss 222–226B)

[30.3] The basic CGT treatment on the disposal of a main residence is that any gain is exempt from CGT providing the property has been the only or main residence throughout the period of ownership, or throughout that period except for all or any part of the last thirty-six months. This is subject to various provisions to cover situations such as other periods of absence, owning two or more residences, using part of the property for business or letting and so on, which are dealt with later in the chapter.

Bear in mind, however, the possibility that private residence relief may be curtailed after several members of parliament were criticised for 'flipping' the designation of their main residence to maximise parliamentary expense allowances and/or the benefit of the statutory CGT relief.

Several MPs offered to pay CGT that they were not liable to pay, even though they denied that they had done anything wrong. In a Finance Bill 2009 debate on an amendment, tabled by the Liberal Democrats but withdrawn, Ian Pearson, the economic secretary to the Treasury, said MPs had raised 'some important points about the abuse of private residence relief, which need further consideration'.

Buying and not moving in immediately

[30.4] If the owner does not move into the house immediately, for CGT purposes HMRC will, by concession, allow them to treat any non-occupation in the first 12 months as covered by the owner occupier exemption if they do not move in because they are having the property built, or are altering or redecorating the property, or because they remain in their old home while they are selling it. HMRC may extend the 12 month period to up to a maximum of 24 months if there are good reasons that are outside the owner's control. (See also **30.15** re second homes and **30.18** re job-related accommodation).

Empty property may be liable to council tax, but newly built or structurally altered property is not subject to the tax for up to six months after the work is substantially completed, and there is no charge on property that is empty and unfurnished for up to six months (see **8.3**).

Periods of absence (TCGA 1992, s 223)

[30.5] Provided that a house has at some time been an individual's only or main residence, the last three years of ownership are always exempt in calculating CGT, whether he is living there or not. Other periods of absence also qualify for exemption provided that the house was his only or main residence at some time *before* the period of absence, that no other residence qualifies for relief during the absence (see **30.15**), and *after* the period of absence there is either a time when the house was his only or main residence, or in a case in (b) to (d) below, he was prevented from resuming residence in the house because the terms of his employment required him to live elsewhere. (This latter rule also applies to a spouse or civil partner living with the individual who was prevented from resuming residence).

These qualifying periods of absence are any or all of the following:

(a)   three years for any reason whatsoever (not necessarily a consecutive period of three years);

(b)   any period of absence abroad where the duties of employment require an individual to live abroad (this applies to a spouse or civil partner who lives with the individual);

(c)   up to four years where the duties of a UK employment require an individual to live elsewhere; and

(d)   up to four years where the individual lives with a spouse or civil partner to whom (c) above applies for that period.

If these periods are exceeded, only the excess is counted as a period of non-residence.

There can thus be long periods of absence without losing any part of the CGT exemption.

Periods of absence before 31 March 1982 are ignored in calculating the chargeable gain, which depends on the proportion of residence/deemed residence to the total period of ownership after 30 March 1982. The exemption for the last three years of ownership still applies, however, no matter whether the period of residence was before or after 31 March 1982.

[30.6] If the individual occupies rented property during his absence, then although the tenancy may have no capital value, the property he is occupying would even so strictly 'qualify for relief' as his dwelling (see **30.15**). In those circumstances HMRC will accept a main residence election for his own property, so that the rules for qualifying periods of absence can apply. By HMRC concession D21, where in these circumstances he did not know at the appropriate time that an election was required, HMRC will accept an out of time election providing he makes it promptly as soon as he becomes aware, the election then taking effect from the time the tenancy was acquired.

[30.7] If an individual acquires an interest in a property from his/her spouse or civil partner when they are living together (including an acquisition as legatee when the spouse or civil partner dies), the individual's period of ownership is treated as starting when his/her spouse or civil partner acquired the property, and the individual's tax position would take into account any part of that period when the spouse or civil partner was not resident in the property.

[30.8] There are no special council tax provisions about permitted absences, other than the exemptions listed at **8.3** and the discount for a property that is no-one's only or main home.

Dwelling occupied by a dependent relative or under a trust (TCGA 1992, ss 225, 226, 226A, 226B)

[30.9] If an individual disposes of a property owned by him on 5 April 1988 that was occupied rent-free by a dependent relative on that date, and the relative continued to live there rent-free until up to three years before the time the individual disposes of the property, any gain arising on the disposal is exempt from CGT. Payment of council tax by the relative does not affect the exemption.

The CGT exemption ceases if there is a change of occupant after 5 April 1988 even if the new occupant is also a dependent relative, but any period from 31 March 1982 which did qualify for the exemption reduces the chargeable period when calculating any chargeable gain.

'Dependent relative' is defined as an individual's own or his/her spouse's or civil partner's widowed mother, or any other relative unable to look after themselves because of old age or infirmity. There is no restriction by reference to income.

The private residence exemption may also be claimed by trustees when they dispose of a property occupied by someone entitled to occupy it under the terms of the trust. Anti-avoidance provisions deny the relief for such disposals where the calculation of the gain would take into account hold-over relief for gifts (see **4.24**) on an earlier disposal, unless the earlier claim is revoked. Where the earlier disposal on which gifts relief was given was before 10 December 2003, the private residence relief is denied only in respect of the period from that date (and the exemption for the last three years of ownership will not include any post-10 December 2003 period). See **33.15** for the use of the trust exemption where couples get divorced.

If the home is let (TCGA 1992, s 223(4); ITTOIA 2005, ss 784–802)

Income tax

[30.10] A 'rent-a-room' relief is available for owner-occupiers and tenants who let furnished rooms in their only or main residence. The relief is available both where the rent comes under the property business rules (see **32.3**) and where substantial services are also provided, for example guest houses and bed and breakfast businesses, so that the rent is charged as trading income (see **CHAPTER 21**). (If part of the property is let unfurnished in the same year, however, the relief cannot be claimed.) The owner must occupy the property as his main home at the same time as the tenant for at least part of the letting period in each tax year or business basis period. No tax is payable if the gross rents for the tax year (or for trades, the accounting year ended in the tax year), before deducting expenses, do not exceed £4,250. If the letting is by a couple, the relief is £2,125 each. The rent taken into account for the relief is the payment for the accommodation plus payments for related goods and services. An election can be made for the relief not to apply for a particular year, for example if the expenses exceed the rent and a claim relief for a loss is made. The time limit for the election is one year from 31 January following the end of the relevant tax year (or longer at HMRC's discretion, see HMRC Property Income Manual PIM4050). The election may be withdrawn within the same time limit. If the rent exceeds £4,250, there is a choice to pay tax either on the excess over £4,250 or on the rent less expenses under the normal rules described below. If the individual wants to pay on the excess over £4,250 he must make an election to do so, and that basis will then apply until the election is withdrawn. The time limit for such an election is the same as that for electing for the relief not to apply at all.

If the 'rent-a-room' relief does not apply, then unless the letting amounts to a trade (see above), the letting income is chargeable to income tax along with other letting income, if any, after setting off appropriate expenses (see **32.5**). It is normally treated as property income, but if the letting qualifies as furnished holiday accommodation (which would be unusual — see **30.13** and **32.22**), the income is treated as trading income.

Capital gains tax

[30.11] As far as the CGT exemption is concerned, the last three years of ownership of the home always count as a period of residence (see **30.5**), so moving out and letting the property during that time it will not affect the exemption.

If the owner continues to live in the property while letting part of it, the CGT exemption is not affected if the letting takes the form of boarders who effectively live as part of the family. It has been confirmed that letting under the rent-a-room scheme would not normally affect the availability of the exemption. Where, however, the letting extends beyond this, or the whole property is let, other than during the last three years of ownership or during another allowable absence period (see **30.5**), the appropriate fraction of the gain on disposal is chargeable but there is an exemption of the smaller of £40,000 and an amount equal to the exempt gain on the owner-occupied part.

Example 1

The gain on the sale of a dwelling in 2010/11 is £80,000. The agreed proportion applicable to the let part is £48,000, the exempt gain being £32,000.

The £48,000 gain on the let part is reduced by the lower of

(a)   £40,000 and
(b)   an amount equal to the exempt gain, i.e. £32,000.

Therefore a further £32,000 is exempt and £16,000 is chargeable. The gain will be reduced by the annual exemption (£10,100 for 2010/11) if not already used.

Where a married couple, civil partners, or any other joint owners jointly let part of the home, each is entitled to the residential lettings exemption of up to £40,000.

The exemption is not available if the let part of the property is effectively a separate dwelling, such as a self-contained flat with its own access. But where part of the home is let, without substantial structural alterations, it will qualify, even if it has separate facilities.

[30.12] The courts have held that the residential lettings exemption was available to the owners of a small private hotel who occupied the whole of the property during the winter months, with one or two guests, but lived in an annexe during the summer. The exemption can be claimed only if the property qualifies as the CGT exempt residence for at least part of the period of ownership, so it cannot be claimed on a property which, although he lives in it sometimes, has never been an individual's only or main residence for CGT purposes. Subject to that, it can be claimed where all of the property has been let for part of the period of ownership, or part of the property has been let for all or part of the period of ownership.

[30.13] The position of furnished holiday lettings is not clear. See **32.22** onwards regarding tax reliefs for such lettings, which are extended for 2009/10 onwards. Gains on such property are specifically eligible for roll-over relief when the property is sold and replaced, but providing the rules outlined above are complied with, it would seem that if the property is the qualifying main residence the residential lettings exemption could apply instead. Where a chargeable gain has been rolled over under TCGA 1992, s 152 or s 153 into the cost of furnished holiday accommodation and a gain on which private residence relief applies accrues on the disposal of that accommodation, that relief will be restricted to the part of the chargeable gain which exceeds the amount of the gain rolled over (see HMRC Capital Gains Manual CG61452). To continue to get the other benefits of the furnished holiday lettings provisions, the rules for such lettings would have to be complied with (in particular ensuring that neither the owner nor anyone else normally occupied the accommodation for a continuous period of more than 31 days for at least seven months of the year).

Council tax and business rates

[30.14] If the let part of the property is self-contained living accommodation that counts as a separate dwelling, the tenants are liable to pay the council tax. But for any period when it is not anyone's only or main home, for example when it is untenanted, the owner is liable to pay up to 90% of the council tax (subject to certain exemptions, for example unfurnished property for up to six months — see **8.3**). If the let part of the home is not self-contained, the owner is liable to pay the council tax, but will usually include an appropriate amount in the rent to cover the proportion applicable to the tenants. If the owner does not live in the property while it is let, the council tax will be paid by tenants who occupy it as their main home, except for multi-occupied property such as bed-sits, where the owner will remain liable. If the let part is let as short-term living accommodation, and is therefore no-one's only or main home, the owner will pay up to 90% of the council tax unless the property is available for short-term letting for 140 days or more in a year (for example self-catering holiday accommodation), in which case he will pay business rates instead. If bed and breakfast facilities are offered in the owner's home, he is not liable to business rates providing he does not offer accommodation for more than six people, lives in the house at the same time and the house is still mainly used as his home. If part of the home is let for business purposes rather than as living accommodation, business rates are payable on that part.

A deduction of an appropriate part of the council tax, or the business rates, paid on let property may be made from the rent in arriving at taxable letting income.

More than one home (TCGA 1992, s 222(5)(6))

Capital gains tax and income tax

[30.15] An individual may notify HMRC within two years after acquiring a second home which of the two is to be the exempt home for CGT. (If he had bought a second home but did not move in immediately because of work being done etc. — see **30.4** — the two year period would not start until the second home became available for use.) The nominated property may be in the UK or abroad (see **30.16**). Only a property used as a home qualifies for the exemption, however, and an individual cannot nominate a property he has never lived in. After nominating the exempt property he may later notify a change of choice from a specified date, which cannot be earlier than two years before the date of the later notification. If no notification is made, and a dispute between the individual and HMRC arises, the main residence will be decided as a question of fact. Provided that both houses have been a qualifying main residence for

CGT at some time, the last three years of ownership of both will in any event be counted as owner-occupied in calculating the exempt gain. An election is not required where the individual has a residence that he owns and a second residence that he neither owns nor leases (e.g. accommodation with relatives, or a hotel room). A property occupied as a tenant would, however, need to be taken into account even if the occupation rights have no capital value (see **30.6**).

The ability to change the election as to which of two homes is the main residence may be helpful where an individual has owned two homes for many years, one of which has never been his qualifying main residence, and he sells that property at a gain. See Example 2. Bear in mind the possibility (see **30.3**) that private residence relief may be curtailed following criticism of the practice of varying the election, even though the practice is in accordance with established HMRC guidance.

Example 2

A taxpayer has owned and occupied two homes, Westcote and Eastcote, for many years and made a valid election for Westcote to be his main residence. He sells Eastcote at a substantial gain in December 2010 and on 10 January 2011 notifies HMRC that Eastcote is to be treated as his main residence from 11 January 2009. On 17 January 2011 he notifies HMRC that Westcote is to be his main residence from 18 January 2009. The elections enable him to obtain the exemption for the last three years' ownership of Eastcote, at the expense of having one chargeable week in respect of Westcote.

A married couple or civil partners living together can only have one qualifying residence and where there are two or more residences owned jointly, or each owns one or more residences, the notice as to which is the main residence needs to be given by both. Where both spouses own a residence when they marry, or a same-sex couple each own a house before registering as civil partners, a new two-year period starts for notifying which is the main residence. A new two-year period does not start if on marriage/registration one spouse or civil partner already owns more than one residence and the other owns no property. If a couple jointly own more than one property before and after marriage or registration, a new two-year period still begins, because the election after marriage or registration must be a joint election.

[30.16] If a second home is abroad, then although it may be nominated as a main home as indicated in **30.15**, and a reduction possibly obtained in the UK tax liability as shown in Example 2, the taxation position in the overseas country would also need to be considered.

A problem arose in relation to overseas property bought through a company, with the UK owners being the shareholders and directors. This has frequently been done in order to avoid possible adverse provisions of foreign tax systems where the property was directly owned. But personal use by the directors of such a company was liable to UK tax and national insurance contributions as a benefit in kind, reduced if the property was only available for part of the year (see **10.20**). Many people were not aware of this liability and it was removed with retrospective effect in FA 2008.

Council tax

[30.17] For council tax, an individual pays up to 90% of the tax on a property which is no-one's only or main home (see **8.5**). The question of which of two or more homes is the only or main home for council tax is a question of fact, decided in the first place by the local authority, but an appeal may be made against their decision. In some circumstances, one of the properties might be the main home of one spouse or civil partner and the other property the main home of the other, in which case the resident partner would be liable to pay the council tax at each property, with a 25% single resident reduction if the property was not also the main residence of anyone else over 18. This could apply, for example, if a wife lived at a house in the country and her husband at a house in town, going to the other house at weekends, etc. But the length of time spent at the property would not necessarily be the deciding factor and all relevant circumstances would be taken into account. If the second home was a holiday property available for short-term letting for 140 days or more in a year, it would be liable to business rates rather than the council tax.

If the second home is a caravan, it will not usually be liable to council tax. The owner of the site where the caravan is kept will pay business rates, which will be included in his charge to caravan owners. Touring caravans kept at home when not touring are not subject to council tax.

Job-related accommodation (TCGA 1992, s 222(8), (8A)–(8D), (9))

[30.18] If an employee lives in accommodation related to employment, for example as a hotel manager or minister of religion, or a trader lives in accommodation related to self-employment, for example as the tenant of licensed premises, that individual may buy a property that is to be the future home. The property qualifies for CGT exemption, even though they do not live there.

If the property is let, a deduction is allowed from the letting income of interest incurred wholly and exclusively for the purposes of the property business.

Unless the property is someone's only or main home (for example if let long-term), 50% of the council tax will be payable on it (see **8.5**).

Moving home (ITEPA 2003, ss 271–289; TCGA 1992, s 223)

[30.19] Owning two houses at the same time is usually covered for CGT purposes by the exemption of the last three years of ownership.

An individual may need to take out a bridging loan when he moves house. Employees earning £8,500 per annum or more and company directors are charged to tax on the benefit of certain low rate or interest-free loans from their employers (see **10.38**). This includes bridging loans, but specific rules apply to removal and relocation expenses and employees are not taxed on qualifying expenses paid by their employers up to a limit of £8,000 (see **10.17**). If the £8,000 limit has not been fully used, any balance is available to cover an equivalent amount of the notional interest chargeable to tax on a low rate or interest-free bridging loan from the employer providing the relevant conditions are met.

See **10.18** for the tax treatment if an employee sells his home to his employer or to a relocation company.

Part use for business purposes (TCGA 1992, s 224)

[30.20] Interest on that part of any borrowing attributable to the use of part of the home exclusively for business is allowed as a business expense. See **19.20** for other allowable expenses when an individual works from home.

Business rates will be paid on the business part of the property (allowable against profits for tax). Where part of the property is used for both business and domestic purposes, and the business use does not prevent the continued domestic use, such as a study where the individual does some work and the children do their homework, business rates are not payable, and a deduction may be claimed against profit for the appropriate proportion of the council tax.

As far as CGT is concerned, the private residence exemption is not available on any part of a property that is used *exclusively* for business purposes. Where a replacement property is acquired that is similarly used partly for business, roll-over relief may be available to defer the gain (see **29.11** to **29.16**) and see also **30.11** to **30.13** for letting businesses. The CGT exemption is not affected if no part of the home is *exclusively* used for business purposes.

Where a person cares for an adult under a local authority placement scheme, their contract with the local authority may require them to set aside one or more rooms exclusively for the use of the adult in care. It is proposed that for disposals on or after 9 December 2009 the private residence exemption will not be prevented from being available on that part of the property.

When an expenses claim against employment income has included part of the home expenses (ITEPA 2003, ss 316A, 336; TCGA 1992, s 158(1)(c); SP 5/86)

[30.21] If it is necessary to work at home, an income tax deduction may be claimed for the appropriate proportion of certain costs. If an employee regularly works at home under homeworking arrangements, reasonable payments by the employer to cover additional household expenses are exempt from income tax (see **10.15**). The treatment of expenses for income tax does not affect the CGT exemption unless a substantial part of the home is *exclusively* used for the purposes of employment. Where there is such exclusive use, a 'just and reasonable' proportion of the gain is chargeable. A claim for roll-over relief (see **29.11** to **29.16**) is then possible where the employer does not make any payment or give other consideration for his use of the property nor otherwise occupy it under a lease or tenancy, thus making it an investment property. Alternatively, any gain might be wholly or partly covered by the annual CGT exemption.

Selling to make a profit, including selling off part of the garden

[30.22] The CGT exemption for the main residence does not apply if the property was acquired with the intention of reselling at a profit, and if after acquiring a property expenditure is incurred wholly or partly to make a gain on sale, an appropriate part of the gain will not be exempt (TCGA 1992, s 224). HMRC have stated, however, that expenditure to get planning permission does not affect the exemption.

The CGT exemption covers grounds not exceeding half a hectare (approximately 1¼ acres), or such larger area as is appropriate to the size and character of the house. If some of the land is sold, perhaps for building plots, the sale is covered by the exemption so long as the land was enjoyed as part of the garden and grounds and is sold before the house and immediately surrounding grounds.

In exceptional circumstances, HMRC may assert that selling part of the garden, or frequent buying and selling of properties (particularly when accompanied by substantial work on them while owned), amounts to a trade, resulting not only in the loss of the CGT exemption but also in the taxation of the profits as trading income.

Death of home owner

[30.23] When the home owner dies, the CGT and IHT aspects need to be considered. There is no CGT charge on death, but gains may arise during the period of administration. See **42.5** for the CGT position of the personal representatives and beneficiaries. The treatment of the home for IHT depends on the terms of the will, as amended by any subsequent variation. For IHT planning in relation to the family home see **35.6** to **35.9**.

Tax points

[30.24] Note the following:

- Since tax relief cannot be claimed for interest on home loans, consideration should be given to reducing the home loan and instead borrowing for other tax allowable purposes on which relief at the top tax rate is available. For allowable interest, see **2.14**. See also **20.16**.

- If a second home is acquired, careful consideration should be given to which is the main residence for council tax purposes and which is to be treated as the CGT exempt residence, remembering that the last three years of ownership of a house which at some time has been a main residence for CGT can in any event be counted as years of owner-occupation in the CGT calculation.

- Where a property has been nominated as the exempt residence for CGT, a change to a different property can be notified and the election can be backdated for two years, and then a further change back to the original property can be notified if wished. But if an election is not made within the permitted two year period from the date of acquiring a second home, the right to make it is lost and the question of the main residence will be decided as a matter of fact.

- An employee living in job-related accommodation should tell HMRC about the acquisition of a dwelling for his own occupation, thus avoiding any doubt that he regards it as his main residence for CGT.

- When considering the business proportion of mixed premises for the purpose of claiming relief for expenses, bear in mind the possibility of CGT when the premises are sold.

- To qualify for 'rent-a-room' relief (see **30.10**), the owner needs to live in the property at the same time as the tenant for at least part of the relevant tax year. The relief can still be claimed for that tax year even if the owner has left the property. But if the owner does not live in the property at all while it is tenanted, rent-a-room relief is not available.

- If the owner takes in a lodger under the 'rent-a-room' provisions, he should make sure he tells his contents insurer. Even so, he will probably be covered for theft only if it is by breaking and entering. He should also check with his mortgage lender that he is not contravening the terms of the loan.

- The maximum £40,000 CGT exemption where the family home has been let (£40,000 each if jointly let by husband and wife or by civil partners or other joint owners) applies where it is wholly let for residential occupation for part of the period of ownership, or partly let for residential occupation at some time during the period of ownership. Because of the residential requirement, it could not exempt a gain that was chargeable because part of the accommodation was used by the family company for trading purposes.

- Where a house has separate buildings to accommodate staff, they may count for the CGT exemption if they are 'closely adjacent' to the main property, but not if they are so far away that the house and buildings cannot really be regarded as a single dwelling.

- If an individual undertakes a barn conversion for his own occupation, he can reclaim the VAT on the building materials.

- Each member of a married couple or civil partnership has a separate annual CGT exemption and gains in excess of the exemption are charged at 18%. Joint ownership of a second home might therefore reduce the CGT on an eventual sale.

- If the owner is selling off part of the garden, he should make sure it is sold before the house and immediately adjoining land.

- If a house sale falls through and the prospective buyer forfeits his deposit, this is treated in the same way as an abandoned option (see **4.36**), so the person who forfeited the deposit cannot claim relief for a capital loss. The seller is taxable on the amount received, reduced by the annual exemption if available. Private residence relief does not apply.
- If following the owner's death the home is to be sold by the personal representatives, there may be a significant increase in value before the sale takes place, and personal representatives may not qualify for the private residence exemption. See **42.5** for the circumstances in which the private residence exemption is available and other planning points.
- If the owner has converted part of the home into a self-contained flat for letting, he will be liable to pay up to 90% of the council tax on it if it is untenanted, except for the first six months if it is unfurnished.
- A bed and breakfast provider will not pay business rates providing he does not offer accommodation for more than six people, still lives there as well and the property's main use is still as his home, and because of the 'rent-a-room' relief there will be no income tax to pay if the gross income does not exceed £4,250 in a tax year.

31

A country life: farms and woodlands

Farming and market gardening profits

[31.1] The profits of farmers and market gardeners are calculated in the same way as those of other businesses, but because of the particular characteristics of farming, various special rules apply, some of which are mentioned below. Proper professional advice on the agreement of taxation liabilities is recommended. Farming typically generates a modest income and the availability of tax credits (see **2.33**) should not be overlooked.

It is common in farming for members of the family to be employed on the farm. As with all businesses, expenses must be incurred 'wholly and exclusively for the purposes of the trade'. The High Court decided in 1981 that a farmer's wages to his young children were pocket money and were therefore neither allowable as an expense in calculating farm trading profits nor to be treated as the children's income to enable their personal allowances to be used. The fact that the children were below legal employment age was taken into account, although it was not conclusive.

HMRC published Business Economic Notes 19 on farming stock valuations in 1993. These have since been superseded by Helpsheet 232 and guidance in HMRC Business Income Manual BIM55410. In their May 1993 Tax Bulletin HMRC gave their view of the treatment to be followed if a change in the basis of valuation was to be made. This has also been superseded and the relevant guidance can be found at BIM55415 and BIM33199. The valuation of cattle bred on the farm can be included at 60% of market value, and likewise that of home-reared sheep and pigs at 75% of market value, but no reduction is permissible for mature bought-in animals.

There are many different grants and subsidies available to farmers. The general tax treatment is that where the amounts are to meet particular costs, they should be set against those costs (and the costs net of such amounts would then be included, where appropriate, in stock valuations). Where they are to subsidise the sale proceeds of a particular crop they should be recognised as income when the crop is sold. Payments received by farmers under the Environmental Stewardship Scheme or its predecessor, the Countryside Stewardship Scheme, will usually be treated as income accruing on a monthly basis, with expenses normally being deducted as they arise. HMRC take the view that while superlevy payments for exceeding milk quota are an allowable expense, purchases of extra quota to avoid superlevy are capital expenditure, and a special commissioner upheld HMRC's refusal of a trading deduction in an appeal. Amounts received for loss of milk quota are treated as income or capital depending on whether they are compensation for loss of profit or of the quota itself. In the event of receipts for loss of milk quota being treated as capital, roll-over relief (see **29.11** onwards) is available. Amounts received by sugar beet growers for the sale of all or part of their contract tonnage entitlement are taken into account in calculating trading profits. For companies, agricultural quotas are dealt with under the intangible assets rules (see **31.23**).

Single Payment Scheme

[31.2] Following the reform of the Common Agricultural Policy, most subsidies were replaced in 2005 by the single payment scheme (SPS). Guidance is available at www.defra.gov.uk/foodfarm/farmmanage/singlepay. DEFRA states that to claim under the SPS an individual must be a farmer, must hold SPS entitlements and must have an eligible hectare of land for each entitlement. There is no requirement to undertake agricultural production but, whether or not the farmer does so, he needs to comply with EU standards in relation to public, animal and plant health, environmental and animal welfare on all his agricultural land.

For those who continue to farm, albeit possibly on only part of their land, or cease production only temporarily, the single payment is part of the trading income. If the farming trade ceases, but the other conditions for receiving the single payment are satisfied, it will be taxed as non-trading income unless another trade is commenced on the land. In that event, any losses in the farming trade would not be allowable against the profits of the new trade.

HMRC have stated that the disposal of an entitlement to receive a single farm payment will normally be a chargeable disposal for capital gains tax (CGT). If such a disposal took place before 1 January 2005, the entitlement was a non-business asset. Thereafter, entitlements under the SPS for those who continue farming are qualifying non-wasting assets for CGT roll-over relief (see **29.12**). Where the land and SPS entitlement are sold together, the proceeds are split between the two assets and the capital gains position computed separately for each asset. For corporation tax the entitlements come within the intangible assets rules (see **20.30** to **20.36**).

For inheritance tax purposes, the single payment entitlement does not qualify for agricultural property relief. The land itself may still qualify as agricultural land depending on the circumstances. Alternatively it may qualify for business property relief if it is an asset of a trading business. The single payment entitlement may similarly qualify as a business asset if it is transferred as part of a trading business. The fact that the single payment entitlement is a separate asset from the farmland should be remembered when wills are being drawn up or amended.

For value added tax, the single payment itself is outside the scope of VAT. The VAT treatment on sale of single payment entitlement will depend on the circumstances. The 'transfer of a going concern' treatment (see **7.41**) will apply where appropriate.

HMRC's Tax Bulletin Special Edition of June 2005 (available at www.hmrc.gov.uk/bulletins/tb-se-june05.pdf) gave information on the tax implications of the SPS. Further information has been published in HMRC Business Income Manual at BIM55125.

Farming as a single trade (ITTOIA 2005, ss 9, 859; CTA 2009, s 36)

[31.3] All farming carried on by one farmer is treated as a single trade, so that several holdings are treated as a single business and a move from one farm to another is not treated as the cessation of one business and the commencement of another. The single trade treatment applies whether the farmer is a sole trader, a partnership or a company, but farming carried on by a partnership is treated as a trade separate from any farming carried on by individual partners.

Loss relief (ITA 2007, Pt 4; CTA 2010, Pt 4)

[31.4] The usual reliefs for losses in early and later years and on cessation of trading are available to farming businesses and the usual restriction applies to prevent losses being set against other income if the business is not operated on a commercial basis (see **CHAPTER 25**). In addition, a loss in the sixth tax year of a consecutive run of farming and market gardening losses (calculated before capital allowances) can only be relieved against later profits of the same trade, unless (very broadly) it can be shown that the taxpayer's farming or market gardening activities are such as would justify a reasonable expectation of profits in the future. The same applies to a loss in a company accounting period following a similar five-year run of losses (before capital allowances).

If losses are required to be carried forward, any related capital allowances are similarly treated. Once one year shows a profit, another six-year period then applies to later losses.

Averaging (ITTOIA 2005, ss 221–225)

[31.5] Averaging enables farmers to lessen the effect of high tax rates on a successful year when preceded or followed by a bad year. The results of an individual farmer or market gardener or of a farming or market gardening partnership may be averaged over two tax years if the profit of one year is less than $^7/_{10}$ths of the profit of the other year, with marginal relief if it is more than $^7/_{10}$ths but less than $^3/_4$.

If profits are averaged, the average figure is then used as the result of the second year and it may again be averaged with the result of the third year and so on. Losses are counted as nil profits in the averaging calculation, with relief for the loss being available separately.

Averaging claims are not made by partnerships. The individual partners may make separate claims on their profit shares if they wish. The time limit for an averaging claim is one year from 31 January following the end of the second tax year, claims being made in the tax return or an amendment to it. Averaging may not be claimed by farming companies nor in relation to any profits charged to tax as property income (see **CHAPTER 32**). An averaging claim cannot be made in the tax year in which a sole trader or partner starts or ceases to trade.

The tax and Class 4 national insurance contributions payable under the various alternatives needs to be calculated, taking into account, if appropriate, the possibility of not claiming plant and machinery capital allowances or claiming a reduced amount (in which case the written-down value carried forward to attract writing-down allowances in later years would be increased).

[31.6] The adjustment to the tax and Class 4 contributions of an earlier year resulting from a farmer's averaging claim is *calculated* by reference to the position of the earlier year, but the adjustment is made in relation to the *later* year. If the adjustment is an increase, it is added to the tax and Class 4 contributions payable for the second year. If it is a decrease, it is treated as a payment on account for the second year. If the adjustment and payments on account for the second year exceed the tax and Class 4 contributions due on the averaged profit for the second year, the excess amount will be repaid (or offset if other tax is due or will become due shortly). Interest on overpaid or underpaid tax and Class 4 contributions relating to the adjustment for the earlier year, where relevant, runs from 31 January following the later year (see **9.6**).

Averaging does not affect the payments on account for the first of the two years that are averaged, which are still based on the previous year's tax and Class 4 contributions, subject to any claim to reduce them to the amount payable on the unaveraged profits. Payments on account for the second year will initially be based on the unaveraged profits of the first year. Once the liability for the second year can be accurately ascertained, based on the averaged profits, a claim can be made to reduce payments on account if appropriate.

The change to the assessable profit of the second year affects the payments on account for the *next following* year. The increase or decrease in the second year's tax and Class 4 contributions as a result of the averaging adjustment for the first year does not, however, enter into the figure for the second year on which payments on account for the next following year are based. See Example 1.

Example 1

Farmer's profits after capital allowances are as follows:

Year ended 31 December		£
2008	Profit	45,000
2009	Loss	(7,000)
2010	Profit	50,000

The farmer is a single man with no other sources of income. The relevant tax rates and allowances are:

	Basic rate limit £	Personal allowance £	Income limit for 40% tax £
2008/09	34,800	6,035	40,835
2009/10	37,400	6,475	43,875
2010/11	37,400	6,475	43,875

Class 4 national insurance contributions are payable as follows:

	Profits between	Chargeable at 8%
2008/09	£5,435 to £40,040	£34,605
2009/10	£5,715 to £43,875	£38,160
2010/11	£5,715 to £43,875	£38,160

In addition, Class 4 contributions are payable at 1% on profits in excess of the upper limit.

Assessable profits may variously be as follows:

	No averaging £	Averaging 2008/09 and 2009/10 only £	All three years averaged £
2008/09	45,000	22,500	22,500
2009/10	—*	22,500*	36,250*
2010/11	50,000	50,000	36,250

* Loss of £7,000 available for relief

The loss of the year to 31 December 2009 is treated as a loss of 2009/10, for which relief may be claimed under ITA 2007, s 64 in 2009/10 or 2008/09. Alternatively it may be carried forward under ITA 2007, s 83 and set off in 2010/11. (Losses are dealt with in **CHAPTER 25**.) Note that following a temporary extension of the carry back of trade losses introduced by FA 2009, if the loss had been greater any balance could also be carried back and set against the profits of the trade for 2007/08 and 2006/07 (see 25.6).

With no averaging, but claiming relief for the loss of £7,000 in 2008/09 to save higher rate tax in that year, higher rate tax would be payable on £6,125 in 2010/11, and the personal allowance and basic rate band of 2009/10 would be wasted.

If 2008/09 and 2009/10 are averaged, and the loss is carried forward to 2010/11, reducing the taxable profit of that year to £43,000, the 2009/10 personal allowance would be utilised, and the higher rate tax of 2008/09 and 2010/11 would be eliminated. The 2009/10 averaged figure of £22,500 would be used to calculate the payments on account for 2010/11.

If all three years are averaged, and loss relief is claimed in 2009/10, again no higher rate tax would be payable in any year and the 2009/10 personal allowance is utilised. Following the first claim, the total tax and Class 4 contributions payable in respect of 2009/10 can be ascertained, comprising a reduction in tax payable for 2008/09 and increase for 2009/10. A claim can then be made to reduce the 2009/10 payments on account (which were originally based on the £45,000 profit for 2008/09) to the amount payable on the averaged 2009/10 figure of £22,500 less the reduction for 2008/09. The 2009/10 averaged figure of £22,500 would be used in arriving at payments on account for 2010/11. This would not alter following the second claim, the increase in tax payable for 2009/10 being treated as extra tax due for 2010/11. This extra tax would not, however, be taken into account in calculating payments on account for 2011/12, which would be based on the 2010/11 averaged figure of £36,250.

The overall tax and NIC payable following either averaging claim is the same because all profits are charged to tax at the basic rate of 20% and to NIC at 8% where chargeable and no personal allowances are wasted. Both give a tax saving over the position if no averaging is claimed. However, there is a slight cashflow advantage in the first claim as it results in more profits being taxable later, in 2010/11 rather than in 2009/10. The position would be different if the basic rate limit and personal allowance were not the same for 2009/10 and 2010/11.

Note that there are proposed changes to the personal allowance, basic rate limit and national insurance rates and thresholds from 6 April 2011 (see 2.15, 13.2 and 24.6).

Herd basis (*ITTOIA 2005, ss 30, 111–129; CTA 2009, ss 50, 109–127*)

[31.7] Farm animals and other livestock are normally treated as trading stock. A production herd may, however, effectively be treated as a capital asset if an election is made for the herd basis. The election is irrevocable. In addition to being available to individuals, companies and partnerships the herd basis is available where animals are held on a shared basis, for instance in share farming. HMRC guidance is available in the Business Income Manual at BIM55501.

For companies, the time limit for making the election is two years from the end of the first accounting period in which the herd is kept. The time limit for individuals and partnerships is one year from the 31 January following the tax year in which the first 'relevant period of account' ends. The first relevant period of account is the first period of account in which the farmer keeps a production herd of the class to which the election relates. If a farmer (other than a partnership) started to carry on the trade in that tax year, the time limit is extended by a year. See Example 2.

Example 2

A production herd is acquired in May 2010 by an established business that makes up its accounts to 31 December.

The time limit for a claim by individuals and partners is 31 January 2013.

The limit would remain the same if the year to 31 December 2010 was the first year of business for a sole trader, because the account ends in the second tax year. If accounts had been made up to 5 April and the year to 5 April 2011 had been the first accounting year of a sole trader, then the relevant account would end in the first tax year of trading, i.e. 2010/11, and the time limit would be 31 January 2014.

A change in the partners in a farming partnership requires a new herd basis election to be made even where the farming business has owned the herd for several years. There are, however, anti-avoidance provisions to prevent the change being used solely or mainly for the purposes of obtaining a benefit resulting from the right to make a herd basis election or flowing from the election. A herd basis election is not affected when a partnership becomes a limited liability partnership.

Under self-assessment, partnerships make a single election for the herd basis, even though partners are assessed separately. HMRC have stated that they will not require farmers to make a separate written election where it is clear from material submitted that the herd basis has been applied.

A production herd is a group of living animals or other livestock kept for obtaining products such as milk, wool, etc. or their young.

The effect of the election is that the initial purchase of the herd and any subsequent purchases that increase the herd attract no tax relief, but a renewals basis applies where animals are replaced, so that the cost of the replacement is charged as an expense and the sale proceeds are brought in as a trading receipt. Where there is a minor disposal without replacement ('minor' usually meaning less than 20% of the herd), profits on the disposal are also brought in as a trading receipt. If the whole or a substantial part of the herd is sold and not replaced, no part of the proceeds is charged as income, because it represents the sale of a capital asset, and CGT does not arise since the animals are wasting assets on which capital allowances are not available and are therefore exempt (see **4.9**).

Compensation for compulsory slaughter

[31.8] By HMRC concession B11, where compensation is paid for compulsorily slaughtered stock to which the herd basis does not apply, the compensation may be left out of account in the year of receipt and brought in over the next three years in equal instalments.

Farm plant and machinery

[31.9] Capital allowances on farm plant and machinery are available in the usual way (see CHAPTER 22 for a summary of the rules). Expenditure should be carefully analysed to make sure that plant and machinery is properly treated as such rather than being treated as part of an agricultural building. This is particularly important now that agricultural buildings allowances are to be phased out (see **31.10**).

Agricultural buildings allowances (ITA 2007, ss 118, 120; CAA 2001, ss 361–393, 570A; FA 2007, s 36; FA 2008, ss 84–88)

[31.10] The owners or tenants of agricultural land may claim agricultural buildings allowances in respect of certain expenditure. However, agricultural buildings allowances (and industrial buildings allowances) are being phased out over a four year period, with no allowances being available from April 2011. From 21 March 2007 (or a later date if the transitional provisions apply), no balancing adjustments are made when agricultural buildings are disposed of, and the new owner takes over the allowances for the years that they remain available. The transitional provisions are the same as those for industrial buildings — see **22.42**.

[31.11] The expenditure that currently qualifies for the allowances is expenditure on the construction of buildings such as farmhouses, farm buildings and cottages, fences and roads, and on the installation of services. In relation to farmhouses, not more than one third of the cost may be included (see **31.21**). Any grants received are deducted from the allowable cost. Farm shops count as agricultural buildings, but the allowable expenditure is restricted if the shops also sell bought-in items.

[31.12] Expenditure is normally relieved at present by *writing-down allowances* at 4% per annum over 25 years, but if agricultural buildings have been disposed of during the writing down period to date, there may have been a recalculation of the allowance (see **31.13**). Where the 4% writing down allowance applied at 21 March 2007, it is to be reduced to 3% from April 2008, 2% from April 2009, 1% from April 2010 and withdrawn altogether from April 2011. The allowances for sole traders and farming partnerships commence in the accounting period in which the expenditure is incurred. For non-trading agricultural landlords they commence in the tax year in which the expenditure is incurred. For both trading and non-trading companies the allowances commence in the accounting period in which the expenditure is incurred. For companies the allowance is proportionately reduced if the accounting period is less than twelve months. For unincorporated businesses the allowance is proportionately reduced or increased according to the length of the period of account (see **22.8** and **22.9**).

Writing-down allowances may be reduced to whatever amount the claimant wishes, but this will rarely have been appropriate and is now unlikely in the remaining years that the allowances remain available.

[31.13] A *balancing allowance or charge* may have been made when agricultural buildings or works were disposed of, demolished or ceased to exist before 21 March 2007, but only if an election to that effect was made by the former and new owners, if there was a disposal, or by the owner, if there was no disposal. The purchaser then received allowances based on the remainder of the 25-year period, normally on what he paid or on what the first user paid, whichever was lower. The time limit for making the election for companies was two years after the end of the relevant accounting period, and for individuals one year from the 31 January following the end of the relevant tax year.

The joint election for the balancing adjustment was not usually made, because it would have been to the advantage of one of the parties at the expense of the other. It will not be relevant in any event for disposals on or after 21 March 2007.

If the election was not made, and in any event for disposals on or after 21 March 2007, the seller gets a final writing-down allowance which is proportionate to the length of the part of his basis period up to the date of sale, and the buyer gets the allowances for the period until their withdrawal at April 2011, with his first writing-down allowance depending on the part of his basis period that occurs after the date of sale.

If a farming tenant vacates his holding and does not receive any consideration for his unrelieved agricultural buildings expenditure from the incoming tenant, the landlord is entitled to relief for the allowances remaining until their withdrawal.

[31.14] In the case of a farming trade, the allowances are given in calculating the trading profits and may therefore increase or create a loss, for which the usual loss reliefs are available (see **CHAPTERS 25** and **26**).

For agricultural landlords, the allowances are treated as expenses of a property business and the property business rules determine how losses may be relieved (see **31.18**).

[31.15] Where a building is sold for more than cost, the full cost is taken into account in the capital gains computation, despite any allowances that have been given against income. Where a building is sold for less than cost, there has previously been no allowable loss for capital gains purposes, because the full value was allowed through the capital allowances system. Once the allowances are no longer available, an allowable loss for capital gains purposes may arise after taking into account the capital allowances that have been given.

VAT

[31.16] For VAT purposes, most of a farm's outputs are zero-rated, but there may also be standard-rated outputs, such as sales of equipment, shooting rights, holiday accommodation, and exempt outputs such as rents for residential caravan sites, possibly leading to partial exemption restrictions. The single payment scheme (see **31.2**) resulted in many farmers diversifying into non-farming activities, and special care needs to be taken in relation to the VAT position. HMRC have paid particular attention to shooting businesses and have found widespread VAT irregularities. The usual input VAT restrictions for entertaining, private use, etc. apply (see **CHAPTER 7**). For the treatment of land and buildings and of the farmhouse, see **31.19** and **31.21**.

If milk quota is sold separately from land, it is standard-rated. If the sale is linked to a supply of land the VAT liability is the same as the liability for the land.

Flat-rate farmers (VATA 1994, s 54; SI 1992/3221; SI 1995/2518, regs 202–211)

[31.17] Farmers may opt to become 'flat-rate farmers' for VAT purposes, regardless of their turnover, providing they satisfy HMRC that the total flat-rate compensation they will be entitled to in the year after they join the scheme will not exceed the input VAT they could have claimed by £3,000 or more. They do not need to register for VAT and therefore make no VAT returns, but they add a fixed flat-rate compensation percentage of 4% to their sale prices when they sell to VAT registered businesses, which they keep to offset the input VAT they have suffered. The registered businesses are able to reclaim on their VAT returns the compensation amount charged to them. Farmers below the registration threshold need not become flat-rate farmers unless they wish to. A flat-rate farmer whose non-farming turnover goes over the registration threshold must leave the scheme and register for VAT.

Agricultural landlords (ITA 2007, ss 118, 120; CAA 2001, ss 361–393; ITTOIA 2005, ss 9–11; CTA 2009, s 36; CTA 2010, ss 62–67)

[31.18] Income from letting agricultural land is taxed in the same way as for any investment property (see **CHAPTER 32**).

For individuals, all rental income is charged as the profits of a property business. If expenses exceed income, the landlord may claim to set the loss against his total income of the same tax year and/or the following tax year, to the extent that the loss consists of capital allowances (see **31.9** and **31.10**) and/or maintenance, repairs, insurance or management expenses (but not loan interest) relating to agricultural land that is managed as one estate. Any part of the loss remaining unrelieved is carried forward to set against later rental income.

Companies are subject to broadly the same rules as individuals, although the treatment of losses is not the same. Companies may set property business losses against their total profits of the same accounting period, or alternatively surrender the losses by way of group relief, any unrelieved balance being carried forward to set against the *total* profits of succeeding periods. For further details see CHAPTER 32.

The occupation of land for farming purposes (such as growing crops and raising farm livestock) is treated as a trade. This will apply where an owner receives income from short-term grazing lets, providing the owner's activities in growing the grass, fertilising, etc., and general upkeep and maintenance of the land, can be regarded as farming. In that event, the land will qualify as a business asset on which roll-over relief for CGT is available if it is sold and the proceeds reinvested in a qualifying replacement asset within one year before and three years after the sale (see **29.11** onwards).

Although gifts relief for CGT normally applies only to business assets or to gifts that are immediately chargeable to inheritance tax (see **4.23** to **4.26**), it applies to agricultural property held as an investment providing the conditions for inheritance tax agricultural property relief are satisfied (see **5.43**).

Value added tax (VATA 1994, Sch 8 Group 5, Sch 9 Group 1 and Sch 10)

[31.19] Grants of long or short leases of agricultural land and buildings, and rents received therefrom, are exempt from VAT, but the landlord has the option to charge VAT. Written notice must be given to HMRC within 30 days. VAT is then charged from the day the landlord exercises his option, or any later date he specifies. (If the landlord is not already VAT registered, he will have to become registered to take this option.) If the option is taken, it can be revoked within six months from the time it takes effect, or twenty or more years after it takes effect. Where a landlord has interests in several different estates, an election can be made for specific discrete areas (such as one farm). The landlord may increase existing rents by the VAT charged if the lease allows VAT to be added or is silent as to VAT. If not, the rent has to be treated as VAT-inclusive.

Following the exercise of the option, VAT must be charged not only on rents and lease premiums, but also on any sale proceeds as and when any of the land and buildings are sold (subject to what is said in **32.39**). An apportionment will be made in each case, however, to exclude any private dwelling/charitable element. Making the election enables the landlord to recover any VAT he suffers, for example on the acquisition of the property, or on repairs, and the farmer tenants will usually be VAT registered and will therefore be able to recover the VAT charged.

FA 2009 introduced provisions to prevent the exercise or revocation of the option to tax or a change in the VAT rate from qualifying as a change of rent for the purposes of the Agricultural Holdings Act. Previously a change in the rate of VAT was treated as a change of rent for these purposes and this prevented the parties to a lease from referring the rent to arbitration for a period of three years from the date of the rate change. The exercise or revocation of the option to tax by the landlord also had the same effect.

Small agricultural holdings

[31.20] The profits of a commercial smallholding are taxed as trading profits, but if losses arise, HMRC may contend that the trade is not conducted on a commercial basis with a view to profit, so that the losses may only be carried forward against future income from the smallholding and not set against any other income. This is quite separate from their right to disallow farming losses from the sixth year onwards (see **31.4**).

The smallholder may seek voluntary VAT registration even though his taxable supplies are less than £70,000 per year (the VAT registration threshold from 1 April 2010, see **7.6**), because he will then be able to reclaim input VAT on his expenditure and he will have no liability on his supplies, which are zero-rated. HMRC are required to register anyone making taxable supplies who seeks voluntary registration. The smallholder may alternatively join the flat-rate scheme (see **31.17**).

The farmhouse (TCGA 1992, ss 222–224; IHTA 1984, s 115(2))

[31.21] The restriction for agricultural buildings allowances of the qualifying capital expenditure on a farmhouse to a maximum of one-third recognises that the domestic and business activities overlap. In arriving at the farm profits, an appropriate part of the establishment charges of the farmhouse is allowed, based on the extent to which the farmhouse is used for business.

HMRC adopt a similar approach in relation to the recovery of input VAT on farmhouse expenses such as light and heat. They may, however, allow a sole proprietor or partner working full-time to recover 70% of the input VAT on repair and maintenance costs where certain conditions are met, under an agreement reached with the NFU. Where farming is not a full-time business, the allowable percentage will need to be agreed with HMRC.

The business expenses deduction will not jeopardise the CGT private residence exemption (see **CHAPTER 30**) provided that no part of the farmhouse has been used exclusively for business purposes. Where part is so used and a chargeable gain arises, roll-over relief may be claimed if the farmhouse is replaced (see **29.11** onwards). The CGT exemption usually extends to grounds up to half a hectare, but for a farmhouse a larger area may be allowed because of the situation and character of the farmhouse and immediately surrounding grounds. The CGT exemptions and reliefs are dealt with in CHAPTER 4.

Agricultural property relief for inheritance tax is available on the farmhouse providing the owner also owns the agricultural land, the farmhouse is 'of a character appropriate to the property', and occupation of the farmhouse is ancillary to that of the agricultural land. These conditions are often considered by HMRC not to be satisfied and decisions in appeals have given support to HMRC's views. Even if it is available, the relief is given on the 'agricultural value' of the property only, not the open market value. Where there is part business use of the farmhouse, for example for bed and breakfast, business property relief will apply on the business proportion.

FA 2009 extended agricultural property relief to qualifying property in other European Economic Area states when an event chargeable to inheritance tax occurs.

Land let by partners to farming partnership, or by directors to farming company (TCGA 1992, ss 152–158)

[31.22] Where land is owned personally by a partner or director, and let to the farming business, any rent paid is allowed as an expense of the business and treated as property income in the partner's or director's hands. If interest is paid on a loan to buy the land it may be deducted in arriving at the net property income (see CHAPTER 32).

CGT roll-over relief may sometimes be claimed if the land is disposed of and the proceeds used to acquire a qualifying asset within one year before and three years after the sale. Charging rent as indicated above does not affect this relief. See **29.11** onwards.

Capital gains tax (TCGA 1992, s 155)

[31.23] Various CGT aspects are dealt with elsewhere in this chapter. As far as roll-over relief for replacement of business assets is concerned, some categories of qualifying asset specifically relate to farming, namely agricultural quotas (see **29.12**). For companies, agricultural quotas acquired on or after 1 April 2002 come within the intangible assets provisions and are dealt with in calculating income rather than under the capital gains rules (see **20.30** onwards). The following provisions now apply only for individuals.

Quota is treated as a separate asset from land, and where nothing was paid for the quota there is no allowable cost to set against the gain on disposal. HMRC regard quotas as being non-depreciating assets for roll-over relief. Where quota and land is transferred in a single transaction, values have to be apportioned on a just and reasonable basis. See also **31.1**.

Where a tenant receives statutory compensation following a notice to quit, or for improvements at the end of the tenancy, the compensation is not liable to CGT.

Farming companies are not qualifying companies for enterprise investment scheme relief (see CHAPTER 29).

Inheritance tax (IHTA 1984, ss 115–124C)

[31.24] When agricultural property is transferred, inheritance tax agricultural property relief is given on the agricultural value, and where the property is also business property, business property relief is given on the non-agricultural value. The detailed rules for each relief are in CHAPTER 5. Farmland that is managed in an environmentally beneficial way under the Environmental Stewardship Scheme or its predecessor, the Countryside Stewardship Scheme, will usually qualify for agricultural property relief providing the land was occupied for agricultural purposes at the time it was brought within the Scheme. Agricultural property relief is not, however, available on farmland converted to woodland under the Woodland Grant Scheme (see **31.27**), but the special provisions for woodlands may apply (see **31.30**).

The rate of relief for some tenanted agricultural property used to be 50%, as against 100% for owner-occupied land, but relief at the 100% rate is now available for all qualifying tenanted property where the letting commenced on or after 1 September 1995, including successions to tenancies following the death of the previous tenant on or after that date (see **5.43**). The grant of the tenancy itself is specifically exempt from inheritance tax so long as it is made for full consideration. Although tenanted property normally has to be owned for seven years to qualify for agricultural property relief (see **5.43**), the period is only two years where the tenant is a partnership in which the donor is a partner or a company controlled by the donor.

The relief applies to lifetime transfers which are not potentially exempt, or which, having been so, become chargeable because the donor dies within seven years, and to transfers on death. The relief is only available in calculating the tax or additional tax payable as a result of the donor's death within seven years if the donee still owns the property (or qualifying replacement property) when the donor dies, or if earlier, when the donee dies.

Where relief at the time of the transfer is at 100%, there will be neither a chargeable transfer nor a potentially exempt transfer at that time, but the transfer will be counted at death if the donor does not survive the seven-year period.

The 100% rate of agricultural property relief discourages lifetime gifts, because a lifetime gift will attract CGT (although payment can be deferred by claiming gifts relief), whereas on death there is a CGT-free uplift in asset values. There is, of course, no certainty that the present favourable regime will continue.

FA 2009 extended agricultural property relief to qualifying property in other European Economic Area states when an event chargeable to inheritance tax occurs.

Stamp duty land tax

[31.25] Stamp duty land tax is payable on the sale of farm land and buildings. It is not usually payable on a gift, but if say mortgaged farmland was transferred from a farmer to a family farming partnership, or from one family partnership to another, and the transferee took over liability for the mortgage, the amount of the mortgage would be subject to stamp duty land tax unless it fell within the zero rate band.

Woodlands and short rotation coppice

[31.26] The tax treatment of woodlands is dealt with below. Short rotation coppice is treated as farming, rather than under the woodlands provisions (see **31.31**).

Income tax (ITTOIA 2005, s 11; CTA 2009, s 37)

[31.27] There is no income tax charge on profits from the commercial occupation of woodlands in the UK, so relief for losses incurred and interest paid in the initial planting period cannot be claimed, but as and when profits arise they are not taxed. Payments under the Farm Woodland Premium Scheme, which are made for ten or fifteen years depending on the type of woodland, are taxable as farming income, even if paid to someone who does not carry on a farming business. Grants under the Woodland Grant Scheme, on the other hand, are not taxable. Both schemes closed to new applicants in 2005 and were replaced by the English Woodland Grant Scheme.

Capital gains tax (TCGA 1992, ss 158, 250)

[31.28] There is no charge to CGT on trees that are standing or felled. Proceeds of sale of timber are therefore not charged to tax at all. The land is, however, a chargeable asset for capital gains purposes. It is therefore important on acquisition and disposal to establish the different values applicable to the timber and the land.

For commercially run woodlands, gains on sale of the land may be deferred by rolling them over against the cost of replacement assets where the land sale proceeds are reinvested in qualifying business assets within one year before and three years after the sale (see **29.11** onwards). If a gain is made on a disposal by way of gift, it will not qualify for gifts relief (see **4.23**) unless the woodlands operation is a trade.

Where woodlands are owned by a company, the land is a qualifying asset for roll-over relief as far as the company is concerned, but an individual shareholder will not get roll-over relief when he sells his shares and reinvests the proceeds (unless he qualifies for enterprise investment scheme relief — see **29.21**). He will not be entitled to gifts relief in respect of the shares unless the company is a trading company and the other conditions for relief are satisfied (see **4.24** to **4.26**).

Value added tax (VATA 1994, Sch 1 para 9)

[31.29] A commercially run woodland is within the scope of VAT, the supply or granting of any right to fell and remove standing timber being standard-rated. It is possible to register for VAT before making taxable supplies, the intention to make taxable supplies being sufficient for registration purposes even though they will not be made for some years (see **7.6**). Having registered, input VAT on goods and services in connection with the woodlands operation can be recovered.

Inheritance tax (IHTA 1984, ss 125–130)

[31.30] Where an estate on death includes growing timber, an election may be made to leave the timber (but not the land on which it stands) out of account in valuing the estate at death. The election must be made within two years after the date of death and is only available if the deceased either had been beneficially entitled to the land throughout the previous five years or had become entitled to it without consideration (for example by gift or inheritance). (Commercially managed woodlands will usually qualify for 100% business property relief, in which case the election would not be made — see below.)

The election cannot be made if the occupation of the woodlands is subsidiary to the occupation of agricultural land, but agricultural property relief would be given if the necessary conditions were fulfilled (except that it will not be available on any part of the land that has been converted to woodland under the Woodland Grant Scheme).

Following the election, when the timber is later disposed of by sale or gift, there will be a charge to inheritance tax on the sale price or, if the disposal is for less than full consideration, the market value, less allowable expenses in both cases. Allowable expenses are the costs of sale and expenses of replanting within three years after disposal, or such longer time as HMRC allow.

The net disposal proceeds or market value are treated as value transferred at the date of death, forming the top slice of the property passing on death, but using the scale and rates current at the time of disposal to find a notional liability on the estate first excluding and then including the timber proceeds, the tax on the timber proceeds being the difference between the two. The tax is due six months after the end of the month in which the disposal takes place, with interest on overdue tax payable from that date. The person entitled to the sale proceeds is liable for the tax. Where there are no proceeds because the disposal is by way of gift, the donee is liable for the tax, which may be paid by instalments over ten years.

FA 2009 extends this relief to qualifying woodlands in other European Economic Area states.

A lifetime gift of woodlands not qualifying for business property relief either attracts inheritance tax or is a potentially exempt transfer (see **CHAPTER 5**). Where the disposal is one on which tax is payable following its being left out of account on an earlier death, the value transferred by the lifetime transfer is reduced by the tax charge arising out of the previous death.

If the person who inherits woodlands on which an election has been made dies before the timber is disposed of, no inheritance tax charge can arise in respect of the first death. Furthermore, a new election may then be made on the second death.

Where woodlands are managed on a commercial basis, despite there being no income tax charge, they qualify for 100% business property relief so long as they have been owned for two years (see **CHAPTER 5**). Where tax is payable, it may be paid by instalments in the case of a death transfer where the value has not been left out of account and where a lifetime transfer is not potentially exempt. If an election is made to leave the timber out of account on a death, business property relief is given on the net sale proceeds when it is disposed of, but only at 50% rather than 100%. This will be relevant where the election has already been made, but clearly no new elections will be made where the 100% business property relief is available.

Short rotation coppice (ITA 2007, s 996; CTA 2010, s 1125)

[31.31] Short rotation coppice, which is a way of producing a renewable fuel for 'green' biomass-fed power stations from willow or poplar cuttings, is regarded as farming for income tax, corporation tax and CGT, and as agricultural land for inheritance tax.

HMRC consider that the initial cultivation costs of the short rotation coppice are capital expenditure, the net amount of which (after deducting any Woodland Grants offset against the expenditure) may be used to roll over gains on disposals of other business assets. The expenditure (net of both Woodland Grants and any rolled over gains) will be allowable in calculating gains when the land is disposed of, providing the coppice stools are still on the land at that time.

Subsequent expenditure after the initial cultivation will be revenue expenditure.

Council tax and business rates

[31.32] Agricultural land and buildings are exempt from business rates. Any buildings or parts of buildings that are for domestic rather than agricultural use attract up to 90% of the council tax if the building or part is no-one's only or main home. If it is someone's only or main home, the residents are liable to pay the council tax. The valuation takes into account the restricted market for the property because of the agricultural use. In Scotland only, unoccupied, unfurnished property previously used in connection with agricultural land or woodlands, etc. is exempt from council tax.

Where farms diversify into non-agricultural activities, business rates are payable.

In small rural communities, post offices and/or village food shops (other than confectionery shops or catering businesses) with rateable values up to £8,500, sole pubs or petrol stations with rateable values up to £12,500, and farm shops etc. on what was previously agricultural land and buildings are entitled to 50% mandatory business rates relief. Councils have the power to increase the relief to 100%, and may also grant relief to other rural businesses important to the community that have rateable values up to £16,500.

Tax points

[31.33] Note the following:

- A smallholding may show consistent losses, and it is unlikely that these can be relieved against other income. A smallholding that amounts to a trade may prejudice the CGT private residence exemption, and it may be worthwhile making a note in the annual tax return that the working of the holding is not by way of trade but only for the maintenance of the holding and that no profits arise.
- Where a smallholding or market garden is clearly a trade, make sure if possible that no part of the dwelling house is used exclusively for business, to avoid any possible loss of the CGT private residence exemption.
- If losses are being made and there is a danger of falling foul of the six-year rule, try to show a small profit in one year, perhaps by delaying repairs or other expenses. The six-year cycle will then start again.
- When buying a holding with agricultural buildings, remember that the price paid for them does not necessarily provide entitlement to any capital allowances. Allowances could not be claimed on any more than that part of the original building expenditure for which relief had not yet been given. The allowances are, in any event, being phased out over a four year period and will not be available after April 2011.
- An individual agricultural landlord who has incurred expenditure on agricultural buildings, may make a claim to set the available allowances against any income to the extent that the total rental income is insufficient. Relief can be given in the tax year itself or the following year. Company landlords may claim to set rental losses (which will include allowances not covered by rental income) against their total profits, including capital gains, of the same accounting period and then succeeding accounting periods.
- Owning agricultural land personally and renting it to his partnership or company will not stop an individual getting CGT roll-over relief (see **29.11** onwards) if the land is sold and replaced. Roll-over relief is not available to other agricultural landlords.
- CGT gifts relief *is* available to agricultural landlords if the conditions are satisfied (see **4.24** to **4.26**).
- A farmer's averaging claim affects income for two or more years, but the claim has no effect on the dates on which tax is due for payment (see **31.5**).

- If ownership of the farm is transferred to the family, but the transferor still lives in the farmhouse, the farmhouse will not qualify for inheritance tax agricultural property relief. The transferor needs to be a partner, with a share, albeit small, in the farm, to remain entitled to the relief.
- Farmers and landowners involved in game shooting should look at the income tax and VAT implications very carefully. HMRC have targeted the shooting industry because they considered there was evidence of non-compliance and misunderstanding.
- A number of specialist organisations advise on an investment in woodlands, not only from the taxation point of view but also on the question of cash grants through the Forestry Commission, and on estate management.

32

Investing in land and buildings

Introduction

[32.1] This chapter deals with both commercial and private investment properties in the UK. The detailed treatment of let agricultural buildings is covered in CHAPTER 31. The tax advantages of investing in enterprise zone buildings and the special provisions relating to the grant of a lease on an enterprise zone building are dealt with in CHAPTER 22 although enterprise zone allowances are to be withdrawn from April 2011. Companies may claim relief equal to 150% of qualifying expenditure on cleaning up contaminated and derelict land that has been acquired for the purposes of a trade or property business (see **20.37**). For anti-avoidance provisions in respect of factoring of taxable receipts which replaced the provisions on rent factoring schemes see **45.7**.

Rental income is charged under the heading of property income, either of a UK property business or an overseas property business as the case may be (see **2.7** for individuals and **3.4** for companies). The treatment of UK property let by those who live abroad and of property abroad let by UK residents is dealt with in CHAPTER 41 and **30.16**.

Landlords of multiple properties will frequently hold service charges and sinking funds on trust. Income from such trust funds held by any UK landlord is taxable at income tax rates and not the trust rate. See **6.17** for special stamp duty land tax provisions for Registered Social Landlords.

Income from land and buildings

[32.2] Income from UK land and buildings is usually charged to tax as property income, except for income from furnished holiday lettings, which is treated as trading income for the purpose of certain reliefs (see **32.22** onwards). The distinction between trading income and property income is important to individuals in relation to pension contributions, although those without earnings may get tax relief on personal pension contributions up to £3,600 a year (see **16.13** and **17.10**). The distinction between trading and property income is also important for capital gains tax (CGT) purposes because an investment property does not qualify for CGT roll-over relief (see **29.11** onwards) when it is replaced (unless it is compulsorily purchased — see **32.30**). Gifts relief (see **4.23**) will not usually be available either. See **29.2** regarding entrepreneurs' relief on qualifying business disposals.

As far as inheritance tax is concerned, business property relief is not available where the business consists of making or holding investments, which includes land which is let (see **5.40**). The relief has been denied in cases before the Special Commissioners even where the owners played a very active role in the letting, management and maintenance of their properties, and one decision by the Special Commissioners in favour of the taxpayer in a case concerning a caravan site was overruled in the High Court (but see **32.27** re furnished holiday lettings). Agricultural property relief is presently available to landlords of let agricultural property (see **31.24**).

Income tax on rents is usually paid as part of the half-yearly payments on account on 31 January in the tax year and 31 July following, with a balancing adjustment on the next 31 January. Companies pay corporation tax on all their profits under self-assessment, the due date normally being nine months after the end of the accounting period, except for certain large companies who are required to pay their tax by instalments (see **3.22**).

The tax treatment of individuals is dealt with from **32.3** to **32.8** and that of companies at **32.9** and **32.10**. The capital allowances provisions for both individuals and companies are dealt with at **32.11** to **32.16**. The treatment of furnished holiday lettings, which applies both to individuals and companies, is dealt with at **32.22** to **32.29**. The treatment of lease premiums, where the treatment is again broadly the same for individuals and companies, is dealt with at **32.17** to **32.21**.

Tax treatment of individuals (ITA 2007, ss 836, 837; CAA 2001, ss 15, 16, 35; ITTOIA 2005, ss 263–275)

[32.3] Special rules apply where furnished rooms are let in an individual's own home, and in some circumstances the letting may amount to a trade. This is dealt with in **30.10** to **30.14**. Profits from the provision of accommodation in hotels or guest houses are wholly trading income and are not property income. With these exceptions, all income from UK property (including the right to use a fixed caravan or permanently moored houseboat) is treated as the profits of a UK property business, whether there is just one letting or a number of lettings, whether the property is let furnished or unfurnished, and no matter whether repairs are the responsibility of the landlord or the tenant (although income from qualifying furnished holiday lettings is kept separate and the provisions outlined at **32.22** to **32.29** apply).

[32.4] Where there are joint owners of a let property, in some cases the letting may form part of a partnership business. More usually each joint owner's share is treated as their personal property business income. HMRC state in their Property Income Manual at PIM1030 that for joint owners other than spouses or civil partners, although normally shares of rental income are equal to the respective shares of ownership of the property, the joint owners may agree to share the income differently. Their taxable share would be the share actually agreed. It would be sensible to have written evidence of any such arrangements. Splitting income differently from capital shares is not possible for spouses or civil partners (see **33.6**).

Calculation of property income

[32.5] The income charged to tax is that of the tax year from 6 April to 5 April. (Different rules apply to partnerships — see **23.4**.) Although the income is investment income, the general accounting rules for working out trading profits apply. Allowable expenses are broadly those that are of a revenue rather than a capital nature and are wholly and exclusively for the purpose of the lettings, so that appropriate adjustments must be made where there is part private use of the let property.

Allowable expenses include business rates or council tax if appropriate (see **32.43**), rent payable to a superior landlord, insurance and management expenses, including advertising for tenants, and maintenance, repairs and redecorations. Allowable expenditure will include that incurred before letting commences, in the same way as for pre-trading expenditure (see **21.8**). This does not, however, include repairs to newly acquired property that were necessary before the property could be brought into use, which form part of the capital cost of the property. Improvement expenditure on, for example, building extensions or installing central heating, is not allowable in calculating income, although it is counted as part of the cost for capital gains purposes. Replacing single glazing with double glazing is, however, accepted as repair expenditure. See the HMRC Property Income Manual at PIM2020 for detailed information on what HMRC accept as allowable repair expenditure. Interest payable, including interest payable to a non-resident lender, is allowed in calculating profits, subject to the 'wholly and exclusively' rule. Because rental income is calculated in the same way as trading profits, it is possible for a landlord to increase the amount borrowed on the let property (the total borrowing not, however, exceeding the original cost of the property) and to withdraw some of the capital he originally invested. See **32.30** for the treatment of a payment for dilapidations by an outgoing tenant.

In calculating the taxable rent, adjustments are made for rent and expenses in arrear or in advance. Where total gross rents do not exceed £15,000 a year, HMRC will accept profit calculations on the basis of amounts received and paid, with no adjustments for amounts in arrear or in advance, providing the cash basis is used consistently and does not give a materially different result from the statutory method.

Where capital allowances are available, they are calculated in the same way as for trades and are deducted as an expense (see **32.14**).

Where total property income before expenses is below £68,000 a year, only total figures of rent, expenses and net income need to be included on the tax return. See www.hmrc.gov.uk/factsheet/three-line-account.pdf.

Landlord's energy saving allowance (ITTOIA 2005, ss 312–314)

[32.6] Landlords who incur capital expenditure before 6 April 2015 to install loft insulation, cavity wall insulation, hot water system insulation, draught proofing, solid wall insulation and floor insulation in residential property may claim an income tax deduction for the expenditure of up to £1,500 per dwelling in any relevant tax year in computing their rental profits. It therefore applies to each dwelling within a building, such as each flat in a block of flats. For joint owners the allowable amount is apportioned in a just and reasonable way. For new property businesses, the deduction is available for expenditure incurred up to six months before the business commenced. The deduction is not available where the property is let under the rent-a-room scheme (see **30.10**) or as furnished holiday accommodation (see **32.22** to **32.29**).

Treatment of losses (ITA 2007, ss 117–127)

[32.7] If losses arise, they are normally carried forward to set against later rental income. Relief is, however, available against other income of the same and/or the following tax year in respect of excess capital allowances (see **22.12**) and certain agricultural expenses (see **31.18**). FA 2010 introduced anti-avoidance provisions to prevent individuals within the charge to income tax obtaining relief for tax-generated losses attributable to the Annual Investment Allowance (see **22.24**) against general income. The legislation is specifically targeted at persons who enter into tax avoidance arrangements on or after 24 March 2010 with a main purpose of obtaining a tax reduction by way of property loss relief attributable to the Annual Investment Allowance.

National insurance contributions

[32.8] Property letting will rarely be regarded as self-employment for national insurance purposes, although if the extent of the landlord's involvement in managing the lettings and looking after the properties is substantial (which might be particularly relevant for furnished holiday lettings — see **32.22** to **32.29**), it is possible that the activities will constitute a business, in which case Class 2 national insurance contributions will be payable (see **24.2**). Class 4 contributions are only payable where income is taxed as trading income. Even though rents are now *treated* as being from a business in calculating property income, this is not the same as saying that a business actually exists, and it does not alter the national insurance position.

Tax treatment of companies (CTA 2009, Pt 4; CTA 2010, ss 62–67)

[32.9] All rental income of companies is treated as the profits of a property business. See **32.30** for the treatment of a payment for dilapidations by an outgoing tenant. Interest paid by a company is dealt with under the 'loan relationships' rules (see **32.10**). Capital allowances are deducted as expenses in arriving at the rental profit or loss as for income tax (see **32.14**). If a loss arises, then providing the business is conducted on a commercial basis, the loss may be set against the total profits of the same accounting period, or surrendered by way of group relief (see **26.16**), any unrelieved balance being carried forward to set against future *total* profits. The landlord's energy saving allowance (see **32.6**) is now available to companies as well as individuals for expenditure incurred on or after 8 July 2008.

Relief for interest

[32.10] Interest on company borrowings is dealt with under the 'loan relationships' rules outlined at **3.5**. Interest relating to furnished holiday lettings (see **32.24**) is deducted from the income from those lettings, since expenses may be deducted as if such lettings were a trade. All other interest relating to let property is taken into account in arriving at the overall non-trading surplus or deficit on loans. If there is a deficit, relief is available as indicated at **26.5**.

Capital allowances (CAA 2001, ss 15, 16, 35, 172–204, 219; FA 1997, s 82 and Sch 12)

[32.11] The capital allowances presently available on let agricultural buildings are dealt with in **CHAPTER 31**, and **CHAPTER 22** deals with allowances on industrial buildings, hotels and buildings in enterprise zones.

[32.12] As far as plant and machinery is concerned, capital allowances are not available on plant and machinery let for use in a dwelling house, except for furnished holiday lettings (see **32.22** to **32.29**), and subject to the exception outlined at **22.40**. For buildings other than dwellings, allowances are available not only on plant and machinery in the let buildings but also on plant and machinery for the maintenance, repair or management of premises. The allowances are calculated in the same way as for trades — see **CHAPTER 22**. With regard to expenditure on fixtures, the expenditure may be incurred either by the landlord or by the tenant, or the items may be leased from an equipment lessor. There are special provisions to deal with the various possibilities (see **22.40**). See also the provisions at **22.5** relating to finance leases and at **22.38** relating to long-life plant and machinery.

[32.13] Although there is no relief for plant and machinery in dwelling houses as indicated above, relief for wear and tear of furniture etc. may be claimed under HMRC concession B47, either on a renewals basis (so that nothing is allowed when furniture, etc. is first bought, but as and when any item is replaced the full cost of the renewal is allowed), or more usually by way of a wear and tear allowance of 10% of rents. Any additions to rent for council tax, water charges and other sums for services which would normally be borne by a tenant are deducted, if material, before calculating the 10% relief. Where the 10% allowance is claimed, no further deduction is allowed for renewing furniture and furnishings, such as suites, beds, carpets, curtains, linen, crockery or cutlery, nor for items such as cookers, washing machines or dishwashers. But an additional deduction may be claimed for renewing fixtures such as baths, washbasins and toilets. To qualify for the concession, the property must be sufficiently furnished to enable it to be occupied without the tenant necessarily having to buy any furniture of his own.

[32.14] Capital allowances are deducted as an expense and are thus taken into account in arriving at the letting profit or loss. See **22.12** for the relief available to individuals for excess allowances. No separate relief for excess allowances is available to companies (see **32.9**).

Conversion of parts of business premises into flats (CAA 2001, ss 393A–393W)

[32.15] Capital allowances are available for expenditure by property owners and occupiers on the renovation or conversion of empty or underused space above qualifying shops and other commercial premises to provide residential flats for short-term letting (i.e. on a lease for not more than five years). The allowances are deducted as expenses of a property letting business. The available allowances are an initial allowance of 100%, which may be claimed wholly or in part, and writing-down allowances of 25% of cost per annum (or lower amount claimed) until the expenditure is fully relieved. A balancing charge or balancing allowance will be made if there is a balancing event (sale, long lease, flat ceasing to be available for letting etc.) within seven years from the time the flat is available for letting. There will be no clawback of allowances if a sale, lease etc. occurs after that time. The allowances are not transferable to a purchaser. Anti-avoidance provisions prevent a balancing allowance being claimed where the proceeds have been artificially depressed as a result of a tax avoidance scheme.

In order to qualify, the properties must have been built before 1980 and must satisfy detailed conditions, including a requirement that the ground floor must be currently rated for business use, there must be not more than four floors above ground level and they must originally have been constructed mainly for use as dwellings, the renovated or converted part of the building must have been empty or used only for storage for at least a year, the new flats must be self-contained with not more than four rooms (excluding bathroom, kitchen, hallway etc.), and the rental value must be within prescribed limits.

Business premises renovation allowance (CAA 2001, ss 360A–360Z4)

[32.16] A new business premises renovation allowance scheme has been introduced in respect of expenditure incurred between 11 April 2007 and 10 April 2012 (or such later date as is prescribed by statutory instrument). The allowances are subject to EU state aid controls and anyone claiming any other state aids must ensure that the total amount claimed does not exceed a stipulated ceiling. The allowances are available to both individuals and companies. The provisions of the scheme are outlined below.

Under the scheme, 100% capital allowances will be available for the costs of renovating or converting qualifying business properties that have remained empty for at least a year in designated disadvantaged areas known as Assisted Areas into qualifying business premises. Qualifying business premises are those used for the purposes of a qualifying trade, profession or vocation or as offices. Qualifying trades exclude fisheries, shipbuilding, coal and steel, synthetic fibres and the production of certain agricultural and milk products. The 100% initial allowance need not be taken in full. Where the full allowance is not taken, writing down allowances of 25% per annum on the reducing balance basis will be available on the unclaimed residue of expenditure (again being reduced to whatever amount is required).

Balancing allowances or charges will be made where there is a 'balancing event', e.g. the building is sold, let on a long lease, demolished or destroyed, or ceases to be a qualifying building, or the person who incurred the qualifying expenditure dies. No balancing adjustments will be made if the balancing event occurs more than seven years from when the premises were first brought back into use or made suitable and available for letting. Unclaimed allowances cannot, however, be transferred to a subsequent purchaser.

Where a premium is payable (TCGA 1992, Sch 8; ITTOIA 2005, ss 60–65, 99–103, 277–283, 287–295, Sch 2 para 28; CTA 2009, ss 62–67, 96–100, 217–223)

[32.17] A premium is a sum paid on the creation of an interest in a property. Premiums may be payable by an incoming tenant to an outgoing tenant when a lease is assigned. They may also be paid by a tenant to a landlord when a lease or sublease is granted. A third type of payment is a payment by a landlord to induce a potential tenant to take out a lease — usually called a reverse premium.

A distinction is made between a premium paid for the grant of a lease and a capital sum paid on the sale of a lease. A sale (or assignment) of a lease is usually a capital gains tax matter. For example, a payment to an outgoing tenant from an incoming tenant is dealt with under the CGT rules.

Premium paid to landlord on grant of lease or sublease

[32.18] The treatment of premiums paid to landlords on the grant of a lease or sublease depends on the length of the lease. If a lease is granted for more than 50 years, it is treated as a part disposal for CGT purposes (see **4.19** and **4.20**). The cost of the part disposed of is the proportion of the total cost that the premium paid bears to the sum of the premium paid and the reversionary value of the property. See Example 1.

Example 1

Individual buys a freehold property for £200,000 in May 2010 and grants a 60 year lease of the property for £250,000 in December 2010. The value of the freehold reversion is £40,000. The capital gain is calculated as follows:

	£
Premium received	250,000
Less: $\quad$ Cost $200,000 \times \dfrac{250,000}{250,000 + 40,000}$	172,414
Capital gain	77,586

The gain will be reduced by the annual exemption if not otherwise used.

There are both capital and income aspects on the grant of a lease of 50 years duration or less (known as a short lease), in that the premium is partly treated as income and partly as disposal proceeds for CGT. The income portion is treated as additional rent and is the amount of the premium less 2% for each complete year of the lease except the first. The amount by which the premium is reduced is treated as the proceeds of a part disposal for capital gains, the cost of the part disposed of being the proportion of the total cost that the capital portion of the premium bears to the full premium plus the value of the freehold reversion. See Example 2.

The income portion of a premium on a short lease is wholly charged in the year the lease is granted, although the lease may run for anything up to 50 years.

Since the income part of the premium is treated as additional rent, any expenses of the letting can be relieved against it. The premium might in fact have been charged to recover some extraordinary expenses, perhaps necessitated by a previous defaulting tenant.

[32.19] Where a premium on the grant of a short lease is paid by a business tenant, he may deduct the income portion (i.e. after the 2% deduction) as a business expense, but spread over the term of the lease rather than in a single sum (see Example 2). A similar deduction may be claimed by a tenant who sublets, his deduction depending on the length of the sublease. Any deductions allowed in calculating income are not allowed in calculating the capital gain if the lease is disposed of.

[32.20] Any expenditure on the acquisition of a lease is treated for capital gains purposes as wasting away during the last 50 years (or shorter period for which the lease was granted) and only the depreciated cost (using a special table in TCGA 1992, Sch 8) may be used. If a lease is held for its full term, no allowable loss may be claimed for the unrelieved expenditure on acquisition, so that any expenditure for which relief has not been given in calculating income will not have been allowed for tax at all.

Example 2

Individual charges a premium of £80,000 on granting a lease for 21 years commencing 20 June 2010. The cost of the freehold was £150,000 in 1990. The value of the freehold reversion after the grant of the lease was £240,000.

	£
The amount treated as additional rent for 2010/11 is:	
Premium	80,000
Less Treated as part disposal for capital gains (21 – 1) = 20 years at 2% = 40%	32,000
Amount treated as additional rent	£48,000
The chargeable gain is:	
Capital proportion of premium	32,000
Less Allowable proportion of cost	
$150,000 \times \dfrac{32,000}{80,000 + 240,000}$	15,000
	£17,000

If the tenant was a business tenant, he could claim a deduction in calculating taxable profits for £48,000 spread over 21 years, i.e. £2,286 per annum, in addition to the deduction for the rent paid.

If he subsequently assigned the lease within the 21 years, the allowable cost for capital gains would be arrived at by reducing the premium paid of £80,000 by the total annual deductions allowed to the date of assignment as a business expense, and depreciating the reduced amount according to the table in TCGA 1992, Sch 8, as indicated in 32.20.

Payments from landlord to tenant — reverse premiums

[32.21] Where a landlord pays a sum to induce a potential tenant to take a lease (a reverse premium) then, unless the payment reduces expenditure qualifying for capital allowances, it is treated as income for income tax or corporation tax in the hands of the tenant (either trading income or letting income as the case may be). The tax charge is spread over the period in which the premium is recognised in the tenant's accounts. The tax charge does not apply where the premises are to be the tenant's main residence or to sale and leaseback arrangements.

As far as the landlord is concerned, the reverse premium paid will be a capital payment, which will normally be regarded as enhancement expenditure in computing a capital gain on disposal of the property. It will not be deductible from the rental income. A reverse premium paid by a builder or developer, on the other hand, will normally be an income payment allowed as a deduction from trading profits.

For VAT, HMRC used to take the view that tenants were making taxable supplies when they received an inducement payment, but they now accept that this will rarely be the case and that the majority of such payments will be outside the scope of VAT (see Business Brief 12/05).

Furnished holiday lettings (ITA 2007, s 127; CAA 2001, ss 17, 249; ITTOIA 2005, ss 322–328; TCGA 1992, s 241; CTA 2010, s 65)

[32.22] As indicated in **32.2**, the furnished holiday lettings provisions apply to both individuals and companies, although clearly many of the provisions dealt with in this section are applicable only to individuals.

[32.23] As with other furnished lettings, the 'rent-a-room' relief exempting gross rent of up to £4,250 a year is available to individuals who let rooms in their homes (see **30.10**) and this may be more beneficial than the furnished holiday lettings treatment described below.

[32.24] Historically, income from qualifying furnished holiday lettings of UK property has been broadly treated as trading income, although it remains chargeable as property income. Furnished holiday lettings (FHL) elsewhere in the European Economic Area (EEA) did not qualify for this treatment. However, the Government was advised that this may not be compliant with European Law and HMRC will regard the treatment as applying to FHL elsewhere in the EEA. This revised treatment is optional but if it is requested it will apply to the property for all relevant tax purposes. HMRC will accept any claims for relief or requests for FHL treatment to apply provided, broadly, that the letting meets the relevant requirements of the FHL rules (see below) and, where a claim or amendment of a return is required, that it is made within the relevant normal time limits. The normal time limit for amending an income tax return is one year after 31 January following the tax year to which it relates. The normal time limit for amending a corporation tax return is generally two years after the end of the accounting period to which it relates. If the return cannot be amended but the normal time limit for making the claim in question has not been exceeded the claim should be made in writing to HMRC. This applies broadly to claims for hold-over relief, roll-over relief, relief for losses carried forward, terminal loss relief and Landlord Energy Saving Allowance, which must be claimed by individuals on or before four years after the end of the tax year in question, or within four years of the end of the accounting period for companies.

In the case of FHL treatment in respect of relief for pension contributions and the substantial shareholdings exemption, a claim does not have to be made before a specific time limit and HMRC will accept a request to apply the treatment if it is made by the time limits referred to above for specific claims. The normal rules for late claims will apply (see **9.5**).

This change of treatment will not result in a new activity for loss relief or capital allowances purposes. Any unused losses from the previous year may still be brought forward and set against profits of the following year and any existing capital allowances pools will continue, without a deemed disposal and reacquisition at market value. For capital allowances purposes an asset on which qualifying expenditure is incurred will be treated as being brought into use on the latest of the following three dates, at its market value at that time, provided the expenditure was incurred before that date:

- when the property was first used as a qualifying FHL;
- the date on which the country in which the property is situated joined the EEA; and
- 1 January 1994.

For capital gains tax purposes assets used for the purposes of a qualifying FHL business situated in the EEA may be treated as a trade asset from the latest of the three dates referred to above.

The FHL treatment of properties both in the UK and the EEA described in this article was intended to be repealed from 6 April 2010. This was announced in the 2009 Budget and provisions were included in the Finance Bill 2010. However these provisions were subsequently dropped from the Finance Act 2010 and therefore the rules below continue to apply at present. However, the current Government intends to consult on a proposal to change the eligibility thresholds and restrict the use of loss relief. It is intended that any changes will take effect from April 2011.

The tax treatment of furnished holiday lettings is broadly as follows. If interest is paid on a loan to purchase or improve the property, it is allowed as a trading expense (restricted if necessary by any private use proportion). Capital allowances (see **CHAPTER 22**) on plant and machinery, such as furniture and kitchen equipment, and loss relief (see **CHAPTERS 25** and **26**) may be claimed, and the income qualifies as relevant earnings for personal pension purposes (although non-earners may get tax relief in any event on personal pension contributions of up to £3,600 a year — see **CHAPTER 17**). Income tax is payable under the self-assessment provisions (see **2.29**). Except for instalment paying companies (see **3.22**), corporation tax is payable nine months after the end of the accounting period. Despite the trading treatment, individuals do not have to pay Class 4 national insurance contributions, because Class 4 contributions only apply where profits are actually charged as trading income. Class 2 contributions would, however, usually be payable unless already paid by reference to other self-employment or the landlord's activities in managing the properties were insufficient to be regarded as carrying on a business (see **24.3**).

[32.25] Furnished holiday letting property is eligible for capital gains roll-over relief either when it is itself replaced, or as a qualifying purchase against which gains on other assets may be set, and for business gifts hold-over relief (see **4.26** and **29.11**). If the property has been the main residence for CGT, it may also be possible to claim the residential lettings exemption (see **30.11**).

[32.26] To qualify, the accommodation must be let on a commercial basis. HMRC look at this aspect very carefully, and will often ask for business plans and accounts to support the contention that the letting is a business venture.

Many HMRC enquiries have been raised in this connection, particular relating to the letting of holiday caravans. The accommodation must be available to the public as holiday accommodation for at least 140 days in the tax year, and actually let as such for at least 70 of those days. The 70 days test may be satisfied by averaging periods of occupation of any or all of the holiday accommodation let furnished by the same person. Accommodation is not normally regarded as holiday accommodation for any period during which it is in the same occupation for a continuous period of more than 31 days. Any such periods of longer term occupation must in any event not exceed 155 days in the tax year. Where only part of the let accommodation is holiday accommodation, apportionments are made on a just and reasonable basis. Where there is part private use of the property, the normal rules for restricting allowable expenditure apply. In these circumstances, great care must be taken to ensure that the letting can be shown to be commercial, rather than producing income merely to offset costs.

[32.27] As far as inheritance tax is concerned, property used for holiday lettings does not qualify for agricultural property relief and it may not qualify for business property relief (see **32.2**). HMRC previously thought that business property relief would probably be available if the lettings were very short-term (say a week or a fortnight) and the owner, personally or through someone acting for him, was substantially involved with the holidaymakers' activities (see HMRC's Inheritance Tax Manual at IHTM25278). However, they have been advised to reconsider this approach and in particular they will now be looking at the level and type of service provided rather than who provided them.

[32.28] The letting of holiday caravans is, depending on the scale, either treated as a trade or as a furnished letting. In the latter case, the income may be treated as trading income from furnished holiday accommodation if the conditions are satisfied. Long-term lets would accordingly not qualify. Caravans occupying holiday sites are treated as plant and machinery qualifying for capital allowances, even if they are on hard standings and not required to be moved.

Income from letting caravan sites is charged as property income, unless the activity really amounts to a trade, embracing services, shops, restaurants, etc. in which all income will be treated as arising from a trade. See the HMRC Capital Allowances Manual at CA32402 regarding the possibility at present of claiming capital allowances under the 'hotels' provisions for capital expenditure on holiday camps. This is subject to the provision that industrial building allowances will be withdrawn from April 2011 (see **22.42**).

Even where caravan sites are accepted as trading businesses, inheritance tax business property relief has usually been denied because the rent from caravan pitches was regarded as being from holding investments. The Court of Appeal has held, however, that business property relief was available for a caravan park with a wide range of activities, of which the pitch letting was only one.

[32.29] For the treatment of furnished property, including holiday property and caravans, in relation to council tax and business rates (see **32.43**).

Capital gains on sale of investment properties (TCGA 1992, ss 243–248; HMRC statement of practice SP 13/93)

[32.30] The usual CGT principles apply (see **CHAPTER 4**), including the relief dealt with in **30.11** to **30.13** where part of the property is owner-occupied, and that dealt with in **32.22** to **32.29** where the property is let as furnished holiday accommodation. Apart from those instances, there is no roll-over relief on disposal and replacement of investment properties except where the disposal is occasioned by compulsory purchase. In this case, there is no tax charge if the proceeds are reinvested in another property, provided that the reinvestment is made within the period beginning one year before and ending three years after the disposal. The replacement property cannot, however, be the investor's CGT exempt dwelling house (see **30.3**) at any time within six years after its acquisition. As an alternative to roll-over relief where part of a holding of land is compulsorily purchased, small proceeds (not defined but taken in practice to mean not exceeding 5% of the value of the holding) may be treated as reducing the CGT cost of the holding rather than being charged as a part disposal.

Compulsory purchase includes not only purchase by an authority but also purchase of the freehold by a tenant exercising his right to buy.

If a lease is surrendered and replaced by a new lease on similar terms except as to duration and rent payable, by HMRC concession D39 the surrender is not treated as a disposal for CGT so long as a capital sum is not received by the lessee and certain other conditions are met. When the extended lease is disposed of, it will be treated as acquired when the original lease was acquired. There are anti-avoidance provisions to prevent people escaping tax by abuse of this concession — see **4.29**.

Where at the end of a lease a tenant makes a payment to a landlord in respect of dilapidations, a decision needs to be made as to whether the amount received by the landlord is a capital or income receipt. If the landlord sells the property, the receipt will probably be regarded as compensation for a breach of the terms of the lease and will be treated as additional proceeds. If on the other hand the landlord carries out the repairs, or relets at a reduced rental, the amount received will probably be treated as letting income.

See **31.18** for the availability of CGT gifts relief for agricultural landlords.

HMRC have two separate schemes relating to valuations for large property portfolios. The first applies to taxpayers who dispose of 30 or more interests in land in one tax year or company accounting period. HMRC use a sampling process in order to avoid, if possible, the need to agree individual valuations for all the properties disposed of. The second relates to pre-disposal valuations. Companies or groups with a property portfolio including either 30 or more properties held since 31 March 1982 or properties held since 31 March 1982 with a current aggregate value higher than £20 million may ask HMRC to agree 31 March 1982 values for all relevant property. For notes on these schemes see HMRC's Tax Bulletin 67 of October 2003 and HMRC Capital Gains Manual CG74080.

Property dealing, etc.

[32.31] The income from letting is assessed as income of a property business. Any surplus on disposal of a property may be liable to income tax or corporation tax, either specifically under ITA 2007, ss 752–772 or CTA 2010, ss 815–833 (see **45.21**), or as a trading transaction, instead of as a chargeable gain. Whether or not a trade may be inferred is dealt with in **CHAPTER 20**, but the letting, whilst not conclusive, will at least indicate an investment motive and be influential in the surplus being treated as a capital gain.

Real Estate Investment Trusts (CTA 2010, Pt 12)

[32.32] A Real Estate Investment Trust (REIT) is a limited company or group that invests mainly in property and distributes at least 90% of its rental business profits to investors. The REIT tax regime shifts the burden of taxation from the company to the investors, and enables investors to obtain returns broadly similar to those they would have obtained by direct investment.

The REIT's rental business income and gains are exempt from corporation tax. Dividends are treated as property income in the investor's hands. Companies and groups have been able to elect to join the REIT regime with effect for accounting periods beginning on or after 1 January 2007. HMRC have produced a 'Guidance on Real Estate Investment Trusts' manual.

[32.33] The qualifying rental income of REITs and their capital gains on investment properties are exempt from corporation tax. Any distributions made out of such tax-exempt property income or capital gains are treated as UK property income and tax is deducted at the basic rate and accounted for to HMRC. Other income and gains of the REIT are taxed at the main rate of corporation tax, and dividends paid out of such profits are treated like any other dividends. For accounting periods ending on or after 22 April 2009 a business with tied premises can treat the rental income from those premises as part of the property rental business of a REIT. Previously the income would have been trading income and not eligible to be in the REIT regime. It is proposed to allow REITs to issue stock dividends in lieu of cash dividends in meeting the requirement to distribute 90% of their rental business profits. The investors will be taxed on the stock dividends in the same way as on cash dividends.

[32.34] The main requirements for a company to qualify as a REIT are that the company must be UK resident, its shares must be listed on a recognised stock exchange, and no investor must be entitled to 10% or more of the company's distributions, or control 10% or more of the share capital or voting rights. 75% or more of the company's assets must be investment property and 75% or more of its income must be rental income. The property letting business must be ring-fenced. A tax charge may be made if the amount of debt financing of the business exceeds a specified level.

[32.35] To join the REIT regime, companies or groups must pay a corporation tax entry charge of 2% of the market value of their investment properties at the date of joining. The charge will be collected with the corporation tax due for the accounting period in which they join the scheme. If they prefer, companies may elect when they join the scheme to pay this charge by instalments of 0.5%, 0.53%, 0.56% and 0.6% over the first four years.

[32.36] A company may give notice that it wishes to leave the REIT regime, and HMRC may give notice that the company must leave if it has repeatedly failed to meet the conditions or been involved in tax avoidance. Certain breaches will trigger automatic termination. Anti-avoidance provisions were introduced in FA 2009 to prevent exploitation of the rules where businesses restructure to gain the benefits of the regime.

VAT (VATA 1994, Sch 4, Sch 7A, Sch 8 Group 5, Sch 9 Group 1 and Sch 10; FA 2007, s 99; SI 2008/1146; SI 2009/1966; SI 2010/485)

[32.37] The VAT position on land and buildings is very complex and the legislation very tortuous, and what follows is a brief summary only.

Sales of commercial buildings that are either new or less than three years old are standard-rated. Sales or leases for more than 21 years of new residential properties (including dwellings created by the conversion of non-residential property) and new buildings occupied by charities for charitable purposes are zero-rated. In the case of leases for more than 21 years, however, the building will be subject to the capital goods scheme (see **7.20**) and input VAT will have to be adjusted if there is a later VAT exempt disposal. (Shorter leases are exempt and cannot be subject to the option to charge VAT — see **32.39**.) The sale of renovated houses that have been empty for ten years or more is zero-rated.

Otherwise, unless the vendor has exercised his option to charge VAT (see **32.39**), all sales of buildings that are more than three years old are exempt, and grants of long or short leases (other than those mentioned above) are also exempt, except for holiday accommodation (see **32.40**). Rents received are exempt unless the landlord has opted to charge VAT.

Most landlords letting domestic property are exempt from VAT. Any VAT on their expenditure therefore forms part of their costs, and must be taken into account in fixing their rents. Landlords letting commercial property are in the same position, unless they opt to charge VAT (see **32.39**). If the expenditure is revenue expenditure, such as repairs, the unrecovered VAT may be claimed as part of the expense in calculating the rental profit. If it is capital expenditure, such as on property conversion, reconstruction, extension, improvement, etc., no deduction can be claimed in calculating the rental profit, but the unrecovered VAT will form part of the cost for CGT purposes when the property is disposed of.

See **7.15** for the reduced rate of VAT of 5% on the installation of energy saving materials, and on central heating systems etc. if funded by Government grants.

Where there is non-business use of commercial land and buildings, HMRC previously required the input VAT to be apportioned at the outset to reflect the private use. As a result of a decision of the European Court, they then permitted businesses to use an alternative method (Lennartz accounting) under which input VAT may be claimed in full at the outset and output VAT is then accounted for on non-business use as it arises. The output VAT is calculated by spreading the cost of the land and buildings over their economic life, and accounting for VAT on the appropriate non-business proportion of the cost in each return period. The deemed economic life of land and buildings was previously taken by HMRC to be 20 years, but following another EU decision, the period was to be reduced to 10 years from 1 September 2007, thus increasing the annual non-business use VAT charges. From 1 January 2011 this method will once again not be available to permit full input tax recovery on the purchase of land and property. Instead input tax will be restricted to the business use proportion (see **20.22**).

Residential conversions, renovations and alterations

[32.38] VAT is charged at the reduced rate of 5% on the supply of services and building materials for the conversion of non-residential property into dwellings, conversion of residential property into a different number of dwellings, conversion of residential or non-residential property into a multiple occupancy dwelling (e.g. bed-sit accommodation), conversion of non-residential property or one or more residential properties into a care home, children's home, hospice etc. (where the services are supplied to the person who intends to use the property for that purpose), the conversion of a care home etc. into a multiple occupancy dwelling, and the renovation or alteration of dwellings, multiple occupancy properties and care homes etc. that have been empty for three years or more. Constructing a garage, or turning a building into a garage, as part of a renovation also qualifies for the reduced rate. Where someone buys a house that has been empty for three years or more and lives in it while it is being renovated, the 5% rate will still apply to the building work providing it is completed within one year from the date the property was purchased.

From 1 July 2007 the reduced rate also applies to the installation of certain mobility aids in the homes of elderly people.

Option to charge VAT

[32.39] The provisions of VATA 1994, Sch 10, dealing with the option to tax supplies in relation to land and buildings, were rewritten in simpler language and the revised schedule applies broadly to supplies made on or after 1 June 2008. The revised Sch 10, set out in the Value Added Tax (Buildings and Land) Order 2008 (SI 2008/1146), introduced the right to revoke an option to tax within a 'cooling off period' of six months, and makes other, minor changes. Under the new regime an option can be revoked (a) in the six-month cooling-off period, subject to certain conditions; (b) automatically, where six years have lapsed since anyone had a relevant interest in the property; and (c) where more than 20 years have lapsed since the option first had effect. The provisions were updated from 1 August 2009 (SI 2009/1966) and as a result of the amendments the procedure in relation to (c) above has been simplified. Other minor amendments to Sch 10 ensure greater flexibility for businesses in relation to the option to tax rules without creating avoidance opportunities. SI 2010/485 further amends Sch 10 Part 1 with effect from 1 April 2010. The amendments enable the use of the option to tax by certain businesses which could not previously use it, and amend the definition of 'relevant housing association' for these purposes.

Guidance is available in an updated VAT Notice 742A, VAT Information Sheet 14/09 and HMRC Brief 51/2009. Earlier versions of the book summarise the rules as they applied to earlier supplies.

Holiday accommodation, etc.

[32.40] If turnover is above the VAT registration limit (currently £70,000), the provision of short-term holiday accommodation in hotels, boarding houses, caravans, etc. is charged to VAT at the standard rate (but see **32.41** for off-season letting for more than 28 days). If holiday accommodation, including time share accommodation, that is less than three years old is sold or leased, then both the initial charges and any periodic charges, such as ground rent and service charges, are also standard-rated. If the property is over three years old, the initial charges are exempt from VAT but periodic charges are still standard-rated. The standard rate applies to charges for pitching tents and to seasonal pitch charges for caravans (charges for non-seasonal pitches being exempt). If the pitch charges to the caravan owners include water and sewerage services and the landlord can ascertain how much is provided to the caravans as distinct from the rest of the site (shops, swimming pools, etc.), this can be apportioned between the caravans and shown separately on the bills, and VAT need not then be charged on those services. Similarly, separately metered supplies of gas and electricity are charged at the reduced rate of 5%. VAT is not charged on any part of the pitch charge that represents business rates on the individual caravans (but it is charged on any business rates element that relates to the rest of the site).

The sale of building plots for holiday accommodation is standard-rated.

[32.41] For guests who stay longer than 28 days in a hotel, boarding house etc., a reduced VAT charge is made from the 29th day, by excluding the 'accommodation' element from the amount on which VAT is payable. This has previously applied only where the tenant paid the charges. HMRC now accepts, however, that it applies where hotels etc. contract with a local authority or other organisation to supply accommodation, for example to homeless people. Claims for VAT overpaid in earlier periods may be made, subject to the normal three year time limit (see **7.33**).

Where holiday accommodation is let as residential accommodation for more than 28 days in the off-season (providing the accommodation is in a 'seasonal' area), the whole of the letting (including the first 28 days) may be treated as exempt.

Stamp duty land tax

[32.42] See CHAPTER 6 for the general stamp duty land tax ('SDLT') provisions. Subject to the following provisions, no SDLT is payable if residential property is purchased for £125,000 or less, or if non-residential property is purchased for £150,000 or less. However for transactions made between 3 September 2008 and 31 December 2009 no SDLT applied if residential property was purchased for £175,000 or less and for transactions between 25 March 2010 and 25 March 2012 no SDLT will apply for purchases by first-time buyers of residential property between £125,000 and £250,000. If the purchase price exceeds the relevant amount, SDLT is payable on the whole of the purchase price at 1%, 3%, 4%, or 5% depending on the consideration. The jump in the rate of SDLT from 1% on a property purchased for £250,000, amounting to £2,500, to 3% on a property purchased for £251,000, amounting to £7,530, means that it is obviously sensible to consider in marginal cases whether part of the purchase price could legitimately be allocated to the purchase of fixtures and fittings. Clearly this must be substantiated by the facts, as HMRC would look carefully at such transactions. See **6.10** to **6.15** for the SDLT provisions in relation to leases. Any SDLT paid forms part of the cost for CGT purposes on a subsequent disposal.

Where VAT is included in the cost of property, SDLT is charged on the VAT-inclusive amount. See **6.14** for the position relating to the option to charge VAT.

Certain transfers of land and buildings involving Registered Social Landlords are exempt (see **6.17**).

Council tax and business rates

[32.43] The detailed council tax and business rates provisions are in CHAPTER 8, which outlines the exemptions and discounts available.

When considering liability to council tax and/or business rates, each self-contained unit is looked at separately. Where there is mixed business and domestic use, business rates are payable as well as the council tax, even if there is no separate business part of the property, unless the business use does not materially detract from the domestic use. Any charges that fall on a landlord are allowable in calculating tax liabilities according to the normal expenses rules.

Let property that is domestic property and is not someone's only or main home is liable to a council tax charge of up to 90%, unless any other discount or exemption applies (see CHAPTER 8). Where let property is someone's only or main home, that person is liable to pay the council tax and there are no council tax or rates implications for the landlord, unless the property is multi-occupied property, such as bedsits, with rent paid separately for different parts of the property, in which case the council tax is payable by the landlord.

Non-domestic property, such as commercial property, boarding houses, etc., is liable to business rates. Staff accommodation, however, is domestic property. If the owner lives there as well, he is liable to pay the council tax. If he does not live there, the staff are liable to council tax if it is their only or main home. If the domestic accommodation was no-one's only or main home, the owner would be liable to pay up to 90% of the council tax. In the case of self-catering holiday accommodation, business rates are payable if it is available for short-term letting for 140 days or more in a year. This is independent of the number of days for which the property is actually let. Bed and breakfast accommodation is not subject to business rating providing it is not offered for more than six people, the provider lives there at the same time and the bed and breakfast activity is only a subsidiary use of the home. Where holiday property is not business rated, the council tax charge of up to 90% is payable on any self-contained accommodation that is not someone's only or main home.

If someone lives in a caravan as his or her only or main home, he or she pays the council tax. For other caravans, the site owner pays business rates on the caravans and pitches, passing on the charge to the caravan owner in the site rents. (Note that this part of the site rent is not liable to VAT — see **32.40**.)

Time shares

[32.44] Owners of time shares need to consider the taxation aspects of receiving income from it, or of making a capital gain on the sale of it.

The nature of the rights acquired depends on the particular agreement, but most time share agreements do not give any rights of ownership over the property itself, but merely a right to occupy it at a certain time.

If the time share is let, the individual will be liable to tax on the rental income less expenses. Where time share property is abroad, income is charged as overseas property income (see **41.13** and **41.24**). Many people will not have any time share income, but will sometimes exchange time shares. If this is done on a temporary basis, there are no tax implications, but a long-term arrangement could be treated as a part disposal for CGT.

When a time share is sold, the individual is liable to CGT on the gain. If the time share has less than 50 years to run, a depreciated cost must be used (on a straight line basis).

Time share property in the UK is usually subject to business rates. The owner of time share property charges VAT on the selling price for the time share if it is less than three years old and on any service charges made, including business rates. If the property is over three years old, the sale proceeds for the time share, but not the service charges, are exempt from VAT.

HMRC's view is that in most cases the timeshare agreement will be a form of personal contract which constitutes a licence to occupy land and is not a chargeable interest for SDLT purposes, see HMRC Stamp Duty Land Tax Manual SDLTM10022. Exceptionally where the agreement provides for exclusive and complete occupation of an individual unit of land or property for a defined period it may constitute a lease, the grant or assignment of which is chargeable to SDLT.

Tax points

[32.45] Note the following:

- It is only the interest element of the repayments on a 'buy to let' mortgage, or any other loan relating to let property, that is an allowable deduction in calculating rental profit.

- If interest paid cannot be relieved against rents, individuals cannot set it against a capital gain on disposal of the property but investment companies can — see **32.10** and **26.5**.

- Management expenses are allowed as a lettings expense. This covers a landlord's expenses of travelling to his properties solely for the purposes of property management. The expenses are not allowable if the travelling is for mixed business/private purposes but a deduction may be allowed if any personal benefit is only incidental.

- To benefit from the furnished holiday lettings treatment, an individual must demonstrate the commercial viability of the lettings and show that all the various conditions are satisfied. Taking a very large mortgage such that letting income will not cover costs in the reasonably near future may prevent relief being available for losses.

- The fact that property is being let does not of itself prevent an income tax charge instead of a chargeable gain on a profit on disposal if a trading motive in buying and selling the property can be proved. There are various possibilities for reducing or deferring tax liabilities, but it is important to establish which tax applies so that the proceeds can be invested in an appropriate purchase (see **CHAPTER 29**).

- The value added tax provisions relating to property letting, including holiday letting, are extremely complex. HMRC provide various booklets relating to different circumstances and it should be noted that the rules relating to the option to tax in respect of land and buildings have been rewritten and subsequently updated.

- If property let for residential use is empty for a period of time, it is still liable for council tax, subject to any available discounts and exemptions (see **32.43**).

- Bed and breakfast providers can escape business rates if they offer the facility as a subsidiary use of their own homes for not more than six people. Otherwise, business rates are payable.

- If a rental property has increased in value, this may enable the owner to take out a further loan and get tax relief for the interest against the letting income, providing the total of the original and further borrowing does not exceed the original cost of the property. This would enable the release of some of the capital.

- For loans to buy property for letting abroad, income tax relief is available on the interest.

- An investment in a property in an enterprise zone can be particularly tax-efficient so long as the price is right. See **22.52** and **29.36** but note that enterprise zone allowances are to be withdrawn from April 2011.

- Under self-assessment, individuals are required to keep the records relating to their property income for at least 5 years 10 months after the end of the tax year (see **9.25**). Penalties of up to £3,000 per tax year apply if individuals do not comply. The self-assessment provisions for companies similarly require records to be kept for six years, with the same penalty for failing to do so of up to £3,000 per accounting period.

Tax and the family

33

Family matters

Introduction

[33.1] The members of a married couple or a civil partnership are taxed separately. Same-sex couples who register as civil partners have the same rights and responsibilities under tax law as married couples, in relation to both beneficial provisions and anti-avoidance provisions. They also receive the same treatment for social security benefits such as pensions and tax credits (see **2.33** onwards). Close blood relatives are not permitted to register a civil partnership.

Married couples and civil partners

[33.2] The incomes of married couples and civil partners are taxed separately. Each spouse or partner is entitled to a personal allowance, and married couple's allowance is available where one spouse or partner was born before 6 April 1935 (i.e. attained the age of 65 before 6 April 2000). The detailed provisions on married couple's allowance are discussed at **34.3**.

The capital gains of married couples and civil partners are also taxed separately, each spouse or partner being entitled to the annual exemption, currently £10,100. Losses of one spouse or civil partner may not be set against gains of the other.

Transfers of assets between spouses or civil partners who are living together are not chargeable to capital gains tax (CGT), the acquiring spouse or civil partner taking over the other's acquisition cost. (This has no relevance to assets acquired on the death of a spouse or civil partner, which are treated as acquired at probate value.)

The CGT rules enable couples to plan in advance and make appropriate transfers one to the other before negotiating disposals to third parties, so that, for example, one does not have gains in excess of the annual exemption while the other has unrelieved losses. Such transfers must, however, be outright gifts (see **33.4**). If capital losses are brought forward from before the introduction of independent taxation of husband and wife on 6 April 1990, the losses of each spouse must be separately identified so that they are set only against that person's gains.

Despite the fact that married couples and civil partners are treated independently for tax purposes, they are required to make a joint claim for tax credits and the claim is based on their joint income. (The same requirement applies to couples, including same-sex couples, who are living together as husband and wife or civil partners.) Tax credits are examined at **2.33** to **2.40**.

For inheritance tax purposes, each spouse or civil partner is taxed separately and has a separate entitlement to exemptions and a separate nil rate band. Transfers between the two in lifetime and on death are exempt unless one of them is not domiciled in the United Kingdom (see **5.2**), in which case the transfers to the non-domiciled spouse or civil partner are exempt up to £55,000 and only 'potentially exempt' on the excess over that amount, meaning that they will become chargeable if the donor does not survive for seven years. Where a surviving spouse or civil partner dies after 8 October 2007 any part of the nil rate band unused on the death of the first spouse or civil partner to die may be added to the survivor's own nil rate band, see **35.3**.

Stamp duty/stamp duty land tax is not normally charged on the value of assets transferred between spouses or civil partners, but see **33.6** re mortgaged property.

Using available allowances and basic rate

[33.3] Some people on lower incomes need to make sure that they make the best use of their allowances and the basic rate of tax. The 10% starting rate for savings is not available to most taxpayers on modest incomes (see **2.4**).

There is a cash flow advantage if income equal to the available personal allowance is received in full, without tax being deducted by the payer. Investments that always pay interest gross are national savings and investments accounts and offshore accounts with banks and building societies. The fact that tax is not deducted does not mean that the income is tax free. The tax payable must be worked out according to the individual's circumstances. If he will not be liable to tax *at all*, he can claim to receive interest from other banks and from building societies without tax being deducted rather than having to reclaim the tax later (see **37.4**). The claim to receive it in full cannot be made if he expects some of his income to be liable to tax, even if he will be entitled to reclaim all or most of the tax deducted by the bank or building society.

Transferring property to a spouse or civil partner (ITA 2007, ss 836, 837; ITTOIA 2005, s 626)

[33.4] In order for spouses and civil partners to take best advantage of being taxed separately, it may be sensible for property to be transferred from one spouse or partner to the other. Any such transfers are fully effective for tax purposes providing the transfer is an outright gift of the property with no question of the transferring spouse/partner controlling it or deriving a benefit from it; that the gift carries a right to the whole of the income from the property; and that the gift is not effectively just a right to income.

HMRC have contended in recent years that certain gifts between spouses were caught by the settlements legislation and were not effective for tax purposes because one or more of these provisos did not apply. In July 2007 the House of Lords decided the 'Arctic Systems' case in favour of the taxpayers on the basis that while there was a settlement, the exemption for outright gifts between spouses did apply. The Government had intended to make changes to the legislation to counter 'income shifting' and consulted on the matter. However, it was announced in the 2008 pre-budget report that, given the economic challenges prevailing at the time, the Government would instead keep the matter under review. See **12.10**, **18.7** and **23.25** for further comments. In the meantime, this particular aspect of the tax treatment of married couples and civil partners is causing a great deal of concern and uncertainty. The professional bodies have called on the Government to undertake a review of small business taxation instead of attempting to introduce rules that would, they argue, be unworkable.

It is not possible to transfer a right to income while retaining a right to the capital (but see **33.5** re jointly owned property). The rules do not prevent the spouse or civil partner who gave the property getting it back at some stage in the future as a gift, or on the death of the other spouse or partner, providing there were no 'strings' attached to the initial transfer. Where property is transferred into the joint names of spouses or civil partners and they own it under the normal 'joint tenants' provisions, HMRC do not regard this as breaching the 'outright gift' rules, even though the property goes automatically to the survivor when one dies (see **33.5**).

Such transfers will be beneficial where a spouse or civil partner would otherwise waste their personal allowance, or where one spouse or partner would be paying higher rate tax while the other did not fully use the basic rate band. Evidence of transfers in the proper legal form must be kept.

Stamp duty/stamp duty land tax is not charged on gifts (except possibly in relation to mortgaged property — see **33.6**).

Where spouses or civil partners are living together and one acquires the other's interest in the family home in lifetime or on death, the joint period of ownership is taken into account for the purpose of the capital gains private residence exemption (see **30.7**).

Jointly owned property

[33.5] Spouses or civil partners normally own joint property as 'joint tenants', which means that each has equal rights over the property and when one dies, it goes automatically to the other. The joint tenancy can, however, be severed, and replaced by a 'tenancy in common', in which the share of each is separate, and may be unequal, and may be disposed of in lifetime or on death as the spouse or partner wishes. If this is done, proper documentary evidence of what has been done must be kept. Severing the joint tenancy may be particularly relevant if couples separate. Otherwise one's share of the property would automatically go to the other in the event of their death.

[33.6] Where property is held in joint names, it is generally treated as being owned equally for income tax purposes unless it is actually owned in some different proportion *and* a declaration is made to that effect. Such a declaration can be made only if the beneficial interests in the property correspond with the interests in the income. It takes effect from the date it is made, providing notice of the declaration is given to HMRC on Form 17 within 60 days of the declaration. It is not possible to make a declaration about partnership profit shares, about earned income or income treated as earned such as from furnished holiday lettings, or about dividends on shares in close companies (which would include most family companies, see **3.26**). Form 17 only covers the assets listed on it. Any new assets must be covered by a separate form.

The tax treatment of joint ownership may be useful to overcome one practical difficulty of maximising the benefits of being taxed separately — that the richer spouse or partner may be unwilling to make a significant transfer to the other. The reluctant spouse or partner could transfer an asset (other than family company shares) into joint ownership as tenants in common, retaining 95% ownership and giving the other spouse or partner a 5% share; if no declaration of the actual shares is notified to HMRC, the general rule applies and the income is treated as being shared equally.

This treatment applies to transfers of any sort of property other than family company shares — land and buildings, non-close company shares, bank accounts, etc. When joint bank and building society accounts are opened, a declaration is normally made that they are in joint beneficial ownership. The ownership can be changed to tenants in common later, but this must be done formally, for example by deed. HMRC have stated that evidence of such a change in the way bank etc. accounts are owned must be provided with Form 17. To provide against the bank or building society still acting on the basis of the original declaration, and thus treating the account as belonging to the survivor when one dies, the personal representatives need to be left clear instructions so that they can deal properly with the estate. Another point that needs to be watched is in relation to mortgaged property. If the spouse or partner to whom the property is transferred takes over responsibility for the mortgage, the mortgage debt is treated as consideration for the transfer and is liable to stamp duty land tax unless covered by the £125,000 limit. This will not apply if the spouse or partner who is transferring the property undertakes to pay the mortgage. (See also **33.15** re separation, divorce and dissolution.)

[33.7] Regardless of the way income is treated for income tax purposes, it is the underlying beneficial ownership of assets that determines the CGT treatment. Again, it is essential to have evidence of the proportions in which property is held. See **38.17** for the treatment of disposals of joint holdings of shares where there are also individual holdings of shares in the same company.

[33.8] For inheritance tax purposes, there are special 'related property' rules which require transfers of assets owned by spouses or civil partners to be valued as part of their combined value (see **5.31**). This applies in particular to unquoted shares and freehold or leasehold property. There are also 'associated operations' rules to link a series of transactions as a single transaction (see **5.38**). The combined effect of these two sets of provisions prevents spouses or civil partners obtaining an undue advantage by using the exemption for transfers from one to the other to route a transfer to their children or other family members via the other spouse or partner.

Children

Child tax credit

[33.9] Child tax credit is a means tested social security benefit paid to the main carer. Working tax credit, including a childcare element, may also be payable. See **2.33** to **2.40**.

Children's income (ITTOIA 2005, s 629)

[33.10] Children's income is theirs in their own right, no matter how young they are, and they are entitled to the full personal allowance. For a child under 18 and unmarried, this does not apply to income that comes directly or indirectly from a parent (including income from ISAs for 16- and 17-year olds — see **36.31**), which is treated as the parent's own income with the exceptions (a) to (g) below. A child who is in a civil partnership is not regarded as 'unmarried'.

(a)   Each parent can give each child sums of money from the total of which the child receives no more than £100 gross income per annum (say interest on bank and building society deposits). If the income exceeds the limit, the whole amount and not just the excess over £100 will be taxed on the parent.

(b)   The National Savings 'children's bonus bonds' for under 16-year olds (see **36.11**) can be given in addition because the return on such bonds is tax-exempt.

(c)   A parent may pay premiums (maximum £270 per annum) on a qualifying friendly society policy for a child under 18 (see **40.18**).

(d)   A parent may pay personal pension contributions of up to £3,600 a year on behalf of a child under 18. Such contributions are paid net of basic rate tax, which is retained whether or not the child is a taxpayer (see **CHAPTER 17**). The pension fund is, of course, not available to the child until he/she reaches the qualifying age for personal pensions.

(e)   Parents may contribute towards the permitted £1,200 a year to a Child Trust Fund account for their children, in addition to any gifts under (a) above (see **33.11**).

(f)   Income from an 'accumulation and maintenance' settlement established by a parent for his children is not treated as his income in certain circumstances, but reforms have reduced the tax efficiency of such trusts (see **CHAPTER 42**).

(g)   A lone parent may establish a trust for a child under 18 under the provisions relating to trusts with a vulnerable beneficiary (see **42.43** to **42.47**), the income from which is not treated as the parent's in specified circumstances.

Gifts within (a) to (e) above are not taken into account as far as inheritance tax (IHT) is concerned providing they are regular gifts out of income (see **5.3**).

The above rules do not affect gifts to children over 18, but the IHT provisions need to be borne in mind for children of any age. There would be no IHT effect if any gifts were covered by the regular gifts, family maintenance, small gifts or annual IHT exemptions (see **5.3**). Otherwise the gifts would be reckonable for IHT, either (i) as potentially exempt transfers which would not attract IHT unless the parent died within seven years or (ii) being immediately reckonable in the case of (f) above.

Doubts were expressed as to whether gifts by parents or grandparents to children under 18 might be brought within the revised IHT provisions for trusts that have applied since 22 March 2006. HMRC confirmed that whether a child is under or over 18, outright gifts will be potentially exempt transfers and thus not subject to IHT unless the parent/grandparent dies within seven years.

Many parents help to fund their children through higher education. Although student loans are available, means testing according to the parents' or student's income (including income arising from parental gifts) may reduce available loans. Where parents buy property for the use of a student child, they will be treated as any other landlord if they retain ownership (see **CHAPTER 32**). If the property was given to the child, the IHT effect would need to be considered, but if other students shared the property the child might be able to claim rent a room relief for income tax (see **30.10**) and so long as it remained the child's main residence the property would be exempt from CGT on disposal.

Child Trust Funds (CTFA 2004)

[33.11] Income and capital gains from Child Trust Fund (CTF) investments are exempt from tax (interest being paid gross) and do not affect tax credits. No relief is given for any capital losses. Guidance is available at www-.childtrustfund.gov.uk.

CTFs have been available since April 2005 for eligible children. A child is eligible, broadly, if he was born after 31 August 2002 and either child benefit is payable for him or he is in care.

At present the Government provides a £250 voucher for each child or £500 for a child in care (but see below regarding the proposed changes), which may only be invested in CTF accounts in the beneficial ownership of the child. An additional £250 is provided for a child who is part of a family with a household income not exceeding the income threshold for child tax credit (£16,190 for 2010/11 — see **2.39**). The Government will make a further payment of £250 into the account when the child reaches age seven (and an additional £250 where household income does not exceed the child tax credit income threshold on the child's seventh birthday). The contributions were slightly increased for children born between 1 September 2002 and 5 April 2005 to compensate for the shorter accumulation period before age 18.

However, the Government announced on 24 May 2010 that it intends to introduce legislation to reduce and then stop Government payments to CTF accounts. Full details of the proposed changes are available at www.childtrust-fund.gov.uk. The intention is broadly that children born after December 2010 will not be eligible for a CTF account.

Parents do not need to claim the awards, which are made automatically following the award of child benefit. Where vouchers are not used to open an account within twelve months (or before the child reaches age 18 if sooner), and also for children in care, accounts will be opened by HMRC. A voucher may be delivered to the account provider not later than seven days after its expiry date providing the application to open the account was made before that date.

CTF accounts may only be provided by approved account providers. The permitted investments are similar to those for individual savings accounts (ISAs), i.e. bank and building society accounts, stocks and shares and life insurance policies satisfying specified conditions. Accounts may be transferred from one provider to another.

Additional contributions may be made to CTFs by family, friends and others, up to an annual limit of £1,200. Subscription years run from the day the account is opened to the day before the child's birthday and annually to that date thereafter. The limit of £100 income from funds provided by a parent referred to in **33.10** does not apply to CTF accounts.

No withdrawals may normally be made until the child is 18 (at which stage the child is treated as acquiring the fund at market value), and only the child will be entitled to make such withdrawals. Access to the CTF account will, however, be available for children under 18 who receive disability living allowance because they are terminally ill and on a child's death.

Various penalties may be imposed, including a penalty of up to £300 for fraudulently opening or withdrawing funds from a CTF, and a penalty of up to £3,000 in the case of fraud or negligence by account providers.

The Government has announced that when a CTF matures, which will be from 2020 onwards, it will be possible to rollover the CTF into an ISA, see **36.24** onwards.

Death of a spouse or civil partner

[33.12] Where a spouse or civil partner was born before 6 April 1935, married couple's allowance is available as indicated in **34.3**. For those married before 5 December 2005 the allowance is given to the husband. For couples marrying and civil partners registering on or after 5 December 2005 the allowance is given to the spouse with the higher income. In either case, the other spouse/partner can claim half of a specified part of the allowance (half of £2,670 for 2010/11) or the whole of the specified amount by agreement.

In the tax year of the claimant's death, the surviving spouse or civil partner can receive the benefit of any of the allowance which has not been used against the claimant's tax bill up to the date of death. This might be particularly relevant where the claimant died early in the tax year. The executors must notify HMRC that the surplus married couple's allowance is being transferred to the survivor. Similarly, in the year in which the claimant's spouse or civil partner dies, then if the deceased spouse or partner had insufficient income in the tax year of death to cover the full amount of married couple's allowance to which he or she was entitled, the unused amount can be transferred back to the other spouse or partner, providing the deceased's personal representatives notify HMRC accordingly. The income of a surviving spouse or civil partner will include any he or she is entitled to from the assets in the deceased's estate.

See **30.7** for the capital gains position when a surviving spouse or partner acquires the other's interest in the family home.

Someone who is under state pension age when their spouse or civil partner dies, or whose late spouse or civil partner was not entitled to the state retirement pension, will get a tax-free bereavement payment of £2,000 from the Department for Work and Pensions (DWP), providing the late spouse or partner satisfied the contribution conditions or the death was caused by the spouse's or partner's job. Widowed parent's allowance or bereavement allowance may also be available to widows, widowers and surviving civil partners. These benefits are taxable, apart from additions to the widowed parent's allowance for dependent children. See the section on bereavement benefits at www.direct.gov.uk for further details. A widow who remarries before age 60 may be worse off in terms of her state retirement pension. See **13.9** for the position regarding inheriting the entitlement to the additional state pension of a spouse or partner.

Separation and divorce or dissolution

[33.13] Where a same-sex couple have registered as a civil partnership, the Civil Partnership Act 2004 makes provision for the partnership to be dissolved or for the partners to have a legal separation. The tax treatment therefore follows that of married couples who divorce or separate.

For the treatment of the married couple's allowance for the over 65s in the year of separation or reconciliation see **34.3**.

The tax position of divorced couples or civil partners whose partnership has been dissolved is broadly the same as that of separated couples. There are some provisions, for example the rules for employee benefits and close company associates, that apply up to divorce or dissolution (but not thereafter) even though the couple are not living together.

For policies entered into before 14 March 1984, a divorced person continues to be entitled to life assurance relief on a policy on the spouse's life taken out before the divorce but no relief is available for later policies. Protection against the loss of maintenance on the death of a spouse or civil partner can be obtained by one spouse or partner taking out a policy on his/her own life in trust for the other, or by one spouse or partner taking out a policy on the other's life. There will be no tax relief on the premium.

Maintenance payments (ITA 2007, ss 453–455)

[33.14] Tax relief for maintenance payments is only available where one spouse or civil partner was born before 6 April 1935 (see **34.6** for details). The relief is given at 10% of the lower of (a) the total of qualifying maintenance payments (as defined) falling due in the tax year, and (b) a specified part of the married couple's allowance (£2,670 for 2010/11). All maintenance payments received are free of tax.

The family home (TCGA 1992, ss 222, 223, 225B; FA 1985, s 83; FA 2003, Sch 3; SI 1987/516)

[33.15] For CGT, when a married couple or civil partners separate, the family home will cease to be the main residence of the spouse or partner who leaves it. His or her share of any calculated gain on a subsequent sale will therefore be chargeable to the extent that it relates to the period of non-residence, subject to any available exemptions or reliefs. The last three years of ownership always count as a period of residence, even if a new qualifying residence has been acquired. If the property is disposed of more than three years after a spouse or partner leaves it, part of the calculated gain will be chargeable, but only in the proportion that the excess period over three years bears to the total period of ownership since 31 March 1982. Even then the chargeable gain may be covered by the annual exemption, currently £10,100. Relief is available for absences of more than three years following separation or divorce or dissolution of a civil partnership, but only where the property is eventually transferred to the spouse or partner remaining in it as part of the financial settlement, and an election for a new qualifying residence has not been made by the spouse or partner moving out in the meantime. There is an HMRC concession D26 which may be relevant in some circumstances where a couple who own two residences, each living in only one of them, exchange their interests so that each only owns one property. The detailed provisions need to be looked at carefully.

The private residence exemption can be preserved on divorce or dissolution if a court order known as a Mesher order is made, under which the sale of the home is postponed, with a spouse or civil partner and children remaining in occupation until a specified event, such as the children reaching a specified age or ceasing full-time education. This is treated as a trust, and occupation of the property by a trust beneficiary qualifies for the private residence exemption (see **30.9**). On the sale of the home by the trustees when the trust ends, the proceeds will not be liable to CGT. The rules for trusts introduced in Finance Act 2006 have, however, affected the IHT position (see **CHAPTER 42**). The IHT exemptions for transfers not intended to confer a gratuitous benefit and transfers for family maintenance (see **5.3**) should avoid any IHT charge on the creation of the Mesher trust, but the exit and possibly ten year charges would apply.

If property is transferred from one spouse or civil partner to the other on break-up of a marriage or civil partnership, neither stamp duty nor stamp duty land tax is payable on property of any description, even if the acquiring spouse or civil partner takes over a mortgage.

Other chargeable assets

[33.16] The special CGT rule (see **4.6**) for transfers between spouses or civil partners only applies in a tax year when the couple are married or civil partners and living together at some time during the year. For transfers in later tax years, CGT is chargeable in the normal way, and this must be remembered when considering a matrimonial or civil partners' settlement following separation. If qualifying business assets are transferred from one to the other after separation but before the divorce or dissolution, gains need not be charged to tax at that time if the couple jointly claim the 'business gifts relief' (see **4.24**), under which the recipient takes over the other's original cost for the purpose of calculating the tax payable on an eventual disposal. Where, following divorce or dissolution, assets are transferred under a court order (even a 'consent' order ratifying an agreement made by the couple), HMRC accept that business gifts relief is available for appropriate assets.

Inheritance tax (IHTA 1984, s 18(1))

[33.17] The IHT exemption for transfers to a spouse or civil partner is not lost on separation but continues until the time of divorce or dissolution. Even then there is an exemption for transfers to former spouses or civil partners for the maintenance of themselves and the children. See **CHAPTER 5**.

Pension schemes

[33.18] See **16.28** for the provisions enabling pension rights to be shared on divorce or dissolution.

Cohabiting couples

[33.19] The following relates to couples, including same-sex couples, who are living together as husband and wife or civil partners but are neither married nor registered as civil partners.

As far as child tax credits and working tax credits are concerned, the rules for cohabitees are the same as those for married couples or civil partners, and claims must be made jointly taking into account the incomes of both partners (see **2.33** to **2.40**).

Where the home is in the name of only one of the cohabitees, but they regard it as their joint property and want the survivor to have the property when one of them dies, it is important to ensure that the other cohabitee's rights in relation to the home are safeguarded. This may be done by the property owner making a declaration that the property is held in trust for them both as joint tenants in equal beneficial shares. The lifetime declaration of trust would not be reckoned for IHT to the extent that both parties had contributed, directly or indirectly, to the cost. If a transfer of value remained, it would be potentially exempt and (subject to the transferor not retaining any benefit in respect of the share transferred — see **5.36**) would only become chargeable if the property owner died within seven years. The declaration would ensure that once the seven years had elapsed, the property owner's estate for IHT would only include the market value of a one-half share, which would be discounted because the cohabitee would still occupy the property. If such a declaration was not made, then even if both parties contribute to the cost and upkeep, HMRC may treat the whole property as part of the owner's estate at death. The exemption from IHT for property passing from one spouse or registered civil partner to the other does not apply to cohabitees, so that an unwelcome charge to tax will arise when the IHT threshold is exceeded.

Council tax

[33.20] Couples who are cohabiting but are neither married nor registered as civil partners are jointly liable for payment of council tax in the same way as married couples or civil partners. For all couples, the joint liability only applies for any part of the year when they are living together, and would not apply after separation, divorce or dissolution. A partner is not liable unless the authority has issued a bill to him or her.

Tax points

[33.21] Note the following:

- HMRC require a married couple or registered civil partners to send in a separate Form 17 (notification of unequal shares — see **33.6**) for any new jointly owned assets. This needs to be borne in mind if they have a joint share portfolio, where there may be frequent changes. See also **38.17** for the identification rules where there are both joint and separately owned shareholdings.
- Proper evidence is required if the ownership of bank and building society accounts is changed so that they are held as tenants in common rather than joint tenants.

- Although the CGT private residence exemption applies only to a qualifying main residence, if a married couple or civil partners own a second home jointly they will each be entitled to the annual exemption when they sell it (unless used against other gains). See also **30.15** re changing a qualifying main residence.
- In a bona fide business partnership of husband and wife or registered civil partners, where both play a significant role in the business, profits can be shared so as to maximise the benefit of being taxed separately. However, the risk of such arrangements being challenged under the 'settlements' rules needs to be borne in mind (see **23.25**).
- If joint wealth is substantial, IHT may be saved by rearranging the ownership of assets between spouses or civil partners. See **CHAPTER 35** for details.
- Social security regulations for cohabiting couples are different from those relating to tax. They should be researched before making financial arrangements between the couple, and for children.

34

Especially for the senior citizen

Introduction

[34.1] This chapter deals with various aspects of the tax system that are of particular interest to older people. HMRC guidance is available at www.hmrc.gov.uk/pensioners.

Personal reliefs (ITA 2007, ss 33–58)

Personal allowance

[34.2] Personal allowances are available based on age. They are deducted from taxable income and save tax at the payer's highest tax rate subject to the restriction in value of the personal allowance for individuals with income over £100,000 (see **34.4** and **2.16**). In addition the higher allowances for those over 65 are reduced if income exceeds a certain limit (£22,900 for 2010/11 — see **34.4** for full details of the restriction in age-related personal allowances). The allowances for 2010/11 are:

Under 65	£6,475
65 to 74	£9,490
75 and over	£9,640

Note that even if a woman gets the state pension at 60, she does not get the higher tax allowance until she is 65.

Married couple's allowance

[34.3] Married couple's allowance is available only where one or both of a married couple or civil partnership was born before 6 April 1935. The allowance is based on the age of the older spouse or partner. The allowance is given as a reduction of the tax liability and saves tax at only 10%, the allowances for 2010/11 being as follows:

		Tax saving @ 10%
Elder 71 to 74	£6,865	£686.50
Elder 75 or over	£6,965	£696.50

As anyone born before 6 April 1935 will be 75 or over by 5 April 2010, only the higher of these allowances is now applicable.

As with the personal allowance, these amounts are reduced where income exceeds a certain limit, but they will not be reduced below a specified minimum amount (£2,670 for 2010/11 — see **34.4**).

The available allowance (after taking into account the income limit where appropriate) is reduced in the year of marriage or registration of civil partnership by 1/12th for each complete tax month before the date of marriage or registration (see **2.18**). The allowance is given in full in the year of separation or death of either spouse/partner. If a separated couple become reconciled in a later tax year, the full married couple's allowance is available in the year of reconciliation (unless they had divorced or dissolved the civil partnership). If the reconciliation takes place in the same tax year as the separation, they will usually be taxed as if they had not been separated.

For those married before 5 December 2005, the married couple's allowance is normally given to the husband (the 'old rule'). For those who marry or register a civil partnership on or after 5 December 2005, the allowance will go to the spouse or civil partner with the higher income (the 'new rule'). However, a couple subject to the old rule may elect for the new rule to apply, where for example the wife has the higher income.

In either case the other spouse or partner may claim half of the specified minimum allowance as of right (giving an allowance of £1,335 for 2010/11), or the couple may jointly claim for the other spouse or partner to get the whole amount (£2,670 for 2010/11). The claim for the allowance must be made *before* the tax year in which it is first to apply (except in the year of marriage or registration when the claim may be made within that year). A claim in respect of 2011/12 must therefore be made by 5 April 2011. Claims must be made on Form 18, available at www.hmrc.gov.uk.

The allowance will then be allocated in the chosen way until the claim is withdrawn, or, where a joint claim has been made for the whole of the specified amount to go to the wife or lower income spouse/partner, as the case may be, until the husband or higher income spouse/partner makes a fresh claim for half of that amount. The withdrawal of the claim, or the new claim by the spouse or partner with the higher income as the case may be, must also be made before the beginning of the tax year for which the revised allocation is to take effect.

Spouses and civil partners can use the transferred allowance to reduce any of their tax for the year, even if the tax relates to income arising before the marriage/civil partnership or after the date of separation or of the death of the other spouse or partner.

If the tax bill is too low to use the married couple's allowance available, an individual may notify HMRC that he/she wants to transfer the surplus allowance to his/her spouse or partner. The whole of any surplus allowance may be transferred, and not just the part of the allowance that may be claimed by either spouse/partner. There is a box to tick in the additional information pages to the tax return if an individual wants to have his/her spouse or partner's surplus allowance or he/she wants to transfer his/her own surplus allowance. Notice of the transfer is given on Form 575, also available at www.hmrc.gov.uk. The time limit for making a claim to transfer the surplus is four years from the end of the tax year.

Since the allowance is given as a fixed amount of tax saving, transferring all or half of the specified amount from one to the other does not save tax unless one has insufficient income to pay tax, or has dividend income and the tax bill would otherwise be lower than the available dividend tax credits. A transfer from one to the other may, however, improve cash flow if, say, one spouse or partner would get the reduction in the tax on self-employed profits that is paid half-yearly as part of the provisional and balancing payments under self-assessment whereas the other is an employee who would pay reduced PAYE tax from the beginning of the tax year.

Income limit for age-related allowances (ITA 2007, ss 36, 37, 43, 58; FA 1990, s 25; FA 2009, s 4)

[34.4] Both the personal allowance and the age-related personal allowance are reduced by £1 for every £2 by which 'adjusted net income' (i.e. taking account of any allowable reliefs and the gross amount of charitable donations and pension contributions, but before deducting personal and blind person's allowances) exceeds the relevant limit. For the personal allowance the limit is £100,000. For the age-related personal allowance the limit is £22,900. However, the age-related personal allowance cannot fall below the amount the individual would be entitled to if he were aged under 65. This means for an individual with income of £100,000 or less it cannot fall below £6,475, which is the basic personal allowance for 2010/11. Where the individual's income exceeds £100,000 the allowance can be reduced further until it is nil as for individuals aged under 65.

The married couple's age allowance is similarly subject to the income limit. For those who have been entitled to the allowance since before 5 December 2005 the amount available depends on the husband's income only, even if the extra allowance is being given because of his wife's age rather than his. For marriages or civil partnerships taking place on or after 5 December 2005, however, the allowance is given to the spouse or partner with the higher income, as indicated in **34.3**. For 2010/11, after the personal allowance has been reduced to £6,475 for individuals whose income is between £22,900 and

£100,000, or otherwise to a figure less than £6,475 (see the above paragraph), the married couple's allowance is similarly reduced by half of the excess of the claimant's total income over £22,900 which has not already been taken into account to reduce the personal allowance, until it reaches the minimum allowance of £2,670 (which may have been transferred to the spouse or partner).

Once income reaches a certain level, therefore, all the benefit of the increased personal allowance, and the excess above £2,670 of the married couple's allowances, is lost.

The reduction of the age allowance by £1 for every £2 of income over £22,900 is sometimes called the age allowance trap, because it has the effect of costing tax at 1½ times the relevant tax rate on the excess income over £22,900. The tax rate on the excess income depends on the nature of the income and may be as high as 30%, i.e. 1/ times 20%, where the extra income is wholly within the basic rate band (see Example 1).

Example 1

		(a) £	(b) £
Single person, aged 68, has income in 2010/11 of:			
Pension		15,900	16,100
Savings income (interest)		7,000	7,000
		22,900	23,100
Personal allowance (over 65):			
Unrestricted		(9,490)	
Restricted by ½ of £200			(9,390)
Taxable income		13,410	13,710
Tax thereon	13,410/ 13,710 @ 20%	£2,682	£2,742

Additional tax payable on extra £200 income is £60, i.e. 30%, which is 1½ times 20%.

Example 2

Facts as in Example 1, but with the savings income including tax-credit inclusive dividends of £2,000 and the extra £200 income being dividends.

	(a) £	(b) £
Pension	15,900	15,900
Savings income:		
Interest	5,000	5,000

Dividends			2,000	2,200
			22,900	23,100
Personal allowance as before			(9,490)	(9,390)
Taxable income			13,410	13,710
Tax thereon:				
Pension	6,410 / 6,510	@ 20%	1,282	1,302
Interest	5,000 / 5,000	@ 20%	1,000	1,000
Dividends	2,000 / 2,200	@ 10%	200	220
	13,410 / 13,710		£2,482	£2,522

> The extra tax of £40 represents 20% on the additional dividend income of £200, made up of 10% tax on the dividends (£200 x 10%) plus a further 10% through the reduction of £100 in the age-related allowance (£100 × 20%). The tax on the dividends @ 10% is covered by the dividend tax credit.

To the extent that income above the age allowance threshold resulted in a reduction of married couple's allowance, the extra tax on that part of the excess income would be only 5%, because the married couple's allowance saves tax at only 10%, so the tax cost of reducing the allowance by half of the excess income would be only 5%.

Individuals caught in the age allowance trap should consider reducing taxable income by switching to tax-exempt investments such as national savings certificates and Individual Savings Accounts (ISAs). For details, see CHAPTERS 36 and 37.

[34.5] As indicated in **34.3**, where a marriage or civil partnership takes place on or after 5 December 2005, and the couple are entitled to married couple's allowance because one or both were born before 6 April 1935, the allowance is based on the income of the spouse or partner with the higher income, and this may affect the amount of the married couple's allowance available. A couple to which the old rule applies may elect for this new rule to apply instead (see **34.3**).

Separation and divorce (ITA 2007, ss 453, 454)

[34.6] When couples separate, get divorced, or dissolve a civil partnership, relief for maintenance payments is available if either or both were born before 6 April 1935.

The relief may be claimed when a marriage or civil partnership is dissolved, in respect of payments made by one of the couple to the other for the other's maintenance. It may also be claimed by one of a separated couple (whether or not they have been married or civil partners) who makes payments to the other for the maintenance of a child of the family under 21 (or a child who has been so treated, other than a child boarded out with the family by a public authority or voluntary organisation). The payments may be made under a court order or written agreement governed by UK (or EU state) law. The claimant is entitled to reduce his/her tax bill by a maintenance relief of 10% of £2,670 (or 10% of the maintenance paid if less).

The full relief is available in the year of separation, as well as the married couple's allowance (as to which see **34.3**). Payments due after a former spouse remarries or former civil partner registers with another partner do not qualify for relief. Maintenance relief is available to qualifying nationals of the European Economic Area (EEA — i.e. the European Union plus Iceland, Liechtenstein and Norway) who are resident in the UK and to qualifying UK nationals paying maintenance by order or written agreement of an EEA country. The relief is given by an adjustment to PAYE codings or in the payer's self-assessment.

All maintenance received is free of tax.

Pensions and state benefits

[34.7] State pensions are taxable but tax is not deducted under the PAYE system, so an increase in state pension results in a larger deduction of tax under PAYE from an occupational or personal pension. The state pension increase takes up another slice of tax allowances, reducing the amount available to set against occupational or personal pension. People with small occupational pensions may find that they do not get the full benefit of their allowances and may need to claim a refund (see Example 5 at **2.32**). See **13.3** for details of entitlement to state pension and **CHAPTER 16** for further points about pensions generally, in particular **16.4** about the possibility of obtaining a lump sum for deferring or suspending the state pension.

Where allowances (in particular married couple's allowance) are restricted to 10%, estimates of income are used to adjust the PAYE code so as to charge the correct amount of tax. Variations in income will lead to under- or overpayments and a taxpayer should let the tax office know if his income varies substantially. Some people may be able to avoid overpaying tax by registering to receive bank and building society interest in full, but an individual is not entitled to register unless he will not be liable to pay tax at all — see **37.4**.

Some state benefits are taxable and others are not (see Table at **10.5**), so care needs to be taken where there is a choice. See **13.9** for details of the inherited additional state pension entitlement of a surviving spouse or civil partner, and **33.12** for the bereavement payment of £2,000 and other bereavement benefits that may be available to widows, widowers and surviving civil partners. For general points on State benefits, see **CHAPTER 13**.

Providing a home for a dependent relative

[34.8] See **30.9** for the capital gains exemption available where there is a disposal of a property provided rent-free to a dependent relative who had occupied the property from 5 April 1988 until up to three years before the date of disposal, and for the capital gains exemption available to trustees where the occupier is entitled to occupy property as a beneficiary of a trust.

Purchased life annuities

[34.9] A purchased life annuity is an annual sum received for life, in exchange for a capital payment. Part of the annuity is regarded as a return of capital and thus escapes tax; tax is deducted from the income element at 20% (see **2.26** and **2.27**). The older the individual, the greater the tax-free capital element of the annuity. The capital required to buy the annuity is sacrificed, and this loss of capital must be weighed against the greater income arising. The loss of capital may be considered worthwhile to enable an improvement in the standard of living, particularly if there are no dependants or others to whom to leave capital. However, it is important to have regard to annuity rates and to get proper professional advice before making this sort of arrangement. See also **36.23** and **40.4**.

Payments for long-term care (ITTOIA 2005, ss 725, 726)

[34.10] Payments made under an 'immediate needs annuity' (which is a special form of life annuity) to a care provider or local authority are exempt from tax. The exemption applies where the annuity is provided to fund long-term care for someone who is unable to live independently because of physical or mental infirmity.

Making the most of the dwelling house

[34.11] The home is often the most significant asset, yet it can be the biggest liability because it has to be maintained, and in most cases it does not produce income.

If an individual decides to let part of his home, he will not have to pay income tax on the rent unless it exceeds £4,250 a year — see **30.10**. The letting will not cause any loss of the capital gains tax private residence exemption (see CHAPTER 30) when the property is sold provided that the gain on the let part does not exceed that on the exempt part, subject to a maximum exempt gain on the let part of £40,000. Taking in boarders who live as part of the family does not affect the capital gains tax exemption at all.

There are numerous schemes, known as equity release schemes, to enable homeowners to realise capital from their property. Some of the schemes are outlined below. Proper financial advice is essential and it must also be ensured that the scheme gives security of income and does not put the home at risk.

[34.12] Sometimes the money to purchase a life annuity (see **34.9**) is raised by a loan secured on an individual's home (a home income plan). If the loan was taken out before 9 March 1999 (or a written offer of the loan had been made before that date), the individual is still entitled to relief on the interest on the first £30,000 of the loan. Relief may be given under the MIRAS scheme despite the general MIRAS relief having been withdrawn (see **2.13**). The rate of relief is 23%. The entitlement to relief for the interest payable continues even if the individual remortgages, or moves to another property or into a nursing home. The interest paid clearly reduces the extra income from the annuity and careful calculations are necessary to see if the result is a meaningful increase in spending money. Another possibility is an arrangement whereby no interest is paid on the loan during lifetime and the compensating interest payable to the lender on death is fixed in advance.

[34.13] A further possibility is a home reversion scheme, under which all or part of the house is sold to the reversion company for much less than its value (the discount usually being at least 50%) in return for the right to live in it until death. Some schemes give lower initial sum but give a share in future increases in value of the property. The initial cash sum does not attract capital gains tax but shares of future increases in value may be liable. The investment of the initial capital sum gives extra spendable income.

[34.14] Yet another possibility is a shared appreciation mortgage, where an individual gets an interest free mortgage equal to a percentage of the value of the property in return for giving up a substantial part of any increase in value of the property when he either sells it or dies. Unlike some earlier home income plans, there is no risk of losing the home if property values fall, because if there is no increase only the amount of the mortgage is repaid.

[34.15] Certain types of equity release scheme are subject to regulation by the Financial Services Authority. This includes home reversion plans from 6 April 2007. The Government has stated that there will not be a tax charge under the pre-owned assets provisions (see **5.37**) for bona fide equity release schemes involving the disposal of all or part of the taxpayer's interest in the property. This also applies to non-arm's length part sales (for example within a family) effected before 7 March 2005 if they were on arm's length terms, and to later similar part sales made for a consideration other than money or readily realisable assets.

Helping the family

[34.16] An individual may be in a position to give financial help to his family rather than requiring help from them. The following gifts may be made without inheritance tax consequences:

(a)   habitual gifts out of income that leave enough income to maintain the usual standard of living;

(b)   gifts of not more than £250 per donee in each tax year;

(c)   the first £3,000 of total gifts in each tax year, plus any unused part of the £3,000 exemption for the previous tax year. This exemption applies to gifts on an 'earliest first' basis, so if an individual gave away nothing last year and gives £5,000 in May and £5,000 in June, the May gift is exempt and £1,000 of the June gift is exempt.

Even if the gift is not exempt, there is still no immediate inheritance tax to pay since lifetime gifts (other than to most trusts) are only brought into account for inheritance tax if the donor does not survive the gift by seven years. In the meantime they are called 'potentially exempt transfers' (see **5.23**). If the donor does not survive the seven-year period, there is still no question of inheritance tax being payable if the gift is within the nil rate band for inheritance tax, currently £325,000. This nil rate band is used against gifts in the seven years before death in the order in which they are made. When the cumulative lifetime gifts exceed the nil rate band, the excess is chargeable, but the tax is reduced on a sliding scale if the donor has survived the gift by more than three years. The tax is payable by the donee. All non-exempt gifts within the seven years before death affect how much of the nil rate band is left to reduce the chargeable estate at death.

Spouses and civil partners are treated separately for inheritance tax, each being entitled to the available exemptions and the nil rate band.

Tax position on death

[34.17] On death, an individual's wealth and the chargeable transfers made in the previous seven years determine whether any, and if so how much, inheritance tax is payable (see **CHAPTER 5**). There is no inheritance tax on assets passing to a spouse or civil partner. There is no liability to capital gains tax on any increase in the value of assets up to the date of death, and those who acquire the assets are treated as having done so at their market value at the date of death. Further details on the position at death are in **CHAPTERS 33** and **35**.

If capital gains have been made in that part of the tax year before death, they are chargeable if they exceed the annual exemption, currently £10,100. Any capital losses in the tax year of death may be carried back to set against gains on which tax has been paid in the three previous tax years, latest first, and, in that event, tax will be repayable to the estate. Interest on the repayment runs from the payment date for the tax year of death (see **9.6**).

As far as income tax is concerned, the income to the date of death is charged to tax in the usual way, and a full personal allowance is available. For married couples and civil partners, if one (or both) was born before 6 April 1935, married couple's allowance is still available, and there are provisions for each spouse or partner to claim part of the allowance (see **2.18**). The treatment of the married couple's allowance in the tax year in which either the main claimant or the spouse or civil partner dies is dealt with in **33.12**.

Council tax

[34.18] Property is exempt from council tax if it is left unoccupied while the owner is a long-term hospital patient, or is being looked after in a residential care home, or is living elsewhere to receive care (see **8.3**). The owner may qualify for a one-band reduction for council tax if the home has special features because he or another resident is disabled (see **8.6**). Other discounts may be available (see **8.5**).

People on low incomes are entitled to council tax benefit of up to 100% (see **8.7**).

Tax points

[34.19] Note the following:

- The structure of tax rates, even for those on modest incomes, can be very confusing. The 10% starting rate for savings is complicated and will not be available to most taxpayers. The 10% tax credit on dividends is not repayable, so if other income does not utilise allowances the dividend tax credits are wasted.
- Those whose income is not fully covered by allowances and deductions cannot register to receive bank etc. interest in full. This means that they may well overpay tax and be required to claim a refund. Many pensioners are unaware of their entitlement and HMRC estimate that there are a large number of pensioners who do not claim the repayments to which they are entitled.
- The marginal tax rate for those over 65 with income over £22,900 but within the basic rate band can be as high as 30%, so that investments that produce tax-free income or capital gains should be considered in those circumstances.
- In reckoning income for age allowances, any investment bond withdrawals over the 5% limit have to be taken into account even though there is no tax to pay on that excess at the higher rate (see **CHAPTER 40**). Conversely, the gross amount of a properly recorded donation to a charity reduces income when calculating whether age allowances are to be restricted. The same applies to a personal pension contribution (see **34.4**).
- If an individual has registered to receive interest in full (see **37.4**), he needs to be careful if he receives rolled-up interest on a National Savings guaranteed equity bond (see **36.13**). Even though he has held the bond for five years, all of the interest is counted as income of the tax year in which the bond matures.
- There is no point in increasing available income now if this jeopardises capital and causes worry and uncertainty for the future.
- If an individual has a pre-9 March 1999 life annuity 'home income plan' and has to leave his home, he can still get tax relief for loan interest for a limited time providing the property is put up for sale. He will not get the relief if he is not trying to sell it.

- Since lifetime transfers (other than those into most trusts) are potentially exempt from inheritance tax and do not have to be reported, it is most important to keep accurate records of gifts out of income and capital so that there can be no doubt about dates and amounts of gifts. Personal representatives are responsible for dealing with the inheritance tax position of lifetime transfers and carefully kept records are essential for the avoidance of doubt.
- If, because of disability, an individual has to provide, adapt or extend a bathroom, washroom or lavatory in his private residence, the cost is not liable to VAT. There is, however, no income tax relief on the cost or on money borrowed to finance the work.
- If an individual's spouse or civil partner does not have enough income to cover his/her personal allowance for income tax, the individual should consider transferring some assets to the spouse or partner if this is practicable, so that the income from them will then be his/hers and not the individual's (see **33.4**). Interest on bank and building society accounts (other than National Savings accounts) can only be paid gross to those who are able to register because they will not be liable to tax at all (see **37.4**). If this does not apply, there will be a cash flow advantage with National Savings accounts, but the rates of interest on offer need to be compared as well. Remember that the personal allowance increases after age 65.
- If it is not appropriate to transfer assets from one spouse or civil partner to the other, placing them in joint ownership but in unequal shares will still have the effect of the income being split equally even if the ownership share of one spouse or partner far exceeds that of the other (see **33.6**). This does not, however, apply to dividends on shares in family companies.
- If an individual makes a lifetime gift not covered by the annual exemptions, it is essential that the donee is aware that he is responsible for the payment of any inheritance tax on it if the individual dies within the next seven years.

35

Making a will and estate planning

Intestate death

[35.1] If a person dies intestate, that is without making a will, the law divides the estate in a particular way. For married couples and registered civil partners, the spouse or civil partner automatically acquires the family home and any other assets such as bank accounts owned as joint tenants (see **35.5**). The intestacy rules apply only to the remainder of the estate. If, on the other hand, the house and other assets were owned either in the sole name of the person who died or jointly with his spouse or civil partner as tenants in common (see **35.5**), the deceased's share would form part of his estate and would be subject to the intestacy rules. The intestacy rules currently applicable in England and Wales are set out in the following table. The spouse or civil partner will not inherit under these rules unless he/she survives the deceased spouse or partner by at least 28 days.

Where there is a surviving spouse or civil partner

[see next page]

Are there any:			Spouse or civil partner takes:	Remainder
Children & their issue*	Parents	Brothers & sisters & their issue*		
No	No	No	The whole estate	n/a
Yes			Personal chattels + £250,000 + life interest in half of residue	Children (or their issue*) share half residue and take spouse's or civil partner's share on his or her death
No	Yes		Personal chattels + £450,000 + half of residue absolutely	Parents share half of residue absolutely
No	No	Yes	Personal chattels + £450,000 + half of residue absolutely	Brothers and sisters (or their issue*) share half of residue absolutely

Where there is no surviving spouse or civil partner

If there are children, or their issue*, they take the whole estate absolutely.

If there are no children or their issue*, the whole estate goes to surviving relatives in the following order of precedence, each category taking the whole estate to the exclusion of any later category:

(a) Parents
(b) Brothers and sisters (or their issue*)
(c) Half brothers and sisters (or their issue*)
(d) Grandparents
(e) Uncles and aunts (or their issue*)
(f) Parents' half brothers and sisters (or their issue*)

If there are none of these relatives, the estate goes to the Crown.

* 'Issue' means children and their children, grandchildren, great grandchildren etc., each such person being entitled to an appropriate proportion of the deceased parent's share.

The share of anyone under 18 is held on trust to age 18.

It is possible for those entitled under an intestacy to vary their entitlement (see **35.14**), but the shares of beneficiaries under 18 cannot be reduced without court consent.

Stepchildren do not have any entitlement under the intestacy rules.

Making a will: tax considerations

General considerations

[35.2] In making the best arrangements from a taxation point of view, it must not be forgotten that the prime objective is to ensure that those left behind are properly provided for in a sensible, practical and acceptable way. There are important tax implications, which it can be expensive to ignore, but they should not be allowed to override the main aim.

It should be borne in mind that wills need to be regularly reviewed to ensure that they remain appropriate. In particular, the effect of marriage or civil partnership, separation, divorce or dissolution, or changes in the legislation, need to be borne in mind. A will is generally revoked by marriage or registration of civil partnership. It is not revoked on divorce or dissolution, although bequests to the former spouse or civil partner would no longer apply, nor any appointment of the former spouse or civil partner as executor. Separation has no effect on a will. If the family home is held as joint tenants, the joint tenancy will not be affected by either separation or divorce/dissolution, so it will usually be appropriate for separating couples to sever the joint tenancy in order to ensure that if one dies before the couple's affairs are settled, the property does not automatically go to the other (see **35.5**).

Inheritance tax: spouses and civil partners (IHTA 1984, ss 8A, 18; TCGA 1992, s 58; FA 2008, s 10 and Sch 4)

[35.3] Gifts between spouses or civil partners are exempt from inheritance tax (IHT) for both lifetime and death transfers (unless the donee is not deemed to be domiciled in the UK, in which case gifts are exempt up to a limit of £55,000 (see **CHAPTER 5**). Transfers between spouses or civil partners in a tax year when they are living together are also exempt from capital gains tax (CGT), and there is no stamp duty or stamp duty land tax on gifts.

Spouses/civil partners are each entitled to the IHT nil rate band, currently £325,000 (see **5.21**). Where a surviving spouse or civil partner dies on or after 9 October 2007, a claim may be made for any part of the nil rate band unused on the death of the first spouse or civil partner to die to be added to the survivor's own nil rate band on his or her death.

The proportion of the first nil rate band to be transferred is calculated by reference to the amount of the nil rate band in force at the time of the survivor's death. In many cases it will now be beneficial, therefore, to arrange for assets to pass to the surviving spouse/civil partner rather than arranging for a chargeable transfer to utilise some of the nil rate band on the first death.

> *Example 1*
>
> H died on 1 May 2007 leaving £75,000 to his children and the remaining estate to his wife W, when the IHT nil rate band was £300,000. The unused proportion of his nil rate band was 75%.

> If W dies on 1 November 2010, when the nil rate band is £325,000, and a claim is made for the transfer of H's unused nil rate band, W's nil rate band will become £325,000 + (75% × £325,000) = £568,750.

The claim is made on form IHT216, available at www.hmrc.gov.uk/cto/iht216.pdf. Since a claim may be made where the first spouse/partner died before 9 October 2007, it may be necessary for claimants to ascertain the unused nil rate band in relation to a death that occurred many years ago. HMRC have published tables showing the nil rate band in force over the years, going back to 1914, for IHT and its predecessors, capital transfer tax and estate duty. The normal time limit for the claim is two years after the end of the month in which the surviving spouse/partner died, although this can be extended at HMRC's discretion.

A will can be drafted to ensure that a spouse/partner enjoys the income but the assets themselves are eventually to go to others, for example children by a previous marriage/civil partnership, This is normally achieved by a will declaring a trust providing for precisely that. The spouse/partner exemption for IHT will still apply so long as the terms of the trust are appropriately drawn. Professional advice is essential.

Where the nil rate band is used by each spouse/partner it may be better on the first death to leave the excess over the nil rate threshold to the surviving spouse/partner so that tax would be paid later rather than earlier, with the survivor being able to make further tax-exempt lifetime gifts. For income tax, it is tax-efficient for each spouse/civil partner to have sufficient capital to produce enough income to use the personal allowance and basic rate bands.

Use of discretionary trusts

[35.4] It is possible, in order to use up the nil rate band, to leave £325,000 or other appropriate amount to a trust where the trustees have a discretion as to what they do with the income and capital, leaving, for example, a spouse/partner as one of the beneficiaries. The supporting capital is thus not transferred to the survivor directly to swell his/her estate for tax purposes on eventual death, but any unexpected need may be made good by the trustees exercising their discretion to pay amounts to him/her. Where land is involved, stamp duty land tax may be payable in connection with nil rate band discretionary trusts. See HMRC's stamp duty land tax manual at SDLTM04045 for detailed comments.

A discretionary trust is also useful where there is some uncertainty at the time of making the will as to who should benefit. A transfer of the capital to one or more individuals by the trustees within two years after death (but not within the first three months of that two years) is treated for IHT purposes as having been made by will, and has the same effect. CGT may, however, be payable (see **35.16**).

Discretionary trusts are dealt with in more detail at **42.27** to **42.36** within the mainstream IHT rules for trusts. The use of trusts in tax planning is a complicated area, and professional advice is essential, particularly in assessing the suitability of discretionary trusts following reforms to the use of the nil rate band discussed at **35.3**.

Jointly owned assets

[35.5] There are two ways in which assets may be held jointly — as joint tenants or as tenants in common. If an asset is held jointly with someone else as a joint tenant, it passes to the other joint tenant(s) through operation of the law by survivorship (i.e. outside the terms of any will) on death. With a tenancy in common, each has a separate share which can be disposed of in lifetime or on death as the person wishes. Spouses and civil partners are normally presumed to own assets as joint tenants, and other people are presumed to own them as tenants in common, although this normal presumption can be varied. It must, however, be done in the proper legal manner appropriate to the asset.

The appropriate share in a jointly held asset still forms part of a person's estate for IHT whether the asset is held on a joint tenancy or as tenants in common, but where assets are held jointly by spouses or civil partners, any assets passing to the other are covered in any event by the spouse/civil partner exemption. Holding as joint tenants has the advantage in the case of a joint bank or building society account that when a spouse or civil partner dies, all that is needed to enable the survivor take over sole ownership of the account is production of the death certificate. There is no need to wait for grant of probate or administration. But a joint account has other tax implications, particularly in relation to income tax, since the shares of income accruing to each spouse or civil partner may not give the best income tax position.

The family home

[35.6] Although most taxation aspects relating to the family home are dealt with in **CHAPTER 30**, there are various points which are of particular importance when making a will, albeit the taxation considerations should never be allowed to get in the way of the security and comfort in body and mind of the surviving spouse/civil partner or other dependants.

Whatever is done will have an impact not only on IHT but also on CGT, income tax and stamp duty land tax, so it is essential that no aspect is considered in isolation. The possibility that the spouse/civil partner or dependant who would normally occupy the property might need to go into care should not be forgotten, bearing in mind that the house value might have to be realised to pay fees which might otherwise be subsidised by the authorities if the spouse/civil partner or dependants did not have an entitlement to occupy the house or receive the sale proceeds.

[35.7] Where the will provides that the home is left to a surviving spouse or civil partner outright, or that he/she is entitled to occupy it for life (see **35.3**), then on the death of the survivor, the value of the home at that time will be reckonable for IHT, but no CGT will be payable on the increase in value to that time. The value on the survivor's death will be the CGT cost for a future disposal.

The uplift in value for CGT will also apply where the house is left absolutely or in trust for a dependant, but the exemption for IHT on the first death will not apply.

[35.8] A spouse or civil partner who inherits the house and is considering giving it away must not fall foul of the clear rule that he/she must not retain a benefit after doing so if the value is not to be reckoned for IHT at his/her death. This could be avoided by the survivor paying a commercial rent to the donee upon which the donee would pay income tax (but perhaps in the process reducing any income surplus of the survivor which would otherwise increase his or her wealth on eventual death). The gift would drop out of the IHT reckoning after seven years.

If, having given away the property, instead of paying rent the survivor paid a market rate lump sum for the right to occupy the property for life, the value of the survivor's estate for IHT would deplete at once by the purchase price of the lease for life, with the gift of the property dropping out of the reckoning after seven years.

A variation on this theme might be the next generation purchasing the house at full market value from the survivor with a commercial loan, the interest being funded by the full market rent received from the survivor and income tax only being paid on the net surplus. This would provide cash to the former house owner who could either use it to produce income or to make capital gifts, the value of the house in the meantime increasing in the hands of the next generation.

But none of the arrangements in the previous three paragraphs would protect the increasing value of the home from CGT, since the property at the time of death of the survivor would neither be owned by him/her nor occupied under the terms of a trust.

[35.9] Mention has been made in **35.4** of the use of a discretionary trust with the survivor being a beneficiary under the trust. Such an arrangement may well be unnecessary now that the surviving spouse or civil partner may benefit from the unused nil rate band on the first death (see **35.3**).

So far as existing arrangements are concerned, where the family home is included in the trust and the survivor allowed to occupy it there is a risk that HMRC might argue that the occupation amounts to a life interest in possession, with the value of the house being reckonable for IHT on the survivor's death as well as having been included earlier in the reckoning for IHT. If instead, the survivor is not a beneficiary under the discretionary trust, he could purchase it from the trustees, thus having the comfort and security of ownership, with the CGT uplift applying at his/her death. If he had insufficient resources for the purchase, the trustees could allow the purchase price to remain on loan from them. This would effectively leave the present value of the house out of the estate of the survivor (i.e. the amount of the loan for the purchase would be a debt deductible in calculating the value of the survivor's estate), but the wealth of the survivor would still include the market value of the house itself. This might, however, attract CGT private residence relief on a subsequent sale by the survivor and there would be no CGT on the increase in value if the property was held until death.

A number of more sophisticated arrangements might be considered, but with these and indeed the others outlined in this section, a word of caution is necessary in that what might be attractive for one purpose is often not so for another, with savings on the one hand sometimes being eroded by costs on the other, and HMRC also being able to challenge arrangements which might be considered to be artificial. Professional advice is essential.

Leaving to charity

[35.10] Bequests to charity reduce the reckonable value of an estate for IHT.

Example 2

An estate at death in December 2010 amounted to £950,000. There were bequests of £50,000 to registered charities and £400,000 to the surviving spouse. The rest of the estate (the residue) was left to the children. The costs of administration were £10,000.

The estate would be divided as follows:

	£	£	£
Estate at death		950,000	
Exempt legacies:			
Charities	50,000		
Spouse	400,000	450,000	
		500,000	500,000
Threshold for IHT		325,000	
Chargeable to IHT		175,000	
IHT at 40%		70,000	(70,000)
Costs of administration			(10,000)
Residuary legatees (children)			420,000

Legacies and their effect on the spouse/civil partner exemption

[35.11] Unless a will states otherwise, legacies are payable out of the residue of an estate, after IHT has been paid, reducing the amount available to the person entitled to the balance of the estate — called the residuary legatee. The legacies are not themselves reduced by IHT unless the will specifically says so. It follows that the amount available to a residuary legatee is often less than is apparent at first sight.

If the residuary legatee is the surviving spouse or civil partner, this has an effect on the tax payable because the exempt part of the estate (which goes to the spouse/civil partner) is first reduced by the tax.

Example 3

A has made no transfers in the seven years before his death in 2010/11. He leaves an estate of £445,000 as follows:

£86,250 to each of his four children = £345,000

Residue to his wife

The IHT position on A's death is as follows:

	Gross	Tax	Net
	£	£	£
Net legacies up to the nil rate threshold	325,000		325,000
Balance grossed up at 100/60	33,333	13,333	20,000
	358,333	13,333	345,000

The estate will accordingly be divided as follows:

Gross estate	445,000
Legacies to children	(345,000)
IHT payable out of residue	(13,333)
Remainder to widow, covered by spouse exemption	£86,667

Out of a gross estate of £445,000, A's children receive legacies totalling £345,000, leaving an apparent residue of £100,000 for the widow. She does not, however, get £100,000, but only that amount less the tax on the rest of the estate. This is calculated by working out the tax on a figure sufficient to leave the legacies intact, called grossing-up. The tax amounts to £13,333 as shown above, leaving the widow with £86,667. If the will had provided that the children should pay the tax on their legacies, the widow would have received £100,000 and the total tax payable by the legatees on £345,000 would have been £8,000 (40% of the £20,000 excess over £325,000). The children could have provided for this liability by insuring their father's life, using the proceeds of the policy to pay the tax on the legacy.

Deaths in quick succession (IHTA 1984, s 141)

[35.12] Where at the time of someone's death, his estate has been increased by a lifetime or death gift made to him within the previous five years, the tax charge on the second transfer is reduced by quick succession relief. Although the relief is deducted from the tax payable on the second transfer, it is calculated as a percentage of the tax paid on the earlier transfer (see **CHAPTER 5**).

Quick succession relief is therefore not relevant in the case of assets received from a spouse or civil partner by gift, in lifetime or by bequest on death, or where they have been acquired otherwise than from a spouse or civil partner in lifetime but no tax has been paid by reference to that transfer. While not losing sight of the overriding principle of family provision, there are cases where it is clearly not sensible to increase a person's estate by lifetime gifts or bequests on death, if they have adequate resources already. Thus it will often be more tax-efficient to leave to grandchildren instead of to children. This gives the added advantage that the income arising is then that of the grandchildren in their own right, on which they will not have to pay tax if it is covered by their available income tax allowances.

Simultaneous deaths and survivorship clauses (IHTA 1984, s 92)

[35.13] Where two closely related people die at the same time, or in circumstances in which it is impossible to decide who died first, neither estate has to be increased by any entitlement from the other in calculating the IHT payable. This is not so if it is clear who died first. It is therefore often advisable to include a survivorship clause in a will making a bequest conditional on the beneficiary outliving the deceased by a given period, and this is effective for IHT providing the period does not exceed six months. This is particularly useful to spouses or civil partners who wish to leave their estates to each other to make sure that there is adequate provision for the survivor's lifetime. If the wills include an appropriate survivorship clause, then if they both die within six months, the estate of the first will not pass to the second, IHT being payable at each death on the value of the separate estates. This will often attract less tax than if no tax was paid on the first death (because of the spouse/civil partner exemption), but tax was calculated on the combined estates for the second, with the survivor having had little or no benefit from the assets in the meantime. The assets in each estate and the extent to which the IHT nil rate band is available need to be taken into account.

A 28-day spouse/civil partnership survivorship period is also prescribed under the intestacy rules (see **35.1**).

Variations and disclaimers etc (IHTA 1984, ss 17, 142–144, 218A; TCGA 1992, s 62)

[35.14] It is possible for those entitled to a deceased's estate (either under a will, on an intestacy or otherwise) to vary the way in which it is distributed, or to disclaim their entitlement, provided that they do so within two years after the death. The variation or disclaimer then takes effect as if it had applied at the date of death and IHT is charged as if the revised distribution had operated at death. For variations (but not disclaimers) this applies only if the variation contains a statement by those making it, and by the personal representatives if additional tax is payable, that they intend the variation to have that effect. Where additional tax is payable, then within six months after the date of the variation the personal representatives must notify the amount of additional tax to HMRC and send a copy of the variation. Court consent is needed for a variation that adversely affects the shares of beneficiaries under 18. If an original beneficiary has died, his personal representatives can act in his place but there may be restrictions on what they are able to vary.

Such a variation or disclaimer can also be effective for CGT purposes (subject to what is said below about trusts) providing, in the case of a variation, the document specifies that it is to apply for CGT. The ultimate beneficiary then takes the asset at the market value at the date of death, so that any increase in value since death is not charged to CGT until the beneficiary disposes of the asset. The original entitlement under the will, while the estate is in administration, is itself a right (a chose in action), and but for the specific application of the variation to CGT, the variation might itself be regarded as a disposal of that right, causing a liability to CGT.

As far as income derived from the assets is concerned, the personal representatives will have paid income tax on it at the trust rate (see **42.4**), but the income is regarded as having been received not by the person who actually receives it following the variation but by the original beneficiary, and any tax due in excess of the amount paid on the income up to the date of variation or disclaimer will be calculated by reference to the original beneficiary's tax rates. It may be appropriate for the person actually receiving the income to agree to pay any income tax at excess rates. Where a variation includes the setting up of a trust, those whose entitlement but for the variation goes into the trust are regarded as settlors of the trust fund for income tax and CGT, so that, for example, parents whose share is given up in favour of infant children will still be taxed on the income so long as the children are under 18 and unmarried (or not in a civil partnership), and trustees' capital gains may be treated as the original beneficiary's gains if that person is a beneficiary under the trust.

[35.15] A deed of variation or disclaimer could be used to advantage where, for example, an estate has been left to the surviving spouse/civil partner without the deceased's nil rate band having been used. If the survivor is already adequately provided for, part of the estate could be diverted to, say, the children. It could also be useful where, for example, children have sufficient assets of their own and would prefer legacies to go to their own children, subject to what is said above about trusts.

Where quoted shares fall in value within the twelve months after death and are sold, cancelled, or dealings are suspended within that period, the lower value may be substituted in calculating tax on the death estate (see **5.30**). The reference to cancellation is apparently intended mainly to apply to liquidations, but it may be that the liquidation is not completed within the twelve-month period, so that the relief cannot be claimed. One way of avoiding the tax liability on the higher death value of the shares would be to use a deed of variation to re-direct the shares to an exempt beneficiary, such as a spouse or civil partner, so that there would be no tax payable on that higher value.

Deeds of variation and disclaimer can be used to lessen the overall tax burden on death, but it is necessary for all concerned to consent to the arrangement, and they should usually be regarded as something in reserve rather than a substitute for appropriate planning.

[35.16] Two other ways of building flexibility into a will are worth consideration. It is possible for someone making a will to leave a 'letter of wishes' asking the personal representatives to give effect to the requests in the letter. This is particularly useful for dealing with chattels and personal effects, and is treated for IHT purposes as if it had been part of the will. The letter of wishes is not, however, binding upon the personal representatives. The other useful provision is the ability to create a discretionary trust by will, out of which the trustees can make distributions within two years after the death, which are again treated as having been made by the will, providing they are not made within the first three months after the death. This can, however, have capital gains consequences if the assets have grown in value since the date of death and the gift relief normally available for transfers out of discretionary trusts does not apply because IHT is not reckonable on the distribution. It is possible for the capital gains charge to be avoided if the trustees appoint assets out of the trust to beneficiaries *before* the personal representatives transfer the assets to them. Where the assets are redirected in a settlement, the deceased is regarded as the settlor for CGT and income tax purposes. This is a complex area and professional advice is essential.

Court orders (IHTA 1984, s 146)

[35.17] Where the court considers that the terms of a will or the intestacy rules do not make reasonable financial provision for certain people, such as a spouse or civil partner, former spouse or civil partner who has not remarried or registered a new civil partnership, child, or cohabitee, they may make an appropriate order, for example for the payment of a lump sum or maintenance. Such orders take effect as if they had applied at the date of death and override the provisions of the will or intestacy rules.

Insurance

[35.18] Life insurance may often be useful in planning for IHT. It is not always possible to reconcile making adequate provision for the family with reducing the tax liability, and insurance may then be used to cover the anticipated liability.

If the proceeds of life insurance belong to an estate, they will attract IHT. Furthermore, they will not be available until the grant of probate or administration is obtained. If, however, a policy on the deceased's life is arranged and funded by someone with an insurable interest, say his children, the funds will not belong to the deceased's estate and hence will not be liable to IHT. Funds will also not be taxable in the deceased's estate if he takes out a policy himself and pays the premiums, with the proceeds in trust for someone else, again say his children. In that event each premium payment is a separate gift, but the deceased will usually be able to show that it was normal expenditure out of income, and thus exempt from IHT, or, if not, covered by the annual exemption of £3,000 for transfers out of capital. Further details are at **40.14**.

Tax points

[35.19] Note the following:

- The regime allowing a surviving spouse or civil partner to utilise any of the IHT nil rate band remaining unused on the first death means that a good deal of routine tax planning is no longer necessary, but changing legislation as well as family circumstances make it important to review wills and potential tax liabilities regularly.

- If an entire estate is left to a spouse or civil partner, he/she can make lifetime transfers out of the combined wealth to an extent which he/she sees as sensible depending on the family circumstances from time to time. Those transfers may be completely exempt if they are covered by annual or marriage/civil partner exemptions, or potentially exempt, becoming completely exempt if the spouse or civil partner survives for seven years after making them (and where they exceed the nil rate threshold any tax arising would be subject to tapering relief on survival for three years). It is not possible for the deceased to ensure that his spouse or civil partner will carry out his wishes, since if his estate is left to him/her unconditionally, he or she is free to decide what to do with it. See above regarding transferability of the nil rate band.

- Where tax at death cannot be avoided, consider covering the liability through life insurance, the policy being written so that the proceeds belong to those who will have to bear the tax.

- A further advantage of paying regular premiums on an insurance policy which provides a lump sum outside an estate is that the estate does not grow by the unspent income, thus effectively saving the further 40% IHT which would arise on unspent accumulated income.

- If a person is apprehensive about leaving outright bequests to certain people, but still wants them to benefit, an amount could be left in trust for them to receive the income it produces, and in certain circumstances, the capital. This may provide the comfort of knowing that, for example, an adult child, whilst able to benefit immediately from the income, does not have an outright capital sum until a later stage when he/she is better able to manage it. The IHT consequences depend on the circumstances.

- Since all gifts to a spouse or civil partner are exempt from IHT, it may be more tax effective to leave agricultural and/or business property to someone else to avoid wasting agricultural and business property relief. Again, the transferability of the nil rate band should be borne in mind and in any event the tax position should not override family and commercial considerations.

- Where IHT business property and agricultural property reliefs are at the rate of 100%, deferring gifts of such property until death avoids any charge to CGT and also any problems of the IHT relief being withdrawn at death because the donee has disposed of the property. But today's reliefs may not be available tomorrow, and a person may still prefer to make lifetime gifts now, deferring any CGT under the gift relief provisions (see **4.23**).
- Wealth left to the next generation is liable to IHT on a person's death, whereas it is not liable if left to a spouse or civil partner. However, if the next generation inherits at the death of the first rather than the second, IHT is avoided on any increase in value between the first death and that of the spouse/civil partner.
- If shares are held through a nominee holding with a broker, the broker has the legal right to sell them before probate is granted. The broker may be willing to do this at the executors' request in order to raise sufficient funds for the executors to pay the IHT due without borrowing. See also **42.2** for provisions enabling personal representatives to arrange for banks etc. holding the deceased's funds to pay IHT direct to HMRC.
- It will make the executors' task far easier if an up-to-date schedule of investments, mortgages, pensions etc is kept, with the will, showing where all the relevant documents are kept. Any potentially exempt gifts for IHT (see **CHAPTER 5**) should also be recorded.
- Although those entitled to the deceased's estate have the right to vary the way it is to be distributed, it is sometimes useful for a will to contain authority for a deed of variation, since this may help the beneficiaries to accept that they would not be acting against the deceased's wishes.
- When varying the provisions of a will or intestacy, it is important to remember that the variation must not be in consideration of something outside the estate being received instead by the individual whose entitlement decreases.
- Where unmarried heterosexual couples or same-sex couples who have not registered as civil partners are cohabiting, it should be remembered that the spouse/civil partner exemptions for IHT and CGT do not apply to them. It should be established whether joint assets are held under a joint tenancy or a tenancy in common. Careful thought and action is necessary to deal with each of those problems.
- A direct bequest to grandchildren is better than a bequest to their parent who then disclaims it in their favour since, while there is no effect on the IHT payable on death, in the latter case the variation would be regarded as a parental settlement for income tax and CGT purposes if the children were under 18 and unmarried or not in a civil partnership. The parent would be charged on the income where the child's total income from parental gifts exceeded £100, and on chargeable gains on disposal of the assets.
- For further post-death planning points see **CHAPTER 42**, which deals with the administration of a deceased's estate.

Choosing investments

36

Tax on investments

Introduction

[36.1] This chapter outlines the tax position on the main forms of investment available to the majority of taxpayers. More detailed information is given in **CHAPTER 37** on investing in banks and building societies and in **CHAPTER 38** on stocks and shares. The following investments are not dealt with in this chapter but are covered in the chapters indicated:

(a)   Industrial buildings (**CHAPTER 22**).
(b)   Shares in unquoted trading companies through the enterprise invest-ment scheme (**CHAPTER 29**).
(c)   Single premium life insurance policies — investment bonds and guar-anteed income bonds (**CHAPTER 40**).
(d)   Chattels and valuables (**CHAPTER 39**).

The information given on each type of investment details the effect of taxation on income and capital growth. It is not intended to replace advice on the investments themselves, nor is it offered as guidance on investment strategy, which should be obtained from appropriate sources.

There are various alternative finance arrangements, in particular those de-signed to meet the requirements of Islamic law, that do not involve paying or receiving interest but have a similar effect. The tax treatment of such payments and receipts is equated with the treatment of interest. Several different types of alternative finance arrangements have been added, and may be added in the future, to the range covered by the original legislation.

If investments are made through an authorised investment adviser, and a loss is suffered as a result of bad advice, poor investment management or the adviser going out of business, it is possible to claim compensation under the Financial Services Compensation Scheme (FSCS, see **37.1**). Further information is provided at www.fscs.org.uk. Any interest included in the compensation payment made to individuals by the FSCS when a financial institution defaults is to be taxed in the same way as if it were paid by the financial institution which defaulted.

Tax on investment income

[36.2] For individuals, if taxable income is below the higher rate threshold of £37,400 investment income is charged to tax at 10% if it is dividend income and at 20% (i.e. the basic rate) otherwise. If taxable income exceeds the higher rate threshold of £37,400 but is less than £150,000, dividends are taxed at 32.5% and other income at 40%. If taxable income exceeds £150,000 dividends are taxed at 42.5% and other income at 50%.

In many cases tax at the 20% rate is deducted at source and dividends carry a 10% tax credit. Higher rate taxpayers then have further tax to pay and non-taxpayers are entitled to a repayment (other than on dividends). See **36.20** for further points on dividends.

Tax on interest received gross, and higher rate tax on taxed income, is included in the half-yearly payments on account on 31 January in the tax year and 31 July following for continuing sources (unless covered by the de minimis limits), with any balance being part of the overall balancing payment due on 31 January following the tax year. An employee or pensioner with small amounts of untaxed interest may have the tax collected through PAYE coding.

For companies, where tax is deducted from income, the company still has to pay corporation tax on the income, but gets a credit against the tax payable for the income tax deducted. See also **36.17** for interest on government stocks.

Investing in building societies and banks

[36.3] The majority of investors in building societies and banks invest in normal interest-bearing accounts. The interest on such accounts is received after deduction of tax at 20%, unless the recipient has registered to receive interest without deduction of tax because, for example, total income will not exceed personal allowances (see **37.4**). A repayment of tax can be claimed from HMRC, if after the end of the tax year the tax deducted is more than the recipient's liability. A repayment can be claimed before the end of the year if it amounts to £50 or more. If interest has been received without deduction of tax and it is found at the end of the tax year that some tax is due, the tax will have to be paid.

For detailed commentary on the tax treatment of bank and building society accounts other than ISAs, see **CHAPTER 37**.

National Savings and Investments

[36.4] National Savings and Investments (NS&I) is a government agency, with the Post Office acting as a distributor for its products. NS&I offers various savings accounts (see **37.7**) and a range of other investments backed by the Treasury, as outlined below. See also www.nsandi.com.

National Savings fixed interest savings certificates

[36.5] These certificates may be attractive to those paying income tax at the higher rate, since the interest, at rates guaranteed for either two or five years, accumulates over the period of the investment, and when the certificates are cashed the increase in value is totally free from income tax and capital gains tax. They may also be attractive to someone whose income would otherwise exceed the income limit for age-related personal allowances (see **34.4**). The minimum purchase is £100 and the maximum is £15,000 per issue, but in addition an unlimited amount may be reinvested from matured certificates. New issues are made fairly frequently, so it will be necessary to check the details of the issue currently on offer. The certificates may be wholly or partly repaid before maturity, so that regular withdrawals could be made to provide an effective tax-free income, although at a lower rate of return. The certificates are repaid at their purchase price in the first year (except for reinvested certificates, which carry interest for each complete three months in the first year), but after that, the tax-free yield rises each year, with the increases biased to discourage early repayment. On maturity, the certificates may be rolled over for the same term at new rates of interest, or reinvested for a different term or into a different type of certificate, or cashed in. Some of the earlier issues attract only the lower general extension rate on maturity. Holders need to check interest rates to ensure they obtain the best available terms.

National Savings index-linked savings certificates

[36.6] Index-linked certificates provide inflation proofing over a three or five-year period, plus guaranteed extra interest on an increasing scale each year, but biased to discourage early repayment. They are subject to a minimum purchase of £100 and there is a limit of £15,000 on the maximum holding of certificates in each issue, but an unlimited additional amount may be reinvested from matured certificates (including fixed interest and yearly plan certificates). The original purchase price is index-linked in line with the increase in the retail prices index, and the index-linking and extra interest are earned monthly from the date of purchase (subject to the rules for early encashment). At the end of each year, the index increases and extra interest are capitalised, and the total amount then qualifies for index-linking and extra interest in the following year.

The certificates may be wholly or partly repaid. If they are cashed within the first year, only the amount invested is repaid (except for reinvested certificates, which earn index-linking and interest for each complete month). If they are cashed after the first year, they qualify for the index increases plus extra interest for each complete month they have been held since the date of purchase. Although the extra interest rates are guaranteed for only three or five years, the certificates may be held for longer, and after the end of the fixed period they attract interest at an indexed extension rate unless they are reinvested or cashed in. The same maturity options apply as stated above for fixed interest certificates. Any increase in the value when the certificates are cashed is free of income tax and capital gains tax.

These certificates are suitable for taxpayers who are prepared to forgo immediate income to protect their capital in real terms, and the extra interest improves the return and is itself fully index-linked once earned. Those who want regular income could make partial withdrawals of their investment, but at a lower rate of return on the certificates cashed.

National Savings capital bonds and pensioner bonds

[36.7] Capital bonds were withdrawn from sale in February 2008 but existing bonds will continue to earn interest until maturity. They have a five-year term and a guaranteed rate of interest that increases over the term. Interest is added to the bond each year. These bonds may be cashed in early but there is no interest if they are repaid in the first year, and a lower rate is earned if the bond is not held for the full five years.

Although the interest is taxable, it is received in full and tax is accounted for as indicated at **36.2**. The disadvantage for taxpayers is that tax is payable every year even though no income is received from the bond until the end of the five-year period, unless it is wholly or partly cashed in, in which case lower interest rates apply.

Pensioners' guaranteed income bonds were also withdrawn from sale in February 2008 but existing bonds will continue to earn interest until maturity. The interest is paid monthly direct into a bank or building society account. Although the interest is taxable, it is received in full and tax is accounted for as indicated at **36.2**.

National Savings income bonds

[36.8] National Savings income bonds are intended for those who wish to invest lump sums at a reasonable rate of interest, and to receive a regular income from their capital. Interest is paid by monthly instalments, either by post or direct to a bank account. Although the interest is taxable, it is received in full and tax is accounted for as indicated at **36.2**. The bonds are particularly beneficial for those whose income is not high enough for them to be liable to tax. The minimum holding is £500 and the maximum £1 million, for either an individual or joint holding. The bonds may be cashed in at any time without penalty.

National Savings guaranteed income bonds

[36.9] Guaranteed income bonds offer a guaranteed monthly income and normally a choice of investment terms of one, three or five years. Interest is paid to a bank or building society account. The interest is taxable, and tax at

20% is deducted at source. The minimum holding is £500 and the maximum £1 million, for either an individual or joint holding. Withdrawals made before the end of the term are subject to a penalty equal to 90 days' interest on the amount withdrawn.

National Savings guaranteed growth bonds

[36.10] Guaranteed growth bonds offer fixed rates of interest and normally a choice of investment terms of one, three or five years. Interest is added to the bond each year. The interest is taxable, and tax at 20% is deducted at source. The minimum holding is £500 and the maximum £1 million, for either an individual or joint holding. Withdrawals made before the end of the term are subject to penalty equal to 90 days' interest on the amount withdrawn.

National Savings children's bonus bonds

[36.11] Children's bonus bonds for children under 16 are bought in units of £25 and the maximum holding per child is £3,000 in each issue. The investment term is five years at a time, and the bonds earn a fixed rate of interest guaranteed for each five year period plus a guaranteed bonus. They mature at the holder's 21st birthday and no further returns are earned after that time. The bonds may be cashed in before the child reaches age 21, but no interest is earned if they are cashed in the first year. All returns are exempt from tax, and parents may provide the funds without affecting their own tax liability.

National Savings treasurer's account

[36.12] The treasurer's account was available for investments by non-profit-making organisations such as charities, clubs and societies. The account is no longer on offer and since 10 August 2007 existing account holders have not be able to make any more transactions other than to withdraw funds and close the accounts.

National savings guaranteed equity bonds

[36.13] Guaranteed equity bonds are five-year investments with a return linked to the increase in the FTSE 100 index. The original investment is repaid if the index falls. The FTSE return is paid in full, but is liable to income tax at the rates that apply to savings. Children under 18 cannot invest in the bonds themselves although a bond can be held in trust for a child of any age. Once the five-year investment term starts the bond cannot be cashed in until maturity. The minimum investment is £1,000 and the maximum is £1 million per individual or single trust holding, £2 million for joint investments.

National Savings premium bonds

[36.14] Any person over 16 can buy premium bonds and an adult can buy them for a child under 16. The minimum purchase is £100, and the current maximum holding is £30,000. They do not carry interest, but once a bond has been held for a clear calendar month it is included in a regular monthly draw for prizes of various amounts. All prizes are free of income tax and capital gains tax and the bond itself can be cashed at face value at any time. This gives the holder the chance to win a tax-free prize, but at the cost of any income or protection of the real value of the capital.

Local authority stock, bonds and loans

[36.15] Some local authority stocks are listed on the Stock Exchange and interest on the stocks is paid to individuals after deduction of income tax. Local authorities also raise money by unlisted temporary loans, mortgages and non-negotiable bonds. Interest on these items is usually paid to individuals after deduction of 20% income tax, although it is possible to register to receive interest gross in the same way as with bank and building society interest (see **37.4**). Interest paid by local authorities to companies is paid gross (see **3.21**).

Local authority stocks, bonds and loans that are transferable are subject to the accrued income provisions described at **36.19**. They are also within the definition of 'qualifying corporate bonds' and are exempt from capital gains tax. See **38.6**.

Income, gains and losses relating to a company's holdings of local authority stocks, etc. are taken into account in calculating the company's income, and disposals are not within the capital gains regime (see **3.5** and **38.5**).

Government stocks (ITA 2007, ss 890–897; TCGA 1992, s 115)

[36.16] These represent borrowings by the British government, and they vary considerably in terms of interest. Some are issued on an index-linked basis so that the interest paid while the stock is held and the capital payment when it is redeemed are dependent on increases in the retail prices index. Interest is paid gross on *all* government stocks acquired on or after 6 April 1998, unless application is made for net payment. Payment will also be made gross from that date on taxed stocks acquired earlier, but only if the stockholder makes an application. Otherwise those who acquired taxed stocks before 6 April 1998 will be treated as having applied for net payment. See **36.2** for the way in which tax is accounted for. Special rules apply to companies (see **36.17**).

Government stocks are exempt from capital gains tax. Some stocks have a redemption date upon which the par value, or index-linked value as the case may be, is paid to the holder, so if they are bought below par there will be a guaranteed capital gain at a given date. The gain on non-index-linked stock is fixed in money terms whereas on index-linked stock it is fixed in real terms. In the meantime, the value of the stock fluctuates with market conditions, so that there may be opportunities to make tax-free capital gains before the redemption date. If, however, losses are made they are not allowable for set-off against chargeable gains.

Government stocks can be useful as a means of providing for future known commitments, such as school fees, and for those that are inclined to overspend, the government stock is not so conveniently accessible as a bank or building society account.

Looked at on a pure money return basis, however, a purchase for capital growth may sometimes be no better for a higher rate taxpayer than an investment producing a greater income with no growth prospects. It depends upon the rates of interest being paid from time to time, and the price at which government stock can be purchased.

For individuals (but not companies), interest on government stocks is subject to the accrued income scheme (see **36.19**).

[36.17] As far as companies are concerned, capital gains on government stocks are not exempt from corporation tax (with one exception (see **38.5**)) and both the income from the stocks and profits and losses on disposal of them are taken into account in calculating a company's income. In the case of indexed government stocks held other than for trade purposes, the index increase in each year is not taxed as part of the company's profits at that time, and tax is chargeable on disposal only on the increase in capital value excluding the index increase over the period. Other indexed securities are normally treated in the same way as other loan stock.

Companies receive interest on government stocks in full, accounting for the tax along with the tax on their other profits.

Company loan stock

[36.18] Company loan stock is normally within the definition of 'qualifying corporate bonds' and exempt from capital gains tax in the same way as government stocks, although for companies holding such stock, their gains and losses are brought into account when calculating the company's income (see **38.5**). Most company loan stock is a less attractive investment than government stocks for the individual taxpayer, because it may not be so readily marketable, there is a greater degree of risk, brokers' commission charges are higher and it is not possible for individuals to receive interest without deduction of tax. For individuals, trustees and personal representatives, the 'accrued income' rules for reckoning interest on a day-to-day basis apply (see **36.19**). Company loan stocks may be held in an Individual Savings Account (ISA), see **36.24**.

Accrued income scheme (ITA 2007, Pt 12)

[36.19] The accrued income scheme applies to interest-bearing marketable securities such as government stocks and to most local authority and company loan stock. It also applies to building society permanent interest bearing shares (see **37.6**). It does not apply to ordinary or preference shares in a company, units in unit trusts, bank deposits or securities within the 'discounted securities' provisions at **38.31**.

The accrued income scheme does not apply to companies because they are already taxed on accrued interest under the 'loan relationships' rules (see **3.5**). Nor does it apply to an individual if the nominal value of all accrued income scheme securities held does not exceed £5,000 at any time either in the tax year in which the next interest payment on the securities falls due or in the previous tax year. If, for example, securities were bought or sold in February 2010 on which interest is paid in June and December, the two tax years to look at are 2010/11 (in which the June interest date falls) and 2009/10 (the previous year). If the interest had been payable in March and September the two tax years to look at would have been 2009/10 (the interest date year) and 2008/09.

Where the scheme applies, interest received is included in income according to the amount accrued on a day to day basis, so that selling just before an interest date does not enable income tax to be avoided on the interest by effectively receiving it as part of the sales proceeds. If securities are sold before they go 'ex dividend', the vendor is taxed on the accrued interest to the settlement date and the buyer's taxable income is correspondingly reduced. If securities are sold ex dividend (so that the vendor gets the full interest at the payment date), the vendor's taxable income is reduced and the buyer's increased by the interest applicable to the period between the settlement date and the interest payment date. The accrued income adjustments are made in the tax year in which the next interest payment date falls, the savings income being charged at the taxpayer's marginal rate.

Where a sale is through a bank or stockbroker, the accrued interest is shown on the contract note.

The accrued income scheme applies not only to sales but also to any other transfers, except that it does not apply on death.

Accrued income charges and reliefs must be shown in the investor's tax return. Most securities covered by the accrued income scheme are exempt from capital gains tax (see **38.6**).

Example 1

An individual investor who is a 40% rate taxpayer sells £10,000 12% stock (on which interest is payable half-yearly on 9 June and 9 December) to a buyer who is a basic rate taxpayer. Stock goes ex dividend on 1 June 2010.

If sold for settlement on 25 May 2010 (i.e. sold cum dividend)

Buyer receives the full 6 months' interest on 9 June 2010, but effectively 'bought' part of this within his purchase price. The interest accrued from 10 December 2009 to 25 May 2010 is:

$$£1,200 \times \frac{167}{365} = £549.04$$

Seller's taxable income is increased (by an accrued income charge) and buyer's taxable income reduced (by accrued income relief) of £549.04.

If sold for settlement on 1 June 2010 (i.e. sold ex dividend)

Seller receives the full 6 months' interest on 9 June 2010, but effectively 'bought' part of this by receiving reduced sale proceeds. The interest from 2 June 2010 to 9 June 2010 when he did not own the stock amounts to:

$$£1,200 \times \frac{8}{365} = £26.30$$

Seller's taxable income is reduced (by accrued income relief) and buyer's taxable income increased (by an accrued income charge) of £26.30.

The accrued income adjustments are made in the tax year in which the next interest payment date falls, 2010/11 in this example, and are recorded in the tax returns for that year. In the first instance (sale for settlement 25 May 2010), the seller will pay tax at 40% on the accrued income charge of £549.04 and the buyer will save tax at 20% on that amount. In the second instance (sale on 1 June 2010), the seller will save tax at 40% on the amount of £26.30 by which his income is reduced and the buyer will pay tax at 20% on that amount.

Ordinary shares in listed companies

[36.20] Ordinary shares are 'risk capital' and investors have to be prepared to accept the risk element in return for seeking rising income and capital appreciation. Although listed shares are readily marketable, the price can fluctuate considerably and the capital is not readily accessible.

Dividends attract a tax credit amounting to 1/9th of the cash amount. This represents a rate of 10% on the tax-credit inclusive dividend and basic rate taxpayers have no further tax to pay. Higher rate taxpayers are taxed at 32.5% (or 42.5% if their taxable income exceeds £150,000). Non-taxpayers cannot claim repayment of the tax credits.

Dividends are included in income as they arise and are not subject to the 'accrued income' provisions that apply to government, local authority and company loan stocks.

Investment in ordinary shares can be free of income tax and capital gains tax if the investment is through an Individual Savings Account (ISAs, see 36.24 onwards).

The detailed treatment of shares, and further information on company loan stock and government stocks, is in CHAPTER 38.

Certified SAYE savings arrangements

[36.21] These HMRC-approved schemes enable an employer company to grant to employees and directors an option to acquire shares in the company in the future at today's price, the shares eventually being paid for out of the proceeds of a linked Save as you Earn (SAYE) scheme. For details of such schemes see 11.10.

The employee does not get tax relief for the SAYE contributions, but bonuses (within specified limits) and interest paid under the scheme are tax free. When the shares acquired under the SAYE arrangement are eventually sold, the resulting gain or loss will be subject to capital gains tax, with the base cost of the shares being the actual price (as opposed to the market value) paid for the shares by the participant.

Unit and investment trusts and venture capital trusts

[36.22] The tax treatment of investments in unit and investment trusts is dealt with at **38.24** to **38.30**. Venture capital trusts are dealt with at **29.25**.

Purchased life annuities

[36.23] If a lump sum is paid to a life insurance company to get a fixed annual sum in return, the annual sum is partly regarded as a non-taxable return of capital, thus giving a comparatively high after-tax income. The after-tax income is even higher for basic rate taxpayers since they only pay tax on the income element of the annuity at 20%. However, it must be remembered that capital has been spent to purchase the annual income, which reduces the amount of capital in the death estate.

Purchased life annuities are therefore often acquired in conjunction with life insurance policies, part of the annual income being used to fund the life insurance premium so that at the end of the annuity period the life insurance policy proceeds can replace the purchase price of the annuity. There are numerous variations on this sort of arrangement (see **CHAPTER 40**).

Individual Savings Accounts (ITTOIA 2005, ss 694–701; SI 1998/1870)

[36.24] Individual Savings Accounts (ISAs) provide a tax-free 'wrapper' for investments. They are available to individuals aged 18 or over who are resident and ordinarily resident in the UK. Cash ISAs are available to those 16 or over (see **36.31**). Joint accounts are not permitted. There is no statutory minimum period for which the accounts must be held and there is no lifetime limit on the amount invested.

An ISA may be either a cash account or a stocks and shares account. For 2010/11 it is possible to invest up to £10,200 a year in an ISA (of which £5,100 can be cash). For 2009/10 the total investment limit was £7,200 a year (of which £3,600 could be in cash), although from 6 October 2009, this limit was increased for individuals aged 50 or over to the current 2010/11 limits. It was announced in the March 2010 Budget that from 6 April 2011 these limits will be increased in line with the annual percentage increase in the RPI, rounded to a figure which allows for the easy calculation of monthly payments. The maximum cash element will be 50% of the overall limit.

[36.25] It is possible to invest up to £5,100 in a cash ISA with one provider, and invest the remainder of the £10,200 allowance in a stocks and shares ISA with either the same provider or a different one.

There is no statutory minimum subscription, although interest rates on the cash element may vary according to the amount invested. Investors that become non-resident, may retain the tax-exempt benefits of existing ISAs but no further investments may be made.

[36.26] Although there is no minimum holding period for an ISA, there are restrictions on withdrawals and deposits made throughout the tax year. If any part of the amount invested in a year is withdrawn, that part of the limit for the year is not then available for further investment. If, for example, an individual deposited the full £5,100 in a cash ISA in 2010/11, and unexpectedly needed to withdraw £2,000, the funds can not subsequently be replaced in that tax year. It would only be possible to reinvest in a later year by using the cash limit for that year. If an individual had only deposited £2,600 in 2010/11 and withdrew it, a further £2,500 could be reinvested into the account in order to use up the remainder of the £5,100 limit.

[36.27] ISAs are free of income tax and capital gains tax. Where ISA investments are in shares, there may be no significant tax benefits for many taxpayers, since the capital gains tax exemption will often not be relevant and there will be no tax relief for any capital losses. The ISA tax exemption ceases on the death of the investor, so that tax will be deducted from any interest received during the administration period (see **42.4**).

[36.28] The investments in which stocks and shares ISAs may be invested include shares and securities listed on a recognised stock exchange, gilts, units in qualifying authorised unit trusts, shares in qualifying open-ended investment companies and certain investment trusts, various collective investment schemes specified as stakeholder products, qualifying life insurance products and cash held temporarily for the purpose of investing in qualifying investments. Interest on such cash is not tax free and the account manager has to account for tax at 20% to HMRC. There is, however, no effect on the investor, who is neither treated as having received taxable income nor entitled to a tax refund.

In the case of rights issues, managers may use cash held within the stocks and shares component to take up the rights, or the investor may make further cash subscriptions up to the annual limit. Alternatively an investor may wish to pay cash to enable the manager to take up the rights outside the account, providing the investments are transferred to the investor to be held outside the account.

Shares received from approved profit sharing and savings-related share option schemes and approved share incentive plans (see **CHAPTER 11**) are also qualifying investments and may be transferred within 90 days into the stocks and shares ISA free of capital gains tax, so long as, together with any other investments, they are within the annual subscription limit. There is no facility to transfer shares acquired under a public offer or following demutualisation of a building society or insurer into an ISA.

The shares held in a stocks and shares ISA are kept separate from the investor's other holdings for the purpose of the capital gains rules for matching disposals with acquisitions. If the investor withdraws his investments, their base cost for capital gains tax is the market value at the date of withdrawal.

[36.29] If tax relief on an ISA is found to have been wrongly given, HMRC may make a direct assessment outside the self-assessment system on either the account manager or the investor to recover the relief. In limited circumstances, and with the approval of HMRC, invalid ISAs may be 'repaired' rather than being closed, although any tax relief up to the date of the repair will still be forfeited.

[36.30] Certain ISAs are designated as stakeholder products, which are either cash deposit accounts or medium-term investment products that meet criteria set by government in relation to risks and charges.

The Government's aim with ISAs is to encourage more people to save but equities are not normally considered suitable for those who do not have a firm underlying core of low risk investments. Non-taxpayers cannot benefit from a tax-free account, and basic rate taxpayers may find any other benefits being eroded by the account charges.

16 and 17-year-olds

[36.31] Up to £5,100 a year may be invested in cash ISAs (but not stocks and shares ISAs) by those who are 16 or over at the end of the tax year but under 18. In the tax year in which the investor attains age 18, not more than £5,100 may be invested before the 18th birthday but the normal ISA limits apply thereafter.

If a parent gives money to his/her children to invest in ISAs, then unless the income arising from all capital provided by the parent is within the £100 limit, the income is treated as that of the parent until the child reaches age 18 and it must be reported on the parent's tax return (see **33.10**).

Tax points

[36.32] Note the following:

- If personal allowances are not otherwise fully used up, National Savings accounts still have a cash flow advantage over other bank accounts and building society accounts unless the bank or building society interest is received gross. This needs to be weighed against the interest rates on offer. See **CHAPTER 37**.
- Index-linked National Savings certificates offer inflation proofing plus a minimal amount of guaranteed extra interest, the best return being available on investments for the full term.
- Although investing for the full term shows the highest returns with National Savings certificates, they can be repaid gradually over the period, giving the opportunity to draw an effective tax-free income.
- Some of the National Savings products are attractive to higher rate taxpayers because of the tax-exempt income.

- A cash ISA can be invested in accounts with building societies and banks, including National Savings and supermarket bank accounts.
- There can appear to be a disproportionate extra tax charge on dividends or other savings income if an increase in other income takes the total income over the basic rate threshold. For an illustration, see **2.27**.
- A small investor can benefit from a wide range of investments through a unit or investment trust. The trust is exempt from tax on its gains. The investor pays tax on income and gains in the normal way, unless the investment is through an ISA. See **38.24** to **38.30**.
- If an investor has children under 16, it is possible to invest the maximum £3,000 in *each issue* of children's bonus bonds. See **36.11**.

37

Investing in banks and building societies

Investing in building societies and banks (ITA 2007, ss 850–873; FA 2005, ss 46–57 and Sch 2; FA 2006, s 95; FA 2007, s 53; FA 2009, s 45)

[37.1] Investing in building societies and banks is generally regarded as a low risk investment, despite the difficulties encountered by Northern Rock plc in 2007 as a result of which the Government took the bank into temporary public ownership. Some protection is available under the Financial Services Compensation Scheme. The compensation limit for protected deposits is £50,000 per person for claims against firms declared in default from 7 October 2008. Detailed guidance is available at www.fscs.org.uk.

The compensation scheme does not cover investments in building society permanent interest bearing shares (see **37.6**). Nor does it cover investments in offshore banks and building societies in the Channel Islands and Isle of Man, although some UK banks and building societies may offer their own protection for those who save with their offshore subsidiaries.

There are various alternative finance arrangements, particularly to meet the requirements of Islamic law, under which interest is not received but the arrangements have a similar effect (see **2.10**). Receipts that equate economically with interest are taxed on the same basis as interest.

Building societies and banks, including the National Savings Bank, notify HMRC how much interest has been paid to customers, no matter how small. This includes interest payable to those who are not ordinarily resident in the UK (see **41.25**).

Income tax is not deducted from bank and building society interest paid to companies (see **3.5**), Individual Savings Account managers (see **36.28**) and charities (see **43.4**). Nor is tax deducted from interest on building society permanent interest-bearing shares (PIBS, see **37.6**), because they are within the definition of quoted Eurobonds (see **3.21**).

[37.2] Interest on some bank and building society accounts is exempt from tax. This applies to SAYE accounts linked to an employee share option scheme (see **11.10**) and Individual Savings Accounts (see **36.24** onwards). Interest on some National Savings and Investments products is paid gross (see **CHAP-TER 36**). Otherwise, interest paid to individuals by building societies and banks is paid after deduction of 20% tax, unless the recipient has registered to receive interest gross (see **37.4**) or the interest is paid gross because it arises under one of the following headings:

(a)   Certificates of deposit (including 'paperless' certificates) and sterling or foreign currency time deposits, providing the loan is not less than £50,000 and is repayable within five years.

(b)   General client deposit accounts with building societies or banks oper-ated by solicitors and others.

(c)   Offshore accounts, i.e. held at overseas branches of UK and foreign banks and building societies. (Note that from 22 April 2009, where an offshore fund holds more than 60% of its assets in interest-bearing (or economically similar) form, any distribution will be treated as a payment of yearly interest in the hands of a UK individual investor. This treatment already applies to UK corporate investors).

(d)   Bank and building society accounts held by someone who is not ordinarily resident in the UK and has provided a declaration to that effect stating their principal residential address.

Interest under headings (a) and (b) is taxed in the same way as any other UK interest received in full. Interest on offshore accounts under heading (c) is taxed as foreign income (see **41.13**). Interest under heading (d) usually escapes UK tax (see **41.35**).

Interest counts as income for tax purposes according to the date when it is credited to the recipient's account. It is not apportioned over the period when it accrues. Whether tax has been deducted by the payer or not, the recipient may have to pay some more tax or claim some back, depending on his tax position.

[37.3] Bank and building society interest paid to trustees is also net of 20% tax, unless it is excluded under heading (a) or (c) above or it is paid to non-resident trustees of discretionary and accumulation trusts of which the beneficiaries are not ordinarily resident in the UK, providing the trustees have given the bank or building society a declaration to that effect.

Receiving bank and building society interest gross (TMA 1970, s 99A; ITA 2007, ss 850–873)

[37.4] Although tax is normally deducted from interest paid by banks and building societies, it is possible to register to receive the interest in full if, for example, it is expected that total taxable income will be below available allowances. The relevant forms R85 may be obtained from banks, building societies and local authorities or at www.hmrc.gov.uk/forms/r85.pdf. A sepa-rate form is needed for each bank or building society account held. A parent can register the account of a child under 16 if the child's total income will be less than the personal allowance. Bear in mind that interest may be treated as the parent's for tax purposes (see (a) at **33.10**).

Written notice must be given straight away to banks and building societies that are paying interest gross if the recipient's circumstances change such that interest should no longer be paid gross. The tax office should also be informed of any tax that may have to be paid. Where tax has been underpaid, it will be collected either by adjustment to a PAYE coding or through self-assessment. A penalty of up to £3,000 may be charged if certification to receive interest gross is given carelessly or deliberately or if notification that interest should no longer be paid gross is not given.

It is not possible to register some accounts and not others. It must be expected that the recipient will have *no tax liability at all* in order to be eligible. If registration is not possible because, for example, income is just above available allowances, a refund can be claimed as soon as at least £50 tax is owing. It is not necessary to wait until the end of the tax year.

For 2010/11 a refund is due to the extent that the grossed-up amount of the interest is covered by personal allowances or falls within the 10% rate for savings.

Building societies: conversion to banks, takeovers, mergers (FA 1988, Sch 12; TCGA 1992, s 217)

[37.5] Building societies are able to convert to companies under the Building Societies Act 1986. If they do, they are subject to normal company and bank legislation. Possible adverse consequences of conversion for building society members are prevented by specific rules which provide that members are not liable to capital gains tax (CGT) on rights to acquire shares in the company in priority to other subscribers, or at a discount, or on rights to acquire shares free of charge; these provisions apply whether the rights are obtained directly or through trustees. As and when the shares are disposed of, there will be a capital gain equal to the excess of the proceeds over the amount (if any) paid for the shares which may be covered by the annual CGT exemption if not already used.

Similar rules apply when a building society is taken over by a company rather than being converted.

Where a cash payment is received on a conversion or takeover, the payments are not chargeable to income tax. Cash payments to *deposit* account holders are also exempt from CGT (since such an account represents a loan, i.e. a simple debt, gains on which are exempt (see **4.10**)). Presumably cash payments to borrowers are also exempt, since they do not derive from an asset. Cash payments to share account holders are not exempt but in many cases the amounts concerned will be covered by the CGT annual exemption in any event so that calculations will not be necessary. If taxpayers are unable to make the necessary calculations for their tax returns, HMRC will, if asked, use their computer programme to produce the figures. See HMRC's Tax Bulletin 34 of April 1998 for detailed comments on both free shares and cash bonuses.

As far as building society *mergers* are concerned, HMRC's view is that any payments on the merger (whether paid in cash or credited to an account) are chargeable to income tax. Such payments would be treated in the same way as other income from the building society. Tax would be deducted at 20%, higher rate taxpayers would have to pay further tax and non-taxpayers would be able to claim a repayment. Taxpayers need to make appropriate entries on their tax returns.

Building society permanent interest bearing shares (ITA 2007, ss 619, 850–873; CTA 2009, s 302; TCGA 1992, s 117)

[37.6] Building societies may issue a special type of share — permanent interest bearing shares (PIBS). These shares are acquired through and listed on the Stock Exchange and are freely transferable, dealing charges being incurred on buying and selling. If the building society fails investors are not entitled to compensation, and PIBS are irredeemable, so proceeds received on sale will depend on prevailing interest rates and the soundness of the building society. Interest on PIBS is paid gross. For non-corporate shareholders PIBS are within the definition of qualifying corporate bonds (see **38.6**) and are exempt from CGT, so that no allowable losses may be created. They are also within the accrued income scheme (see **36.19**), so that adjustments for accrued interest are made when they are transferred.

For companies, the accrued income scheme does not apply. Dividends, interest and capital gains on the PIBS are dealt with under the loan relationships rules (see **3.5**).

Where PIBS are issued to existing members in priority to other people the right to buy them does not result in a capital gains tax charge.

National Savings Accounts (ITTOIA 2005, s 691)

[37.7] National Savings & Investments (NS&I) offer easy access savings accounts and investment accounts (and interest is still paid on dormant ordinary accounts). They also offer accounts that are eligible for the cash component of ISAs (see **36.24** onwards).

After 31 July 2004 ordinary accounts became dormant and holders may only access the accounts either to close them or to transfer them to an easy access savings account. So long as ordinary accounts remain open, however, the account balances will continue to earn interest. Interest is credited annually on 31 December without deduction of income tax (see **36.2** for the way in which tax is collected). The first £70 of interest on ordinary accounts is and will continue to be exempt from tax.

The easy access savings account is card based and account holders receive quarterly statements. Accounts may be opened and operated by telephone, by post, on the internet, or at post office branches and may also be operated via

ATM machines. The minimum balance is £100 and the maximum is £2 million (£4 million for joint accounts). Deposits are subject to a £10 minimum, and up to £300 may be withdrawn daily. Interest rates are variable and paid gross on 31 March annually. The rates are tiered depending on the amount deposited. Unlike the ordinary account, there is no exempt slice of interest and the full amount earned must be declared on tax returns.

The investment account is an easy access passbook savings account which pays interest on 31 December annually at varying rates depending on the amount invested. The minimum balance is £20 and the maximum is £1 million. No notice is required for withdrawals. Although the interest is liable to tax, it is paid gross, which gives a cash flow advantage compared with investing in other banks or building societies if interest must be paid net (i.e the investor is not entitled to register to receive interest gross).

In addition to their savings accounts, NS&I have a wide range of other investments. These are dealt with in **36.4**.

Tax points

[37.8] Note the following:

- Failure to register to receive interest gross does not prohibit repayment of overpaid tax and it is possible to make an interim claim before the end of the tax year.
- It is not possible to register to receive interest gross unless it is expected that *all* income will be covered by available allowances (i.e. it is expected that there will be no tax liability at all).
- Even if most of bank and building society interest is covered by allowances, it is not possible to register some accounts and not others. It is all or nothing.
- If a person has registered to receive bank and building society interest gross there is no difference in tax treatment between investing in National Savings accounts and investing in accounts with other banks and building societies. It will therefore be necessary to compare the rates of interest on offer. If a person cannot register but has allowances available to set against interest, there will be a cash flow benefit from a National Savings account, because for other accounts it will usually be necessary to wait for a tax refund.
- If a person has registered to receive interest gross, care will need to be taken in the case of rolled-up interest on, for example, a National Savings guaranteed equity bond (see **36.13**). Even though the bond will have been held for five years, all of the interest is counted as income of the tax year in which the bond matures.
- When filling in a tax return, it is necessary to include interest received on current bank accounts, as well as interest on savings accounts.
- A cash windfall received on a building society takeover/conversion, is liable to CGT, (although the gain may well be covered by the CGT annual exemption). A cash windfall on a building society *merger* is

liable to income tax, and will be received net of 20% tax. Further tax will be due from a higher rate taxpayer, but a non-taxpayer (or those who pay tax at less than 20%) may be entitled to a refund.

- An investor in a building society ISA, is a member of the building society and will thus qualify if there is an offer of free shares on the conversion of the building society to a company.

- It is only the general client deposit accounts maintained by solicitors and others on which interest is received without tax being deducted, and not designated accounts which they have specifically opened for a particular client or their own accounts for office monies.

38

Investing in stocks and shares

Background

[38.1] The term 'quoted securities' has in general been replaced in the tax legislation by 'listed securities'. For EU countries (and Iceland, Liechtenstein and Norway) listed securities means securities listed by a competent authority and admitted to trading on a recognised stock exchange. For other countries it means securities admitted to trading by a recognised stock exchange. AIM securities are unlisted.

Many of the provisions in the capital gains legislation deal with stocks and shares acquired many years ago, in respect of which the old terminology may still apply. For simplicity, the terms 'quoted' and 'unquoted' have been retained in this chapter.

The principal securities that may be acquired when investing through the Stock Exchange are company shares or loan stock, government stocks, local authority loan stock and building society permanent interest bearing shares (see **37.6**). Other investments may include unquoted company stocks and shares and unquoted local authority loans (see **36.15**).

The treatment of foreign stocks and shares is dealt with at **41.25** (with 'foreign' meaning that the issuing company is not resident in the UK).

There are various special provisions relating to trading on the Stock Exchange by broker/dealers, including provisions for stock lending and manufactured payments. Where shares are held as trading assets (either by dealers or others such as banks), dividends and other distributions received, and also manufactured payments treated as received, are treated as trading profits (and manufactured payments made are deducted as trading expenses). The chargeable (or allowable) amount excludes tax credits.

Stamp duty is payable on most transactions in stocks and shares, usually at ½%, but higher rates apply in some circumstances. The provisions are outlined in CHAPTER 6.

Tax treatment of income from stocks and shares

Dividends (CTA 2010, s 1109; ITA 2007, ss 6–21)

[38.2] Dividends paid by companies on their shares represent a distribution of profits to the members. The shareholder receives a tax credit of 1/9th of the cash amount of the dividend, representing 10% of the tax credit inclusive amount. Basic rate taxpayers have no further tax to pay, higher rate taxpayers have to pay a further 22.5% and taxpayers with income in excess of £150,000 have to pay a further 32.5%. Non-taxpayers cannot, however, claim a refund. Tax credits may be available to non-residents under the terms of double tax treaties (see **41.37**).

Scrip options (CTA 2010, s 1049; ITTOIA 2005, ss 410–414)

[38.3] Where scrip shares are taken up by an individual, instead of a cash dividend from a UK resident company (a scrip dividend or stock dividend), the cash dividend forgone is treated as income, unless it is different from the market value of the shares by 15% or more. In that event the deemed income is the market value of the shares on the first day of dealing. The recipient is treated as having a notional tax credit of 1/9th, which is treated in the same way as an actual tax credit.

If scrip dividend options are taken up by personal representatives, the gross equivalent is treated as income of the estate.

Where scrip dividend options are taken up by trustees of discretionary trusts (except trusts in which the settlor retains an interest – see below), the gross equivalent is treated as income liable to the 42.5% dividend trust rate (see **42.28**), with a notional tax credit of 10%. The capital gains tax (CGT) effect is dealt with at **38.20**.

Where scrip dividends are issued to a company, or to a trust in which the settlor retains an interest, they are not treated as income, and have a capital gains base cost of nil. This also applies to scrip dividends issued to a life interest trust unless the scrip dividend is income of the life beneficiary under trust law. If the trustees take the view that the scrip dividend belongs to the life tenant, the shares are effectively treated as acquired directly by the life tenant outside the trust's holding of shares (except in Scotland, where the rules are different — see HMRC Statement of Practice 4/94), and the life tenant is treated as having notional income in the same way as if he had acquired the shares directly.

Some companies have dividend reinvestment plans (DRIPs), under which shareholders use their dividends to acquire shares bought on the market by the company on their behalf. There is, however, a cost to the shareholder because part of the dividend is used to cover the cost of brokers' fees and stamp duty. The dividend is taxable as income, with the cash forgone representing the cost of the new shares.

Interest (ITA 2007, ss 6–21, Pt 15)

[38.4] Interest paid by companies and local authorities on quoted stocks is paid gross. Companies and local authorities may also pay other interest to another company or local authority, or to a pension fund, without deducting tax (see **3.21** for details). Other interest is paid after deduction of tax. Interest on government stocks is paid gross unless the holder applies to receive it net.

Where tax is deducted, those liable at a rate other than 20% will either have further tax to pay or be entitled to a refund. See **36.2** for the way tax is collected and **36.19** for the special accrued income scheme provisions that may apply to individuals in relation to interest-bearing securities. The treatment of interest received by companies is dealt with at **3.5**.

There are some special provisions for discounted securities held by personal investors (see **38.31**).

Capital gains treatment of stocks (TCGA 1992, ss 104–105, 108, 115–117 and Sch 9; FA 1996, s 96)

Companies

[38.5] A company's gains and losses on disposal of most loan stock are brought into account in calculating the company's income under the 'loan relationships' rules outlined at **3.5**. This does not apply to disposals of 5½% Treasury Stock 2008/12, which is outside the 'loan relationships' rules and is exempt under the capital gains rules, so that there can be neither a chargeable gain nor an allowable loss. Nor do the loan relationships rules apply to certain non-trading increases and decreases in the value of derivatives, which are dealt with under the capital gains rules.

As far as loan stock is concerned, the distinction between qualifying and non-qualifying corporate bonds for individuals (see **38.6**) does not apply to a company's holdings, and the definition of a qualifying corporate bond for companies is *any* asset that represents a loan relationship (as to which see **3.5**). See **38.34** for the treatment in takeovers where shares are exchanged for corporate bonds or vice versa.

Individuals

[38.6] As far as individuals, personal representatives and trustees are concerned, government stocks, qualifying corporate bonds and local authority stocks are exempt from CGT, so that there are neither chargeable gains nor allowable losses when they are disposed of (subject to some special rules for losses on qualifying corporate bonds (see **38.36**)).

Qualifying corporate bonds are quoted or unquoted non-convertible sterling loan stock purchased or issued on commercial terms after 13 March 1984. Building society permanent interest bearing shares (see **37.6**) are also within the definition of qualifying corporate bonds for individuals (but not for companies). Profits and losses on certain securities issued at a deep discount are dealt with under the income tax rather than the capital gains provisions (see **38.31**). Index-linked securities that are outside the deeply discounted securities provisions (i.e. those that are linked to the value of a share index) are also outside the definition of qualifying corporate bond and are thus chargeable to CGT.

The capital gains exemption for qualifying corporate bonds cannot be used to avoid income tax by selling just before an interest date, because of the accrued income provisions (see **36.19**). There are special provisions for company reorganisations to ensure that the appropriate exemption is given on loan stock converted into shares or vice versa (see **38.32**).

Disposals of interest-bearing stocks that are not government stocks or qualifying corporate bonds (i.e. non-sterling loan stock, loan stock that may be converted into shares, loans that are not commercial loans and loan stock acquired before 14 March 1984) are subject to CGT (unless they are deeply discounted securities within the income tax charge). The same matching rules apply as for shares (see **38.17**).

Capital gains treatment of shares (TCGA 1992, ss 35, 53–55, 104–110 and Sch 2)

[38.7] The rules governing the CGT implications of share disposals have been changed so frequently that this area has become one of the most complicated in the tax legislation and we now have the situation where there are two separate sets of rules running side by side (one for corporate shareholders (see **38.8**) and one for shareholders other than companies (see **38.17**)). It is not possible for this book to deal with all the complexities of share disposals, and the rules discussed below cover the tax treatment of such disposals in the current tax year.

It must be remembered that the provisions outlined below may well not affect individuals with modest holdings. If a person does not regularly buy and sell, he may acquire shares in a company by a single purchase and sell them by a single sale, so unless there have been rights issues, takeovers, etc., the calculation merely requires a comparison of the cost with the sale proceeds. If any gains arising are below the annual capital gains exemption (£10,100 for 2010/11) it may not be necessary to show calculations of gains in a tax return.

If, however, the transaction produced a loss, calculations would have to be shown in order to claim loss relief.

Example 1

Shareholder acquired 2,000 shares in A plc in June 2001 for £8,000 (including acquisition costs) and sold them in May 2010 for £10,500 (net of selling costs). He had no other capital transactions in 2010/11.

Since the 2010/11 annual exemption is £10,100, any gains arising are clearly exempt. If the proceeds had been £6,500 there would have been an allowable loss of £1,500.

Disposals by corporate shareholders

[38.8] The rules detailed at **38.9** to **38.16** apply to disposals by companies where gains/losses are not otherwise exempt under the substantial shareholding exemption (**3.31**). They also applied to taxpayers other than companies for disposals prior to 6 April 2008 only.

Disposals are matched with acquisitions in the following order (subject to the same treatment as outlined in **38.17** for scrip and rights shares, except for scrip dividend option shares, which are treated as normal scrip shares (see **38.20**)):

(a)   Acquisitions on the same day as the disposal.
(b)   Acquisitions within the previous nine days (and no indexation allowance is available on the disposal).
(c)   The post-1982 pool (**38.9**).
(d)   The pre-1982 pool (**38.11**).
(e)   Pre-6 April 1965 acquisitions that are not included in the pre-1982 pool, latest first (**38.13**) .
(f)   Acquisitions after disposal, earliest first.

Where partly paid shares are acquired, the instalments of the purchase price qualify for any available indexation allowance from the date the shares are issued, unless they are paid more than twelve months later, in which case they qualify from the date they are paid.

Shares acquired on or after April 1982

[38.9] Rules were introduced from 1 April 1985 (6 April 1985 for taxpayers other than companies), to treat each holding of quoted or unquoted shares of the same company and class acquired on or after 1 April 1982 (6 April 1982 for taxpayers other than companies) as a single asset. This asset is called a 'section 104 holding' in the legislation, but it is referred to in this chapter as a post-1982 pool. (Shares acquired by an employee that are subject to disposal restrictions are treated as being of a different class from any other shares held). Post-1982 pools grow with acquisitions and are depleted by disposals.

Indexation

[38.10] Indexation allowance on post-1982 pools is worked out from the month in which the expenditure was incurred. The holdings are maintained at both an unindexed value and an indexed value, and the indexed value is uplifted by further indexation every time an event occurs that alters the value of a holding (such as a purchase or a sale, but not a bonus issue (**38.18**). Unlike other indexation allowance calculations, the indexation adjustment on the post-1982 pool should strictly not be rounded to three decimal places. If the index has fallen since the previous event, no adjustment is made to the indexed value. The post-1982 pool rules were introduced on 1 April 1985 (6 April 1985 for taxpayers other than companies) and an opening figure for the indexed value was required at that date, working out indexation allowance on each acquisition from 1 April 1982 (6 April 1982) onwards. (If the calculation was delayed until the time of the first event affecting the value of the holding, it would not significantly affect the figures).

For individuals, personal representatives and trustees, no further shares are added to post-1982 pools after 5 April 1998 (except for scrip issues and rights shares (see **38.18**)) and each acquisition of shares after that date is treated as a separate, free-standing acquisition. Acquisitions continue to increase post-1982 pools for company shareholders.

Example 2

A corporate investor acquired 5,000 shares in AB plc in May 1987 for £7,500 and a further 2,000 shares in December 1990 for £4,000. All the shares were sold in March 2010 for £28,000. The retail prices index was 101.9 for May 1987, 129.9 for December 1990 and 220.7 for March 2010. The capital gains computation is:

AB plc post-1982 share pool

	Number of shares	Unindexed value £	Indexed value £
May 1987 Bought	5,000	7,500	7,500
Dec 1990 Indexation on £7,500 from May 1987			
$\dfrac{129.9 - 101.9}{101.9}$			2,061
Bought	2,000	4,000	4,000
	7,000	11,500	13,561

March 2010 Indexation on
£13,561 from Dec 1990

$$\frac{220.7 - 129.9}{129.9}$$

			9,479
			23,040
Sold	(7,000)	(11,500)	(23,040)
Amounts c/fwd	—	—	—

CGT computation for March 2010 disposal:

Proceeds	28,000
Indexed cost	(23,040)
Chargeable gain	4,960

It is important to remember that indexation cannot increase or create a loss so if, in this example, the disposal proceeds were say £15,000 (i.e. between the cost and indexed value) then the indexation will simply reduce the gain to nil.

Shares acquired before April 1982

[38.11] When calculating the gain/loss on disposals of shares held on 1 April 1982 (6 April 1982 for taxpayers other than companies) different calculations will have to be made depending upon whether a general rebasing election has been made (see **4.15**).

Where a rebasing election has been made all shares of the same class in the same company held on 1 April 1982 (6 April 1982 for taxpayers other than companies), including any acquired before 6 April 1965, are treated as acquired at their 31 March 1982 market value and are regarded as a single asset. Any such holding is called a '1982 holding' in the legislation, but it is referred to in this chapter as a pre-1982 pool. Any gain/loss on a subsequent disposal is calculated using this March 82 value as the base cost.

If the rebasing election has not been made, then unless some of the shares in the company concerned were acquired before 6 April 1965, the single asset treatment still applies but when calculating a gain/loss on disposal two calculations are performed. The gain/loss is calculated using firstly the March 82 value as base cost and secondly the actual cost as the base cost, with the lower gain/ larger loss being taken for CGT purposes. If one calculation shows a loss and the other a gain, the transaction is treated as giving rise to neither a gain nor a loss. In both calculations, the indexation allowance is based on the *higher* of the cost and 31 March 1982 value. If some of the shares were acquired before 6 April 1965, then they must be kept separate from the pre-1982 pool. This does not apply to *quoted* shares if an election had been made (under provisions introduced in 1968) to treat them as acquired at their market value on 6 April 1965, in which case they are included in the pre-1982 pool at that value. The treatment of unpooled pre-6 April 1965 acquisitions is dealt with at **38.13** to **38.16**.

Where 31 March 1982 valuations of unquoted holdings are needed by several shareholders, HMRC Shares and Assets Valuation department (formerly known as Shares Valuation Division) will open negotiations with the shareholders or their advisers before being asked by a tax office, providing all shareholders with similar holdings will accept the value agreed. Someone with pre- and post-6 April 1965 holdings in the same unquoted company may, by concession, have them valued as a single holding, which may give a higher value per share. This does not affect the rules for matching disposals with acquisitions (see **38.8**).

Indexation

[38.12] For pre-1982 pools of shares the indexation allowance is calculated by taking the increase in the retail prices index between March 1982 and the month of disposal. Where a rebasing election has been made to treat all assets acquired before 31 March 1982 as being acquired at their market value on that date, the indexation allowance is based on that 31 March 1982 value. Where the election has not been made, the indexation calculation is based on the higher of the value of the shares at 31 March 1982 and their cost or, for shares held at 6 April 1965, their 6 April 1965 market value when using that value to calculate the gain or loss (see **38.13**). Where the rebasing election has been made, the pre-1982 pool can be maintained at both unindexed and indexed values in the same way as the post-1982 pool, although this is not provided for in the legislation. This can still be done even if there is no rebasing election, but figures would be required both for indexed cost and indexed 31 March 1982 value, basing indexation allowance in both cases on the higher of those two figures, but not so as to create or increase a loss. (For an illustration, see Example 8 at **38.18**).

Example 3

Quoted shares in CD plc are acquired by a company as follows:

	Number	Cost (£)
Between 6.4.65 and 5.4.82 (pre-1982 pool)	5,000	35,000
31.5.85 (post-1982 pool)	6,000	66,000

Sales	Number	Consideration (£)
16.3.10	10,000	270,000

Market value was £3 per share at 6 April 1965 and £8 per share at 31 March 1982. No election had been made to include shares acquired before 6 April 1965 in the pre-1982 pool nor a rebasing election to treat all assets acquired before 31 March 1982 as being acquired at 31 March 1982 value.

		Gain
	£	£
Sale of 10,000 on 16.3.10:		
Proceeds for sale out of post-1982 pool 6,000/10,000 × 270,000	162,000	
Indexed cost (see Example 4)	(152,988)	9,012
Sale of 4,000 shares in pre-1982 pool:		
Gain (see Example 5)		19,104
Giving total chargeable gains on CD plc shares in 2009/10 of		£28,116

Example 4

CD plc post-1982 pool	Num-ber of shares	Unin-dexed value	In-dexed value
		£	£
Bought: 31.5.85	6,000	66,000	66,000
Indexation from May 1985 to March 2010 (1.318)			86,988
			152,988
Sale: 16.3.10	(6,000)	(66,000)	(152,988)

Example 5

CD plc pre-1982 pool
5,000 shares cost £35,000, value at 31.3.82 £8
each = £40,000.

	£	£
Sale proceeds: 4,000/10,000 × 270,000	108,000	108,000
Cost: 4,000/5,000 × 35,000	(28,000)	
31.3.82 value: 4,000 × 8		(32,000)
Indexation allowance 1.778 on 31.3.82 value	(56,896)	(56,896)
	23,104 or	19,104
Lower gain		£19,104

655

Shares held on 6 April 1965 (TCGA 1992, Sch 2, Parts I and III)

[38.13] If a rebasing election has been made to treat all assets acquired before 31 March 1982 as acquired at their market value on that day, gains and losses are computed on that basis for both quoted and unquoted shares. Where the rebasing election has not been made, the procedure is as follows.

Unquoted securities

[38.14] For unquoted securities, the legislation requires two computations to be made, as follows.

(a) Firstly:

    (i) Calculate the gain or loss over the whole period of ownership.

    (ii) Adjust for the available indexation allowance based either on cost or 31 March 1982 value, whichever is higher (but not so as to create or increase a loss), then calculate the proportion of the resulting gain or loss that relates to the period after 5 April 1965 (but ignoring any period of ownership before 6 April 1945).

    (iii) As an alternative to the result in (ii), the taxpayer may make an irrevocable election to have the result computed by reference to the value of the asset on 6 April 1965, with indexation allowance based on the higher of 6 April 1965 value and 31 March 1982 value (but the indexation allowance cannot create or increase a loss). If this calculation would give a loss instead of a gain, the transaction is deemed to give neither gain nor loss. The election cannot give a greater loss than the amount by which the cost exceeds the sale proceeds.

    (Losses will not usually arise under either calculation because the costs of many years ago are being compared with current sale proceeds).

(b) Secondly, calculate the gain or loss as if the shares had been bought on 31 March 1982 at their market value on that date. The available indexation allowance is based on the higher of 31 March 1982 value and either cost or 6 April 1965 value according to which was used to give the result in the first computation (but not so as to create or increase a loss).

If both computations show a loss, the lower loss is taken, and if both show a gain, the lower gain is taken. See Example 6. If one computation shows a gain and the other a loss, the result is treated as neither gain nor loss. If, however, the first computation has already resulted in no gain, no loss, that result is taken and the 31 March 1982 value calculation is not made. Where a gain arises it will be obvious in many cases that the lower gain will result from using the 31 March 1982 calculation, without making the alternative calculation. As far as losses are concerned, there can only be an allowable loss if the sale proceeds are below both the cost and the 31 March 1982 value.

> *Example 6*
>
> 1,500 unquoted shares were acquired by a corporate investor on 6 October 1962 for £2 per share.

Market value considered to be £2.50 per share at 6 April 1965 and £8 per share at 31 March 1982. No rebasing election had been made to treat all assets acquired before 31 March 1982 as being acquired at 31 March 1982 value.

The shares were sold on 6 April 2010 for £25 per share.

Assume RPI from March 1982 to April 2010 is 1.778.

First computation

Using time apportionment	£	Using 6 April 1965 market value	£
Sale 1,500 shares @ £25	37,500	Sale	37,500
Cost 6.10.62 @ £2	(3,000)	6.4.65 MV	
		1,500 @ £2.50	(3,750)
Indexation allowance (1.778 x March 82 value of £12,000)	(21,336)		(21,336)
Overall gain	13,164		

Proportion after 6.4.65

$$\frac{6.4.65 - 6.4.10}{6.10.62 - 6..4.10} = \frac{45}{47.5}$$

Gain	12,471		12,414
Lower gain is			£12,414

Second computation

Sale 1,500 shares @ £25			37,500
31.3.82 value @ £8			(12,000)
Indexation allowance			(21,336)
Gain			4,164

Both computations produce a gain so the lower gain is taken of £4,164.

Quoted securities

[38.15] For quoted securities, unless a rebasing election has been made, or the shares on hand at 6 April 1965 are included at their value at that date in the pre-1982 pool (see **38.11**), two computations are also made. The procedure is similar to that for unquoted securities, except that time apportionment does not apply. In the first computation, the sale proceeds are compared with both the cost and the 6 April 1965 value and the lower gain or lower loss is taken. If one method shows a gain and the other a loss, the computation is treated as giving rise to neither gain nor loss. The available indexation allowance is deducted in each case (based on the higher of the cost/6 April 1965 value and 31 March 1982 value) but not so as to create or increase a loss. The second computation treats the shares as acquired at 31 March 1982 value (but the available indexation allowance is nonetheless based on cost/6 April 1965 value if it exceeds 31 March 1982 value). The lower gain or lower loss produced by the two computations is then taken. If one computation shows a loss and the other a gain, the result is neither a gain nor a loss. If the first computation has already given a no gain/no loss result, then the second computation is not made. As with unquoted securities, it will often be obvious that the lower gain will result from the 31 March 1982 calculation. Allowable losses will not arise except to the extent that the proceeds are less than the lowest of the cost, 6 April 1965 value and 31 March 1982 value.

Effect of the above rules

[38.16] The examples show that where a taxpayer has acquired shares at various times before and after 31 March 1982 the rules may require several calculations to be made. If the rebasing election has been made, the position is simpler because there are only two share 'pools' for any class of shares in any company, one covering all acquisitions up to 5 April 1982 (the pre-1982 pool) and the other all later acquisitions (the post-1982 pool). Even so, complications arise through scrip and rights issues, takeovers, etc. The calculations can be simplified by using the publications that detail 31 March values and other relevant information.

Disposals by individuals, personal representatives and trustees

[38.17] Finance Act 2008 greatly simplified the rules for share disposals by individuals, personal representative and trustees. For disposals after 5 April 2008 by such shareholders automatic rebasing to 31 March 1982 applies and there is no indexation allowance. Gains accruing on or after 23 June 2010 are instead taxed for individuals at a flat rate of 18% (or 28% for gains that exceed the basic rate band). For personal representatives and trustees, gains accruing on or after 23 June 2010 are taxed at a flat rate of 28%. Gains for individuals, trustees and personal representative that accrued prior to 23 June 1020 were taxed at a flat rate of 18%.

Furthermore, the simpler identification rules set out below have removed much of the complexity associated with CGT computations for companies.

Disposals on or after 6 April 2008 by individuals, personal representatives and trustees are matched with acquisitions in the following order:

(a)   Acquisitions on the same day as the disposal.

(b)   Acquisitions within 30 days after the disposal.

(c)   Assets in the (enlarged) 'section 104 holding'. This is the holding mentioned in **38.9** (and described elsewhere in this chapter as a post-1982 pool) as enlarged, where appropriate, to include shares acquired at any time before the date of the disposal. The allowable cost for this holding is the market value of such shares held at 31 March 1982 plus the cost of shares acquired since that date. Indexation allowance must be excluded because it was abolished for disposals after 5 April 2008. Where part of this holding is sold, a proportion of the allowable cost is deducted from the proceeds.

For the purpose of the matching rules, all the shares acquired on the same day are treated as having been acquired by a single transaction, with scrip and rights issue shares being treated as acquired when the original shares were acquired (see **38.18**). See, however, **11.31** for a special rule where some of the shares are acquired under HMRC approved employee share schemes.

Example 7

Investor (a basic rate taxpayer) acquired 2,000 shares in AB plc in 1981 for £4,000. Their market value at 31 March 1982 was £4,500. He acquired 3,000 shares for £8,000 in 1998 and 5,000 shares for £15,500 in 2003. He sold 5,000 shares for £25,000 in October 2010. There is a single pool (the enlarged 'section 104 holding') of 10,000 shares with an acquisition value of £28,000. Having sold 50% of the shares, he is entitled to set £14,000 of that value against the proceeds, giving a gain of £11,000. No indexation is available, so assuming that the annual exemption of £10,100 is available, CGT is payable at 18% on £900 = £162.

The 30-day rule in (*b*) prevents 'bed and breakfast' transactions, where shares are sold and bought back on the following day in order either to use the capital gains exemption or to produce losses to reduce chargeable gains. The rules do not prevent a spouse or civil partner repurchasing the shares on the market, providing the spouse or civil partner is the beneficial owner of the shares bought. Alternatively, a similar effect could be achieved by acquiring shares in a company in the same business sector. The above matching rules apply not only to shares but also to loan stock that is not exempt from CGT (see **38.6**).

Scrip and rights issues (TCGA 1992, ss 57, 122, 123, 126–132)

Corporate shareholders

[38.18] A scrip issue/bonus issue of shares to a corporate shareholder is treated as acquired at the same time as the shares out of which they arise. Where the original shares were in the post-1982 pool (**38.9**) it is not necessary to increase the indexed value of the pool to the date of the bonus issue— the number of shares in the pool is simply increased.

A rights issue is also treated as being acquired at the same time as the shares out of which they arise. Where the original shares were in the post-1982 pool, the number of shares, amount paid for them and indexation (to the date of the rights issue) is added to the pool. Where the original holding is in the pre-1982 pool (and earlier acquisitions) indexation is only available on the rights issue shares from the date of issue.

If rights are sold nil paid, the proceeds are treated as a part disposal of the holding, unless they are 'small', in which case they are deducted from the cost instead. Proceeds may be treated as 'small' if they are either not more than 5% of the value of the holding or they amount to £3,000 or less. The taxpayer may use the normal part disposal treatment if he wishes. (The value of the holding is arrived at by taking the ex-rights value of the existing shares plus the proceeds for the rights shares sold. If not all the rights shares were sold, those retained would also be valued at nil-paid price in this calculation.)

Example 8

A corporate taxpayer acquired 2,000 shares in EF plc on 23 February 1986 for £2,000. On 10 December 1987 there was a scrip issue of 1 for 2. On 19 October 2007 there was a rights issue of 1 for 6 at £2 per share. The ex-rights value of the shares was £3.00, giving a value of £9,000 for 3,000 shares.

EF plc post-1982 pool
If rights are taken up:

	Shares	Unindexed value £	Indexed value £
23.2.86	2,000	2,000	2,000
10.12.87 Scrip	1,000		
	3,000		
19.10.07 Rights	500		
Indexed February 1986 to October 2007 1.163			2,326
Rights cost		1,000	1,000
Pool values carried forward	3,500	3,000	5,326

If rights are sold nil paid for £1 per share = £500, which is 'small' being less than £3,000, even though more than 5% of (£9,000 + £500 =) £475:

	Shares	Unindexed value £	Indexed value £
Pool values bought forward	3,500	3,000	5,326
Less: Rights shares	(500)	(1,000)	(1,000)
Rights proceeds		(500)	(500)
Pool values carried forward	3,000	1,500	3,826

Example 9

In addition to the post-1982 pool in Example 8, the taxpayer had acquired 3,000 shares for £1,500 on 11 April 1979. These shares comprise the pre-1982 pool. The 31 March 1982 value of the shares was 75p per share. Rebasing election not made.

EF plc pre-1982 pool
If rights are taken up:

	Shares	Unin-dexed cost £	In-dexed cost £	Unin-dexed 31.3.82 value £	In-dexed 31.3.82 value £
At 31.3.82	3,000	1,500	1,500	2,250	2,250
10.12.87 Scrip	1,500				
	4,500				
19.10.07 Rights	750				
Indexn. March 1982 to Oct 2007 (1.630 × £2,250)			3,668		3,668
Rights cost		1,500	1,500	1,500	1,500
Pool values carried forward	5,250	3,000	6,668	3,750	7,418

If rights are sold nil paid for £1 per share:

	Shares	Unin-dexed cost £	In-dexed cost £	Unin-dexed 31.3.82 value £	In-dexed 31.3.82 value £
Pool values bought forward	5,250	3,000	6,668	3,750	7,418
Less: Rights shares	(750)	(1,500)	(1,500)	(1,500)	(1,500)
19.10.07 rights proceeds		(750)	(750)	(750)	(750)
Pool values carried forward	4,500	750	4,418	1,500	5,168

Although Examples 8 and 9 show small proceeds on a sale of rights being deducted from the value of the holding, if treating them as a part disposal would produce a gain covered by other capital losses (or for individuals etc the annual exemption), the part disposal treatment would be better. The part of the cost of the holding that is taken into account against the cash proceeds is arrived at in the same way as for cash on a takeover (see **38.32**).

Individual, personal representative or trustee shareholders

[38.19] For individual, personal representative or trustee shareholders, the rules detailed above for corporate shareholders apply equally, but within the greatly simplified regime that applies to such shareholders. Consequently any scrip/bonus or rights issue shares will enter the enlarged 'section 104 holding' and be taxed accordingly on a subsequent disposal.

Scrip dividend options (TCGA 1992, s 142)

[38.20] If individuals, personal representatives or trustees of discretionary trusts take scrip shares (stock dividends) instead of a dividend, the CGT cost is the amount treated as their net income (see **38.3**), not the grossed up equivalent. Scrip shares issued in lieu of dividends are treated as free-standing acquisitions.

Where scrip shares in lieu of a dividend are issued to a company, they are treated in the same way as ordinary scrip shares, i.e. there is no deemed cost and the shares are treated as acquired when the original shares were acquired.

The same applies if the recipient is a life interest trust unless the trustees treat the shares as income of the life tenant (see **38.3**). Where trustees adopt that treatment, the scrip shares do not go into the trust's holding at all, and are regarded as belonging to the life tenant directly, so that the life tenant is treated in the same way as other individuals, even if the shares are held by the trustees (except in Scotland, where the treatment is different).

Reliefs

Shares of negligible value (TCGA 1992, s 24)

[38.21] Where shares (or any other assets) have become of negligible value, it is possible to establish an allowable loss by claiming for them to be treated as if they had actually been disposed of either on the date of the claim or at a stipulated time within the two tax years before the tax year in which the claim is made, providing the shares were of negligible value on the chosen date. Details of quoted shares that are regarded as being of negligible value, and the date from which that applies, are published by HMRC. In the case of unquoted shares, the fact that the shares are of negligible value has specifically to be agreed with HMRC. Even though shares are on HMRC's list, it is not necessary to make a negligible value claim. If a claim has not been made before the time when the shares cease to exist, they are treated as disposed of at that time and a normal loss claim, rather than a negligible value claim, may then be made.

Relief against income for losses on shares in qualifying trading companies (ITA 2007, ss 131–151; CTA 2010, ss 68–90)

[38.22] Where an individual disposes of shares at a loss, or the shares become valueless, the loss is normally relievable, like any other capital loss, against gains on other assets. However, relief may be claimed instead against any other *income* of the tax year of loss or of the previous tax year if the shares disposed of are ordinary shares or stock:

(a)   in a 'qualifying trading company' for which the individual subscribed. (Where some shares were acquired other than by subscription, there are rules to identify which shares have been disposed of); or

(b)   which would have qualified for EIS income tax relief (see **29.17**), although the relief is not restricted to EIS shares.

A qualifying trading company is essentially a company that has, throughout the 6 years before the sale, been an unquoted trading company or the parent of such a trading group and its gross assets before and after the sale do not exceed £7 million and £8 million respectively. Note if a company has ceased to trade prior to sale, the relief is still available provided the cessation is not more than three years before the date of sale and in the three year period the company has not been an investment company or carried out non-trading activities). The claim to set off such losses takes priority over any claim for relief for trading losses. Claims must be made within one year from 31 January following the tax year of loss (e.g. by 31 January 2013 for a 2010/11 loss).

Where an investment company realises a loss on a disposal of ordinary unquoted shares in a qualifying trading company it may claim relief for the loss by setting it against its income (as opposed to its chargeable gains) of the same or preceding year provided the company making the disposal is an investment company on the date of the disposal and either:

(a)   has been an investment company for a continuous period of six years ending on that date; or

(b)   has been an investment company for a shorter continuous period ending on that date, and must not have been, before the beginning of that period, a 'trading company' or an 'excluded company'.

A claim for this relief must be submitted within two years of the end of the accounting period in which the loss arose.

Disposal by gift (TCGA 1992, ss 67, 165)

[38.23] Where shares or securities are disposed of by gift, the proceeds are regarded as being their open market value. If a gain arises, the donor and donee may make a joint election for the donee to adopt the donor's base cost for CGT purposes, but this right is only available if the gift is made by an individual or trustees and comprises shares or securities in an unquoted trading company, or in a quoted trading company in which the donor owns 5% of the shares, or the gift is immediately chargeable to inheritance tax, or would be if it were not covered by the donor's annual inheritance tax exemption and/or inheritance tax nil rate band (see **4.23** to **4.26**).

If a loss arises on a gift to or other transaction with a connected person — which broadly means close family of the donor and of his spouse or civil partner, trustees of family trusts and companies controlled by the donor — the loss is not allowed against gains generally but only against a gain on a subsequent transaction with the same person. This does not apply to gifts between spouses or civil partners, which are treated as made at neither a gain nor a loss (see **4.6**).

Investment funds/trusts and savings schemes

Authorised investment funds (CTA 2010, ss 612–620; CTA 2009, ss 487–497; ITA 2007, ss 504, 941–943: TCGA 1992, ss 99–99AA, 100; FA 1995, s 152; F(No 2)A 2005, ss 17, 18; SI 2006/964)

[38.24] Authorised investment funds (AIFs) consist of open-ended investment companies (OEICs) and authorised unit trusts (AUT). An OEIC is a company in which the shares may be continuously created or redeemed, depending on investor demand. An AUT is a professionally managed fund which enables an investor to obtain a wide spread of investments. There are various types of funds to suit particular circumstances, for example some aimed at capital growth and some at maximising income. This chapter deals only with authorised unit trusts (i.e. trusts authorised under the Financial Services and Markets Act 2000 or earlier legislation, which places certain restrictions on the investments the trust is able to make). Both OEICs and AUTs are treated essentially the same way for taxation purposes.

AIFs pay corporation tax at 20% on their taxable income (essentially interest income as they do not pay tax on dividends) and they are exempt from tax on capital gains (subject to various anti-avoidance provisions). Relief for management expenses is given against profits chargeable to corporation tax. Distributions to unit holders may be dividend distributions or interest distributions. An AIF can only pay interest distributions where its interest-bearing investments comprise more than 60% of the total market value of the trust fund. Where certain conditions are met, an AIF can elect to be treated as a tax elected fund (TEF). This essentially means that there will be no corporation tax levied on its taxable income provided such income is distributed to its shareholders. This is achieved by the TEF receiving a deduction, for tax purposes, equal to the amount of interest distributions made.

[38.25] The tax treatment of individual investors is broadly similar to the position had they invested directly. Dividend distributions (whether from a TEF or an AIF) carry a tax credit of 1/9th of the cash amount, whether they are from equity based funds or from funds that invest wholly or partly in interest-bearing securities. Interest distributions (whether from a TEF or an AIF) are paid net of 20% tax. Foreign investors are able to receive interest free of UK tax in some circumstances, or may be able to claim double tax relief. See **41.11** for the inheritance tax treatment of those not domiciled in the UK. An individual investor's gains are similarly taxed as if the funds had been invested directly, except that gains on sales of gilt units are taxable, whereas gains on gilts themselves are not. 'Equalisation' payments received on the acquisition of new units are not taxed as income. They reduce the cost of an individual's units for CGT.

[38.26] Dividend distributions paid to companies from the AIF are franked investment income and are not liable to corporation tax, unless part of the AIFs income is not dividend income, in which case an equivalent part of the dividend distribution from the AIF is treated as interest received net of 20% tax. This amount is stated on tax vouchers. Any such amount is brought into account along with interest distributions as part of the company's income chargeable to corporation tax. The income tax suffered at source is deducted from the tax payable by the company, but if the investor company is claiming an income tax repayment, the repayment cannot exceed the company's proportion of the AIFs corporation tax liability on the gross income. The trustees are required to state their net liability to corporation tax on the distribution statement sent to the company and this is usually expressed as an amount per unit held so that the company can calculate the maximum income tax available for repayment. Gains and losses on disposals of a company's unit trust investments also form part of the corporation tax profit or loss (see 3.5). Anti-avoidance provisions apply from 22 June 2010 to ensure that a corporate investor cannot make use of an AIF to create a credit for UK tax where no UK tax has been paid.

Investment trusts (CTA 2010, ss 1158–1165; ITA 2007, ss 276–277; TCGA 1992, s 100; FA 2009, s 45)

[38.27] Investment trusts are actually companies and not trusts, and investors buy shares in them in the usual way. Some trusts with a limited life are split level trusts, i.e. they have income shares that receive most of the trust's income and a fixed capital sum on liquidation, and capital shares that receive little or no income but get most of the capital surplus (if any) on a liquidation.

Investment trusts are exempt from tax on their capital gains if they are approved investment trusts (approval has to be given every year by HMRC) but the gains may only be reinvested and cannot be distributed as dividends. There are anti-avoidance provisions to prevent the exemption being exploited either by transferring a company's business to a company that is, or later becomes, an investment trust, or by transferring assets intra-group to a company that is, or later becomes, an investment trust. Investment trusts are normally charged to corporation tax in the normal way, which puts them at a disadvantage as against unit trusts. However, from 1 September 2009 an investment trust can opt to receive a deduction, for tax purposes, for the interest distributions made to its shareholders. This enables it to invest in interest producing assets tax efficiently and moves the point of taxation for income received from the investment trust to the shareholder with the result that shareholders face broadly the same tax treatment as they would have had they owned the interest bearing assets directly. The income and gains of UK Real Estate Investment Trusts are exempt from tax in certain circumstances (see 32.32).

Venture capital trusts

[38.28] Individuals may invest in qualifying unquoted trading companies through a venture capital trust, one of a number of government incentives to promote investment and enterprise. See **29.25** to **29.29**.

Savings schemes

[38.29] Unit trusts, open-ended investment companies and investment trusts operate monthly savings schemes, which give the investor the advantage of 'pound cost averaging', i.e. fluctuations in prices are evened out because overall investors get more units/shares when the price is low and fewer when it is high.

Individual Savings Accounts (ITTOIA 2005, ss 694–701; TCGA 1992, s 151; SI 1989/469; SI 1998/1870)

[38.30] Investors can invest up to £10,100 a year in unit and investment trusts and open-ended investment companies through the stocks and shares component of ISAs. For details of ISAs generally see **36.24** to **36.31**.

Personal Equity Plans (PEPs) were introduced in January 1987, but no further PEP investments have been permitted since 5 April 1999. Existing PEPs became stocks and shares ISAs from 6 April 2008.

Deeply discounted securities (ITTOIA 2005, ss 427–460)

[38.31] The provisions for deeply discounted securities outlined below do not apply to companies, because a company's gains and losses are dealt with under the 'loan relationships' rules (see **3.5**).

Special rules apply to all securities issued at a discount to private investors. The accrued income scheme (see **36.19**) does not apply to securities within these provisions. Securities are deeply discounted securities where their issue price is lower than the redemption price by more than ½% per year between issue and redemption, or, if that period exceeds 30 years, by more than 15%. The provisions do not cover shares, gilt-edged securities (except for gilt strips, for which there are special rules), indexed securities that are linked to the value of a share index, life assurance policies and capital redemption policies.

There is no CGT charge on deeply discounted securities, and investors are charged to income tax in the tax year of disposal or redemption on the profit made. For securities acquired before 27 March 2003 the expenses of acquisition and disposal may be deducted. If a loss arises on securities acquired before that date, a claim may be made by the first anniversary of 31 January following the relevant tax year to set the loss against the total income of that tax year. Trustees may only set losses against income from discounted securities of the tax year of loss or, if that is insufficient, of a later tax year. When someone dies, they are treated as disposing of the securities to the personal representatives at market value at the date of death, income tax being chargeable accordingly. Transfers from personal representatives to legatees are treated as at market value at the date of the transfer, with income tax being charged on the estate on the difference between the value at death and the value at the date of the transfer.

Takeovers, mergers and reconstructions (TCGA 1992, ss 57, 116, 126–131, 135, 136, 138A and Sch 5AA)

Share and cash consideration

[38.32] An exchange of new shares for old does not normally involve a chargeable gain, instead the new shares are treated as standing in the shoes of the old both as regards acquisition date and cost. This often happens when one company (whether or not its shares are quoted on the Stock Exchange) acquires another (either quoted or unquoted) by issuing its own shares to the holders of the shares in the company which is being taken over (known as 'paper for paper' exchanges).

Where both cash and new shares are received, a partial disposal arises, in the proportion that the cash itself bears to the market value of the securities acquired in exchange.

Part of a takeover package may take the form of shares or securities to be issued at some future date, the number of such shares or securities depending for example on future profits (known as an earn-out right). For the treatment of such transactions, including the treatment where the future consideration is to be in cash, see **28.8** to **28.10**.

Example 10

X Ltd owns 10,000 shares in a company, A, which cost £6,000 in September 1983. The shares do not qualify for the substantial shareholding exemption.

Company A is taken over by company B on 6 March 2010, indexation allowance from September 1983 to March 2010 being 1.564.

Scenario (a)
12,000 shares in company B, valued at £30,000, are received in exchange for the 10,000 shares in company A.
No chargeable gain arises on the £24,000 excess value of the company B shares over the cost of the company A shares.
Instead the 12,000 shares in company B are regarded as having the same £6,000 base value as the 10,000 company A shares which they replace.

Scenario (b)
12,000 shares in company B, valued at £24,000, together with £6,000 in cash are received in exchange for the 10,000 shares in company A, the shares in company A having an indexed cost of £15,384. The cash represents 20% of the total consideration and the shares 80%.

The 12,000 shares in company B have base values as follows:

Unindexed value 80% × £6,000	£4,800
Indexed value 80% × £15,384	£12,307

The indexed cost to set off against the £6,000 cash received for the part disposal is 20% × £15,384 = £3,077 reducing the gain to £2,923.

If X had been an individual, the treatment would have been the same, except that indexation allowance would not be available and the gain would have been taxed at a flat rate (of either 18% or 28%, depending upon his personal tax position (see **4.2**)).

Corporate bonds

Qualifying corporate bonds

[38.33] As indicated at **38.6**, qualifying corporate bonds are not chargeable assets for CGT, and can create neither a chargeable gain nor allowable loss (subject to the special rules at **38.36**). Sometimes on a takeover or reorganisation qualifying corporate bonds may be exchanged for shares or vice versa. When qualifying corporate bonds are exchanged for shares the shares are treated as acquired at their market value at the date of the exchange. If shares are exchanged for qualifying corporate bonds, the gain or loss on the shares at the date of the exchange is calculated and 'frozen' until the qualifying corporate bonds are disposed of, when the frozen gain or loss crystallises. No gain or loss can be established on the bonds themselves (with the exception stated at **38.36**). In some cases, this could mean that a gain is chargeable even if the qualifying corporate bonds have become virtually worthless. One solution may be to give them to a charity. The frozen gain on the shares would not then be charged, nor would the charity have any tax liability when it disposed of the bonds. A frozen gain escapes being charged to tax if the taxpayer dies. If a frozen gain arises on shares held by personal representatives, however, it is charged when the loan stock is disposed of by the personal representatives, or when disposed of by a legatee following the transfer of the stock to him by the personal representatives.

Where a frozen gain would otherwise become chargeable, it may be deferred if an equivalent investment is made by subscribing for unquoted shares under the enterprise investment scheme provisions (see **29.20**). Where shares are exchanged partly for cash and partly for qualifying corporate bonds, the enterprise investment scheme deferral relief may be claimed on the gain on the cash element.

It is possible that when shares are exchanged for qualifying corporate bonds, a gain on the disposal of the shares could have qualified for entrepreneurs' relief (see **29.2** to **29.10** for full details of the relief). Under the previous operation of the relief which applied before 23 June 2010 (see **29.9**) if entrepreneurs' relief was claimed, the frozen gain was reduced by 4/9ths when it crystallised. However, where the exchange takes place on or after 23 June

2010 different rules apply. An election can be made for the gain not to be deferred but instead brought into charge at that time and entrepreneurs' relief claimed (see further **29.9**). If no election is made and the gain is deferred it is unlikely that the frozen gain will qualify for entrepreneurs' relief when it crystallises. Where gains were deferred on an exchange of shares for qualifying corporate bonds before 6 April 2008, when the frozen gain comes into charge entrepreneurs' relief can be claimed on the first disposal of qualifying corporate bonds after that date.

[38.34] For company investors, all loan stock is included within the definition of a 'qualifying corporate bond' (see **38.6**). Where a company receives shares in exchange for corporate bonds, the gain or loss on the bond is taken into account in computing the company's income under the 'loan relationships' rules (see **3.5**). If a company receives corporate bonds in exchange for shares, the 'frozen gain or loss' treatment outlined above applies, with the frozen gain or loss on the shares being brought in as a *capital* gain or loss when the bonds are disposed of. (Any gain or loss on the disposal of the bonds themselves will be brought into account under the 'loan relationships' rules).

Non-qualifying corporate bonds

[38.35] If, on a takeover, shares are exchanged for non-qualifying corporate bonds, the bonds stand in the shoes of the shares as regards date and cost of acquisition, with a later disposal of the bond giving a capital gain or loss at that time.

Losses on qualifying corporate bonds (TCGA 1992, ss 254, 255)

[38.36] Since qualifying corporate bonds are exempt from CGT, no allowable loss can arise under the normal rules. For qualifying corporate bonds issued before 17 March 1998, relief for losses may be claimed according to the rules outlined at **4.28** if the claimant made the loan to a UK resident trader. Someone to whom the bond has been assigned cannot claim the relief. A claim may also be made when the value of such a loan has become negligible (see **4.27**). The relief for losses outlined above does not apply to individuals for bonds issued on or after 17 March 1998. Nor does it apply to companies, because a company's gains and losses are dealt with under the 'loan relationships' rules (see **3.5**).

See **38.33** and **38.34** for the treatment of losses on qualifying corporate bonds acquired on a takeover and **38.35** for the treatment of non-qualifying corporate bonds.

Tax points

[38.37] Note the following:

- It is not possible to sell shares and buy them back the next day (bed and breakfast) to use the annual capital gains exemption (currently £10,100), although a person's spouse or civil partner could repurchase them on the open market.
- Investment managers frequently prepare capital gains reports for clients at the tax year end. Care needs to be taken with the thirty day rule for matching disposals with acquisitions where disposals take place shortly before the end of the tax year.
- For a small investor, unit and investment trusts can be a useful way of getting the benefit of a wide spread of investments, with the added advantage of expert management. Such trusts are exempt from tax on their capital gains. CGT is due in the usual way on the disposal of the investment in the trust. The investment is particularly tax-efficient when made through an Individual Savings Account (ISA), although the tax exemption has sometimes been more than offset by falling investment values.
- Investing regular amounts on a monthly basis into a unit or investment trust evens out the ups and downs of share prices.
- When an ISA investor dies, his personal representatives should notify the ISA manager promptly, because the tax exemption ceases at the date of the investor's death.
- If shares are given away, they are regarded as disposed of for market value, but tax does not have to be paid at that time if they qualify for gift relief and a claim is made for the relief to apply (see **4.24**).
- It is possible to avoid a frozen gain crystallising on qualifying corporate bonds that were acquired on a takeover, etc. and have since become valueless by giving them to a charity (see **38.33**).
- If shares have become virtually worthless, it may be advantageous to make a negligible value claim as soon as they have been included on HMRC's list (see **38.21**). But if, for example, making the claim immediately would reduce gains and cause annual exemption to be wasted, it is possible to defer the claim to a later year, but not later than that in which the shares cease to exist.
- If there is some control over the time of payment of a dividend, as with a family or other small company, watch that the date of payment does not aggravate an already high taxable income where the income of the major shareholders varies from year to year.
- On an investment in government stocks, interest is received gross and the income tax paid later, rather than receiving the interest net as with some other loans. The end result is the same but cash flow is improved.
- If not more than £5,000 nominal value of government stock or other securities are held to which the accrued income scheme applies, remember that the accrued interest is neither charged to nor relieved from income tax (see **36.19**). The securities will usually be exempt from CGT (see **38.6**). If they are not, the accrued interest is taken into account for CGT in arriving at the cost or proceeds as the case may be.
- If more than £5,000 nominal value of accrued income scheme securities are held, it will be necessary to consider what adjustment is required on a disposal of any of them. Details must be shown on a tax return. If

dealings are through a bank or stockbroker, the amount of accrued interest will be shown on the contract note. Accrued income charges or reliefs are taken into account in the tax year in which the next interest payment is made on the stock.

- Since spouses and civil partners are each entitled to an annual CGT exemption, currently £10,100, it may be appropriate to split share portfolios so that each may take advantage of it. Transfers between spouses or civil partners are not chargeable disposals. If shares are held jointly in unequal proportions, watch the provisions about notifying HMRC for income tax purposes (see **33.6**).

39

Chattels and valuables

What are chattels? (TCGA 1992, ss 21, 262, 263, 269)

[39.1] Chattels are tangible movable property, for example coins (**39.2**), furniture, jewellery, works of art, motor vehicles. Motor cars (other than one-seater cars) are specifically exempt from CGT. One-seater cars and other motor vehicles are exempt as wasting assets unless they have been used in a business.

Coins

[39.2] Although coins come within the definition of a chattel, sterling currency is specifically exempt from capital gains tax (CGT), as is foreign currency for personal expenditure abroad.

Coins that do not fall within these exemptions are chargeable to CGT in the normal way. Demonetised coins (which include pre-1837 sovereigns) fall within the definition of a chattel, and if they have a predictable life of more than 50 years, which obviously applies to collectors' items, the wasting asset exemption for chattels does not apply but the £6,000 exemption is available.

Collectors' coins are normally liable to VAT at the standard rate, whether they are legal tender or not, unless they are dealt with under the special scheme for antiques and collectors' pieces or under the global accounting scheme for second-hand goods (see **7.22**). Subject to certain special rules, coins that are 'investment gold' as defined are exempt from VAT and are not eligible to be sold under the second-hand schemes.

Income tax

[39.3] When investing in valuable objects, the appreciation in value does not generally attract income tax (see below regarding CGT), but on the other hand there is no tax relief for expenses of ownership such as insurance or charges for safe custody.

A succession of profitable sales may suggest to HMRC that chattels and valuables are being held for trading purposes rather than investment, particularly where the scale and frequency of the sales, or the way in which they are carried out, or the need for supplementary work between purchase and sale, suggest a trading motive. Indeed, even a single purchase and sale has on occasion been held to be a trading transaction. However, an important indicator of trading is the lack of significant long term investment value or pride of ownership.

Capital gains tax on sales of chattels (TCGA 1992, ss 44–47, 262)

[39.4] The CGT treatment of a chattel depends on the nature of the chattel, and sometimes on its value, as follows:

(a)   The following chattels are exempt;
- motor cars, sterling currency, and foreign currency for own use abroad are completely exempt;
- chattels with a predictable life of 50 years or less (called wasting assets), are totally exempt from CGT unless they are used in a business and capital allowances have been, or could have been, claimed on them. Plant and machinery is always regarded as having a predictable life of 50 years or less. So privately owned items such as greyhounds and yachts (and even collectors' items if they are 'machinery') are exempt because they are wasting assets;

(b)   Chattels that do not fall within (a) will potentially be chargeable but may be eligible for chattels relief. This relief provides that a gain on such chattels is exempt if the sale consideration is £6,000 or less. If there are joint owners, such as husband and wife or civil partners, each has a separate £6,000 limit to compare with their share of the sale proceeds. Where the proceeds exceed £6,000, the chargeable gain cannot exceed 5/3rds of the excess proceeds over £6,000. If the chattel is sold at a loss for less than £6,000, it is treated as sold for £6,000 to calculate the allowable loss. This means that there can only be an allowable loss if the chattel cost more than £6,000, and if it is a business chattel there will not be an allowable loss in any event (see below).

Example 1

	£
An antique collector's sale proceeds for an antique dresser in June 2010 are	7,200
Cost was	4,570
Chargeable gain	£2,630
But limited to 5/3 × (7,200 − 6,000)	£2,000

The gain would be eliminated completely if the annual exemption of £10,100 had not been used against other gains.

No allowable loss could arise on the dresser, no matter what the sale proceeds, because proceeds of less than £6,000 are treated as £6,000 to calculate a loss.

Example 2

A painting that had cost a collector £11,000 in January 1990 was sold for £8,000 in June 2010. The allowable loss is £3,000. If the painting had been sold for £4,000, it would be treated as sold for £6,000, giving an allowable loss of £5,000 rather than £7,000.

Chargeable chattels comprising a set or collection are treated as separate assets unless they are sold to the same or connected persons (see **4.8**), in which case the sales are added together for the purposes of the £6,000 exemption. Chattels form a set if they are essentially similar and complementary and their value taken together is higher than if they were considered separately. Where the set is sold over a period spanning more than one tax year, the gain is calculated on the total sale proceeds but it is then apportioned between the different tax years according to the respective amounts of sale proceeds in each tax year. Splitting up a set and selling it to different unconnected people would usually not be sensible because it would substantially reduce its value. See **39.6** re chargeable chattels given away by a series of transactions with connected persons.

As far as business chattels are concerned, capital allowances are taken into account in computing income liable to income tax or corporation tax. If the chattel is sold for more than cost, the capital allowances will be withdrawn by means of a balancing charge, so that they will not affect the computation of a capital gain. Where a business chattel is sold for less than cost, the capital allowances computation will automatically give relief for the loss on sale in arriving at taxable income, so there will be no allowable loss for CGT purposes.

[39.5] For HMRC comments on the treatment of wines and spirits and pairs of shotguns, see HMRC RI 208, and RI 214 respectively.

Gifts of chattels

[39.6] A gift of a chargeable chattel is treated as a disposal at open market value at the date of the gift. In order to arrive at an estimated valuation, some evidence of the transaction in the form of correspondence, etc. is advisable. If the value is below the £6,000 exempt level, no tax charge will arise, but the market value at the time of the gift counts as the cost of the asset to the donee when calculating his CGT position on a subsequent disposal.

There are provisions similar to the rules for sets of articles in **39.4** where chargeable assets are given away or otherwise disposed of by a series of transactions with connected persons within a period of six years, and they are worth more together than separately. These provisions apply not only to chattels but also to any other assets, particularly unquoted shares and land and buildings. See **4.23** for details.

If the value of the gifted chattel exceeds the £6,000 exempt level and there is a chargeable gain, tax may not even so be payable because the gain, together with other gains, may be covered by the annual exemption (£10,100 for 2010/11). For gifts of business assets, certain other gifts for public benefit, etc. and gifts into and out of certain trusts, it is possible for donor and donee to claim gift relief (see **4.23** to **4.26**).

[39.7] For inheritance tax purposes, a gift of a chattel may be covered by the annual exemption. If not, it will either be a potentially exempt transfer, or a chargeable transfer in the case of transfers to a company or some trusts. If the donor does not survive the gift by seven years, the potential exemption will be lost and the value at the time of the gift will be taken into account in calculating the inheritance tax payable at death. The person who received the gift will be primarily responsible for the inheritance tax triggered by the death within seven years, including any additional inheritance tax payable on a lifetime chargeable transfer because the death rate applies rather than the lifetime rate originally used. HMRC have the right to look to the estate of the donor if necessary. There will not be any potential liability if the value of the gift was within the nil rate band, but, if there is a potential liability it may be worth insuring against by a term assurance policy on the life of the donor in favour of the donee.

Tax points

[39.8] Note the following:

- HMRC have the power to require auctioneers to provide details of all chattel sales exceeding £6,000.
- Details of chattel acquisitions are frequently required at a later date, perhaps for CGT purposes or to demonstrate that funds for some other investment or business enterprise were available from their sale. Evidence can be provided by purchase invoices that identify the object, and/or by having substantial items included specifically on a household contents insurance policy when they are acquired.
- A profit on the sale of a vintage or classic car is exempt from CGT (unless it is 'unsuitable to be used as a private vehicle') unless it is bought and sold with the aim of making a profit (in which case it is likely that the transaction will be viewed as a trading transaction and liable to income tax (or corporation tax)).
- 'Machinery' is always regarded as a wasting asset and is therefore exempt from CGT unless it is used in a business. A private individual will therefore not pay tax on a gain on a valuable antique machine, such as a clock. The same would apply to a gain by a private individual on a vintage or classic vehicle not covered by the cars exemption.

- It is important to be aware of the trading trap if regularly buying and selling chattels and valuables.

40

Sensible use of life insurance

Qualifying policies (TA 1988, ss 266, 267, 274 and Sch 15)

[40.1] Certain reliefs etc are available in respect of qualifying life policies, as detailed below. The definition of a 'qualifying policy' is complex, but broadly the policy must be on the individual's own life or the life of his spouse or civil partner; it must secure a capital sum payable either on death or earlier disability or not earlier than ten years after the policy is taken out; the premiums must be reasonably even and paid at yearly or shorter intervals; and there are various requirements as to the amount of the sum insured and sometimes as to the surrender value. The offer of a free gift on taking out a policy could breach the 'qualifying policy' rules, but gifts costing up to £30 are ignored.

Income tax relief on premium payments (TA 1988, ss 266, 274)

[40.2] It is not possible to get tax relief on life insurance premiums paid unless the policy was taken out before 14 March 1984 and has not subsequently been amended (whether or not by a clause in the policy) to increase the benefits or extend the term. The rate of relief available on a pre-14 March 1984 qualifying policy is 12½% of the premiums paid, subject to maximum allowable premiums of either £1,500 or one-sixth of total income, whichever is higher. Premiums are paid net of the tax relief.

Capital gains tax treatment of qualifying policies (ITTOIA 2005, ss 498–514)

[40.3] When a qualifying policy matures (provided it has not been varied etc in the meantime), the policy proceeds are tax-free, unless the policy is surrendered etc early. Where a qualifying policy is varied, surrendered or assigned less than ten years after the policy is taken out (or, for endowment policies, before the expiry of three-quarters of the term if that amounts to less than ten years), any profit arising is charged to tax at the excess of higher rate tax over the basic rate of 20% to the extent that the profit falls within the taxpayer's higher rate income tax band (but top-slicing relief is available (see **40.10**)). See **40.5** for the way in which the profit is taken into account where there is savings income.

Details of gains must be shown on the tax return, as for non-qualifying policies (see **40.5**).

A variation which acknowledges the exclusion of an exceptional risk of critical illness or disability, with a consequent effect upon the future premium or the sum insured, does not cause a policy to lose its qualifying status.

The provisions charging gains on qualifying and non-qualifying policies do not apply to someone who was not resident in the UK when the gain arose. See **40.14** for the position for policies held in trust.

Purchased life annuities (ITTOIA 2005, ss 717–726)

[40.4] A qualifying policy is sometimes useful to higher rate taxpayers in conjunction with a purchased life annuity (see **36.23**).

Only part of the purchased annuity is liable to income tax, tax being deducted at the basic rate of 20%, with further tax payable or repayable depending on the annuitant's tax position. The remainder of the annuity is regarded as a return of capital.

Instead of making a conventional investment and losing a substantial part of the income in tax, a higher rate taxpayer could purchase a life annuity and use the net income arising to fund a qualifying life policy, the profits on maturity of the policy being tax-free. Whilst the reduction in tax rates has reduced the advantages of this form of investment, it can still be attractive in some circumstances, but specialist advice is essential.

For an older taxpayer, a variation is available under which only part of the net annual sum from the annuity is used to pay the premiums on a qualifying policy to replace the initial cost of the annuity, the remainder being retained as spendable income.

Anti-avoidance provisions apply to prevent life insurance companies manipulating the purchased life annuity rules to obtain an excessive deduction against their profits in respect of annuities taken out by financial traders.

Non-qualifying policies (ITTOIA 2005, ss 461–546; FA 2009, s 69)

[40.5] If a policy is not a qualifying policy, there is no relief for premium payments, even for policies taken out before 14 March 1984. Whenever the policy was taken out, the proceeds are not wholly tax-free. They are free of capital gains tax (CGT) so long as they are received by the original policy holder, but such of the capital appreciation that comes within the higher rate tax band when it is added to income in the tax year of surrender or assignment, is chargeable to income tax at the excess of higher rate tax over the basic rate of 20% subject to certain special provisions which are outlined below.

Investment bonds

[40.6] A non-qualifying policy usually takes the form of a single premium investment bond. When invested by the life insurance company, the single premium should ideally grow more rapidly than an equivalent amount in the hands of a higher rate taxpayer reinvesting net income from a conventional investment. It is possible to make withdrawals of not more than a cumulative 5% per annum of the initial investment in each policy year (ending on the anniversary of the policy) without attracting a tax liability at that time, such withdrawals being treated as partial surrenders which are only taken into account in calculating the final profit on the bond when it is cashed in. The 5% is a cumulative figure and amounts unused in any year swell the tax-free withdrawal available in a later year, which could be useful for some particularly heavy item of future expenditure. If more than the permitted 5% figure is withdrawn, the excess is charged to tax, but only if, taking into account the excess, and also the top-slicing rules in **40.10**, taxable income exceeds the basic rate limit. Therefore if the excess occurs in a year when, after adding in the excess, taxable income does not exceed the basic rate limit, no charge will arise. The same applies when the bond is finally cashed in, because if this can be arranged in a year when income, even with the addition of the appropriate 'slice' of the bond profit, does not attract the higher rate, no tax is normally payable. Thus it may be possible to surrender in a year when income is low, for example, because of business losses or following retirement. Rather than surrendering the bond, it is possible to defer any tax liability by extending the period of the policy and thus its maturity.

[40.7] An astute investor will usually want to switch investments from time to time, say from equities to properties, then to gilts and so on. For a small administration charge, a life insurance company will allow investors to switch the investments underlying the bond, and the switch has no adverse tax effect.

To give added flexibility in the timing of bond surrenders, it is possible to take out a number of smaller bonds, so that they need not all be cashed in the same tax year. Not only can the original investment be cashed in over a number of years but the amount liable to tax in any year is itself top-sliced (see **40.10**) in arriving at the tax payable. This type of arrangement may be used as an alternative to a purchased life annuity in order to pay the premiums on a qualifying policy, and also to pay large items of anticipated recurrent expenditure such as school fees.

Guaranteed income bonds

[40.8] Guaranteed income bonds are another form of single premium life policy and the tax treatment is the same as in **40.6**. They offer a fixed income (or growth) over a fixed term. No tax is payable on annual income within the 5% limit and the tax payable at the end of the term will depend on the bondholder's tax position in that year.

Calculation of tax due on life policy gains

[40.9] A taxable life policy gain is treated as part of the total income of an individual in the year in which the chargeable event occurred, with a non-repayable deemed tax payment of 20%. For individuals that are not higher rate taxpayers, no further tax is due. For higher rate taxpayers, top slicing relief is available to lessen the impact of the tax charge. Although savings income is treated as the top slice of income for all other purposes (except for calculating tax on payments covered by the 'golden handshake rules' (see **15.6**)), life policy gains (including any gains chargeable on qualifying policies) are added in last of all in order to calculate any tax liability.

Anti-avoidance provisions apply where premiums totalling more than £100,000 have been invested over a specified period in short to medium-term policies. The amount of premiums allowable in calculating the gain is reduced by commission that has been rebated or reinvested.

Gains must be shown on the tax return. The insurance company should provide the taxpayer with the relevant details (see **40.11**). HMRC provide a comprehensive tax calculation guide, which deals with the tax on the life insurance gains.

Note that the cashing-in of a bond, or an earlier chargeable event, may result in a tax charge, even for basic rate taxpayers, if they are entitled to a higher age related personal allowance and/or a married couple's allowance. Although the bond profit or excess withdrawn is only chargeable to tax if taxable income exceeds the basic rate limit, taking into account top-slicing relief, the full profit counts as part of the total income for the purposes of age-related allowances. Any loss of age-related allowances thus indirectly results in a tax charge.

If the bond is cashed in on death, any mortality element of the profit as distinct from the surplus on the underlying investments is not taxable, and since the income of the year of death will usually not cover a full tax year, even on the taxable portion there may be little tax liability at the higher rate.

There is no relief if there is a loss when the bond is cashed in, but if any deficiency on the bond in the tax year in which that event occurs exceeds the cumulative 5% tax-free withdrawals from the bond, a higher rate taxpayer may deduct the excess from his income of that tax year in calculating the amount of extra tax payable on income above the basic rate threshold. The relief is given at the taxpayer's marginal rate. For policies taken out or varied on or after 3 March 2004, relief for a deficiency is only available where the earlier taxable withdrawals formed part of the taxable income of the bondholder. This is to counter avoidance schemes where earlier gains were made by a different person, such as a spouse. Legislation was also introduced by FA 2009 to ensure that no loss relief can be claimed when an offshore life insurance policy is cashed in. Anti-avoidance provisions apply to 'personal portfolio bonds'. These are aimed particularly at offshore bonds, but they also apply to UK bonds. For details see **45.18**.

The provisions charging gains on qualifying and non-qualifying policies do not apply to someone who was not resident in the UK when the gain arose. See **40.14** for the position for policies held in trust.

Top-slicing relief for chargeable events (ITTOIA 2005, ss 535–538)

[40.10] In the tax year when a chargeable event arises on a qualifying or non-qualifying policy (for example when a bond is cashed in) top-slicing relief is available to lessen the impact of the charge to income tax at the higher rate. The surplus on the policy is divided by the number of complete policy years (ending on the anniversary of the policy) that the policy has been held, and the amount arrived at is treated as the top slice of income to ascertain the tax rate, which is then applied to the full profit. The amount chargeable is the excess of higher rate tax over the basic rate of 20%. The longer the policy has been held the smaller the annual equivalent on which the tax charge is based.

Example 1

		£
Taxpayer purchases investment bond in 2003/04 for		10,000
He takes annual withdrawals of £500 for six years (covered by 5% rule)	3,000	
He cashes in bond in 2010/11 for	11,800	14,800
Profit liable to tax in 2010/11		£4,800

His taxable income after all allowances and reliefs is £37,100, leaving £300 available within the basic rate limit of £37,400.

			£
Annual equivalent of bond profit (1/6th × £4,800)			800
Tax thereon as extra income:	300 @ 20%	60	
	500 @ 40%	200	260
Less basic rate tax on £800 @ 20%			160
Tax at excess rates on £800			£100
Tax charge on full profit of £4,800 is £100 × 6, i.e.			£600

It might be possible to avoid paying higher rate tax on the bond profit by taking steps to reduce taxable income. Note, however, that a gift aid donation to charity does *not* reduce taxable income for top-slicing purposes.

Example 2

Taxpayer in Example 1 makes a personal pension contribution of £400 net, £500 gross, in March 2011, which increases his basic rate limit to £37,900. The bond profit does not then attract higher rates (because the annual equivalent of £800 is within the increased basic rate band). This saves tax of £600, which is £200 more than the amount of the pension contribution.

Top-slicing relief is only available when paying tax above basic rate. It does not enable an individual to avoid losing age-related allowances if the taxable profit or excess withdrawal takes total income above £22,900. It is possible, however, to reduce income for *age allowance* purposes by making a personal pension contribution or gift aid donation to charity.

Provision of information by insurers (TA 1998, ss 552, 552ZA)

[40.11] Where gains on policies are chargeable to tax, insurers are required to inform the policyholder. They are also required to inform HMRC if the chargeable event is the sale of the policy or if the aggregate gains in a tax year exceed half the basic rate income threshold.

Second-hand life policies

[40.12] When a life policy is assigned, the assignee may have an income tax liability as in **40.5** to **40.10** if the policy proceeds exceed the premiums paid. In addition, an assignee who receives a policy as a gift is subject to the capital gains rules if *someone else* has previously purchased the policy. (There is an exception for consideration paid by one spouse or civil partner to the other, or paid in connection with a divorce or dissolution of civil partnership, or on an intra-group transfer.) The assignee will be deemed under the normal capital gains rules to have acquired the policy at open market value. Furthermore, the loss allowable for CGT cannot be greater than the loss actually incurred by comparing the assignee's proceeds and cost. The assignee might still have an income tax liability on the difference between the amount of the premiums paid by the original policy holder to the insurance company and the assignee's disposal proceeds.

Transferring shares in life policies (ITTOIA 2005, ss 498–514)

[40.13] Where a life policy is changed from joint to single names or vice versa, such as in marriage or divorce settlements, or forming or dissolving civil partnerships, no tax is payable if a share in a policy is transferred for no consideration, nor do the chargeable events rules apply to assignments between spouses or civil partners living together or to the transfer of rights under a court order as part of a divorce/dissolution settlement.

Trust policies

[40.14] Where a life policy matures on the death of the person who took it out, and that person remained the beneficial owner, the policy proceeds are included in his estate for inheritance tax (IHT).

Where, under a lifetime trust created before 22 March 2006, someone is entitled as of right to the trust income (i.e. he has an interest in possession), the trust fund itself is regarded as belonging to that person for IHT purposes (see **42.23**).

If, therefore, an individual has taken out such a policy on his own life in trust for, say, his children, the policy is treated as belonging to them, and, when the proceeds are received by the trustees, there is no IHT charge because the children have held an interest in the trust fund throughout, which now comprises cash instead of a life policy. Nor is there any IHT when the trustees pay the cash to the children, because the trust fund, embracing whatever was within it for the time being, was always regarded as belonging to them (the interest in possession).

Example 3

In 2002 a taxpayer took out a qualifying policy on his own life assuring £100,000 on his death and paid the first annual premium of £5,000. The policy was gifted to trustees for the benefit of his son, but the taxpayer continues to pay the annual premiums of £5,000 out of his income. The effect is that (a) the gift of the annual premiums is covered by the IHT exemption for gifts out of income, and (b) the son will receive the eventual proceeds when the taxpayer dies without any tax charge whatsoever.

In the case of a married couple or civil partnership a policy will often have been written so that the proceeds do not arise until the second death. This enabled the survivor to take the whole of the deceased's estate at the first death without IHT (because of the surviving spouse/civil partner exemption), with the liability to IHT on the second death being covered by the policy proceeds in the hands of the policy beneficiaries.

This useful way of providing for an anticipated IHT liability by putting funds in the hands of those who will inherit the estate has fallen foul of the FA 2006 changes relating to trusts, since interest in possession trusts created in lifetime on or after 22 March 2006 are not excluded from the mainstream IHT rules unless they provide for the future disability of the settlor. Hence any new arrangements would be within the mainstream IHT rules, albeit with the policy proceeds still outside the estate of the deceased (because he never had an interest in the policy). HMRC indicated that straightforward policies in place at 22 March 2006 should not be affected, despite premiums to maintain the policy having been paid after that date. Insurance companies are always considering the consequences of changing legislation and how they might adapt their products to provide sensible IHT protection. Whatever future changes are made, the principle of providing a lump sum outside the estate by means of suitable life cover enabled by affordable premiums within normal expenditure or the annual £3,000 exemption still holds good (see **CHAPTER 42** for new trust rules).

The rules for charging income tax on gains on non-qualifying policies outlined at **40.5** apply to life policies held in trust, but they are taxed on the settlor if he is UK resident. If the settlor is either dead or non-resident when the gain is made, but there are UK resident trustees, the gains are taxed on the trustees. If the trustees are non-resident, UK beneficiaries are taxed as and when they receive benefits from the trust funds under the anti-avoidance rules re transferring assets abroad (as to which see **45.17**).

Where a life policy is held in a bare trust for a minor, HMRC take the view that minors who have an absolute entitlement to trust income and capital have unimpaired beneficial ownership of the life insurance policies held under a bare trust. Therefore the beneficiaries, rather than the settlor, are taxable on any gains arising. However, where the child's parents are settlors of the bare trust, the parents may still be taxable on the gains under the settlements legislation (see **42.15**).

Specially adapted trust policies

[40.15] There are several tailor-made insurance products which are aimed at mitigating IHT liabilities whilst giving financial comfort in the meantime. These are very specialised areas requiring advice in each case from appropriately qualified advisers, with the insurance companies themselves providing helpful explanatory literature and guidance. Here again the provisions of FA 2006 caused insurance companies to reconsider what they were able to offer. Reference to their literature and expert views is essential in considering appropriate ways forward.

Endowment mortgages

[40.16] Endowment mortgages are a combination of a loan on which interest is paid, plus a qualifying life insurance policy which is intended to pay off the loan when it matures, although there have been very many instances recently where the policy proceeds have proved woefully inadequate. No capital repayments are made to the lender, so the interest cost never falls because of capital repaid. The profit element in the policy when it matures is not liable to tax.

Policies taken out before 14 March 1984 still attract 12½% life insurance tax relief on the premiums.

If the mortgage is reduced because capital becomes available, or is repaid early, usually on change of residence, it is worth considering whether the existing insurance policy should be retained, either in order to preserve tax relief on the premiums because it is a pre-14 March 1984 policy or because to cash in the policy would have an adverse effect on its value. If the existing policy were surrendered and a new policy taken out to cover the whole borrowing, no life insurance relief would be available on the premiums and the comparative cost would be higher because of the individual's increased age.

If the early surrender causes the rules for qualifying policies to be breached, tax may be payable (see **40.3**).

Any compensation received because a qualifying policy is held to have been mis-sold is not liable to income tax or CGT.

Pension mortgages

[40.17] Some lenders will grant mortgages or loans with no capital repayments, but with an undertaking that the borrowing will eventually be repaid out of the capital sum received from a pension fund (see **CHAPTERS 16** and **17**), the borrowing in the meantime being covered by appropriate life insurance. The lender cannot take a legal charge on the pension fund, but the borrower can give an undertaking to use the lump sum from the fund to discharge the loan.

The effect is that tax relief at the borrower's various marginal rates while building up his pension fund is obtained on the capital repayment since the fund used to make the repayment has resulted from pension contributions upon which the tax relief has been obtained at the time of payment. Unless these arrangements are part of an overall plan to provide adequately for retirement, it must be remembered that part of the money that was intended to finance retirement will be used to pay off a mortgage.

Friendly societies (TA 1988, ss 459–466)

[40.18] Whereas the profits of other life insurance companies are taxable, the profits of friendly societies arising from life or endowment business are generally exempt from income tax and corporation tax. The exemption applies where the premiums in respect of the policies issued by the friendly society, generally assuring up to about £2,500 over a ten-year term, do not exceed £270 a year, or the annuities which they grant do not exceed £156 a year.

Policies taken out by children under 18 qualify for the exemption and payment of the premiums by a parent does not contravene the income tax rules about parental gifts (see **33.10**); there is therefore no tax charge on the parent.

The society's tax exemption gives an added advantage to a qualifying policy with a registered friendly society, although the restrictions on premiums and annuities limit the scope accordingly and as with all life assurance products the society's operating charges may significantly reduce the benefit of the tax exemption.

Friendly societies are able to offer their insurance policies within the stocks and shares component of Individual Savings Accounts (ISAs) (see **36.24** onwards).

Where, on or after 17 July 2007, a friendly society transfers its business to a life insurance company, any of its policies that are tax-exempt will retain their exempt status, providing there is no increase in premiums. The life insurance company will not, however, be able to issue any new tax-exempt policies.

Demutualisation

[40.19] If an insurance company demutualises, and as a result investors receive either free shares or cash or a mixture of the two, the tax treatment depends on the circumstances. There will usually be no immediate tax consequences on the issue of free shares, which will have a nil cost. Cash payments to compensate members for loss of membership rights are not treated as 'unauthorised payments' under the pension regime that came into effect on 6 April 2006. Cash payments are, however, chargeable to CGT. Gains may be covered by the annual exemption (currently £10,100) if it is not used elsewhere. See HMRC's Tax Bulletin 34 of April 1998. HMRC stated in relation to the Scottish Widows windfall payments that where there were joint holders, then even though such payments were made only to the first-named holder, they could be treated as received equally, with the gain being divided between the joint holders. Presumably the same treatment will apply to any other insurance windfall payments.

Group policies (ITTOIA 2005, ss 480–483)

[40.20] It is sometimes commercially sensible and convenient to insure a group of lives within one policy, e.g. a number of borrowers. Gains on such policies which provide only death benefits are generally exempt from a tax charge.

Gains on policies held by charitable and non-charitable trusts

[40.21] Gains on life policies held by charitable trusts are treated as the trustees' gains, liable to tax at the basic rate of 20%. Gains accruing to non-charitable trusts are taxed on the trustees if no other person is liable, and sums lent to trustees by or at the direction of the insurer are deemed to be part surrenders equal to the amount of the loan.

Compensation scheme

[40.22] If an insurance company goes out of business, compensation may be payable under the terms of the Financial Services Compensation Scheme (FSCS). Guidance is available at www.fscs.org.uk. HM Treasury have authority to make regulations in connection with how taxes apply after an intervention by the FSCS in relation to insurance contracts.

Tax points

[40.23] Note the following:

- While there is no tax relief on premiums on life insurance policies taken out after 13 March 1984, trustees of a pension fund may take out life cover on the lives of the beneficiaries so as to produce sufficient liquidity within the fund as to enable lump sum benefits to be paid upon death in service (see **16.31**).

- Life insurance relief at 12.5% is only available on premiums paid on a qualifying policy taken out before 14 March 1984. Whether or not the policy is linked to a mortgage, this should be taken into account in considering early surrender.

- A policy on an individual's own life forms part of his estate unless the benefits are payable direct to others. Proceeds falling within the estate will increase IHT payable, and moreover will not be available until a grant of probate or administration has been obtained. A policy on an individual's life for the benefit of someone else will escape tax in the individual's estate if the arrangements are outside the FA 2006 mainstream IHT rules for trusts. The policy monies will be available to the beneficiary on production of the death certificate and appropriate claim form.

- A wide range of methods of investing through life insurance and purchased annuities is on offer by the various life insurance companies who are constantly reviewing their products to ensure continued tax efficiency. An arrangement can often be tailored to specific requirements. Specialist advice is essential.

- A single premium bond can be a simple and convenient way of investing without the need for any complex records such as those required when investing on the Stock Exchange.

- Bonds are also a convenient way to get into and out of the property market by choice of appropriate funds, and it is possible to give away one of a series of property fund supported bonds much more easily than giving land itself, with no IHT charge if the gift is covered by exemptions, or if the donor survives for seven years after making the gift.

- Many people with endowment mortgages may be considering surrendering their policies because of concerns as to whether sufficient will be realised to pay off the mortgage. The tax consequences need to be taken into account if the surrender is within ten years (or within three-quarters of the term if less). Care also needs to be taken with selling the policy on the open market, because the same tax consequences will occur if the sale is within that period.

- There is no magic way of paying school fees. Sensible use of the types of life insurance contracts mentioned in this chapter will help, but early planning is essential, and contracts should be taken out soon after the child is born.

- There is a limit to the lump sum that can be taken from a pension fund on retirement. If this lump sum is to repay a loan, the lender needs to be satisfied that the level of contributions is sufficient to produce a high enough lump sum to discharge or substantially reduce the debt (leaving the remainder of the fund to provide income).

- Friendly society policies for children are a tax-efficient way of using income for children's benefit, although if the charges are relatively high they may offset the tax advantages. For other tax-efficient parent/child arrangements, see **33.10**.

- An insurance company may rebate commission to investors, net it off against the premium, or invest it on the investors' behalf. The rebated commission does not count as income for tax purposes. See **40.9**, however, for anti-avoidance provisions in relation to rebated or reinvested commission.

Miscellaneous

41

The overseas element

Overview

[41.1] Today's global business environment presents many challenges for personal and business taxpayers wishing to manage their tax affairs effectively, making use of available reliefs and avoiding 'double taxation'. At the same time, governments are keen to protect against loss of revenue through tax evasion and avoidance.

The treatment of the overseas aspects of the tax affairs of individuals and companies is complex, and this chapter gives no more than a brief overview of the various provisions.

Professional advice is likely to be essential for UK resident individuals who are eligible for the 'remittance basis' of taxation for foreign income and gains. A major reform of the remittance basis was enacted in FA 2008, including the imposition of a flat £30,000 charge for remittance basis users. The provisions are lengthy and complex, and a very brief summary is provided at **41.14**. FA 2009 made a number of minor amendments to the remittance basis rules.

This chapter focuses on the tax position of individuals but matters relevant to companies (see **41.44**) and trusts (see **41.64**) are outlined briefly.

Persons affected

[41.2] There are two main aspects to the overseas element — the tax treatment of UK-resident individuals and companies with income or assets abroad, and the tax treatment of non-resident (or non-UK domiciled) individuals and non-resident companies with income or assets in the UK. The overseas element also affects the taxation of trusts, see **41.64 to 41.67**.

The tax liability determined under domestic tax law may be affected by double taxation relief, so the relevant double tax agreement needs to be looked at to see if the tax treatment is varied under the provisions of the UK's agreement with the country concerned. Double taxation agreements normally provide for the profits of a trade to be taxed only in the country of the taxpayer's residence, unless there is a 'permanent establishment' (defined, broadly, as a fixed place of business or an agency) in the other country. In relation to electronic commerce, HMRC's view is that websites and servers do not of themselves constitute permanent establishments.

Determination of liability

[41.3] An individual's liability to UK tax depends on whether he is resident, ordinarily resident and domiciled in the UK. A company's tax liability depends on its residence.

Legislation concerning the residence etc. of individuals is not comprehensive and it is has been necessary to look to published HMRC guidance based on court decisions and practice established over many years. The Government indicated during the Finance Bill 2008 debates that it was willing to consider introducing a 'statutory residence test', and in April 2009 the Treasury was reported to be working on a number of possible tests for consideration by ministers.

HMRC's normal practice in relation to the meaning of residence, ordinary residence and domicile is outlined in HMRC6, 'Residence, Domicile and the Remittance Basis', which is available at www.hmrc.gov.uk/cnr/hmrc6.pdf. It has no legal force and does not seek to 'set out regulation or practice'.

HMRC's Centre for Non-Residents (see www.hmrc.gov.uk/cnr) offers guidance to non-residents and their agents on various aspects of liability to UK tax and national insurance contributions.

HMRC have the power to obtain relevant tax information from taxpayers and third parties in order to counter tax evasion, and for such information to be exchanged with tax authorities of jurisdictions with which the UK has made a double taxation agreement or a tax information exchange agreement. EU member states provide mutual assistance in collecting taxes, and one state may require another to take proceedings to recover taxes owed to its tax authority. An EU Savings Directive requires paying agents to report details of savings income payments made to certain non-residents. See also **CHAPTER 45** regarding anti-avoidance provisions.

Administration

[41.4] If a person leaves the UK permanently or indefinitely they are asked to complete form P85 (Leaving the United Kingdom), available at www.hmrc.gov.uk/cnr/p85.pdf. Prior to 1 June 2010 it was also necessary to complete form P86 (Arrival in the United Kingdom), see www.hmrc.gov.uk/cnr/p86.pdf, on returning to the UK. From 1 June 2010, this is no longer necessary.

UK resident individuals: determination and effect of residence

Residence and ordinary residence (ITA 2007, ss 829–833; TCGA 1992, s 9)

[41.5] Residence usually requires physical presence in a country. An individual will always be regarded as resident in the UK if he is physically present here for 183 days or more in the tax year. The residence status of a spouse or partner is determined separately. An individual can be resident in more than one country for tax purposes.

Ordinary residence is broadly equivalent to habitual residence. HMRC consider that the word 'ordinary' indicates that residence in the UK is 'typical and not casual'. It is therefore possible to be regarded as remaining resident and ordinarily resident in the UK despite a temporary absence abroad, or it is possible to be resident but not ordinarily resident here.

Strictly an individual is either resident or non-resident for the whole of a tax year, but by HMRC concession A11 a tax year may be split for income tax purposes into resident and non-resident periods as indicated in **41.6**, and there is a similar concession for capital gains tax (CGT) (see **41.28**).

In the event of a dispute regarding residence status it is possible to request a review by an HMRC officer other than the one who made the decision, or ask for an independent appeal tribunal to hear an appeal (see **1.5**).

An individual is treated as spending a day in the UK, in calculating days spent here to determine residence status, if he is present here at midnight at the end of that day. This is subject to an exception for passengers in transit between two places outside the UK.

Leaving the UK

[41.6] Although strictly an individual is either resident or non-resident for the whole of a tax year, by virtue of concession A11, the tax year can be split (so that an individual is regarded as not resident and not ordinarily resident in the UK from the day after departure) if an individual leaves the UK for:

(a)   full-time service under a contract of employment abroad and both the absence from the UK and the employment itself span a complete tax year; or

(b)   permanent residence abroad. HMRC must be notified if leaving the UK 'permanently or indefinitely'. Their guidance says 'By leaving the UK "permanently" we mean that you are leaving the country to live abroad and will not return here to live. By leaving "indefinitely" we mean that you are leaving to live abroad for a long time (at least three years) but you acknowledge that you might eventually return to live here.'

In both situations, return visits to the UK must amount to less than 183 days in any tax year and average less than 91 days a tax year. See **41.16** regarding the conditions for this treatment.

HMRC consider that links with the UK that continue after leaving the country may mean that an individual remains resident or ordinarily resident here. Residence and ordinary residence may be affected by several factors, including the reason for leaving the UK, the visits made to the UK after departure, and connections that are kept in the UK, e.g. 'family, property, business and social connections'. Evidence will usually be required by HMRC to demonstrate non-residence.

If an individual accompanies a spouse or civil partner who goes abroad to work full-time (but does not work full-time himself), his liability for the tax years in which he leaves and returns is based on the time spent in the UK in each year, in the same way as for the employed spouse or civil partner, providing the absence spans a complete tax year and subject to the same rules for intervening UK visits (concession A78).

Individuals that spend time abroad, may remain liable to pay council tax either as owner-occupier or, where there are no residents, as owner (see **8.4**). An exemption or a discount (see **8.3** and **8.5**) may be available.

Arriving in the UK

[41.7] Although strictly an individual is either resident or non-resident for the whole of a tax year, by virtue of concession A11, the tax year can be split (so that an individual is regarded as resident and ordinarily resident in the UK from the day of arrival) where an individual comes to live in the UK permanently or to stay for at least two years. This treatment might be revised if circumstances change and the UK stay is in fact short-term.

In all other situations HMRC will regard individuals as either 'short-term visitors' or 'longer-term visitors', depending on the circumstances. A short-term visitor is someone who is not going to remain in the UK for an 'extended period' and will visit for limited periods in one or more tax years. A longer-term visitor is someone who has not come to the UK permanently, but has come here indefinitely or for an 'extended period' which might cover several tax years. Such visitors will fall to be treated as resident in the UK if they are physically present here for 183 days or more in the tax year and will be regarded as resident and ordinarily resident in the UK from the beginning of the relevant tax year.

Domicile

[41.8] Domicile is relevant only if an individual has non-UK income or gains. It is not the same as nationality, and unlike residence for tax purposes it is possible to have only one domicile at any one time. An individual's domicile is usually the country in which he has his permanent home. A domicile of origin is acquired at birth, and under UK law this is normally the father's domicile (or the mother's domicile where the parents are not married).

It is possible to acquire a new domicile of choice. This necessitates positive action, e.g. settling in a different country and making a will under the law of the new country. A high standard of proof is required to establish a change of domicile, but HMRC may seek to establish that someone who has settled in the UK has acquired a domicile of choice here. This is a difficult area where professional advice is recommended. Domicile has an extended meaning for inheritance tax (see **5.2**). It has no relevance for companies except in very limited circumstances.

Effect of residence, ordinary residence and domicile

[41.9] UK resident individuals are charged to income tax, broadly, on their worldwide income, subject to certain deductions (e.g. a foreign earnings deduction for seafarers) and special rules for individuals who are not ordinarily resident or not domiciled in the UK.

Individuals are normally charged on the full amount of foreign income arising abroad, whether it is brought into the UK or not (the 'arising basis'). However, if an individual is resident in the UK, but either not domiciled here or not ordinarily resident here, he may choose to be taxed either on the arising basis (see **41.13**) or on the 'remittance basis' (see **41.14**), which taxes UK income as it arises but taxes foreign income only as it is brought into the UK. The remittance basis must be claimed, except in some circumstances.

[41.10] Different rules apply for capital gains tax. Individuals who are resident *or* ordinarily resident in the UK and have a UK domicile are liable to CGT on gains arising anywhere in the world. Individuals who are resident *or* ordinarily resident in the UK but have a domicile elsewhere may be taxed either on the arising basis or on the remittance basis, which taxes UK gains as they arise but taxes foreign gains only as they are brought into the UK (see **41.14**).

A person who is resident or ordinarily resident in the UK can roll over a gain arising on a disposal of assets which qualify for rollover relief on replacement of business assets (see **29.11**) against the acquisition of new qualifying assets situated either in the UK or overseas. HMRC will not seek to deny relief if the person has ceased to be resident or ordinarily resident in the UK when the new assets are acquired, so long as the various conditions for the relief are met (see HMRC's Capital Gains Manual at CG 60253). If the replacement assets are sold in a tax year when the individual is not resident and not ordinarily resident in the UK (and not carrying on a business in the UK through a branch or agency) there will be no UK tax on the rolled over gains (unless on a later return to the UK liability is established under the temporary residence rules outlined at **41.28**). There may, however be liability in the new country of residence.

If an individual becomes not resident and not ordinarily resident within six years after receiving a gift on which CGT was deferred under the gift relief provisions, the deferred gain is chargeable to tax (see **4.25**). Becoming non-resident within a specified period also triggers gains deferred under the enterprise investment scheme or venture capital trust provisions (see **CHAPTER 29**).

[41.11] Residence has no bearing on inheritance tax (except in relation to the extending meaning of 'domicile', see **5.2**). IHT applies to worldwide property if an individual is domiciled in the UK and to UK property only if an individual is domiciled elsewhere. Holdings in authorised unit trusts and open-ended investment companies (see **38.24** to **38.26**) are, however, not liable to IHT for people who are not domiciled in the UK.

Owning property abroad may lead to problems on death because foreign probate may be required before the assets can be dealt with by the executors. For jointly held assets this will normally occur only on the second death, because the ownership normally passes by survivorship to the other joint owner. The costs involved should be borne in mind when considering investing abroad.

[41.12] As far as VAT is concerned, when returning from a non-EU country, it is possible to bring personal possessions into the UK free of VAT and Customs duty providing the individual has been abroad for at least a year, paid VAT or duty on the items abroad and has owned and used them for at least six months prior to returning to the UK. When returning from an EU country, VAT will have been paid abroad when purchasing the possessions, except for new motor vehicles, boats, aircraft, etc., on which UK VAT must be paid on returning to the UK.

UK resident individuals: basis of charge for foreign income and gains (ITTOIA 2005, ss 829–845)

Arising basis

[41.13] Income and gains accruing to UK residents are taxed on the arising basis (i.e. taxed on the full amount of foreign income arising abroad, whether it is brought into the UK or not) where an individual is not eligible for, or does not claim, the remittance basis outlined at **41.14**.

Where the arising basis applies, tax on foreign income (other than the profits of a foreign business) is charged on the income arising in the current tax year. Where a business is carried on wholly abroad, tax is charged according to the same rules as for UK businesses, i.e. generally on the profits of the accounting year ending in the tax year.

Income that is locked into a foreign country is treated as not arising until it can be brought to the UK (but as and when it can be extracted, it is taxable at that time whether or not it is in fact brought to the UK).

See **41.15** for the treatment of certain specific sources of income.

Remittance basis

[41.14] If an individual is resident in the UK but is either not ordinarily resident or not domiciled here, income arising abroad may be taxed on the remittance basis rather than the arising basis. The remittance basis is also available for capital gains for individuals who are not domiciled in the UK. The effect of the remittance basis, broadly, is that income or gains arising abroad are charged to tax if and when they are remitted to the UK. There are complex rules to decide whether or not income or other sums are being remitted. The remittance basis applies automatically in some cases, but in other it must be claimed.

The remittance basis applies automatically (to otherwise eligible individuals) if:

(a)   their unremitted foreign income and gains are less than £2,000 in a tax year; or

(b)   they have no UK income or gains, do not remit any foreign income or gains to the UK, and are either under 18 or have been UK resident in fewer than seven of the previous nine tax years. In these circumstances such individuals also retain entitlement to personal allowances and the CGT annual exemption. (This rule ensures that an individual does not have to complete a self assessment return only so that they may claim the remittance basis and then have no tax to pay).

The remittance basis must be claimed in all other cases. If a claim for the remittance basis is made a 'remittance basis charge' or RBC (an annual tax charge) of £30,000 may also need to be paid if the claimant has at least £2,000 of unremitted foreign income and gains, is 18 or over *and* has been UK resident in at least seven of the previous nine tax years. If a claim is made for the remittance basis for a tax year, and the individual has at least £2,000 of unremitted foreign income and gains, it is not possible to use the income tax personal allowance, married couple's allowance, blind person's allowance, or the CGT annual exemption. This rule is subject to an exception for certain 'dual residents' of the UK and one of a number of specified countries that have particular provisions in their double tax agreements.

It is necessary to nominate the foreign income and/or capital gains to which the RBC applies. HMRC guidance indicates that if untaxed foreign income and/or gains from outside the UK are used to pay the RBC, then the payment should be made direct to HMRC by means of electronic transfer or a cheque drawn on a foreign bank account, in order to prevent the payment itself being regarded as a taxable remittance.

UK resident individuals: specific sources of income (ITEPA 2003, ss 573–576; ITTOIA 2007, s 402)

[41.15] Specific sources of income are subject to special rules. In particular employment income (see 41.16), trading profits (see 41.19), property income (41.24 but see 32.44 regarding time shares), savings and investment income and other miscellaneous items (41.25).

Foreign savings income is taxed at the same rates as UK savings income (see 2.5). Dividends from non-resident companies carry a tax credit of 1/9th of the dividend, providing certain conditions are met. Foreign pensions are subject to UK tax but the amount charged to tax is normally only 90% of the actual amount arising. A pension or annuity paid to a victim of Nazi persecution is exempt from income tax.

UK residents with earnings from employment abroad (ITEPA 2003, ss 20–41E, 378–385)

[41.16] Non-residents escape UK tax on all overseas earnings. UK residents are liable to tax on earnings from employment both in the UK and abroad unless they are seafarers (see 41.17).

If an individual's employment abroad is full time and both his absence from the UK and the employment abroad span a complete tax year, he may be treated by concession (see the conditions in 41.6) as non-resident from the day after departure and as a new resident on return.

Note that it is not the length of the absence but whether it spans a tax year that is important. Therefore if, for example, an individual was working away from 1 April 2010 to 30 April 2011, a period of thirteen months spanning a complete tax year, he would be non-resident for that period. However if he was working away from 1 July 2010 to 31 December 2011, a period of eighteen months that does not span a complete tax year, he would remain UK resident throughout.

Seafarers

[41.17] Seafarers are entitled to a deduction of 100% in respect of earnings abroad during a qualifying period of at least 365 days. A qualifying period is one consisting either wholly of days of absence or of days of absence, linked by UK visits, where those visits do not exceed 183 consecutive days and also do not in total exceed one-half of the days in the period. A day counts as a day of absence if the individual is absent at the end of it, i.e. midnight.

If a seafarer who satisfies the 365-day qualifying period rules has both overseas earnings and UK earnings the 100% deduction is limited to a reasonable proportion of the earnings, having regard to the nature of the duties, and the time devoted to them, in the UK and overseas.

Duties performed on a ship that is engaged on a voyage beginning or ending outside the UK (but excluding any part of it beginning and ending in the UK), or engaged on a part beginning or ending outside the UK of any other voyage, are treated as performed outside the UK.

The 100% deduction also applies to earnings in a period of paid leave at the end of the employment, but if the paid leave is spent in the UK it cannot be counted as part of the 365-day qualifying period.

The 100% deduction is given where possible through the PAYE system, but where this is not possible the relief due is taken into account in the employee's self-assessment. It is claimed in the additional information pages and claimants are required to name the ships on which they have worked.

It has been announced that this seafarers' earnings deduction will be extended to EU and EEA-resident seafarers with effect from 6 April 2011.

Travelling and board and lodging expenses (ITEPA 2003, ss 341, 342, 370, 371, 376)

[41.18] For an employee resident and ordinarily resident in the UK, the costs of travelling from and to the UK when taking up and ceasing an employment wholly abroad, and the costs of travelling between a UK employment and a foreign employment and between foreign employments, are allowed as a deduction from earnings. The costs of any number of outward and return journeys whilst serving abroad are also allowed so long as the expense is met by the employer (thus offsetting the tax charge on the employee in respect of the employer's expenditure). If the employer pays or reimburses the employee's board and lodging costs for an employment wholly abroad, the amount paid or reimbursed is also offset by an equivalent expenses allowance, but no deduction is given for board and lodging payments that an employee bears himself.

If an absence lasts for 60 days or more (not necessarily in one tax year) an employee can claim a deduction for the travelling expenses of two outward and two return journeys per person in any tax year for his or her spouse or civil partner and children (under 18 at the start of the journey) to visit him or her, but only where the travelling expenses are paid or reimbursed by the employer (so that the deduction offsets the benefits charge on the expenditure) and not where the employee bears them personally.

A round sum expenses allowance cannot be treated as payment or reimbursement of expenses by an employer, so care must be taken that the expenses are paid in a way that entitles the employee to an equivalent deduction.

Earned income from self-employment abroad (ITA 2007, s 95; IT-TOIA 2005, ss 17, 92–94, 849–858)

[41.19] Where a business is carried on wholly abroad, the expenses of travelling to and from it are allowed in computing profits. A deduction is also allowed for board and lodging expenses at any place where the trade is carried on and, where the trader's absence spans 60 days or more, for not more than two visits in any tax year by a spouse or civil partner and children (under 18 at the start of the journey). Expenses of travelling between an overseas business and another business carried on wholly or partly abroad are similarly allowable.

[41.20] If a sole trader is resident in the UK, it would be highly unlikely for him to be able to show that his business was carried on *wholly* abroad. The main instance would be where he was only technically resident in the UK and normally lived and carried on the business abroad. If, exceptionally, that was the case, it would not make any difference to the calculation of his profits. If the business made a loss, however, the loss could be relieved only against the profits from the same or any other foreign business, and against foreign pensions and, if the trader was not domiciled in the UK, any employment earnings from a foreign employer.

[41.21] As far as partners are concerned, the profit shares of UK resident partners include both UK profits and profits earned abroad. For a foreign-controlled partnership, this does not apply to a UK resident partner who is not ordinarily resident and/or not domiciled in the UK. Such a partner is charged on the full amount of his share of UK profits, and on the part of his share of foreign profits that is remitted to the UK. (Non-resident partners are taxed on their shares of UK profits — see **41.31**).

The UK tax on a UK resident partner's share of the profits of a partnership resident abroad cannot be reduced or eliminated by double tax relief, even though the terms of the double tax agreement exempt the profits of the foreign partnership.

[41.22] When someone who carries on business wholly or partly abroad becomes, or ceases to be, UK resident, he is treated as ceasing one business and starting another. This does not prevent the carry-forward of any losses before the change if they cannot otherwise be relieved.

[41.23] Class 4 national insurance contributions are not payable where the trader is non-resident in the UK.

Income from overseas property (ITA 2007, ss 117–124; ITTOIA 2005, ss 265, 269)

[41.24] If investment property is purchased abroad, the foreign rental income is calculated in a similar way to UK rental income (see **CHAPTER 32**). Profits and losses for all foreign let properties are aggregated, any overall profit being treated as the profits of an 'overseas property business'. The profit or loss for properties in different countries needs to be calculated separately, however, in order to calculate the amount of double tax relief available (see **41.26**). Allowable expenses include interest on borrowings to buy or improve the foreign property. If there is an overall loss, the rules at **32.7** apply, so that the loss is normally carried forward to set against the total foreign letting profits of later years.

If an individual is UK resident but not UK domiciled (or not ordinarily resident in the UK) and the remittance basis applies (see **41.14**), then the rental income will be chargeable only when it is remitted to the UK.

Other sources of foreign income (TMA 1970, s 17; ITA 2007, ss 6–21)

[41.25] Other sources of foreign income apart from business profits and rents are taxed as outlined at **41.13**.

Offshore bank and building society accounts have the advantage that tax is not deducted at source from the interest, although for those required to make half-yearly payments on account under self-assessment, those payments are based on the amount of tax paid directly for the previous tax year, so an amount is included for continuing sources of untaxed interest.

Interest on foreign government stocks, and also some other interest and dividend income, is received through a UK paying or collecting agent, such as a bank. UK tax is not deducted from such income, so the full amounts received will be charged to UK tax, subject to any claim for double tax relief (see **41.26**). Under arrangements with the EU and various other countries, individuals may also receive interest in full from overseas paying agents. Alternatively a special withholding tax may be deducted. The gross amount is chargeable to UK tax, subject to any claim for double tax relief (see **41.26**).

Foreign fixed interest stocks are subject to the accrued income scheme (see **36.19**), unless the recipient is only liable to tax on income remitted to the UK (see **41.14**). The special rules for scrip dividends (see **38.3**) do not apply to scrip dividends from non-UK resident companies. There are anti-avoidance provisions to counter the rolling-up of income in an offshore fund with the intention of realising it in a capital form. The provisions are dealt with briefly at **45.16**.

Banks, building societies and other paying and collecting agents are required to provide information to HMRC on interest paid to investors, including investors who are not ordinarily resident in the UK. HMRC exchange information on savings income on a reciprocal basis with other countries. HMRC recently used their powers to obtain information from major UK banks about offshore accounts. As a result of the large volume of information received, HMRC announced an Offshore Disclosure Facility (ODF), under which those with undisclosed tax liabilities could notify HMRC. For details see **9.57**.

UK resident individuals: double taxation relief (ITA 2007, ss 29, 1026; TCGA 1992, s 277; TIOPA 2010, ss 2–145)

[41.26] Where the same income and gains are liable to tax in more than one country, relief from double taxation is given either under the provisions of a double tax agreement with the country concerned or unilaterally. The relief is calculated separately for each source of income or capital gains. There are anti-avoidance provisions to prevent manipulation of the double taxation rules, but they should not affect the majority of double tax relief claimants.

Where there is a double tax agreement, it may provide for certain foreign income and gains to be wholly exempt from UK tax. If not, UK tax is charged, but a claim may be made for a credit to be given against the UK tax for the lower of the overseas tax liability and the UK tax liability.

UK paying and collecting agents do not deduct UK tax from foreign interest and dividends (see **41.25**). Taxpayers must therefore pay any amount by which the UK tax exceeds the foreign tax. If the foreign tax exceeds the UK tax, the double tax relief will be restricted to the amount of the UK tax. Where the overseas company pays dividends with tax credits, as in the UK, the tax credits are not eligible for double tax relief unless specifically provided for by the double tax agreement. If the agreement does not so provide, the amount charged to UK tax is the net dividend received.

As stated in **41.25**, UK taxpayers will sometimes receive interest in full from overseas paying agents in the EU and certain other countries. Alternatively, a special withholding tax may be deducted. In that event double tax relief may be claimed. The withholding tax will not be deducted if the UK taxpayer authorises the foreign paying agent to report information about the payments made or provides him with a certificate from HMRC.

Where there is no double tax agreement, unilateral relief may be claimed against the UK tax of the lower of the UK tax and the overseas tax. If double tax relief is not claimed, the income or gain, net of the overseas tax suffered, is charged to UK tax but this would rarely be advantageous.

Additional tax credit relief is given for overlap profits arising when a business starts and on changes of accounting date, and the additional relief is recovered as and when overlap relief is given.

If the amount of foreign tax payable is later adjusted, the amount of double tax relief claimed is similarly adjusted. If an adjustment to foreign tax results in too much relief having been claimed, HMRC must be notified within one year after the adjustment.

Where credit is claimed for foreign tax and a payment is made either to the claimant or a connected person, the foreign tax relief will be restricted to the net amount.

Non-UK resident individuals: tax position and personal allowances (ITA 2007, ss 33–58, 811–814)

Income tax

[41.27] Non-residents are liable to income tax only on income that arises in the UK (they are not liable to UK tax on income arising outside the UK), unless it is specifically exempted etc.

Non-residents are exempt from UK tax on UK government stocks (see **41.35**) and may be exempt on other sources of income under a double tax agreement. Tax is not usually deducted from bank and building society interest (see **41.35**), or from social security benefits (see **41.32**), although such income is not actually exempt from tax. The 10% tax credit rate normally applies to dividend income (see **41.35**). If the other income is from property, tax may have been deducted at the basic rate (see **41.34**).

Certain classes of non-resident are eligible to claim UK personal allowances. These include EEA nationals, residents of the Isle of Man or the Channel Islands, those who have previously resided in the UK but are resident abroad for the health reasons, Crown employees (and their bereaved spouses or partners) and those in the service of a territory under the protection of the British Crown or in the service of a missionary society. Additionally, a claim for allowances may be provided for by the terms of a double tax agreement. Prior to 6 April 2010 personal allowances were also automatically available to citizens of the Commonwealth; this was withdrawn from 6 April 2010. Where allowances are available, they are given in full against the UK income.

The *maximum* tax payable by a non-resident is the tax, if any, deducted from interest, dividends (dividend tax credits being treated as tax deducted) and social security benefits plus the tax on any other taxable income, calculated as if personal allowances were not available. If a claim is made for personal allowances, all non-exempt income is taken into account. This may limit or eliminate the benefit of making a claim.

Example 1

In 2010/11 a non-resident British national who is a single person aged 70 has untaxed income from UK banks and building societies amounting to £2,000 and a state pension of £8,000. No UK tax is payable, since the maximum tax on such income is the tax, if any, deducted from it.

If the non-resident also had rental income of £2,400, from which tax of £480 was deducted, his maximum liability would be tax on that income as if it were his only UK income. He could not benefit from a claim for personal allowance, because his untaxed income of £10,000 would have to be taken into account in such a claim and that income exceeds the age-related personal allowance of £9,490.

If in addition to the rental income of £2,400 the only untaxed income had been the pension of £8,000, the position would be:

	£
Total income	10,400
Personal allowance at age 70	(9,490)
	910
Tax at 20%	182
Tax deducted at source	480
Tax repayable	298

Capital gains tax

[41.28] As a general rule an individual is not liable to CGT if he is not resident and not ordinarily resident in the UK. HMRC concession D2 allows a 'split year' treatment (similar to that available for income tax, see **41.5**) for the tax years of departure and return. Where the conditions for this concession are met, gains on disposals made after the date of departure and before returning to the UK are treated as exempt. This rule is however subject to a number of exceptions:

(a)   individuals that have been resident or ordinarily resident in the UK for any part of at least four of the previous seven tax years, and become not resident and not ordinarily resident for less than five tax years, will be treated as temporarily non-resident. Such individuals will be liable to tax on gains realised on the disposal of assets owned before they left the UK. All such gains in the tax year of departure are chargeable in that year. Gains on such assets arising while abroad are charged in the tax year in which the individual becomes UK resident again. Losses are allowed on the same basis as gains are taxed. If an individual has an interest in a non-resident trust, he will also be taxed on his return on gains during his absence that would have been taxed on him as settlor had he not been non-resident (see **41.66**). Gains on assets acquired while the individual is resident abroad that are realised in the years between the tax year of departure and the tax year of return are exempt (subject to certain anti-avoidance provisions);

(b)   non-residents carrying on a business in the UK through a branch or agency are liable to CGT on gains arising on assets used in the business (see **41.36**);

(c)   special rules apply to the CGT position on a private residence when absent abroad (see **30.5**).

Spouses and civil partners

[41.29] The residence and ordinary residence status of spouses and civil partners is determined independently. If a spouse or civil partner remains in the UK while the other spouse or partner is working abroad for a period which spans a tax year, he or she will be taxed as a UK resident on UK and foreign income, and the spouse/partner will normally be exempt as a non-resident from UK tax on income arising outside the UK and will be able where appropriate (see **41.27**) to claim personal allowances as a non-resident against UK income.

If a non-resident spouse or civil partner is entitled to personal allowances but his or her UK income is insufficient to absorb the married couple's allowance (if available (see **2.18**)), the surplus may be transferred to the other spouse or partner providing the spouse or partner is entitled to allowances either as a resident or a qualifying non-resident.

Non-UK resident individuals: earned income (ITEPA 2003, ss 20–41, 373–375)

Income from employment

[41.30] The treatment of a non–resident's UK earnings depends on the length of his visit. Where he does not remain long enough to be classed as resident he is nonetheless liable to UK tax on UK earnings (although sometimes he may be exempt under the provisions of a double tax treaty (see **41.37**)). UK personal allowances are available only to certain non-residents (see **41.27**).

Expenses of travel and of visits by spouses or civil partners and children are allowed if they are paid or reimbursed by the employer (thus offsetting the benefits charge) in the same way as described at **41.18** for a UK resident working abroad. This only applies, however, where the employee was either not resident in the UK in either of the two tax years before the tax year of his arrival in the UK, or was not in the UK at any time during the two years immediately preceding his arrival. Where this condition is satisfied, the expenses are allowed for a period of five years beginning with the date of arrival in the UK to perform the duties of the employment.

A non-resident who remains in the UK long enough to be classified as resident but not ordinarily resident in the UK, is liable to tax on UK earnings as they arise, but he may be able to claim the remittance basis in respect of foreign income (see **41.14**). It is important for visitors to keep records (for example, separate bank accounts for capital and for different sources of income) to enable them to demonstrate whether or not remittances out of foreign earnings have taken place.

Employers may make special PAYE arrangements for foreign national employees (known as tax equalisation arrangements) under which the employers meet all or part of the employees' tax. Details are in HMRC Help Sheet HS212. See also HMRC's Tax Bulletin 81 (February 2006) regarding tax equalised employees and Tax Bulletin 50 (December 2000) on benefits and expenses provided to employees sent on secondment by overseas employers.

Income from a UK business

[41.31] Non-residents who carry on business in the UK either on their own or in partnership are charged to tax on the UK business profits in the same way as UK residents. Tax due on the profits is dealt with under the self-assessment rules and is paid by the non-resident or, where the business is carried on through a UK branch or agency, by a UK representative.

State pensions, other pensions and state benefits

[41.32] Non-residents receive state pensions and other relevant social security benefits in full, and tax is not charged on them (but see **41.27** in relation to tax repayment claims). As far as occupational and personal pensions paid to non-residents are concerned, such pensions are chargeable to UK tax unless (as will usually be the case) they are exempt under a double taxation agreement. Tax is deducted from such pensions under PAYE where the payer has been instructed to do so by the tax office. In this event, the code number may take personal allowances into account.

Non-resident performers (ITTOIA 2005, ss 13, 14; ITA 2007, ss 965–970; CTA 2009, s 1309)

[41.33] Basic rate tax may be deducted by the payer from the UK earnings of non-resident entertainers, sportsmen and sportswomen. Royalty payments received from the sale of records are excluded (as they are already exempt under many double taxation agreements).

Tax need not be deducted where the person making the payment does not expect to pay more than a total of £1,000 to the individual in question during that tax year. Where tax is deducted, HMRC may agree a rate below the basic rate. The tax deducted is set against the final tax liability for the year, or repaid to the extent that it exceeds that liability. The rules are administered by HMRC's Foreign Entertainers Unit and guidance is provided in Help Sheet 303.

Non-UK resident individuals: rental income of non-resident landlords (ITA 2007, ss 971, 972; SI 1995/2902)

[41.34] Where UK property is let, the rental income from all let properties is treated as being from a single property business, as outlined in **CHAPTER 32**. There are, however, special regulations dealing with the taxation of rental income of non-resident landlords. The reference to a non-resident landlord is not in fact accurate, because the legislation refers to someone whose 'usual place of abode' is outside the UK, the aim being to make it easier to collect tax from someone who is usually abroad. HMRC's interpretation is to regard an individual as having a usual place of abode outside the UK if he is away for more than six months. Companies will not be so treated if they are UK resident for tax purposes. References to non-residents in the remainder of this section should be read accordingly.

A UK agent handling let property for a non-resident landlord, or the tenant where there is no such agent, must notify HMRC's Centre for Non-Residents (CNR). The agent or tenant must then deduct basic rate tax from the property income (net of allowable expenses paid by the agent or tenant and net of VAT on the rent where this has been charged), and pay it over to HMRC within 30 days after the end of each calendar quarter. The agent or tenant must give the non-resident an annual certificate showing the tax deducted by 5 July following the tax year and must also send in a return to HMRC by the same date. These provisions apply whether the non-resident landlord is an individual, trustee or a company, except that they do not apply to the rental income of a UK permanent establishment of a non-resident company (see **41.49**).

Tax does not have to be deducted at source if the agent or tenant receives written notice to that effect from CNR. Tenants paying rent of, broadly, £100 a week or less do not have to deduct tax unless told to do so by CNR. The non-resident landlord is required to pay any excess of tax due over the tax deducted at source (or claim a refund) under the self-assessment provisions, so that unless the tax paid directly to HMRC for the previous tax year was below the de minimis thresholds, payments on account should be made on 31 January in the tax year and 31 July following, with the balance due at the same time as the tax return on 31 January following the end of the tax year.

A landlord may apply to CNR to receive his rental income in full providing his UK tax affairs are up to date, or he has never had any UK tax obligations, or he does not expect to be liable to UK tax. He must undertake to complete tax returns if required and pay any tax due on time. Unless covered by the de minimis thresholds, the non-resident landlord will be required to make payments on account in the same way as landlords who receive taxed rent (see above). CNR have stated that they will not normally issue self-assessment returns to non-resident individual landlords who have no net tax liability, although returns may still be sent occasionally to ensure that the tax position remains the same.

Non-UK resident individuals: other income and capital gains (ITA 2007, ss 811–814, 911–913; TCGA 1992, ss 2, 10, 12, 25)

Other income

[41.35] Non-residents have no liability to UK tax on foreign income. If they are not ordinarily resident in the UK they are also exempt from tax on UK income from government securities, interest on which is paid gross. Other UK income is not exempt but special provisions apply as indicated below. The treatment of income and gains may be varied by the provisions of a double tax treaty (see **41.37**).

Interest on quoted Eurobonds (i.e. interest-bearing stock exchange listed securities issued by a company) is paid gross. UK bank and building society interest is also paid without deduction of tax to those who provide the bank or building society with a declaration stating that they are not ordinarily resident in the UK and giving their principal residential address. As far as UK dividends are concerned, under the terms of most double tax agreements, non-residents are entitled to reclaim the excess of the tax credits over 15% of the tax credit inclusive dividend. Since the tax credit rate on dividends is only 10%, very few non-residents will be entitled to any repayment (see **41.37**). Non-residents are not liable to pay tax on investment income other than rents, except to the extent that tax is deducted at source (tax credits on dividends being treated as tax deducted at source). Non-residents therefore escape UK tax altogether on interest received in full as indicated above, and do not have to self-assess, unless they have other taxable income and are claiming a repayment. In calculating how much tax is repayable, however, any UK income that is not exempt from tax may have to be taken into account (see **41.27**). Tax is normally deducted at the basic rate from patent royalties paid to overseas companies and individuals. A paying company may, however, pay royalties gross, or deduct tax at a reduced rate according to the terms of the double tax agreement, if it believes the recipient to be entitled to double tax relief (see **41.37**). The company will have to pay the tax shortfall, plus interest and possibly penalties, if its belief turns out to be incorrect.

Those completing tax returns must show any non-exempt income, whether tax is payable or not, otherwise the return will be incomplete. (The UK tax liability of someone who is non-resident for only *part* of a tax year (see **41.5**) is calculated by reference to *all* taxable income of the year and the treatment indicated above does not apply).

As far as bank accounts are concerned, if UK bank and building society accounts are replaced with foreign accounts, the interest will be free of UK tax while non-resident, and will not be taken into account in calculating relief under a non-resident's personal allowances claim. Closing foreign accounts before a return to the UK will prevent any of the foreign interest being subject to UK tax. If offshore roll-up funds (see **45.16**) have been invested in there is no UK tax if they are disposed of before UK residence is resumed. See **45.18** for the anti-avoidance provisions in relation to personal portfolio bonds.

For individual savings account (ISA (see **36.24** onwards)) the tax exemption on the investment is not lost on becoming non-resident but it is not possible to contribute further or take out a new ISA.

If an individual is in the UK long enough to be classed as resident, he will be liable to income tax on foreign as well as UK sources of income although the remittance basis (see **41.14**) may apply. It might be appropriate to invest abroad and leave the income there. An alternative for those of foreign domicile who are resident and ordinarily resident in the UK is an individual savings account (ISA) (see **36.24** onwards).

Capital gains

[41.36] An individual does not escape liability to CGT unless he is both not resident and not ordinarily resident in the UK. Even then, if he carries on a trade in the UK through a branch or agency, he will be charged to CGT on the disposal of assets in the UK used for the business or by the branch or agency. See also **41.28** for a CGT charge on 'temporary non-residents'.

Non-UK resident individuals: double tax relief (ITTOIA 2005, ss 397–401)

[41.37] Income or gains may be exempt from UK tax under a double tax agreement.

As far as earned income is concerned, many treaties provide that someone working in the UK on a short-term basis will be taxed only in their own country. HMRC broadly operate a '60 day' rule in this connection (see their Tax Bulletin 68 of December 2003 for detailed comments).

Sometimes a double tax agreement may provide for income that is not exempt from UK tax to be charged at a reduced rate, for example, interest may be taxed at only 10%. The tax on dividends is frequently restricted in the agreement to a maximum of 15%, but as the UK tax credit rate on dividends is only 10% repayments will rarely arise.

Non-residents who claim UK personal allowances (see **41.27**) are entitled to dividend tax credits in calculating tax payable whether or not they are entitled to them under a double tax agreement. If no claim for personal allowances is made, a non-resident's UK tax liability on dividend income is covered by the dividend tax credit (see **41.27**).

National insurance contributions and social security

[41.38] The detailed national insurance and social security provisions are complex, so whether leaving or coming to the UK, it is advisable to contact HMRC and the Department for Work and Pensions to establish the liability to make NICs and the overall benefits position. Contact details for HM-RC's centre for non-residents, and the DWP's international pensions centre, are provided in leaflet NI 38.

Leaving the UK

[41.39] If an individual leaves the UK his liability to pay national insurance contributions (NICs) will normally cease unless he works abroad for an employer who has a place of business in the UK, in which case Class 1 NICs continue for the first 52 weeks. Where there is no liability to pay Class 1 NICs, it may be to an individual's advantage to pay Class 3 voluntary NICs. Alternatively if an individual is employed or self-employed abroad, it is possible to maintain a contributions record for certain benefits by paying the lower Class 2 NICs, providing certain conditions are satisfied. See HM-RC's leaflet NI38 for details.

[41.40] If an individual is working temporarily abroad, or moving from one foreign location to another, he may be required to continue to pay Class 1 NICs. The position is different if an individual goes to a country with which the UK has a reciprocal social security agreement, when home country liability may sometimes continue for several years. The position is also different if an individual goes to a country in the European Economic Area, in which case there will usually be liability in the country of employment from the outset, except (from 1 May 2010) for a short-term visit of up to 24 months. (Prior to 1 May 2010, a short term visit was a 12 month period, with an ability to apply for an extension of up to a further 12 months. The change has simply done away with the need to apply for an extension at 12 months). During the short term visits an individual will remain liable in the UK.

If a person normally works in more than one EEA country, he will, from 1 May 2010, be liable in his state of residence, provided he performs a substantial part of his duties in that state. (This rule applies even if he has multiple employments and the employers are in different member states). If he does not perform a substantial amount of his work in his state of residence, then he will be liable in the state that his employer resides. Prior to 1 May 2010 it was provided that for such a person, who continued to be habitually resident in the UK (and worked in the UK), UK liability could continue. It was also provided that if a person was not resident in any of the states in which he worked he was to be liable where the employer was registered or had a place of business.

Employers should ensure that where UK liability continues, they account for the appropriate amount of NICs on all relevant pay and benefits. HMRC provide details of the pre and post 1 May 2010 rules at http://www.hmrc.gov.uk/nic/work/new-rules.htm.

[41.41] If an individual leaves the UK and is self-employed abroad, there is not normally a *requirement* to pay Class 2 NICs but there may be an *entitlement* to pay them in some circumstances to maintain contribution records. Again, the position is subject to variation for workers in the EEA or in a country with which the UK has a reciprocal social security agreement. A self-employed person who is not resident in the UK in a tax year is not liable to pay Class 4 NICs. Class 4 contributions do not apply where a trader is not UK resident.

Arrival in the UK

[41.42] Visitors to the UK and new permanent residents who are employees are normally not liable to pay Class 1 NICs for the first twelve months. This does not apply to those coming from an EEA country or a country with which the UK has a reciprocal social security agreement, who will either be liable to UK NICs from the outset or remain liable under their home country's rules. Where an employee is liable, the employer is liable to pay employer's secondary NICs. This applies to all overseas employers, subject to special rules for EEA countries and countries with which the UK has a reciprocal social security agreement.

People coming to the UK who are self-employed are only *required* to pay Class 2 NICs if they are ordinarily resident in the UK, or have been resident in the UK for 26 or more weeks out of the last 52. They are *entitled* to pay Class 2 NICs if they are *present* in the UK for the relevant contribution week. Again, the general rules are varied for EEA countries and countries with which the UK has a reciprocal social security agreement. Class 4 NICs are payable where relevant unless the person is not resident in the UK for the tax year concerned.

State pension

[41.43] As far as the state pension is concerned, if an individual emigrates, he is normally entitled to a pension based on contributions made, but it is frozen at the rate payable when leaving the UK or when first becoming entitled to the pension, if later. This may be varied by the provisions of reciprocal social security agreements. Again, the position needs to be checked with the DWP's pensions service.

UK resident companies: determination and effect of residence (CTA 2009, ss 5, 13–32)

[41.44] Under UK tax law, any company that is incorporated in the UK is treated as being UK resident no matter where it is managed and controlled. Companies incorporated abroad are regarded as UK resident if they are managed and controlled here. Where, however, a company is treated as non-resident under the terms of a double tax treaty, this overrides these rules and the company is regarded as not being UK resident.

A company that is UK resident is liable to corporation tax on all 'profits', i.e. income and chargeable gains, wherever they arise.

A company may have more than one country of residence. Anti-avoidance provisions apply to dual resident investment companies (see **45.14**). HMRC provide guidance on company residence in their International Manual.

UK resident companies: basis of charge (CTA 2009, ss 931A–931W; CTA 2010, ss 66, 67, 111–128, 1141; TIOPA 2010, ss 18–104)

Overseas property income

[41.45] A company's income from letting of overseas property is treated as the profits of an 'overseas property business' and computed in broadly the same way as for UK lettings, but with the profit or loss computed separately for properties in different countries in order to calculate the amount of any available double tax relief (see **41.48**). Interest on any borrowing to acquire foreign property is deducted under the 'loan relationships' rules in the same way as for UK property (see **32.10**). Providing the lettings are on a commercial basis, any losses arising may be carried forward to set against later profits from the overseas property business.

Overseas permanent establishments/subsidiaries

[41.46] The losses of a foreign 'permanent establishment' (broadly, a fixed place of business) of a UK resident company are not available for surrender to other UK group companies under the group relief provisions to the extent that the loss could be relieved for foreign tax purposes in the country in which it arose. Special rules apply to the calculation of branch profits (see **41.49**), which may alter the amount of double taxation relief available.

Where business is carried on through a foreign subsidiary, the UK company's liability will arise only on amounts received from the subsidiary by way of interest or, in some cases, dividends. However, from 1 July 2009 the majority of foreign dividends received by UK companies are not taxable, provided they fall into an exempt class and anti-avoidance provisions do not apply.

Group companies resident (or with a permanent establishment) in another state in the European Economic Area may surrender losses to UK group companies if the losses would otherwise be unrelievable either in the country in which they were incurred or any other country. The amount of loss available for surrender must be recomputed according to UK tax principles. Loss relief will not be available where there are arrangements the main purpose (or one of the main purposes) of which is to obtain UK tax relief.

Controlled foreign companies and dual resident companies

[41.47] The controlled foreign company legislation provides that in certain circumstances tax is charged on a UK company in respect of profits of a foreign company in which the UK company has a stake of 10% or more. They are outlined very briefly at **45.15**. There are also anti-avoidance provisions in relation to dual resident companies, which are outlined at **45.14**. Companies are required to declare amounts taxable under the controlled foreign companies rules in their tax returns.

UK resident companies: double tax relief

[41.48] Double tax relief is available in respect of the foreign tax suffered on both income and gains. Normally, only direct foreign taxes are taken into account for double tax relief but if a UK company receives dividends from a foreign company in which it owns 10% or more of the voting power, underlying taxes on the profits out of which the dividends are paid are taken into account as well. In this case the amount included in UK profits is the dividend plus both the direct and underlying foreign taxes. However, from 1 July 2009 the majority of foreign dividends received by UK companies will not be taxable, provided they fall into an exempt class and anti-avoidance provisions do not apply. Double tax relief is also available both for direct and underlying foreign tax suffered by UK permanent establishments of non-resident companies, other than tax paid in the taxpayer company's home state.

Unrelieved foreign tax on permanent establishment profits and, where applicable, foreign dividends (but see the paragraph above) may be carried back to the previous three years or carried forward indefinitely for offset against tax on income from the same source (providing, in the case of underlying tax, that the required 10% interest continues to be held). Unrelieved foreign tax may also be surrendered within a group of companies (including group companies that are dual-resident).

Double tax relief is given either unilaterally or under the provisions of a double tax agreement.

The relief on overseas income cannot exceed the UK corporation tax payable on the overseas income, after all deductions (other than advance corporation tax set off under the provisions of the shadow ACT system). It is, however, provided that in deciding how much corporation tax is attributable to the overseas income, any available deductions may broadly be set against any source of profits in the most beneficial way (although not so as to turn profits into a loss for which loss relief is claimed). The main point to bear in mind on interest relating to the trade is that it should be set against UK trading profits in priority to foreign trading profits. As far as non-trading interest is concerned, if there is a non-trading deficit for which relief is claimed against total profits (see **26.5**), the deficit must be set against the same profits for both loss relief and double tax relief. Any non-trading deficit brought forward (see **26.6**) must be regarded for double tax relief as reducing non-trading profits.

Double tax relief in respect of foreign tax paid on chargeable gains is limited to the UK corporation tax payable thereon.

If double tax relief is restricted because it exceeds the UK tax, then, apart from the provisions mentioned above in relation to unrelieved tax on permanent establishment profits and foreign dividends, the unrelieved foreign tax is wasted and cannot be carried forward or back.

If the amount of foreign tax payable is later adjusted, the amount of double tax relief claimed is similarly adjusted. If an adjustment to foreign tax results in too much relief having been claimed, HMRC must be notified within one year after the adjustment.

Where credit is claimed for foreign tax and a payment is made either to the claimant or a connected person, the foreign tax relief will be restricted to the net amount.

There are various anti-avoidance provisions that restrict the amount of relief available for underlying tax, and also prevent financial traders getting excessive relief for foreign tax paid on overseas interest. All traders with foreign profits must take expenses into account on a just and reasonable basis, and there is a general anti-avoidance provision relating to 'prescribed schemes and arrangements designed to increase relief'.

Non-resident companies: basis of charge (TCGA 1992, ss 25, 171; ITA 2007, ss 815, 816; CTA 2009, ss 5, 19–32; CTA 2010, s 968)

UK permanent establishment

[41.49] A non-resident company is chargeable to corporation tax only if it carries on a trade in the UK through a permanent establishment (broadly, a fixed place of business) in the UK. The company is liable to tax on profits, wherever they arise, that are attributable to the permanent establishment.

A permanent establishment is treated as having the amount of equity and other capital it would need if it were operating as a separate company. This restricts the amount of interest that may be deducted in calculating taxable profits. The permanent establishment is responsible for dealing with the UK tax liabilities on the company's profits. The rules relating to non-resident landlords at **41.34** do not apply. The company is liable to income tax on any UK sources of income not connected with the permanent establishment in the same way as companies not operating through a permanent establishment (see below).

If the UK trade ceases, or the assets are removed from the UK, the company is treated as if it had disposed of the assets, and gains are charged to tax accordingly. If, however, the permanent establishment is converted into a UK subsidiary, the assets are transferred from the parent to the subsidiary on a no gain/no loss basis. The subsidiary may also take over stock at cost, and be treated for losses and capital allowances as if there had been no change.

[41.50] If a non-resident company does not trade in the UK through a permanent establishment, it is not liable to corporation tax but is liable to income tax (at the basic rate) on UK sources of income, e.g. on rental income from UK property, subject to an overriding limit where certain disregarded company income is received. The charging provisions for rental income are the same as those for individuals (see **41.34**). A gain on the disposal of such a let property would not be charged to tax. For companies liable to income tax, interest paid is dealt with under the income tax rules rather than the loan relationships rules.

UK subsidiary (CTA 2010, s 1109)

[41.51] A UK resident subsidiary of a foreign company is liable to corporation tax in the same way as any other resident company. An overseas parent is not normally entitled to a tax credit on dividends, although some double tax treaties provide for a limited credit. See **41.52** re group relief for losses.

Group relief for losses etc. (TA 1988, ss 402–413; CTA 2010, ss 111–128, 973–980)

[41.52] A UK permanent establishment of an overseas company may claim group relief against its UK profits in respect of losses surrendered by UK resident subsidiary companies of the overseas parent, and may surrender its losses as group relief to such companies, providing the losses relate to UK activities and are not relievable in the overseas country.

Tax payable by a non-resident company within a group that remains unpaid for six months after the due date may be recovered from another company within the same group.

Non resident companies: cessation of residence (TCGA 1992, ss 185, 187)

[41.53] If a foreign-registered company that is resident in the UK ceases to be so resident, it is charged to tax as if it had disposed of all its assets at that time, unless they are retained in a UK permanent establishment. The tax charge is postponed if the company is a 75% subsidiary of a UK resident company and the two companies so elect within two years. The parent company is then charged to tax on the net gains on the deemed disposal as and when the subsidiary disposes of the assets, or ceases to be a subsidiary.

Transfer pricing (TIOPA 2010, ss 146–230)

[41.54] The transfer pricing provisions require non-arm's length transactions (including interest on 'excessive' debt finance) between associated persons to be adjusted for tax purposes to the normal arm's length price. These provisions apply not only where one of the companies is non-resident but also where both are UK resident. There are, however, exemptions for most small and medium-sized companies. The transfer pricing provisions are covered briefly in **45.19**.

Computations relating to foreign exchange matters (see **41.63**) are in any event made using arm's length principles and are outside the transfer pricing rules. Taxpayers may make 'advance pricing arrangements' with the tax authorities that their transfer pricing arrangements are acceptable to those authorities. Such agreements are mainly made by multinational companies.

European Union

[41.55] The EU is playing an increasing part in the taxation of member states, and its directives and regulations must be taken into account in UK tax legislation. The EU's executive body, the European Commission, provides information on the EU tax policy and strategy at www.ec.europa.eu/taxation_customs.

[41.56] The European Commission has put forward proposals for a consolidated corporate tax base for all of a company's EU-wide activities and a 'one-stop shop' system to enable a trader to fulfil his EU-wide VAT obligations in his home state. These are part of wider aims to boost competitiveness, reduce compliance costs and encourage research and development. Clearly some of the proposed changes would take a considerable time both to devise and implement, and indeed they may never come to fruition.

The Commission has also announced a series of initiatives to promote better co-ordination of direct tax systems in EU states.

European Economic Interest Groupings (ITA 2007, s 842; CTA 2010, s 990)

[41.57] A European Economic Interest Grouping (EEIG) is a form of business entity that may be set up by enterprises of states in the European Economic Area (i.e. the European Union plus Iceland, Liechtenstein and Norway) for activities such as packing, processing, marketing or research.

The EEIG's profits are taxable and losses allowable only in the hands of the members. The EEIG cannot be formed to make profits for itself. Any trade carried on by the members is treated as carried on in partnership, with the normal rules of income tax, corporation tax and CGT applying.

The 'fiscal transparency' of the EEIG does not apply to provisions other than those charging tax on income and gains, so that an EEIG registered in the UK is required to collect and account for tax on interest, etc. and under PAYE.

European Company

[41.58] Companies operating in more than one EU member state may form a 'European Company' (Societas Europaea — SE) or a European Co-operative (Societas Co-operative Europaea — SCE). Various provisions in the UK tax legislation have been amended to incorporate references to SEs and SCEs.

Such companies may effect a merger, under which the SE or SCE could be within or outside the charge to UK corporation tax. The UK legislation has already been amended to ensure that various UK tax provisions that could have an effect on the merger, i.e. provisions relating to capital gains, intangible assets, loan relationships, derivative contracts, capital allowances and stamp taxes, will operate broadly on a tax neutral basis, and provision is made in FA 2007 for further provisions to be included in regulations. There are anti-avoidance provisions to ensure that the merger is for bona fide commercial reasons and not as part of a tax avoidance scheme. Advance clearance may be obtained that this condition is met.

Interest and royalty payments (ITTOIA 2005, ss 757–767)

[41.59] Under an EU Directive, companies may pay interest and royalties without deducting tax where the payments are made to an associated company in another EU state. Companies are associated where one directly owns 25% of the capital or voting rights in the other or a third company directly owns 25% of both. Such payments from a UK company to an EU associate are exempt from tax. For interest, but not for royalties, the paying company must apply for an exemption notice from HMRC. Certain EU countries will be allowed to continue to apply a withholding tax to such payments for a transitional period.

Transfer of a trade (TCGA 1992, ss 140–140D; FA 2010, s 37)

[41.60] A claim can be made for the transfer of a UK business to be made on a no gain/no loss basis if the transfer is to an EU resident company in exchange for shares or securities issued by the transferee company and provided certain conditions are satisfied.

There are similar provisions to permit a claim to be made to defer a capital gains charge on the transfer of a non-UK business to a company resident overseas. The deferred gain is brought back into charge on either a subsequent disposal by the UK company of any of the securities in the overseas company (by treating the disposal as a separate chargeable transaction) or the disposal by the overseas company of any of the assets transferred, within six years of the transfer. Alternatively, if the transfer is of a non-UK business to a company resident in another EU state it is possible instead to claim a tax credit for any tax that would have arisen were it not for the mergers directive.

Value added tax

[41.61] The VAT treatment of transactions between European Union countries is outlined at **7.29**. If a trader suffers VAT in another EU state on goods or services bought and used there (say while participating in a trade fair), it cannot be treated as input VAT in the UK, but it may be recoverable from the other EU state. Details are in HMRC Notice 723.

Single currency — the euro (FA 1998, s 163; SI 1998/3177)

[41.62] Businesses may pay their taxes and national insurance contributions in euros, although liabilities will still be calculated in sterling and under- or overpayments may arise because of exchange rate fluctuations before payments are actually credited by the tax authorities. There is legislation to prevent unintended tax consequences arising as a result of the adoption of the euro by other EU states.

Foreign currency (CTA 2010, s 1127 and Sch 2 paras 11–15)

[41.63] Both trading and non-trading companies use the currency of their accounts (or branch financial statements) to calculate their taxable profits and determine their exchange gains and losses, so long as the use of that currency follows generally accepted accounting practice. Generally accepted accounting practice means either UK generally accepted accounting practice (GAAP) or, where appropriate, generally accepted accounting practice in accordance with international accounting standards (IAS). There are provisions to prevent groups of companies gaining a tax advantage through one company using UK GAAP and the other using IAS.

Where a company computes its profits or losses for corporation tax purposes in a currency other than sterling, any losses carried either forwards or back are translated into sterling at the same exchange rate as the profits they are offsetting.

For UK resident companies, the treatment of profits and losses arising from exchange rate fluctuations is broadly as follows. Foreign exchange gains and losses on monetary assets and liabilities (such as cash, bank deposits and debts), and on forward contracts to buy or sell currency, are taxed as income or allowed as deductions as they accrue. Exchange differences on monetary items are taken into account as they accrue. Unrealised gains above certain limits on long-term capital items may be partly deferred. Exchange differences on borrowing that 'matches' a non-monetary asset are deferred until the asset is disposed of, and then dealt with under the CGT rules. See HMRC's Statement of Practice 2/02 for the detailed provisions. There are anti-avoidance provisions to prevent companies from sheltering an exchange gain from tax whilst still obtaining relief for an exchange loss.

Gains and losses on certain financial instruments for managing currency risk are also taken into account in calculating income profits and losses.

As far as VAT is concerned, HMRC consider that in general, forex transactions are supplies for VAT purposes if the registered person adopts a spread position (a difference between a bid price and a sell price from which a person would expect to derive a profit) over a period of time when buying and selling currency. In relation to such supplies, the consideration would be the net result of all forex transactions over a period and would be VAT exempt (see Revenue & Customs Brief 05/07).

Trusts (ITA 2007, ss 474–476; TCGA 1992, ss 2, 10A, 13(10), 68–73, 79A–98A and Schs 5, 5A)

[41.64] Trustees are treated, both for income tax and CGT, as a single person unless the context otherwise requires. From 6 April 2007, that notional person is treated as resident and ordinarily resident in the UK if either (a) all the trustees are UK resident or (b) at least one trustee is UK resident (at least one trustee being non-UK resident) and the settlor was resident, ordinarily resident or domiciled in the UK either when he made the settlement or, for settlements created on death, immediately before his death. Anti-avoidance provisions prevent trustees exploiting the residence terms of double taxation agreements to reduce or eliminate a CGT charge (see **45.24**). HMRC guidance to assist in the determination of the residence of trustees can be found at http://www.hmrc.gov.uk/cnr/trustee-res-guidance.pdf.

Trustees are not directly chargeable to UK income tax for a tax year throughout which they are non-resident. Income from a UK source is paid to them under deduction of tax.

Non-resident trusts are dealt with by HMRC's Centre for Non-Residents. Special provisions apply to reduce or eliminate the tax advantages of offshore trusts as indicated in **41.65** to **41.67**. See **40.14** in relation to the income tax charge on gains on offshore life policies held in trust and **45.24** for brief notes on other anti-avoidance provisions.

Exit charge when trust becomes non-resident

[41.65] Where a trust becomes non-resident, all the trust assets (except any that remain within the scope of UK tax, for example assets that continue to be used in a UK trade) are treated as disposed of and reacquired at market value, and gains are charged to CGT. Rollover relief on replacement of business assets (see **29.11 TO 29.16**) cannot be claimed if the new assets are acquired after the trust becomes non-resident and are outside the UK tax charge. These provisions also apply to dual resident trusts that are exempt from UK tax on gains because of a double tax treaty.

The acquisition cost of a beneficiary's interest in an emigrating trust for CGT is normally uplifted to the market value at the time of the trust's emigration. This uplift is, however, prevented by anti-avoidance provisions where the trust has a stockpile of gains that have not been attributed to beneficiaries.

Charge on settlor (TCGA 1992 s 86; ITTOIA 2005, s 624; ITA 2007, ss 721–724)

[41.66] Where gains are made by a non-resident trust (or a dual resident trust outside the UK capital gains charge), the settlor may be taxed on the gains. This applies where the settlor has an interest in the trust in the tax year in which the gains arise, and in that year he is UK domiciled and is either UK resident at some time during the year or is ordinarily resident. The gains can be reduced by the settlor's unused personal capital losses for the current year and earlier years. Any chargeable gains are treated as forming the highest part of the gains on which the settlor is chargeable for that year. The settlor has the right to recover from the trustees any tax charged on him.

A settlor is treated as having an interest in a trust if his or her spouse or civil partner, or his or her children or their spouses or civil partners have an interest, or an interest is held by a company controlled by the settlor and/or those persons. The settlor is also treated as having an interest in a trust in which grandchildren have an interest, if the trust was set up on or after 17 March 1998, or it was set up before that date but became non-resident, or funds were added, or grandchildren became beneficiaries, thereafter.

Where a settlor who is ordinarily resident in the UK settles property on a non-resident trust and has power to enjoy income therefrom, either immediately or in the future, that income is broadly deemed to be the settlor's income. Certain exemptions may apply and there are provisions to prevent double charging.

Charge on beneficiaries (TCGA 1992, s 87)

[41.67] Where gains are not charged on a settlor as indicated above, UK domiciled beneficiaries are charged to CGT on their share of the gains of a non-resident trust if they receive capital payments from the trust when they are resident or ordinarily resident in the UK. The tax on a capital payment to a beneficiary is increased by a supplementary charge if gains are not distributed to the beneficiaries in the tax year in which they are made or the following year. The charge runs from 1 December in the tax year following that in which the trustees' gains arose to 30 November in the tax year after that in which the gain is distributed to the beneficiary. The charge is at an annual rate of 10% of the tax on the capital payment, with a maximum of six years, giving an overall maximum possible rate of $60 \times 18\% = 10.8\%$, in addition to the CGT already payable.

Gains realised by beneficiaries on *disposal* of their interests in a non-resident trust are taxable if the trust is, or has at any time been, an offshore trust.

In arriving at the gains to be attributed to beneficiaries under these provisions, the beneficiaries' own losses cannot be set against the trustees' gains.

Income from a non-resident trust attributable to a beneficiary resident in the UK is chargeable as miscellaneous income. Credit will be available for any tax suffered by the trustees.

Various schemes have been devised to avoid the tax charge on the beneficiaries and specific anti-avoidance legislation has been introduced to counteract them. See **45.24** for brief details.

Tax points

[41.68] Note the following:

- Taxpayers, other than short-term visitors to the UK, who are eligible for the remittance basis may be able to claim the benefit of that basis only if they pay an additional tax charge of £30,000 (see **41.14**). They need to consider carefully the pros and cons of making the claim.

- An employee whose work is wholly carried out abroad, should try to arrange for the employer to meet the cost of overseas board and lodging, so that the taxable benefit can then be offset by an expenses claim; otherwise the employee will get no tax relief on it.

- If UK property is let out it is not necessary to be *non-resident* to be within the rules requiring tax to be deducted from the rents. The rules apply if the landlord's 'usual place of abode' is abroad — see **41.34**.

- An individual who is resident, ordinarily resident and domiciled in the UK, has to pay tax on all income wherever in the world it arises. It is not possible to escape income tax by investing in offshore roll-up funds — see **45.16**.

- Many people invest in offshore bank and building society accounts to get the benefit of receiving gross income (although tax is still payable unless covered by reliefs and allowances). Much of the cash flow benefit is lost for those making half-yearly payments on account under self-assessment. There are also problems in the event of death, because of the possible need to take out probate of the will abroad. These points need to be borne in mind when considering whether the investment is worthwhile.

- Individuals that are taxed on income or gains remitted to the UK, might consider keeping funds abroad separate where possible, supported by detailed records, so that it can be demonstrated, where appropriate, that remittances do not represent either income or chargeable gains. FA 2008 contained detailed changes aimed at closing 'loopholes' in this area.

42

Trusts and estates

Background

[42.1] A trust, or settlement, arises when someone transfers assets to trustees who hold them and the income from them for the benefit of one or more persons.

A trust can be created in lifetime, or on death by a will or under the intestacy rules where a person does not leave a will (sometimes referred to as a statutory trust). See **CHAPTER 35**, which also deals generally with planning points relating to a deceased's estate.

The overseas aspect of trusts is dealt with at **41.64** to **41.67**. See also **40.14** regarding gains on offshore life policies held in trust.

There are a number of anti-avoidance provisions that specifically relate to trusts. The rules for gains on disposal of a private residence occupied under the terms of a trust are dealt with in **30.9**. The 'pre-owned assets' income tax charge on benefits received by those who continue to enjoy a benefit from property they have disposed of, including the disposal of property to a trust, is dealt with briefly in **5.37**. See **29.33** for the special tax provisions where trustees receive a distribution arising out of the purchase by a company of its own shares and **45.24** for other trust anti-avoidance provisions.

HMRC's work on UK resident trusts and the administration of deceased's estates is dealt with by HMRC Trusts, except for some small estates where no trust is involved, which are dealt with in local tax offices. Non-resident trusts are dealt with by the Centre for Non-Residents. HMRC guidance is available at www.hmrc.gov.uk/trusts.

The tax law and practice relating to estates and trusts is complex and was made more so by Finance Act 2006. It is essential to seek appropriate professional advice.

Administration of an estate

[42.2] Where a trust is created on death, the personal representatives must first complete the administration of the estate. They need to deal with the deceased's tax position for the year of death (and earlier years if returns have not been submitted) and also their own tax position as personal representatives until the administration of the estate is completed. The normal time limit for enquiring into a tax return for 2007/08 onwards is 12 months after the date on which the return is filed (see **9.31**). To minimise delays in winding up estates and trusts, and distributing estate or trust property, HMRC will, on request, issue tax returns before the end of the tax year of death, or of winding up an estate or trust, and will give early confirmation if they do not intend to enquire into the return. See **9.40** re limits in relation to HMRC enquiries into the tax position of a deceased taxpayer.

The personal representatives will not usually be able to settle the deceased's tax liabilities until probate is obtained, and the inheritance tax (IHT) due must be paid before probate is granted. Under an agreement between HMRC and the British Bankers' and Building Societies' Associations, participating institutions accept instructions from personal representatives to transfer sums standing to the credit of the deceased direct to HMRC in payment of IHT before the issue of the grant. This is of considerable practical help where the personal representatives do not have ready access to other funds outside the estate, such as the proceeds of an insurance policy on the life of the deceased which do not belong to the estate. The deceased's tax office should be asked to arrange for the HMRC Accounts Office not to issue any further self assessment statements pending probate being obtained, since they can often cause needless distress to the family. By HMRC concession A17, interest on tax falling due after death will not start to run until thirty days after the grant of probate.

The administration period during which the personal representatives deal with the collection of assets and payment of liabilities and the distribution of the estate may last some months or even years if the estate is complex.

[42.3] Personal representatives deal with the estate of a deceased either under the terms of the will, according to the rules of intestacy where there is no will, or under a deed varying the will or entitlement in the intestacy. (For the way an intestate person's estate is distributed see **35.1**.) Income tax is payable on the income of the deceased up to the date of death, with a full year's allowances, any unused married couple's age allowance of the deceased spouse or civil partner being transferable to the other if the personal representatives notify HMRC (see **33.12**). If the deceased had chargeable gains in excess of the annual exemption in the tax year of his death, capital gains tax (CGT) is payable but there is no CGT on the increase in the value of assets held at death. If there are capital losses in the year of death, they may be carried back to set against gains of the three previous tax years, latest first (ignoring any gains already covered by the annual exemption), and tax will be repaid accordingly (but interest on the repayment will run from the payment date for the tax year of death — see **9.6**).

IHT is payable if transfers of wealth by the deceased in the seven years before death which were either then chargeable or potentially exempt, together with the amount chargeable at death, exceed the threshold (currently £325,000). See **35.3** regarding the transfer of any unused part of the IHT nil rate band, on the death of the first spouse or civil partner to die, to the survivor on the survivor's own death after 8 October 2007.

See **9.21** to **9.51** for further details, including the provisions under which an IHT account does not have to be submitted for small estates. Assets to which a surviving spouse or civil partner becomes entitled either absolutely, or to enjoy the income with the assets being predestined for others upon the death of the survivor, are not chargeable to IHT at that time, but will be included in the survivor's estate for IHT upon his or her death or earlier lifetime transfer. The value of business and agricultural property can be eliminated from the calculation of IHT in some circumstances. The way in which the tax is calculated is dealt with in **CHAPTER 5**.

Personal representatives need to be aware that HMRC take a harsh view in relation to provisional figures included without proper enquiry in calculating IHT for the purpose of obtaining probate, even though those calculations can be revised later and any additional tax paid (called a 'corrective' account). Before including such figures, personal representatives are required to make 'the fullest enquiries that are reasonably practicable in the circumstances' and in a case before the Special Commissioners HMRC sought (although without success) to exact a penalty despite the fact that accurate figures were submitted long before the due date for payment of IHT. (The due date is often meaningless because of the need to pay the IHT before obtaining probate.) HMRC announced in their December 2004 IHT Newsletter that they would be paying close attention to the values included for IHT in respect of household and personal goods and may open an enquiry to satisfy themselves that all of the goods have been included and that they have been valued on the correct 'market value' basis.

Where the deceased's property is rebanded after death for council tax purposes, any refund arising from an earlier overpayment will be subject to IHT, although the value of the refund may be reduced by 50%.

Where property is transferred to those entitled under a will or intestacy, neither stamp duty nor stamp duty land tax is payable. Nor is stamp duty land tax payable when personal representatives dispose of a deceased's home to a property trader.

Income during the administration period (ITA 2007, ss 11, 14, 403–405; ITTOIA 2005, ss 649–682; CTA 2009, ss 934–968)

[42.4] Personal representatives are liable to income tax at 10% on dividend income and at the basic rate on other income. Personal representatives are not taxed at the starting rate or the higher rate, nor can they claim personal allowances. If the deceased held individual savings accounts (ISAs), the tax exemption ceases at the date of death (see **36.27**), so that the basic rate (prior to 2008/09, the savings rate) of 20% will be charged on any subsequent interest. Where the personal representatives have borrowed to pay IHT other than on land and buildings, preparatory to obtaining a grant of probate, interest payable for up to one year from the date of the loan may be deducted from the estate income of the tax year of payment. If the interest exceeds the estate income of that tax year, it may be carried back against estate income of preceding tax years, and any remaining amount may be carried forward against future estate income.

The income during the administration period will be distributed to the beneficiaries entitled to it either because they are entitled absolutely to the assets or because, while the assets remain in trust, they are entitled to the income. Any payments to a beneficiary on account of income during the administration period are net of the 'applicable rate' of tax, i.e. the dividend ordinary rate of 10% or the basic rate (prior to 2008/09, the savings rate) of 20% according to the income they represent. The gross equivalent is included in taxable income in the tax year when it is received by the beneficiary from the personal representatives. Payments to beneficiaries are treated as being made first out of brought-forward and current income charged at the basic rate, then dividends carrying a non-repayable tax credit at the dividend ordinary rate of 10%. Dividend income includes normal dividends, scrip dividends, loans written off by close companies and bonus issues of redeemable shares or securities. The total income will first have been apportioned between beneficiaries on a just and reasonable basis, the personal representatives being required to provide a certificate showing the types of income and the tax deducted.

The rate of tax treated as deducted from payments to beneficiaries is not necessarily the same as that borne by the personal representatives, since the relevant rate is the applicable rate in force at the time of the payment to the beneficiaries, rather than the rate in force when the income was received. When the administration period is completed and the final amount of income due to each beneficiary ascertained, the beneficiary is treated as having received the balance due to him in the tax year in which the administration is completed (or, for someone with a life entitlement whose interest ceased earlier, say because of his death, in the tax year when the interest ceased). The amount due to each beneficiary is grossed up at the relevant rate in force at the time according to the income it represents.

Capital gains during the administration period (TCGA 1992, ss 3(7), 4, 62, 225A; F(No.2)A 2010, s 2 and Sch 1)

[42.5] No CGT arises on the transfer to legatees of assets comprising specific legacies, the legatees acquiring them at market value at the date of death. Assets that pass to the personal representatives (out of which they pay debts due and distribute the residue of the estate) are also acquired by them at market value at the date of death. Any gains arising on a disposal of assets by the personal representatives are calculated by reference to the sales proceeds less the value at death. The personal representatives are entitled in their own right to the annual exemption, currently £10,100, against any gains on their disposals in the tax year of death and the next two tax years, but not thereafter. In 2010/11 gains in excess of the exempt limit are taxed at 18% for disposals before 23 June 2010 and at 28% for disposals thereafter. If any losses arise, they may only be set against gains of the personal representatives and cannot be transferred to beneficiaries. However, for 2010/11, where gains are taxable at more than one rate, the annual exemption and losses can be applied in a way that produces the lowest possible tax charge. Therefore, where the personal representatives have gains both before and after 23 June 2010, the exemption and any losses should be applied to the gains arising on or after 23 June 2010. This is subject to any existing legislation that limits the way in which certain losses may be set off.

If the private residence is to be sold by the personal representatives, a chargeable gain may arise between death and sale. The private residence exemption is available following a claim by the personal representatives where the property has been used immediately before and after death as the main residence of individuals who are entitled to at least 75% of the net sale proceeds either absolutely or for life. Where the exemption was not available for a disposal prior to 6 April 2008 it might have been appropriate for personal representatives to consider a transfer of the property to beneficiaries, so that the gain was charged at their personal tax rates rather than the flat 40% rate then applicable to the personal representatives on gains above the annual exemption. Now that the rate of CGT payable by personal representatives has been reduced the incentive for such a transfer has been reduced (but a transfer might still be effective if, for example, the personal representatives have used their annual exemption but the beneficiaries have not, or the beneficiaries' tax rates are less than those of the personal representatives).

Personal representatives do not qualify for gift hold-over relief, but trustees do. Where the residue of the estate is left on trust, the personal representatives should ensure that assets on which gift hold-over is available and is appropriate to be claimed have been formally appropriated by the personal representatives to the trustees (which will usually but not necessarily be themselves, but then acting in a different capacity) before being allocated to those entitled under the trust.

End of administration period

[42.6] The administration period ends either when the whole estate is finally distributed if no trust has been created, or when the residue of the estate after payment of debts and legacies is transferred to a trust fund. There is no chargeable gain on personal representatives when they transfer assets to beneficiaries or trustees, the assets transferred being regarded as acquired by the beneficiaries or trustees at market value at the date of death or the cost to the personal representatives if acquired later.

Types of trust

[42.7] Apart from a bare trust, which effectively means that someone holds an asset as nominee for another (see **42.15**), trusts broadly come within the following categories for taxation purposes:

(a) Trusts in which before 22 March 2006 one or more individuals were entitled under a lifetime settlement or by will or intestacy to the income (called the 'interest in possession'), with the capital being predestined elsewhere at a future point, and the trustees sometimes having overriding powers. The person entitled to the interest is called the life tenant (see **42.16**).

(b) As in (a) but either:

   (i) the present life interest came to an end by death or otherwise before 6 October 2008, with a new life tenant then being entitled to the interest in possession, or

   (ii) the present life interest comes to an end on or after 6 October 2008 on the death of the life tenant and a surviving spouse or civil partner then becomes entitled to an interest in possession.

   An interest arising under (i) or (ii) is called a 'transitional serial interest'. Finance Act 2006 provided for a transitional period up to 5 April 2008 but Finance Act 2008 extended that period (in relation to interest in possession trusts only) by six months.

(c) Trusts in which from 22 March 2006, one or more individuals are entitled under a will or intestacy to the income, with the capital being predestined to go to one or more individuals or to remain in an appropriate trust at a future point — called an immediate post-death interest.

(d) Accumulation and maintenance trusts (see **42.37** to **42.42**). Before 22 March 2006 these trusts received favourable IHT treatment where they provided for children of a common grandparent to have income used for their benefit or accumulated, with a child being entitled to his or her share at age 25. It was sufficient for the child's entitlement at that age to be the right to his or her share of the income whilst the capital remained in trust.

   New accumulation and maintenance trusts from 22 March 2006 only fall within the special provisions for such trusts if they are established for bereaved minors either on an intestacy, under the will of a deceased parent or under the Criminal Injuries Compensation Scheme. The requirement for beneficiaries to have a common grandparent no longer applies. Under the new provisions, the beneficiary must be entitled to his or her share of the capital at age 18 in order for IHT not to be chargeable. Where the child has a right only to income at that age, but has an entitlement to his or her share of the capital by age 25, special IHT provisions apply.

   For trusts in existence at 22 March 2006, the terms could be changed by 5 April 2008 to bring them within the new rules. If such changes were not made, the trusts now come within the 'mainstream' IHT rules (as to which see (g)).

(e) Trusts for a vulnerable beneficiary, i.e. a disabled person or a child under 18, one or both of whose parents have died (see **42.43** to **42.46**).

(f)   Self-settlements under which from 22 March 2006 an individual with a condition expected to lead to disability can settle assets on himself/herself for lifetime (see **42.47**).

(g)   Trusts within the 'mainstream' IHT rules for trusts (see **42.27** to **42.36**). Before 22 March 2006 these rules were generally known as the rules for discretionary trusts, i.e. trusts where the trustees had a discretion as to what they did with the income and capital. FA 2006 gave the rules the label 'mainstream' and extended their coverage so that they apply in all cases except those listed in (a) to (f) above.

Prior to FA 2006, on the death of a life tenant entitled to the income under (a) above, the capital supporting that interest was included in his estate at death for IHT. This still applies where that life tenant, or one with a transitional serial interest under (b) above, dies (see Example 2 in **42.23**). It also applies on the death of the life tenant under (c). In all of these cases the value of the assets for CGT purposes is increased to the value at the date of death, without any CGT being payable.

For trusts under (d) and (g) above, the value of the capital within a trust fund will not be reckoned for IHT at the death of a beneficiary, and neither will the value of the trust assets be uplifted to the value at a death in calculating the CGT payable on a later disposal by the trustees.

For trusts falling within (g) above, there is a charge to IHT every ten years, based on the value of the trust funds at that point, together with a further charge when capital is distributed to beneficiaries (called an 'exit charge'). There is no CGT effect at the ten-year anniversary. There is a disposal by the trustees for CGT purposes when they distribute assets to beneficiaries, but hold-over relief may be available (see **4.24**).

There is no IHT ten-year or exit charge on an accumulation and maintenance trust where the capital is required to be distributed to beneficiaries at age 18. Where that is not so, there will be an exit charge, the calculation of which is restricted by reference to the years after age 18 (see **42.42**). There will be a disposal for CGT where the trustees distribute assets to beneficiaries, but hold-over relief (see **4.24**) is available.

Trusts for vulnerable beneficiaries and qualifying self-settlements (see (e) and (f) above) are broadly dealt with as if the assets and income belong to the beneficiary, and the trust assets will be included in the beneficiary's estate at death.

Further details on each type of trust, including the income tax position, are given in the remainder of this chapter.

Powers over trusts (IHTA 1984, ss 47A, 55A, 272)

[42.8] Trusts may include a general power for the settlor to dispose of trust property as he sees fit. Powers over trusts are normally not treated as part of a person's property for IHT purposes. This is subject to anti-avoidance rules where such powers are purchased.

Trusts in which the settlor retains an interest — income tax and capital gains tax position (ITTOIA 2005, ss 619–648; TCGA 1992, Schs 4A–4C; FA 2000, s 44)

[42.9] The settlor remains liable for income tax on the trust income if he or his spouse or civil partner retains a present or future right to the income or assets of the trust, or where the settlement transfers income but not capital (see 12.10, 18.7 and 23.25 for detailed comments). 'Spouse or civil partner' does not include a future, former, separated or deceased spouse or civil partner.

Even though a settlement is of capital in which the settlor does not retain an interest, if income of the settlement is paid to or for the benefit of an unmarried child of the settlor who is under 18, it is treated as the settlor's income, subject to the exceptions at 33.10 (see also 42.15 and 42.38). The settlor is entitled to recover the tax paid by him from the trustees, or from the person who received the income. The income tax liability on the settlor does not apply to the extent that the trustees give the income to charity, or a charity is entitled to the income under the trust.

The settlor may receive a repayment of tax if he is taxable at a lower rate than the trustees. If the repayment arises because of an allowance or relief available to him he must pass the repayment to the trustees. It is proposed that from 6 April 2010 any repayment received must be passed to the trustees regardless of how it arose.

[42.10] As far as CGT is concerned, see 42.14 regarding the denial of gift hold-over relief on transfers to a settlor-interested trust. Prior to 2008/09, gains made by the trustees of settlor-interested trusts were taxed as if they were the settlor's personal gains. The settlor could, however, recover from the trustees any CGT paid by him. Finance Act 2008 abolished this rule with effect from 2008/09.

[42.11] Where a beneficiary disposes of an interest in a trust in which the settlor has an interest (or had an interest at any time in the two previous tax years), there is a deemed disposal and reacquisition by the trustees at market value, and the settlor is charged on the resulting gains. Gift hold-over relief is not available. See 45.24 for anti-avoidance provisions to counter a tax avoidance device known as the 'flip flop'.

Tax liability on setting up a trust (IHTA 1984, s 200; TCGA 1992, ss 165, 169B–169G, 260)

Inheritance tax

[42.12] The appropriate amount of IHT is charged on a deceased's estate before property is transferred to a trust created by his will or on intestacy.

The only lifetime transfers to trusts which do not come within the mainstream rules for IHT (see 42.27) are those for the disabled and by the settlor for himself to provide for his future disability (see 42.46). Otherwise the settlor is liable to IHT on the property transferred to the trust at one-half of the scale rate, except to the extent that the transfer is within the nil rate band. The transfer has to be grossed up if the settlor also pays the IHT (see CHAPTER 5). If the settlor dies within the next seven years, tax on the lifetime transfer is recalculated using the full rate and scale applicable at the date of death less a credit up to the amount of any tax already charged in lifetime.

Capital gains tax

[42.13] As indicated in 42.6, no CGT arises when property is transferred to trustees by personal representatives.

When assets are placed into trust in lifetime, they are treated as disposed of at market value for CGT, but where the mainstream IHT rules for trusts apply, the gains may be held over under the gift hold-over relief provisions (see 4.24 to 4.26).

Where gift hold-over relief has been claimed, the effect is to increase the chargeable gain when the donee disposes of the asset.

[42.14] Gift hold-over relief is not available on disposals to a trust in which either a settlor (who need not be the transferor) has an interest or there are arrangements under which a settlor will acquire an interest. Gift relief is also denied in respect of a gain on a disposal to a trust if the expenditure allowable in calculating the gain is reduced by gift relief on an earlier disposal, and immediately after the disposal the transferor has an interest in the trust, or there are arrangements under which he will acquire an interest. Where gift relief is not available, the transferor will be entitled to the annual exemption.

Where a disposal is made to a trust that is not initially a settlor-interested trust, any gift relief on the disposal is clawed back if the settlor acquires an interest within six years after the disposal.

Bare trusts (ITTOIA 2005, ss 629–631)

[42.15] A bare trust is one in which the beneficiary has an absolute right to the assets and income, but the trustees are the legal owners and hold the property effectively as nominee. The transfer to the bare trust is a potentially exempt transfer for IHT, becoming completely exempt if the donor survives the seven-year period. Following the changes to trust taxation in FA 2006, HMRC initially took the view that a transfer to such a trust was no longer potentially exempt, but they have now confirmed that the pre FA 2006 treatment still applies.

A bare trust could simply be a bank or building society account in the settlor's name as trustee for the beneficiary, and in that event the trust income would not be depleted by administration expenses.

The tax position of the trust depends on the beneficiary's circumstances rather than those of the donor or the trustee, so that the trust income is included with that of the beneficiary in calculating how much of the beneficiary's income tax personal allowances and starting rate band are available. Likewise the question of whether any CGT reliefs and exemptions are available on the disposal of chargeable assets depends upon the circumstances of the beneficiary. Beneficiaries must show their income and gains from a bare trust in their own tax returns and trustees are not required to complete returns. HMRC have, however, stated that the trustees may, if they wish, send in a return of income (but not capital gains). This will not affect the liability of the beneficiaries to send returns of both income and gains. Any tax deducted at source will be refunded if covered by reliefs and allowances.

The income tax treatment described above applies to bare trusts created before 9 March 1999 even if such a trust was made by a parent in favour of a child (and the parent could be the trustee), providing the income is not actually paid to or for the benefit of the child while the child is unmarried and under 18. If it is, the income would then be treated as the parent's under the provisions at **42.9**. The child cannot be prevented from having the property put into his own legal ownership at age 18.

For bare trusts created by parents on or after 9 March 1999 in favour of their children under 18, and for income on funds added to existing trusts on or after that date, income is taxed as that of the parent, unless covered by the £100 limit dealt with at **33.10**. Bare trusts created by a parent's will are still effective to treat income as that of the beneficiary, and also bare trusts created by other relatives, although it is not possible to make a reciprocal arrangement for someone to create a trust for his relative's children and for the relative to do the same for his children.

Bare trusts created by parents are effective for capital gains purposes, so that it is possible to use such trusts to acquire investments for children that produce capital growth rather than income. Where capital gains are made, a bare trust is entitled to the full annual exemption (currently £10,100) rather than half of that amount as applies to other trusts (or proportionate amount where several trusts are created by the settlor).

Trusts with an interest in possession

Income tax (TA 1988, s 689B; ITA 2007, ss 6–21, 484–487)

[42.16] Where there is an interest in possession, one or more beneficiaries has a right to the trust income.

The trustees are charged to tax on dividend income at the dividend ordinary rate of 10% and on other income at the basic rate (currently 20%). Trustees are not liable to higher rate tax. Income is calculated in the same way as for an individual. There are, however, no deductions for personal allowances. There is no relief in calculating the tax payable by the trustees for expenses of managing the trust, which are therefore paid out of the after-tax income. Expenses are treated as paid out of savings income in priority to non-savings income and out of dividend income before other savings income.

The income beneficiaries are personally liable to income tax on that income less the trust expenses, whether they draw the income or it remains in the trust fund as an amount owed to the beneficiary (except where the settlor has retained an interest and the tax is payable by him — see **42.9**). The beneficiaries are entitled to a credit for the tax paid by the trustees on that part of the trust income that has not been used to pay trust expenses, but the tax credit on dividends is non-repayable.

Example 1

Trust's income in 2010/11 comprises rents of £3,195 gross, £2,556 net after tax of £639. The trust expenses are £156. The beneficiary will receive (2,556 – 156 =) £2,400, which is equivalent to gross income of £3,000. If he is a basic rate taxpayer he will have no further liability and will retain the £2,400. If he is not liable to tax he will reclaim tax of (3,000 @ 20% =) £600, if he is a higher rate payer he will have an additional liability of 20% of £3,000, i.e. £600, and if he is an additional rate taxpayer he will have a liability of 30% of £3,000, i.e. £900.

If instead the trust's net income comprised rents of £1,278 after tax of £319, and cash dividends of £1,278 with tax credits of £142, the trust expenses would reduce the dividend income to £1,122, with a tax credit of £125. The beneficiary would still receive £2,400, but the gross income would be (1,597 + 1,247 =) £2,844. A basic rate taxpayer would retain the £2,400. A non-taxpaying beneficiary would be able to reclaim only £319. A higher rate payer would have to pay 20% of £1,597 = £319 plus 22.5% of £1,247 = £280, giving a total of £599. An additional rate taxpayer would have to pay 30% of £1,597 = £479 plus 32.5% of £1,247 = £405 giving a total of £884.

The need to pay expenses out of the taxed income of the trust may be minimised if specific income is paid direct to the beneficiary, for example, by a mandate to a building society to pay interest direct, with a consequent saving in administration expenses. This will improve the position of a beneficiary who is entitled to a tax repayment, but for a higher rate or additional rate taxpayer it will deny relief on the trust expenses at the excess of the higher rate or additional rate over that paid by the trustees.

Capital gains tax (TCGA 1992, ss 4, 71–74, 79A, 165 and Schs 1, 7; F(No.2)A 2010, s 2 and Sch 1)

[42.17] The only interest in possession trusts created in lifetime after 21 March 2006 which are not subject to the mainstream IHT rules are a trust for a disabled person and a trust in favour of the settlor to provide for his future disability (see **42.46**). For such a self-settlement, if the settlor transfers chargeable assets to the trust, he is liable to CGT. The gift hold-over relief is not available since he retains an interest in the trust (see **42.14**). Gains on a disposal of chargeable assets by the trustees prior to 6 April 2008 would be treated as the settlor's gains (see **42.10**). Anti-avoidance provisions apply to counter a tax avoidance device known as the 'flip flop', which aimed to reduce or eliminate the tax on disposals from a trust. These are outlined at **45.24**.

[42.18] Trust gains are reduced by an annual exemption (£5,050 for 2010/11) and in 2010/11 the remaining gains are taxed at 18% for disposals before 23 June 2010 and at 28% for disposals thereafter. However, in 2010/11, where gains are taxable at more than one rate, the annual exemption and losses can be applied in a way that produces the lowest possible tax charge, so where the trustees have gains both before and after 23 June 2010, the exemption and any losses should be applied to the gains arising on or after 23 June 2010. This is subject to any existing legislation that limits the way in which certain losses may be set off. Where there are a number of trusts created by the same settlor, the annual exemption of £5,050 is divided equally between them, subject to a minimum exemption of £1,010 for each trust. Trusts for the disabled qualify for the full annual exemption of £10,100, reduced where the same settlor has created several disabled trusts, with a minimum exemption for each disabled trust of £1,010.

Where losses arise on disposals by the trustees, they cannot be set against any gains made by the trustees on assets that had been transferred to the trust if the transferor or someone connected with him had bought an interest in the trust and had claimed gift hold-over relief on the transferred assets (see **45.24**).

[42.19] When a beneficiary becomes absolutely entitled to trust property following the death of the person entitled to the income, the trustees are regarded as disposing of the property to the beneficiary at its then market value, but no CGT liability arises. Any increase in value up to that time escapes CGT (and any losses are not allowable). Where the CGT cost of the property had been reduced by gift holdover relief (see **4.23** to **4.26**), there is a chargeable gain equal to the held over amount. If the property is still qualifying business property for gift hold-over relief, a further claim to defer the tax liability may be made by the trustees and beneficiary, so that the gain will be treated as reducing the acquisition cost of the beneficiary.

Broadly gift relief applies to settled property if the trustees make a non-arm's length disposal of a specified business asset and a claim is made by the trustees and the transferee, or the trustees alone where they are also the transferee. The specified assets are:

(a)   an asset, or interest in an asset, used for the purposes of a trade, profession or vocation carried on by the trustees, or by a beneficiary who had an interest in possession in the settled property immediately before the disposal; or

(b)   shares or securities of a trading company, or of a holding company of a trading group, where either the shares are unlisted or the trustees held at least 25% of the voting rights at the time of the disposal.

[42.20] When a life interest terminates other than on death, for example because a widow remarries, but the property remains in trust, there is neither a chargeable gain nor any change in the base value of the property for future CGT disposals by the trustees.

When, however, a beneficiary becomes absolutely entitled to trust property other than on the death of the person entitled to the income, this is regarded as a disposal at market value at that date, and CGT is payable on the increase in value. The same provisions for deferring the gain apply as stated above if the property still qualifies for business gift hold-over relief. Where the deemed market value disposal to the beneficiary results in an allowable loss that the trustees cannot use against gains arising at the time of the transfer or earlier in the same tax year, the loss is treated as made by the beneficiary who has become absolutely entitled to the asset, but the beneficiary can use the loss only to reduce a gain on the disposal of the asset, or in the case of land, an asset derived from the land, thus restricting his chargeable gain to that which would have arisen had he adopted the base value of the trustees as his own (see **45.24**).

[42.21] If when a life interest ends, the property goes back to the settlor, the trustees are only chargeable to tax to the extent that gains have been held over, and even then, the special rules for assets acquired before 31 March 1982 (see **4.15**) may apply. The settlor is treated as acquiring the property at its cost (and as having held it on 31 March 1982 if it was settled before that date, enabling him to use 31 March 1982 value to compute a gain if appropriate).

[42.22] If a beneficiary under a trust transfers his interest to someone else, this is not normally treated as a chargeable disposal for CGT, whether he is transferring a life interest or a reversionary interest (i.e. the right to the capital of the trust when those with life interests die or give up their interests). There is a chargeable disposal if the beneficiary had bought the interest from someone else, or had acquired it by gift from someone who had bought it.

See **42.11** for the position where a beneficiary sells an interest in a settlement in which the settlor has an interest (or has had an interest at any time in the two previous tax years). See also **41.67** for disposals of an interest in an overseas trust.

Inheritance tax (IHTA 1984, Pt III)

[42.23] Someone who became entitled to the income for the time being from a trust fund established before 22 March 2006, or became so entitled on or after that date and the interest is a transitional serial interest (see **42.7** at (b)), or an immediate post-death interest (see **42.7** at (c)), or a disabled person's interest (see **42.46**), is regarded for IHT purposes as entitled to the underlying capital, so that he is treated as making a chargeable transfer of that capital on his death. This will also apply to an interest in possession to which a person becomes beneficially entitled after 8 December 2009 where it is purchased at full value. This is an anti-avoidance provision introduced by FA 2010 to prevent the avoidance of IHT on assets transferred into a trust where the individual purchases an interest that had not been subject to UK IHT when the property was originally transferred into it. Although any tax is calculated by reference to his own chargeable position, it has to be paid by the trustees. The fact that trust funds are treated as belonging to the beneficiary entitled to the income prevents wealth being protected from IHT through the use of an interest in possession trust. It may also result in IHT being paid on the income

beneficiary's own estate whereas his estate would have been below the nil band
if the trust funds had not been included.

Example 2

A taxpayer died on 30 September 2010, having made no transfers in lifetime
other than a potentially exempt transfer of £226,000 after annual exemptions of £6,000 in June 2008. At his death, his own assets less liabilities
(called his free estate) were valued at £100,000. He had also been entitled
for many years to the income from trust funds, the value of which were
£50,000 and to which his daughter became absolutely entitled. He was a
widower, his estate being left to his son.

The IHT payable on his death is:

		Gross	Tax
Lifetime transfer*		226,000	—
Free estate at death	100,000		
Trust funds at death	50,000	150,000	20,400**
		£376,000	£20,400

** (376,000 − 325,000) = £51,000 @ 40% = £20,400

The tax is payable as
follows:

From free estate (pay- able by personal repre- sentatives)	$\dfrac{100,000}{150,000} \times £\,20,400$	13,600
From trust funds (pay- able by trustees)	$\dfrac{50,000}{150,000} \times £\,20,400$	6,800
		£20,400

If the trust fund had not counted as part of the chargeable estate, the amount
reckonable for IHT on the estate would have been (326,000 − 325,000) =
£1,000 @ 40%, i.e. £400.

*Although potentially exempt in lifetime, the transfer must be taken into
account at death because the taxpayer died within seven years after making
it.

Where there are successive IHT charges on the trust property within five years,
the tax payable on the later transfer may be reduced by quick succession relief
(see **5.45**).

[42.24] Where the individual entitled to a life interest gives it up in favour of another individual or a disabled trust, or the life tenant changes under the rules for a transitional serial interest (see **42.7** at (a)), this will be a potentially exempt transfer in so far as that individual is concerned. This will also apply where someone with an immediate post-death interest (see **42.7** at (c)) gives it up in favour of a bereaved minor's trust (see **42.7** at (d)). But otherwise, the transfer of the interest will be regarded as an immediately chargeable lifetime transfer by the former life tenant, and will fall within the mainstream IHT rules.

[42.25] Prior to FA 2006 the creation of a trust fund in which someone was entitled to the income was a potentially exempt transfer for IHT, and only attracted tax if the settlor died within seven years. This provided the settlor with an efficient means of tax planning, since the individual entitled to the income could not access the capital. This is no longer possible for lifetime settlements from 22 March 2006 (except for settlements for a disabled person — see **42.46**), because the settlement comes within the mainstream IHT rules, so that the transfer of funds itself will be a chargeable transfer attracting IHT at the lifetime rate of 20% (rising to 40% if death occurs within seven years) and the charges every subsequent ten years and on distribution of the capital to the beneficiary will apply. It follows that the capital value of such a settlement is no longer included alongside the free estate of the income beneficiary as illustrated in Example 2.

[42.26] For a pre 22 March 2006 interest in possession settlement (including one with a transitional serial interest), or a disabled person's settlement, IHT is not chargeable if the settled property reverts to the settlor, or if his/her spouse or civil partner (or surviving spouse/civil partner if the settlor had died less than two years earlier) becomes beneficially entitled to the property and is UK domiciled. The value of the capital supporting the life interest is also excluded from the reckoning on a life tenant's death if the interest is an immediate post-death interest (see **42.7** at (c)), the settlor died less than two years earlier than the life tenant and the settlor's spouse or civil partner then takes the assets.

Subject to certain exceptions, the capital supporting a life interest will not be reckoned as a chargeable transfer upon the cessation of the life interest in possession if the person entitled to the life interest then becomes entitled to the capital itself.

Where an individual transfers property into a trust in which they or their spouse or civil partner retains a future interest (a reversionary interest) or where the individual purchases such a reversionary interest there will be an IHT charge when the interest comes to an end and they become entitled to the property or if they gift the reversionary interest. It applies to reversionary interests in relevant property to which the individual becomes entitled after 8 December 2009 (and does not therefore apply to certain interests in possession such as a disabled person's interest).

Tax rules for trusts within the mainstream inheritance tax regime

[42.27] What are now referred to as the 'mainstream' IHT rules for trusts previously applied only where the trustees had discretionary power over the distribution of income and appointment of capital. From 22 March 2006 the provisions were extended to all trusts except qualifying interest in possession trusts, qualifying accumulation and maintenance trusts and trusts for the disabled.

Income tax (TA 1988, ss 689B, 832; ITA 2007, ss 479–503)

[42.28] Even though many life interest trusts are now within the mainstream IHT rules, the income tax treatment of such trusts remains as stated in **42.16**. For trusts in which the trustees have discretionary power over the distribution of income and no-one is entitled to it as of right, income tax is chargeable at 50% from 6 April 2010, previously 40% (known as the trust rate) on income other than dividend income. Dividend income is charged at the dividend trust rate of 42.5% from 6 April 2010, previously 32.5%, of which 10% is covered by the tax credit, leaving an additional 32.5% of the tax credit inclusive dividend income to pay (36% of the cash dividend received). The first £1,000 of the trust's income (known as the 'basic rate' band) is not, however, taxable at these special rates but is taxable instead at the basic rate of 20%, or the dividend ordinary rate of 10%. Although this enables trusts with a small amount of income to avoid a tax liability at the 50% or 42.5% rate, the 50% rate would still apply to any distribution of the income (see **42.29** and Example 3). In arriving at the amount chargeable at the 42.5% or 50% rate, trustees are entitled to deduct their expenses. Expenses are set first against dividend income then against other income, so that the part of the trust's income used to pay expenses will bear tax at 10% if it is dividend income, or the basic rate if it is other income. If the trust has any exempt income, either because the trustees are not resident or are treated as being non-resident under a double tax treaty, the allowable expenses are proportionately restricted. The trustees are not chargeable if the income is treated as the settlor's income (see **42.9**). In that event the settlor may recover from them (or from beneficiaries who receive the income) the tax he pays.

[42.29] Any income paid to beneficiaries (other than any that is treated as the settlor's income) is net of 50% tax, the beneficiary being entitled to an income tax repayment to the extent that the income is covered by available personal allowances or chargeable at less than 50%.

Even though the trustees are charged to tax at 42.5% (or, where appropriate, the dividend ordinary rate of 10%) on tax credit inclusive dividend income, the rate of tax regarded as deducted from payments to beneficiaries is still 50%, and non-taxpaying beneficiaries will still be able to recover that tax. The trustees cannot, however, count the dividend credit as tax paid by them when calculating how much of the tax deducted from the beneficiaries' income has to be accounted for by them. The result is that unless the trust has a pool of unused tax from earlier years (see **42.48**), the maximum gross amount that can be paid out without depleting the trust fund will be the amount of the cash dividend. The position is illustrated in Example 3.

Example 3

The following example ignores the effect of trust expenses and assumes that the trust has other income that has utilised the £1,000 'basic rate band' (see 42.28) and has no pool of unused tax.

Dividend of £180 plus tax credit of £20 was received by a discretionary trust in 2010/11 and distributed to the beneficiaries. The tax position is as follows:

	£
Tax on trust income of (180 + (1/9) 20) @ 42.5%	85
Less: Dividend tax credit	20
Tax payable by trustees @ 32.5% of £200 (tax credit inclusive dividend)	65
Leaving net income of (180 – 65) = £115	
Distribution to beneficiaries equal to cash dividend	180
Tax at 50%	90
Net payment to beneficiaries	90
Further tax to be accounted for by trustees (90 – 65)	25

Net payment to beneficiaries of £90 plus further tax payable of £25 = net trust income of £115.

Non-taxpaying beneficiaries could recover the tax of £90, so that their income would be £180.

If the dividend ordinary rate of 10% had applied to the dividend, the trustees would have had no tax to pay on the trust income. But they could still only distribute an amount equal to the cash dividend of £180, because they would have to account for tax at 50% on the whole amount, the trust not having paid any tax. This would amount to £90, leaving a net amount of £90 available for the beneficiaries as above.

Capital gains tax (TCGA 1992, ss 165, 260; F(No.2)A 2010, s 2 and Sch 1)

[42.30] The settlor is chargeable to CGT on any gains on chargeable assets transferred to the trust, but gains may instead be treated as reducing the trustees' acquisition cost under the gift hold-over relief provisions (see **4.24** to **4.26**). The hold-over relief is not restricted to business and other qualifying assets, the reasoning being that there is an immediate reckoning for IHT (see **42.31**). The settlor cannot, however, claim gift hold-over relief if he retains an interest in the trust (see **42.14**).

Gains on disposals of chargeable assets by the trustees are calculated in the normal way. The trustees are entitled to an annual exemption of £5,050 for 2010/11 (or proportionate part thereof where there are associated trusts). For 2010/11 the rate of tax on any remaining gains is 18% on disposals before 23 June 2010 and 28% on disposals thereafter. However, in 2010/11 the annual exemption and losses can be applied in a way that produces the lowest possible tax charge, so where the trustees have gains both before and after 23 June 2010, the exemption and any losses should be applied to the gains arising on or after 23 June 2010. This is subject to any existing legislation that limits the way in which certain losses may be set off.

When a beneficiary becomes absolutely entitled to any chargeable assets of the trust, the trustees are treated as disposing of the assets at market value at that date for CGT purposes (subject to the special rules for assets acquired before 31 March 1982), but if a gain arises the trustees and beneficiary may jointly elect for the tax liability to be deferred by treating the gains as reducing the beneficiary's acquisition cost for CGT, unless the distribution from the trust takes place within three months after its creation or within three months after a ten-year anniversary for IHT (see **42.31**). If the distribution takes place within such a three-month period, gift relief will still be available if the assets are qualifying business assets (see **4.24**). It may not be possible to defer CGT where a distribution is made out of a discretionary will trust as described in **35.16**. See **42.39** re accumulation and maintenance trusts.

Inheritance tax (IHTA 1984, Pt III)

[42.31] A trust within the mainstream IHT rules has its own threshold for IHT, with tax being charged every ten years by reference to the value of the trust funds, and also upon distribution of capital sums to beneficiaries (called an 'exit charge'). The rate of tax is 30% of the 20% scale rate, giving a maximum of 6% on the amount chargeable, and in the case of the exit charge this is discounted pro rata according to how many *complete* quarters have elapsed in the ten-year period. The rules apply to trusts set up in lifetime or on death.

A useful way of utilising the IHT threshold at death by means of a discretionary trust is illustrated at **35.4**.

Gifts into a lifetime trust within the mainstream IHT rules are not potentially exempt, so that if the nil rate threshold of the settlor is exceeded, IHT is payable at the 20% lifetime rate, increased to the full 40% rate if the settlor dies within seven years.

Business and agricultural property reliefs are available where the trust assets include qualifying property.

[42.32] If an exit charge arises within the first ten years, the IHT payable is calculated by reference to the chargeable transfers of the settlor before he settled the funds, and the initial value of the trust funds. See Example 4.

Example 4

A settlor, having made a transfer of £55,000 four years earlier that was a chargeable transfer rather than being potentially exempt, settled £300,000 on discretionary trusts on 1 October 1997, personally paying the IHT so that the trustees received the full £300,000.

If the trustees distributed £100,000 to a beneficiary on 10 June 2002 (which is 18 complete quarters after trust commenced), the IHT payable (assuming that the tax was payable out of the £100,000 so that no grossing up (see 5.24) was necessary) would be:

Previous chargeable transfer of settler	55,000
Initial value of trust fund	300,000
	355,000
Trust's nil rate threshold (2002/03 scale)	250,000
	£105,000
IHT at 20% lifetime rate	£21,000

Representing an effective tax rate of: $\dfrac{21,000}{300,000} = 7\%$

Of which 30% (the rate applicable to discretionary trusts) =	2.1%
£100,000 @ 2.1%	2,100
Less: $\dfrac{22 \text{ quarters/part quarters remaining in 10-year period}}{40 \text{ quarters in 10-year period}}$	1,155
IHT payable out of the £100,000 distribution is	£945

[42.33] The charge at the first ten-year anniversary is found by reference to the settlor's chargeable transfers before he settled the funds, plus the distributions liable to exit charges in the first ten years and the value of the fund at the ten-year anniversary. See Example 5.

Example 5

Say that at 30 September 2007 the value of the trust fund in Example 4 was £500,000. The tax payable by the trustees is calculated as follows:

Previous chargeable transfer of settlor	55,000
Distributions in the first ten years	100,000
Value of fund at 10 year anniversary	500,000
	655,000
Nil rate threshold at 30.9.2007	300,000
	£355,000
IHT at 20% lifetime rate	£71,000

Representing an effective tax rate on fund of: $\dfrac{71,000}{500,000} = 14.2\%$

Of which 30% (the rate applicable to discretionary trusts) = 4.26%

Giving tax payable on the £500,000 trust fund of	£21,300

[42.34] Following a ten-year charge, exit charges in the next ten years are based on the effective rate at the last ten-year anniversary, that rate, however, being recalculated by reference to the nil rate threshold at the date of the distribution.

Example 6

Say the trustees at Example 5 made a distribution of £100,000 to a beneficiary on 8 April 2010, at which time the nil rate threshold was £325,000.

Rate applicable on distribution is:

10 year total as in Example 5	655,000
Nil rate threshold	325,000
	£330,000
IHT at 20% lifetime rate	£66,000

Representing an effective tax rate of: $\dfrac{66,000}{500,000} = 13.2\%$

Of which 30% (the rate applicable to discretionary trusts) = 3.96%

£100,000 @ 3.96%	3,960

Less: $\dfrac{\text{30 quarters/part quarters in period}}{\text{40 quarters in 10-year period}}$	2,970
IHT payable out of the £100,000 distribution is	£990

[42.35] Where a discretionary trust is created at death in order to utilise but not exceed the then threshold, a distribution within the first ten years will not attract any IHT. See Example 7.

Example 7

	£
Initial value of settled fund at death on 31 August 2010	325,000
Trustees' nil rate threshold at time of distribution will not be less than	325,000
Amount on which rate on distribution will calculated	—

So rate on distributions in the first 10 years is 0%.
The 10-year charge will apply to the value of the fund at 31 August 2020, and exit charges on distributions in the 10 years after that will be based on the rate at the 10 year anniversary, as reduced by the quarterly discount.

[42.36] Another use of a discretionary trust created by a will is to leave the estate on discretionary trusts, with the trustees being aware of (but not bound by) the preferred wishes of the testator as to its distribution. Distributions within two years after death are regarded as under the will. This includes distributions to a trust for a bereaved minor (see **42.46**), an accumulation and maintenance trust within the 18–25 years of age rules (see **42.42**) and an immediate post-death interest (see **42.7** at (c)). The distributions must not be made within the three months after death but must be made before there is an interest in possession in the property.

Accumulation and maintenance trusts

[42.37] These are a special sort of discretionary trust giving flexibility to a parent or grandparent in providing funds for the benefit of children. The position of such trusts was changed from 22 March 2006 as indicated in **42.7**. Further details of the tax position are given below.

Income tax (ITA 2007, ss 479–483; ITTOIA 2005, ss 629, 631)

[42.38] The rule that a parent remains chargeable to income tax on income from funds settled on his own unmarried children under age 18 does not apply where the capital and income are held on qualifying accumulation and maintenance trusts for the benefit of the children, except to the extent that any income is paid to or for the benefit of the child (for example for education or maintenance). Payments of capital to or for the benefit of the child are also treated as income to the extent that the trust has any undistributed income. Any such income or capital payments are treated as the parent's income and taxed on him (unless, together with any other income from the parent, they do not exceed £100 in any tax year).

Since the trust is a discretionary trust, the trustees pay income tax at 42.5% from 6 April 2010 (previously 32.5%) on tax credit inclusive dividend income and 50% from 6 April 2010 (previously 40%) on other income accumulated within the fund (see **42.28**). When the accumulated income is transferred when the child reaches the appropriate age, it does so as capital and thus does not attract any further income tax at that time.

Capital gains tax (TCGA 1992, ss 165, 260)

[42.39] Gifts from 22 March 2006 into an accumulation and maintenance trust no longer qualify as potentially exempt transfers for IHT, so that capital gains gift hold-over relief (see **4.24**) is available to the settlor at that point.

Gains made by the trustees are calculated in the normal way, with an annual exemption of £5,050 being available. The exemption is proportionately reduced where there are associated trusts, subject to a minimum exemption of £1,010 for each trust. When a distribution from a trust is reckonable for IHT (see **42.40**), gains may be held over and treated as reducing a beneficiary's CGT cost.

Inheritance tax (IHTA 1984, ss 70, 71, 71A–71H; FA 2006, Sch 20)

[42.40] As indicated in **42.7** at (d), the treatment of accumulation and maintenance trusts has changed from 22 March 2006. Such trusts are within the mainstream IHT rules for trusts if created in lifetime from 22 March 2006. Trusts in existence at that date will come within the mainstream rules from 6 April 2008 unless by then they change their constitution so that beneficiaries have an absolute entitlement to their share of the assets at age 18. For both pre and post 22 March 2006 trusts, however, the mainstream rules are modified for 'age 18 to 25 trusts' as indicated in **42.42**.

Many settlors/trustees may decide to accept the new regime rather than take what they regard as unacceptable risks within their planning for the family. For trusts existing at 22 March 2006 that do not make the necessary changes to their constitution, there is no immediate IHT effect. The first ten year charge will apply on the first ten year anniversary after 5 April 2008, with only the time apportioned amount from that date being payable.

Example 8

An accumulation and maintenance trust set up on 29 September 1996 does not modify its constitution to come within the new rules. The first ten year

> charge after 5 April 2008 is on 29 September 2016. The tax payable will be limited to the time apportioned amount since 5 April 2008, that is 33 complete quarters, and hence 33/40ths of the ten year charge, calculated on the basis in Example 5 in **42.33**.

In calculating any subsequent exit charges (see **42.34**) within ten years after the first post 5 April 2008 anniversary, the calculation of the effective rate will take into account a full ten years, and not just the complete quarters since 5 April 2008.

[42.41] Trusts that comply with the rules of the new regime receive favourable treatment for IHT. During the period until the beneficiary becomes absolutely entitled to the capital at age 18, the trust income must either be accumulated or used for the beneficiary's benefit. There is no ten-yearly charge on the trust funds and no exit charges when a distribution is made to a beneficiary or when a beneficiary becomes absolutely entitled to the trust property or to the income from it. The transfer of property from the settlement to the beneficiaries is thus free of tax in these circumstances.

[42.42] Special treatment is available where there is an income entitlement at age 18 but a capital entitlement does not arise until age 25. These rules apply to trusts created both before and after 22 March 2006. The provisions are relevant where the settlors/trustees wish to retain the capital within the trust until the beneficiary reaches age 25 but are prepared for the beneficiary to have the right to income at age 18. For such trusts, the IHT exit charge will apply at age 25 when the beneficiary becomes entitled to the capital, but the charge will be based on only 7/10ths of the normal calculation (representing the seven years from 18 to 25). In view of the charge to IHT, CGT hold-over relief (see **42.39**) will be available.

Example 9

On 1 February 2006 taxpayer transferred £300,000 into an accumulation and maintenance trust for his three children aged 8, 10 and 14, each being entitled to an equal share of the capital or to the income arising from it upon attaining age 25 but the trustees being able to make advances of capital in the meantime. He had not made any gifts in the previous three years.

The IHT position is:

Settlor

1.2.2006	Gift to accumulation and maintenance trust			300,000
	Annual exemption	2005/06	3,000	
		2004/05	3,000	6,000
	Potentially exempt transfer			£294,000

Accumulation and maintenance trust

There will be a ten year charge at the tenth anniversary on 1 February 2016 (calculated pro rata from 6 April 2008), an exit charge on capital advances and a final charge on distribution, unless the entitlement of each beneficiary is changed before 6 April 2008 to an absolute entitlement in his/her share of the assets at age 18. There will be no IHT charges on any of these occasions if that modification is made.

Had the transfer into trust been a year later, on 1 February 2007, it would not have been potentially exempt, IHT of £1,800 (£294,000 − £285,000 = £9,000 @ 20%) being payable. The mainstream IHT rules for trusts would apply, with none of the advantages of an accumulation and maintenance trust being available.

Trusts with a vulnerable beneficiary (FA 2005, ss 23–45 and Sch 1; IHTA 1984, ss 89, 89A, 89B)

[42.43] New income tax and CGT provisions were introduced with effect from 6 April 2004 for trusts with a vulnerable beneficiary, i.e. a disabled person or a 'relevant minor' (which means someone under 18 one or both of whose parents have died). An election for vulnerable beneficiary trust treatment must be made by the trustees and (strangely) the vulnerable person, no later than 12 months after 31 January following the tax year for which the treatment is to take effect (i.e. no later than 12 months after 31 January 2013 for 2010/11). The election is irrevocable, but it no longer has effect if the beneficiary is no longer a vulnerable person or the trust fails to qualify or comes to an end. Claims for the special tax treatment must be made each year.

[42.44] In order to qualify, a trust for a disabled person must provide that during the disabled person's lifetime (or, for protective trusts, the period for which the property is held on trust for him), or until the termination of the trust if earlier, neither trust property nor income may be applied for the benefit of anyone other than the disabled person. A trust for a relevant minor must either be a statutory trust arising on intestacy, or a trust established under the will of a deceased parent or under the Criminal Injuries Compensation Scheme. For non-statutory trusts, the relevant minor must become absolutely entitled to the property at age 18, and until that time neither trust property nor income may be applied for the benefit of anyone other than the relevant minor.

[42.45] The broad effect of vulnerable person trust treatment is that the income tax and CGT charged on the trustees is the amount that would have been charged had the trust's income and gains accrued directly to the beneficiary. There are special provisions where a beneficiary is non-resident.

[42.46] The term 'vulnerable beneficiary' is not used in the IHT legislation, and trusts for disabled persons and for bereaved minors are dealt with separately.

A trust for a disabled person does not come within the mainstream IHT rules for trusts, so that there will be no ten year or exit charges, the disabled individual effectively being treated as one who owns the assets. The definition of disabled person for this purpose includes the settlor of a self-settlement made because the settlor has a condition expected to lead to a disability.

Also excluded from the mainstream IHT rules for trusts are those established under the Criminal Injuries Compensation Scheme for a bereaved minor and where a fund is held in trust for a bereaved minor under the will of a deceased parent or the intestacy rules. In these cases the minor becomes entitled to the capital at age eighteen but the special treatment for age 18 to 25 trusts is also applicable (see **42.42**).

Where the trust has been established on death, IHT will have been paid before arriving at the available fund. For transfers in lifetime the value transferred will be a potentially exempt transfer.

[42.47] Where a self-settlement is made on or after 22 March 2006 otherwise than as indicated in **42.46**, the mainstream IHT rules for trusts will apply, with the transfer of funds into the settlement being a chargeable transfer and the ten year and exit charges applying. This is so even though the settlor has simply predestined the funds upon a later event (for example death or remarriage) and retained the income in the meantime. (Self-settlements created before 22 March 2006 come within the rules for interest in possession trusts and 'transitional serial interests' — see **42.7** at (a) and (b).)

There is an obvious anomaly in that a settlor will clearly have retained a benefit from the assets which he has settled upon himself, with their value arguably being reckonable for IHT upon the cessation of his income entitlement. It remains to be seen how the anomaly is resolved.

Trusts and estates — self-assessment

[42.48] Trustees and personal representatives are subject to the normal self-assessment rules in relation to their tax liabilities (see **CHAPTER 9**). They are required to make payments on account half-yearly on 31 January and 31 July, based on the previous year's net income tax (unless covered by the de minimis thresholds), and a balancing payment, including any CGT, on the following 31 January (the due date for submission of the tax return).

There is a special tax return (SA900) for trusts and estates. The format of the return broadly follows that for individuals, with supplementary pages for various types of income and gains and a tax calculation working sheet. Only some supplementary pages are sent with returns. Others need to be requested from HMRC. Trust returns require certain additional information to be provided, such as details of capital added to a settlement, capital payments to minor children of the settlor, discretionary payments to beneficiaries, and changes in personal representatives and trustees.

Discretionary trusts liable at the dividend trust rate of 42.5% and/or the 50% rate (see **42.28**) have to maintain details of the 'pool' of tax they have paid, which covers an equivalent amount of tax deducted from subsequent payments made to beneficiaries. Details of the tax pool are included in the tax calculation working sheet. Any tax paid directly in respect of the dividend trust rate or the 50% rate enters into the calculation of the half-yearly payments on account for the following year.

Position of infants

[42.49] Where income is paid to beneficiaries (and is not treated as a parent's income), it is after deduction of tax at 10% if it relates to dividends, and at the basic rate for other income, except for discretionary trusts where the rate on all income is 50%. If the beneficiaries are infants, a repayment of tax is often due because of their personal allowances, although the 10% tax on dividend income is not repayable. The parent or guardian can make the repayment claim, or it may be made by the beneficiary himself in respect of the previous six years on his reaching age 18.

Married couples and registered civil partners

[42.50] The spouse/civil partner exemption for IHT applies where a capital sum is put into trust for the benefit of the survivor under a *will or intestacy*, so long as the capital goes absolutely on the death of the survivor to one or more individuals or to an appropriate trust. The spouse/civil partner exemption is otherwise denied.

The trust will come within the rules for an immediate post-death interest (see **42.7** at (c)), with the income being included within that of the surviving spouse or civil partner for income tax purposes (as the life tenant in possession) and the capital value being reckonable for IHT on his/her death together with the free estate (see Example 2 at **42.23**).

The spouse/civil partner exemption does not apply where a capital sum is put into trust for a spouse or civil partner during *lifetime*. In this event, the mainstream IHT rules for trusts apply (see **42.31** to **42.36**), with IHT being payable at the lifetime rate when the assets are placed into trust, rising to the death rate if death occurs within the next seven years, and the periodic exit and distribution charges also applying. The same applies where a settlor settles assets on himself/herself for life with the surviving spouse or civil partner taking an absolute or life interest on the settlor's death unless the self-settlement comes within the rules for providing for future disability. For pre 22 March 2006 trusts these rules are subject to the provisions for 'transitional serial interests' (see **42.7** at (b)).

In the case of lifetime settlements, the income will be taxed on the settlor during his lifetime, with there being no hold-over relief for CGT when the assets are placed into trust and the settlor being taxed on any capital gains arising in the hands of the trustees.

Stamp duty and stamp duty land tax (FA 2003, ss 49, 105 and Schs 3, 16)

[42.51] Stamp duty applies only to transactions relating to shares and securities (see **6.2**). For stamp duty land tax purposes, the acts of bare trustees are treated as those of the person who is absolutely entitled as against the trustees. For trustees other than bare trustees, the stamp duty land tax provisions apply to acquisitions of land and buildings by the trustees as if they had acquired the whole interest in the property, including the beneficial interest. Stamp duty land tax is not payable where land and buildings are transferred to a beneficiary. If trustees receive consideration for exercising a power of appointment or a discretion in relation to a land transaction, the consideration is treated as chargeable consideration for stamp duty land tax. In some circumstances, stamp duty land tax may be payable in connection with nil rate band discretionary trusts. (See HMRC's Stamp Duty Land Tax Manual at SDLTM04045 for HMRC's detailed comments.)

Tax points

[42.52] Note the following:

- Personal representatives have to include in their IHT account details of earlier transfers affecting the IHT liability. Providing they have done everything possible to trace potentially exempt transfers made by the deceased in the seven years before his death and disclose them to HMRC, then once they have received a certificate of discharge and distributed the estate, they will not usually be asked to pay the tax if untraced transfers subsequently come to light.
- Where a person entitled to trust income has unused personal allowances, it is better to arrange for income to be paid direct to him, because the income will not then be depleted by trust expenses, and he will get a higher income tax repayment where tax has been deducted.
- Since IHT is less where the value transferred is lower, it is usually beneficial to transfer assets that are growing in value earlier rather than later. Even if the donor dies within seven years the benefit of transferring assets when their value was lower is retained.
  Assets transferred into or out of a trust may qualify for capital gains gift hold-over relief (see **4.23** to **4.26**) unless the settlor has an interest in the trust (see **42.14**).
- Where assets are put into a trust, the trustees may pay the IHT rather than the settlor. If they do, and dependent upon the type of asset, the tax may be payable by instalments (see **5.48**). The requirement to treat the amount settled as its gross equivalent when calculating the tax is also avoided.
- If, since before 22 March 2006, an individual has been the beneficiary of an interest in possession trust and does not need all the income, he could disclaim his entitlement to the income on an appropriate amount of capital which could be released early to the individual eventually entitled to it. Part of the disclaimed amount would be covered by IHT

annual exemptions if not otherwise used and the balance would be treated as a potentially exempt transfer, so there would be no immediate tax charge. If the potentially exempt transfer was within his nil rate band, no tax would be payable even if he died within seven years (although in that event the nil rate band available on death would be correspondingly reduced). If the potentially exempt transfer was above the nil rate band, tax would be payable by the donee if the donor did not survive the seven-year period, but it would be reduced if the donor had survived for more than three years (see **5.27**).

- For CGT purposes, those entitled to the assets in a deceased's estate acquire them at market value at the date of death. If assets have fallen in value since death, losses made by the personal representatives on disposal cannot be used by the beneficiaries. If, on the other hand, the assets themselves, rather than cash proceeds from their sale, are transferred to beneficiaries, losses on disposal by the beneficiaries will be their own allowable losses for capital gains purposes.

- Where a trust in which a settlor has an interest realises gains that are covered by available losses, there is no charge on the settlor and the trust's available losses will be used only to the extent necessary to leave gains covered by the trust's annual exemption of £5,050. If, however, gains exceed losses, the gains net of the full amount of the available losses will be taxed on the settlor and the trust's annual exemption will be wasted.

- To obtain the spouse/civil partner exemption on death, assets must be left absolutely to the survivor or in trust for him/her to have the income for life with one or more individuals or an appropriate trust taking the capital on the death of the life tenant or earlier.

- A lifetime settlement in favour of one's spouse/civil partner is a chargeable transfer for IHT. For a gift to be potentially exempt, the assets must be given outright.

- Where the settlor, spouse or civil partner retains an interest in a settlement, hold-over relief for CGT is not available despite the transfer of the asset being immediately reckonable for IHT.

- In the case of an accumulation and maintenance settlement set up before 22 March 2006, the exemption of the trust from the exit charges applicable to discretionary trusts will only apply if the trust was modified before 6 April 2008 so that each beneficiary is entitled to his/her share of the capital at age 18.

  The ten year charge (but not the exit charge) can be avoided if the right to income applies at age 18, with the absolute entitlement to capital applying at age 25.

- The IHT ten year charge will apply to a trust established after 21 March 2006 which holds a lifetime insurance policy for the purpose of paying IHT on the death of the settlor. The principles of valuation of the policy and the available IHT threshold will usually eliminate any tax payable. But since the policy proceeds will not be available until the death of the settlor a means will have to be found of paying any IHT that does become due in the meantime.

- For additional tax points on trusts, see **CHAPTER 35**.

43

Charities and charitable trusts

Definition of a charity (ITA 2007, s 989; FA 2010, s 30 and Sch 6)

[43.1] Currently a 'charity' is defined in Income Tax Act 2007 as 'a body of persons or trust established for charitable purposes only'.

FA 2010 introduced a new definition of a charity, essentially to widen the scope of the UK charitable tax reliefs to organisations equivalent to charities and community amateur sports clubs (**43.33**) in the EU and in the European Economic Area (EEA) countries of Norway and Iceland following a judgment in the European Court of Justice in January 2009. This new definition will not apply to most provisions until a commencement order is made by the Treasury, but it does apply from 6 April 2010 to donations by individuals under Gift Aid (**43.19**). The FA 2010 definition provides that an organisation will be eligible for UK charity tax reliefs if:

(a)   it is established for charitable purposes only;

(b)   it is located in the UK or a member state of the EU or a specified country;

(c)   it meets the registration condition (i.e. where the organisation is required under the law of its home country to be registered with a charity regulator similar to the Charity Commission for England and Wales, it must be so registered); and

(d)   all persons in the organisation having control and management responsibilities are 'fit and proper' persons (this phrase not being further defined, but guidance is provided by HMRC at http://www.hmrc.gov.uk/charities/guidance-notes/chapter2/fp-persons-test.htm).

In order to register a charity, it is necessary to satisfy the Charity Commissioners in England and Wales, or HMRC in Scotland and Northern Ireland, that the purposes or objects of the organisation are of 'charitable purpose', and not only must the purpose be one of those listed but must be for the public benefit. All new charities must meet this requirement and some existing charities will be asked to show how they meet the requirement. Charities will not be registered if their annual income does not exceed £5,000.

A charity may be a limited company with a separate legal existence independent of its members, or an unincorporated association which has no separate status so that assets must be held on its behalf by trustees.

Guidance is available at www.charity-commission.gov.uk for England and Wales, and www.oscr.org.uk for Scotland.

How the tax system operates for charities

[43.2] Detailed guidance on how the tax system operates for charities is provided at www.hmrc.gov.uk/charities.

[43.3] The tax status of charities is outlined below. Charities are within the self-assessment system, although HMRC issue returns only to a sample of charities each year. If a charity that does not receive a return has a tax liability, it is under the usual obligation to notify HMRC.

Income tax and corporation tax (ITA 2007, ss 518–564; CTA 2010, ss 466–517)

[43.4] Investment and rental income is exempt from income tax if it is the income of a charitable trust, or it is required (for example, by law or trust deed) to be applied to charitable purposes only. However, the tax credit attached to a dividend is not repayable.

Profits of a trade carried on by a charitable trust are exempt if the profits are applied solely for the purposes of the trust and the trade is a 'charitable trade'. Broadly, a trade is a charitable trade if it is conducted in the course of carrying out a primary purpose of the trust, or the work is mainly done by beneficiaries.

Where a trade is conducted only partly for a primary purpose of the charity, or is conducted partly but not mainly by beneficiaries of the charity, the parts of the trade that are and are not carried on for a primary purpose, or the parts that are and are not carried on by beneficiaries, are treated as two separate trades, with income and expenses being apportioned appropriately. This avoids the loss of tax relief that might otherwise occur. Smaller charities whose profits are not otherwise exempt from income tax are exempt from tax on trading income used solely for charitable purposes if it is less than the lower of £50,000 and 25% of the charity's income, or in any event if it is less than £5,000 (the amounts of £50,000 and £5,000 being reduced pro rata for accounting periods of less than twelve months). This may remove the need in some cases for charities to have a trading subsidiary (as to which see **43.30**), although charities must still consider their position under charity law. The profits of a charity's fundraising events such as bazaars, jumble sales, etc., are exempt providing the events would be covered by the VAT exemption (see **43.7**) and the profits are used for charitable purposes. There are corresponding exemptions for charitable companies in respect of income applied to charitable purposes only.

If a charity deposits money with a bank or building society, the bank or building society will pay the interest in full without deducting income tax.

Charities and other non-profit making bodies have previously been able to use National Savings Treasurers' Accounts, but they are no longer available from 10 August 2007 (see **36.12**).

See **40.21** for the provisions relating to life policies held by charitable trusts.

Capital gains tax (TCGA 1992, ss 256–256D)

[43.5] A charity is not liable to capital gains tax (CGT), or corporation tax on chargeable gains, on gains applied for charitable purposes.

Value added tax (VATA 1994, Sch 8 Groups 4, 12 and 15)

[43.6] The general tax exemption for charities does not extend to VAT, and the detailed provisions need to be looked at carefully to ensure that the rules are complied with.

Where a charity makes taxable supplies it must register for VAT, subject to the normal rules relating to exempt supplies and taxable turnover (see **CHAPTER 7**). Where funds raised by donation are used to fund business activities, any input VAT on fundraisers' fees may be recovered. Where funds are used for both business and non-business activities, or for making taxable and exempt supplies, the VAT will need to be apportioned under the partial exemption rules.

If a charity has a number of branches which are virtually autonomous, each branch having control over its own financial and other affairs, each branch is regarded as a separate entity for VAT purposes and is required to register only if its taxable supplies exceed the VAT threshold of £70,000 (£68,000 before 1 April 2010).

[43.7] Income from one-off fundraising events, including admission charges, is normally exempt. Exemption is also available in respect of a series of events, providing not more than 15 events of the same kind are held in any one location in any year. (Small events do not count towards the limit providing aggregate takings for such events do not exceed £1,000 a week). Where income is exempt, there is a corresponding restriction in the recovery of VAT on purchases and expenses for the event. Except for fund-raising events, admission charges are normally standard-rated. Where a charity supplies goods or services consistently below cost for the relief of distressed persons, for example, meals on wheels, such supplies are not regarded as being made in the course of business and hence are not liable to VAT. Sales of donated goods to the general public at charity shops etc. and donated goods sold only to disabled people or people receiving means tested benefits are zero-rated. Sales of bought-in goods are standard rated. VAT Leaflet 701/1 explains in detail the VAT treatment of charity challenge events.

[43.8] Membership subscriptions to 'bodies with aims of a political, religious, patriotic, philosophical or philanthropic nature' are exempt from VAT if the conditions are satisfied. Exemption does not apply where free admission is provided in return for the subscription. Where the members receive publications as part of their subscriptions, the relevant part of the subscription is treated as zero-rated, enabling the bodies to recover an appropriate part of their input VAT.

Certain national museums and galleries who offer free admission are able to claim a refund of the VAT they incur in connection with the provision of the free admission.

[43.9] Supplies of nursery and crèche facilities by charities are not treated as business activities for VAT in specified circumstances — see HMRC Business Brief 02/05 for details.

[43.10] Certain supplies to charities may be zero-rated in specified circumstances, such as media advertising, building work (see below), motor vehicles, mechanical products and equipment supplied to those who provide care for the handicapped, aids for disabled people, medicinal products, and bathrooms provided for disabled people in day centres and other charity premises. From 1 July 2006 the 5% reduced rate applies to the provision by charities of advice or information connected with or intended to promote the welfare of elderly or disabled people or children.

[43.11] As far as buildings are concerned, zero-rating does not apply to new buildings bought by charities or to services provided in the construction of buildings for charities, unless the charity uses the building solely for charitable purposes (which means otherwise than in the course of a business), or as a village hall, or to provide social or recreational facilities for a local community. Any other use strictly falls foul of these provisions (for example, allowing someone to rent a room for a children's party), but by concession before 1 July 2010 business use can be ignored where the non-business use of the building covers 90% or more of the time the building is normally available or of the available floor space, or where 90% or more of the people using the building are engaged solely on non-business activities. This concession was withdrawn from 1 July 2010 but a charity will still be able to ignore business use provided the building is intended to be used 95% or more for a relevant charitable purpose. Transitional rules apply for one year from 1 July 2009. Even if zero-rating applies, it does not apply to the services of architects and surveyors, which are standard-rated.

[43.12] In relation to repair and maintenance work the UK has a special grant scheme (the Listed Places of Worship Grant Scheme) enabling churches to receive grants to cover all VAT incurred on the repair and maintenance of listed places of worship. The UK also has a Memorials Grant Scheme which provides grants to charities and faith groups for the VAT incurred in building and maintaining memorials. Both schemes were due to end in 2008, but the Government announced that they would continue until 2011.

[43.13] When buildings are rented, landlords have the option to charge VAT on rents except for buildings or parts of buildings used for charitable purposes (but the exception does not cover the charity's offices). The landlord is entitled to add VAT to existing rents unless the agreement specifically prevents him from doing so. In that event, the rent would have to be treated as VAT inclusive until such time as the landlord has a right under the agreement to increase it.

[43.14] Various leaflets are available from HMRC on the subject of charities and guidance is available online at www.hmrc.gov.uk/charities/vat.

Stamp duty and stamp duty land tax (FA 1982, s 129; FA 2003, s 68 and Sch 8)

[43.15] No stamp duty is payable on documents transferring assets to charities. Exemption also applies to the stamp duty land tax transactions of charities, providing the land is to be held for qualifying charitable purposes and is not being acquired for tax avoidance reasons. This also applies to acquisitions by trusts and unit trusts where all the beneficiaries or unit holders are charities. The relief must be claimed in a stamp duty land tax return or amendment to a return, and it will be withdrawn if within three years the purchaser ceases to be a charity or the land is used other than for charitable purposes.

National insurance

[43.16] Charities receive no special treatment. Employers' national insurance is dealt with in CHAPTER 13.

Business rates

[43.17] There is both mandatory and discretionary relief from business rates on premises occupied by a registered charity and used for charitable purposes. 'Charitable purposes' includes shops used for the sale of goods donated to the charity. The mandatory relief is 80% and discretionary relief can increase this to 100%, so that no rates are payable. Discretionary relief up to 100% may be awarded by local authorities to various non-profit-making organisations such as schools and colleges, societies concerned with literature and the arts, and recreational clubs and societies.

Restriction of charity tax reliefs (ITA 2007, ss 518–564; CTA 2010, ss 492–517; SI 2009/1029; FA 2010, s 32 and Sch 8)

[43.18] A charity's tax relief may be restricted if it uses its funds for non-charitable purposes, or makes payments to overseas bodies without taking reasonable steps to ensure that they are used for charitable purposes, or makes certain loans or investments for tax avoidance rather than for the benefit of the charity. In such situations, the amount of income and gains eligible for tax relief is reduced by an amount equal to the amount of any non-charitable expenditure.

Certain transactions with substantial donors (i.e. donors giving £25,000 or more in a single year or £150,000 or more over a six year period) are treated as non-charitable expenditure. Where a charity receives a grant from another charity, the grant is chargeable to tax unless it is used for charitable purposes.

Any claim that a payment overseas qualifies for relief as charitable expenditure must be supported by evidence sufficient to satisfy HMRC that the charity's trustees took reasonable steps to ensure the money would be spent charitably. In practice this will mean that charities will be required to maintain records of how charitable funds are spent overseas and be able to produce evidence of charitable works undertaken. The level of record keeping required will depend upon the circumstances relating to the expenditure. For example, it may not be possible for a charity providing aid during an emergency to maintain the same level of record keeping as for routine overseas expenditure.

Giving to charity: individuals

Gift aid donations by individuals: money gifts (ITA 2007, ss 413–430; ITTOIA 2005, s 627; FA 1990, s 25; SI 2000/2074; FA 2008, s 53 and Sch 19; FA 2010, s 32 and Sch 8)

[43.19] Tax relief at the payer's top tax rate is available for money given to charities under the gift aid scheme. The scheme covers both single donations and a series of donations, including covenanted payments. There is no minimum limit for gift aid payments, although charities may stipulate their own minimum limit for donations to be brought within the scheme. Gift aid relief is available not only to UK residents but also to non-residents who are liable to pay sufficient UK tax to cover the basic rate on the grossed up amount of the donation (e.g. £20 UK tax for a cash donation of £80). Tax returns contain notes about gift aid. A claim may be made in the return for relief to be given in the tax year to which the return relates for gift aid payments made between 6 April following that tax year and the date the return is submitted (see **43.24**). Taxpayers expecting a tax repayment may indicate in their returns that they want a nominated charity to have all or part of the repayment. They may also indicate that gift aid should apply to the donation. The donation will be regarded as made when the charity receives the payment and it is not possible to treat the gift as made in the tax year to which the return relates. HMRC have a special process enabling charities to reclaim tax on gift aid donations without completing a tax return.

Finance Act 2008 provides a transitional relief for charities to compensate for a reduction in their income following the reduction of the income tax basic rate from 22% to 20%. A supplement will be added to tax repayments relating to gift aid donations made between 6 April 2008 and 5 April 2011.

[43.20] If individuals give goods to charities the gifts do not qualify for gift aid (see **43.29** re gifts of stocks and shares). The charity may, however, sell the goods on behalf of the donor, who may then donate the proceeds to the charity. The conditions for relief in these circumstances are set out in HMRC's guidance notes. The charity will normally obtain a gift aid declaration in advance, which will not, however, relate directly to the goods that are being sold. The individual must have the opportunity of changing his mind about the donation when the charity notifies him that the goods have been sold.

[43.21] Donations do not qualify for relief if the donor receives a benefit from the gift, unless the benefits come within stipulated limits, i.e. 25% of a gift up to £100, £25 for a gift between £100 and £1,000, and 5% of a gift in excess of £1,000 up to a maximum benefit limit of £500. An unrestricted right of admission for at least a year to charity premises in return for a donation is not treated as a benefit for these purposes. For shorter periods or single visits, there is no benefit providing the cost to the donor is at least 10% higher than the amount charged to other members of the public. If any additional benefits are provided, they must fall within the benefits limits stated above.

[43.22] To qualify for gift aid relief, donors are required to make a declaration. The declaration may cover any number of donations already made or to be made. The declaration need not be written, and may be made by telephone or over the internet, providing the donor's name and address is obtained. Where a donation is given by oral declaration, the charity must maintain detailed auditable records.

In view of the fact that tax relief on gift aid donations is given at the payer's top rate of tax, a higher rate taxpayer may be persuaded to increase his donation, thus making a larger contribution to the charity.

Example 1

Taxpayer who is liable to 40% tax makes a cash gift to charity of £1,000. The tax position is:

	£	£
Cash gift	1,000	1,000
Basic rate tax treated as deducted (20/80)	250	250
Amount received by charity*	1,250	1,250
Tax saved at 40%		500
Net cost to donor		750

* See **43.19** regarding a supplement payable to the charity in respect of transitional relief for loss of income due to the reduction in the basic rate.

If the donor was prepared to contribute £1,000 out of his after-tax income, he could increase the cash gift to £1,334, as follows:

	£	£
Cash gift	1,334	1,334
Basic rate tax treated as deducted (20/80)	333	333
Amount received by charity	1,667	1,667
Tax saved at 40%		667
Net cost to donor		1,000

Thus the charity would receive extra income of (1,667 – 1,250 =) £417 at an extra net cost to the donor of £250.

> The tax saving to a higher rate taxpayer may be even higher where the donations are paid out of dividends (see Example 3).

[43.23] Donations are treated as being net of basic rate tax, but in order to retain the tax relief, donors must be liable to pay an equivalent amount of income tax (including tax at rates below the basic rate) and CGT. In order to put this into effect, donations are not deducted from income in calculating the tax position for the year. Instead the basic rate threshold is increased by the gross amount of the donations. (The gross charitable donations are, however, regarded as reducing income for age-related allowances — see **34.4**).

Where the amount of income tax and CGT chargeable after deducting personal allowances does not cover the tax deducted from the donation, the personal allowances are restricted accordingly. If despite the restriction of personal allowances there is still insufficient tax payable, the donor is liable to pay tax equal to the shortfall. For gifts made on or after 6 April 2010, this treatment applies to both UK resident and non-resident donors. (For gifts made prior to 6 April 2010, the treatment only applied to UK resident donors. If a non-resident donor had not paid enough UK tax to cover the gift, the donation was not treated as a gift aid donation at all). In calculating the shortfall the amount of tax taken into account is before deducting the 10% relief on married couple's age allowance and dividend tax credits. Any unused married couple's allowance is available to transfer to the spouse or civil partner. HMRC have the right to issue an assessment to collect the tax due. They may not do so if the amount involved is small but where a tax repayment is being claimed, the repayment is restricted to cover the amount due because of the charitable payment.

Example 2

In 2010/11 an unmarried taxpayer aged under 65 has income as shown below and makes charitable donations of £800 net, £1,000 gross.

	£
Interest	14,475
Dividends (tax credit inclusive)	2,000
	16,475
Personal allowance	6,475
Taxable income	10,000

Tax thereon:	Interest	8,000	@ 20%	1,600.00
	Dividends	2,000	@ 10%	200.00
		10,000		1,800,00

Since the tax chargeable exceeds the £200 retained out of the donations, the taxpayer is entitled to keep that amount.

Example 3

In 2010/11 an unmarried taxpayer aged under 65 has income as shown below and makes charitable donations of £2,400 net, £3,000 gross.

	£
Earnings	32,235
Interest	5,000
Dividends (tax credit inclusive)	10,000
	47,235
Personal allowance	6,475
Taxable income	40,760

Tax thereon:	£		£
	30,760	@ 20%	6,152.00
Dividends (part)	9,640	@ 10%	964.00
	40,400*		
Dividends (balance)	360	@ 32.5%	117.00
	40,760		7,233.00

* Basic rate band extended by £3,000 because of charitable donation.

The extension of the basic rate band has saved tax of £3,000 @ 22.5% = £675, in addition to the £600 basic rate relief given by deduction, because an extra £3,000 of dividend income is below the basic rate threshold. The net cost of the gift is therefore (3,000 − 600 − 675 =) £1,725. The tax saving amounts to 42.5%, i.e. basic rate tax 20% + dividend tax (32.5% − 10% =) 22.5%.

Had all the income been earned income, the tax saving would have been 40%, i.e. the basic rate of 20% plus the reduction of 20% in the tax on the earnings (40% − 20%).

Carry back election for gift aid payments (ITA 2007, ss 426–427)

[43.24] A taxpayer may treat a gift aid donation as made in the previous tax year provided, broadly, that the grossed up amounts of donations made in that year, when added to donations carried back, do not exceed chargeable income and gains. The claim must be made on or before the date the tax return for the previous year is sent in and not later than 31 January in the tax year in which the gift was made. Provision is made in tax returns for the claim to be made (see **43.19**). The relief for the carried back amount will reduce the tax payable for the previous year and the normal treatment of backdated claims in **9.6** will not apply.

Gift aid donations by individuals: shares, securities and real property (ITA 2007, ss 431–445; FA 2010, s 31 and Sch 7)

[43.25] In addition to cash gifts, relief is available against income for gifts to charities of shares and securities that are listed on a recognised stock exchange or dealt in on any designated UK market (AIM shares thus being included), units in unit trusts, shares in open-ended investment companies and interests in offshore funds. Relief is also available for gifts of UK land and buildings.

In general, the amount of the relief is the market value of the gifted assets (the net benefit received by the charity), plus any incidental costs of making the gift. However, for disposals on or after 15 December 2009, this is restricted to the donors acquisition cost where the:

(a)   qualifying investment gifted to the charity (or anything from which the investment derives) was acquired within four years of the date of disposal; and

(b)   main purpose(s) of acquiring the qualifying investment was to dispose of it to a charity and claim the tax relief.

The relief for the gift is given to individuals by deducting the value of the gifted assets from income, rather than extending the basic rate band. If the donor receives a benefit from the gift, the amount deductible from income is reduced accordingly.

Payroll deduction scheme (ITEPA 2003, ss 713–715; CTA 2009, ss 72, 1236; FA 2010, s 32 and Sch 8)

[43.26] Employees can authorise participating employers to deduct a stipulated amount from their earnings before tax, for passing on to charities chosen by the employee, through HMRC approved charity agencies with which the employer has made an arrangement. The employee thus receives full tax relief for the contributions made. There is no limit on the amount that may be deducted under the scheme. The charity agencies are required to pass on the donations to the relevant charities within 60 days of receiving them. Voluntary payments to the agency by the employer to cover running costs are allowed in calculating the employer's taxable profits. Government grants have previously been given to employers with fewer than 500 employees who set up a payroll giving scheme, but the grants are no longer available.

Gifts made under payroll giving on or after 24 March 2010 will be exempt from tax in the hands of the charity only to the extent the income is spent on charitable purposes (this provision was introduced to align the treatment of donation income under payroll giving with the treatment of other donation income).

Inheritance tax (IHTA 1984, ss 23, 58, 70, 76)

[43.27] All gifts to charity are exempt for inheritance tax purposes whether made in lifetime, on death or at the discretion of trustees. Where the charity is a discretionary trust, inheritance tax is not payable by the trustees unless property leaving the trust is used for a non-charitable purpose.

Giving to charities: companies

Gift aid donations by companies: money gifts (CTA 2010, ss 191–202)

[43.28] The gift aid provisions enable companies to obtain tax relief when they make payments to charity. As for individuals, payments under the gift aid provisions by companies include covenanted payments. Companies are not required to deduct tax from any of their charitable payments and the full amount of the payment is deducted from the profits of the company in calculating corporation tax payable for the accounting period in which the payment was made. (See **43.30** for the special provisions for payments by a company owned by a charity).

The same provisions apply as for individuals (see **43.21**) where a company receives a benefit from the gift, including the allowability of benefits within stipulated limits. Additional restrictions apply to prevent the company receiving a repayment of the gift or either the company or a connected person receiving benefits in excess of stipulated limits. See **43.29** for the treatment of gifts in kind.

The after-tax cost to the company depends on whether the company is paying tax at the full rate, the small profits rate or the marginal rate. The cost may indeed be 100% if the company has no taxable profits, because in that case loss relief cannot be claimed for charitable payments (except within a group of companies by way of group relief).

Gift aid donations by companies: shares, securities and real property (TCGA 1992, s 257; CAA 2001, s 63; CTA 2009, s 105; CTA 2010, s 203–217)

[43.29] If businesses make gifts of their stock or plant and machinery to charities, they do not have to bring amounts into account as trading receipts or disposal proceeds for capital allowances.

Relief is available against income for gifts to charities of shares and securities that are listed on a recognised stock exchange or dealt in on any designated UK market (AIM shares thus being included), units in unit trusts, shares in open-ended investment companies and interests in offshore funds. Relief is also available for gifts of UK land and buildings.

In general, the amount of the relief is the market value of the gifted assets (the net benefit received by the charity), plus any incidental costs of making the gift. However, for disposals on or after 15 December 2009, this is restricted to the donors acquisition cost where the:

(a) qualifying investment gifted to the charity (or anything from which the investment derives) was acquired within four years of the date of disposal; and

(b) main purpose(s) of acquiring the qualifying investment was to dispose of it to a charity and claim the tax relief.

The relief for the gift is given by deducting it as a qualifying donation to charity. If the donor receives a benefit from the gift, the amount deductible from income is reduced accordingly.

Gifts in kind to charities are exempt for capital gains purposes, so neither a chargeable gain nor allowable loss will arise.

Companies owned by charities (CTA 2010, s 199)

[43.30] Many charities have fund-raising subsidiaries that gift their entire profits to the charity. As indicated in **43.28**, relief is available for gift aid payments made during a company's accounting period, but the total profits will not be known until after the end of the period. Special rules apply to charity-owned companies. A claim may be made by such companies for gift aid donations to be treated as made within an accounting period falling wholly or partly within the nine months before the payment was made.

Employees seconded to charities etc. (ITTOIA 2005, s 70; CTA 2009, ss 70, 1235)

[43.31] The salaries of employees temporarily seconded to charities, local education authorities or other approved educational bodies may be deducted as a business expense even though, because of the secondment, the salaries are not paid wholly and exclusively for the purposes of the trade.

Intermediary charities

[43.32] Individuals and companies may want to give regularly to several charities, but may not want to commit themselves to any one of them. As well as making one-off payments under the gift aid provisions (see **43.19**), there are two ways of achieving this and still retaining the tax advantages. The simplest way is to make payments to an intermediary organisation such as the Charities Aid Foundation. It is possible to tell the organisation which particular charities are to benefit. The organisation will, if requested, make annual payments to the chosen charities by standing order. Alternatively, and especially where the size of the donation is more significant, it is possible for individuals or companies to set up their own intermediary charity. A simple charitable trust can be set up relatively easily although it is essential to have proper professional advice. Additionally, for small amounts, the payroll deduction scheme may enable the recipient charity to be varied.

Community amateur sports clubs (CTA 2010, ss 658–671)

[43.33] Some sports clubs may be able to satisfy the tests for charitable status. For those who do not, or who do not wish to apply to be charities, they may be able to register with HMRC as community amateur sports clubs (CASCs), which will entitle them to various tax exemptions and reliefs. Registration is available to non-profit making amateur sports clubs that are open to the whole community and provide facilities for, and promote participation in, one or more eligible sports. CASCs are exempt from corporation tax on all interest and gift aid income, trading income (before expenses) of up to £30,000, property income (before expenses) of up to £20,000 and capital gains on the disposal of assets.

Donations to a CASC qualify for tax relief under the gift aid provisions (see 43.19), and the relief for business gifts of stock or plant and machinery applies (see 43.29). The capital gains exemption for gifts in kind to charities and the inheritance tax exemption for gifts to charities also apply (see 43.29 and 43.27). CASCs are entitled to 80% mandatory relief from business rates.

Tax points

[43.34] Note the following:

- If a donor sets up his own charitable trust, the trustees must not profit from their position or allow their duties and responsibilities to conflict with their personal interests. It is possible, however, to appoint a professional trustee, such as a solicitor or accountant, and an appropriate charging clause in the trust deed will enable his fees to be paid.
- Although gift aid donations may be evidenced by a simple declaration (possibly made by telephone or online), the donor must be a taxpayer to be able to retain tax relief on the donation. If an oral donation is made, the charity must keep detailed records to enable HMRC to check that the conditions for relief have been satisfied. Charities receiving regular amounts in cash (for example church collections) must have a system that demonstrates that the donations have been received.
- For the paying company to get relief from corporation tax for an accounting period on a charitable payment, the payment must be made in that accounting period, except for charity-owned companies, who obtain relief for payments made up to nine months after the end of the accounting period.
- 'Charity affinity cards', i.e. credit cards on which some of the money spent goes to a charity, will not cause the charity to have a tax liability if the money is channelled through a trading subsidiary that donates its

income to the charity. For VAT purposes, HMRC will usually treat at least one-fifth of the charity's initial payment from the card provider as being liable to VAT as income from promotional activities, with the remaining four-fifths or less, plus all subsequent payments based on turnover, not attracting VAT.

44

Contractors and subcontractors in the construction industry

Employed or self-employed?

[44.1] Although this chapter deals with the special scheme for contractors and subcontractors in the construction industry, the scheme has no relevance where the worker concerned should in fact be classified as an employee. The IR35 provisions requiring personal service companies to account for tax and national insurance contributions (NICs) on deemed pay if an employee would have been treated as employed by a client of the company had he contracted directly with the client (see **19.6**) also need to be taken into account. Where the IR35 rules apply, the tax and NICs on the deemed payment is due by 19 April (or 22 April for electronic payments) following the tax year, whereas subcontractors may also have suffered tax under the construction industry scheme, such tax not being repayable until accounts have been submitted. Since 6 April 2006 it has also been necessary to consider whether payments to a participator in a managed service company are to be treated as employment income (see **19.15**).

The decision as to whether someone is employed or self-employed is often difficult to make (see **19.1**), particularly in the construction industry, but the consequences of getting it wrong can be extremely serious. HMRC's factsheet CIS349 'Are your workers employed or self-employed? – advice for contractors' outlines the factors to be taken into account, and HMRC provide an employment status indicator tool at www.hmrc.gov.uk/calcs/esi.htm which they consider can be used in 'all but the most complex cases' (see **19.2**). However, it is only an 'indicator' and the accompanying HMRC notes state that it will not give a definitive or legally binding opinion.

The Treasury and HMRC launched a consultation in July 2009 on a proposal to address the problem of 'false self-employment' in construction. The consultation paper invited comments on how to develop the best legislative approach to 'ensure that construction workers engaged in an employment relationship are taxed appropriately'.

It was proposed that, where a person ('the engager') whose main business involves the carrying out or commissioning of 'construction operations' (as defined) uses the services of a worker to carry out such operations, payments received in respect of those services will be deemed to be employment income unless the worker fulfils one of three statutory criteria in relation to provision of plant and equipment, provision of all materials, or provision of other workers.

In the event of reclassification, the worker's self-employed business will cease in the tax year of reclassification. See **10.2** for the treatment of construction industry employees supplied by agencies.

If contractors are found not to be complying with the PAYE regulations for those who should properly be treated as employees, they will have to account to HMRC for the amount of the unpaid tax and NICs.

The consequences of reclassification are far-reaching and potentially extremely costly for contractors, not only in relation to tax but also in relation to employment law and health and safety law.

Contractors' monthly returns (see **44.6**) include a declaration that the employment status of each worker has been considered and that payments have not been made under contracts of employment.

Construction industry scheme (FA 2004, ss 57–77 and Schs 11, 12; SI 2005/2045)

[44.2] The current construction industry scheme came into operation on 6 April 2007. Broadly it requires subcontractors to register either to receive payments from contractors gross or net of 20% tax. If contractors make payments to unregistered subcontractors they must deduct 30% tax at source.

This scheme is aimed at reducing the regulatory burden on construction businesses, improving compliance with tax obligations and helping construction businesses to get the employment status of their workers right.

Registration of contractors

[44.3] New contractors must register with HMRC before taking on their first subcontractor.

A 'contractor' has a wider meaning than just a construction company and covers many other businesses involved in construction work. Gangleaders who organise labour for construction work are included. Non-construction businesses are also included if they spend on average more than £1 million a year over a three year period on construction-related work. Private householders and smaller non-construction businesses are excluded. Construction work includes repairs, decorating and demolition. Work outside the UK is not included, but the scheme applies to UK construction work even if the subcontractors and/or contractors are non-resident, and even if payment is made abroad.

Registration of subcontractors

[44.4] Subcontractors need to register with HMRC. Those seeking registration must contact HMRC by telephone or online. If they are not already paying tax or NICs they will need to take specified identification documents to a local HMRC office.

There are two types of registration, registration for gross payment and registration for payment under deduction of tax at 20% (see **44.5**). HMRC may cancel the registration at any time if the qualifying conditions no longer apply or the rules have been breached. The subcontractor has a right of appeal against HMRC's decision. If a subcontractor does not register, the contractor is required to deduct 30% tax at source from payments made to the contractor.

The registration system replaced the registration cards used under the pre-6 April 2007 scheme. Subcontractors registered under the old scheme do not need to re-register if they had a tax certificate, or a permanent or unexpired registration card, at 6 April 2007.

Payment of subcontractors

[44.5] Contractors must obtain basic identification details from subcontractors (e.g. name, taxpayer reference number and national insurance number) and must verify the status of their subcontractors with HMRC, either by telephone or online. This must be done before any payments are made. Contractors may assume that the subcontractor's status remains unchanged unless HMRC notify them to the contrary.

Registered subcontractors can either be registered for:

(a)   payments to be made gross. To be registered for such payments subcontractors must comply with detailed conditions. They must have complied promptly with all tax obligations for the previous year. Sole traders need to have a turnover (net of materials) under contracts relating to 'construction operations' of at least £30,000 in the previous year. The minimum turnover for partnerships and companies is the smaller of (a) £30,000 multiplied by the number of partners/directors (and, for close companies, shareholders), or (b) £200,000. The business must operate in the UK and be run 'to a substantial extent' through a bank account; or

(b)   payments to be made net of 20% tax deducted at source.

Contractors may pay unregistered subcontractors, but tax must be deducted from payments at 30%.

Administration

[44.6] Where contractors deduct tax from payments to either registered or unregistered subcontractors, they must supply them with statements showing the gross amount and the tax deducted. Deductions under the scheme are normally paid over to the HMRC Accounts Office each month. Payments may instead be made quarterly if contractors expect their average payments of amounts due under the PAYE system and subcontractor deductions to be less than £1,500 a month. Interest is charged on underpayments as for PAYE (see **10.46**), and penalties will apply if the tax is not paid by a specified date.

Contractors must submit monthly returns (even if they make payments quarterly) and must provide details of recipients and payments made, together with a 'status declaration' confirming that 'employment status' has been considered (see **44.1**). The returns must be sent in every month (by post or online), even if no payments have been made (except where the contractor has told HMRC that he will make no further payments under construction contracts within the following six months), and penalties will apply if a return is not submitted. Nil returns may be made on paper, online or by telephone.

Tax position of non-corporate subcontractors

[44.7] The subcontractor's earnings are brought into the self-employed accounts of the subcontractor, and the amount deducted becomes a payment on account of the tax and Class 4 NICs due. The deduction by the contractor does not absolve the subcontractor from preparing accounts and submitting returns, and if his liability is greater than the amount deducted there is the possibility of interest and penalties if he has not complied with time limits for submission of returns and payment of tax and NICs. Where tax and Class 4 NICs have been overpaid, a repayment may be claimed in the subcontractor's tax return. For subcontractors who make up accounts to a date earlier than 5 April, repayment claims may be made before the end of the tax year, but before making a repayment HMRC will ensure that the subcontractor's tax affairs are up to date and that all tax and Class 4 NICs due for earlier years has been paid.

Tax position of corporate subcontractors

[44.8] Tax deducted under the subcontractors' scheme from payments to companies is set off against monthly or quarterly amounts due to be paid by the company to HMRC in respect of PAYE, NICs etc. and, where the subcontractor itself uses further subcontractors, subcontractors' scheme deductions.

Tax points

[44.9] Note the following:

- Where tax is deducted from the full labour content of a payment to a subcontractor, an overpayment will normally arise because of the expenses of the trade and because individuals will normally have personal allowances available (but, on the other hand, Class 4 NICs will increase the liability).
- The definition of operations covered by the scheme is wide. It is important to check the legislation to see if the contractors operations are included. If the scheme is not applied when it should have been, all

the tax that should have been deducted from payments to subcontractors plus interest may be due. If the workers should have been treated as employees, the position is even worse (see below).

- New businesses need to be able to satisfy turnover requirements in the previous twelve months in order to obtain registration for gross payment. In the meantime, tax will be deducted at 20%. If the new business's own subcontractors are registered for gross payment, those gross payments will have to be made out of net payments received.

- Contractors should be very careful to ensure that the terms under which workers operate bring them within the self-employed category if they are to treat them as subcontractors. Bear in mind also the possibility of a change in the rules following the consultation launched in July 2009 (see **44.1**).

- If workers are wrongly classified, the contractor could be held liable for the PAYE tax that should have been deducted, plus employers' and employees' NICs, and possibly penalties as well. Where a subcontractor company is caught by the IR35 personal service company rules, it is the subcontractor company rather than the contractor who suffers the burden of employer's PAYE and NICs.

- See also **19.15** for the special rules introduced in 2007 which treat payments to participators in managed service companies as employment income.

45

Main anti-avoidance provisions

Background

[45.1] HMRC's ability to counter what they regard as unacceptable tax avoidance has been strengthened by various court decisions and the introduction, in 2004, of rules requiring the disclosure to HMRC of tax avoidance schemes meeting certain criteria. Promoters as well as users are required to notify avoidance schemes. A good deal of specific anti-avoidance legislation pre-dated these developments but the Government has continued to introduce measures to counter arrangements notified under the disclosure rules.

Schemes that include steps inserted purely for tax avoidance may well prove unsuccessful, although bona fide commercial arrangements will usually be effective provided that they do not breach any of the specific provisions.

It is important to bear in mind that tax avoidance is legal and tax evasion is illegal (see **1.7**). Anti-avoidance rules are necessarily complex, and what follows is only a brief outline of some of the more common rules. It should not be regarded as an exhaustive list of anti-avoidance measures. Much of the legislation granting reliefs has anti-avoidance measures within it. Examples include the rules relating to demergers; companies purchasing their own shares; the enterprise investment scheme; capital allowances; the revised remittance basis rules enacted in FA 2008 and relief for trading losses.

The present anti-avoidance rules are largely piecemeal and targeted at specific areas. The Government has considered introducing a general anti-avoidance rule or GAAR, and while such a rule has not been enacted yet it remains an option. A GAAR does apply, however, for stamp duty land tax (see **45.25**).

Much of the present legislation is intended to prevent income being converted into a capital gain, and this is likely to become of greater significance now that gains are taxed at a flat rate of 18% (or 28%, if appropriate (see **4.2**)), significantly lower than the 50% higher rate of income tax.

As well as measures affecting direct taxes, there are anti-avoidance provisions relating to VAT. Examples include provisions relating to multinational groups of companies, transfers of businesses as going concerns, business splitting, charity reliefs, the option to charge VAT on buildings, the treatment of staff hire, the margin scheme for second-hand goods, cash accounting, the treatment of credit vouchers, the capital goods scheme and rules to counter exploitation by commercial sports clubs of the exemption for non-profit making organisations. There is also an anti-avoidance provision requiring non-UK businesses that reclaim UK VAT and then dispose of goods in the UK to be registered in the UK regardless of their turnover.

Disclosure of tax avoidance schemes (TMA 1970, s 98C; SSAA 1992, s 132A; FA 2004, ss 306–319)

[45.2] 'Promoters' who market certain tax avoidance schemes and arrangements are required to make a disclosure of information about them to HMRC. The types of schemes and arrangements that came within the provisions include:

(a) (from August 2006) any income tax, corporation tax, or capital gains tax (CGT) scheme, where the main benefit expected under the scheme is a tax advantage and the arrangement bears one or more 'hallmarks';

(b) (from May 2007) national insurance saving schemes, where the main benefit is the obtaining of a NIC advantage and the scheme bears one or more 'hallmarks;

(c) (from August 2005) schemes intended to avoid stamp duty land tax on UK property transactions, where the schemes are made available or implemented on or after 1 August 2005 (SI 2005/1868). They apply to commercial property with an aggregate market value of £5 million or more.

A 'promoter' is anyone who provides taxation services in the course of a trade if he has responsibility for designing such schemes, or markets or promotes schemes designed by someone else. The provisions do not apply to legal advisers in relation to anything covered by legal professional privilege (unless the clients have waived privilege, allowing the promoter to make the disclosure).

The scheme promoter must make the disclosure to HMRC within five business days. HMRC register all such schemes and give each a reference number, which promoters must provide to their clients together with information specified in regulations. Taxpayers have to provide details of schemes themselves where they have purchased the scheme from an offshore promoter who has not made a disclosure, where the promoter is protected from disclosure by legal professional privilege or where the scheme was devised in-house. The time limit for taxpayers to provide such details to HMRC is 5 days, (extended to 30 days where the scheme was devised in-house) after the first transaction forming part of the arrangements. Neither individuals nor businesses that are small or medium-sized enterprises, however, have to disclose in-house schemes. A 'small or medium-sized' enterprise for this purpose is as defined by the European Union, i.e. a business that has fewer than 500 employees, with a turnover of less than €100 million and/or balance sheet total of less than €86 million.

Taxpayers using the schemes will usually only be required to include the reference number of the scheme on their tax returns (except where they are required to disclose as indicated above).

There are penalties for failure to disclose a scheme, or to provide a client with a reference number.

The disclosure requirements have resulted in a number of avoidance schemes being notified, which have resulted in anti-avoidance legislation in subsequent Finance Acts.

Disclosure of VAT avoidance schemes (VATA 1994, s 58A and Sch 11A; SI 2004/1933)

[45.3] Businesses that use certain VAT avoidance schemes must disclose their use to HMRC. There is a statutory register of VAT avoidance schemes, each of which has a reference number. Businesses with an annual turnover of £600,000 or more that continue to use such listed schemes must notify HMRC. There is also a statutory register of 'hallmarks' of avoidance. Businesses with a turnover of £10 million or more that use arrangements that include such a hallmark and have as a main purpose the obtaining of a tax advantage must also notify HMRC. Penalties are imposed for failure to notify use of a scheme.

Notification must be made within 30 days from the last day for submission of the relevant return, or within 30 days after the date of a relevant claim for a refund of output VAT or increase of allowable input VAT.

Cancelling tax advantage from transactions in securities (ITA 2007, ss 682–713; CTA 2010, ss 731–751)

[45.4] Where in consequence of a transaction in securities a person has obtained a tax advantage, then unless he shows that the transaction was for bona fide commercial reasons or in the course of making or managing investments, and that none of the transactions had as their main object, or one of their main objects, the realising of a tax advantage, that tax advantage may be nullified.

These provisions have been used particularly where elaborate schemes have been devised with the aim of extracting the undistributed profits of companies in a capital form. In view of the far reaching implications there is an appropriate clearance procedure which it is wise to follow wherever shares are being sold in closely controlled companies with significant distributable reserves.

The provisions do not apply until HMRC serve a notice specifying the adjustment to be made, and taxpayers are not required to deal with the liability in their self-assessment returns, nor are HMRC bound by the self-assessment enquiry time limits. See HMRC Tax Bulletin 46 (April 2000).

Avoidance relating to financial products

[45.5] Schemes relating to financial products are routinely notified under the disclosure provisions outlined in **45.2** and are usually blocked by legislation. A few of these rules are outlined below, but in general this type of anti-avoidance legislation is beyond the scope of this book and professional advice should be sought in such situations.

Transfer of an income stream (CTA 2010, ss 752–757)

[45.6] There is a general principle, set out in statute, that consideration received for the sale or transfer of an income stream on or after 22 April 2009 is subject to tax in the transferor's hands in the same way that the income itself would have been (so there is no possibility of converting income into capital). These provisions only apply where certain conditions are met. Similar provisions also apply for income tax purposes, which essentially mirror the corporation tax rules with a few minor exceptions simply to cater for the different structure of income tax.

Finance agreements (CTA 2010, ss 758–776)

[45.7] Specific provisions counter cases where:

(a)   a taxpayer sells the right to income receipts for a predetermined period in return for a lump sum payment which is treated as a capital receipt for the purposes of corporation tax on chargeable gains, or where the taxpayer is within the charge to income tax, capital gains tax; and

(b)   the transaction is, in economic substance, a financing transaction and this is how the transaction is accounted for in the taxpayer's accounts.

In such cases, subject to certain exceptions, the transfer of the asset is disregarded in computing the taxpayer's taxable income and the taxpayer is able to obtain tax relief for the financing charge which it reflects in its accounts in respect of the transaction, provided that its accounting treatment is in accordance with generally accepted accounting practice.

Miscellaneous (CTA 2010, ss 780–804)

[45.8] There are provisions to prevent the rules relating to manufactured payments in respect of UK securities (which are largely relevant to companies trading in the financial markets) being used by individuals to generate tax-deductible manufactured payments coupled with non-taxable receipts.

There are also provisions preventing the purchase and sale of securities being used to create tax allowable trading losses or to enable tax-exempt persons to claim repayments.

Change in ownership of a company etc

Trading losses (CTA 2010, ss 673–676)

[45.9] Trading losses may not be carried forward where within a period of three years there is both a change in ownership of a company and a major change in the nature or conduct of its trade. The rules also apply where ownership changes after activities have sunk to a low level and before any significant revival. Similar provisions apply to prevent trading losses of an accounting period ending *after* the change of ownership being carried back to an accounting period beginning *before* the change. Statement of Practice SP 10/91 sets out HMRC's interpretation of a 'major change in the nature or conduct of a trade'. See **26.19**.

Capital loss buying and capital gains buying (TCGA 1992, ss 16A, 177A, 184A–184F and Sch 7A)

[45.10] There are detailed and complex provisions to prevent groups of companies avoiding tax on capital gains by acquiring a company with capital losses and using the intra-group no gain/no loss rules to transfer assets to the purchased company before disposing of them outside the group. The provisions broadly operate where there is a change of ownership of a company that, amongst other things, occurs in connection with arrangements to secure a tax advantage. The rules provide that unused losses brought forward at the time the company joins the group, (or later losses realised on the disposal of assets owned by the company before the change in ownership) cannot be offset against gains realised by the company after the change in ownership.

There are parallel provisions to prevent the reverse procedure, i.e. acquiring a company with realised gains in order to utilise unrealised group losses. Capital gains (realised or unrealised) on assets held by a company before a change in ownership cannot (once realised) be offset against a capital loss accruing to the company where, amongst other things, the change of ownership occurs in connection with arrangements to secure a tax advantage.

Schemes to avoid corporation tax liabilities (CTA 2010, ss 710–715)

[45.11] There are provisions to counteract schemes under which a company's trading assets are transferred to another group company prior to the sale of the first company and the new owners strip the company of the remaining cash assets, leaving the company unable to pay its corporation tax. Corporation tax liabilities arising before the sale of a company may in prescribed circumstances be collected from the previous owners. The provisions also apply to corporation tax liabilities arising after the sale if it could reasonably have been inferred at the time of the sale that they were unlikely to be met.

Pre-sale distributions etc. (CTA 2010, ss 157–182; TCGA 1992, ss 31–33, 170)

[45.12] There are provisions to prevent companies reducing or eliminating capital gains by reducing the value of a subsidiary before its sale. Where unrealised gains are distributed by a subsidiary to its parent company as group income prior to the sale of the subsidiary, the parent company is treated as if it had received additional consideration of an equivalent amount. The provisions also cover the transfer of a subsidiary to a non-resident company in the group prior to its onward sale, where the subsidiary leaves the group within six years after being transferred to the non-resident company.

There are also provisions to prevent companies retaining a subsidiary within a group for capital gains purposes by means of issuing special types of shares, while selling commercial control of the company.

Change in ownership of, or change in interest in, plant or machinery leasing business (CTA 2010, ss 382–436; FA 2010, s 61 and Sch 18)

[45.13] Legislation targets changes in the economic ownership of a plant or machinery leasing business carried on by a company on its own or in partnership. It applies to both simple sales of shares in a leasing company and changes in partnership sharing arrangements, in addition to any other route by which the economic ownership of a business could be changed. The legislation aims to prevent an unacceptable permanent deferral of tax. It had previously been possible for a leasing company to generate losses in the early years of a long leasing contract as a consequence of the availability of capital allowances, such losses being available for group relief. In the later years of the lease the capital allowances would be reduced and the company would become profitable. If the leasing company was sold in the interim to a loss-making company or group, the leasing company's profits would be covered by the new owner's losses. Thus, an acceptable temporary deferral of tax became a permanent deferral of tax.

The legislation acts by bringing into charge an amount of income which is calculated by reference to the difference between the commercial position of the company and the tax position. The charge is calculated by comparing the sum of the balance sheet values of the net investments in the leases and the plant and machinery with the tax written down value of the plant and machinery. Consequently the tax benefit derived by the leasing company from the capital allowances is recovered.

Alternatively, from 9 December 2009, companies can opt for a different treatment which replaces the charge and relief with a ring fence that preserves the profits of the leasing business by restricting the set off of losses. As a consequence of these restrictions tax is collected on the deferred profits over time.

Overseas issues

Dual resident investment companies (CTA 2010, s 109; TCGA 1992, ss 171, 175)

[45.14] Where an investment company is resident both in the UK and in another country, that company cannot surrender losses etc. under the group relief provisions (see **3.29**). Such companies are also unable to take advantage of the various capital allowances provisions that would normally prevent transfers to them being treated as being at open market value.

For capital gains purposes, assets may not be transferred intra-group on a no loss/no gain basis if the transferee is a dual resident investment company. Nor may business assets rollover relief be claimed within a group in respect of assets acquired by a dual resident investment company.

Controlled foreign companies (TA 1988, ss 747–756 and Schs 24–26; ITA 2007, s 725; SI 1998/3081)

[45.15] A UK resident company is charged to tax in respect of the profits of a foreign company if the foreign company is controlled to a significant extent by companies or individuals resident in the UK, and pays tax in its country of residence at less than 75% of the amount that a UK resident company would pay, where the UK company and associates have at least a 25% stake in the foreign company. Companies paying tax under what are known as 'designer rate' tax regimes are automatically treated as being subject to a lower rate of taxation. The relevant designer rate regimes are specified in regulations and are in the Channel Islands, the Isle of Man and Gibraltar. The controlled foreign companies (CFC) rules do not apply if the foreign company satisfies one or more of certain tests as to exempt activities, motive, or if its profits for a twelve-month period were less than £50,000. Companies are excluded from the CFC provisions if they are resident and carrying on business in a country listed in the 'Excluded Countries' regulations, providing they satisfy specified requirements as to income, gains etc. There are provisions to prevent the CFC and excluded countries rules being exploited by artificial schemes. HMRC have the power to issue regulations designating certain foreign jurisdictions in which all controlled foreign companies will automatically be covered by the rules, regardless of whether one of the exemptions would otherwise apply.

UK resident companies that are regarded as non-resident under the provisions of a double tax treaty are nonetheless regarded as resident for the CFC rules. Special rules apply to companies that were non-resident under a double tax treaty before 1 April 2002.

Companies are required to make any necessary adjustments relating to the CFC provisions in their self-assessment tax returns. A clearance procedure is available to both trading and non-trading controlled foreign companies, and HMRC publish comprehensive guidance notes to help companies comply with the rules.

Offshore funds (TIOPA 2010, ss 354–363; SI 2009/3001; SI 2009/3139)

[45.16] New regulations for offshore funds came into force on 1 December 2009. However, the purpose of both the original and replacement regimes is the same. Realisation of an interest in an offshore fund investment is charged to tax as income rather than chargeable gains, unless certain conditions are met.

Under the regulations, funds are recognised as either reporting funds or non-reporting funds. Reporting funds must comply with strict guidelines laid down in the regulations in order to qualify as such.

Broadly UK resident investors in reporting funds will be taxable on their share of the funds' reported income each year, regardless of whether it is distributed to them, and any gain or loss on disposal will be treated as a capital gain or loss.

UK investors in non-reporting funds remain chargeable to income tax or corporation tax on any distributions made to them. Alternatively if the fund is transparent for income purposes they will be chargeable to tax on the underlying investments. Untaxed accumulated income and gains in a non-reporting fund are treated as offshore income on realisation. A disposal of an interest in a non-reporting fund will give rise to a gain chargeable to income tax (an offshore income gain).

Transfer of assets abroad (ITA 2007, ss 714–751)

[45.17] The purpose of the transfer of assets provisions is to prevent an individual ordinarily resident in the UK avoiding UK tax by transferring income-producing property abroad in circumstances which enable him to benefit from the property either immediately or in the future, such as a transfer to trustees of a foreign settlement made by him, of which he is a beneficiary. The provisions also impose a charge when benefits go not to the transferor but to someone else, such as his children or grandchildren. The provisions apply to life policies held in trust in certain circumstances (see **40.14**).

Personal portfolio bonds (ITTOIA 2005, ss 515–526)

[45.18] Special provisions apply to 'personal portfolio bonds', which are insurance policies where the policyholder or his adviser may select and vary the underlying investments. Such bonds are within the 'chargeable events' provisions for life insurance policies. Although particularly aimed at offshore bonds, the provisions also catch UK bonds. The effect of the rules is that there is an annual income tax charge on the bonds for each policy year other than the last year. The annual charge is equal to 15% of a deemed gain equal to the total of the premiums paid and the total deemed gains from previous years, net of any taxable amounts withdrawn in earlier years. The gains are charged in the same way as other gains on insurance bonds (see **40.6**), i.e. on the excess, if any, of higher rate tax over the basic rate of 20%, but top slicing relief is not available. The total amount of gains taxed under the yearly provisions is deducted from any gain arising when the policy terminates. If gains arising during the life of a policy are reversed when the policy comes to an end, a compensating deduction will be made from taxable income.

Most bonds taken out before 17 March 1998 are excluded from the provisions, and policyholders who were not UK resident on 17 March 1998 will have at least 12 months after becoming resident to change the terms of the policy so that they also are excluded.

Transfer pricing (TIOPA 2010, ss 146–217)

[45.19] Where any sales take place between persons connected with each other, including partnerships and companies, at a price other than open market value, the sale price of the one and purchase price of the other must be adjusted to the open market value for tax purposes. Similarly, adjustments may be required in relation to interest on 'excessive' debt finance.

The transfer pricing rules apply to transactions between UK parties, as well as transactions between UK and overseas parties. There are exemptions for most small and medium-sized companies. Any transfer pricing adjustments must be made in the self-assessment tax returns. The normal penalties for careless or deliberate actions apply.

The transfer pricing rules apply where parties that could collectively control a business act together to finance that business.

Transfers between dealing and non-dealing companies

[45.20] Transfers of assets between dealing companies and associated non-dealing companies are covered by the transfer pricing scheme.

Special rules apply where a dealing company makes a payment etc to an associated non-dealing company which is tax deductible for the dealing company but not taxable for the non-dealing company. In such situations the non-dealing company is deemed to receive income of an amount equal to the deduction allowed to the dealing company.

Artificial transactions in land (CTA 2010, ss 815–833; ITA 2007, ss 752–772)

[45.21] The aim of this provision is 'to prevent the avoidance of income tax by persons connected with land or the development of land'. It enables land transactions to be taxed as trading or other income instead of as a capital gain.

Sale and lease-back

Land (CTA 2010, ss 838, 849–862)

[45.22] Where land is sold and leased back, the deduction allowed for rent is limited to a commercial rent. A sale at an excessive price (subject to CGT) cannot therefore be compensated by an excessive rent payment allowable in calculating taxable income.

Further, if a short lease (less than 50 years) is sold and leased back for 15 years or less, part of the sale price is treated as income, that part being $(16 - n)/15$ where n is the term of the new lease.

Assets other than land (CTA 2010, ss 865, 870–886)

[45.23] If assets other than land are sold and leased back similar rules will apply to those for sale and leaseback of land. Furthermore, if a deduction has been received in relation to a lease of an asset other than land and a capital sum is received by the lessee in respect of his interest in the lease, then the lower of the deduction obtained and the capital sum received will be charged as income.

Avoidance using trusts (TCGA 1992, ss 71, 76B, 79A, 83A, 85A and Schs 4B, 4C; FA 1986, ss 102, 102ZA and Sch 20)

[45.24] There are provisions to prevent artificial schemes under which capital losses generated within trusts are sold to purchasers to reduce their capital gains on other assets. A loss on an asset transferred to a trust beneficiary may be used only against gains on the disposal of the same asset (or in the case of land, an asset derived from the land). Further anti-avoidance provisions apply to a variation of the above schemes. Losses arising on disposals by trustees cannot be set against any gains made by the trustees on assets that have been transferred to the trust if the transferor or someone connected with him had bought an interest in the trust and had claimed gift holdover relief on the transferred assets.

It used to be possible to reduce or avoid CGT by using a device known as the 'flip flop'. It is now provided that where the trustees of any trust except a UK trust in which the settlor does not have an interest borrow money and advance it to another trust, the trustees are deemed to dispose of the trust assets and reacquire them at market value, and no claim for gift holdover relief may be made, thus crystallising the chargeable gains in the first trust.

There are provisions to ensure that UK beneficiaries of offshore trusts cannot escape CGT on capital payments. Anti-avoidance provisions were introduced in 2005 to prevent trustees who are within the charge to UK CGT at some time in a tax year avoiding that tax by realising gains at a time when they are resident in a country with which the UK has a double tax agreement, and thus taxable on the gain in that country (but with little or no liability arising on the gain). The gain will be chargeable to UK tax, with the usual double taxation relief available.

IHT anti-avoidance provisions prevent married couples and civil partners using trusts to get round the rules in **5.36** about retaining benefits from a gift.

Other anti-avoidance provisions relating to trusts are mentioned in CHAP-TERS 41 and 42.

Stamp taxes (FA 2000, ss 117–122, 128 and Sch 33; FA 2002, ss 111–115 and Schs 34–36; FA 2003, ss 62, 75A–75C, 104, 109, 120 and Schs 7, 15, 17A; FA 2010, s 55)

[45.25] There is a general anti-avoidance provision in relation to stamp duty land tax (SDLT) at FA 2003, s 75A. There are also various specific provisions to counter SDLT avoidance schemes in relation to group relief, leases and partnerships. In addition HMRC have power to issue regulations to counter stamp duty and SDLT avoidance devices as they arise. Specific provisions treat a series of linked transactions as a notional land transaction, and amend the SDLT rules for partnerships. FA 2008 contained SDLT measures to counter avoidance by groups of companies; to counter 'misuse' of rules designed to encourage use of alternative finance structures; and to amend some of the FA 2007 provisions retrospectively.

There are also a large number of specific stamp duty and stamp duty reserve tax avoidance provisions, some of which are mentioned briefly in CHAPTER 6, in particular at **6.5**.

Other measures

[45.26] There are also measures to counter avoidance in the following circumstances.

- Companies leaving a group and taking out a chargeable asset acquired intra-group on a no loss/no gain basis within the previous six years (TCGA 1992, ss 179–181).
- Group companies seeking to avoid tax by channelling disposals of assets through tax-exempt bodies such as venture capital trusts and friendly societies (TCGA 1992, s 171).

- Claiming group relief for losses when arrangements exist where a company may leave the group (CTA 2010, ss 154–156).
- Companies avoiding tax through the use of tax arbitrage (i.e. exploiting differences between or within national tax codes) (TIOPA 2010, ss 231–259).
- Transfers of plant and machinery between associated persons in order to obtain capital allowances (CAA 2001, s 215).
- Losses arising from depreciatory transactions, e.g. dividend-stripping (TCGA 1992, ss 176, 177).
- Value passing out of shares, which could have been avoided by a controlling shareholder (TCGA 1992, ss 29–33A).
- Individuals realising capital gains abroad through a non-resident close company (TCGA 1992, s 13).
- Transferring relief for partnership losses which would otherwise relate to a partner who is a company (CTA 2010, ss 958–962).
- Annual payments for non-taxable consideration (ITA 2007, ss 843, 898–905).
- Transfer of chargeable assets on which holdover relief for CGT is obtained into dual resident trusts (TCGA 1992, s 169).

Subject index

Index entries are to paragraph numbers in the chapters, and to page numbers (Roman numerals) in the preliminary pages.

Retirement benefits schemes – *cont.*
stakeholder pensions *see* Stakeholder pension schemes
Retraining 10.42
Returns
company law requirements 9.20
construction industry
contractors 44.6
subcontractors 44.7
employee share schemes 11.2
failure to make, penalties
corporation tax 9.47
income tax 9.46
inheritance tax 9.48
income tax 9.13
inheritance tax 9.21–9.23, 9.48
late 9.11
notification of liability 9.27–9.28
partnerships 23.5–23.10
self-assessment *see* Self-assessment
VAT 7.33, 7.35
Revaluations
business rates 8.10
Revenue and Customs Division (RCD), Crown Prosecution Service 1.3, 9.36
Reverse charge, VAT 7.42
Reverse premiums 32.21
Reversionary interests
trusts 42.26
Right to Enfranchisement (RTE) companies 30.2
Right to Manage (RTM) companies 30.2
Rights issues *see* Shares
Rollover relief *see* Capital gains tax
Royalties
associated companies, payments to 41.59
double taxation relief 41.33
intangible fixed assets rules 20.32
patents 3.21
record sales 41.33
RPI (retail prices index) xvii–xviii
RSL (registered social landlords) 6.17
RTE (Right to Enfranchisement) companies 30.2
RTM (Right to Manage) companies 30.2

S

S2P (State Second Pension Scheme) *see* State pensions
SAI (Standard Accounts Information) 23.6
Salaried partners 23.32

Salaries *see* Pay
Sales and leasebacks
anti-avoidance 45.22–45.23
stamp duty land tax 6.15
SAP *see* Statutory adoption pay
Savings certificates 4.9, 36.5, 36.6
Savings income
overseas 41.15
tax rates 2.24
SAYE
contracts, capital gains tax 4.9
employee share schemes 11.10–11.11, 17.12, 36.21
SCE (Societas Co-operative Europaea) 41.58
Scholarships
benefits to parents 10.24
employees 10.40
Scientific research allowance 22.59
Scotland
local enterprise companies (LEC) 29.37
Parliament 1.2
Scrip dividends *see* Dividends
Scrip issues *see* Shares
SDLT *see* Stamp duty land tax
SDRT *see* Stamp duty reserve tax
SE (Societas Europaea) 3.28, 41.58
Seafarers, employment income 41.17
Second homes 8.5, 30.15–30.17
Second-hand life insurance policies 40.12
Second-hand margin scheme, VAT 7.22
Securities
accrued income on 36.19, 38.4
anti-avoidance 45.4–45.7
artificially depressed or enhanced market values, with, employee share schemes 11.6
convertible, employee share schemes 11.6
discounted 38.31
disposal of for more than market value, employee share schemes 11.6
employee schemes *see* Employee share schemes
government *see* Government securities
listed *see* quoted *below*
options 10.19
see also Employee share schemes
post acquisition benefits from 11.6
qualifying corporate bonds *see* Qualifying corporate bonds
quoted
capital gains tax 4.32, 38.15
inheritance tax valuation 5.30, 35.15
readily convertible assets 10.19
restricted 11.6
tax points 38.37

Shares – *cont.*
market values, share awards
and 11.5–11.6
negligible value, of 38.21
non-qualifying corporate bonds exchange
for 38.35
options *see* Employee share schemes
ordinary 36.20
own, companies purchasing 29.32
permanent interest-bearing shares
(PIBS) 3.5, 37.6
personal pension schemes, transfers
into 17.12
priority allocations for employees 11.33
qualifying corporate bonds exchange
for 38.33–38.34
readily convertible assets 10.19
quoted
meaning 38.1
capital gains tax 4.32
rights issues
capital gains tax
corporate shareholders 38.18
individuals, personal representatives
or trustees 38.19
disposals 38.17
share incentive plans 11.26
sold nil paid 38.18
scrip issues
capital gains tax
corporate shareholders 38.18
individuals, personal representatives
and trustees 38.19
disposals 38.17
dividend alternatives *see* Dividends: scrip
selling family companies 28.1, 28.2
shareholders' concessions 3.20
tax points 38.37
traded options 4.36
transfer of businesses to companies 27.14
unquoted 38.1
capital gains tax 4.32, 38.14
loss relief 38.22
valuations 38.11
value passing out of, anti-avoidance 45.26
see also Securities
Short-life assets
capital allowances 22.35
Short rotation coppice 31.26, 31.31
Sickness
benefits 10.5
employment and support allowance xx,
10.5
incapacity benefits 10.5
insurance 10.5

Sickness – *cont.*
statutory sick pay *see* Statutory sick pay
Sideways relief 25.6, 25.13
Simultaneous deaths 35.13
Single payment scheme (SPS), farming 31.2,
31.16
Sinking funds held on trust by landlords 32.1
SIP *see* Share incentive plans
**SIPPS (self-invested personal pension
schemes)** 17.1, 17.19
Skills Funding Agency (SFA) 29.37
Sleeping partners 23.33
Small business rate relief 8.10, 8.12
Small companies
family companies *see* Family companies
research and development expendi-
ture 29.39
Small profits rate, corporation tax 3.13–3.14,
26.9
**Small self-administered pension schemes
(SSAS)** 16.37
Smallholdings 31.20
SMP *see* Statutory maternity pay
**SOCA (Serious Organised Crime
Agency)** 9.30
Social housing, registered providers of 6.17
Social security
benefits
funding 13.1
non-residents 41.32, 41.43
pensions *see* State pensions
rates of xx–xxi
senior citizens 34.7
tax treatment 10.5
income, taxable 2.7
see also National insurance contributions
Societas Co-operative Europaea (SCE) 41.58
Societas Europaea (SE) 3.28, 41.58
Sole traders *see* Self-employed persons
Special annual allowances
pension contributions 16.13
**Special Civil Investigations Office,
HMRC** 9.36
Specialist information powers, HMRC 9.29
**'Spinout' companies to develop intellectual
property**
employee share schemes and 11.4
Split level capital investment trusts 38.27
Sports clubs, community amateur 43.33
Sports facilities 10.24
Sports grounds
safety expenditure, capital allow-
ances 22.20
Sports pavilions
capital allowances 22.43